Madeira
(Portugal)

Rabat

Algiers

TUNISIA

Mediterranean Sea

Tripoli

Cairo

Canary Is
(Spain)

MOROCCO

ALGERIA

LIBYA

EGYPT

Red Sea

WESTERN
SAHARA

MAURITANIA

NIGER

CHAD

Khartoum

ERITREA

DJIBOUTI

Dakar

SENEGAL

THE GAMBIA

GUINEA-
BISSAU

GUINEA

BURKINA
FASO

Kano

Ndjamena

SUDAN

Addis
Ababa

SIERRA LEONE

CÔTE
d'IVOIRE

GHANA

BENIN

NIGERIA

CAMEROON

CENTRAL AFRICAN
REPUBLIC

ETHIOPIA

SOMALIA

LIBERIA

Lagos

TOGO

Bangui

Kisangani

UGANDA

KENYA

Abidjan

EQUATORIAL GUINEA

CONGO

DEM. REPUBLIC
of

Nairobi

Libreville

GABON

Brazzaville

CONGO

Dodoma

Zanzibar

ATLANTIC

CABINDA

Kinshasa

(ZAIRE)

TANZANIA

Dar es Salaam

Luanda

Lubumbashi

COMOROS

OCEAN

ANGOLA

ZAMBIA

MALAWI

MOZAMBIQUE

MALAGASY
REPUBLIC

Harare

NAMIBIA

ZIMBABWE

Windhoek

BOTSWANA

Pretoria

Maputo

SWAZILAND

R RWANDA B BURUNDI

SOUTH
AFRICA

LESOTHO

Cape Town

| 0 | 500 | 1000 miles |
| 0 | 500 | 1000 | 1500 km |

AFRICA : 2005

THE STATE OF
AFRICA

THE STATE OF
AFRICA

A History of Fifty Years
of Independence

MARTIN MEREDITH

London · New York · Sydney · Toronto

First published in Great Britain by The Free Press, 2005
An imprint of Simon & Schuster UK Ltd
A Viacom Company

1 3 5 7 9 10 8 6 4 2

Simon & Schuster UK Ltd
Africa House
64–78 Kingsway
London WC2B 6AH

www.simonsays.co.uk

Simon & Schuster Australia
Sydney

PICTURE CREDITS
1, 2, 3, 7, 9, 10, 11, 12, 19, 20, 21, 25, 26, 29, 30, 31, 32,
34, 35, 36, 37, 39, 40, 41, 53, 56, © Getty Images
4, 5, 8, 13, 14, 15, 16, 17, 18, 22, 38, 43, 44, 45,
47, 48, 49, 50, 51, 55, 57, 58, © Corbis
6, 23, 24, © Popperfoto
27, 42, 46, 54 © Magnum Photos
28, 52 © Associated Press
33 © Camera Press

A CIP catalogue record for this book is available
from the British Library

Hardback ISBN 0-7432-3221-6/EAN 9780743232210
Trade paperback ISBN 0-7432-6842-3/EAN 9780743268424

Typeset by M Rules
Printed and bound in Great Britain by
Mackays of Chatham plc

CONTENTS

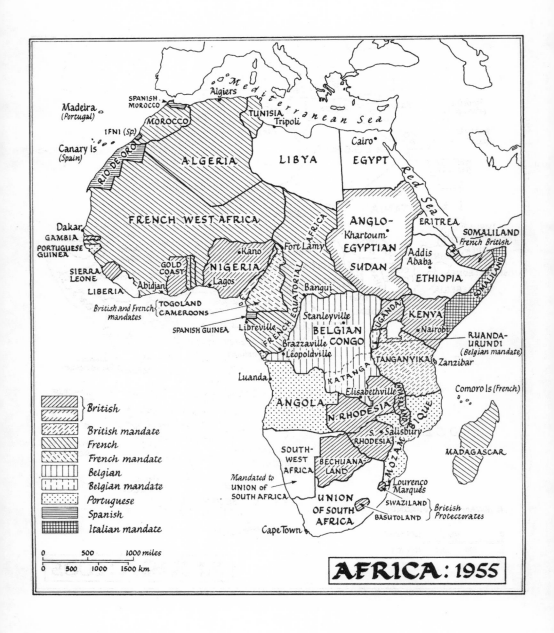

Madeira
(Portugal)

SPANISH
MOROCCO

IFNI (Sp)

Canary Is
(Spain)

RIO DE ORO

Algiers

Mediterranean Sea

MOROCCO

TUNISIA
Tripoli•

ALGERIA

LIBYA

Cairo•

EGYPT

Red Sea

FRENCH WEST AFRICA

ANGLO-
Khartoum•
EGYPTIAN

ERITREA

SOMALILAND
French British

Dakar•

GAMBIA

PORTUGUESE
GUINEA

SIERRA
LEONE

LIBERIA

•Kano

GOLD
COAST

NIGERIA

•Abidjan   Lagos•

British and French
mandates   TOGOLAND
CAMEROONS

SPANISH GUINEA

Fort Lamy•

FRENCH EQUATORIAL AFRICA

Bangui•

SUDAN

Addis
Ababa•

ETHIOPIA

SOMALILAND

Libreville•

Stanleyville•

BELGIAN
CONGO

Brazzaville•
•Léopoldville

UGANDA

KENYA

•Nairobi

RUANDA-
URUNDI
(Belgian mandate)

TANGANYIKA

•Zanzibar

Luanda•

KATANGA

•Elisabethville

Comoro Is (French)

ANGOLA

N. RHODESIA

MOZAMBIQUE

S.   •Salisbury
RHODESIA

MADAGASCAR

SOUTH-
WEST
AFRICA

Mandated to
UNION of
SOUTH AFRICA

BECHUANA-
LAND

Lourenço
Marques•

UNION
OF SOUTH
AFRICA

SWAZILAND

BASUTOLAND

British
Protectorates

Cape Town•

British

British mandate

French

French mandate

Belgian

Belgian mandate

Portuguese

Spanish

Italian mandate

0   500   1000 miles

0   500   1000 1500 km

AFRICA: 1955

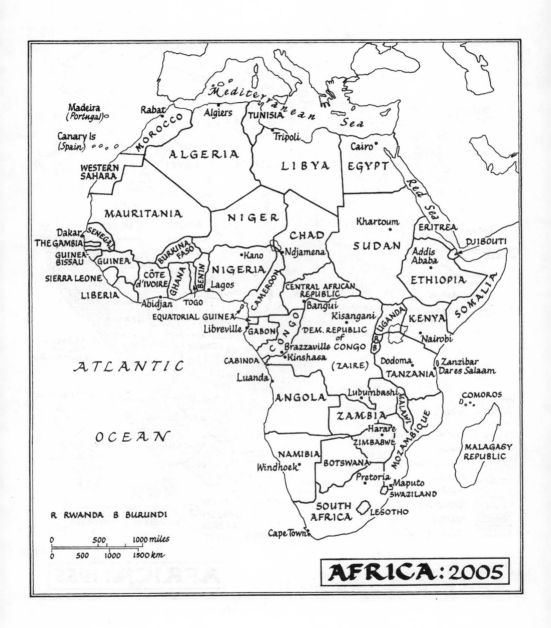

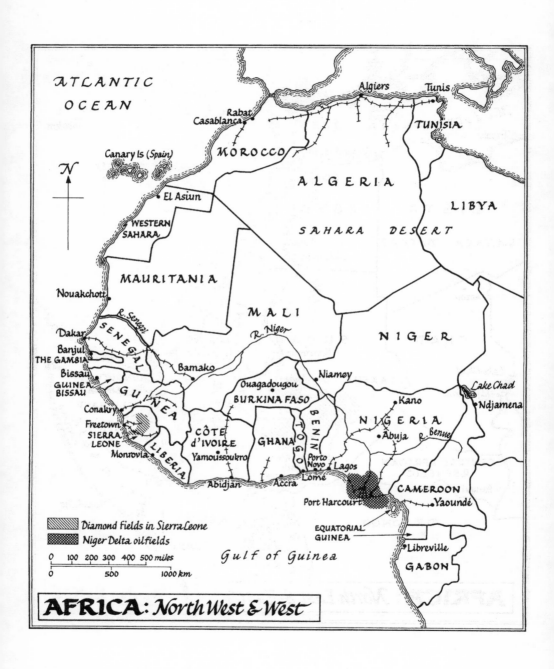

ATLANTIC
OCEAN

N

Canary Is (Spain)

Rabat
Casablanca
MOROCCO

Algiers
Tunis
TUNISIA

ALGERIA

LIBYA

El Asiun

WESTERN
SAHARA

SAHARA   DESERT

MAURITANIA

Nouakchott

MALI

R. Senegal

Dakar
Banjul
THE GAMBIA
Bissau
GUINEA
BISSAU

SENEGAL

R. Niger

NIGER

Bamako

Niamey

GUINEA

Ouagadougou

Lake Chad

Conakry

BURKINA FASO

Kano

Ndjamena

Freetown
SIERRA
LEONE

CÔTE
d'IVOIRE

GHANA

BENIN

NIGERIA

Abuja

R. Benue

Monrovia

LIBERIA

Yamoussoukro

TOGO

Porto
Novo

Lagos

Abidjan

Accra

Lomé

CAMEROON

Port Harcourt

Yaoundé

EQUATORIAL
GUINEA

Diamond fields in SierraLeone
Niger Delta oilfields

Gulf of Guinea

Libreville

0   100 200 300 400 500 miles

GABON

0   500   1000 km

AFRICA: *North West & West*

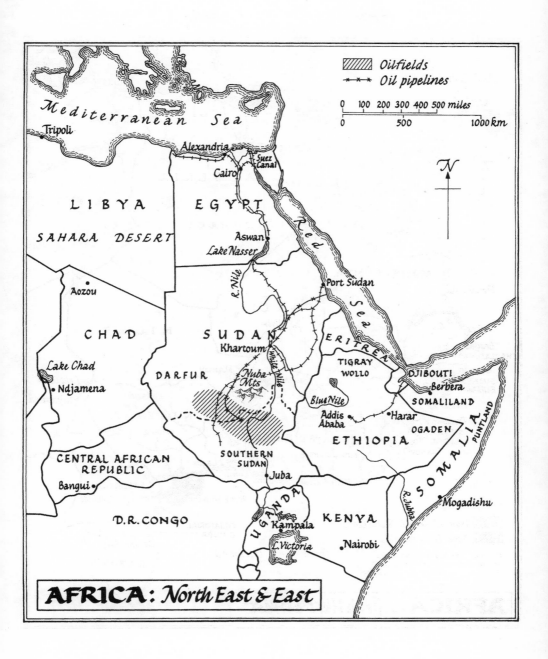

Oilfields

Oil pipelines

0 100 200 300 400 500 miles

0 500 1000 km

N

Mediterranean Sea

Tripoli

Alexandria
Cairo
Suez Canal

LIBYA

EGYPT

SAHARA DESERT

Aswan
Lake Nasser

R. Nile

Red Sea

Port Sudan

Aozou

CHAD

SUDAN

ERITREA

Lake Chad

Ndjamena

DARFUR

Khartoum

Nuba
Mts

White Nile

TIGRAY
WOLLO

DJIBOUTI
Berbera

SOMALILAND

Blue Nile

Addis
Ababa

Harar

OGADEN

CENTRAL AFRICAN
REPUBLIC

Bangui

SOUTHERN
SUDAN

ETHIOPIA

SOMALIA

PUNTLAND

Juba

D.R. CONGO

UGANDA
Kampala

L.Victoria

KENYA

R. Juba

Mogadishu

Nairobi

AFRICA: *North East & East*

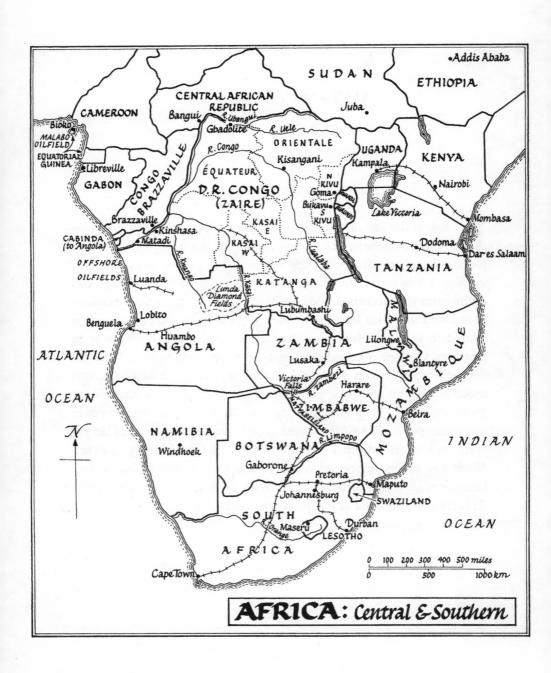

AFRICA: Central & Southern

AUTHOR'S NOTE

In 1964, at the age of twenty-one, I set out from Cairo travelling up the Nile on a journey to central Africa. In many ways, my African journey has continued ever since. As a young reporter on the *Times of Zambia*, I was fortunate enough to witness the surge of energy and enthusiasm that accompanied independence. As a foreign correspondent based in Africa for fifteen years, my experience was more often related to wars, revolution and upheaval. As a research fellow at St Antony's College, Oxford, and as an independent author, I sought deeper perspectives on modern Africa. Along the way I have met with much generosity and goodwill. Many people on many occasions have given me valued help and assistance. To list them here would cover too many pages. But for the innumerable acts of kindness, of hospitality and of friendship I have received, I am profoundly grateful. What has always impressed me over the years is the resilience and humour with which ordinary Africans confront their many adversities. This book is intended as testimony to their fortitude.

Ex Africa semper aliquid novi – *Out of Africa always something new*

Pliny the Elder

INTRODUCTION

During the Scramble for Africa at the end of the nineteenth century, European powers staked claims to virtually the entire continent. At meetings in Berlin, Paris, London and other capitals, European statesmen and diplomats bargained over the separate spheres of interest they intended to establish there. Their knowledge of the vast African hinterland was slight. Hitherto Europeans had known Africa more as a coastline than a continent; their presence had been confined mainly to small, isolated enclaves on the coast used for trading purposes; only in Algeria and in southern Africa had more substantial European settlement taken root.

The maps used to carve up the African continent were mostly inaccurate; large areas were described as *terra incognita*. When marking out the boundaries of their new territories, European negotiators frequently resorted to drawing straight lines on the map, taking little or no account of the myriad of traditional monarchies, chiefdoms and other African societies that existed on the ground. Nearly one half of the new frontiers imposed on Africa were geometric lines, lines of latitude and longitude, other straight lines or arcs of circles. In some cases, African societies were rent apart: the Bakongo were partitioned between French Congo, Belgian Congo and Portuguese Angola; Somaliland was carved up between Britain, Italy and France. In all, the new boundaries cut through some 190 culture groups. In other cases, Europe's new colonial territories enclosed hundreds of diverse and independent groups, with no common history, culture, language or religion. Nigeria, for example, contained as many as 250 ethno-linguistic groups. Officials sent to the Belgian Congo eventually identified six thousand chiefdoms there. Some kingdoms survived intact: the French retained the monarchy in Morocco and in Tunisia; the British ruled Egypt in the name of a dynasty of foreign monarchs founded in 1811 by an Albanian mercenary serving in the Turkish army. Other kingdoms, such as Asante in the Gold Coast (Ghana) and Loziland in Northern Rhodesia (Zambia) were merged into larger colonial units. Kingdoms that had been historically antagonistic to one another, such as Buganda and Bunyoro in Uganda, were linked into the same colony. In the Sahel, new territories were established across the great divide between the desert regions of the Sahara and the belt of tropical forests to the south – Sudan, Chad and Nigeria – throwing together Muslim and non-Muslim peoples in latent hostility.

As the haggling in Europe over African territory continued, land and peoples became little more than pieces on a chessboard. 'We have been giving away mountains and rivers and lakes to each other, only hindered by the small impediment that we never knew exactly where they were,' Britain's prime minister, Lord Salisbury, remarked sardonically to a London audience. Britain traded the North Sea island of Heligoland with the Germans for Zanzibar, and parts of northern Nigeria with the French for fishing rights off Newfoundland. France exchanged parts of Cameroon with Germany in return for German recognition of the French protectorate over Morocco. By the time the Scramble for Africa was over, some 10,000 African polities had been amalgamated into forty European colonies and protectorates.

Thus were born the modern states of Africa.

On the ground, European rule was enforced both by treaty and by conquest. From their enclaves on the coast, officials moved ever deeper into the interior to proclaim the changes agreed in the chancelleries and country mansions of Europe. The task was a prolonged one: French claims extended over about 3.75 million square miles; those of Britain over about 2 million square miles. Many treaties were duly signed. The Basuto king, Moshoeshoe, fearful of the encroachment of white settlers into his mountain terrain in southern Africa, appealed for the protection of Queen Victoria, imploring that his people might be considered 'fleas in the Queen's blanket'. Several of his neighbours – the Swazi and the Tswana chiefdoms of Bechuanaland (Botswana) – followed suit.

But episodes of resistance occurred in parts of nearly every African colony. Some were settled by short, sharp actions. The powerful Muslim emirs of the Sokoto Caliphate, ruling from crenellated palaces of red clay on the edge of the Sahara desert, soon came to terms with a small British expeditionary force sent to incorporate them into northern Nigeria. But other episodes were more prolonged. After occupying the Asante capital, Kumasi, the British were besieged there for four months until reinforcements suppressed resistance. Elsewhere in West Africa, Samori Ture, the founder of a Mandingo empire, waged an eight-year campaign of remarkable tenacity and military skill against the French. In Rhodesia (Zimbabwe) the Ndebele and Shona fought ferociously against white settlers who had seized large areas of land. In Kenya, the Nandi bore the brunt of six punitive expeditions by British forces. In German East Africa (Tanganyika) and South West Africa (Namibia), German administrations inflicted fearful repression to stamp out rebellions, annihilating more than three quarters of the Herero people and half of the Nama people between 1904 and 1908. In Angola Chief Mandume of the Ovambo mustered an army of forty thousand to defy the Portuguese.

Scores of African rulers who resisted colonial rule died in battle or were executed or sent into exile after defeat. Samori of the Mandingo was captured and died in exile two years later; the Asantehene, King Agyeman Prempeh, was deposed and exiled for nearly thirty years; Lobengula of the Ndebele died in flight; Behazin of Dahomey and Cetshwayo of the Zulu were banished from their homelands.

In the concluding act of the partition of Africa, Britain, at the height of its imperial power, set out to take over two independent Boer republics, the Transvaal and the Orange Free State, and incorporate them into the British Empire, assuming that a war of conquest would take at most a matter of months. It turned into a gruelling campaign lasting three years, required nearly half a million imperial troops to finish it, and left a legacy of bitterness and hatred among Afrikaners that endured for generations. Faced with guerrilla warfare for which they were unprepared, British military commanders resorted to scorched-earth tactics, destroying thousands of farmsteads, razing villages to the ground and slaughtering livestock on a massive scale, reducing the Boers to an impoverished people. Women and children were rounded up and placed in what the British called concentration camps, where conditions were so appalling that some 26,000 died there from disease and malnutrition, most of them under the age of sixteen. All this became part of a Boer heritage passed in anger from one generation to the next, spawning a virulent Afrikaner nationalism that eventually took hold of South Africa.

Small-scale revolts against colonial rule continued for many years. The Baoulé of Côte d'Ivoire fought the French village by village until 1911; the Igbo of Nigeria were not fully defeated until 1919; the Jola of Senegal not until the 1920s; the Dinka of southern Sudan not until 1927. In the desert wastelands of Somaliland a fiery Muslim sheikh, Muhammad 'Abdille Hassan, dubbed by his adversaries the 'Mad Mullah', led Dervish warriors in a holy war against the British for twenty years until his death in 1920. Bedouin resistance against Italian rule in Libya ended only in 1931 after nine years of guerrilla warfare. By the 1930s, however, the colonial states of Africa were firmly entrenched; they had, moreover, acquired a legitimacy in the eyes of their inhabitants.

A reshuffle of territory occurred as a result of the First World War. German colonies were shared out among Britain, France, Belgium and the Union of South Africa, a British dominion founded in 1910. Tanganyika was handed over to Britain; South West Africa to South Africa; the tiny territories of Rwanda-Burundi were passed to Belgium; and Togoland and Cameroon were divided up between Britain and France. As a reward for Italian support in the First World War, Britain gave Jubaland to Italy to form part of Italian Somaliland, moving the border of Kenya westwards. But otherwise the boundaries of Africa remained fixed.

Only one African state managed to stave off the onslaught of European occupation during the Scramble: Ethiopia, an ancient Christian kingdom, once ruled by the legendary Prester John. In 1896, when the Italians, with 17,000 European troops, invaded

Ethiopia from their coastal enclave at Massawa on the Red Sea, they were routed by the emperor, Menelik. The Italians were thus forced to confine themselves to occupying Eritrea. Forty years later, however, the Italian dictator, Benito Mussolini, took revenge. Determined to construct an East African empire, he ordered the conquest of Ethiopia, using half a million troops, aerial bombardment and poison gas to accomplish it. After a seven-month long campaign, Italian forces captured the capital, Addis Ababa; the emperor, Haile Selassie, fled into exile in England; and Ethiopia was turned into an Italian province to add to Italian possessions in Eritrea and Somaliland.

Having expended so much effort on acquiring African empires, Europe's colonial powers then lost much of their earlier interest in them. Few parts of Africa offered the prospect of immediate wealth. Colonial governments were concerned above all to make their territories financially self-supporting. Administration was thus kept to a minimum; education was placed in the hands of Christian missionaries; economic activity was left to commercial companies. The main functions of government were limited to maintaining law and order, raising taxation and providing an infrastructure of roads and railways. There seemed to be no need for more rapid development. Colonial rule was expected to last for hundreds of years.

In much of Africa, therefore, the colonial imprint was barely noticeable. Only a thin white line of control existed. In northern Nigeria, Frederick Lugard set out to rule 10 million people with a staff of nine European administrators and a regiment of the West African Frontier Force consisting of 3,000 African troops under the command of European officers. By the late 1930s, following the amalgamation of northern and southern Nigeria into one territory in 1914, the number of colonial administrators for a population of 20 million people was still less than 400. The Sudan Political Service consisted of 140 officials ruling over 9 million people. The whole of French Equatorial Africa in the mid-1930s was run by 206 administrative officers. French West Africa, comprising eight territories with a population of 15 million, was served by only 385 colonial administrators. The whole of British tropical Africa, where 43 million people lived, was governed by 1,200 administrators. Belgium ran the Congo in 1936 with 728 administrators. Scattered across vast stretches of Africa, lone district administrators became virtually absolute rulers of their domain, functioning simultaneously as police chief, judge, tax collector, head of labour recruitment, special agent and meteorological observer. In French Africa they were known as *rois de la brousse* – kings of the bush. A veteran native commissioner in Southern Rhodesia remembered being told that his duties as a district officer were to: 'Get to know your district, and your people. Keep on eye on them, collect tax if possible, but for God's sake, don't worry headquarters.'

With so few men on the ground, colonial governments relied heavily on African chiefs and other functionaries to collaborate with officials and exercise control on their behalf. The British, in particular, favoured a system of 'indirect rule', using African authorities to keep order, collect taxes and supply labour, that involved a minimum of staff and expense. The model for indirect rule was devised by Lugard in northern Nigeria where Fulani emirs had governed in accordance with Islamic traditions of law and discipline stretching back for centuries. Lugard posted British Residents at their courts but allowed the emirs to continue to police, tax and administer justice on their behalf much as before. Similar methods of indirect rule were adopted in Buganda, in Loziland and in other parts of Britain's African empire.

In many cases, however, African chiefs came to constitute no more than a new class of intermediaries paid to transmit government orders. As agents of colonial rule, the role they played was far removed from their traditional position at the apex of authority, balancing many diverse interests. Some chiefs were members of old royal families carefully selected for their willingness to collaborate; others had no traditional legitimacy at all. The *chefs de canton* appointed by the French were effectively administrative officers chosen from the ranks of the more efficient clerks and interpreters in government service. In some cases where chiefs did not exist, as among the acephalous village societies of the Igbo of southern Nigeria, chiefdoms were invented. In other cases, 'traditional' chiefs were left bereft of all functions.

Year by year the new colonies gradually took shape. Railway lines snaking into the interior from the coast reached Lake Victoria in 1901, Katanga in 1910, Kano in northern Nigeria in 1912 and Lake Tanganyika in 1914. New patterns of economic activity were established. African colonies became significant exporters of minerals and agricultural commodities such as groundnuts, palm oil, cotton, coffee, cocoa and sisal. By 1911 the Gold Coast (Ghana) had become the world's leading exporter of cocoa. In the highlands of eastern and southern Africa and along the Mediterranean coast of Algeria and Tunisia, European settlers acquired huge landholdings, establishing the basis of large-scale commercial agriculture. In Kenya the fertile White Highlands were designated for their exclusive use. In 1931 half of the entire land area of Southern Rhodesia was stipulated for the use of white farmers who at the time numbered no more than 2,500. In South Africa some 87 per cent of the total area was declared white land.

Through the efforts of Christian missionaries, literacy and primary education were slowly introduced throughout Africa south of the Sahara. By 1910 about 16,000 European missionaries were stationed there. With government support, a handful of secondary schools were established, becoming the nurseries of new African elites: Achimota College in the Gold Coast; the Ecole Normale William Ponty in Senegal; Makerere in Uganda; Kaduna in Nigeria; Lovedale and Fort Hare in the Eastern Cape of South Africa. North Africa's first Western-style university opened in Cairo in 1909.

The small educated elites that colonial rule produced in the 1920s and 1930s were preoccupied primarily with their own status, seeking to gain for themselves a role in administration in preference to the chiefs whom they regarded as rivals for power. They paid little attention to the welfare of the rural masses. Few espoused nationalist ambitions.

In 1936 Ferhat Abbas, a political activist and writer, who had studied pharmacology at Algiers University, summed up his view on Algerian nationalism in a weekly publication he had founded:

> If I had discovered an Algerian nation, I would be a nationalist and
> I would not blush for it as though it were a crime. Men who die for

a patriotic ideal are daily honoured and regarded. My life is worth
no more than theirs. Yet I will not die for the Algerian homeland,
because such a homeland does not exist. I have not found it. I have
questioned history, I have asked the living and the dead, I have visited the cemeteries; no one has told me of it . . . One does not build
on the wind.

A prominent Northern Nigerian, Abubakar Tafawa Balewa, who was
destined to become the first federal prime minister, remarked in 1948:
'Since 1914 the British Government has been trying to make Nigeria
into one country, but the Nigerian people themselves are historically
different in their backgrounds, in their religious beliefs and customs
and do not show themselves any signs of willingness to unite . . .
Nigerian unity is only a British invention.' In a book published in
1947, the Yoruba leader, Obafemi Awolowo, who dominated Western
Nigerian politics for more than thirty years, wrote: 'Nigeria is not a
nation. It is a mere geographical expression. There are no "Nigerians"
in the same sense as there are "English", "Welsh", or "French". The
word "Nigerian" is merely a distinctive appellation to distinguish
those who live within the boundaries of Nigeria and those who do
not.'
    The Second World War, however, brought profound change to
Africa. Showing a purpose and vigour never seen on the continent
before, colonial governments built airports, expanded harbours, constructed roads and supply depots and demanded ever greater
production of copper, tin, groundnuts – any commodity, in fact,
useful in the war effort. Bases such as Freetown, Takoradi, Mombasa
and Accra became a vital part of the Allied network. Thousands of
African troops were recruited for war service. From British territories,
some 374,000 Africans served in the British army. African units
helped to defeat the Italians in Ethiopia and to restore Emperor Haile
Selassie to his throne. African regiments were sent to India and fought
with distinction in Burma. In India and Burma, African soldiers
learned how nationalist movements there had forced promises of self-
government from the British government even though their
populations were mainly poor and illiterate.

From French Africa some 80,000 African troops were shipped to France to fight the Germans. But for France the war brought the spectacle of a nation not only defeated but divided into opposing camps – Free French and pro-Vichy – which fought each other for the loyalty of the empire. Much of French Africa sided with the Vichy regime. But French Equatorial Africa, responding to General de Gaulle's appeal for help in exile, rallied to the cause of the Free French. For two and a half years, Brazzaville, a small town on the north bank of the Congo river, became the temporary capital of what purported to be the government of France.

The war also threw up decisive shifts in power, away from Europe and its colonial powers. As European influence declined, the emerging superpowers, the United States and the Soviet Union, competed for ascendancy. For different reasons, both were anti-colonial powers. When Winston Churchill and President Roosevelt drew up the Atlantic Charter in 1941, supporting the right of all peoples to choose their own government, Churchill had in mind self-determination only for the conquered nations of Europe, not for British territories. But Roosevelt was adamant that postwar objectives should include self-determination for all colonial peoples. Roosevelt's views about British rule hardened considerably during the war, when, on his way to the 1943 Casablanca conference, he stopped briefly in Gambia. Appalled by the poverty and disease he witnessed there, he wrote to Churchill describing the territory as a 'hell-hole'. About the French he was even more scathing. To the indignation of the French, when Roosevelt subsequently reached Casablanca, he made the point of telling Sultan Mohammed V that the Atlantic Charter applied to Morocco as well as to all other colonies, giving impetus to the idea of Moroccan nationalism.

The aftermath of the war brought frustration and restlessness, in Africa as much as in other parts of the world. African elites took the Atlantic Charter to constitute some form of official encouragement to demand political rights, yet faced obstruction. Ex-servicemen returning home with new ideas and skills, wider experiences and high expectations about the future, many believing they had earned the right to demand some share in the government of their own countries, found few openings. In the towns there was a groundswell of discontent over unemployment, high prices, poor housing, low wages and consumer shortages. In the wartime boom the towns had swollen. Around cities such as Lagos, Accra, Dakar, Nairobi and Léopoldville (Kinshasa), shanty-towns, slums and *bidonvilles* proliferated as a constant flow of migrants arrived from rural areas in search of work. Labour unrest was common. In many African towns there was an air of tension. Tribal disciplines were weakening; old religions were losing ground. The spread of primary school education, particularly in West Africa, created new expectations. A new generation was emerging, ambitious and disgruntled. In Accra and Lagos 'youth' movements and African newspapers blamed every social ill on the authorities, denounced the whole colonial system and demanded self-government. The colonial authorities dismissed these critics as a handful of urban 'agitators' without popular support, confident that local chiefs and hence the bulk of the population remained loyal. Yet a tide of events had begun to flow that would eventually sweep away the African empires that Europe so proudly possessed.

In 1945 there were four independent states in Africa: Egypt, nominally independent, headed by a corrupt monarch, but subject to British political interference and obliged by treaty to accept the presence of British military forces; Ethiopia, a feudal empire newly restored to Haile Selassie after five years of Italian occupation; Liberia, a decaying republic founded on the west coast in 1847 for freed American slaves, the only African state left untouched by European colonial rule, but in reality little more than a fiefdom of the American Firestone Company, which owned its rubber plantations; and the Union of South Africa, the richest state in Africa, holder of the world's largest deposits of gold, given independence in 1910 under white minority rule. The rest were the preserve of European powers, all confident about the importance of their imperial mission.

Britain was the only colonial power even to contemplate the possibility of self-government for its African territories, having established precedents in Asia. It nevertheless expected to hold sway there at least until the end of the twentieth century. In the postwar era, partly for reasons of self-interest, but also because a more enlightened mood about the conduct of colonial affairs prevailed, it embarked on major programmes of development, of agriculture, transport, education and health services. Universities were opened in the Gold Coast, Nigeria, Uganda and Sudan. But with plans for political advancement, the British government was far more cautious. A long apprenticeship was envisaged. There would be no short cuts. Africans needed to be introduced to the business of government with careful preparation, step by step. To give the colonies their independence, said one senior Labour politician, Herbert Morrison, would be 'like giving a child a latch-key, a bank account and a shot-gun'.

Each of Britain's fourteen African territories was governed separately. Each had its own budget, its own laws and public services. Each was under the control of a governor powerful enough in his own domain to ensure that his views there prevailed. Britain's West African territories were the most advanced. In the Gold Coast, Nigeria and Sierra Leone, the black professional elite — lawyers, doctors, teachers and merchants — had been given some role to play in ruling institutions since the end of the nineteenth century. During the Second World War, Africans had been admitted to executive councils advising governors and, in the case of the Gold Coast, a few had been elevated to the senior ranks of the administration. After the war, new constitutions were introduced for the Gold Coast and Nigeria, providing for elections for a handful of members of legislative councils. These constitutions were expected to satisfy political aspirations for the next decade.

In Britain's colonies in east and central Africa, political activity revolved around the demands of white settlers for more political power. In Southern Rhodesia the white population, numbering no more than 33,000, had won internal self-government as far back as 1923. In Kenya they had vigorously pursued the same aim. But Britain, having set the Rhodesian precedent, then stuck to the notion that African interests should be properly protected. In practice this did not always amount to much. Because of their much later contact with Europe, the African populations of east and central Africa were considered to be several generations behind West Africa. The British government took the view that future prosperity there depended largely on encouraging white communities. White immigration soared in the postwar era; in Southern Rhodesia and Kenya the white population doubled. In the White Highlands of Kenya more farming land was made available to former British soldiers, even though African land grievances were mounting. Bolstered by rising numbers and foreign investment, white politicians in Salisbury (Harare) and Nairobi confidently set their sights on establishing new white-led British Dominions in the heart of Africa.

The French, too, embarked on major development programmes in the postwar era and introduced political reform, giving African populations greater representation. Unlike the British, the French regarded their colonies not as separate territories but as part of *la plus grande France*. Political advancement thus meant according Africans a higher number of representatives in the French parliament. Since the nineteenth century, African residents in four coastal towns in Senegal had exercised the right to participate in the election of a representative to the French parliament. The first African deputy elected from Senegal arrived in Paris in 1914 and rapidly rose to the rank of junior minister. In 1945 the number of deputies from French Africa elected to represent African interests was raised to twenty-four. Local assemblies were also established for each territory, and federal assemblies for the two federal regions of French West Africa and French Equatorial Africa. Nevertheless, however much French Africa benefited from political and economic development, the central objective of the '*Union Française*', as the postwar Empire was called, was to bind the colonies tightly to metropolitan France. The links were said to be *indissoluble*.

Of the two other colonial powers, neither Belgium nor Portugal permitted any kind of political activity in their African territories. Belgium regarded the Congo essentially as a valuable piece of real estate that just required good management. The Congo's affairs were directed from Brussels by a small group of Belgians who simply passed down edicts to officials on the ground; neither Belgians living in the Congo nor the Congolese had a vote. Portugal, the poorest country in Europe, remained in the grip of Salazar's dictatorship which dealt ruthlessly with critics and dissidents of any kind. Anyone suspected of agitation in Africa was either jailed or sent to a penal colony or into exile.

The advent of the Cold War introduced a new factor to the African equation. In 1948, after the communist seizure of power in Prague, Western governments became convinced that communists were embarked upon a campaign of world mastery in which African colonies were prime targets. When, a few days later, riots erupted in the Gold Coast, hitherto regarded as Britain's 'model' colony, the governor, Sir Gerald Creasy, who had only recently arrived from London, was quick to detect what he believed was a communist conspiracy. In radio broadcasts, he referred to the danger of a communist takeover and of new forms of terrorism.

A commission of enquiry into the riots found little evidence of communist subversion, but pointed instead to profound political and economic grievances and recommended swift political advancement as the solution. The British government concurred. A new governor, Sir Charles Arden-Clarke, was despatched to the Gold Coast in 1949, with the warning that 'the country is on the edge of revolution' and with instructions to implement a new constitution giving Africans not only increased legislative responsibilities but executive power, in order to avert it.

The new system of government was regarded as being in the nature of 'an experiment', one that could be carefully controlled and monitored, and delayed and halted if something went wrong. The reality, however, was different. One senior British official involved in the Gold Coast experiment later described the process as 'like laying down a track in front of an oncoming express'.

This book follows the fortunes of Africa in modern times, opening in the years that it sped towards independence and encompassing the half-century that has since passed. It focuses in particular on the role of a number of African leaders whose characters and careers had a decisive impact on the fate of their countries. It examines, too, the reasons why, after the euphoria of the independence era, so many hopes and ambitions faded and why the future of Africa came to be spoken of only in pessimistic terms. Although Africa is a continent of great diversity, African states have much in common, not only their origins as colonial territories, but the similar hazards and difficulties they have faced. Indeed, what is so striking about the fifty-year period since independence is the extent to which African states have suffered so many of the same misfortunes.

PART I

1

THE GOLD COAST
EXPERIMENT

At his headquarters at Christiansborg Castle, a seventeenth-century slaving fort from where British governors had ruled the Gold Coast for fifty years, Sir Charles Arden-Clarke awoke on the morning of 9 February 1951 to face the most difficult decision of his career. His problem concerned a 41-year-old prisoner in James Fort in Accra serving a three-year sentence for subversive activities. In the eyes of the colonial authorities, Kwame Nkrumah was a dangerous troublemaker. Official reports referred to him as 'a thorough-going Communist'. He had launched his own political party, the Convention People's Party, in June 1949, demanding 'Self-Government Now' and threatening to wreck Britain's carefully laid plan for constitutional reform if it was not granted.

British officials considered their plan, drawn up in consultation with a committee of distinguished Africans, to be far-reaching enough. It proposed the most advanced political framework for any colony in Africa, offering the Gold Coast what was called 'semi-responsible government'. For the first time in the country's history, there would be a general election, a national assembly with an African majority and a new executive council, consisting largely of African ministers who would run internal affairs.

In devising this plan, British officials expected to find themselves collaborating in government with an elite group of Gold Coast lawyers and businessmen – the intelligentsia, as they were called locally – who had long been pressing for this kind of reform. Known as 'men of property and standing', they had formed in 1947 their own political party, the United Gold Coast Convention, choosing the slogan 'Self-Government in the shortest possible time'. Their leader, Dr Joseph Danquah, was much admired by the British. He had gained a doctorate at London University, qualified as a barrister at the Inner Temple and written a highly regarded book on Akan law and religion. As part of the drive for political advancement, he had come up with the idea of dropping the colonial name of Gold Coast and changing it to Ghana, an African empire that had flourished in West Africa in the eleventh century.

Hoping to build up popular support for their cause, Danquah and his colleagues decided to hire a full-time organiser. One name recommended to them was Kwame Nkrumah. About Nkrumah the lawyers knew virtually nothing. He had been living abroad for twelve years, an itinerant student, invariably penniless but politically ambitious. In the United States he had collected degrees in economics, sociology and philosophy. To earn a living during student vacations, he had worked as a labourer in a soap factory and as a ship's steward; he had even tried selling fish on street corners in Harlem. Moving to London in 1945, he had intended to study law, but soon became caught up in left-wing politics, befriending leading British communists and avidly participating in anti-colonial protests. 'There was nothing to stop you getting on your feet and denouncing the whole British Empire,' he recalled. He abandoned his law studies but found it difficult to make ends meet as a political activist. Short of money, he would spend hours discussing politics in cheap cafés in Camden Town, only occasionally able to afford a cup of tea and a bread roll. When the offer of a job with the United Gold Coast Convention reached him, Nkrumah leapt at the opportunity.

With his left-wing views and ambitious nature, Nkrumah soon fell out with Danquah and his colleagues. Eighteen months after returning to the Gold Coast, he broke away and threw himself with restless energy into the task of turning his new party, the Convention People's

Party (CPP), into a modern political machine, organising youth groups, using flags, banners and slogans and setting up newspapers which vilified the colonial authorities at every opportunity. In fiery speeches across the country, he promised that 'Self-Government – Now' would solve all the grievances and hardships inflicted by colonial rule and bring a new world of opportunity and prosperity. His flamboyant manner and winning smile earned him the nickname of 'Showboy'. To the young, to the homeless 'verandah boys' who slept on the verandahs of the wealthy, he became an idol, a political magician whose performances generated a sense of excitement, of hope, of expectation. His radical appeal spread to trade unionists, ex-servicemen, clerks, petty traders and primary school teachers, to a new generation, frustrated and impatient, seeking a better way of life. To those without money, without position, without property, Nkrumah's call of 'FreeDom' was an offer of salvation. 'Seek ye first the political kingdom,' Nkrumah told them, 'and all else will follow.'

Growing ever bolder, Nkrumah denounced the British plan for constitutional reform as 'bogus and fraudulent' and announced the start of a campaign of 'Positive Action' – strikes, boycotts, agitation and propaganda – intended to force Britain to agree to immediate self-government.

As violence broke out, the governor, Arden-Clarke, declared a state of emergency, imposed curfews and ordered the arrest of Nkrumah and other party leaders. The objective of CPP militants, he claimed, was 'to seize power for themselves by creating chaos'. Nkrumah was brought before a criminal court and convicted on three charges of incitement and sedition and sentenced to a total of three years' imprisonment. As Danquah put it, 'the wolf had been driven away'. In a private family letter, Arden-Clarke wrote: 'Sorry I have been so bad about writing but I have been rather preoccupied in dealing with our local Hitler and his putsch'.

But far from hindering the CPP, the arrest of Nkrumah and his lieutenants turned them into heroes. The 'prison graduate cap' became a possession admired and respected. Those who completed their sentences were welcomed back rapturously and returned to the fray with renewed enthusiasm. As the election scheduled for February

1951 drew near, there was every indication that the CPP would gain a majority of seats.

In his prison cell in James Fort, spending his time making fishing nets and weaving baskets, Nkrumah was at first resigned to missing the election. He discovered, however, that, under the law, any prisoner sentenced to a term of imprisonment not exceeding one year was still entitled to be registered on the electoral roll. Although his total sentence amounted to a period of three years, it consisted of three separate terms of imprisonment of one year each. He duly managed to get his name on the electoral roll, and then announced to the prison authorities that he had decided to stand as a candidate for election.

Nkrumah's participation in the election raised the level of popular excitement even higher. In Christiansborg Castle, Arden-Clarke noticed 'a great wave of enthusiasm' spreading through the CPP. The final result was a victory for the CPP which exceeded even their expectations. Of thirty-eight popularly contested seats, the CPP won thirty-four, Danquah's Convention, three. Nkrumah's personal triumph was similarly spectacular. Standing for an Accra constituency, he won the seat with 20,780 votes out of a total of 23,122. The news was relayed to him by the prison authorities at 4 a.m. on the morning of 9 February.

The dilemma facing Arden-Clarke was whether to release Nkrumah – a convicted criminal – from prison. There was no precedent for releasing him on political grounds. Furthermore, he had threatened disruptive action unless the Gold Coast was granted immediate self-government. He could be as troublesome if set free as if he was kept locked up.

That morning, while shaving, Arden-Clarke made up his mind. 'There were pros and cons aplenty,' he recalled, 'and plenty of pressures being applied. It was, however, obvious that the CPP would refuse to cooperate in working the Constitution without their leader. Nkrumah and his party had the mass of the people behind them and there was no other party with appreciable public support to which one could turn. Without Nkrumah, the Constitution would be still-born and if nothing came of all the hopes, aspirations and concrete proposals for a greater measure of self-government, there would no longer be any faith in the good intentions of the British government and the Gold Coast would be plunged into disorder, violence and bloodshed.'

So Arden-Clarke ordered his release, describing it as 'an act of grace'. After fourteen months' imprisonment, Nkrumah walked out of James Fort at midday on 12 February to a tumultuous welcome from his supporters and an invitation to pay a call on the governor the following morning at Christiansborg Castle.

The castle was an imposing building that Nkrumah was to come to know well. Built on a rocky promontory on the outskirts of Accra, with stone imported from Denmark as ballast in incoming slave ships, its foundations were continually pounded by the roaring surf. Salt moisture seeped endlessly into its deep dungeons, once filled with slaves awaiting their fate across the Atlantic. Its high walls were painted a dazzling white; tall palm trees leant against the crenellated battlements; and the gardens were ablaze with cannas – maroon, salmon-pink, scarlet and pale-yellow.

Walking into the courtyard, Nkrumah was not sure of what to expect. He had never met Arden-Clarke and was suspicious of him. Arden-Clarke was equally wary. 'We knew each other only by reputation, and my reputation was, I think, as obnoxious to him as his was to me,' Arden-Clarke remembered. 'That meeting was redolent of mutual suspicion and mistrust. We were like two dogs meeting for the first time, sniffing around each other with hackles raised trying to decide whether to bite or to wag our tails.'

They rapidly got down to business and concluded their meeting cordially enough. Nkrumah left Christiansborg Castle, having been asked to form a government. He had made the leap from convict to prime minister in less than a day. 'As I walked down the steps it was as if the whole thing had been a dream, that I was stepping down from the clouds and that I would soon wake up and find myself squatting on the prison floor eating a bowl of maize porridge.'

It was to become a familiar experience for British governors in Africa to have to come to terms with nationalist politicians whom they had previously regarded as extremist agitators. But, at the time, the election victory of Nkrumah, a man who described himself as a 'Marxian Socialist' implacably opposed to imperialism and who was bent on securing full self-government, sent a shockwave across Africa, causing alarm in some quarters, inspiring awe in others.

In British eyes, however, the Gold Coast had always stood out as a special case. It had advantages of wealth and attainment unrivalled in tropical Africa. As the world's leading producer of cocoa for forty years, it possessed a large and prosperous farming community. Its education system was the most advanced, and its reservoir of trained personnel the largest, of any African colony. The country was relatively homogenous, seemingly free of ethnic and religious tension; half of the population was of Akan origin and spoke related dialects. British officials therefore considered the Gold Coast to be an exception from other territories and adapted themselves accordingly.

At their second meeting at Christiansborg Castle, Arden-Clarke and Nkrumah began to establish a measure of trust. 'Although much was left unsaid,' recalled Arden-Clarke, 'we both understood that there were two men who could break the Constitution and the whole experiment in five minutes – Nkrumah and I – and that that would advantage no one. We believed that we had the same objective, the attainment of full self-government for the country, and though we might differ as to the how and the when – and we did differ – we both felt, I think, that it would be in the best interests of the country and of ourselves if we worked with and not against each other.'

Though new to the business of government, Nkrumah constantly pressed for faster change and for more power. The new constitution, which he had been obliged to accept, left control of the police, the judiciary, finance, defence and external affairs in the hands of the governor and his senior officials; the governor, moreover, was entitled to preside over cabinet meetings and to veto or enforce legislation as he deemed fit. Impatient with this 'period of probation', Nkrumah introduced a motion in parliament in July 1953 demanding full self-government without delay. 'We prefer self-government with danger to servitude in tranquillity,' he declared. Though the British government had strong misgivings about the pace of change, the following year it granted the Gold Coast a new constitution providing for full internal self-government under an all-African cabinet.

With his flair for publicity, Nkrumah was forever in the limelight, dominating the headlines. His life was a whirlwind of meetings, speeches, tours and rallies. Party newspapers built up the image of a man of supernatural powers, a prophet, a new Moses who would lead his people towards the cherished land of independence. 'Man of Destiny, Star of Africa,' proclaimed the *Evening News* on 19 June 1954. 'Hope of Millions of down-trodden Blacks, Deliverer of Ghana, Iron Boy, Great Leader of Street Boys.' Ordinary people came to regard him as a messiah capable of performing miracles. He was venerated in hymns and prayers; supporters recited phrases like, 'I believe in Kwame Nkrumah'. From early morning, queues would form outside his home, people seeking advice on anything from marital disputes to sickness, infertility, job recommendations, financial assistance and settlement of debts. No matter how busy he was, Nkrumah always endeavoured to find time for them.

He possessed a magnetism evident to all who encountered him. A lithe figure of medium height and slim build, with a prominent forehead, receding hairline and soulful eyes, he exuded vitality. An American writer, John Gunther, who met him at a dinner given by Arden-Clarke at Christiansborg Castle in July 1953, was struck by his charisma. Nkrumah was wearing national costume: a Roman-like toga in silk *kente* cloth, with the left arm and shoulder left bare. 'His movements and gestures have power, ease and an almost animal-like magnetism,' wrote Gunther. 'He neither struts nor shows exaggerated reserve.'

His whole life was dominated by politics. A bachelor, he took no interest in sport, or food, or personal comfort. Baptised a Catholic, he had once seriously considered a career as a Jesuit priest and was still attracted by the sense of single-minded purpose it involved. He did not smoke or drink. When Gunther asked him what he did for relaxation, he replied: 'Work.' He was fond of music, both classical and the local dance music called highlife. When a friend suggested he should listen more often to classical music to help him relax, he promptly ordered two hundred records. But the only one he listened to, over and over again, was the 'Hallelujah Chorus' from *The Messiah*.

Behind all the hurly-burly, Nkrumah was a lonely figure, distrust-ful of his close colleagues, rarely confiding in them. He enjoyed the company of women, but feared intimacy and declared he had no time to get married. One of the most trusting relationships he formed was with the governor's private secretary, Erica Powell, an Englishwoman who had arrived in the Gold Coast in 1952. When he first invited her to dinner at his home, Powell consulted Arden-Clarke who encour-aged her to accept. 'You know, Erica,' said Arden-Clarke, 'Nkrumah is a very lonely man. A *very* lonely man.'

Nkrumah often telephoned her late at night. 'Sometimes I listened while he became more and more drowsy and slurred his speech,' she recalled in her memoirs. 'But if I suggested hanging up he would immediately come to life.' He arrived at her flat unexpectedly one evening, complaining about the crowd of people hanging around his own home and promptly fell asleep. She encouraged him to find a quieter residence, and also coaxed him into taking an interest in food and personal fitness.

In 1955 she joined his staff as his private secretary. The gossip in Accra at the time was that she was his mistress but she always denied it. In her memoirs she portrays Nkrumah as moody, erratic, impatient and volatile, but also charming and considerate when it suited him. 'The trouble was that his moods could change so rapidly,' she wrote. Despite all the frustrations and the exhausting pace of his schedule, she remained a key figure in his entourage, working closely with him for more than ten years. Nkrumah once confided to her that she was the only person on whom he could rely for unbiased advice.

After winning the 1954 election, Nkrumah seemed set to make rapid progress towards independence. But he encountered unexpected resistance centred on his conduct of government. In the final stages of colonial rule, the Gold Coast, once a model colony, was riven by such bitterness, division and violence that it appeared in danger of break-ing up.

At the core of the crisis was cocoa money. To protect cocoa farm-ers from price fluctuations, the colonial authorities had established a

Cocoa Marketing Board (CMB) which each year fixed a guaranteed price for farmers and acted as the sole buyer, grader, seller and exporter of cocoa. Once in office, Nkrumah instructed the CMB to keep the price as low as possible, aiming to raise funds for development projects. But the CMB soon became notorious for corruption and mismanagement; it was regularly exploited to distribute credit, contracts, commissions, licences and jobs to CPP supporters. An official investigation revealed that the CPP used a CMB subsidiary to enrich the party's coffers, to coerce farmers into joining the party and to control petty commerce.

Soon after the 1954 election, Nkrumah announced that the price paid to farmers would be fixed for a period of four years at a level less than one-third of ruling world prices. This decision provoked a surge of anger across Asante, the central forest region where half of the country's cocoa crop was grown. Not only farmers but cocoa traders, merchants and businessmen based in the Asante capital, Kumasi, resented the loss of income. A new opposition party, the National Liberation Movement (NLM), sprang up, proclaiming to defend Asante interests and culture against a central government it portrayed as corrupt, dictatorial and bent on undermining the beliefs and customs of the Asante people. With the blessing of the Asante paramount chiefs and backed by fervent support in the Asante heartland, the NLM demanded a federal constitution prior to independence, giving Asante and other areas that wanted it a substantial measure of local autonomy.

Nkrumah saw the issue as a struggle between a modern democratic government and the feudal power of traditional chiefs trying to protect the old order. But he misjudged the extent of popular support for Asante institutions. As the NLM and Nkrumah's CPP struggled for ascendancy, violent disturbances broke out. A bomb attack was made on Nkrumah's house in Accra. Alarmed by the disorders, the British government refused to set a date for independence and eventually insisted on resolving the issue by calling another general election. At the polls in July 1956, Nkrumah's CPP won an outright majority, 72 of 104 seats, though only 57 per cent of the votes cast. While the CPP received 398,000 votes, the opposition tally was

299,000 votes. Satisfied with the result, Britain finally pronounced a date for independence: 6 March 1957.

It was a date that marked the beginning of a new era for Africa. The advent of independence for Ghana was seen as a portent watched and admired around the world. No other event in Africa had previously attracted such attention. Nor was there an occasion when the feeling of euphoria was so strong.

Messages of congratulations came from an array of world leaders, from Eisenhower, Bulganin, Nehru and Zhou En-lai. Delegations from fifty-six countries arrived, exuding warmth and goodwill. From Britain, representing Queen Elizabeth, came her aunt, the Duchess of Kent; the Chinese sent a general in a turquoise blue uniform; the Russians, a junior minister, with a fistful of invitations to Moscow; the South Africans, an all-white delegation. But the most enthusiastic visitor was Richard Nixon, then the United States vice-president. From the moment he touched down in Accra, he rushed about shaking hands, hugging paramount chiefs, fondling black babies and posing for photographs. It was not always to good effect. Surrounded by a crowd of Ghanaians at an official ceremony, he slapped one man on the shoulder and asked him how it felt to be free. 'I wouldn't know, sir,' replied the man. 'I'm from Alabama.'

The celebrations lasted for six days. There were sailing regattas, race meetings, garden parties, church services, a Miss Ghana competition and a number of hidden dramas. The prime minister's new residence, where a visiting dignitary was due to stay, was discovered at the last minute to contain numerous faults. A lavatory cistern on the first floor overflowed, flooding the prime minister's study below, saturating the new carpet and damaging hundreds of books lying on it, waiting to be sorted. Just before a reception at the new State House building was due to begin, all the stewards were found to be drunk, sprawled across the kitchen floor. A few managed to stagger to their feet and weaved about dreamily carrying trays at a dangerous angle.

At the centre of all the festivities, Nkrumah remained an engaging host, alert and dynamic even though he managed to snatch little sleep. When he first learned that he was expected to lead the dancing with the Duchess of Kent at the State Ball, he groaned, complaining that he could only dance the highlife. But Louis Armstrong's wife, Lucille, came to the rescue, teaching him the basic steps of the waltz, the fox-trot and the quickstep, and on the night Nkrumah managed a creditable performance.

At midnight on 6 March as crowds danced and sang in Parliament Square, the Union flag was lowered and the new flag of Ghana, red, green and gold, was hoisted in its place. Wearing a convict's white skull cap embroidered on the front with the letters 'PG' – his 'prison graduate' badge – Nkrumah was borne from parliament on the shoulders of his colleagues to the nearby polo ground where a small wooden platform had been erected. Under the glare of floodlights, he performed an impromptu dance and then, with tears streaming down his face, he spoke of the moment of freedom that had arrived. 'Today, from now on, there is a new African in the world,' he declared.

No other African state was launched with so much promise for the future. Ghana embarked on independence as one of the richest tropical countries in the world, with an efficient civil service, an impartial judiciary and a prosperous middle class. Its parliament was well established, with able politicians in both government and opposition. The prime minister, himself, then only forty-seven years old, was regarded as a leader of outstanding ability, popularly elected, with six years of experience of running a government. The country's economic prospects were equally propitious. Not only was Ghana the world's leading producer of cocoa, with huge foreign currency reserves built up during the 1950s cocoa boom, but it possessed gold, timber and bauxite.

As if to mark the capture of the citadel of colonial power, Nkrumah chose Christiansborg Castle as his official residence. It was a strange decision. Nkrumah's domestic staff were convinced the place was haunted by ghosts from its past as a slaving fort and refused to stay there overnight. Arden-Clarke, when he was governor, was kept awake by a persistent knocking but could find no cause for it and declined to sleep in the same room again. Nkrumah had his own experiences. Soon after moving into the castle, he was awakened one night by a piercing yelp from his devoted Alsatian which normally slept in a corner of his bedroom. When he turned on the light, the dog was trembling, its fur on end. Despite coaxing, the dog refused to

set foot in the room again. But even more striking about Nkrumah's
decision to move to the castle was the distance it put him from people.
For Christiansborg was a place of solitude and remoteness, where the
most familiar sound was the insistent roar of the surf pounding against
its ancient walls.

With his customary energy, Nkrumah soon made his mark in international circles. In June 1957 he attended the Commonwealth
conference in London, creating a favourable impression among fellow
prime ministers. He was particularly thrilled at the prospect of meeting Queen Elizabeth at Buckingham Palace – 'agog with excitement',
according to Erica Powell. His staff explained that normally an audience would last about half an hour. 'It's no good talking to me about
time, you know it means nothing to me,' he retorted. 'If I am bored
I shall want to leave after two minutes. If I'm interested I may stay an
hour or two without realising it.' Horrified, his staff advised that the
Queen would give some kind of indication when the audience was at
an end.

The following morning he returned from the palace, exhilarated by
the experience. 'She's an amazing woman!' he declared. 'So small and
so simple and modest.'

'How long did you stay?' his staff asked eagerly.

'My goodness! It was terrible! We were talking so much and it was
all so interesting for me that when I at last looked at my watch I saw
that I had been there an hour! I exclaimed: "Oh! Is that really the
time?" And I got worried in case I might not have noticed the sign
that she may have made for me to leave. Anyhow, I looked for my
stick, but I couldn't see it. Then the Queen asked me if I had lost
something, and I said: "Yes, my stick." And can you imagine what she
did? She actually got down on her knees to help me find it. It had
fallen at the back of my chair. I felt so ashamed of myself.'

Queen Elizabeth was as fascinated by Nkrumah as he was by her.
On a subsequent occasion, he was invited as her personal guest to the
royal residence at Balmoral, a rare favour for a foreign head of government. There, after a walk on the moors to watch Prince Philip
shooting grouse, he was affirmed a member of 'Her Majesty's Most
Honourable Privy Council'. The picture taken of him with the

Queen at Balmoral became a favourite possession. He ordered thousands of copies to be printed.

Nkrumah's main ambitions, however, focused on Africa. He was determined to turn Accra into a centre of African liberation, to provide a base from which nationalist leaders from colonial Africa could draw support and encouragement. 'Our independence is meaningless unless it is linked up with the total liberation of the African continent,' he proclaimed before the vast crowds assembled at the polo ground on Independence Day.

In 1958 he brought together an array of political parties, trade unions and student groups from across the continent with the aim of coordinating 'the African non-violent revolution'. Gathered in State House amid the Italian marble, silks, brocades and crystal chandeliers, some three hundred African representatives attended the All-African People's Conference. Many were later to achieve prominence: Julius Nyerere came from Tanganyika (Tanzania); Joshua Nkomo from Southern Rhodesia (Zimbabwe); Kenneth Kaunda from Northern Rhodesia (Zambia); Hastings Banda from Nyasaland (Malawi); Patrice Lumumba from the Belgian Congo; Amilcar Cabral from Portuguese Guinea; Holden Roberto from Angola. The young Kenyan trade unionist Tom Mboya was chosen as the conference chairman.

For a week they drew in the intoxicating draught of revolutionary rhetoric and departed eager for the fray. In his concluding speech to the conference, Tom Mboya reflected the belligerent mood. The colonial powers, he said, should now reverse the Scramble for Africa. 'Your time is past,' he declared. 'Africa must be free. Scram from Africa.'

2

REVOLT ON THE NILE

On a sultry night in July 1952, King Farouk of Egypt was enjoying one of his habitual gambling sessions with rich socialites in the summer coastal resort of Alexandria when he was urgently called away to the telephone. The call was from his prime minister, Hussein Sirry, warning that a small group of dissident officers within the army was planning a coup d'état. When told of the identity of the plotters, Farouk laughed. 'A bunch of pimps,' he retorted, and went back to the gaming tables.

Arrogant, vain and pampered from birth, Farouk was supremely confident of the loyalty of his generals, of his control of the army and his position as monarch. He was one of the richest men in the world, famous for his spending sprees, gargantuan appetite and endless procession of mistresses. His fortune included the largest landholding in Egypt, four palaces, two yachts, thirteen private aircraft, two hundred cars and a huge collection of pornographic artefacts. At the age of thirty-two he had become an inveterate playboy, obese and balding, addicted to pleasure-seeking.

To escape from the heat and hubbub of Cairo, he had decamped with his family and household staff to the Montazah palace on the beachfront at Alexandria, 125 miles away, intending to stay there for the summer. The problems of government seemed intractable. Time and again he had shuffled prime ministers and cabinets. But Cairo remained in ferment, a cauldron of conspiracy, assassination, rioting and press agitation, where communists, nationalists, royalists and Muslim extremists competed for ascendancy. In rural areas there were gusts of violence as impoverished peasants rebelled against feudal landowners. Though Farouk was oblivious to it, the old order was on the verge of collapse.

On the morning after receiving the telephone warning, Farouk installed a new prime minister, appointed his brother-in-law as minister of war, telling him to round up the conspirators, and then adjourned to the beach. At army headquarters in Cairo on the evening of 22 July, his generals duly assembled to prepare a plan of action.

Tipped off that moves against them were imminent, the conspirators advanced their own plans to strike. For three years they had plotted in secret, forming a clandestine network within the army called the Society of Free Officers – *Dhobat el-Ahrar* – determined to establish a new political order. Initially, their principal aim had been to rid Egypt of Britain's military presence. But they had since become convinced of the need to remove Farouk and his entourage as well. Farouk had come to represent the old imperialism as much as the British did.

Their leader, Colonel Gamal Abdel Nasser, was a 34-year-old war hero from the 1948 Arab–Israeli conflict over Palestine, deeply embittered, like his colleagues, by the incompetence and corruption of Farouk's high command which he blamed for Egypt's humiliating defeat. A taciturn, studious officer, with a taste for intrigue and dissimulation, secretive by nature and driven by fierce personal ambition, he was the mastermind behind the Free Officers' conspiracy, both its theoretician and organiser, though he preferred to operate in obscurity.

Their numbers were few. Organised by Nasser into cells of four or five members, unknown to each other, the Free Officers comprised no more than a hundred men in all. Though their identity remained secret, they announced their existence in a series of underground leaflets denouncing Farouk's regime, pushing them under the doors of officers' private houses or sending them through the mail. Many were written or edited by Nasser himself.

Nasser also tried his hand at assassination. On 9 January 1952, together with two fellow officers, he ambushed the car of the army's corrupt chief of staff, General Hussein Sirri Amer, outside his house. But he found the experience distasteful. 'The sound of shots, followed immediately by the piercing cries of women, the whimpering of a child, shouts for help, haunted me all the way to my bed and kept me awake all night,' he wrote in his *Philosophy of the Revolution*. 'A kind of remorse filled my heart . . . I stammered, "If only he does not die." By dawn I had arrived at the point where I prayed for the life of the man I had tried to kill – how great was my joy when, feverishly searching the morning newspaper, I discovered that the man had not succumbed.'

The date that Nasser and his executive committee had originally set for the coup was in August 1952. Their aims were ambitious but vague. The 'six principles' they drew up included: 'the liquidation of colonialism and the Egyptian traitors who supported it'; 'the liquidation of feudalism'; 'an end to the domination of power by capital'; the formation of 'a powerful popular army'; and the need to establish 'social equality' and 'a healthy domestic life'. In a final underground leaflet which they distributed just before the coup, the Free Officers declared: 'The army's task is to win the country's independence.' What Nasser was determined to ensure above all was that the Free Officers should both lead and control the revolution.

When they learned Farouk's generals were meeting at army headquarters, the Free Officers decided to attack the building while they were there. 'It will save us time and trouble,' said Nasser. 'We can take them all together, instead of one by one at their homes.'

Nasser drove around Cairo in a small black Austin car, dressed in civilian clothes, moving from unit to unit to give them instructions. At one point he was stopped by a traffic policeman for having defective lights. In another incident he was almost shot by mistake by troops from his own side who failed to recognise him.

With revolvers in hand, Nasser and his companions stormed into army headquarters. After token resistance the generals surrendered. By the early hours of 23 July the Free Officers were in control of the radio station, the telegraph office, police posts and government buildings. An armoured convoy was despatched to block the road from the Canal Zone in case British troops there tried to intervene on behalf of Farouk. In a radio broadcast at 7 a.m., the Free Officers issued their first communiqué, announcing that the army had seized power in order to purge itself and the country of 'traitors and weaklings'. The announcement was made in the name of General Mohammed Neguib, a distinguished 54-year-old war hero, benign-looking, pipe-smoking and affable, who had been drawn into the conspiracy at a late stage and who was used by the Free Officers as a respectable figurehead.

The fate of Farouk now became a matter of fierce debate among the coup leaders. Some wanted his execution; others favoured exile. Nasser and Neguib voted in favour of exile, tipping the balance. In a note Nasser wrote to his colleagues at the time, he gave his reasons:

> The liberation movement should get rid of Farouk as quickly as possible in order to deal with what is more important – namely, the need to purge the country of the corruption that Farouk will leave behind him. We must pave the way towards a new era in which the people will enjoy their sovereign rights and live in dignity. Justice is one of our objectives. We cannot execute Farouk without a trial. Neither can we afford to keep him in jail and pre-occupy ourselves with the rights and wrongs of his case at the risk of neglecting the other purposes of the revolution. Let us spare Farouk and send him into exile. History will sentence him to death.

So Farouk's life was spared. On 26 July, with his palaces in Alexandria surrounded by troops, the king signed an act of abdication and prepared for exile. Dressed in an admiral's uniform, he boarded the royal yacht *Mahroussa* with members of his family, taking with him sixty-six trunks hastily packed with gold, jewellery and priceless objects, heading for the fleshpots of Europe.

★

In historical terms, the changes wrought by the army coup in 1952 were dramatic. It not only brought an end to the 140-year-old Turkish dynasty founded by Farouk's great-great-grandfather Mohammed Ali; it meant that for the first time since the Persian conquest twenty-five centuries before Egypt was ruled by native Egyptians.

But apart from Neguib, little was known about the secretive group of officers that had carried out the coup. They usually met at night in what had been Farouk's yacht house on an island in the Nile, keeping their identities hidden. Nor did they have any detailed plan of what was to follow.

They started by implementing measured reforms. They rounded up Farouk's palace clique, abolished the old Ottoman titles of Pasha and Bey, and initiated a modest land reform programme, limiting the holdings of the rich elite who owned more than half of all cultivable land. They claimed they wanted no more than a supervisory role for themselves over government, holding out the prospect of parliamentary elections once political parties had purged their ranks of corrupt aristocrats.

After six months in power, however, the Free Officers – now calling themselves the Revolutionary Command Council (RCC) – began to consolidate their own control, laying the foundations for an army dictatorship, excluding and eliminating all rivals along the way. They abolished the old constitution and banned political parties, confiscating their funds and other assets. Hundreds of army officers, career diplomats, government officials, university professors and politicians connected to the Farouk era were removed. Trade unions, student organisations, the media, professional syndicates and religious organisations were similarly purged of opposition elements. Rival groups such as communists, the Muslim Brotherhood and ultra-nationalist factions were ruthlessly suppressed. In June 1953 the RCC abolished the monarchy and proclaimed a republic, signifying their intention to hold power permanently. In an attempt to mobilise popular support, they launched their own political movement, the Liberation Rally. Emerging from the shadows, Colonel Nasser was nominated as its secretary-general.

Nasser also moved decisively to obtain Britain's withdrawal both from the Canal Zone and from neighbouring Sudan. Since 1899 Sudan had been run nominally as a condominium, with control shared jointly by Britain and Egypt. In practice it had been ruled by Britain alone. But the Egyptians had constantly pressed their own claims to full sovereignty. For much of the nineteenth century it had been part of their own empire, conquered by Mohammed Ali's forces in 1819. Its capital, Khartoum, lying at the confluence of the Blue Nile and the White Nile, had originally been founded as an Egyptian army outpost. In Cairo the idea of the 'unity of the Nile Valley', encompassing both Egypt and Sudan, was still a prominent objective. Many Egyptians regarded control of the Nile, on which the Egyptian economy was largely based, to be imperative. In a fanciful gesture in 1951, designed to put pressure on Britain, King Farouk had proclaimed himself 'King of Sudan'.

Britain, however, aware of the rising tide of Sudanese nationalism, insisted on the right of the Sudanese to self-determination. For several years the issue of Sudan's future remained at an impasse. The Free Officers, when planning their coup, were just as adamant as other Egyptian groups in demanding the unity of the Nile Valley.

Once in power, however, Nasser accepted the need for self-determination, fully expecting that, when the time came, the Sudanese would favour linking up with Egypt. Left with little room for manoeuvre, Britain was obliged to reach a swift agreement. On 12 February 1953 Sudan was set on the road to independence, scheduled for 1956 after a three-year transitional period. The timing was determined not by any notion of Sudan's 'readiness' for independence but by the exigencies of Britain's Middle East policy.

There were inherent dangers in such a pace of change. Sudan was a country of two halves, governed for most of the colonial era by two separate British administrations, one which dealt with the relatively advanced north, the other with the remote and backward provinces of the south. The two halves were different in every way: the north was hot, dry, partly desert, inhabited largely by Arabic-speaking Muslims and containing three-quarters of the country's population; the south was green, fertile, with a high rainfall, populated by diverse black tribes, speaking a multitude of languages, adhering mostly to traditional religions but including a small Christian minority which had graduated from mission schools.

What links of history there were between the north and the south provided a source of friction. In the nineteenth century northern traders had plundered the south in search of slaves and ivory. Tales of the slave trade, passed from one generation to the next in the south, sustained a legacy of bitterness and hatred towards northerners which still endured. Northerners, meanwhile, tended to treat southerners as contemptuously as they had done in the past, referring to them as *abid* – slaves.

Only in 1946, when ample time still seemed to be available, did the British begin the process of integration, hoping that the north and the south would eventually form an equal partnership. From the outset, however, southern politicians expressed fears that northerners, because of their greater experience and sophistication, would soon dominate and exploit the south. The south was ill-prepared for self-government. There were no organised political parties there until 1953, nor any sense of national consciousness uniting its disparate tribes. When negotiations over independence for Sudan were conducted in 1953, southerners were neither consulted nor represented. While Sudan's march towards independence in 1956 was greeted with jubilation by northerners, among southerners it precipitated alarm and apprehension.

Negotiations over Britain's withdrawal from the Canal Zone were more protracted. To the British, it was a symbol of their imperial might, the largest overseas military base in the world, dominating the crossroads of Europe, Asia and Africa, a veritable nexus of empire where the Union flag still flew. A huge complex of dockyards, airfields, warehouses and barracks, it stretched along the Suez Canal for two-thirds of its length, and covered more than 9,000 square miles. Some 80,000 British troops were stationed there. In the postwar era Britain's military chiefs regarded the Canal Zone as an indispensable part of their global interests.

To the Egyptians, Britain's presence there was an intolerable affront to national sovereignty. The area included three major cities – Port

Said, Ismailia and Suez. One million Egyptians lived there. Moreover, under the terms of a 1936 treaty, the British were supposed to restrict their Suez garrison to no more than 10,000 men. The Egyptians used Britain's occupation there as a pretext for incessant anti-British agitation; guerrilla raids in the Canal Zone, aided and abetted by the authorities in Cairo, were a common occurrence. 'We cannot feel free and sovereign until they go,' said Nasser.

By the early 1950s, British politicians had come to doubt the value of retaining a military base in such hostile territory. Of the total garrison, 50,000 troops were needed to protect the 30,000 who actually ran the base. Furthermore, anti-British agitation in Egypt undermined Britain's attempts to exert influence elsewhere in the Arab world.

In October 1954 Britain and Egypt reached a compromise. Britain agreed to withdraw all British troops from the Canal Zone by 18 June 1956; while Egypt accepted that British civilian technicians could remain on the base for a period of seven years to operate ordnance depots and army workshops retained for Britain's use; the base was thus to be shared. Nasser further agreed to a 'reactivation' clause, entitling Britain to return to the base in the event of global hostilities in the region involving the Soviet Union or some other 'outside power'.

Nasser took an intense interest in the details of the agreement, as Anthony Nutting, the British minister leading the negotiations, recalled :

> On one occasion, after he had demanded that all the houses then occupied by British generals should be reserved for Egyptian senior officers, I asked rather testily where our technicians were expected to live. Nasser, kneeling on the floor beside me and poring over a map of the base, pointed to a vacant lot. 'Thank you for nothing,' I said. 'That happens to be the football field.' He then tried again, indicating an area with a building on it. 'And that,' I said, 'is the Methodist Church.' Nasser collapsed with laughter and it was some time before we got back to serious discussions.

Britain's agreement to withdraw from its Suez base represented a milestone in Egypt's history. For the first time since 1882, Egypt would have no British garrison on its territory. And for the first time in twenty-five centuries, it would have complete national sovereignty. Nasser was naturally jubilant. 'A dark page in Anglo-Egyptian relations has been turned,' he declared. 'Another page is now being written. Great Britain's prestige and position in the Middle East have been reinforced and now there remains virtually no reason why Great Britain and Egypt cannot work together in a constructive fashion.' Yet within two years, Nasser and Britain were to become protagonists in the biggest international crisis since the Second World War.

By the end of 1954, after a protracted internal struggle within the army, Nasser had emerged in sole control of the government, ousting Neguib and opening the way for himself to rule as president under a new constitution which endowed him with massive powers. A referendum in which he was the only candidate gave him 99.8 per cent of the vote. To make sure that any sign of opposition was snuffed out, he made use of an increasingly repressive security and intelligence service. By 1955 more than 3,000 political prisoners were held in prisons and concentration camps.

He became ever more ambitious, determined to modernise Egypt's economy through industrialisation and to turn Egypt into a regional power. His grandest scheme was to construct a new dam at Aswan that would regulate the flow of the Nile throughout the year, release a million acres for reclamation, provide a source of irrigation and generate electricity. At three miles long, the Aswan High Dam was to be one of the largest engineering projects in the world. To ensure success, Nasser needed foreign funds and expertise. In the initial stages he was encouraged by signs that both the United States and Britain might support the scheme.

Nasser's regional ambitions, however, drew him into increasing conflict with the West. Nasser saw himself as the champion of Arab unity and African liberation, intent on freeing the region from foreign influence. Cairo Radio broadcasts were used incessantly as a weapon to spread the message, urging Arabs to 'throw off the yoke of foreign occupation'. Nasser's targets were not solely 'imperialist' powers but 'reactionary regimes' in the Arab world which acted on their behalf.

When Britain asked for Egyptian cooperation in setting up a Western-controlled Middle East defence pact to oppose the Soviet Union, Nasser refused to join, proposing instead an Arab defence pact, with no outside powers involved. In place of Western links, he advocated a 'non-aligned' course in foreign policy, avoiding entanglements in the Cold War. But Britain and the United States regarded his form of neutralism as no more than a cloak for anti-Western hostility, in effect a shift towards the Soviet Union. Britain retaliated by restricting its supply of arms to Egypt.

The sequence of events that led eventually to war started in March 1955 when Israeli forces launched a sudden strike on three Egyptian army camps in the Gaza Strip, blowing up their headquarters building there. Nasser saw the attack as part of a concerted Western conspiracy to destroy his government. From that moment on, his overriding priority became to rearm the ill-equipped Egyptian army, acquiring weapons from whatever sources were available. When the West turned him down, Nasser approached the Soviet Union, signing a deal for fighter aircraft, bombers and tanks paid for in exchange for Egyptian cotton. News of the deal produced a shockwave in London and Washington. Both condemned Nasser for giving the Russians an opportunity to establish themselves in the Middle East theatre, an area hitherto regarded as a preserve of Western influence. Nasser insisted that, having just got rid of the British, he had no intention of allowing the Russians to gain a foothold. But suspicions of his intentions remained high.

As nationalist demonstrations against 'Western imperialism' gathered momentum in the Arab world, the British government cast Nasser as the mastermind seeking to drive out British influence from the Middle East altogether. In March 1956, when King Hussein of Jordan suddenly dismissed Sir John Glubb, the British commander of his army, Britain's prime minister, Anthony Eden, was convinced it was Nasser's handiwork, spurning all the evidence that the young king had decided the issue on his own account. Eden, in ill health, physically exhausted and facing domestic political difficulties, became obsessed with Nasser. His friend Anthony Nutting was present in Downing Street when Eden heard the news of Glubb's dismissal.

'Eden's reaction to Glubb's dismissal was violent,' Nutting recalled. 'He blamed Nasser and he decided that the world just wasn't big enough to hold both of them. One had to go. He declared that night a personal war on Nasser.' Nutting tried to reason with him, but to no avail. 'Driven by impulses of pride and prestige and nagged by mounting sickness, he began to behave like an enraged elephant charging senselessly at invisible and imaginary enemies in the international jungle,' wrote Nutting in his account *No End of a Lesson*.

When Nutting attempted to take a calmer approach, drawing up proposals with the help of Foreign Office officials to 'quarantine' Nasser's influence, Eden reacted in fury. 'I was horrified to get a telephone call over an open line to the Savoy Hotel in which Anthony Eden said: "What is all this poppycock you have sent me about isolating and quarantining Nasser? Can't you understand that I want Nasser murdered." He actually used that word.'

The United States too was annoyed by Nasser's neutralist policies that officials in Washington deemed to be pro-Soviet Union, and even more so by his decision in May 1956 to establish diplomatic relations with 'Red China'. In July 1956 the Americans withdrew their offer to help finance the Aswan High Dam, publicly citing 'the weakness of the Egyptian economy' and 'the instability of the regime', believing it would 'cut Nasser down to size'. Eden quickly followed suit.

Nasser's response on 26 July 1956 stunned the world. Even his cabinet ministers, told of it a few hours in advance, were nonplussed. Addressing a crowd in the main square in Alexandria, to mark the fourth anniversary of Farouk's abdication, Nasser announced the nationalisation of the Suez Canal Company, an Egyptian-registered company owned by British and French shareholders which had run the canal since its construction was completed in 1866. Linking Europe with Middle East oilfields and with Asia, the canal was the world's most important international waterway, used by 12,000 ships a year from forty-five nations, the main artery of oil for Europe, carrying more than 20 million tons of oil a year for Britain alone, half of its supplies. The company's concession to run the canal was due to continue until 1968.

'Today, in the name of the people, I am taking over the company,' declared Nasser. 'Tonight, our Egyptian canal will be run by Egyptians. *Egyptians!*'

Revenues which had previously gone to the canal company would be used to finance the building of the High Dam, he said. But he also promised full compensation to shareholders, including the British government which had a 44 per cent holding in the company, and insisted that there would be no interference with normal traffic.

Britain's reaction, in the words of Anthony Nutting, 'bordered on panic and hysteria'. Politicians from all sides demanded the strongest measures to force the 'upstart dictator of Egypt' to disgorge his prize before other British and Western interests were taken over in a similar fashion. Convinced that Britain's entire commercial stake in the Middle East, including its oil resources, was at risk, Eden ordered his military chiefs to prepare to seize the canal by force and to despatch troops to Britain's bases in the Mediterranean in readiness. Britain, he said, could not tolerate having Nasser's 'thumb on her windpipe'.

The reaction in France was similar. The French government was already as hostile to Nasser as Britain was, blaming him for fomenting nationalist rebellion in Algeria. At a meeting with Eden in March 1956, the French prime minister, Guy Mollet, a socialist, had compared Nasser to Hitler. 'Nasser [has] the ambition to recreate the conquests of Islam,' Mollet claimed. In the wake of Nasser's nationalisation coup, Mollet too saw an opportunity for a military showdown with Egypt.

The Americans, however, though regarding Nasser as a menace, did not share the Anglo–French enthusiasm for war and preferred to use economic pressures against Egypt. They wanted the dispute over nationalisation to be resolved by a negotiated settlement. The only justification for military action, they argued, was if traffic through the canal was stopped. But under Egyptian management, a steady flow of traffic continued, even increasing from an average of forty-two ships a day to forty-five. The Americans favoured a system of international control of the canal. While Nasser argued that international control would infringe Egyptian sovereignty, negotiations nevertheless made progress. There seemed every prospect that a settlement could be reached.

But Eden and Mollet were bent on destroying Nasser's regime. While negotiations with Egypt were underway, they engaged in a secret conspiracy to invade Egypt in collusion with Israel and seize the canal. On 29 October 1956 Israeli forces crossed into Sinai and raced towards the canal. On the pretext of trying to separate the combatants, Britain and France issued an ultimatum to Egypt to withdraw its forces west of the canal. When Nasser rejected the ultimatum, Britain and France launched their own attack, bombing Egyptian airfields to destroy Nasser's air force, landing troops at Port Said and dropping leaflets on Cairo urging Egyptians to overthrow his government.

The folly of this exercise in imperial bullying was swiftly evident. Nasser promptly sunk forty-seven ships in the canal, blocking all traffic and cutting the main route for Europe's oil supplies, thereby bringing about the nightmare scenario that Eden's actions were supposed to prevent. With unexpected suddenness, Britain faced a storm of condemnation, a sterling crisis and the prospect of petrol rationing.

The United States, deceived about the conspiracy, was furious. At the United Nations General Assembly the US put forward a resolution demanding withdrawal, gathering support from sixty-four other nations. The Soviet Union threatened to intervene with missiles. The Arab world erupted in uproar; Saudi Arabia broke off diplomatic relations and imposed an oil embargo. In desperate need of emergency loans to help it over the sterling crisis, Britain could no longer turn to the US for support. On 6 November, less than forty-eight hours after British troops had landed in Egypt, with Nasser facing disaster, Eden was forced to call a halt to the campaign. 'I cannot hold out any longer,' Eden told Mollet.

Far from precipitating Nasser's downfall, the Suez invasion propelled him to a pinnacle of prestige and influence. He was acclaimed and idolised as a latter-day Saladin, the architect of Western defeat and humiliation, the *Rayyes* or leader who had withstood 'the triple aggression', as the Suez war was called in the Arab world, and broken the spirit of imperialism, a miracle-worker possessed of extraordinary vision and wisdom. His photograph was displayed in souks, cafés, taxis and shops not only in Egypt but throughout the Middle East and North Africa.

Basking in the adulation, Nasser set out to impose Egypt's leadership on the Arab world. He became a master of propaganda, the most successful communicator with the Arab masses in modern times, discovering he could sway and manipulate crowds with oratory that sent them into paroxysms of applause. Once renowned as a tedious, shy and awkward speaker, sticking to prepared texts written in neo-classical Arabic, he now captivated audiences on radio and television and at huge rallies using the language of the streets, mocking Western politicians and denouncing 'imperialism' and 'reactionaries' at every opportunity. The Nasser cult soon took hold, both in Egypt and in the rest of the Arab world. It made Cairo the fountainhead of a new nationalism, spreading the message of an Arab 'revolution' across the region.

The Suez crisis also enabled Nasser to sweep away at a stroke layers of foreign influence in Egypt's commercial, academic and social life. All British and French banks and companies were sequestrated, a total of 15,000 enterprises. New laws were passed requiring banks, insurance companies and other commercial businesses to be Egyptian-registered, with majority Egyptian shareholding and Egyptian management. In October 1958 Nasser concluded a deal with the Soviet Union enabling the Aswan Dam project to proceed. By the end of the decade he had become the leading exponent of Arab socialism.

For Britain, the Suez debacle marked the end of its imperial ambitions. It had forfeited much of its influence in the Arab world; and its willingness to hold on to its African colonies, in the face of the rising tide of nationalism there, was much diminished. The 'retreat from Empire' gathered momentum.

The French, however, still believed in the importance of their imperial mission in Africa and were determined to defend African territories they still regarded as part of *la plus grande France*.

3

LAND OF THE SETTING SUN

In the early hours of 1 November 1954, a day when French *colons* were due to celebrate the festival of All Saints, bands of nationalist guerrillas launched a series of coordinated attacks, seventy in all, across a wide area of Algeria. Their targets included police posts, barracks, bridges, farm buildings and telephone lines. Leaflets scattered on the streets announced that a new nationalist movement called the *Front de Libération Nationale* (FLN) had embarked on a revolutionary struggle for independence and would fight on until it had won.

The attacks caught the French administration by surprise. Algeria enjoyed a reputation for being a relatively tranquil part of France's empire in the Maghreb – the Arabic name for north-west Africa, meaning 'land of the setting sun'. Algeria was also unique in that its three northern *départements*, Algiers, Constantine and Oran, where most of the European population lived, were considered to be a part of France itself, having the same status as *départements* in mainland France as, say, Seine-et-Oise or Alpes-Maritimes. There was an unmistakable French character to the towns of Algeria. Algiers, the capital, cradled in steep hills dotted with red-tiled villas overlooking one of the most spectacular bays in the Mediterranean, seemed just like a Riviera resort. Its broad boulevards and avenues were lined with expensive shops, kiosks, *trottoir* cafés and bookshops; along the waterfront stood grand, arcaded buildings housing banks and mercantile companies. One third of the population in Algiers was white. In the hinterland lay vast vineyards and cereal and citrus farms owned mainly by *colons*.

The tranquillity, however, was deceptive. After 124 years of *la présence française* in Algeria, French *colons* – or *pieds noirs*, as they were called – had achieved a total grip on political power, commerce, agriculture and employment, effectively relegating the majority Muslim population – Arab and Kabyle – to a subservient status and stubbornly resisting all attempts at change. Both groups sent deputies to the National Assembly in Paris, but Muslims numbering 8 million were allocated no more than fifteen seats, the same as for the 1 million *pieds noirs*. Moreover, the *pieds noirs* could always rely on support from other political parties in the National Assembly as well as powerful French groups in commerce, banking and the press to protect their interests. In the turbulent postwar era, as a succession of French governments struggled to survive amid strikes, inflation, austerity and a debilitating war in Indo-China, none was willing to risk antagonising the *pied noir* population and their supporters for the sake of reform in Algeria. Moderate Algerian nationalists seeking reform were consequently given short shrift.

In Algeria itself the local assembly was effectively subject to the control of the French administration. Elections were blatantly rigged to ensure that amenable Muslim candidates – '*Beni-Oui-Oui*', as government collaborators were known derisively – won their seats. The upper echelons of the administration were virtually an exclusive French preserve: of 864 higher administrative posts, no more than eight were held by Muslims. In rural areas a thin layer of 250 French administrators ruled over 4 million Muslims.

The gulf between the two communities was huge. The vast majority of *indigènes* were illiterate, poor and unemployed. In general, they were seen as an inferior race, treated with disdain, indifference or outright abuse. Their numbers were fast growing. In fifty years the Algerian population had nearly doubled, prompting fears among *pieds noirs* that they were in danger of being 'swamped'. In urban areas, most lived in wretched *bidonvilles* – tin-can slums – on the outskirts of towns. Algiers in 1954 harboured 140 *bidonvilles* built on wasteland and demolition sites and in the ravines that ran down to the sea. In the Casbah, the old fortress-palace of Algiers, some 80,000 Muslims were packed into an area of one square kilometre, an Arab town embedded in a European city. There were limited job prospects for Muslims; preference was usually given to *petits-blancs*. Nearly two-thirds of the rural population was officially classified as 'destitute'. Unable to find employment in Algeria, half a million *indigènes* worked in France, mainly as unskilled labourers.

The plight of Algerians and their frustration at being blocked at every turn was fertile ground for militant nationalists. In 1947 they formed a revolutionary group, *Organisation Spéciale,* a prototype of the FLN, dedicated to armed struggle. Among the founder members was Ahmed Ben Bella, a 29-year-old former warrant officer in the French army, who had been awarded both the Croix de Guerre and the Médaille Militaire for bravery in the Second World War. In 1949, in the first important action undertaken by the group, Ben Bella organised a raid on the main post office in Oran, which netted 3 million francs. With poor security, the *Organisation Spéciale* was soon broken up by French intelligence. Ben Bella himself was arrested and sentenced to eight years' imprisonment. In 1952, however, he managed to escape from prison, after sawing through the bars of his cell with a blade hidden in a loaf of bread, and made his way to Cairo, establishing a base there under Nasser's auspices.

In the spring of 1954 the militants regrouped. A committee of nine leaders – subsequently known as the *chefs historiques* – was formed to organise armed rebellion: six were based in Algeria; three, including Ben Bella, were exiles living in Cairo where they looked to Nasser to provide them with arms. Under the noses of French intelligence, they proceeded to draw in recruits and to collect weapons. To their intense disappointment, Nasser, despite all the rhetoric about Arab liberation poured out by Cairo Radio, failed to deliver any material support until the war was well under way. To launch their rebellion, they possessed no more than about 400 miscellaneous weapons, most of them sporting guns. A network of bomb factories set up in the labyrinth of alleys in the Casbah produced only primitive devices.

The targets were carefully chosen: government installations, French military personnel and gendarmes, private property of *grands colons* and Muslim 'collaborators'. Strict instructions were issued to avoid white civilian casualties. But despite all the preparations, many of the attacks launched on All Saints Day failed. None of the main targets in Algiers – the radio station, the telephone exchange, the gasworks, a petroleum depot and a French-owned warehouse – was seriously damaged. When police, army and intelligence chiefs met at an emergency conference in Algiers on the morning of 1 November, all were agreed that the government was facing isolated incidents rather than a general insurrection.

They nevertheless ordered severe reprisals. Police made indiscriminate mass arrests, incarcerating hundreds of Muslims, including moderate nationalists uninvolved with the rebellion. As paratroop reinforcements arrived from France, punitive expeditions were launched in the Aurès mountains, a traditional bandit stronghold which the FLN had made the main focus of its guerrilla operations. Security forces repeatedly conducted *ratissages* against Algerian communities, brutally 'raking' them over for signs of guerrilla support. In Algiers the FLN network was crushed within two weeks. Only in the Aurès did the French face a significant military problem. But as winter set in, the FLN contingent there was reduced to no more than 350 active *maquisards*. After the initial shock of the All Saints Day attacks, life for the *pieds noirs* resumed much as before. No one seriously thought that France had entered a new war.

In Paris the government remained adamant. 'The Algerian *départements* are part of the French Republic,' declared the prime minister, Pierre Mendès-France, in November 1954. 'They have been French for a long time and they are irrevocably French.'

Having survived the harsh winter months, the FLN renewed its offensive in the spring of 1955, concentrating on 'soft' targets. Hundreds of Muslim officials were tortured, mutilated and murdered. The French poured in reinforcements, expanding their forces to 100,000 men, double the number stationed in Algeria at the start of the rebellion. Their *ratissages* became ever more brutal; collective punishment was enforced against villagers; thousands were sent to internment camps. Both sides resorted increasingly to the use of terror tactics.

In August 1955 the war exploded in full horror. Abandoning their policy of avoiding white civilians in the conflict, the FLN now made them a direct target. 'To colonialism's policy of collective repression we must reply with collective reprisals against the Europeans, military and civil, who are all united behind the crimes committed,' declared Youssef Zighout, a guerrilla leader in the Constantine area. 'For them, no pity, no quarter!' In the harbour city of Philippeville an FLN mob swarmed into the streets, hurling grenades into cafés, dragging white motorists from their cars and slashing them to death. In a small mining centre in the Philippeville district, FLN groups went from house to house, slaughtering all the occupants including women and children. In all, seventy-one whites died.

French forces took savage reprisals, shooting Muslims at random; *pieds noirs* formed vigilante groups, executing Muslims summarily. According to official French figures, 1,273 'insurgents' died. The FLN, giving names and addresses, claimed the figure was as high as 12,000.

In this ferocious struggle, there was no longer any hope of compromise. The middle ground fell apart. Moderate nationalists who had striven for years to achieve concessions from the French threw in their lot with the FLN. Among them was Ferhat Abbas, a leading liberal, former deputy to the National Assembly, a middle-class *évolué* married to a Frenchwoman, for whom the idea of negotiation had once been all-important. When the insurrection had begun, he had denounced it. 'We continue to be persuaded that violence will settle nothing,' he had said. Now he declared his support for the FLN.

> They know in Paris that I am honest, that I work only for a return to peace. Today I can do nothing inside my own country or in France. I have knocked on all the doors, I have spoken to all the politicians able to understand me, to understand us. Those who have really understood can do nothing. I cannot continue any longer to stand bail for a situation of which I entirely disapprove.

My departure will show at last to my fellow citizens that I have
withdrawn from ineffectual politics . . . I am simply joining the
organisation which struggles for the liberation of Algeria, because
there is no other way.

Thus Algeria descended into an inferno of violence, an endless cycle
of repression and revenge that was eventually to destroy the Fourth
Republic.

France's determination to hold on to Algeria meant reappraising its
involvement in the rest of the Mahgreb – in Morocco and Tunisia –
where French rule was also under challenge from nationalist movements but where French interests were less deep-rooted. Both
Morocco and Tunisia were governed as 'protectorates' under international treaties which obliged France to act in the name of their
indigenous rulers: the Sultan of Morocco, and the Bey in Tunisia.
Though both territories possessed large European communities, as
vociferous and demanding as Algeria's whites, they had never been
allowed to acquire political rights. The struggle in both territories
revolved around settler demands for representation and nationalist
demands for independence.

France had ruled Morocco since 1912 when the sultan surrendered control of external affairs but not internal sovereignty. Instead of
a governor-general, France was represented by a resident-general tech-
nically attached to the sultan's court. In practice, the French
administration controlled every aspect of government. As the number
of *colons* increased over the years, eventually reaching 400,000, they
persistently pressed for a share in power, in effect, for co-sovereignty.
They were supported by powerful lobbies in Paris and retained a virtual stranglehold over the administration in Morocco, enabling them
to exert strong pressure on the resident-general.

The reigning sultan, Mohammed ben Youssef, however, was not
amenable. Educated by French tutors, he had reached the throne in
1927 at the age of seventeen, the eighteenth member of the Alaouite
dynasty in north-west Africa to become monarch, mainly because the
French considered he would be politically malleable. But though

avaricious and extravagant, he had nevertheless turned out to be hard-working, profoundly attached to Islam and inclined to support nationalist demands for independence. In a dramatic speech in 1947, he proclaimed Morocco's affiliation to the Arab world and demanded recognition of Morocco's national aspirations, drawing him into open conflict with France. He then further infuriated the colonial power by withholding his signature to French decrees, thereby causing administrative deadlock.

The French retaliated by encouraging the sultan's rivals, Berber chieftains, to organise a vast march demanding that he be deposed. Using this as a pretext, the French government on 20 August 1953 duly deposed him, sending him into exile with his youngest wife and concubines, first to Corsica, then to Madagascar, and replacing him with an elderly uncle, a wealthy landowner who had previously played no role in political life.

The exiled sultan, however, swiftly became the focus of nationalist agitation, uniting the urban and rural populations, the middle class and the peasantry, behind a common cause. Violence and disorder afflicted towns and the countryside, culminating in the formation of a liberation army.

In Tunisia, which France had occupied since 1881, the French faced similar nationalist ferment. Frustrated by the resistance of the white community of 250,000 to any political reform, nationalists organised violence across the country. In this struggle the Bey of Tunis played no role. An eccentric figure who filled his palace with clocks and kept a private troupe of dwarfs, he spent much of his time indulging his passion for astronomy and alchemy, mixing secret brews and potions in his laboratory.

The impetus for change came instead from an articulate middle class. Their leader, Habib Bourguiba, an energetic lawyer, born in 1903, trained in Paris and married to a Frenchwoman, had been in and out of prison for much of his career. Shortly after founding the Néo-Destur party in 1934, he had been exiled to the Sahara for twenty months. Upon his release he had travelled to Paris pressing his demand for 'the replacement of the despotic regime by a constitutional regime which permits the people to participate in power'. Arrested again in

1938, he spent the next four years in prisons in Tunisia and France. In 1945, as France resumed its grip over Tunisia, Bourguiba fled in a smuggler's boat, making his way to Cairo, endeavouring to raise help from the Arab world, but finding little support there. Returning to Tunisia in 1949, he cajoled the French into implementing reform. A new French administration in Paris agreed in 1950 to measures moving Tunisia towards internal autonomy. But the reforms were thwarted largely by pressure from *colons*. Bourguiba planned to take the issue to the United Nations, but was arrested, taken first to a prison in the Sahara, then transferred to La Galite, an island in the Mediterranean, forty miles north of Bizerte, uninhabited except for a few lobster fisherman. After two years he was taken to another island, Groix, off the coast of Brittany, and interned there until a new French administration decided to move him to Chantilly, near Paris. In the meantime, political violence in Tunisia steadily mounted.

Rather than face a contagion of wars in North Africa, the French government decided to adjust its priorities. Morocco and Tunisia were ultimately dispensable. Algeria, the centre of French interests and investment, considered as much a part of France as the mainland itself, would be held at all costs.

In June 1955 Bourguiba returned to Tunis in triumph, welcomed by cheering crowds lining the quayside and the avenues leading to the bey's palace. Two days later an agreement granting internal autonomy to Tunisia was finally signed. In November 1955 Ben Youssef returned from exile to the throne in Morocco amid popular acclaim, duly recognised by the French government as His Majesty Mohammed V. In March 1956, both Morocco and Tunisia were granted independence.

For Algeria, six more years of terrible civil war lay ahead.

Under pressure from *pied noir* 'ultras' demonstrating on the street of Algiers, the French prime minister, Guy Mollet, agreed in 1956 to increase French forces in Algeria to 500,000 men in a bid to crush the rebellion. To find the extra manpower, he had to extend military service for conscripts to thirty months and call up reservists. At the same time, the government acquired 'special powers' enabling it to suspend individual rights in its pursuit of military victory. In effect, France was committing itself to 'total' war.

The military grew ever more powerful. In a spectacular escapade in October 1956, they succeeded in hijacking a plane carrying Ben Bella on a flight from Morocco to Tunisia. Ben Bella had been visiting Morocco to take possession of a shipment of arms for the FLN. He had been due to leave for Tunis on a personal plane provided by Mohammed V to attend a meeting to discuss a possible truce, an initiative encouraged by Mollet and supported by Morocco and Tunisia. But at the last minute, told that there was insufficient room on the king's plane, he had taken off in an Air Maroc aircraft with a French crew. Tipped off that Ben Bella was no longer flying under the protection of the king, French generals in Algiers decided to force down the Air Maroc plane on Algerian soil. Ben Bella subsequently spent five years without trial in French prisons.

The hijacking of Ben Bella, in flagrant breach of international law, was greeted with jubilation by the *pied noir* population, but caused an international furore. It infuriated Bourguiba and Mohammed V, cut short their willingness to mediate and made them all the more determined to support the FLN. It also removed from the scene a possible 'interlocuteur', an Algerian leader ready to contemplate negotiation. Fearful of the reaction of the military and the *pieds noirs*, Mollet possessed neither the will nor the power to release him.

In 1957 the focus of the war moved from rural areas to the city of Algiers. After an upsurge of assassinations and bombings of bars and cafés by the FLN and a violent backlash against the Muslim population by *pied noir* mobs, the governor-general, Robert Lacoste, handed over responsibility for order in the city to the military. It was a fateful decision, effectively relinquishing civilian control of Algeria. Under the command of General Jacques Massu, a veteran combat officer, four paratroop regiments moved into Algiers, sealing of the Casbah, carrying out house-to-house searches, arresting thousands of suspects and taking them to detention centres for interrogation. In scenes reminiscent of French experience under Nazi occupation, the city was divided into sectors, sub-sectors, blocks and buildings, each bearing a number or letter, and kept under constant surveillance by warders and informers. Muslim districts were isolated behind barbed wire and subjected to searchlights. When the FLN launched a general strike, it was brutally broken up.

At their interrogation centres, the military readily resorted to torture. A favourite method was the *gégène*, a term used for the generators which delivered electric shocks. Other methods included water torture and mock-drownings. In a letter of resignation, Paul Teitgen, secretary-general of the Algiers police, a former resistance hero who had himself been tortured on nine occasions by the Nazis during the Second World War, wrote: 'In visiting the [detention] centres, I recognised on certain detainees the deep marks of cruelties and tortures that I personally suffered fourteen years ago in the Gestapo cellars.' He estimated the number of victims who had 'disappeared' during military interrogation at 3,000.

Despite censorship and a shroud of secrecy surrounding what was described as a 'peacekeeping' operation in Algeria, the steady stream of disclosures about the use of torture caused growing public disquiet in France and raised doubts about the whole purpose of France's mission there. A distinguished colonial expert, Robert Delavignette, wrote prophetically at the end of 1957: 'The most serious problem is not the atrocities themselves, but that as a result of them the state is engaged in a process of self-destruction. What we are witnessing in Algeria is nothing short of the disintegration of the state; it is a gangrene which threatens France itself.'

Nevertheless, General Massu's paratroops and intelligence units were effective in destroying the FLN's network of bomb factories, arms caches and combatant groups. The number of attacks fell from 112 in January to 29 in March. Surviving members of the FLN command in Algiers were forced to flee the country and seek sanctuary in Tunisia. In June there was a brief resurgence of attacks, including the bombing of the dance hall of a casino crowded with *pieds noirs*. But by the autumn the last of the bombers had been tracked down. The Battle of Algiers, as it was called, had ended in French victory. Life for the *pieds noirs* swiftly returned to normal.

By early 1958 the French command judged that the war was virtually won. Terrorist attacks in the cities had been defeated; in rural areas 'pacification' programmes were well under way; a network of resettlement camps for a million peasants was being built to deprive the FLN of rural support. The army was also successful in recruiting thousands of Algerian auxiliaries – *harkis* – to help the French war effort. To prevent FLN infiltration from bases in Tunisia and Morocco, the military constructed a system of *barrages* – electrified wire fences, minefields and radar alarms – running the length of Algeria's frontiers, with formidable effect.

Moreover, the French had a powerful new motive to hold on to Algeria: oil. After ten years of prospecting, oil had been discovered at Hassi-Messaoud deep in the sands of the Sahara, shortly after the beginning of the war. In January 1958 the first oil started to flow to France.

The FLN command, meanwhile, was in serious disarray. Forced out of Algeria, it regrouped in Tunisia. Its policy of urban warfare had proved disastrous, and in rural areas it was no match for the French military. It was beset by leadership feuds, low morale and an internecine struggle with a rival nationalist group, the *Mouvement National Algérien*. Its survival now was largely dependent on the support and protection given by Tunisia. But even though Bourguiba was willing to provide a headquarters base, a route for arms supplies, sanctuary for the FLN army and training facilities, FLN guerrillas faced severe difficulty trying to penetrate the *barrages*. In the first seven months after the *barrages* were completed in 1957, the FLN estimated its losses there as 6,000 men.

While the military managed to gain the ascendancy in Algeria, however, metropolitan France was besieged by crisis. Buffeted by strikes, economic turmoil and international criticism of the Algerian conflict, successive French governments struggled in vain to shore up the Fourth Republic. In May 1957, after the fall of Guy Mollet's administration, France was left without a government for twenty-two days; in October and November there was no government for thirty-five days. The next administration collapsed in April 1958, leaving France once more without a government. The vacuum of leadership, the climate of impotence, the plunge of France's prestige around the world, all caused mounting disgust at the antics of its politicians.

Nowhere was this felt more strongly than among the military. Haunted by memories of their defeat by communists in Indo-China and the catastrophe of Dien Bien Phu, resentful of the humiliating retreat from Suez forced upon them by world opinion, the military were determined not to let victory in Algeria slip from their grasp as the result of a betrayal by weak-willed politicians in Paris. They saw the nationalist struggle in Algeria as evidence of the steady encroachment of communism and believed the battle to keep Algeria French was an essential part of the wider struggle to defend Western values. Their mission therefore was not only to restore the grandeur of France but to halt the decadence of the West. They were convinced they could finish the job in Algeria by striking directly at FLN targets in Tunisia and Morocco and were held back only by politicians fearful about the international repercussions.

What further infuriated the military were signs that some prominent politicians in Paris were prepared to forsake the cause of *Algérie française*. During the desperate efforts in April and May to find a prime minister for a new administration, the leading candidate, Pierre Pflimlin, announced his intention to open negotiations with the FLN once he was appointed, prompting the commander-in-chief in Algeria, General Raoul Salan, to make an official protest. The army, said Salan, would accept nothing less than the total defeat of the rebels. In a telegram to the chief of the general staff in Paris on 9 May, he warned of army intervention in national politics: 'The army in Algeria is troubled by recognition of its responsibility towards the men who are fighting and risking a useless sacrifice if the representatives of the nation are not determined to maintain *Algérie française*.'

Later that day came an event which detonated this explosive mixture of anger, resentment and suspicion and propelled French Algeria into rebellion. In Tunis, the FLN announced that, as a reprisal for the execution of FLN fighters by the French, it had executed three French soldiers, young conscripts captured four months before.

A wave of outrage swept through the army and the *pied noir* population. Salan announced that an official ceremony would be held to pay tribute to the three dead soldiers on 13 May. *Pied noir* groups prepared for mass demonstrations on the same day. On 10 May the governor-general, Robert Lacoste, departed for consultations in Paris, sensing he would never return. Algiers was left without a governor-general; Paris still had no government.

On 13 May, shortly after Salan had laid a wreath at the *monument aux morts*, a *pied noir* mob, led by students, stormed the offices of the Gouvernement-Général, seizing control and demanding the army take power. Appearing on the balcony, Salan and Massu, the hero of the Battle of Algiers, agreed to form a committee of public safety in conjunction with *pied noir* representatives. 'I could not act otherwise,' Massu told Lacoste in a phone call to Paris. 'Or we would have had to fire on the mob.' Galvanised into action by the rioting, the French parliament finally voted Pflimlin into office in the early hours of 14 May. The following day, Pflimlin imposed a blockade of Algeria, severing communications links.

In Algiers the new Committee of Public Safety, now ensconced in the Gouvernement-Général building, demanded the return to power of General Charles de Gaulle, the legendary wartime leader of the Free French. The military joined in. Addressing crowds gathered at the Gouvernement-Général on 15 May, Salan spoke of his attachment to the soil of Algeria. 'What has been done here will show the world that Algeria wants to remain French,' he declared. He concluded with a rallying cry of '*Vive la France! Vive l'Algérie française! . . .*' pausing to add, '*et Vive de Gaulle!*'

For the past twelve years, since abruptly abandoning the presidency, de Gaulle had led a reclusive life in Colombey-les-Deux-Eglises, south-east of Paris, content with writing his memoirs. At the age of sixty-seven, aloof and enigmatic, though convinced of his ability to save France from turmoil and restore its grandeur, he had not expected to hear the call for his return. His supporters, however, both in metropolitan France and in Algeria, had been working assiduously for just such a moment. Responding to the growing clamour, de Gaulle broke his silence. 'In the face of the ordeals once more mounting' in the country, he declared on 15 May, he stood 'ready to assume the powers of the Republic'.

On 1 June, after two weeks of coup plots and tense negotiations, de Gaulle was invested as prime minister by the National Assembly with full powers to rule by decree for six months and a mandate to draw up a new constitution for France. His return to power was greeted with jubilation by the army and the *pied noir* population in Algeria, all convinced that he would stand unwaveringly behind the cause of *Algérie française*.

Arriving in Algeria on 4 June, de Gaulle was fervently acclaimed a saviour. On the balcony of the Gouvernement-Général, Salan introduced him to the crowd, declaring: 'Our great cry of joy and hope has been heard!' The crowd erupted in celebration. Stretching his arms in a V-sign above his head, de Gaulle responded: *'Je vous ai compris!'* – 'I have understood you!'

4

L'AFRIQUE NOIRE

Whatever difficulties the French faced in Algeria, in the rest of their African empire – *l'Afrique Noire* – they remained confident of the loyalty of the fourteen territories they governed. In conducting their 'civilising mission' in Africa, they had been highly successful in cultivating a small black elite to whom they accorded full rights as citizens on condition that they accepted assimilation into French society and rejected their African heritage, family law and customs. In outlook, members of the elite saw themselves, and were seen, as Frenchmen, brought up in a tradition of loyalty to France, willingly accepting its government, its language and culture, and taking a certain pride in being citizens of a world power. Their political aspirations centred on securing for the African populations of *l'Afrique Noire* the same rights and privileges enjoyed by metropolitan Frenchmen. No one campaigned for independence. Political debate tended to reflect metropolitan tastes. The writer Thomas Hodgkin noted in 1954: 'In British West Africa, everyone who is politically conscious is a nationalist of some kind. In French West Africa, there are Catholics and anti-clericals, Communists and Gaullists, Socialists, Syndicalists and Existentialists.'

Two men personified the close relationship that France strove to establish with its African elite: Léopold Senghor of Senegal and Félix

Houphouët-Boigny of Côte d'Ivoire. Both rose to become ministers in the French government; both acted as staunch advocates of the 'Union Française'; and both ensured that French influence prevailed even when the empire began to disintegrate.

Senghor achieved distinction not only as a political leader, but as a gifted poet and as an intellectual in the grand French manner, familiar with a vast range of Western literature and philosophy. Born in 1906 into a prosperous Serer trading family, he had been taught by Catholic missionaries in Senegal to scorn his ancestral culture as worthless and to look solely to France for enlightenment. By the time he left Senegal for France at the age of twenty-one, with a government scholarship to pursue his literary studies, he had become the epitome of an alienated but 'civilised' black Frenchman. Seven years of study in Paris completed his 'Frenchification'.

'With docility we accepted the values of the West; its discursive reason and its techniques,' he recalled in 1961. 'Our ambition was to become photographic negatives of the colonisers: "black-skinned Frenchmen". It went even further, for we would have blushed, if we could have blushed, about our black skin, our frizzled hair, our flat noses, above all for the values of our traditional civilisation . . . Our people . . . , secretly, caused us shame.'

Along with other young black intellectuals living in the Latin quarter of Paris, however, Senghor soon began to react against assimilation. 'Paradoxically, it was the French who forced us first to seek and then to reveal ourselves to ourselves,' he remembered. 'We had been able to assimilate the French language and mathematics, but we weren't able to slough off either our black skin or our black soul. Thus we were led in search of a passionate quest for a Holy Grail: our *collective soul*.'

What Senghor and his companions in Paris eventually formulated was a philosophy they termed '*négritude*', a black consciousness which asserted the unique contributions, values and characteristics of black people and black civilisation. *Négritude* served as an intellectual precursor to nationalism. But while Senghor stressed the importance of cultural liberation, he nevertheless remained committed to the French empire. 'To be "a Frenchman above all" is an excellent prescription on the political level,' he declared.

Remaining in France as a teacher, he became the first African ever to win an *'agrégation'*, a coveted postgraduate degree qualifying him to teach at a lycée. As a naturalised Frenchman, he spent a year on compulsory military service, and when war with Germany broke out, he left the lycée near Paris where he was teaching, to become 'a second-class soldier', as he put it, denied a commission because of his race.

When his unit was taken prisoner by the Germans, all the blacks in it were pulled out of the ranks and lined up against a wall. Senghor quickly understood that the Germans intended to execute them on the spot. Just as the firing squad was about to shoot, he recalled, 'we called out, "*Vive la France, Vive l'Afrique Noire*"'. At that very moment, the Germans put down their guns. A French officer had persuaded them that such slaughter would be a stain on German honour. Senghor spent eighteen months in prisoner-of-war camps, using his spare time to learn German well enough to read Goethe's poetry in the original. On his release in 1942, he resumed teaching as a *professeur*.

Senghor's political career began in the postwar era. Elected to represent Senegal in the Constituent Assembly in 1945, one of nine African deputies among a throng of nearly six hundred others, he helped draft the new constitution of the Fourth Republic, endorsing the emphasis it placed on the 'indivisible' nature of the *Union Française*. In recognition of his expertise in the French language, he was employed as the official grammarian.

He played an influential role in the Socialist Party in the National Assembly, but eventually became disillusioned with the preoccupations of French socialists. In 1948 he formed his own political party, the *Bloc Démocratique Sénégalaise* (BDS). As a Catholic in a predominantly Muslim country, and as a Serer rather than a member of the dominant Wolof group, Senghor became adept at building coalitions, seeking support without appealing either to religious or ethnic affiliation. He forged close links with Senegal's *grands marabouts*, Muslim religious leaders who exerted strong discipline over their communities; he also gained a reputation as 'a man of the people', attentive to the needs of rural masses, content to sit on the floor of peasants' huts, listening to their complaints and eating whatever he was served; he managed too to reflect the concerns of young radical activists. His inclination for persuasion and compromise became part of Senegal's political culture, with lasting impact.

Alongside his political activities, Senghor pursued his ambitions in the literary world, meeting regularly with writers and poets at the fashionable Brasserie Lipp on the Left Bank. In 1947 he helped to establish a literary journal, *Présence Africaine*, which was devoted to promoting black culture; and the following year he published his own *Anthologie* of new poetry by black writers which included a preface by the French writer Jean-Paul Sartre, entitled 'Black Orpheus', examining the notion of *négritude*. Senghor also began to develop ideas about 'an African road to socialism', reworking European socialism into an African idiom, emphasising the importance of African communal traditions.

Even when the winds of nationalism gathered momentum elsewhere in Africa, Senghor remained staunchly loyal to the French cause. He scorned Nkrumah's ideas as 'too radical', advised the Tunisians to keep close ties with France, voted for war appropriations in Algeria and approved the despatch of Senegalese troops to fight the FLN. 'What I fear,' he said a few days before the opening of the Bandung conference of non-aligned states on colonial independence in 1955, 'is that, in the future, under the fatal pressure of African liberation, we might be induced to leave the French orbit. We must stay not only in the French Union but in the French Republic.'

Instead of independence, he advocated a new political federation between France and Africa. Independence for small political entities, with weak economies and few resources, would be no more than 'pseudo-independence', he argued. The future lay in large groupings of states working in cooperation with European powers. What was needed was the mobilisation of European resources to help Africa combat poverty, disease and ignorance.

Senghor's vision of the future, however, was overshadowed by growing friction with Houphouët-Boigny of Côte d'Ivoire. The conflict between them concerned the destiny of the *Union Française*, not their common loyalty to it but the direction it should take.

★

A year older than Senghor, Houphouët had taken a more conventional route to prominence. The son of a prosperous, chiefly Baoulé family, born in 1905 in the small village of Yamoussoukro, he had gained an elite education, studying at the École Normale William Ponty in Senegal and graduating as a *médecin africain* from the School of Medicine in Dakar, the first in his class. Returning to Côte d'Ivoire, he had served in the colonial medical service for fifteen years. After inheriting large landholdings in Yamoussoukro, he had quickly established himself as one of the richest African cocoa planters in the country. He had also been appointed *chef de canton* of his home district.

His entry into politics came in 1944 when he led a group of African planters, the *Syndicat Agricole Africain*, in opposing the French policy of discriminating in favour of French planters in Côte d'Ivoire. Elected as a deputy to the Constituent Assembly in 1945, he made it his special task to campaign for an end to forced labour. When in April 1946 he succeeded, by sponsoring a law which became known as the *Loi Houphouët-Boigny*, he established himself as a national leader, with a popular following in Côte d'Ivoire and beyond. His achievement was celebrated in dances and songs throughout the colony. With this triumph, he was able to turn his *Parti Démocratique de la Côte d'Ivoire* (PDCI) into the first mass political party in black Africa. He also extended his influence throughout *l'Afrique Noire*, heading an interterritorial alliance of radical parties, the *Rassemblement Démocratique Africain* (RDA).

To ensure more effective political representation in the National Assembly in Paris, Houphouët chose an alliance with the communists. Initially, the arrangement had its advantages. The communists were represented in the coalition government. Like other French political parties, they valued the empire. They showed no enthusiasm for demands for autonomy for the colonies, but stressed the need for colonial peoples to unite with the French working class, through which they would gain their own emancipation. They were ready to provide practical assistance, funds, training and personnel, both in Paris and in the colonies.

The drawback came in 1947 when the communists abandoned the

government in favour of a policy of 'revolutionary' action, urged the RDA to follow suit and tightened their grip over RDA activities. The RDA was thus dragged into the politics of Europe's Cold War and into deadly conflict with the French administration. From Paris, 'tough' administrators were sent out to Africa with instructions to suppress it. Aided enthusiastically by local officials and *colons*, the French administration eventually brought the RDA to its knees. Government employees, village chiefs, teachers sympathetic to the RDA were dismissed; RDA meetings were banned; elections were blatantly rigged.

The brunt of the repression, as it was called, fell on Côte d'Ivoire, the RDA stronghold. Party officials were imprisoned en masse; pro-PDCI villages found their taxes raised; even pilgrims to Mecca known to be party members were prevented from leaving. The PDCI retaliated with hunger strikes, boycotts, mass demonstrations, street fighting and sabotage. But they were no match for the French. The repression succeeded. In 1950, after a meeting with the Minister of Overseas France, François Mitterrand, Houphouët broke with the communists, sued for peace and decided to collaborate with the government.

All through this turbulent period, Houphouët constantly affirmed his loyalty to France. The RDA was neither anti-French in its policy, nor did it at any time demand independence. It aimed at equality for Africans within the *Union Française* and concentrated attacks on the dual system of voting and other forms of discrimination. The source of the conflict, Houphouët acknowledged, had been his proximity to the communists. Now that it had ended, the way was open for cooperation. 'A new page has been turned,' he said in 1951. 'On it let us write a resolution to make Africa the most splendid and most loyal territory in the French Union.'

In stark contrast to Nkrumah in neighbouring Gold Coast, Houphouët made economic development rather than political reform his priority. Independence, he said, was not the best solution for Africa. He forged an alliance with the French business community, encouraging the flow of public and private French capital into Côte d'Ivoire. As the largest planter in the country, he also recognised the benefits that France could provide for his fellow farmers through trade deals. Under a 1954 agreement, coffee, which then accounted for 57 per cent of total exports, received both a quota guarantee and a price floor in metropolitan markets.

Economic growth in Côte d'Ivoire, based on coffee and cocoa exports, advanced in leaps and bounds in the postwar era. Between 1950 and 1956, the area of land devoted to cocoa production rose by 50 per cent; coffee production doubled. By 1956, Côte d'Ivoire had become by far the largest exporter of all the territories in French West Africa, providing 45 per cent of the total; Senegal came second, providing 35 per cent, mainly peanuts.

The growing prosperity of Côte d'Ivoire, however, aroused resentment there about the taxation system used by the French to support their two federations in black Africa, *Afrique Occidentale Française* (AOF), consisting of eight West African territories, including Côte d'Ivoire and Senegal, and *Afrique Equatoriale Française*, a group of four territories in equatorial Africa. As the richest country in the AOF, Côte d'Ivoire paid the highest contribution. Each year it received back on average no more than 19 per cent of the money it remitted to the AOF. It calculated that if it had retained revenues sent to the AOF, it would have been able to double its budgetary income without increasing taxes.

Houphouët was determined to break the link with the AOF, to decentralise the federation. But he met strong opposition from Senghor. Senegal, where the headquarters of the AOF were based, stood to lose considerable benefits. But Senghor's main argument was that a political federation of eight territories with a combined population of 20 million would evolve into a powerful force capable of attaining economic self-sufficiency, whereas individual countries with populations of only 3 million, like Côte d'Ivoire and Senegal, would become little more than pawns.

All sides recognised the need for reform of the *Union Française*. French ministers were concerned that the kind of violence afflicting Algeria might surface elsewhere in Africa. The clamour for independence in Ghana and other British colonies in West Africa added to the momentum for change. 'The natives are restless,' the new Minister of Overseas France, Gaston Defferre, told the National Assembly in Paris in March 1956. 'The question is not whether we should plagiarise the British, but there is no doubt that the fact that they transformed the political and administrative regime of their territories has contributed to the growth of the impatience of the people of French West and French Equatorial Africa.'

The initiative was seized by Houphouët-Boigny. As a result of the 1956 elections, his RDA group had emerged as the largest African party in the National Assembly. He was consequently awarded a full cabinet post in the new French government, able to exert considerable influence over the direction the reforms took. With Houphouët's support, Defferre pushed through the National Assembly a *loi-cadre*, a 'framework law' enabling the government to take action by decree, thus avoiding the delays that resulted from protracted parliamentary wrangling. In the reforms subsequently introduced, France conceded universal franchise and a single college for elections. But even more important, it allowed its African territories a considerable measure of internal autonomy. Each territory acquired its own prime minister, cabinet and assembly with control over matters such as budgets, the civil service, public works and primary education.

In the process the two federations of French West Africa and French Equatorial Africa were broken up. France had no intention of permitting the development of federations of African territories with enhanced powers, capable of wielding significant influence in the metropolitan parliament. Senghor accused the French government of wanting to 'balkanise' Africa, to maintain its control there by keeping African countries small, divided and therefore dependent. But his protests were in vain.

Nevertheless, neither Senghor nor Houphouët-Boigny nor any other African leader in *l'Afrique Noire* voiced support for independence from France. Africa's involvement in the French system brought considerable benefits. In 1956 the number of deputies that black Africa sent to Paris increased to thirty-three. A year later the French government included four Africans as ministers or secretaries of state. The financial benefits bestowed by the *Union Française* were also of major importance. The French government paid a substantial part of administrative costs and provided subsidies for export crops. Between

1946 and 1958, more than 70 per cent of total public investment and more than 30 per cent of annual running costs were financed by France. Vast sums were spent on roads, bridges, schools, hospitals and agriculture. 'Independence has no positive content,' said Senghor. 'It is not a solution.'

In April 1957, in the Ivorian capital Abidjan, a wager was made between Houphouët-Boigny, in his role as minister in the French government, and Kwame Nkrumah, paying his first official visit abroad as prime minister of newly independent Ghana. Houphouët predicted that ten years hence Côte d'Ivoire, with the assistance of France, would have surpassed its neighbour in economic and social progress. 'You are witnessing the start of two experiments,' Houphouët told his compatriots. 'A wager has been made between two territories, one having chosen independence, the other preferring the difficult road to the construction, with the metropole, of a community of men equal in rights and duties . . . Let us undertake this experiment in absolute respect for the experiment of his neighbour, and in ten years we shall compare the results.'

When the Fourth Republic collapsed in 1958 and Charles de Gaulle assumed power, Houphouët became a fervent Gaullist. Though de Gaulle was preoccupied more with reaching a constitutional settlement for France to enable him to deal with Algeria, he also sought a new arrangement with l'Afrique Noire, willing to give its ruling elites more local power – internal autonomy – while leaving France effectively in control of foreign affairs, defence and overall economic policy. Under the Fifth Republic's constitution, the name of the Union Française became the Franco-African Community, but little else changed.

Houphouët was in full agreement with de Gaulle's strategy. He was convinced that the only effective way to safeguard the interests of Côte d'Ivoire or any other French African territory was to maintain union with France. When the draft proposals for the new constitution dealing with the Franco-African Community were being drawn up, Houphouët was the principal architect. The proposals made no mention of any territory's right to independence. Nor did they include any scope either for a looser confederation of states or for an inter-African federation within the Community, which Senghor and others advocated.

To settle the constitutional issue, de Gaulle announced that a referendum would be held on 28 September 1958. African territories would be given a choice of voting 'Yes' which would commit them to permanent membership of the Community, or 'No' which would mean their 'secession' and the loss of all French assistance, effectively consigning them to economic ruin and administrative chaos. 'Of course, I understand the attractions of independence and the lure of secession,' he said in August. 'The referendum will tell us whether secession carries the day. But what is inconceivable is an independent state which France continues to help.' Given such a stark choice, virtually all African leaders could see no alternative but to accept de Gaulle's conditions.

There was, however, one notable exception: the young Guinean leader, Ahmed Sékou Touré. He came from a different background from the intellectual Senghor and the aristocratic Houphouët-Boigny. His route to power had been not through the closeted world of the African elite but through the rough and tumble of trade union politics. From a trade union base, he had managed to build up the *Parti Démocratique de Guinée* (PDG) into a powerful mass movement. In the 1957 elections in Guinea the PDG had won fifty-six out of sixty seats and Touré, at the age of thirty-five, had become Guinea's prime minister. An admirer of Nkrumah, he was far more interested in ideas of Pan-African unity than in the Franco-African Community and quickly made clear his dislike of de Gaulle's plan. It was, he said dismissively, 'a French Union re-baptised – old merchandise with a new label'.

When de Gaulle arrived in the Guinean capital Conakry on 25 August at the end of an African tour to campaign for a 'Yes' vote, he was greeted by well-marshalled crowds lining the streets from the airport shouting independence slogans. At the old white Assembly Hall he was subjected to a brash speech from Touré, attacking France's colonial record and demanding complete decolonisation before Guinea joined the Franco-African Community. 'We prefer poverty in freedom to riches in slavery,' he declared to enthusiastic applause.

Deeply affronted, de Gaulle rose in reply to defend France's record and he repeated his offer: 'I say it here, even louder than elsewhere: independence is at Guinea's disposal. She can take it by saying "No" to the proposal which is made to her, and in that case I guarantee that metropolitan France will raise no obstacles . . .' He already acknowledged what the result would be. Turning to his entourage, he is said to have remarked: 'Well gentlemen, there is a man who we shall never get on with. Come now, the thing is clear: we shall leave on 29 September, in the morning [after the referendum].' On the way back to the airport in the same car, the two men sat tightlipped, in silence. They shook hands for the last time and de Gaulle departed with the words: '*Adieu la Guinée!*'

Soon after de Gaulle had left, Touré summed up his position. 'Between voting "Yes" to a constitution which infringes the dignity, unity and freedom of Africa, and accepting, as General de Gaulle says, immediate independence, Guinea will choose that independence without hesitating. We do not have to be blackmailed by France. We cannot yield on behalf of our countries to those who threaten and put pressure on us to make us choose, against heart and reason, the conditions of marriage which could keep us within the complex of the colonial regime.'

In the referendum on 28 September, the vote in eleven territories went overwhelmingly in favour of de Gaulle's proposals for a Franco-African Community. In Guinea, the vote was no less overwhelming: 95 per cent said '*Non*'. Four days later, on 2 October 1958, Guinea was proclaimed an independent republic.

De Gaulle's reaction to Guinea's vote was swift and vindictive. Despite polite overtures from Touré, all French aid was terminated. French civil servants and army units, including army doctors largely responsible for providing health services to the civilian population, were withdrawn. In a mass exodus, some 3,000 administrators, teachers, engineers, technicians and businessmen left the country. They took with them any French government property they could carry and destroyed what had to be left behind. Government files and records were burned; offices were stripped of furniture and telephones, even of their electric light bulbs. Army doctors took away medical supplies; police officers smashed windows in their barracks.

When Touré moved into the former governor's house, he found that the furniture and pictures had been removed and the crockery smashed. Only 150 French government employees, mostly volunteers, stayed behind.

Cast into isolation, Touré turned to the Soviet Union and other communist countries for assistance. Legions of technicians from Eastern Europe arrived. Nkrumah was ready with a large loan and proposals for a union between Ghana and Guinea. In the anti-colonial world at large, Touré was acclaimed a hero. Western mining groups expressed interest in Guinea's mineral resources. Far from being daunted by the severe disruption Guinea faced, Touré urged other members of the Franco-African Community to demand their independence.

De Gaulle's Community soon encountered difficulty. While France expected to run the Community as it had done in the past, African leaders wanted greater control. Senghor decided to form a federation linking Senegal with Soudan (Mali) and pressed for independence within the Community. De Gaulle at first resisted the demands, but he came to recognise that independence was, as he said 'a sort of elementary psychological disposition'. Houphouët-Boigny held out in favour of the French Community for longer than any other African leader. 'It is not the shell of independence which counts; it is the contents: the economic contents, the social contents and the human contents.' But he too was swept along on the same tide.

In 1960 the eleven members of the Community, along with Cameroon and Togo, two trust territories administered by France under a United Nations mandate, were launched as independent states. French delegations hopped from one colonial capital to another to attend ceremonies lowering the *tricolore* and hoisting independence flags: Dahomey (later Benin) on 1 August; Niger on the 3rd; Upper Volta (later Burkina Faso) on the 5th; Côte d'Ivoire on the 7th; Chad on the 11th; the Central African Republic on the 13th; the French Congo (Brazzaville) on the 15th; Gabon on the 17th; and Senegal on the 20th. Mali followed in September and Mauritania in November.

Hardly any of these new states were economically viable. Countries like Chad, Niger and Mali were landlocked, mostly desert, thinly populated and desperately poor. Mauritania consisted of no more than desert inhabited by nomads which until 1954 had been ruled from the Senegalese city of Saint Louis. Upper Volta had only become a separate territory in 1947. Even Senegal, the second wealthiest colony in *l'Afrique Noire*, relied heavily on French subsidies. Only Côte d'Ivoire was thought to be economically viable on its own. The new states were also deprived of the cohesiveness that the two giant federations of French West Africa and French Equatorial Africa had lent them for the past fifty years. Coastal states lost important markets; landlocked states suffered economic disruption. Instead of cooperating, they became weak rivals.

To ensure that the new states survived and that French interests there were protected, de Gaulle adopted a benevolent stand, signing agreements covering a wide range of financial and technical assistance. France supplied presidential aides, military advisers and civil servants to staff government ministries. The French treasury supported a monetary union, underwriting a stable and convertible currency. French troops were stationed permanently in several African capitals under defence agreements designed to provide a guarantee of internal security. France also operated an extensive intelligence network in Africa controlled from the Élysée Palace by de Gaulle's African adviser, Jacques Foccart. The French continued to dominate industry, banking and trade as thoroughly as before. In the post-colonial era, *l'Afrique Noire* was regarded as part of France's *chasse gardée* – a private estate, jealously guarded against encroachment by other world powers.

Indeed, the changes that occurred were largely ceremonial. In place of a French-controlled administration, the new states were now run by elite groups long accustomed to collaborating with the French and well attuned to French systems of management and culture. Though popularly elected, they were separated by a wide social and cultural gulf from the mass of the population. Their ambitions lay more in accumulating positions of power, wealth and status, more in developing a high bourgeoisie, than in transforming society.

No one illustrated this sense of continuity, or the benefits to be derived from it, better than Houphouët-Boigny. After serving in six successive French governments, he returned home to concentrate his attention on running Côte d'Ivoire. A glimpse of his lifestyle was provided in 1961, shortly after independence, by a correspondent for the magazine *West Africa*.

> Far and away the most splendid residence in Africa is that of the Ivory Coast's President, M. Houphouët-Boigny . . . Over £3 million has already been spent – out of French aid funds – and further work on the landscaping of the grounds is likely to cost a further million at least. In keeping with Houphouët's unflamboyant nature, the palace doesn't look so extraordinary from the street. It is in three separate buildings: the Presidency, the Residence and the reception halls. Not until the dinner-jacketed guest penetrates to the latter, past fountains, cascades, statues and descends a regal staircase into a vast marble reception hall, there to shake hands with his host and his beautiful wife, does the extent and beauty of the place register. Nothing is missing: from chandeliers and antique-style furniture in subtly contrasted colours to embossed chinaware and cutlery for over 1,000 guests, and a single table that seats hundreds . . . Many visitors – both tax-paying Frenchmen and delegations from less favoured African states – were, I am told, shocked at such extravagance. But an Ivorian journalist who inspected the palace on the day after the big reception, exclaimed: 'My God, anyone could live here – the Queen of England, President Kennedy. It makes me thrilled to be an Ivory Coast citizen.'

★

In Algeria, meanwhile, the war dragged on. For all his determination to resolve the issue, de Gaulle made little progress. Five times he visited Algeria in the summer months of 1958, but, caught between the conflicting demands of the *pieds noirs*, the army and the Algerian nationalists, he was able to offer no clear way forward. Under the 1958 constitution, Algeria remained a group of twelve *départements* of France. To restore metropolitan control in Algeria, de Gaulle curbed the activities of *pied noir* 'ultras' and purged the army of dissident officers. He also announced a programme of massive economic aid, in the hope of encouraging the emergence of a 'third force' of moderates in the Algerian community with whom he could negotiate a viable settlement and bypass the FLN. But the middle ground had long since collapsed.

The FLN reacted to de Gaulle's programme by intensifying guerrilla action, organising terrorist raids in France and setting up a government-in-exile, based in Tunis, appointing as its figurehead the moderate francophile Ferhat Abbas. When de Gaulle offered what he called 'a peace of the brave', suggesting that if FLN combatants were 'to wave the white flag of truce', they would be 'treated honourably', he was curtly rebuffed. 'The problem of a ceasefire,' retorted Ferhat Abbas, 'is not simply a military problem. It is essentially political and negotiation must cover the whole question of Algeria.'

It was not until September 1959, fifteen months after his initial 'tour of inspection', that de Gaulle endeavoured to break the logjam. In a national broadcast he offered Algeria 'self-determination', setting out three possible options: Algerians would be able to choose either 'secession', by which he meant independence, shorn of all French assistance, like Guinea; or total integration, which he termed *françisation*; or a measure of internal self-government in 'association' with France. The outcome would be decided by a referendum to be held within four years after the restoration of peace. De Gaulle made clear his own views about how 'disastrous' secession would be: secession, he said, 'would bring with it the most appalling poverty, terrible political chaos, widespread slaughter, and soon after the bellicose dictatorship of the Communists'. The most sensible course, he implied, would be 'association'.

Whatever de Gaulle's preference, the genie of 'self-determination' was now out of the bottle. In Paris his offer was widely acclaimed: the National Assembly passed a vote of confidence by a huge majority. But in Algeria it provoked fury, both within the *pied noir* community and within the army. For by conceding the majority Muslim population the right to decide Algeria's fate, de Gaulle in effect signalled his willingness to accept the end of *Algérie française*.

After weeks of plotting, paramilitary 'ultra' groups took to the streets of Algiers in January 1960, setting up barricades, determined to force de Gaulle to withdraw his offer of self-determination, expecting the army to join them. But the president stood firm, demanding obedience from the army, and the insurrection – 'Barricades Week', as it was called – petered out.

Throughout 1960 – the sixth year of the war – de Gaulle held fast to the belief that 'association' could still be made to work, that he could carry the bulk of the Muslim population with him and thwart the FLN. To the FLN he renewed his offer of an 'honourable' ceasefire and authorised preliminary talks, but when the FLN discovered they were required to lay down arms before substantial negotiations could begin, the talks soon foundered. The FLN insisted not only on discussing political issues prior to any ceasefire but demanded recognition as the sole representative of Algerian opinion.

Striving to restore momentum, de Gaulle announced in November 1960 'a new course' that would lead eventually, he said, to an *Algérie Algérienne* associated with France. He spoke of a *République Algérienne* with 'its own government, its own institutions, its own laws', within the French orbit. Once again, the *pied noir* population vented their fury. During a 'tour of inspection' de Gaulle made in December, riots erupted in Algiers and Oran. But what was even more significant about his visit was that the Muslim population used it as an occasion to demonstrate their support for the FLN and the cause of Algerian independence. Thousands of green-and-white FLN flags appeared in the Muslim quarters of Algiers. With unexpected ferocity, Muslim riots broke out. No longer were the French able to claim that the FLN represented nothing more than a minority clique terrorising the Algerian majority.

Concluding that there was no alternative but to negotiate with the FLN, de Gaulle agreed in February 1961 to open peace talks. The backlash this time came from within the army. In April a group of retired generals, including General Salan, the former commander-in-chief in Algeria, led a revolt against de Gaulle, seizing control of Algiers. De Gaulle stood firm once more and, after four days, the putsch collapsed.

The failure of the putsch, however, brought dissident officers into alliance with 'ultra' groups. Using the name *Organisation Armée Secrète* (OAS), they launched a campaign of terror targeted mainly at the Muslim population, trying to provoke FLN reprisals against the French that would lead to the intervention of the army and the collapse of de Gaulle's entire strategy. The OAS gained the support of much of the *pied noir* population in cities such as Algiers and Oran. For month after month, the killing and bombing continued. OAS terror was matched by counter-terror carried out both by French *'barbouzes'* – underground government agents – and by the FLN. The gulf of hatred between Muslim and European widened ever further. Metropolitan France was caught up in a similar cycle of violence. Numerous attempts were made to assassinate de Gaulle.

Negotiations meanwhile proceeded in fits and starts. De Gaulle at first tried to keep hold of the Sahara with its huge oil and gas reserves. He demanded a special status for the *pieds noirs*, even proposing partition at one stage. But with his negotiating position steadily weakening, he was forced to yield on one issue after another. By early 1962, as the carnage continued, he resolved to get rid of the 'Algerian problem' at the earliest possible date. On 18 March a deal agreeing to Algeria's independence was signed at Evian. De Gaulle told his cabinet it was 'an honourable exit'.

But the agreement did not bring peace. In a final paroxysm of violence, the OAS took revenge on the Muslim population, bombing and murdering at random, destroying schools, libraries and hospital facilities, attacking florists' stalls and grocery shops, determined to leave behind nothing more than 'scorched earth'. Whatever slim chance of reconciliation between *pieds noirs* and Algerians there had been was snuffed out.

In the mass exodus that followed, more than a million *pieds noirs* fled to France, many leaving with no more than what they could carry in suitcases. Farms, homes and livelihoods were abandoned en masse. Amid the retreat, thousands of *harkis* – Muslims who had fought on France's side – were slaughtered by FLN groups in an orgy of revenge.

Thus the French departed, in chaos and confusion, after eight years of war which had cost half a million lives. On 5 July 1962 Algeria attained its independence under the control of a revolutionary government.

WINDS OF CHANGE

Following in Ghana's footsteps, Britain's other territories in West Africa – Nigeria, Sierra Leone and even the tiny sliver of land known as The Gambia, a miniature colony consisting of little more than two river banks – made their way up the independence ladder. The timetable for independence was determined not so much by any British reluctance to set them free but by local complications on the ground.

The birth of Nigeria as an independent state proved especially difficult. The most populous country in Africa, it was beset by intense and complex rivalries between its three regions, each of which was dominated by a major ethnic group with its own political party. No national party emerged.

The North, with an area comprising three-quarters of Nigeria's territory and containing more than half the population, was largely Muslim and Hausa-speaking, accustomed to a feudal system of government run by the Fulani ruling class. Both Hausa and Fulani looked disdainfully on the people of the South. After travelling to Lagos for the first time in 1949, the principal Northern leader, the Sardauna of Sokoto, observed: 'The whole place was alien to our ideas and we found the members of the other regions might well belong to another world as far as we were concerned.' Few traces of the modern world –

in education or economic life – had been allowed to intrude in the North. By 1950 there was only one Northern university graduate – a Zaria Fulani convert to Christianity. Southerners who migrated to the North were obliged to live in segregated housing and to educate their children in separate schools; they were also prevented from acquiring freehold titles to land. Northern Muslims were taught to regard Southerners as 'pagans' and 'infidels' and forbidden on both religious and administrative grounds to associate with Southerners.

The West, which included the capital, Lagos, was dominated by the Yoruba, who traditionally had been organised into a number of states ruled by kingly chiefs. Because of their early contact with Europeans and long experience of city life, the Yoruba had progressed far in education, commerce and administration and absorbed a high degree of Western skills.

In the Eastern region, on the other side of the Niger river, the Igbo, occupying the poorest, most densely populated region of Nigeria, had become the best educated population, swarming out of their homeland to find work elsewhere as clerks, artisans, traders and labourers, forming sizeable minority groups in towns across the country. Their growing presence there created ethnic tensions both in the North and among the Yoruba in the West. Unlike the Hausa-Fulani and the Yoruba, the Igbo possessed no political kingdom and central authority but functioned on the basis of autonomous village societies, accustomed to a high degree of individual assertion and achievement.

In addition there were some 250 ethnic minority groups, each with its own language, occupying distinct territories, amounting in total to one-third of the population. In the North the Hausa-Fulani constituted only about half of the population; some 200 other linguistic groups lived there, most of them in the lower North or 'Middle Belt', as it was called. In the West the Yoruba constituted about two-thirds of the population; and in the East, the Igbo, about two-thirds. In each region, minority groups resented the dominance of the three major ethnic groups and the neglect and discrimination they suffered as minorities and harboured ambitions to obtain their own separate states within Nigeria and the resources that would go with them. Some non-Muslim minorities in the North had long been engaged in struggles to overthrow their feudal Muslim overlords; Tiv resistance exploded in riots in 1960. In the West the Edo-speaking people of Benin province yearned to restore the old autonomy of the kingdom of Benin, once renowned for its artistic achievement. In the East the Ibibio and Efik hankered for the former glory of the Calabar commercial empire.

There was also an immense development gap between the North and the two Southern regions. At independence, after expanding its education system, the North, with 54 per cent of the population, still produced less than 10 per cent of the country's primary school enrolments and less than 5 per cent of secondary enrolments. Only fifty-seven students at the University College in Ibadan out of a total of more than one thousand came from the North. The shortfall in qualified Northerners meant that many government positions were filled by highly educated Southerners, notably Igbos. On a national level, barely 1 per cent of Nigerian officials in higher executive posts were Northerners. A constant fear in the North was that its own traditions and conservative way of life would be undermined by Southern encroachment; the ruling aristocracy in particular were determined to protect their own position against radical change.

Finding a constitutional arrangement that satisfied so many diverse interests was a protracted business. The 1951 constitution lasted for no more than three years. The 1954 constitution was more durable. Each region was given its own government, assembly and public service and allowed to move separately towards self-government. The West and the East attained self-government in 1957 but then had to wait until 1959 for the North to catch up. The independence constitution provided for a federal structure that was regarded as an effective compromise balancing regional interests, though it left the North, because of the size of its population, in a commanding position, with a potential stranglehold over the political process, capable of dominating the combined weight of the other two regions.

Nevertheless, when Nigeria was finally launched as an independent state in 1960, it was with a notable sense of optimism. Led by popularly elected politicians, endowed with a strong, diversified economy and an efficient civil service, Nigeria, by virtue of its size, population and resources, was marked out as one of Africa's emerging powers.

In Britain's colonies in east and central Africa, because of the presence of vociferous and powerful white minorities, a different timetable was envisaged. Britain's aim in postwar years was to develop what it called 'multiracial' societies there, a 'partnership' between white and black, albeit under white leadership. White leadership was regarded as indispensable for economic development. The white populations were the economic mainstay of each colony; they constituted the only reservoir of professional skills. Because the African peoples of the region had come into contact with European colonisation relatively recently, compared to West Africans, they were considered to be several generations behind in terms of political advancement. Whereas the first African nominated to the local legislature in the Gold Coast made his debut in 1888, the first African to sit in the legislative council in Kenya was appointed in 1944, in Tanganyika and Uganda in 1945, in Northern Rhodesia (Zambia) in 1948, and in Nyasaland (Malawi) in 1949.

At any sign that Africans or Asian immigrants might advance at the expense of the white community, the white reaction was invariably hostile. Protracted battles were fought over the exact balance of representation between each community. In Kenya the British eventually decided on a ratio of two European representatives to one African and one Asian – 2:1:1. In Uganda, with a different population mix, the ratio was 1:2:1. In Tanganyika it was initially to have been 1:2:1, but as a result of strong European pressure, it was finally fixed at 1:1:1.

Determined to entrench white rule, the region's white communities campaigned vigorously for the British government to establish two new dominions in Africa – one in East Africa comprising Kenya, Uganda and Tanganyika, and one in Central Africa comprising Southern Rhodesia, Northern Rhodesia and Nyasaland. They made little headway in East Africa. But in Central Africa, by stressing the economic benefits to be derived from closer association and their commitment to the idea of 'partnership', they eventually won the approval of the British government for the establishment of the Federation of Rhodesia and Nyasaland, even though there was persistent opposition from African populations who feared being placed under the control of reactionary whites intent on entrenching white minority rule. When explaining their idea of 'partnership', white Rhodesians invariably spoke of senior and junior partners, or, as the Southern Rhodesian prime minister, Sir Godfrey Huggins, put it more memorably, 'the partnership between the horse and its rider'. But for the British government, the federation seemed a progressive step forward with its plans for developing 'multiracial' societies.

The whole strategy was blown off course by a rebellion against colonial rule in Kenya. The rebellion grew out of anger and resentment at the mass expulsion in postwar years of Kikuyu peasants from the White Highlands, an area of 12,000 square miles of the best agricultural land in the country, set aside for the exclusive use of white farmers. It spread to other sections of the Kikuyu people, to the Kikuyu reserves where long-standing grievances over land were already festering, and to Nairobi, where militant activists set up a central committee to direct the violence.

Taken by surprise by the scale of the rebellion, the colonial authorities ordered outright repression. They blamed the violence on the nationalist leader, Jomo Kenyatta, portraying him as a criminal mastermind who employed witchcraft and coercion in his drive for power and profit, and proceeded to rig his trial to justify their claims. But the repression they ordered, far from crushing the rebellion, turned into a full-scale war. At the height of the Emergency, as it was called, the government employed eleven infantry battalions, 21,000 police, air force heavy bombers and thousands of African auxiliaries to contain it. It took four years before the army was able to withdraw. With such a massive commitment needed to protect Kenya's small white minority, British officials began to rethink their strategy.

No other revolt against British rule in Africa gained such notoriety as the Mau Mau rebellion in Kenya. It was cited for years to come as an example of the atavistic nature of African politics lying just beneath the surface. White settlers, colonial officials, missionaries and the British government were unanimous in regarding Mau Mau as a sinister tribal cult affecting a largely primitive and superstitious people, confused and bewildered by their contact with the civilised world and prey to the malevolent designs of ambitious politicians. In the words of the official Colonial Office report published in 1960, Mau Mau was a subversive movement 'based on the lethal mixture of pseudo-religion, nationalism and the evil forms of black magic'.

All the fear and hatred that the white community felt facing this threat focused intensely on the person of Kenyatta. No other figure in colonial Africa was so reviled. Everything about him – the grip he appeared to exert over the Kikuyu, the hypnotic effect of his eyes, his suspicious visits to the Soviet Union, his left-wing connections in London – increased their sense of loathing. Tracing the signs of African unrest back to the time of his return to Kenya in 1946 after a period abroad of fifteen years, they were convinced that he had brought with him an evil scheme to subvert the Kikuyu and drive out the whites.

British officials held fast to the same view. In 1960, a year after Kenyatta had completed his sentence of seven years' imprisonment for 'managing' Mau Mau, the British governor, Sir Patrick Renison, refused to release him, describing him as 'the African leader to dark-ness and death' and claiming he still posed a threat to national security. Even though the British were soon thereafter obliged to release Kenyatta and, as they had done with other nationalist opponents, subsequently came to value his judgement and leadership, the stigma of Mau Mau and Kenyatta's involvement in it remained as marked as before. The reality, however, was somewhat different.

Kenyatta's career as a political activist had been one of the most adventurous of all nationalist leaders in Africa. Born in about 1896, educated by missionaries at the Church of Scotland headquarters near Nairobi, he had taken sundry jobs before becoming a full-time gen-eral secretary of the Kikuyu Central Association (KCA), a pressure group set up by the first generation of Kikuyu nationalists to campaign over land grievances. It was on behalf of the KCA that Kenyatta first travelled to London in 1929 bearing a petition on land grievances to the Colonial Office. The impression that he made on the missionary network in London who took an interest in his work was highly unfavourable. There were concerns about his poor English and shock at his unwholesome taste for expensive clothes and loose women. It was thought best that he should return to Kenya as soon as possible. But a West Indian talent-spotter for Comintern, George Padmore, who met him in London, recognised his potential. Within a few months of reaching London, Kenyatta had been taken on an extended tour of Europe and Russia. He returned to Russia in 1932 to study at Moscow's special revolutionary institute for colonial candidates, the University of the Toilers of the East.

Being a Moscow-trained revolutionary, however, was only one of the roles that Kenyatta was adept at playing. After his return to London in 1933, he joined Professor Bronislav Malinowski's classes in anthropology at the London School of Economics and duly published a study of Kikuyu life and customs entitled *Facing Mount Kenya*. He also worked briefly as an extra in Alexander Korda's film *Sanders of the River*. During the war he retreated to a village in Sussex, worked as an agricultural labourer and lectured to British troops. He even volunteered to join the Home Guard. Outwardly, he seemed as much at home whether gossiping with local villagers in the pub in Sussex or striding down Piccadilly dressed flamboyantly in a red sports jacket and carrying a silver-headed cane. He had an English family, a wife, Edna, and a son.

By the end of the war, however, approaching the age of fifty, he hankered to return to Kenya, anxious to engage in the nationalist struggle. 'I feel like a general separated by 5,000 miles from his troops,' he once exclaimed with exasperation to Edna. By the time he reached Kenya in September 1946, the first stirrings of rebellion amongst the Kikuyu had already begun.

They were an industrious, able and acquisitive people, with a deep attachment to the land, numbering more than 1 million, the largest tribe in Kenya, and fast expanding. Living close to Nairobi and almost surrounded by the White Highlands, they had felt the impact of colonial rule more fully than most others. More than 100 square miles of Kikuyuland in the vicinity of Nairobi had been alienated for European settlement, a constant source of grievance. The cry for the return of 'lost lands' was the main demand of the Kikuyu Central Association. At the outbreak of war, the KCA's opposition to government policies was deemed subversive and the movement was banned.

Another grievance over land was burgeoning in the main part of the White Highlands, the Rift Valley province. The land there had been cleared for white occupation largely by removing the pastoral Maasai people. As well as white landowners who established farms there, large numbers of Kikuyu peasants from Kikuyuland emigrated to the Rift Valley, keen to use the vast, undeveloped area for themselves. The Kikuyu 'squatters', as they were called, were welcomed by white farmers who needed a regular supply of labour. A system of labour tenancy emerged. In return for a plot of land to grow crops and graze their sheep and goats, Kikuyu squatters paid rent in labour and in kind. Many squatters were born and grew up in the Rift Valley and looked on the White Highlands as their home. Despite growing friction with white farmers, the squatters managed to survive as independent producers. By the mid-1940s, the population of Kikuyu squatters and their families had risen to about 250,000, one-quarter of the Kikuyu people.

In the postwar era, however, the squatter communities came under increasing threat. White farmers needing more land for their expanding operations, and requiring only wage labourers, imposed tight restrictions on squatter activities, forcing thousands to leave in destitution. The British government added to the pressure, setting aside a quarter of a million acres in the White Highlands for use by British ex-servicemen. In the three years following the end of the Second World War, some 8,000 white immigrants arrived in Kenya, escaping postwar austerity in Europe, bringing the total white population to 40,000.

Facing the loss of land and grazing rights and the destruction of their communities, the squatters embarked on a resistance campaign, binding themselves together with secret oaths. The Kikuyu traditionally used oaths for a variety of social purposes. In the 1920s, KCA leaders, impressed by the ceremonial accompanying the oath of allegiance to the Crown that the British employed, introduced their own oath of loyalty to the Kikuyu people. The oath involved holding a Bible in the left hand and a handful of earth in the right hand pressed to the navel, while swearing to serve the Kikuyu people faithfully. In the postwar era, members of the banned KCA, meeting in secret, devised a new oath of loyalty using only Kikuyu symbols: the meat of a goat replaced the Bible. The oathing campaign spread throughout the squatter communities in the Rift Valley. White farmers reported a mood of increasing truculence and incidents of cattle-maiming and sabotage.

In 1948 the District Commissioner of Nakuru in the Rift Valley, in his annual report, made the first official mention of the name *Mau Mau*. It was a name which in the Kikuyu language was meaningless. Its origin was lost in the Kikuyu passion for riddles. The authorities, convinced that it was a sinister secret society, outlawed the 'Mau Mau Association' in August 1950. But what they were really facing was an incipient revolt among the Kikuyu for which Mau Mau became, by common usage, the fearsome expression.

On his return to Kenya, Kenyatta rapidly assumed command of the Kenya African Union (KAU), a nationalist group formed in 1944 to campaign for African rights. His forceful personality, his powers of oratory and his flamboyant manner soon captivated the crowds who flocked to listen to him. Preferring a rural base in Kikuyuland to Nairobi, he bought a small farm, built a spacious house, filling it with books, pictures and mementoes from Europe, and married into the most powerful family in southern Kikuyuland, the Koinanges. His headquarters at Githunguri, where he was appointed principal of an independent teachers' training school, became the centre of an extensive political network. His aim was to develop the KAU into a truly national movement. But the mass support that KAU won came largely from the Kikuyu tribe, as did its leadership. It was among the Kikuyu that the mood of anger against the government and against the whites was at its most intense.

Not only squatters in the Rift Valley were on the verge of rebellion. In the heavily populated Kikuyu reserves there was growing resentment of new conservation measures enforced by the government to prevent land degradation, adding to old grievances over 'lost lands' and government restrictions on African production of lucrative cash crops like coffee. The pressure on land in the Kikuyu reserves was aggravated further by senior tribal figures accumulating ever more land for themselves. Landless peasants from Kikuyuland, along with dispossessed squatters from the Rift Valley, poured into the slums of Nairobi.

In postwar years the African population of Nairobi doubled in size. More than half of the inhabitants were Kikuyu, their ranks swelled by a growing tide of desperate, impoverished vagrants. Adding to their numbers were groups of ex-servicemen returning from the war with high expectations of a new life but finding little other than poverty and pass laws. Unemployment, poor housing, low wages, inflation and homelessness produced a groundswell of discontent and worsening crime. Mixing politics and crime, the 'Forty Group' – Anake wa 40 – consisting largely of former soldiers of the 1940 age group who had seen service during the war in India, Burma and Ethiopia and other militants were ready to employ strong-arm tactics in opposing the government's policies and in dealing with its supporters. The trade unions, gathering strength in Nairobi, carried the agitation further, conducting a virulent campaign against the granting of a royal charter to Nairobi. In the African press, too, the tone was becoming increasingly strident. By 1948, the oathing campaign, started by squatters in the Rift Valley and taken up in the Kikuyu reserves and in Nairobi, was in full swing. At fervent gatherings, Kikuyu songs, adapted from church hymns, were sung in praise of Kenyatta and prayers recited to glorify him. In all, several hundred thousand Kikuyu took the oath.

The rising temper of the Kikuyu made little impression on the British governor, Sir Philip Mitchell, a solitary, unapproachable figure from the old colonial school, contemptuous of African nationalists, more preoccupied with the recalcitrant white community than with signs of African discontent, and singularly ill-equipped to deal with the crisis unfolding before him.

Kenyatta, too, found difficulty in controlling the surge of militancy. He favoured constitutional means to oppose colonial rule but was outflanked by militant activists prepared to use violence. In 1951 a hardened group, including two prominent trade unionists, Fred Kubai and Bildad Kaggia, captured control of the Nairobi branch of the KAU, proceeded to gain a virtual stranglehold over the national executive and then formed their own secret central committee with plans for an armed uprising. Kaggia, a former staff sergeant in the army, had seen wartime service in Africa, the Middle East and England. Outbreaks of violence – murder, sabotage, arson and forced oathing – became more frequent.

The move towards violence split the Kikuyu people. Both the old Kikuyu establishment – chiefs, headmen and landowners – and the aspiring middle class – businessmen, traders, civil servants and government teachers – opposed violence. So did large numbers of Christian Kikuyu. But by 1952, much of the Kikuyu tribe was caught up in rebellion.

Kenyatta tried to ride out the turbulence, seeking to defuse the crisis rather than to stir it up. Leading activists in Nairobi, while using his name to justify their actions, regarded him with profound suspicion. When the government asked him to denounce Mau Mau publicly, he duly obliged, using a traditional Kikuyu curse. 'Let Mau Mau perish for ever,' he told a huge crowd in Kiambu in August 1952. 'All people should search for Mau Mau and kill it.' His speech infuriated the central committee. Summoned to a meeting of the central committee at KAU headquarters in Nairobi, he was clearly surprised to discover who its members were. 'We said, "We are Mau Mau and what you have said at this Kiambu meeting must not be said again",' recalled Fred Kubai. 'If Kenyatta had continued to denounce Mau Mau, we would have denounced him. He would have lost his life. It was too dangerous and he knew it. He was a bit shaken by the way we looked at him. He was not happy. We weren't the old men he was used to dealing with. We were young and we were serious.'

As the violence grew worse, with daily incidents of murder, forced oathing and intimidation, a new governor, Sir Evelyn Baring, on the advice of his officials, concluded that the best way to deal with it was to lock up all KAU leaders. In October 1952, shortly after his arrival, Baring declared a state of emergency and ordered the detention of Kenyatta and 150 other political figures, a move taken by Mau Mau activists as tantamount to a declaration of war. In growing panic, white farmers in the Rift Valley expelled some 100,000 squatters, providing Mau Mau with a massive influx of recruits. Many headed straight for the forests of the Aberdares and Mount Kenya to join armed gangs recently established there. Far from snuffing out the rebellion, Baring's action intensified it. It was only after the emergency was declared that the first white settler was murdered.

The brunt of the war, however, fell not on the whites but on loyalist Kikuyu. They became the target of Mau Mau leaders determined to enforce complete unity among the Kikuyu people before turning on the whites. Nearly 2,000 loyalists died. The official death toll of rebels and their supporters was listed as 11,500, though modern researchers put the real figure far higher. Some 80,000 Kikuyu were detained in camps, often subjected to harsh and brutal treatment. As the tide against Mau Mau turned, gang leaders in the forests tried to keep control by employing ever more perverted oaths, horrifying to the Kikuyu and to whites alike. By comparison, the white community escaped lightly. Though white farmers in isolated farmsteads often lived in fear of attack, after four years only thirty-two white civilians had been killed, less than the number who died in traffic accidents in Nairobi during the same period.

Baring was determined to pin the blame for all this on Kenyatta. 'He desperately wanted a conviction and a quick one at that,' wrote Baring's biographer, Charles Douglas-Home. The difficulty was the lack of evidence and the shortage of witnesses. Baring authorised 'rewards' to be paid to witnesses willing to testify. Informing the Colonial Office of his decision, he wrote: 'Every possible effort has been made to offer them rewards and to protect them, but no one can tell what will happen when they are confronted in court by Kenyatta's formidable personality.' The main prosecution witness, Rawson Macharia, was offered two years' study at an English university, with all expenses paid, and, on his return to Kenya, a government job. Macharia testified that he had witnessed Kenyatta administer oaths to several people in 1950. Kenyatta denied the story and so did nine defence witnesses. However, the magistrate, a retired High Court judge, Ransley Thacker, regarded as a 'sound chap' by the white community, chose to accept Macharia's evidence as the truth. 'Although my finding means that I disbelieve ten witnesses for the defence and believe one for the prosecution, I have no hesitation in doing so. Rawson Macharia gave his evidence well.' What was not known at the time was that on Baring's instructions Thacker had been promised an ex gratia payment of £20,000 to compensate him for having to leave Kenya after giving his verdict, to avoid reprisal. For his part, Macharia subsequently admitted that his evidence against Kenyatta was false.

Thacker's verdict was that Kenyatta was the mastermind behind Mau Mau who had used his influence over the Kikuyu to persuade them in secret to murder, to burn, to commit evil atrocities, with the aim of driving all Europeans out of Kenya. 'You have let loose upon this land a flood of misery and unhappiness affecting the daily lives of the races in it, including your own people.'

Duly convicted, Kenyatta was imprisoned at an inaccessible spot in the northern desert called Lokitaung, and the government did its best to erase memory of him. Githunguri was turned into an administrative centre; Kenyatta's house was pulled down and his small farm turned into an agricultural station. Baring publicly promised that never again would Kenyatta and other convicted leaders be allowed to return to Kikuyuland, not even when their sentences were finished.

In the aftermath of the rebellion, the British government recognised the need for more rapid African advancement if its strategy of developing a multiracial partnership was to survive. Notable progress was made with agrarian reform: restrictions preventing African farmers from growing a range of cash crops were removed; and in October 1959 the White Highlands were formally opened to all races. But political advancement was still hampered by white objections. The first African elections in 1957 brought eight elected Africans to the legislative council; they included the trade unionist Tom Mboya, and a minority Kalenjin leader, Daniel arap Moi. The following year the number of Africans increased to fourteen, giving them parity with white representatives, but this racial balance was expected to remain unaltered for ten years.

There still seemed ample time available to lay out long-term plans. When Britain's Colonial Secretary, Alan Lennox-Boyd, and the governors of East Africa gathered for a conference at Chequers in the English countryside in January 1959, they considered some likely dates for independence. Tanganyika, they agreed, would come first, but not before 1970; Uganda and Kenya would follow by about 1975.

★

Less than two months later, there was another explosion of violence, this time in Nyasaland, which rendered the idea of long-term planning obsolete. The root cause of the violence was mounting African opposition to the Federation of Rhodesia and Nyasaland and to plans by its white leaders to obtain independent dominion status. The opposition was led by an elderly medical doctor, Hastings Banda, who had only recently returned to Nyasaland after spending forty-two years abroad, most of them in England. Before leaving London in 1958, Banda had called on the Colonial Secretary, Alan Lennox-Boyd, an enthusiastic supporter of the Federation. Of their meeting, Lennox-Boyd recalled: 'Banda said to me, "I go back to break up your bloody Federation." I said: "This may well end in your detention." We got on very well.'

Banda was an intensely conservative figure, an Elder of the Church of Scotland, with puritanical views on dancing and dress. As a doctor in north London, he enjoyed a prosperous middle-class life, owned a house, drove a small car, dabbled on the stock market and took to wearing a black homburg hat and carrying a rolled umbrella. He was renowned for many acts of generosity and so highly respected that patients in the waiting room of his surgery would stand up when he entered. In politics he tended not to venture beyond anything respectable. But from the time the idea was first promoted, he was vehemently opposed to Nyasaland's inclusion in the Federation, campaigning tirelessly against it. When the British government gave the Federation its approval, Banda complained bitterly of the 'cold, calculating, callous and cynical betrayal of a trusting, loyal people'.

Welcomed home as the saviour of his people, Banda, at the age of sixty, threw himself with remarkable energy into the task of building up the Nyasaland African National Congress into a mass movement. Touring one district after another, invariably dressed in a dark three-piece suit and black homburg hat even under a hot midday sun, he discovered, to his surprise, that he had a talent for mob oratory. Wherever he went, there were excited, cheering crowds, relishing his attacks on the 'stupid' Federation. 'Things are hot here,' he wrote to a colleague in November 1958. 'I have the whole of Blantyre and Zomba on fire. Very soon I hope to have the whole of Nyasaland on fire.'

His campaign soon led to violence and disorder. Convinced that the government was facing a widespread conspiracy, including a plot to murder whites, the governor, Sir Robert Armitage, summoned Rhodesian troops in February 1959 to help keep order, thus exacerbating the crisis. He then declared a state of emergency, arrested Banda and hundreds of his supporters and banned the Nyasaland African National Congress. Far from restoring order, however, the emergency measures provoked greater disorder. Riots and demonstrations broke out, in which nearly fifty Africans died.

The report of an official inquiry into the violence had a devastating impact. Though finding that the governor was justified in taking emergency measures, it pointed out that they had turned Nyasaland into 'a police state'. Moreover, the report challenged the British government's contention that nationalist agitation over the Federation was confined to 'a small minority of political Africans, mainly of self-seekers'. Opposition to the Federation, it said, was 'deeply rooted and almost universally held'.

Britain's entire strategy for the region was now in disarray. The report's description of Nyasaland as 'a police state' reverberated around the world, severely damaging Britain's reputation for progressive colonial management. Plans for the future of the Federation were also thrown in doubt. No longer were British ministers able to portray the Federation as a bold experiment in racial partnership. The difficulties of colonial rule were multiplying. In Northern Rhodesia, the authorities, fearing disorders in the 1959 election there, banned one militant group advocating a boycott of the polls and arrested its leader, Kenneth Kaunda. In Kenya there was uproar over the death of Mau Mau detainees in a prison camp. Where Britain had once been in the vanguard of progress towards colonial emancipation, now it was seen to be trailing behind France, its standing much impaired. But what British ministers feared above all, in the wake of the Nyasaland emergency, were further outbreaks of anti-colonial violence that available British forces would be stretched to control.

The change of course in 1959 was abrupt. Britain jettisoned all long-term plans for independence and accelerated the whole process. No longer would African political progress be held up by the objections of white settlers. 'Any other policy would have led to terrible bloodshed in Africa,' maintained the Colonial Secretary Iain Macleod, who pushed through the new programme. Prime Minister Harold Macmillan sounded the retreat in January 1960 during an African tour to Ghana, Nigeria, Southern Rhodesia and South Africa. 'The wind of change is blowing through the continent, and whether we like it or not, this growth of national consciousness is a political fact,' he said in Cape Town. 'We must all accept it as a fact and national policies must take account of it.'

Neither Macmillan nor Macleod believed that the remaining African colonies were ready for independence. Most were economically weak; all were inadequately prepared. But the risks of moving rapidly in Africa were now outweighed by the dangers of moving too slowly. Macmillan was especially fearful of the advance of communist influence. 'As I see it,' he said, 'the great issue in the second half of the twentieth century is whether the uncommitted peoples of Asia and Africa will swing to the East or the West.' To drive nationalism back, he maintained, would be to drive it into the hands of the communists.

In short order, Kenya's white community were told they would have to accept African majority rule. Opening a constitutional conference in London in January 1960, Macleod declared: 'We intend to lead Kenya to full self-government, or, if I may use a plainer word, to independence.'

When African politicians pressed for the release of Kenyatta, the authorities eventually agreed. Released in 1961, Kenyatta made strenuous efforts to overcome the fear and suspicion with which whites regarded him, making clear his disdain for Mau Mau. 'We are determined to have independence in peace, and we shall not allow hooligans to rule Kenya,' he said in 1962. 'We must have no hatred towards one another. Mau Mau was a disease which has been eradicated, and must never be remembered again.' In his book *Suffering without Bitterness*, published in 1968 when he was president, he was even more forthright in denouncing Mau Mau: 'Those who built up an organisation of unbridled violence in Kenya were never the political associates or executive colleagues of Kenyatta.'

Banda too was released and quickly won British assent to African majority rule in Nyasaland. The battle over the Federation, however, was protracted. It raged on for three years as white politicians fought tooth and nail to keep it intact, railing against British treachery. Its demise in 1963 added to the mood of distrust and bitterness among Rhodesian whites who regarded Britain's withdrawal from Africa as an act of surrender to the forces of black extremism with dangerous implications for their own position.

The speed of the change meant that colonies in east and central Africa advanced towards independence with a minimum of trained local manpower. Whereas the Gold Coast could boast some sixty lawyers by the late 1920s, Kenya's first African lawyer did not begin to practise his profession until 1956. In Northern Rhodesia only thirty-five Africans had gained higher education by 1959; in Nyasaland the figure was twenty-eight. Not until 1957 was an African appointed a district officer in Tanganyika. In 1961, the year of Tanganyika's independence, every senior civil servant in Dar-es-Salaam, every provincial commissioner and fifty-five out of fifty-seven district commissioners were still British expatriates.

Using the old Colonial Office criteria for self-government, British officials estimated at the time that a minimum period of between ten and fifteen years of intensive training was needed to prepare reasonably efficient and stable modern administrations. But in the rush to transfer power, all previous rules were discarded. In West Africa the Nigerians had participated in elections to the legislature thirty-eight years before independence; in Ghana it had been thirty-two years. In Tanganyika the period between the first national election and independence was a mere thirty-nine months. Whereas Nigeria had nine years of 'responsible' government before independence and Ghana six years, in the case of Tanganyika it was nineteen months.

So rapid was the pace of change that in some cases British officials dealing with arrangements for the transfer of power – new constitutions, elections and parliamentary legislation – were hard pressed to complete them in time. The drafting of the Independence Order in Council for Uganda was finished only one week before the independence date. In Northern Rhodesia negotiations over the transfer of mineral rights owned by the British South Africa Company were still going on behind a tea-tent at a garden party in the grounds of Government House a few hours before independence.

For all the unseemly haste, the transfer of power was accomplished efficiently and with a remarkable amount of goodwill. One by one, the new states emerged amid much jubilation and to the world's applause. In 1961 came Sierra Leone and Tanganyika; in 1962, Uganda; in 1963, Kenya and Zanzibar. In 1964 Nyasaland gained independence as Malawi and Northern Rhodesia became Zambia. In 1965 tiny Gambia was set up as an independent state. The three southern Africa territories – the 'fleas in the Queen's blanket' – soon followed: Bechuanaland (Botswana) and Basutoland (Lesotho) in 1966 and Swaziland in 1968.

Whatever their experience of British rule, African leaders were fulsome in the tributes they paid. Dr Banda, commenting on his year's imprisonment by Britain, remarked: 'It was the best turn the British ever did for me.' Kenneth Kaunda, twice jailed by the British author- ities, referred proudly to the fact that independence in Zambia had been achieved without bitterness. Seretse Khama, once banished from Bechuanaland because of his marriage to an English girl, duly became president of Botswana, deeply attached to the British. The Sierra Leone leader, Sir Milton Margai, when asked at a London conference on what date he would like his country to become independent, burst into tears and said he never expected to live long enough to be asked that question. In his independence message, Sir Abubakar Tafawa Balewa of Nigeria spoke warmly of Britain's colonial contri- bution, 'first as masters, then as leaders, finally as partners, but always as friends'. But the most poignant speech, in the circumstances, was made by Kenyatta. 'We do not forget the assistance and guidance we have received through the years from people of British stock: admin- istrators, businessmen, farmers, missionaries and many others. Our law, our system of government and many other aspects of our daily lives are founded on British principles and justice.'

It was all in marked contrast to what happened in the Belgian Congo.

HEART OF DARKNESS

As he sat listening to King Baudouin deliver his address to the
assembled dignitaries in the Palais de le Nation in Léopoldville
on the Congo's independence day on 30 June 1960, the new prime
minister, Patrice Lumumba, became increasingly agitated, scribbling
notes furiously. Baudouin's speech was full of patronising remarks. 'It
is now up to you, gentlemen, to show that you are worthy of our confidence,' he told the Congolese delegates. He praised Belgium's
colonial record, singling out the contribution made by his great-
uncle, Léopold II. 'The independence of the Congo,' he said,
'constitutes the culmination of the work conceived by the genius of
King Léopold II, undertaken by him with a tenacious courage and
continued with perseverance with Belgium.' He went on to offer
advice on how the Congolese should manage their affairs. 'Don't
compromise the future with hasty reforms, and don't replace the
structures that Belgium hands over to you until you are sure you can
do better.'

The Congo's president, Joseph Kasa-Vubu, gave a short speech in
reply, keeping to his prepared text, but, angered by the whole tone of
Baudouin's address, he decided to leave out the final passage which
paid personal tribute to the king.

Lumumba, however, had no intention of letting the matter pass.

Excluded from the official programme, he rose to deliver a tirade against Belgium, being deliberately rude and vindictive, denouncing at length the 'terrible suffering' and 'exploitation' of Belgian rule. What Baudouin had sought to glorify as his great–uncle's masterpiece was nothing more than 'humiliating slavery that was imposed on us by force', he said.

> We have known sarcasm and insults, endured blows morning, noon and night, because we were 'niggers' . . . We have seen our lands despoiled under the terms of what was supposedly the law of the land but which only recognised the right of the strongest. We have seen that the law was quite different for a white than for a black: accommodating for the former, cruel and inhuman for the latter. We have seen the terrible suffering of those banished to remote regions because of their political opinions or religious beliefs; exiled within their own country, their fate was truly worse than death itself . . . And finally, who can forget the volleys of gunfire in which so many of our brothers perished, the cells where the authorities threw those who would not submit to a rule where justice meant oppression and exploitation.

Lumumba's speech was warmly applauded by the Congolese present. But the Belgians were outraged. The official lunch which followed the ceremony was delayed for two hours while Baudouin and his ministers debated whether to boycott it and fly back at once to Belgium. When the lunch eventually took place, it was cold and dis-organised. Lumumba was portrayed in the Belgian press as a dangerous extremist. Lumumba himself was pleased enough with the result to have copies of his speech sent all over the Congo.

The Congo's origins as a state were different from any other African country. It began life not as a colony but as the personal property of Léopold II, an ambitious, greedy and devious monarch whose lust for territory and wealth was largely responsible for igniting the Scramble for Africa among European powers. Determined to obtain what he called 'a slice of this *magnifique gâteau africain*', in 1878 he hired the

Welsh-born journalist-explorer Henry Morton Stanley, who had recently returned from an epic journey across Africa, to carve out a territory for him along the Congo river.

Over a period of five years, Stanley signed 'treaties' with more than 400 African chiefs, persuading them to give up their sovereignty, and proceeded to establish a network of outposts in the equatorial forests of the Congo basin on Léopold's behalf. A hard taskmaster, never slow to hand out severe punishment, Stanley gained the name *Bula Matari* – a Kikongo term meaning 'Breaker of Rocks', derived from the use white engineers made of dynamite to blast a trail through the Crystal Mountains into the interior. The name, with its image of crushing, overwhelming force, soon came to be applied to the Belgian regime in general and the European agents it employed. For the Bakongo, the name signified terror.

In 1885, after much manoeuvring, Léopold obtained international approval for his personal empire, calling it the Congo Free State. It was an area of nearly 1 million square miles, seventy-five times the size of Belgium and one-thirteenth of the African continent. It included a web of interconnecting rivers, navigable by steamboat, running deep into the interior and a wealth of resources such as ivory, palm oil, timber and copper. Pondering a choice of title for himself, Léopold at first considered 'Emperor of the Congo', but he eventually settled for the more modest 'King-Sovereign'.

Léopold's principal aim henceforth was to amass as large a fortune for himself as possible. Ivory was at first his main hope. Company agents paid on commission scoured the country, sending out hunting expeditions, raiding villages, press-ganging porters, employing ever more ruthless means to collect ivory. The symbol of Léopold's rule became the *chicotte* – a whip of raw, sun-dried hippopotamus hide, cut into long, sharp-edged strips, used to flay victims, sometimes to death.

The madness of greed and violence that engulfed Léopold's Congo Free State was immortalised by Joseph Conrad in his novel *Heart of Darkness*, which he wrote after working as a river-boat captain on the Congo for some six months. The central character in the novel, Kurtz, the head of Inner Station, is renowned for his exploits as an ivory-collector. 'Sends in as much ivory as all the others put together', it was said of him. But he is a sick man, haunted by memories of his own savagery, and finally dies, whispering in despair: 'The horror, the horror.'

Léopold's next fortune came from wild rubber. With the invention of the pneumatic tyre, fitted first to bicycles and then to motor cars in the 1890s, demand for rubber and the price for it soared. Using a system of slave labour, concession companies, sharing their profits with Léopold, stripped the Congo's equatorial forests of all the wild rubber they could lay their hands on, imposing quotas on villagers and taking hostages whenever necessary. Villagers who failed to fulfil their quotas were flogged, imprisoned and even mutilated, their hands cut off. Thousands were killed for resisting Léopold's rubber regime; thousands more fled their homes.

The increase in rubber production was impressive. In 1890 the Congo exported 100 tons of rubber; in 1901, 6,000 tons. But Léopold's regime provoked uprisings and revolts and left behind a landscape of burned villages, terrified refugees, starvation and disease. Ultimately, his rule came to depend on the *Force Publique*, an army composed of white officers and African auxiliaries, notorious for its brutal conduct. By the end of his twenty-three-year reign as 'King-Sovereign', Léopold had become one of the richest men in Europe. But the Congo had lost several million people, possibly as many as 10 million, half of its population. In an essay on exploration, Joseph Conrad described the activities of Léopold's Congo Free State as 'the vilest scramble for loot that ever disfigured the history of human conscience'.

This was the man to whom Baudouin referred on independence day in 1960 as a genius.

The public furore that eventually erupted over the Congo's 'rubber terror' forced Léopold in 1908 to hand over his private empire to the Belgian government. The colonial state that replaced it was rigidly controlled by a small management group in Brussels representing an alliance between the government, the Catholic Church and the giant mining and business corporations, whose activities were virtually exempt from outside scrutiny. In essence, the government provided administration, the Church attended to education and moral welfare, and the mining corporations produced the revenue to support the whole enterprise.

The Congo remained an immensely profitable venture. No other colony in Africa possessed such profusion of copper, diamonds and uranium. The mineral riches of Katanga, when first discovered, were memorably described as 'a veritable geological scandal'. By 1959 the Congo was producing nearly 10 per cent of the world's copper, 50 per cent of its cobalt and 70 per cent of its industrial diamonds. All this enabled Belgium to maintain a framework of law, order and develop-ment which far surpassed the efforts of other colonial powers. Even in the more remote rural areas the firm hand of Belgian authority was to be found, ensuring that villagers produced crops efficiently, main-tained the roads and were available for work on mines and plantations. Missionaries were active in building an impressive network of primary schools and clinics across the country; by 1950 more than one-third of the population were professed Christians. Mining companies in the eastern Congo provided their employees with housing, welfare schemes and technical training. The assumption on which Belgian rule was based was that the African population, given strict upbring-ing, wise leadership and enough material benefits would be content with Belgian rule for the rest of their lives.

No Congolese was ever consulted about this system of government. The Congolese had no political voice, no rights to own land or to travel freely. They were subject to curfews in urban areas; in rural areas, to forced labour. Though primary schools abounded, there was no higher education available except in Catholic seminaries. Nor were students allowed to study in Belgium. Only in 1950 were Congolese children seeking higher education permitted for the first time to enter white secondary schools. While Africans were encour-aged to train as clerks, medical assistants or mechanics, they could not become doctors, lawyers or architects. Quite deliberately, the Belgians set out to isolate the Congo from any outside influence and to stifle the emergence of a black elite which might demand a change in the system.

In postwar years, as the economy boomed, a small black elite nev-ertheless emerged. But it was an elite concerned only with demanding more rights and an end to discrimination for themselves. No one challenged Belgium's authority. 'The essential wish of the Congolese elite,' wrote Patrice Lumumba in 1956, 'is to be "Belgians" and to have the right to the same freedoms and the same rights.'

A tall, thin, intense man, born a member of the small Batatela tribe in Kasai province in 1925, Lumumba had a charismatic personality and great powers of oratory but a mercurial, volatile temperament. Though his formal education consisted of only four years at primary school and one year of technical training at a school for postal clerks, he possessed high intelligence and a restless energy. While working as a postal clerk in Stanleyville (Kisangani), he edited the journal of the postal workers' union and contributed articles to other journals and newspapers. Stanleyville became his main political base. Convicted of embezzlement in 1956, he spent a year in prison, using his time to write a book – *Le Congo, Terre d'Avenir* – setting out his views on colonial rule. On his release he moved to the capital, Léopoldville, where he worked as a salesman for a local brewery.

Political activity in Léopoldville at the time was beginning to stir. News of Ghana's independence in 1957 and the growing momentum in neighbouring French colonies towards African rule provided a new stimulus. The first initiative came from a tribal organisation, Abako, originally founded by Bakongo leaders to promote use of the Kikongo language, but which now began to make overt political demands. Abako's leader, Joseph Kasa-Vubu, who had once trained as a priest, set his sights on reuniting the Bakongo people divided by the boundaries of the Belgian Congo, the French Congo and Angola and rebuilding the old Kongo kingdom that had last flourished in the sixteenth century. Among the Bakongo living in Léopoldville and the Lower Congo region, Abako established a strong political base.

Lumumba chose a different road. In 1958 he joined a group of other young educated Congolese - *évolués*, as they were called – to launch the *Mouvement National Congolais* (MNC) to rally support on a national basis. Along with two companions, he was allowed to travel to Accra in December 1958 to attend the All-African People's Conference. Like other delegates present at the conference, he returned home burning with enthusiasm for the struggle against colonial rule and determined to build the MNC into a mass political movement along the lines of Nkrumah's CPP. Addressing a MNC meeting on his return, Lumumba declared: 'The *Mouvement National Congolais* has as its basic aim the liberation of the Congolese people from the colonial regime . . . we wish to bid farewell to the old regime, this regime of subjection . . . Africa is engaged in a merciless struggle for its liberation against the coloniser.'

Seven days later, with a suddenness that shook Belgium to the core, Léopoldville was torn by vicious rioting. The immediate cause of the violence in January 1959 was a decision by the local authorities to refuse permission for Abako to hold a scheduled Sunday afternoon meeting. But Belgian investigations showed that unemployment, over-crowding and discrimination had produced a groundswell of frustration and discontent.

To help restore calm, the Belgian government announced a pro-gramme of political reform, starting with local government elections. It also added a vague promise about independence as being the even-tual goal of Belgian policy. But having taken that momentous decision, it then fell into protracted debate about the wisdom of the move.

Across the Congo, however, political activity burst out in wild and hectic profusion. By November 1959 as many as fifty-three political groups were officially registered; a few months later the number had increased to 120. Almost every party sprang from tribal origins. Some were based on major groups like the Bakongo, the Baluba, the Balunda and the Bamongo; others were of only local importance. In Katanga, the Congo's richest province where the giant copper indus-try was located, a thousand miles south-east of Léopoldville, the main party to emerge was the Lunda-dominated Conakat – *Confédération des Associations Tribales du Katanga*. Led by Moise Tshombe, a shrewd, clever politician, the son of a wealthy Katanga businessman, it favoured provincial autonomy for Katanga, worked closely with Belgian groups pursuing the same interest, and advocated continuing ties with Belgium.

Amid the profusion of tribal rivalry, only the MNC stood out as the champion of Congolese nationalism. Lumumba travelled around the country stirring crowds with his impassioned speeches. As he sought to keep the MNC ahead of other political parties, his demands became increasingly extreme. Moderates within the MNC tried to remove him, then decided to break away to form their own group. At a MNC congress in Stanleyville (Kisangani) in October 1959, delegates agreed to launch a campaign of positive action for the immediate liberation of the Congo. Following Lumumba's speech, riots broke out and twenty-six Africans were killed. Lumumba was arrested and sentenced to six months' imprisonment for inciting violence.

As well as Stanleyville, other key areas of the Congo descended into disorder and violence which the Belgian authorities found difficult to suppress. In the Lower Congo the Bakongo refused to pay taxes and to abide by administrative regulations. In Kasai province a tribal war broke out between the Lulua and the Baluba. Disturbances continued in Stanleyville and when King Baudouin visited the town in December 1959, the mob of demonstrators that greeted him at the airport had to be dispersed with tear gas. Local elections held in December were boycotted in many parts of the country.

Alarmed by the possibility that they might be drawn into an Algerian type of war, the Belgian government sought to regain the initiative by inviting the leaders of thirteen political parties to a conference in Brussels in January 1960 to discuss the terms and timetable for independence. It was the first occasion on which the Belgian authorities had consulted Congolese opinion. Among those who attended were Kasa-Vubu, Tshombe and Lumumba, who had been released from prison especially so that he could be present. The Belgian negotiators had been hoping for an agreement which would lead to a phased transfer of power over a period of about four years, but found themselves faced with a united front of Congolese delegates, excited by the prospect of power and position, demanding immediate elections and independence on 1 June 1960. The most the Congolese were willing to concede was an extra thirty days of Belgian rule. Fearing the alternative would be a colonial war, Belgium agreed to the independence of the Congo on 30 June.

The risks involved were enormous. Except at a local level, no Congolese had acquired any experience of government or parliamentary life. No national or even provincial elections had ever been held. The lack of skilled personnel was acute. In the top ranks of the civil service no more than three Congolese out of an establishment of 1,400 held posts and two of those were recent appointments. By 1960 the sum total of university graduates was thirty. Indeed, the largest complement of trained manpower were priests: of those there were more than six hundred. At the end of the 1959–60 academic year, only 136 children completed secondary education. There were no Congolese doctors, no secondary school teachers, no army officers. The first contingent of Congolese officer cadets to be sent for training in Belgium was not due to return until 1963.

When conceding the Congolese demand for such a swift transfer of power, the Belgian gamble – *le pari Congolais* – was that it would provide Congolese politicians with the trappings of power while purchasing enough goodwill to enable them to continue running the country much as before. Though the Congolese would assume political responsibility for government ministries, the core of the colonial state – the bureaucracy, the army and the economy – would remain in Belgian hands. The gamble was also based on the hope that, with Belgian assistance, 'moderate' pro-Belgium parties would fare well in the elections before independence. 'If we have a little luck,' said Belgium's Minister for the Congo, M. de Schryver, in May 1960, 'we shall have won the independent Congo bet.'

But moderate parties fared badly in the elections. The lead was taken by Lumumba's MNC, which had become increasingly distrustful of Belgian intentions. Of 137 seats, the MNC took 33, the largest single total; together with its allies, it could count on 41 seats. But nearly half of the MNC vote came from just one province, the Stanleyville hinterland. The MNC gained little support in two crucial areas, in Léopoldville and in southern Katanga. In the wheeling and dealing that followed, the Belgian authorities showed themselves unduly reluctant to allow Lumumba to form a government, turning instead to Kasa-Vubu. But when Lumumba managed to obtain majority support in the Chamber of Deputies – 74 out of 137 seats – they were obliged to call on him.

The final result achieved five days before independence was a

cumbersome coalition of twelve different parties, which included
bitter rivals. Kasa-Vubu was chosen as a non-executive president; and
Lumumba, then only thirty-five years old, ill-prepared for office and
harbouring deep resentment about Belgian intrigues during the election, became the Congo's first prime minister. '*Nous ne sommes plus vos
singes*,' Lumumba told King Baudouin, in his speech at the Palais de la
Nation – 'We are no longer your monkeys.'

It was only a few days before the first disaster struck. Among the ranks
of the *Force Publique*, the Congo's 25,000-man army, resentment over
low pay and lack of promotion had been simmering for months.
Soldiers contrasted their own dismal prospects with the sudden wealth
and influence of civilian politicians, former clerks and salesmen, now
driving around in large cars and spending money freely. While the
government was run by Congolese, the army remained under the
control of the same 1,100-strong Belgian officer corps. The *Force
Publique* commander, General Emile Janssens, a tough right-wing
career officer, was adamant that there would be no acceleration in the
Africanisation programme. After an incident of indiscipline at an army
barracks in Léopoldville on 4 June, Janssens summoned officers and
men on duty at army headquarters and lectured them on the need for
absolute obedience. To make his point clear, he wrote on a blackboard
the words: 'Before independence = after independence.' A protest
meeting of soldiers held in the army camp that night demanded the
dismissal of Janssens and ended in a riot. Troops at another garrison
were ordered to intervene, but mutinied and went on the rampage
attacking European civilians.

   Lumumba publicly accused Belgian officers of fomenting rebellion
and dismissed Janssens and other senior officers. In subsequent negotiations with the army, Lumumba decided that the entire officer corps
should be replaced by Congolese. The new army commander he
appointed, Victor Lundula, was a former sergeant who had last served
in the army in the Second World War. As chief of staff, Lumumba
chose his trusted personal aide, Joseph Mobutu, who had spent seven
years in the *Force Publique* working mainly as a clerk, rising to the rank
of sergeant-major, the highest rank open to Congolese. Discharged

from military service in 1956, Mobutu had taken up freelance journalism; he had also become a paid informer for the Belgian police, providing detailed reports on the activities of fellow Congolese.

Despite these changes, the mutiny spread. In scores of incidents, whites were humiliated, beaten and raped; priests and nuns were singled out for special insults. Seized by panic, the white population fled in thousands. The Belgian government at first tried to persuade Lumumba to permit Belgian troops stationed in the Congo to restore order, but when Lumumba refused, it unilaterally ordered Belgian forces into action and arranged to fly in reinforcements. As Belgian troops took control of key points like Léopoldville airport, Lumumba became convinced that Belgium was trying to reimpose its rule. He broke off diplomatic relations and declared that, as far as he was concerned, the Congo was now at war with Belgium.

On 11 July the crisis escalated. With the connivance of Belgium and the support of Belgian mining and commercial firms, the Katanga leader, Moise Tshombe, grasped the opportunity of the chaos to declare Katanga an independent state. Belgian troops were used to disarm and expel Congolese army units from the province; Belgian regular officers formerly attached to the *Force Publique* began training a new Katangese *gendarmerie*; and a Belgian technical assistance mission was sent to Elisabethville, the Katanga capital, to act, in effect, as a shadow government. Belgium stopped short of according Katanga official recognition; it still favoured a unified Congo. Its main purpose was to insulate the province from the disorder and militant nationalism sweeping the rest of the Congo and to safeguard Western investment there. But it was also intent on using Katanga as a base from which to establish a pro-Belgian government in Léopoldville.

Within a fortnight of independence, the Congo's plight was critical. Internal security had collapsed; the army had degenerated into a rabble; the exodus of whites had left the administration bereft of expertise; Léopoldville was in turmoil; the secession of Katanga threatened to break the country apart; and Belgium was actively looking for ways of ousting Lumumba's government.

In desperation, Lumumba appealed to the United Nations for help. Acting with remarkable speed, within days the UN organised a major

airlift of foreign troops, mainly from African countries, and set in
motion plans for a large civilian task force to run public services.

But Lumumba wanted more. In an increasingly volatile mood, he
demanded that the UN force be used to expel Belgian troops. After
meeting him in Léopoldville on 16 July, the head of the UN operation in the Congo, Ralph Bunche, an African-American awarded the
Nobel Peace Prize for his United Nations work, reported that
'Lumumba was crazy and that he reacted like a child'. The following
day, Lumumba issued an ultimatum threatening that if the UN did not
remove all Belgian troops from the Congo by midnight on 19 July,
then he would invite the Soviet Union to intervene. At a time when
Cold War rivalry was at one of its peaks, Lumumba's threats infuriated
the United States and pitched the Congo into the middle of a Cold
War confrontation. US officials feared the possibility of 'another
Cuba' – a Communist takeover, similar to Fidel Castro's Cuban revolution in 1959, that would provide the Soviet Union with a base in
the heart of Africa. At a meeting of the US National Security Council
in Washington on 22 July, presided over by President Eisenhower, the
Central Intelligence Agency chief, Allen Dulles, described Lumumba
as 'a Castro or worse', adding: 'It is safe to go on the assumption that
Lumumba has been bought by the Communists.'

A visit that Lumumba paid to Washington in late July went badly.
The US under-secretary of state, Douglas Dillon, assessed Lumumba
as 'an irrational, almost "psychotic" personality'. At their meeting at
the State Department, according to Dillon, 'he would never look
you in the eye. He looked up at the sky. And a tremendous flow of
words came out . . . And his words didn't ever have any relation to the
particular things we wanted to discuss. You had the feeling that he was
a person that was gripped by this fervour that I can only characterise
as messianic. He was just not a rational being.' He concluded: 'The
impression that was left was very bad, that this was an individual
whom it was impossible to deal with.' Dillon subsequently became
convinced that Lumumba was 'working to serve the purposes of the
Soviets' to oust the UN from the Congo and take it over on their
behalf.

Lumumba's personal behaviour in Washington did not help. The

State Department's Congo desk officer, Thomas Cassily, reported that Lumumba had asked him to provide a female companion for him at Blair House where he was staying. Taken aback, Cassily asked him what exactly had the prime minister in mind. '*Une blanche blonde*', replied Lumumba. Lumumba's request was passed on to the CIA who duly procured a suitable woman. But before she could be delivered, the White House put a stop to the matter.

Belgian troops were eventually withdrawn from the Congo. But Lumumba issued new demands, insisting that UN troops be used to end the secession of Katanga, by force if necessary. When UN officials made clear to him that their mandate precluded interfering in the Congo's internal conflicts and that they wanted a negotiated settlement in Katanga, Lumumba reacted in fury, accusing the UN of collaboration with Belgium and attacking the whole UN operation. Key UN officials came to share the US and Belgian view that Lumumba was too erratic and irrational to be trusted. 'His dealings with the UN quickly deteriorated into a bewildering series of pleas for assistance, threats and ultimatums,' recalled Brian Urquhart, a senior UN official. 'He issued impossible demands and expected instant results.' Lumumba's diatribes against the UN both jeopardised the safety of UN personnel working in the Congo and alienated foreign governments which had provided troops to support the UN's Congo operation. The UN Secretary-General, Dag Hammarskjöld, feared that Lumumba's actions might wreck not only the Congo but the United Nations as well.

Congolese politicians in Léopoldville and the Catholic hierarchy were similarly exasperated by Lumumba's incessant quarrelling, his dictatorial habits and impetuous decisions. Often he listened neither to argument nor to advice, driving colleagues to rage and despair.

On 15 August, obsessed by the need for military victory in Katanga and facing another secession in south Kasai, the main source of the Congo's diamond riches, Lumumba took the fateful decision to ask the Soviet Union for immediate military assistance. With the support of Soviet aircraft, trucks, crews and technicians, he planned to send a military force first to regain control in south Kasai and then to march on Elisabethville to overthrow Tshombe.

At a meeting of the US National Security Council three days later, President Eisenhower, when told by his advisers that Lumumba might succeed in forcing the UN to leave the Congo, authorised the CIA to 'eliminate' Lumumba. 'The President would have vastly preferred to have him taken care of some way other than by assassination,' recalled Richard Bissell, the CIA operations chief at the time. 'But he regarded Lumumba as I did and a lot of other people did: as a mad dog . . . and he wanted the problem dealt with.'

On 26 August the head of the CIA, Allen Dulles, sent a telegram to Lawrence Devlin, the CIA station chief in Léopoldville, saying: 'In high quarters here it is the clear-cut conclusion that if [Lumumba] continues to hold high office, the inevitable result will be at best chaos and at worst pave the way to Communist takeover of the Congo with disastrous consequences for the prestige of the UN and for the interests of the free world generally. Consequently we concluded that his removal must be an urgent and prime objective.'

Lumumba's military expedition to Kasai meanwhile resulted in the massacre of hundreds of Baluba tribesmen and the flight of a quarter of a million refugees. News of the atrocities in Kasai added to the alarm spreading among Lumumba's growing band of critics and opponents. Hammarskjöld described the events in Kasai as having 'the characteristics of the crime of genocide'. Colonel Mobutu, now the army's chief of staff, fell out with Lumumba over the expedition and joined the ranks of his critics.

As moves to get rid of Lumumba gathered momentum, the focus of attention settled on President Kasa-Vubu. An indolent politician, he had hitherto shown no inclination to intervene. 'In my opinion,' the US ambassador, Clare Timberlake, told the State Department, 'he is naïve, not very bright, lazy, enjoying his new found plush living and content to appear occasionally in his new general's uniform.' But, urged on by Congolese supporters, by his Belgian advisers and by US diplomats, Kasa-Vubu finally roused himself.

In a radio broadcast on 5 September, he accused Lumumba of governing arbitrarily and plunging the Congo into civil war, and announced that he had 'revoked' his appointment as prime minister and appointed Joseph Ileo, a widely respected moderate, in his place.

He then returned to his residence and went to bed. The UN force commander, General van Horn, recalled in his memoirs how, after the broadcast, the atmosphere changed to one of 'relief, almost of satisfaction'.

Lumumba, however, was not so easily thwarted. On hearing the news, he rushed to the radio station to announce that he had dismissed Kasa–Vubu as president, accusing him of treason. In the confusion that followed, some parts of the Congo declared for Lumumba, other parts for Kasa–Vubu and Ileo. Parliament voted to annul both decisions. Western governments sided with Kasa–Vubu; the Soviet bloc with Lumumba. The United Nations, loudly criticised by all sides, was caught in the middle. As Lumumba and Ileo competed for support from the army and the populace, arrests and counter-arrests began. The UN mission chief in Léopoldville, Andrew Cordier, warned Hammarskjöld of the imminent possibility of a 'complete disintegration of authority'.

The outcome was decided on 14 September. With the active encouragement of the CIA and the connivance of UN officials, Colonel Joseph Mobutu, the 29-year-old army chief of staff, who controlled the Léopoldville troops, stepped forward and declared that he was neutralising all politicians until the end of the year and assuming power himself. He then ordered the expulsion of all Russian and Czech personnel.

At the time of his first coup in September 1960, Mobutu appeared as a nervous and hesitant figure clearly daunted by the chaos into which the Congo had sunk. Worried about his safety, he often sought the company of UN officials, paying nocturnal visits to '*Le Royal*', the UN headquarters in Léopoldville, arriving there exhausted and sometimes in despair, and staying late into the night, drinking heavily. The chief UN representative in the Congo, Rajeshwar Dayal, saw him at the time as 'a young man who was so troubled by his unfamiliar and onerous responsibilities and overwhelmed by the problems of his country'. In his memoirs, Dayal wrote: 'Mobutu gave the impression of Hamlet torn between opposing loyalties, unsure of himself and full of doubts and fears. His mobile face was gloomy and preoccupied, his dark glasses adding to his mournful appearance.'

Nevertheless, Mobutu was a willing accomplice in the intrigues of Western governments. 'From time to time,' wrote Dayal, 'Western military attachés would visit Mobutu with bulging briefcases containing thick brown paper packets which they obligingly deposited on his table.' The CIA station chief, Lawrence Devlin, struck up a particularly close relationship with him, providing him with funds to secure the loyalty of his troops. In later years, Mobutu's fortunes would come to depend heavily on his links with the CIA.

Mobutu's coup led to further division in the Congo. He formed an interim government, retaining Kasa-Vubu as president but excluding all Lumumba's supporters. Lumumba himself, after seeking UN protection, continued to live at the prime minister's residence in Léopoldville, a mansion situated on a bluff overlooking the Congo river, guarded by an inner ring of UN troops in the garden to prevent his arrest and surrounded by an outer ring of Mobutu's soldiers on the perimeter to prevent his escape. His conduct remained erratic. On one occasion he threatened that Soviet troops would be used to expel 'brutally' the UN from the Congo. 'If it is necessary to call on the devil to save the country, I will do it without hesitation, confident that with the total support of the Soviets, I will, in spite of everything, emerge victorious.' Four days later, he asked for UN assistance to secure a reconciliation with Kasa-Vubu.

The CIA, meanwhile, fearing that Lumumba might return to power, continued with its assassination schemes. At a meeting of the National Security Council on 21 September, chaired by President Eisenhower, CIA chief Allen Dulles stressed that 'Lumumba . . . remained a grave danger as long as he was not disposed of'. A senior CIA scientist, Dr Sidney Gottlieb, put together an assassination kit that included a poison designed 'to produce a disease indigenous to that area of Africa and that could be fatal'. Gottlieb sent the kit by diplomatic pouch to Léopoldville, then travelled there himself on 27 September to instruct Larry Devlin on how to use it. Gottlieb explained to Devlin that the poison had to be put in Lumumba's food or on his toothbrush. But the poison reached its expiry date before Devlin had worked out a scheme to infiltrate Lumumba's residence. According to Devlin, he dumped the poison kit into the Congo river.

The Belgians were also working on assassination schemes. In a telegram to Belgian officials in Elisabethville on 6 October, the Minister of African Affairs, Count Harold d'Aspremont Lynden, the chief architect of Katanga's secession, summed up Belgian intentions: 'The main aim to pursue in the interests of the Congo, Katanga and Belgium, is clearly Lumumba's *élimination définitive.*'

According to a memorandum written by a Belgian officer recording a subsequent meeting between Mobutu, Tshombe and their expatriate advisers, the general consensus among them was that Lumumba should be 'neutralised, physically if possible'. The memorandum, dated 19 October, was passed on to King Baudouin who noted in the margin: 'One cannot allow the achievements of the past eighty years be destroyed by the hate-filled policies of one man.'

UN officials in Léopoldville, well aware of how hazardous Lumumba's position was, warned him that they would only be able to provide protection if he remained in his residence in the capital. But in November, shortly after the UN General Assembly bowed to American pressure and accorded recognition to Kasa-Vubu's administration, Lumumba decided to head for Stanleyville, his main political base, to set up a rival regime there. 'If I die, *tant pis,*' he told a friend, Anicet Kashamura. 'The Congo needs martyrs.' On the evening of 27 November, during a tropical downpour, Lumumba left his residence, crouching in the back of a Chevrolet taking his servants home for the night. But for his insistence on stopping along the way to harangue local villagers whenever the opportunity arose, he might have reached Stanleyville safely. On 1 December, however, he was arrested in Kasai province, halfway to Stanleyville. Denied protection by UN troops, he was severely beaten, flown back to Léopoldville and handed into the army's custody. According to an account by Cléophas Kamitatu, a former minister, when Lumumba was brought to Mobutu's residence in the Binza paracommando camp, Mobutu 'scrutinised Lumumba with a malicious air, spat in his face, then said to him, "Well! You swore to have my skin, now it is I who have yours."'

While Lumumba languished in an army prison at Thysville, about 100 miles south-west of Léopoldville, his supporters in Stanleyville led by Antoine Gizenga established their own government – the 'Free

Republic of the Congo' – and raised an army. The Congo, six months after independence, was divided into four regimes, each with its own army and each with its foreign sponsors. Mobutu and Kasa-Vubu in Léopoldville were supported by Western governments; Gizenga in Stanleyville received help from the Soviet bloc and from radical leaders such as Nasser in Cairo; Tshombe in Katanga, though still not formally recognised, relied on Belgian assistance; and in south Kasai, the ramshackle 'Diamond State' led by Albert Kalonji also received help from Belgian interests. Only the presence of UN troops and civilian personnel provided some semblance of national order. But the UN operation itself was constantly buffeted by rows and disputes among rival delegations in New York and by fierce tensions in the Congo.

The fate of Lumumba was central to the Congo crisis. Even in prison he remained a potent force – a rallying symbol to his supporters, a persistent danger to his enemies. While the Léopoldville government led by Mobutu and Kasa-Vubu stumbled on ineffectively, propped up by the United Nations and Belgian advisers, the new Stanleyville regime formed in Lumumba's name grew from strength to strength. In late December the provincial government of Kivu, in the eastern Congo, fell into Stanleyville's hands. Mobutu despatched troops to regain control but the expedition ended in disarray. A week later Stanleyville troops drove into north Katanga and attempted to set up a separate 'Province of Lualaba'. These advances in the eastern Congo produced a wave of alarm in Léopoldville. In the army and police there was mounting unrest. Rumours abounded about the possibility of a coup in Lumumba's favour.

The Belgian government and Congolese politicians in Léopoldville alike became increasingly fearful of the impact that Lumumba's release would have. On 4 January 1961 Count d'Aspremont Lynden in Brussels sent a telegram to André Lahaye, the Belgian adviser to Mobutu's head of security, Victor Nendaka, drawing 'special attention' to 'the disastrous consequences of releasing Lumumba'. A few days later d'Aspremont Lynden stressed again that Lumumba's release had to be avoided 'at all cost, I repeat, at all cost'.

Then on 13 January, at the Thysville army camp where Lumumba was imprisoned, troops mutinied demanding higher pay. Kasa-Vubu and Mobutu rushed to the barracks and with offers of more pay and privileges they managed to restore order. But the effect that Lumumba had on troops guarding him was clearly unsettling. Mobutu's adviser, Colonel Louis Marlière, the senior Belgian official in Léopoldville at the time, was convinced that 'Lumumba had to be eliminated'. It was, he said years later, 'a public health measure'. Both he and Lahaye, he admitted, had been 'intimately involved in the preparation of this operation'.

The coterie of Congolese running the Léopoldville regime, among them Mobutu, Kasa-Vubu and Nendaka, were equally convinced of the need to get rid of Lumumba. The plan they devised, along with their Belgian advisers, was to send him to Elisabethville, Tshombe's capital, knowing that it was tantamount to a death sentence.

In Brussels, d'Aspremont Lynden gave his imprimatur to the scheme. On 16 January he sent a telegram to the Belgian consulate in Elisabethville, marked for the attention of President Tshombe. It read: 'Aspremont personally urges President Tshombe to allow Lumumba to be transferred to Katanga with the least possible delay.' Kasa-Vubu phoned Tshombe the same day to discuss the transfer.

In the early morning of 17 January 1961 Lumumba and two colleagues were collected by Nendaka from the army camp at Thysville. They were taken to an airfield at Moanda, accompanied by three Baluba soldiers from Kasai, specially chosen for their hatred of Lumumba. On the six-hour flight to Elisabethville the prisoners were savagely beaten by their guards. Their clothes torn and bloodstained, they were met at the airport by a large contingent of Belgian officers and Katangese soldiers, hit with rifle butts, thrown into the back of a truck and taken to an empty house two miles from the airport, guarded by troops and police under the command of a Belgian officer. Held in the bathroom, they were repeatedly beaten and tortured. Tshombe and other Katangese ministers came by to taunt them, joining in the savagery. When Tshombe returned to his official residence, he was, according to his butler, 'covered in blood'. During a drunken session at Tshombe's residence later that night, the Katangese decided that Lumumba and his companions should be executed at once.

At about 10 p.m., according to an authoritative account by the Dutch journalist Ludo de Witte, the three prisoners were taken in a convoy of vehicles to a remote clearing in the bush thirty miles away. Among those in the convoy were Tshombe, several other Katangese ministers, three Belgian military policemen and a Belgian police commissioner, Frans Verscheure.

When they arrived, their graves had already been dug. The prisoners were barefoot and dressed only in their trousers and vests. As he was led to the graves, Lumumba spoke to Verscheure: 'You're going to kill us, aren't you?' he asked. 'Yes,' replied Verscheure. Lumumba was the last to die, shot by a firing squad under the command of a Belgian officer.

During the night the Belgians, increasingly worried about the implications of their involvement in Lumumba's murder, began to concoct a cover story about how Lumumba and his companions had been killed by 'patriotic' villagers after escaping from detention. They also decided to get rid of the bodies. The following night two Belgians and their African assistants dug up the corpses, transported them to Kasenga, 120 miles north-east of Elisabethville, hacked them into pieces and threw the pieces into a barrel of sulphuric acid. Then they ground up the skulls and scattered the bones and teeth during the return journey, so that no trace of Lumumba and his companions would ever be found.

The murder of Lumumba turned him into one of the most famous political martyrs of modern times. It sent shockwaves through much of the Congo and led to worldwide protest. The Belgian embassy in Cairo was sacked and there were demonstrations in more than thirty cities including Washington, New York and London. To many protesters he was a heroic figure struggling to free his country from the iron grip of imperialism, the victim of a neo-colonial conspiracy, cut down by Western powers because he challenged their hegemony. Overnight he entered the pantheon of liberation heroes.

Certainly, the difficulties that Lumumba faced were immense. Belgium's abject failure to devise any coherent policy for bringing independence to the Congo meant that this vast and complex country passed into the hands of ill-assorted politicians lacking all experience of government, parliamentary life and administration and suddenly required to deal simultaneously with a mutinous army and a secessionist movement intent on appropriating the main source of its wealth.

Yet Lumumba himself contributed much to the cauldron of chaos, fear and violence into which the Congo descended. The coalition government that he headed was shaky from the start; his own party held no more than a quarter of parliamentary seats. He possessed no plan of action or strategy and his habit of taking impulsive and arbitrary decisions quickly alienated many of his Congolese allies. In the frenetic atmosphere he created, conspiracy and hatred flourished around him.

Carried away by his own anti-colonial rhetoric, he also managed within a few weeks to set not only Belgium but the United States and the United Nations against him, just when the Congo most needed their assistance. His appeal to the Soviet Union was no more than a piece of opportunism but it unleashed a bout of Cold War rivalry with dangerous ramifications. The Soviet Union's response was similarly opportunistic; it possessed few means in 1960 to project its power to central Africa and to influence the course of events, but it nevertheless relished the opportunity to meddle in an 'anti-imperial' struggle there. The threat it posed to Western interests was exaggerated. In 1962 the CIA director, Allen Dulles, admitted on television that the United States had 'overrated the Soviet danger in the Congo'. But by acting precipitately to involve the Soviet Union in the first place, Lumumba convinced Western governments of the advantages of being rid of him. United Nations officials, given the task of holding the Congo together but subjected to constant attacks from Lumumba for their efforts, took much the same view. When his own colleagues Kasa-Vubu and Mobutu agreed to move against him, there was a palpable sense of relief. In the sixty-seven days that Lumumba had held office as prime minister, he had squandered all goodwill and accumulated a powerful array of adversaries.

It took many years for the details of Lumumba's murder and the many accomplices involved in it to emerge. The Belgian government claimed for forty years that it was an exclusively Congolese affair. Only in 2000, as a result of the work of the Dutch journalist Ludo de Witte, did the Belgian authorities set up an official inquiry. The outcome was that in 2001 Belgium formally admitted 'its share of responsibility'. As for Mobutu, one of the principal conspirators in the murder, he subsequently tried to cloak himself in Lumumba's mantle, acclaiming him as 'this illustrious Congolese, this great African'.

Yet the Congo paid heavily for the chaos surrounding the advent of independence. For years to come it became a battleground for warring factions, marauding soldiers, foreign troops, mercenary forces, revolutionary enthusiasts and legions of diplomats and advisers. Katanga struggled to maintain its secession for another two years, until in 1963 the United Nations put an end to it.

Then, in 1964, revolt and rebellion broke out in the eastern Congo, Lumumba's former stronghold, on a scale that surpassed anything the Congo had experienced before. In the space of three months the Léopoldville government lost control of half of the entire country. In Stanleyville former Lumumba supporters set up a 'People's Republic of the Congo' and ordered the mass executions of clerks, teachers, civil servants, merchants – men deemed to be 'counter-revolutionaries' or 'intellectuals'; at least 20,000 Congolese died, many of them executed with appalling cruelty in public at the foot of monuments to Lumumba. Support for the Stanleyville regime came from China, Cuba, Algeria and Egypt.

To prevent the Congo from disintegrating, the United States and Belgium undertook a massive rescue operation, supplying combat aircraft, transport planes, counter-insurgency experts and hundreds of technicians. Under the auspices of the CIA, Cuban refugee pilots and European mechanics were hired to staff a combat air force. A mercenary force was assembled – a rough assortment of adventurers, desperadoes and misfits, together with some professional soldiers, recruited mainly in Rhodesia and South Africa.

Facing defeat, the Stanleyville regime seized some three hundred Belgian and American hostages. Belgian paratroops, transported by American planes, were dropped on Stanleyville to rescue them. In all, some 2,000 whites were evacuated from the eastern Congo. Three hundred others, some of them missionaries living in remote outposts, were murdered. As mercenary groups and government troops beat back rebel opposition, they left behind a terrible trail of repression and plunder. Overall, a million people were estimated to have died in the 1964 rebellions.

In Léopoldville the politicians resumed their bickering and intrigue once more until in 1965 Mobutu, the army commander, stepped forward for a second time, suspended all political activity and assumed the presidency for himself. At the time, it seemed to offer some prospect of respite.

7

THE WHITE SOUTH

As the tide of African nationalism swept through Africa, white-minority governments in southern Africa tightened their control, determined to bring it to a halt and to keep political power and wealth in white hands. To the white populations of South Africa, South West Africa, Rhodesia and the Portuguese colonies of Angola and Mozambique, the notion of African rule spelt disaster. All saw themselves as bastions of Western civilisation, striving to uphold standards in a continent prone to strife and instability. Time and again, the chaos in the Congo was cited as an example of what happened when the guiding hand of Europeans was removed from Africa. The advent of African independence to the north was attributed not only to the decline and weakness of Europe's colonial powers but to the insidious advance of communism, posing grave threats to their own security. Communists, they maintained, were using African nationalists for their own ends – their ultimate aim being to gain a strategic hold over southern Africa and to capture its vast mineral riches. White governments argued it was imperative, therefore, to curb the activities of African nationalist groups that threatened white rule. In one country after another, political activists were harassed and imprisoned, their organisations banned. Across Africa, a new frontier was drawn, dividing the black north from the white south, marking out southern Africa as a seemingly impregnable fortress of white power.

To ensure that South Africa's whites retained power permanently, white politicians constructed the most elaborate racial edifice the world has ever seen. At the end of the Second World War, South Africa's racial policies differed in detail rather than in essence from the discriminatory practices employed elsewhere in Africa under European rule. But in 1948 Afrikaner Nationalists came to power bearing their own version of racial rule they called apartheid, determined to ensure white supremacy for all time and to destroy the *swart gevaar*, the black peril they said white society faced.

Stage by stage, the black population was subjected to a vast array of government controls and segregated from whites wherever possible. Every facet of their life – residence, employment, education, public amenities and politics – was regulated to keep them in a strictly subordinate role. In the name of apartheid, more than three million people were uprooted from their homes to satisfy government planners; millions more were imprisoned for infringing apartheid regulations. There was no pretence about the objective. 'Either the white man dominates or the black man takes over,' the prime minister, Hans Strijdom, told parliament in 1956. 'The only way the Europeans can maintain supremacy is by domination . . . And the only way they can maintain domination is by withholding the vote from Non-Europeans.'

In their early campaigns to press for African rights, African nationalists organised petitions, deputations and appeals. For thirty years the efforts of the African National Congress (ANC), founded as a small elite movement in 1912, proved ineffective. Despite African protests, African voters were struck from the common roll in the Cape Province in 1936, losing a right they had held for more than eighty years. As the historian Cornelis de Kiewiet noted, the effect was 'to destroy the most important bridge between the worlds of two races'.

Then, in the early 1940s, a militant mood began to affect the African population. Massive numbers of Africans moved to industrial centres on the Witwatersrand, driven there by poverty and hunger in the African 'reserves' and by harsh conditions on white farms, hoping to find work in booming wartime industries, but often meeting little else but hardship and squalor. The housing shortage reached crisis levels. Squatter camps proliferated on the outskirts of Johannesburg, in defiance of municipal authority. The cost of food soared. African trade unions led a sudden rash of strikes in support of demands for a minimum wage. In 1946 African mineworkers launched the largest strike in South Africa's history in protest against pay and conditions.

The militant mood prompted ANC politicians to sharpen their own stance. In 1943 they presented the government with a document entitled 'African Claims' which demanded full citizenship rights and an end to all discriminatory laws, in accordance with the Atlantic Charter drawn up by Churchill and Roosevelt. It was formally adopted as an ANC policy statement in 1945.

A group of young activists, however, scorned such polite methods of political activity and demanded radical action. Among them was Nelson Mandela, a law student connected to the Thembu royal family. Born in 1918 in the simple surroundings of a peasant village in Thembuland, he had won a coveted place at Fort Hare College, the leading educational institute for Africans in southern Africa, but left to escape an arranged marriage. Making his way to Johannesburg, he had fortuitously found work as a clerk with a white law firm, enabling him to complete his university degree by correspondence course. A tall, athletic figure with dark, piercing eyes and an engaging laugh, he had a commanding presence, a patrician manner, but a tendency to act impulsively. A close friend, Oliver Tambo, remembered him at the time as 'passionate, emotional, sensitive, quickly stung to bitterness and retaliation by insult and patronage'. His circle of friends and acquaintances was unusually wide and included many whites and Indians, but Mandela identified himself with the Africanist wing of black politics whose supporters favoured slogans like 'Africa for the Africans' and 'Hurl the White man to the sea'. Mandela recalled: 'While I was not prepared to hurl the white man into the sea, I would have been perfectly happy if he had climbed aboard his steamships and left the continent of his own volition.'

In 1949 radicals in the ANC succeeded in ousting the old guard. A new generation of activists took control and duly announced a 'Programme of Action' including civil disobedience, boycotts and 'stay-at-home' strikes on a mass scale.

The new National Party government reacted forcefully to signs of growing opposition. Claiming that much of the dissent was caused by the activities of communists, it introduced legislation called the Suppression of Communism Act which gave it powers to suppress not only the small, multiracial Communist Party but other opponents it deemed to be troublesome. The Act was the first weapon in an arsenal of security measures acquired by the government that would eventually provide it with totalitarian control. So wide was the Act's definition of communism that it could be used to silence anyone who opposed government policy simply by 'naming' them. The government was empowered to place them under house arrest, to restrict their movements, to prohibit them from attending public or even social gatherings and to proscribe their writing and their speeches. No reason had to be given when 'naming' communists; nor was there any right of appeal.

Undaunted by the threat of government repression, the ANC helped organise a 'Defiance Campaign' in 1952 in protest against the growing encroachment of apartheid laws. Volunteers were asked to deliberately court arrest and imprisonment by contravening selected laws and regulations such as using railway coaches, waiting rooms and platform seats marked for Europeans only or by parading in streets after curfew. The idea was to fill the courts and prisons so that they overflowed with petty offenders, thereby causing the system to break down. The campaign quickly caught the public imagination, transforming the ANC into a mass movement. In five months more than 8,000 people went to prison for periods of one to three months. Thirty-five organisers of the campaign, including Mandela, were charged with promoting communism and found guilty. Some were subjected to banning orders preventing them from participating in political activity for life. New legislation was introduced which laid down severe penalties of fines, imprisonment and corporal punishment for anyone inciting others to commit civil-disobedience offences and which empowered the government to declare a state of

emergency and use emergency regulations whenever 'the maintenance of public order was endangered'. The effect was to make protest
virtually illegal. For years to come, political activists were harassed by
police raids, surveillance, banning orders, restrictions, arrests and ban-
ishments. Informers and agents provocateurs penetrated their inner
ranks.

Still the ANC persevered. In conjunction with Indian activists and
a group of radical whites, many of them secretly members of the
underground Communist Party, it drew up a 'Freedom Charter' in
1955, pointing the way ahead to a multiracial society. 'South Africa
belongs to all who live in it, black and white,' the Charter declared. It
demanded the right of all citizens to vote, to hold office and to be
equal before the law. The economic clauses of the Charter advocated
nationalisation of the mines, land and banks. In an article explaining
the purpose of the Charter, Mandela denied it was a blueprint for a
socialist state, but acknowledged its radical nature. 'It is a revolutionary document precisely because the changes it envisages cannot be
won without breaking up the economic and political set-up of present
South Africa.'

The government thought so too and set out to prove that the
Charter's aims could not be achieved without violence. In 1956 it
arrested 156 activists, including almost all the senior ANC leaders as
well as prominent white radicals, and charged them with high treason,
claiming that they had been preparing 'for the overthrow of the existing State by revolutionary methods, involving violence and the
establishment of the so-called People's Democracy'. The trial dragged
on for four years, sapping the energy of the movement and its leaders,
ending in the acquittal of all the accused.

The juggernaut of apartheid meanwhile gathered momentum. In
1958, after the death of Hans Strijdom, the National Party chose as
prime minister Hendrik Verwoerd, a Dutch-born ideological fanatic
with ambitions to put apartheid into practice on a scale never
previously envisaged. Verwoerd cast himself in the role of a leader
chosen by God and proceeded to act accordingly, allowing nothing to
deflect him from his purpose. 'I do not have the nagging doubt of ever
wondering whether perhaps I am wrong,' he declared.

Verwoerd believed that he had found the ultimate solution for South Africa: total territorial separation between black and white. The central part of his strategy was division of the black population. He decreed that the African population would be divided into separate ethnic groups or 'nations' and given control of their own homelands where they would enjoy full social and political rights – 'separate freedoms' – under a system of government suited to their own tribal background. All blacks would become citizens of the new homelands, including blacks resident in 'white' areas, regardless of how many generations had lived there.

Divided into separate ethnic groups, the blacks would be inhibited from acting as a single community against outnumbered whites. Because each 'national' group was a minority of the whole, no one 'nation' could claim rights on the basis of numerical strength. Thus the demands for majority rule by African nationalists were irrelevant; and whites would be guaranteed supremacy in their own area for ever more.

Verwoerd acknowledged that his 'ideal' of total territorial separation would not be reached for many years, but the goal needed to be set. The only solution to the 'rivalry and clashes' endemic between the races was to give each one 'mastery' over its own area. At the end of this grand design, Verwoerd confidently expected South Africa would consist of flourishing black homelands living side by side in peace with an ever-prosperous white state. Unveiling his master plan in 1959, he announced that henceforth South Africa would become a 'multinational' state with separate homelands for eight black 'nations'.

Facing the onslaught of white supremacy, the ANC held fast to its multiracial principles. Mandela, who had once aligned himself to the Africanist wing within the ANC, was now fully committed to a multiracial future for South Africa, impressed in particular by the dedication shown by radical whites to the cause, notably white communists. Africanists, however, had become increasingly critical of the direction taken by the ANC, condemning the alliances it was willing to make with other racial groups to oppose apartheid. They especially resented the clause in the Freedom Charter declaring that South Africa belonged to 'all who live in it, black and white'. In the

Africanist view, the only true 'owners' of South Africa were Africans. Others had merely 'stolen' the country.

In 1959 the Africanists broke away from the ANC to form their own group, the Pan-Africanist Congress (PAC), demanding 'government of the Africans, by the Africans, for the Africans' and promising militant action to achieve it. Competing for support with the ANC, they announced a campaign of mass protest against the hated pass law system, the mainstay of government control of the African population, which required every African over the age of sixteen to carry a pass proving their right to be in a 'white' area; thousands went to prison every week for failing to produce a passbook on demand. On 21 March 1960 police in Sharpeville, a black township fifty miles south of Johannesburg, opened fire indiscriminately on a crowd of PAC demonstrators, killing 69 and wounding 186. Most of the casualties were shot in the back as they fled the gunfire.

The Sharpeville massacre became a permanent symbol of the brutality of the apartheid regime. It provoked a storm of African protest – marches, demonstrations, strikes and violence. Many whites feared that South Africa might be on the verge of revolution. An outburst of international condemnation added to the atmosphere of crisis. Western attitudes towards South Africa, hitherto ambivalent, became markedly more hostile. A United Nations Security Council resolution blamed South Africa's racial policies for causing 'international friction'. Foreign investors, fearing imminent upheaval, deserted in droves.

To all criticism, both domestic and foreign, Verwoerd remained impervious. Nothing was to shake his faith in apartheid. Far from being willing to make concessions, he ordered a massive crackdown. Using emergency powers, the government banned the ANC and the PAC and detained thousands of anti-apartheid dissidents. Few activists escaped the dragnet. Within weeks, the back of African resistance was broken.

Despite being driven underground, the ANC still believed that mass action might yet shake the government. In 1961 ANC activists devised plans to stage a three-day national strike to be followed by a wave of 'mass non-cooperation'. The key figure in this new campaign was Nelson Mandela. Abandoning his legal practice and forsaking all chance of a family life with his young wife, Winnie, and their two children, he decided to commit himself wholeheartedly to working as an underground leader.

A warrant for Mandela's arrest was soon issued. But with the help of a network of Communist Party supporters, who had years of experience of working underground undetected, he evaded capture for month after month, moving from town to town, urging support for the strike and advertising his activities through telephone calls to newspapers. Much of the work he carried out at night, growing used to spending his days in hide-outs. He disguised himself with different outfits, dressing in workmen's overalls or chauffeur's clothes, growing a beard and wearing round, rimless spectacles. After dark he often appeared as a night-watchman, dressed in a large grey overcoat and cap pulled over his eyes and occasionally sporting large earrings. Because of his success in dodging the police, the press dubbed him the Black Pimpernel, an African version of the Scarlet Pimpernel, a fictional character who evaded capture during the French Revolution.

To counter the strike threat, the government passed new laws enabling it to detain anyone without trial and ordered the largest mobilisation of the army and police since the war. Night after night, police carried out raids in African townships; all political meetings were banned; and employees threatened with mass dismissals. Despite the display of might, thousands of workers in major towns answered the strike call. But the overall result did not match Mandela's expectations. On the second day he called off the campaign.

The failure of the strike convinced Mandela that there was nothing further to be gained from continuing with protest action and that the only alternative available was to resort to violence. Years of demonstrations, boycotts, strikes and civil disobedience had achieved nothing. Each occasion had been met with government reprisals. Mandela believed that a limited campaign of sabotage would scare off foreign investors, disrupt trade and cause sufficient damage to force the white electorate and the government to change course.

Mandela's thinking was influenced strongly by revolutionary enthusiasts in the underground Communist Party who had already decided to form armed groups as a prelude to engaging in guerrilla warfare. With ready access to the Soviet bloc and China, they were planning to send recruits outside the country for training. The armed struggle, they believed, would receive massive support from the oppressed African population and soon bring the apartheid regime to an end. They cited the example of Cuba where Castro's revolution had shown how a small group of revolutionaries could gain mass support to win power. What made a particular impact from the Cuban example was Che Guevara's 'detonator' theory of revolution, the idea that armed action on its own would create a momentum among the population.

But while Mandela was persuaded about the need for an armed struggle, other ANC leaders were vehemently opposed to it. At a secret meeting in June 1961, the arguments raged back and forth. By the end of it a compromise was reached. It was agreed that the ANC would remain committed to non-violence, but that it would not stand in the way of members who wanted to establish a separate and independent military organisation.

The new organisation – *Umkhonto we Sizwe*, meaning Spear of the Nation – rapidly took shape. With Mandela as chairman, it was essentially a joint venture between the ANC and the Communist Party, an elite group consisting of no more than a few hundred conspirators but with access to all the Communist Party's resources and its international connections. The difficulties the conspirators faced were enormous. None of them had any experience of sabotage or guerrilla action. Mandela embarked on the armed struggle knowing literally nothing about what was involved in practice. From the outset, there was a large degree of amateurism about Umkhonto.

Its operational headquarters were a spacious farmhouse on a smallholding called Lilliesleaf in the Rivonia area, ten miles north of Johannesburg, a property originally bought by the Communist Party in July 1961 for use as its own underground headquarters. Mandela lived there in a thatched cottage in the grounds for several months while police scoured the country searching for him, staying there during the day, leaving for assignments at night and spending weekends there with his wife and children. Numerous meetings were held at Rivonia. Indeed, the comings and goings of the conspirators were so frequent that it resembled more a business enterprise than the secret headquarters of a revolutionary movement.

The date set for the start of the sabotage campaign was 16 December 1961, a day then known as the Day of the Covenant, on which whites celebrated their victory over the Zulu king Dingane at the Battle of Blood River in 1838. Leaflets dropped on the streets announced the formation of *Umkhonto we Sizwe* with the warning: 'The time comes in the life of any nation when there remain only two choices: submit or fight. That time has now come.' Bombs were set off at government buildings in Johannesburg and other cities. Over the course of the next eighteen months, sabotage attacks continued sporadically, mainly on public buildings, railway lines and power installations. Most of the attacks were clumsy and ineffectual, none causing any lasting damage.

Three weeks after the start of the campaign, Mandela left South Africa surreptitiously, crossing the border into Bechuanaland, to seek support for the armed struggle from African states, remaining abroad for six months. During his travels, he took the opportunity to undergo a brief course of military training in Ethiopia. 'If there was to be guerrilla warfare,' he said, 'I wanted to be able to stand and fight with my people and to share the hazards of war with them.' But less than two weeks after his return to South Africa in July 1962, careless about his own personal security, he was captured by police while travelling by car between Durban and Johannesburg. Whatever suspicions the police may have had, however, they possessed no evidence to link Mandela to Umkhonto and the sabotage campaign. In court he was charged with no more than inciting African workers to strike illegally, and leaving the country without a valid travel document.

Mandela's trial attracted worldwide attention. He conducted his own defence and his manner and bearing before the court was judged impressive. Found guilty on both charges in November 1962, he took the opportunity, when speaking in mitigation of sentence, to deliver a searing indictment of the government. Every attempt that the ANC had made to seek peaceful solutions to the country's ills had been treated with contempt and met with force, he said. 'They set the scene for violence by relying exclusively on violence with which to answer our people and their demands.' And he warned of more violence to come. 'Government violence can do only one thing and that is to breed counter-violence.' He was sentenced to five years' imprisonment.

The net was meanwhile closing in on other conspirators. Reacting to the sabotage campaign, Verwoerd appointed a new minister of justice, John Vorster, a former Nazi sympathiser who had been interned without trial during the Second World War, with instructions to root out all resistance. The security police were given virtually unlimited powers of arrest and detention. Scores of men and women vanished into prison, to be subjected to solitary confinement and prolonged interrogation. When interrogation methods failed, the security police resorted to physical assaults and torture. With information obtained from detainees and informers, police soon identified Lilliesleaf as a suspect location. On 11 July 1963 they raided the farm and captured a whole set of leading conspirators. They also acquired a massive haul of documents relating to arms production, guerrilla recruitment and training, contacts with China and the Soviet bloc, and evidence about the involvement of Mandela.

The trial of Mandela and other leading conspirators lasted from October 1963 to June 1964. They were charged under the Sabotage Act which carried the death penalty. Once again, it was Mandela's bearing before the court and the impassioned speech he made about the reasons for his participation in Umkhonto which caught worldwide attention. 'It was only when all else had failed,' he said, 'when all channels of peaceful protest had been barred to us, that the decision was made to embark on violent forms of political struggle, and to form *Umkhonto we Sizwe*. We did so not because we desired such a course but solely because the Government had left us with no other choice.'

He explained the aims of the African population:

Africans want a just share in the whole of South Africa, they want a security and a stake in society. Above all, we want equal political rights, because without them our disabilities will be permanent. I know this sounds revolutionary to the whites in this country, because the majority of voters will be Africans. This makes the white man fear democracy. But this fear cannot be allowed to stand in the way of the only solution which will guarantee racial harmony and freedom for all.

For five hours Mandela continued reading his statement. Then he put down his papers and turned to face the judge, speaking his final words from memory:

During my lifetime I have dedicated myself to this struggle of the African people. I have fought against white domination, and I have fought against black domination. I have cherished the ideal of a democratic and free society in which all persons live together in harmony and with equal opportunities. It is an ideal which I hope to live for and to achieve. But if needs be, it is an ideal for which I am prepared to die.

On 12 June 1964 Mandela, then forty-five years old, was sentenced to life imprisonment. Eight of his colleagues were given the same sentence. That night they were flown to Cape Town and taken by ferry to Robben Island. Known as prisoner no. 466/64, Mandela spent his time labouring in the island's lime quarry, collecting seaweed for fertiliser and studying Afrikaans.

In terms of the objectives that Mandela had set, Umkhonto's sabotage campaign was a total failure. The impact on the economy was negligible. Foreign investors, far from being frightened away during the early 1960s, became more deeply involved. The white electorate reacted in support of the government not in opposition to it. The government, instead of changing course, was spurred into taking ever more repressive counter-measures, obliterating fundamental civil rights on the ground that it was dealing with a communist-inspired conspiracy to overthrow the state. All that was proved, ultimately, was that a collection of amateur revolutionaries were no match for the brute strength of the South African state.

In trying to explain the collapse of Umkhonto, revolutionary enthusiasts spoke of 'an heroic failure'. But it was more a fatal miscalculation about the power of the government and the ways in which the government was willing to use it. The price for this miscalculation was huge. With the nationalist movement destroyed, a silence descended for more than a decade.

The Rhodesian government faced similar nationalist agitation and dealt with it in a similar fashion. The first major nationalist organisation, the African National Congress, launched in 1957, soon succeeded in establishing a mass movement both in urban and rural areas. Poverty and frustration in the towns and overcrowding in rural areas had already produced strong undercurrents of discontent. There was particular resentment in rural areas over the government's land policies: over a period of thirty years, more than half a million Africans had been uprooted from their homes on land designated to be in 'white' areas.

To avoid alarming the white population, the African National Congress set out to project a moderate image. The central theme of its platform was non-racialism and economic progress; it suggested the abolition of discriminatory laws, reform of land allocation and an extension of the franchise. Although the franchise was non-racial, the qualifications for a vote, based on income, were so high at the time that, of an electorate of 52,000, only 560 were Africans.

The ANC's leader, Joshua Nkomo, was chosen because of his moderate credentials. Born in 1917, the son of a relatively prosperous teacher and lay preacher who worked for the London Missionary Society, he had proved a skilful negotiator as a railway union official and was known for his work in multiracial and church circles; on Sundays he performed as a lay preacher in the British Methodist Church.

Although there was no open disorder at the time, the government banned the ANC in February 1959 on the grounds that it was inciting the black population to defy the law and ridicule government authority. More than 500 Africans were arrested and 300 detained, some for a period of four years. To control any future African opposition, the government devised a series of laws so sweeping and severe that the Chief Justice, Sir Robert Tredgold, resigned in protest, accusing the government of turning Rhodesia into 'a police state'.

Determined to press ahead, the nationalists in January 1960 launched a new organisation, the National Democratic Party (NDP), putting forward a more radical platform. They demanded not simply the redress of grievances over land and discrimination but political power as well. 'We are no longer asking Europeans to rule us well,' said Leopold Takawira, one of the founders. 'We now want to rule ourselves.' Convinced that the key to their advancement lay with Britain, the nationalists spent much of their energy trying to persuade the British government to intervene to curb the white politicians in Salisbury.

The opportunity for the nationalists to advance their cause came in 1961 when the British government convened a constitutional conference in Salisbury which NDP officials were invited to attend. The purpose of the conference was to settle on a new constitution that reconciled white demands for independence under white minority rule with African demands for political progress.

The fatal error the nationalists made was to equate their own situation with that of other British colonies. They assumed that any agreement at the conference would assist the nationalist cause and lead towards African rule, as other constitutional conferences that the British had arranged for their African colonies had done. But the British government's objectives with Rhodesia were discernibly different. Even though Britain had retained certain reserve powers since granting self-government in 1923, no British government had ever shown any intention of trying to change the structure of white rule. Indeed, successive governments had stood by impervious as the whites consolidated their control. The British were now anxious to disengage from Rhodesia and willing to hand Rhodesians virtual autonomy provided African advancement was recognisably established.

The deal eventually worked out was remarkably favourable to the Rhodesian government. Under the 1961 constitution, Britain withdrew virtually all its reserve powers. The remaining safeguards were described by Britain's Commonwealth Secretary Duncan Sandys as trifling. In exchange, the Rhodesian government conceded to the nationalists fifteen out of sixty-five parliamentary seats, based on a complex franchise that would have delayed majority rule for several decades, in effect guaranteeing white rule for the foreseeable future. It was a miracle, said Sandys, that the nationalists had accepted it.

No sooner were the results known than a storm of African protest erupted. Joshua Nkomo, who had negotiated the terms of the 1961 constitution on behalf of the NDP, faced severe criticism from his own officials and after ten days he was obliged to repudiate the agreement. Since it was then too late for the nationalists to stop the passage of the 1961 constitution, they refused instead to participate in any activity related to the new constitution and resorted to reckless violence to prevent African voters from registering for the 1962 elections. African homes, schools, beer halls and shops were looted and burned; gangs of youths roamed the black suburbs seeking out victims who were identified with the government or who were not party members.

In December 1961 the government banned the NDP. One week later a new nationalist organisation, the Zimbabwe African People's Union (Zapu), was formed, with identical aims and tactics. The violence increased and included white targets; forests and crops were burned, cattle maimed, attacks carried out on schools and churches and sabotage attempts made on railway lines. From mid-1962, youths were sent out of the country to Ghana, Algeria and communist countries for training in sabotage techniques, and small supplies of arms and ammunition started filtering across the northern border. In September 1962 Zapu was banned and its officials placed under restriction.

Other than violence the nationalists offered no coherent plan. Nkomo's strategy was based on the notion that eventually the scale of violence would force Britain to intervene, as it had done after similar agitation in Nyasaland and Northern Rhodesia. Most of the time he spent touring the world seeking international support for the nationalist cause, leaving the party's organisation in Rhodesia in disarray. His prolonged absences, his reluctance to face the issues at home, his indecisiveness all caused mounting dissatisfaction among party officials. Confrontation in Rhodesia was what was needed, they argued, not pseudo-diplomacy.

In 1963 the nationalist movement split into two irreconcilable camps. Nkomo relaunched the loyal contingent of Zapu as the People's Caretaker Council. His critics formed the Zimbabwe African National Union (Zanu), choosing as leader Ndabaningi Sithole, a mission-educated teacher and church minister who had studied divinity in the United States for three years; his book, *African Nationalism*, published in 1959, had stressed the need for equality of human rights and a genuine multiracial society. Zanu's secretary-general, Robert Mugabe, had more radical leanings. Also a mission-educated teacher and holding three university degrees, he had given up a teaching post in Ghana in 1960 to join the nationalist cause as a full-time official, already convinced of the need for an armed struggle.

The differences between Zapu and Zanu were at first negligible. Both advocated the same goal of majority rule; both continued to seek foreign support and to lobby the British government; both established external bases in Africa to coordinate their foreign activities, and recruited members for guerrilla training outside the country. Initially, tribal allegiances were not affected. But as each group tried to assert itself, their rivalry developed into internecine warfare. Gang raids, petrol bombing, arson, stoning and assaults became commonplace.

The threat that African ferment within Rhodesia posed to white rule produced a growing backlash. Many whites were convinced their survival depended on smashing the nationalist movement before it became too deeply rooted. A new right-wing party, the Rhodesian Front, was launched in 1962 promising to deal ruthlessly with the nationalist menace and to entrench white control permanently. Within a matter of months, it managed to consolidate a disparate collection of conservative factions into a single, effective political organisation. Supported by white farmers worried about their right to land and by white workers who feared black competition, the Rhodesian Front swept to victory in the December 1962 election, setting Rhodesia on a perilous course.

Once in power, the Rhodesian Front government became obsessed with the need for independence. In other African colonies, Britain was seen to be abandoning white communities to the hazards of black nationalist rule. As the same policy was being applied to Rhodesia, according to the Rhodesian Front, the remaining links with Britain were a threat to white survival. Rhodesia, after forty years of self-government, had earned the right to independence, the government maintained – far more so than had other African states with less experience of self-government which were already independent. With high standards of justice, order and government, it could be relied on to defend Western interests. Moreover, without independence, neither the whites nor foreign investors would have any confidence in the country's future.

For three fruitless years the Rhodesians pressed these arguments on the British government. The dispute during this time was never over the question of Britain granting independence to a white minority government, for the British government raised no objection to that prospect; it centred on whether the Rhodesians should make constitutional concessions that Britain demanded to ensure that no independent government could thwart African progress once it was set free from British control. The Rhodesian Front saw no reason to pay such a price.

The first prime minister whom the Rhodesian Front installed to wrest independence from Britain was clearly the wrong choice. Winston Field was a conservative gentleman farmer, born in the English counties, who had a reputation for being cautious and fair-minded. When, after sixteen months in office, he had failed to make any headway in negotiations with Britain and balked at the idea of seizing independence unilaterally, he was removed.

His successor, Ian Smith, was at the time a relatively unknown right-wing politician, with no obvious talent or flair, whose career both in politics and farming had so far met with little success. As a member of parliament for sixteen years, his contribution had been insignificant. His brief record as finance minister in Winston Field's government had been equally colourless. He was a dull speaker with a limited, repetitive vocabulary and narrow interests. His parochial nature, however, concealed an astute tactical mind, an appetite for political infighting and a remarkable tenacity.

There was never any doubt about what he stood for. Shortly after assuming office as prime minister in April 1964, a few days after his forty-fifth birthday, Smith declared: 'I cannot see in my lifetime that the Africans will be sufficiently mature and reasonable to take over.' From then on, the slogan of 'no majority rule in my lifetime' became a guarantee for those who had any doubts. In pursuing this goal, Smith was ready to deal forcefully with any opponents who stood in his way, whether they were African nationalists or the British government.

The nationalists, in the end, sealed their own fate. After months of internecine warfare, Smith banned both nationalist parties in August 1964 in the name of law and order, and sent Nkomo, Sithole, Mugabe and hundreds of others to detention camps. Many remained there for ten years.

In his dealings with the British government, Smith remained intransigent. Unwilling to make any concessions, he set out to convince Rhodesia's whites that the choice they faced was between black rule and a unilateral declaration of independence (UDI). With relentless propaganda, the government portrayed Smith as a man of unwavering determination who would save Rhodesia from 'the forces of evil' and keep the country in 'civilised and responsible' hands for all time. In a general election that Smith called in May 1965, asking for a decisive vote of confidence to strengthen his hand in negotiations with Britain, he achieved a resounding victory: all fifty white seats went to the Rhodesian Front.

The warnings against UDI came from many quarters, from South Africa as well as Britain. But Smith was convinced his position was secure enough. The government had the overwhelming support of the white population, some 220,000 strong. It was backed by an efficient administration, a well-equipped defence force and an effective security apparatus capable of dealing with any internal threat. It also had control of radio and television, invaluable for propaganda purposes. Smith minimised the possible repercussions, suggesting that UDI would be no more than a 'three-day wonder'.

So it was that on 11 November 1965 Smith and his ministers signed their Proclamation of Independence. It was a curious document, drawn up in archaic language intended to resemble the American

Declaration of 1776 and embellished with red, green and gold scrolls. In his independence message Smith portrayed his act of defiance in grandiose terms. 'I believe that we are a courageous people and history has cast us in a heroic role,' he said. 'To us has been given the privilege of being the first Western nation in the last two decades to have the determination and fortitude to say "So far and no further" . . . We Rhodesians have rejected the doctrinaire philosophy of appeasement and surrender . . . We have struck a blow for the preservation of justice, civilisation and Christianity.'

By outward appearances, the Portuguese colonies of Angola and Mozambique under Dr António Salazar's dictatorship were tranquil backwaters enjoying increasing prosperity and seemingly free from the ferment of African nationalism sweeping other African territories. In Angola the discovery of oil, the expansion of mining and the buoyant coffee industry had produced boom conditions. Both Angola and Mozambique were attracting new foreign investment. The cities of Portuguese Africa – Luanda, Lourenço Marques, Beira, Lobito, Benguela – were among the most modern on the continent, well served by their own newspapers, broadcasting stations, sports clubs and museums. By 1960, Luanda, the capital of Angola, had become the third largest city in the Portuguese domain after Lisbon and Oporto; and the white population of Angola had risen to 200,000. Like France, Portugal regarded its African colonies as overseas 'provinces', as inalienable a part of the Portuguese nation as metropolitan Portugal. Having ruled his country with an iron fist since 1932, Salazar had no intention of changing course. 'We have been in Africa for four hundred years, which is rather more than to have arrived yesterday,' he told Portugal's National Assembly in November 1960. 'We are present there with the policy that authority is steadily effecting and defending, which is not the same as to abandon human destiny to the so-called "winds of history".'

What signs of political opposition to Salazar's regime there were, among whites as well as blacks, were quickly snuffed out by his secret police. In 1956 a group of radical Angolan intellectuals founded the *Movimento Popular de Libertação de Angola* (MPLA) with the aim of overthrowing Portuguese rule. Its leaders were mostly *mestiços* (mixed race) but included a number of white Angolans; some had links to the underground Angolan Communist Party. The MPLA attracted a following among dissident civil servants and students in Luanda and other towns in the Kimbundu hinterland. For several years it managed to operate clandestinely, but most of its leading members were caught in a wave of arrests carried out by the secret police in 1959 and in 1960. The MPLA thus became an organisation in exile, establishing offices first in Paris, then moving in 1959 to Conakry, the capital of Guinea, then in 1961 transferring to Léopoldville in the Congo, close to the Angola border. Its leader, Agostinho Neto, a medical doctor and accomplished poet, was widely admired abroad for his opposition to Portuguese rule. But the MPLA itself was regarded as a largely ineffective organisation, debilitated by internal power struggles and dissension, and kept alive largely by support from the Soviet bloc.

The tranquillity of the empire was abruptly shattered in 1961 by an explosion of violence in northern Angola which caught the Portuguese administration completely unprepared. In mid-March roving bands of Africans armed with machetes, home-made muskets and other crude weapons attacked isolated European settlements and plantations, killing several hundred whites, including women and children, and massacring African migrant workers. Some fifty administrative posts and settlements were overrun. It took six months for the Portuguese to regain control.

The uprising had been organised in part by an Angolan exile group, based in the Congo, the *União das Populações de Angola* (UPA), with the aim of driving the Portuguese out of Angola. Formed in 1957 in Léopoldville by Angolan Bakongo, the UPA had started out as a Bakongo tribal organisation with the idea of resurrecting the old Kongo kingdom, but had subsequently proclaimed nationalist objectives. Its leader, Holden Roberto, named after a Baptist missionary, had spent most of his life in exile in the Congo, working for eight years as an accountant in the Belgian administration. He had been converted to the nationalist cause while attending the All-African People's Conference in Accra in 1958. Party agents had been sent across the border into Angola with instructions to foment an uprising.

But more lay behind the uprising than the work of Bakongo activists. The sudden and spontaneous character of much of the violence indicated massive discontent with Portuguese rule. There were strong grievances in northern Angola over the loss of African land acquired by Portuguese farmers for their coffee and palm plantations, and over the harsh treatment meted out by Portuguese settlers and traders. The area had also been affected by the independence of the Congo, which raised expectations that the Portuguese, like the Belgians, would leave rather than fight to stay, if faced with violence.

The magnitude of the 1961 uprising shook the very foundations of the Portuguese empire. As well as ordering outright repression, in which some 20,000 Africans died, Salazar authorised the first major reforms to colonial policy for more than sixty years. Decrees were issued abolishing all forms of compulsory labour and prohibiting illegal land expropriation. Equal rights were accorded to 'civilised' and 'non-civilised' citizens of the empire. A programme of social rehabilitation, education and economic development was launched in northern Angola. But Salazar still refused to contemplate any political reforms or to relax his grip over political activity.

The UPA meanwhile soon fell into disarray. Roberto ran the movement as his personal fiefdom, controlling all finance and administration and tolerating no rivals. He rarely ventured into Angola, preferring a comfortable emigré lifestyle in Léopoldville where he had extensive business interests. In 1962 the UPA changed its name to the *Frente Nacionale de Libertação de Angola* (FNLA). Support was forthcoming from Tunisia and the Algerians. The Americans, too, showed an interest. Under the Kennedy administration, US officials took a sympathetic view of African nationalism and sought out nationalist leaders free from communist association. Roberto's group was cleared by the Central Intelligence Agency as being a suitable venture for covert assistance in the form of money and arms, much to the fury of the Portuguese when they found out. Roberto himself received an annual retainer from the CIA of $10,000. But despite such help, the FNLA's campaign in northern Angola, weakened by splits and desertions, came to a virtual halt.

Elsewhere in Portugal's African empire, however, Salazar's refusal to initiate political reform led nationalist movements to embark on guerrilla warfare to end Portuguese rule. Guerrilla wars broke out in Guinea-Bissau, a small West African colony, in 1963, and in Mozambique in 1964. In both cases they were started by exile groups using neighbouring African territories as their bases from which to recruit and train supporters and to gather arms – the *Partido da Independência da Guiné e Cabo Verde* (PAIGC) in Guinea-Bissau; the *Frente Libertação de Moçambique* (Frelimo) in Mozambique. Guerrilla attacks were confined initially to border areas. The Portuguese army had little difficulty in containing them. The guerrilla movements themselves were frequently wracked by bouts of internal dissension, personal feuds and tribal antagonisms. Yet the breaches that had occurred in the citadels of white power were eventually to have profound consequences for the whole of southern Africa.

PART II

THE BIRTH OF NATIONS

The honeymoon of African independence was brief but memorable. African leaders, riding the crest of popularity, stepped
forward with energy and enthusiasm to tackle the tasks of development and nation-building; ambitious plans were launched; bright
young men went quickly to the top. Expectations were high; the
sense of euphoria had been raised to ever greater heights by the lavish
promises of nationalist politicians campaigning for power, pledging to
provide education, medical care, employment and land for all. 'Seek
ye first the political kingdom,' Nkrumah had told his followers, 'and
all else shall be added unto you.' The march of African nationalism
seemed invincible. Africa, so it was thought, once freed from colonial
rule, was destined for an era of unprecedented progress. African leaders even spoke of building new societies that might offer the world at
large an inspiration.

The circumstances seemed auspicious. Independence came in the
midst of an economic boom. In the postwar era, world prices for
African commodities – cash crops like cocoa and coffee and mineral
products like copper – soared to new levels. Between 1945 and 1960
the economies of colonial Africa expanded by between 4 and 6 per
cent per annum. West African groundnut production doubled
between 1947 and 1957; cotton production trebled. Tea production in

southern Africa doubled. In Kenya, once government restrictions were lifted, peasant output between 1954 and 1964 rose on average by more than 7 per cent per annum. The terms of trade were favourable; oil at the time cost less than $2 a barrel. Public debt was low; foreign currency reserves in many cases were relatively high. Moreover, Western governments stood ready to provide substantial amounts of aid. In 1964 the level of aid to sub-Saharan Africa in the form of grants or cheap loans from Western Europe and North America alone reached more than $1 billion. Given the extent of the vast mineral resources that Africa was known to possess – oil, gas, uranium, bauxite, diamonds, gold – the potential for economic development seemed enormous. In his book *The Economics of African Development*, published in 1967, the World Bank economist Andrew Kamarck concluded: 'For most of Africa, the economic future before the end of the century can be bright.'

Even the rainfall pattern – a key factor in determining Africa's fortunes – was propitious. Good rains fell throughout the 1950s, boosting agricultural production. In 1961 Lake Chad and Lake Victoria reached their highest levels in the twentieth century.

The advent of independence also brought a cultural revival. African music, art and literature expanded into new forms; African novelists and dramatists made their debut. In 1966 President Senghor of Senegal hosted the first World Festival of African Arts and Culture in Dakar, bringing writers, musicians, sculptors, artisans and *griots* – traditional storytellers – from every corner of Africa for two weeks of performances, celebrations, lectures and debates.

The study of Africa – its history, archaeology, sociology and politics – became a serious discipline in universities around the world. What attracted particular interest was new evidence discovered in 1959 that Africa had been the cradle of mankind. After years of exploring the Olduvai Gorge, a hot, desolate, stony canyon in northern Tanganyika (Tanzania), a Cambridge archaeologist, Louis Leakey, and his wife, Mary, uncovered the skull of an australopithecine, a hominid ancestor whose remains have been found only in Africa. Officially known as *Zinjanthropus boisei*, but more affectionately referred to in the trade as Dear Boy, it was immediately acclaimed the earliest known tool-making ancestor of mankind, about 1.8 million years old.

On the global stage, African states excited the attention of the world's rival power blocs. The position that each newly independent country adopted in its relations with the West or the East was viewed as a matter of crucial importance. Africa was considered to be too valuable a prize to lose. While the old colonial powers sought to strengthen the special relationship they had mostly formed with their former colonies, the Eastern bloc embarked on major campaigns to gain influence in the new states. There was often intense competition between the two sides at a time when the Cold War in other parts of the world was at one of its peaks. 'We see Africa as probably the greatest open field of manoeuvre in the worldwide competition between the [communist] bloc and the non-communist,' said President Kennedy in 1962, echoing Harold Macmillan's earlier view. The West tended to regard with suspicion and distrust any links between Africa and the socialist world. An even fiercer contest for influence was waged between the Russians and the Chinese.

With both the West and the Soviet bloc vying for their support, African politicians became adept at playing off one side against the other. The more idealistic leaders, such as Tanganyika's Julius Nyerere, preferred that Africa should stand aloof from the sterile quarrels of the Cold War. But others sought to gain maximum advantage from it.

A sign of Africa's growing international ambitions came in 1963 when representatives from thirty-one African governments established an Organisation of African Unity. The OAU was launched with many high ideals and a hotchpotch of aims, including the liberation of southern Africa from white minority rule, but also the hope that it would provide Africa with a powerful independent voice in world affairs.

As they set out to achieve their goals of economic development and social progress, African leaders settled on a variety of blueprints for the future. Most believed that development and modernisation depended on strong government control and direction of the economy, a strategy inherited from the colonial era and encouraged by an influential school of Western development economists. The private sector was

considered too weak to make much difference. 'Throughout most of
Africa today, you can count the number of effective African businessmen on two hands,' wrote Barbara Ward, one of the most influential
development economists in Africa, in 1962. Only state power and
planning could produce the degree of rapid change required to deliver
the promises that African leaders had made before independence. A
'big push' was needed to break the mould of poverty and to move
Africa towards sustained growth. The imperative of development thus
justified greater government control and intervention, an outcome
that African leaders actively sought for their own purposes.

The route most favoured by African governments and development
economists alike was industrialisation. Industrialisation, it was
thought, would enable African states to break out of their colonial
trading patterns, ending their dependence on a narrow range of commodity exports and manufactured imports. It would have a far more
'modernising' impact than agriculture, providing higher productivity
and creating urban employment. Agriculture was considered incapable of providing the engine of economic growth. The
recommended form of industrialisation was import–substituting
industry; it would replace the need for imported goods by developing local manufacturing production for domestic markets, thereby
improving the balance of payments position and saving foreign
exchange. What was envisaged in essence was a shift from low-
productivity agriculture to high-productivity manufacturing. 'The
circle of poverty', declared Nkrumah, 'can only be broken by a massively planned industrial undertaking.'

In defining their ideological stance, most governments opted for
the umbrella of African socialism, believing that it held the potential
for fast growth after years of exploitation by Western capitalists.
Drawing a comparison between socialism and colonial capitalism,
Nkrumah remarked:

> Ghana inherited a colonial economy . . . We cannot rest until we
> have demolished this miserable structure and raised in its place an
> edifice of economic stability, thus creating for ourselves a veritable
> paradise of abundance and satisfaction . . . We must go forward

with our preparations for planned economic growth to supplant the
poverty, ignorance, disease and illiteracy left in the wake by discredited colonialism and decaying imperialism . . . Socialism is the
only pattern that can within the shortest possible time bring the
good life to the people.

What particularly influenced Nkrumah and other leaders impressed by
the potential of socialism was both the experience of the Soviet Union
which seemed to show that socialism produced rapid modernisation,
and the record of socialist parties in Western Europe after the Second
World War in establishing welfare states.

African societies, it was commonly claimed, traditionally included
many indigenous aspects of socialism: the communal ownership of
land; the egalitarian character of village life; collective decision-
making; extensive networks of social obligation; all were cited as
examples. 'We in Africa,' asserted Nyerere, a leading proponent of
African socialism, 'have no more need of being "converted" to socialism than we have of being "taught" democracy. Both are rooted in
our past, in the traditional society which produced us.'

In an essay on African socialism that he wrote in 1962, Nyerere
gave an idyllic account of pre-colonial society. 'Everybody was a
worker . . . Not only was the capitalist, or the landed exploiter
unknown . . . [but] capitalist exploitation was impossible. Loitering
was an unthinkable disgrace.' The advent of colonialism had changed
all this. 'In the old days the African had never aspired to the possession
of personal wealth for the purpose of dominating any of his fellows.
He had never had labourers or "factory hands" to do his work for
him. But then came the foreign capitalists. They were wealthy. They
were powerful. And the African naturally started wanting to be
wealthy too.' There was nothing inherently wrong with that, said
Nyerere, but it led to exploitation. There was now a need for Africans
to 're-educate' themselves, to regain their former attitude of mind,
their sense of community. 'In rejecting the capitalist attitude of mind
which colonialism brought into Africa, we must reject also the capitalist methods which go with it.'

Yet despite all the time and energy spent on explaining it, African socialism was little more than a potpourri of vague and romantic ideas lacking all coherence and subject to varying interpretations. For some governments it was merely a convenient label. Kenya entitled its key policy document as *African Socialism and its Application to Planning in Kenya* while vigorously pursuing a capitalist strategy. Côte d'Ivoire was one of the few which admitted to a policy of 'state capitalism'. While Nyerere argued that socialist ideals would eventually produce socialist structures, Nkrumah aimed to build socialist structures in the first place. Modibo Keita of Mali described his vision of socialism as 'a system where there will be no unemployed, and there will be no multimillionaires . . . a system where there will be no beggars, and where each will eat if hungry'. Whatever formula they chose, most socialist-minded governments placed high value on the role of the private sector and on foreign investment. What they wanted essentially was to avoid both the evils of capitalism and the pitfalls of doctrinaire socialism. Almost all remained wary of the idea of nationalisation. Only Nasser in Egypt, Ben Bella in Algeria and, for a short time, Sékou Touré in Guinea, went in for wholesale nationalisation.

More radical views about Africa's future were often aired. Marxist economists and theoreticians argued that because colonial rule had made Africa so dependent on the international capitalist system – restricting its role to producing commodities, enabling foreign operators to export their profits and thereby limiting the possibilities for development – only a clean break with the past would release its full potential. They advocated that Africa should cut its ties to international capitalism altogether, opt out of world markets and become 'autonomous'.

Another school of thought believed that Africa required revolutionary violence to throw off the shackles of its colonial past in order to attain true socialism. The leading proponent was Frantz Fanon, a black psychotherapist, born in 1925 on the Caribbean island of Martinique, who had fought in the French army during the Second World War, earning the Croix de Guerre with bronze star for his actions against the Germans in northern France. After qualifying as a doctor in 1952, Fanon took a post as head of the psychiatric department at a hospital at Blida in Algeria, but resigned in 1956 in protest against the brutality of the Algerian war and joined the FLN, becoming a prominent spokesman for its cause. He attended the All-African People's Congress in Accra in 1958 as an FLN representative and in 1960 became its permanent ambassador there, gaining glimpses of how the newly independent states of West Africa were being run. Diagnosed with leukaemia in 1960, he spent his dying days in 1961 based in Europe writing a ferocious tirade attacking not only colonialism but the bourgeois regimes that had inherited power in Africa. Published in 1961 as *Les Damnés de la Terre* – 'The wretched of the earth' – Fanon's polemic became a bible for revolutionary enthusiasts around the Third World.

Fanon argued that Africa had achieved only a 'false decolonisation', leaving real power in the hands of foreigners and their 'agents' among the ruling elites. What was needed was a violent overthrow of the entire system. Drawing on his experience of the Algerian war, he maintained that violence had 'positive and creative qualities'.

> Violence alone, violence committed by the people, violence organised and educated by its leaders, makes it possible for the masses to understand social truths and gives the key to them. Without that struggle, without that knowledge of the practice of action, there's nothing but a fancy-dress parade and the blare of trumpets. There's nothing save a minimum of readaptation, a few reforms at the top, a flag waving; and down there at the bottom an undivided mass, still living in the Middle Ages, endlessly marking time.

On a national level, violence helped nation-building; it unified people, providing 'a cement mixed with blood and anger'. It also benefited individuals. 'At the level of individuals, violence is a cleansing force. It frees the native from his inferiority complex and from his despair and inaction; it makes him fearless and restores his self-respect.'

Fanon believed fervently in the coming African revolution. He pinned his hopes principally on the peasantry. He regarded workers in towns as a 'labour aristocracy', too compromised by the colonial system, to be of use. But he envisaged that the spearhead of the revolution would be formed by the dispossessed masses living in *bidonvilles* on the fringes of towns – the wretched of the earth, or the lumpen-proletariat, as he called them. 'This lumpen-proletariat is like a horde of rats; you may kick them and throw stones at them, but despite your efforts, they'll go on gnawing at the roots of the tree.'

A number of foreign players actively sought out revolutionary opportunities in independent Africa, notably China. Lacking the economic resources to compete with Russia on trade and aid, the Chinese hoped to gain more by spreading revolutionary ideology. They focused on dissident groups, such as the Sawaba movement in Niger, Tutsi exiles in Burundi and opposition factions in Kenya. After setting up embassy quarters in a Greek-owned hotel in Bujumbura, the capital of Burundi, in 1964, they dabbled extensively in rebel activities in neighbouring Congo, lending support to Lumumbist leaders like Gaston Soumialot in Kivu and Maniema and Pierre Mulele, a former Lumumbist minister who, after fifteen months' training in Maoist teaching and guerrilla tactics in China in 1962–3, set up a revolutionary group in Kwilu province.

China's presence in Africa was small, insignificant when placed alongside the West's many contingents. Yet the reputation the Chinese gained throughout much of Africa at the time, in African eyes as much as in the Western view, was of a dangerous breed of men, capable of any feat of subversion. When China's premier, Zhou En-lai, made a tour of African states between December 1963 and February 1964, his very appearance was taken as an ominous sign. The Lagos *Daily Times* described him as 'one of the world's most dangerous men'. His parting speech in Mogadishu, the capital of Somalia, in February 1964, seemed to confirm the worst fears about China's intentions. Speaking of the 'earth-shaking changes' that had already occurred in Africa, Zhou En-lai went on to assert that 'revolutionary prospects are excellent throughout the African continent'. In the version more commonly used, his words were translated as 'Africa is ripe for revolution'.

Another foreign player keen to find a revolutionary role in Africa was Cuba. Encouraged by the Algerians, Fidel Castro decided in 1965 to despatch an expeditionary force to eastern Congo to assist rebel groups operating there. The expedition was intended to be part of what was called an 'International Proletarian Army', an alliance of revolutionary groups aimed at confronting 'imperialism' around the world, notably American imperialism.

A team of 120 Cuban fighters was recruited for the eastern Congo mission, all volunteers and virtually all black. Their leader was the legendary Argentinian revolutionary, Ernesto 'Che' Guevara, who had become bored with life as a minister in Castro's government and was eager for a new adventure. During the preliminary stages of setting up the mission, Guevara travelled to Algiers to consult Ben Bella, to Beijing to consult Zhou En-lai and to Cairo to consult Nasser. 'I shall go to the Congo,' Guevara told Nasser, 'because it is the hottest spot in the world now . . . I think we can hurt the imperialists at the core of their interests in Katanga.' Nasser was sceptical about Guevara's intention to lead the mission himself. According to an account of their meeting given by the journalist Mohammed Heikal, Nasser's son-in-law, Nasser warned Guevara not to become 'another Tarzan, a white man among black men, leading them and protecting them'. He shook his head sadly: 'It can't be done.'

The group that Guevara chose to support operated in the mountains along the western shore of Lake Tanganyika. It was led by Laurent Kabila, a 26-year-old assembly member from north Katanga, a former student in Paris and Belgrade, who hoped to establish 'a provisional government for the liberated territories of the east'. Guevara's plan was to use this liberated zone as a training ground not only for Congolese rebels but for members of liberation movements from southern Africa. He recognised that the task might take up to five years.

In April 1965, at the age of thirty-four, Guevara arrived in Dar es Salaam, in secret and in disguise, as part of an advance party of Cuban fighters en route to the eastern Congo, a thousand miles away. Travelling in three Mercedes-Benz, they reached the lakeside town of Kigoma, then crossed Lake Tanganyika by boat to the Congo, landing there on 24 April.

The expedition was a fiasco. Guevara found Kabila's rebels to be untrained, undisciplined, disorganised, riven by tribal rivalry and petty squabbles, and led by incompetent commanders who preferred the safety and comfort of bars and brothels in Kigoma on the other side of the lake to revolutionary action. 'The basic feature of the People's Liberation Army', Guevara subsequently recorded, 'was that it was a parasite army; it did not work, did not train, did not fight, and demanded provisions and labour from the population, sometimes with extreme harshness.'

Kabila himself put in only one appearance, arriving with copious supplies of whisky, but left for Kigoma after only five days in the field, preferring to spend his time on international travel or at his base in Dar es Salaam. His brief visit left Guevara unimpressed. 'He let the days pass without concerning himself with anything other than political squabbles, and all the signs are that he is too addicted to drink and women,' Guevara noted in his field diary. He dismissed Kabila as a man lacking in 'revolutionary seriousness'.

Despite the efforts of the Cubans, guerrilla activity tended to end in disarray, with rebels fleeing in panic, abandoning their weapons and leaving their wounded to fend for themselves. 'Often it was the officers who took the lead in running away,' Guevara recorded. Harassed by the Congolese army and white mercenaries, the rebels suffered one reverse after another. After seven months of fruitless endeavour, weary and demoralised, Guevara organised the Cuban retreat, crossing the lake to Kigoma in November 1965. His scathing account of what had happened was written in a small upstairs room in the Cuban embassy in Dar es Salaam during December 1965 and January 1966, but it remained secret for thirty years. His opening words were candid. 'This is the history of a failure,' he wrote.

The difficulties that African states faced as they embarked on independence were daunting. Africa was the poorest, least developed region on earth. Its climate was often harsh and variable. Drought was a constant hazard, sometimes lasting several years; two droughts earlier in the twentieth century – in 1913–14 and 1930–3 – proved catastrophic. Rainfall in half of the continent was generally inadequate. African soils in many areas were thin, deficient in nutrients and low in organic content, producing limited yields. Most of Africa's population – some 80 per cent – were engaged in subsistence agriculture, without access either to basic education or health services. Disease proliferated among humans, animals and plantlife. Although modern medicine had tamed epidemic diseases like smallpox and yellow fever, endemic diseases like malaria and sleeping sickness (trypanosomiasis) took a heavy toll; the tsetse fly, causing sleeping sickness among humans and cattle alike, prevented some 10 million square kilometres of potentially productive land from being utilised effectively for livestock and mixed agriculture. Locusts and red-billed quelea birds regularly devastated crops. River blindness (onchocerciasis) affected more than 1 million people living in the riverine areas of the interior of West Africa. Bilharzia (schistosomiasis), absent from a large part of the continent at the turn of the twentieth century, by 1960 had spread to almost every water area below a few thousand feet. Death rates for children in Africa in 1960 were the highest in the world; life expectancy, at thirty-nine years on average, was the lowest in the world.

There was an acute shortage of skilled manpower. Most African societies were predominantly illiterate and innumerate. Only 16 per cent of the adult population was literate. In black Africa in the late 1950s, just as the independence era was beginning, the entire region, containing a population of about 200 million, produced only 8,000 secondary school graduates, and nearly half of those came from two countries, Ghana and Nigeria. No more than 3 per cent of the student-age population obtained an education at secondary level. Few new states had more than 200 students in university training. In the former French colonies there were still no universities. Only about one-third of the student-age population at primary level went to school. More than three-quarters of high-level manpower in government and private business were foreigners.

The rate of population growth added new difficulties, stretching government services to the limit. As a result mainly of health measures, the growth rate rose from about 1 per cent in 1945 to nearly 3 per cent in 1960. Each woman in Africa contributed on average six children to the next generation. In Kenya in the 1970s the figure rose to eight children. Between 1950 and 1980, Africa's population tripled. Nearly two-thirds of the increase occurred in rural areas, aggravating land shortages. Millions migrated to urban areas, notably to capital cities, some driven by landlessness and poverty, others attracted by the hope of a new life with regular wages, a share in the money economy, football and movies.

The urban population in Africa expanded faster than on any other continent. In thirty-five African capitals, the population increased annually at 8.5 per cent – a rate which meant that they doubled in size every ten years. In 1945 there were only forty-nine towns in the entire continent with a population exceeding 100,000. More than half were in North Africa: ten in Egypt; nine in Morocco; four in Algeria; one in Tunisia; and one in Libya. Eleven others were in South Africa. Between the Sahara and the Limpopo, only thirteen towns had reached a population on 100,000, four of them in Nigeria. In 1955, the population of Lagos numbered 312,000; of Léopoldville (Kinshasa), 300,000; of Addis Ababa, 510,000; of Abidjan, 128,000; of Accra, 165,000. By the early 1980s, Lagos and Kinshasa had populations of about 3 million each, while Addis Ababa, Abidjan and Accra had all passed 1 million. Most urban inhabitants lacked basic amenities like running water, sanitation, paved roads and electricity. Millions lived in slums and squatter settlements, in shacks made from sheets of plastic, packing crates, cardboard boxes and pieces of tin. For most there was no prospect of employment. On average less than 10 per cent of the African population at independence earned a wage.

The economic resources available to African governments to fulfil their dreams were limited. Africa's share of world trade was no more than 3 per cent. The assets of three US corporations – General Motors, Du Pont and the Bank of America – exceeded the gross domestic product of all Africa, including South Africa. Government revenues were subject to sharp fluctuations. In Ghana, over an eight-year period between 1955 and 1963, the average year-to-year fluctuation in revenue from export duties was plus or minus 28 per cent. Only a few islands of modern economic development existed, most of them confined to coastal areas or to mining enterprises in areas like Katanga and the

Zambian Copperbelt. Much of the interior remained undeveloped, remote, cut off from contact with the modern world. Fifteen African states were landlocked, relying on long and often tenuous links to the sea, hundreds, sometimes a thousand miles away.

The colonial legacy included an infrastructure of roads, railways, hydro-electric schemes and a revenue system based on commodity exports and imported goods. But much of the economies of African states had been developed in accordance with the needs of colonial powers, as Sylvanus Olympio, the first president of Togo, noted:

> The effect of the policy of the colonial powers [he wrote] has been the economic isolation of peoples who live side by side, in some instances within a few miles of each other, while directing the flow of resources to the metropolitan countries. For example, although I can call Paris from my office telephone here in Lomé, I cannot place a call to Lagos in Nigeria only 250 miles away. Again, while it takes a short time to send an air-mail letter to Paris, it takes several days for the same letter to reach Accra, a mere 132 miles away. Railways rarely connect at international boundaries. Roads have been constructed from the coast inland but very few join economic centres of trade. The productive central regions of Togo, Dahomey (Benin) and Ghana are as remote from each other as if they were on separate continents.

Africa's economies were largely owned or controlled by foreign corporations – almost all modern manufacturing, banking, import–export trade, shipping, mining, plantations and timber enterprises. They remained heavily dependent on foreign markets, supplies of capital and technology. But except for mining and trade, foreign investors found little to attract them: the risks were regarded as high; the markets of Africa were tiny. The manufacturing sector, on which so many hopes were pinned, was only a small fraction of gross domestic product, usually less than 5 per cent.

Political systems too were recent transplants. Africans had little experience of representative democracy – representative institutions were introduced by the British and the French too late to alter the established character of the colonial state. The more durable imprint they left behind was of authoritarian regimes in which governors and their officials wielded enormous personal power. The sediment of colonial rule lay deep in African society. Traditions of autocratic governance, paternalism and dirigism were embedded in the institutions the new leaders inherited.

The most difficult task facing Africa's new leaders was to weld into nations a variety of different peoples, speaking different languages and at different stages of political and social development. The new states of Africa were not 'nations'. They possessed no ethnic, class or ideological cement to hold them together, no strong historical and social identities upon which to build. For a relatively brief period, the anti-colonial cause had provided a unity of purpose. Nationalist leaders had successfully exploited a variety of grievances among the urban and rural populations to galvanise support for the cause. But once the momentum that they had achieved in their drive for independence began to subside, so other loyalties and ambitions came thrusting to the fore. 'We have all inherited from our former masters not nations but states,' remarked Félix Houphouët-Boigny, 'states that have within them extremely fragile links between ethnic groups.' Indeed, as the result of a long historical process during the colonial era, the engine of ethnic consciousness – the tribal factor – was more potent than it had ever been before.

African societies of the pre-colonial era – a mosaic of lineage groups, clans, villages, chiefdoms, kingdoms and empires – were formed often with shifting and indeterminate frontiers and loose allegiances. Identities and languages shaded into one another. At the outset of colonial rule, administrators and ethnographers endeavoured to classify the peoples of Africa, sorting them out into what they called tribes, producing a whole new ethnic map to show the frontiers of each one. Colonial administrators wanted recognisable units they could control. 'Each tribe must be considered as a distinct unit,' a provincial commissioner in Tanganyika told his staff in 1926. 'Each tribe must be under a chief.' In many cases, tribal labels were imposed on hitherto undifferentiated groups. The chief of a little-known group in Zambia once ventured to remark: 'My people were not Soli until 1937 when the Bwana D.C. [District Commissioner] told us we were.' When local government was established under colonial rule, it was frequently aligned with existing 'tribal areas'. Entirely new ethnic groups emerged, like the Abaluyia or Kalenjin of western Kenya, formed from two congeries of adjacent peoples. Some colonial rulers used tribal identities to divide their subjects, notably the British in southern Sudan and the French in Morocco. Chiefs, appointed by colonial authorities as their agents, became the symbol of ethnicity.

Missionary endeavour added to the trend. In the process of transcribing hitherto unwritten languages into written forms, missionaries reduced Africa's innumerable dialects to fewer written languages, each helping to define a tribe. The effect was to establish new frontiers of linguistic groups and to strengthen the sense of solidarity within them. Yoruba, Igbo, Ewe, Shona and many others were formed in this way.

Missionaries were also active in documenting local customs and traditions and in compiling 'tribal' histories, all of which were incorporated into the curricula of their mission schools, spreading the notion of ethnic identity. African teachers followed suit. In southern Nigeria, young men from Ilesha and Ijebu who attended school in Ibadan or Oyo were taught to write a standard form of the Yoruba language and to identify themselves as Yoruba – a term previously reserved for subjects of the Oyo empire. As mission stations were largely responsible for providing education, educational achievement tended to depend on their locality and thus to follow ethnic lines.

Migration from rural areas to towns reinforced the process. Migrants gravitated to districts where fellow tribesmen lived, hoping through tribal connections to find housing, employment or a niche in trading markets. A host of welfare associations sprang up – 'home-boy' groups, burial and lending societies, cultural associations, all tending to enhance tribal identity. Certain occupations – railwaymen, soldiers, petty traders – became identified with specific groups which tried to monopolise them.

It was in towns that ethnic consciousness and tribal rivalry grew apace. The notion of a single Igbo people was formed in Lagos among the local 'Descendants' Union'. The Yoruba, for their part, founded the *Egbe Omo Oduduwa* – a 'Society of Descendants of Oduduwa', the mythical ancestor of the Yoruba people; its aim was 'to unite the various clans and tribes in Yorubaland and generally create and actively foster the idea of a single nationalism throughout Yorubaland'. Ethnic groups became the basis of protest movements against colonial rule.

In the first elections in the postwar era in Africa, nationalist politicians started out proclaiming nationalist objectives, selecting party candidates regardless of ethnic origin. But as the number of elections grew, as the number of voters expanded, as the stakes grew higher with the approach of independence, the basis for campaigning changed. Ambitious politicians found they could win votes by appealing for ethnic support and by promising to improve government services and to organise development projects in their home area. The political arena became a contest for scarce resources. In a continent where class formation had hardly begun to alter loyalties, ethnicity provided the strongest political base. Politicians and voters alike came to rely on ethnic solidarity. For politicians it was the route to power. They became, in effect, ethnic entrepreneurs. For voters it was their main hope of getting a slice of government bounty. What they wanted was a local representative at the centre of power – an ethnic patron who could capture a share of the spoils and bring it back to their community. Primary loyalty remained rooted in tribal identity. Kinship, clan and ethnic considerations largely determined the way people voted. The main component of African politics became, in essence, kinship corporations.

The formation of one ethnic political party tended to cause the formation of others. In Nigeria the National Council of Nigeria and the Cameroons, the first modern political organisation in West Africa launched in 1944, started out with the aim of establishing a broad-based national movement, but after tribal dissension it became an Eastern regional party, dominated by Igbo politicians. Yoruba politicians left to form the Action Group, building it around the nucleus of *Egbe Omo Oduduwa*. In Northern Nigeria, the Hausa-Fulani, while disdaining the nationalist cause which Southerners espoused, nevertheless formed in 1949 the Northern People's Congress as a political offshoot of a predominantly Hausa cultural organisation, *Jam'yyar*

Mutanen Arewa – Association of the Peoples of the North. In a more extreme example, in the Belgian Congo rival tribal parties were launched by the score. In most countries, political leaders spent much time on 'ethnic arithmetic', working out alliances that would win them power and keep them there.

Few states escaped such divisions. In Tanganyika, Julius Nyerere was helped, as he himself acknowledged, by the fact that the population was divided among 120 tribal groupings, none of which was large enough or central enough to acquire a dominant position. He bene-fited too from the common use of the Swahili language, spread initially by Arab traders, then taken up by the Germans and the British as part of their education system. Other states had to contend with a variety of languages, sometimes numbering more than a hundred. In all, more than 2,000 languages were in use in Africa.

There was a widespread view at the time of independence that once the new states focused on nation-building and economic devel-opment, ethnic loyalties would wither away under the pressure of modernisation. 'I am confident,' declared Nigeria's first prime minis-ter, Abubakar Tafawa Balewa, during a 1959 debate over the motion to ask for independence, 'that when we have our own citizenship, our own national flag, our own national anthem, we shall find the flame of national unity will burn bright and strong.' Ahmed Sékou Touré of Guinea spoke in similar terms in 1959. 'In three or four years, no one will remember the tribal, ethnic or religious rivalries which, in the recent past, caused so much damage to our country and its popula-tion.' Yet African governments were dealing not with an anachronism from the past, but a new contemporary phenomenon capable of erupting with destructive force.

An example of the potentially explosive nature of ethnic rivalry occurred just before independence in the fertile green hills of Rwanda and Burundi, two ancient kingdoms in the heart of Africa, adminis-tered under Belgian rule as a joint colony called Ruanda-Urundi. The two kingdoms were both occupied by a Hutu majority and a Tutsi minority, speaking the same language, sharing the same customs and living intermingled on the same hillsides. In the pre-colonial era the royal elite, chiefs and aristocracy of the Tutsi, a cattle-owning people

numbering no more than 15 per cent of the population of both territories, had established themselves as a feudal ruling class over the
Hutu who were predominantly agriculturalists. In Rwanda the Hutu
were required to submit to bonded labour service — *uburetwa* — from
which all Tutsi were exempt. Discrimination between Tutsi and Hutu
was part of everyday life. By appearance, Tutsis tended to be taller and
slimmer than their Hutu neighbours, with longer faces and narrower
noses. But generations of intermarriage, migration and occupational
change had blurred the distinction. Hutu and Tutsi alike moved from
one group to the other. Some Hutu were wealthy in cattle; some Tutsi
farmed. Though ethnic divisions were well entrenched, what mattered as much as ethnicity was status. Beneath the pinnacle of the royal
elite, relationships were determined by a pyramid of immensely complex pecking orders. Central rule in Rwanda was based on a tripartite
structure — Tutsi cattle chiefs, Hutu land chiefs and a separate category
of army chiefs, all appointed by the king. Loyalty to the Tutsi kings
was widely shared.

Under colonial rule, first by the Germans then by the Belgians,
more rigid definitions were imposed. German officials in the early
1900s identified Hutu and Tutsi as distinct and separate ethnic groups.
With few staff of their own on the ground, they relied on the Tutsi as
the ruling aristocracy to enforce control, enabling them to extend
their hegemony over the Hutu.

The Belgians went further. In the 1920s they introduced a system
of identity cards specifying the tribe to which a holder belonged. In
cases where appearance was indecisive or proof of ancestry was lacking, a simple formula was applied: those with ten cows or more were
classified as Tutsi, those with fewer were Hutu. The identity cards
made it virtually impossible for Hutus to become Tutsi.

Belgian officials established a Tutsi bureaucracy and favoured Tutsi
education. The Catholic Church was especially influential in promoting the Tutsi cause. Its resident bishop, Monsignor Léon Classe,
who had arrived in Rwanda as a simple priest in 1907, was regarded
as a leading expert and consulted regularly by the Belgian authorities.
What Classe envisaged, as he made quite clear, was a medieval-style
Rwanda, with a ruling Tutsi aristocracy and a Hutu peasantry,

working hand-in-hand with the colonial administration and with the Catholic Church guiding the whole enterprise. When the Catholic Church was given responsibility for the entire educational system in the early 1930s, government and church officials were in full agreement on what was required. 'You must choose the Batusi [Tutsi],' Monsignor Classe, told missionaries, 'because the government will probably refuse Hutu teachers . . . In the government the positions in every branch of the administration, even the unimportant ones, will be reserved henceforth for young Batusi.' The Hutu were not entirely disregarded, but a streaming system ensured that Tutsi were given the best opportunities in education. Primary schools were segregated. The only Hutu able to escape relegation to the labouring masses were those few permitted to study in seminaries. In the forced labour regime that the Belgians ran, developing it from the previous Tutsi system, Tutsi were employed as taskmasters over Hutu labourers. Tutsi chiefs were used to enforce order and discipline. By the late 1930s the Belgians had made ethnicity the defining feature of ordinary life in both Rwanda and Burundi. Whatever sense of collective identity had previously existed in the two kingdoms shrivelled and died.

The reaction in Rwanda came during the 1950s. A period of Hutu political agitation culminated in 1957 in the publication of a *BaHutu Manifesto*, written by a group of nine Hutu intellectuals, all former seminarists, which challenged the entire administrative and economic system in Rwanda. The central problem, said the authors, was 'the political monopoly of one race, the Tutsi race, which, given the present structural framework, becomes a social and economic monopoly'. They demanded measures to achieve 'the integral and collective promotion of the Hutu'. Church leaders, including Tutsi priests, were prominent in advocating reform. Belgian officials conceded that 'the Hutu–Tutsi question posed an undeniable problem' and proposed that official usage of the terms 'Hutu' and 'Tutsi' – on identity cards, for example – should be abolished. The Hutu, however, rejected the proposal, wanting to retain their identifiable majority; abolition of identity cards would prevent 'the statistical law from establishing the reality of facts'. The idea gained ground that majority rule meant Hutu rule. Ethnic obsession took hold among the small stratum of the educated elite. Political parties were formed on an ethnic basis. Hutu parties campaigned for the abolition of the Tutsi monarchy and the establishment of a republic.

The first violence erupted in November 1959, after a Hutu sub-chief, a prominent political activist, was beaten up by a band of Tutsi militants. In what became known as 'the wind of destruction', roving bands of Hutu went on the rampage, attacking Tutsi authorities, burning Tutsi homes and looting Tutsi property. Hundreds of Tutsi were killed; thousands fled into exile. The terminology used by Hutu extremists for the killing was 'work'.

At this critical juncture the Belgians decided to change sides. A Belgian army officer, Colonel Guy Logiest, appointed to take charge of Rwanda as Special Resident, believed it necessary to be 'partial against the Tutsis' in order to reconstruct the system. In a report to Brussels he declared: 'Because of the force of circumstances, we have to take sides. We cannot remain neutral and passive'. Recalling his mission in a book published in Brussels in 1988, Logiest spoke of his desire 'to put down the arrogance and expose the duplicity of a basically oppressive and unjust aristocracy'.

In early 1960 Logiest began dismissing Tutsi chiefs, appointing Hutus in their places. The new chiefs immediately organised the persecution of Tutsis in districts they controlled, precipitating a mass exodus in which some 130,000 Rwandan Tutsi sought refuge in the Congo, Burundi, Uganda and Tanganyika. In local government elections, held in June and July 1960 amid continuing violence, the all-Hutu *Parti du Mouvement de l'Émancipation Hutu* – Parmehutu – won 2,390 out of 3,125 council seats, gaining a dominant position in almost every commune. The Belgian authorities then colluded with Hutu leaders in organising what was subsequently described as a 'legal coup'. In January 1961 Rwanda's newly elected *bourgmestres* (mayors) and councillors were summoned to a meeting at Gitarama, the birthplace of the Hutu leader, Grégoire Kayibanda, where they declared the abolition of the monarchy and the establishment of a republic. Legislative elections in September confirmed Hutu supremacy. But a report by the United Nations Trusteeship Commission warned in 1961: 'The developments of these last eighteen months have brought about the racial dictatorship of one party . . . An oppressive system has been replaced by another one . . . It is quite possible that some day we will witness violent reactions on the part of the Tutsi.'

On 1 July 1962 Rwanda became an independent state under a republican government led by Grégoire Kayibanda, a politician devoted to the cause of Hutu hegemony and determined to keep the Tutsi in a subordinate role. On the same day Burundi gained its independence with seemingly more stable prospects. Though there were similar tensions between Tutsi and Hutu, the Tutsi monarchy in Burundi survived. Yet Burundi and Rwanda alike were to endure a series of massive upheavals.

THE FIRST DANCE OF
FREEDOM

As founding fathers, the first generation of nationalist leaders –
Nkrumah, Nasser, Senghor, Houphouët-Boigny, Sékou Touré,
Keita, Olympio, Kenyatta, Nyerere, Kaunda, Banda – all enjoyed
great prestige and high honour. They were seen to personify the states
they led and swiftly took advantage to consolidate their control. From
the outset, most sought a monopoly of power; most established a
system of personal rule and encouraged personality cults. 'The president personifies the Nation as did the Monarch of former times his
peoples,' explained Senghor. 'The masses are not mistaken who speak
of the "reign" of Modibo Keita, Sékou Touré and Houphouët-
Boigny, in whom they see, above all, the elected of God through the
people.'

Kwame Nkrumah's ambition soared above all others. Having successfully challenged the might of British rule in Africa and opened the
way to independence for a score of other African countries, he saw
himself as a messianic leader destined to play an even greater role. At
home he wanted to transform Ghana into an industrial power, a
centre of learning, a model socialist society which other states would
want to emulate. He also dreamed of making Africa a giant, in economic, political and military terms, as united and as powerful as the
United States or the Soviet Union, with himself as leader. Believing

himself to possess unique ability, capable of achieving for Africa what Marx and Lenin had done for Europe and Mao Tse-tung for China, he created an official ideology, calling it Nkrumahism, and built an ideological institute in his name costing millions of dollars. A staff of mostly left-wing expatriates worked there diligently, constructing elaborate political theories. But despite their efforts, 'Nkrumahism', though frequently quoted in public, was never clearly defined. When it was launched in 1960, 'Nkrumahism' was defined as a 'complex political and social philosophy' to which Nkrumah would add from time to time. A few years later it was said to be based on 'scientific socialism'. After four years of study, the Kwame Nkrumah Ideological Institute announced:

> Nkrumahism is the ideology for the New Africa, independent and absolutely free from imperialism, organised on a continental scale, founded upon the conception of One and United Africa, drawing its strength from modern science and technology and from the traditional African belief that the free development of each is conditioned by the free development of all.

Gamal Abdel Nasser controlled Egypt through what was known as 'Nasserism'. Nasserism was neither a movement nor an ideology but a system of personal rule. The organisation of the state and its policy was determined by his will alone. All power was concentrated in his hands; every aspect of government came under his remit. He decreed the nationalisation of industry, transport, financial institutions, large hotels and department stores and introduced central planning of the economy, all enhancing his personal ability to control the state. 'He managed to abolish the difference between state and government, between those two and himself,' his biographer, Professor P. J. Vatikiotis, observed. 'Instead of separating the powers of government, he fused them.' His control extended to the media, trade unions, professional syndicates, youth organisations and religious institutions. Some Egyptians likened him to a modern Pharaoh.

Personal loyalty was what Nasser required from his officials. 'The Council of Ministers under his chairmanship became an audience,'

recalled Fathi Radwan, one of Nasser's ministers. 'Ministers listened
dutifully and took down notes, received instructions. If one of them
wished to comment or speak he had to ask his permission.' He tolerated no opposition, crushing communists and Muslim Brethren alike,
relying on his secret police – the *mukhabarat* – to track down dissenters. 'Their main task – and source of livelihood – comprised in
suggesting to their chief, Nasser, the existence of conspiracies against
him, and that they were protecting him from them,' recalled another
of Nasser's ministers, Dr Abdul Wahhab Al-Burullusi. Thousands of
his opponents suffered detention in concentration camps at the hands
of the *mukhabarat*. Many others lived in constant fear of them. Writing
from prison in October 1965, Kamal El-Din Hussein, one of the
original group of conspirators, remarked: 'I regret the revolution has
been transformed into one of terror. No person is certain of his fate
once he utters a free opinion.' The paradox was that despite running
a police state, Nasser was still idolised by the masses.

In Guinea, Sékou Touré deified himself in a similar fashion. His
main title was *Guide Suprème de le Révolution*, but he also liked to be
known as 'The Great Son of Africa'; 'The Terror of International
Imperialism, Colonialism and Neo-Colonialism'; and 'The Doctor of
Revolutionary Sciences'. He was portrayed as an expert in every field,
from agriculture to philosophy to soccer. More than twenty volumes
of his speeches and reflections upon Guinea and African development
were published and made compulsory reading. Students were required
to memorise his long didactic poems to ensure success in their examinations. No major decision could be taken without his approval. He
was the source of all authority, ruling by decree, intervening at his
own discretion in legal cases and deciding the verdict when necessary
in the name of the people. Guinea, wrote Lansiné Kaba, was 'a one-
man show, in which Touré was the sole actor, while others danced,
applauded or sang in his honour according to his whim'.

In Malawi, Hastings Banda's grip extended not just over the government and the economy of the country but even over the moral
standards under which the population was required to live. Within
weeks of independence in 1964, in a blaze of anger he dismissed
ministers who dared to challenge his authority and went on to run

Malawi as his personal fiefdom, demanding not just obedience but servility. No other African leader imposed his personality with such
vigour and force on the country he ruled. He insisted on directing
even the smallest details of Malawi's affairs. 'Everything is my business.
Everything,' he once said. 'The state of education, the state of our
economy, the state of our agriculture, the state of our transport, everything is my business.' He was equally blunt about what power lay at his
disposal. 'Anything I say is law. Literally law. It is a fact in this country.' He tolerated neither dissent nor criticism. No one was permitted
to question his authority or his decisions. His quest for absolute control extended to interference with the courts. The strict puritan code
which he so much admired became the nation's way of life. Men were
forbidden to wear long hair; women were forbidden to wear short
skirts or trousers. Films, foreign newspapers, magazines and books
were strictly censored to prevent 'decadent' Western influences from
harming the population. The position that Banda held in Malawi was
sometimes likened to that of one of the old Maravi kings, complete
with divine right and absolute authority.

In Côte d'Ivoire, Houphouët's 'reign' was more benign but similarly autocratic. An avid admirer of de Gaulle, he took control at
independence in 1960 under a constitution which he himself had
designed to ensure that one-man rule prevailed. He remained
unapologetic about his style: 'Democracy is a system of government
for virtuous people,' he said. 'In young countries such as our own, we
need a chief who is all-powerful for a specified period of time.'

In one country after another, African leaders acted in contempt of
constitutional rules and agreements they had sworn to uphold to
enhance their own power. Constitutions were either amended or
rewritten or simply ignored. Checks and balances were removed.
Nkrumah's first amendment to the constitution – abolishing regional
assemblies – was introduced only two years after independence.

In their quest for greater control, the device they commonly
favoured was the one-party system. In some cases, one-party systems
were achieved by popular verdict. In pre-independence elections in
francophone Africa in 1959, Houphouët-Boigny's *Parti Démocratique
de la Côte d'Ivoire* won all seats in the Legislative Assembly; so too did

Senghor's *Union Progressiste Sénégalaise*, Keita's *Union Soudanaise* in Mali and Bourguiba's *Neo-Destour* in Tunisia. In East Africa, Nyerere's Tanganyika African National Union won all open seats in parliament in 1960; and in the 1964 elections, Banda's Malawi Congress Party also swept the board. In other cases, one-party systems were arranged by negotiation, whereby opposition parties accepted a merger with ruling parties. Sékou Touré's *Parti Démocratique de Guinée* won fifty-six seats in Legislative Assembly elections in 1957, and the following year he arranged for opposition politicians to join the PDG. In Kenya in 1964, Kenyatta persuaded opposition politicians from the Kenya African Democratic Union to cross the floor and take up prominent posts in the government. There were many other examples, however, of where one-party systems were imposed simply by suppressing opposition parties – as in Ghana, Niger, Dahomey, Togo, Mauritania, Central African Republic and Upper Volta (Burkina Faso).

Not all attempts to impose one-party rule were successful. When Abbé Fulbert Youlou announced plans to install a one-party system in Congo-Brazzaville in 1963, trade unions and youth groups took to the streets in anti-government demonstrations which lasted for three days. A former Catholic priest, Youlou ran a regime that was notoriously corrupt. Most ministers were heavily involved in their own business affairs, setting up ventures like bars and nightclubs in Brazzaville and running diamond-smuggling rackets. A television station was established for three hundred sets. Critics of his regime were dealt with vigorously. Once when the opposition tabled a motion of censure against his government in the National Assembly, Youlou pulled out a revolver from under his soutane and pointed it at the deputies responsible. When demonstrations against his plans for a one-party system erupted, Youlou telephoned de Gaulle pleading with him to order French troops stationed in Congo-Brazzaville to intervene, but de Gaulle refused. Congolese army officers went to Youlou to demand his resignation. He signed, then fell into a faint and, upon recovering, telephoned de Gaulle. '*J'ai signé, mon général*,' he announced tearfully. He later sought exile in France, but was turned away and settled in Madrid.

There were many arguments used to justify one-party systems.

New states facing so many challenges, it was said, needed strong governments which were best served by concentrating authority with a single, nation-wide party. Only a disciplined mass party, centrally directed, was an effective means to overcome tribal divisions, to inspire a sense of nationhood and to mobilise the population for economic development. Some proponents of one-party systems held an ideological conviction that an elite political party was the supreme instrument of society. Multi-party politics, it was argued, usually deteriorated into a competition between tribal blocs and alliances. Since opposition parties tended to rely on tribal groups for support, they undermined the cause of nation-building and weakened the efficiency of the state. They were thus a luxury which new states with limited resources could ill afford. Some African leaders argued that opposition parties were in fact alien to African practice and that a one-party system, if properly managed, provided a democratic outlet just as adequate as did a multi-party system.

Julius Nyerere was one of the most eloquent advocates of a one-party system. He maintained that the two-party system had evolved in the West as a result of competition between socio-economic classes. But since African society was essentially classless, there was no basis for two parties, and parliamentary systems of the kind bequeathed to Africa by Europe's departing colonial powers were misplaced.

> The British and American tradition of a two-party system is a reflection of the society from which it evolved. The existence of distinct classes and the struggle between them resulted in the growth of this system. In Africa, the Nationalist movements were fighting a battle for freedom from foreign domination, not from domination by any ruling class of our own. Once the foreign power – 'the other Party' – has been expelled, there is no ready-made division among the people. The Nationalist movements must inevitably form the first Governments of the new states. Once a free Government is formed, its supreme task lies ahead – the building up of the country's economy. This, no less than the struggle against colonialism, calls for the maximum united effort by the whole country if it is to succeed. There can be no room for difference or division.

Opposition parties, said Nyerere, were no more than a distraction, with dangerous potential. 'The only voices to be heard in "opposition" are those of a few irresponsible individuals who exploit the very privileges of democracy – freedom of the press, freedom of association, freedom to criticise – in order to deflect the government from its responsibilities to the people by creating problems of law and order.'

> There can only be one reason for the formation of such [opposition] parties in a country like ours – the desire to imitate the political structures of a totally dissimilar society. What is more, the desire to imitate where conditions are not suitable for imitation can easily lead us into trouble. To try and import the idea of a parliamentary opposition into Africa may very likely lead to violence – because the opposition parties will tend to be regarded as traitors by the majority of our people, or, at best, it will lead to the trivial manoeuvrings of "opposing" groups whose time is spent in the inflation of artificial difference into some semblance of reality "for the sake of preserving democracy". The latter alternative, I repeat, is an over-sophisticated pastime which we in Africa cannot afford to indulge in; our time is too short and there is too much serious work to be done.

Moreover, claimed Nyerere, a one-party system could offer an even better framework for democracy than a multi-party system which resulted in endless bouts of political warfare. 'Where there is one party – provided it is identified with the nation as a whole – the foundations of democracy can be firmer, and the people can have more opportunity to exercise a real choice, than when you have two or more parties.'

In practice, one-party systems were used by politicians in power mostly to suppress any sign of opposition to their regimes and to keep themselves in office. Mass parties, once founded upon popular support, simply withered away, leaving, as Frantz Fanon remarked, nothing but the shell, the name, the emblem and the motto; they served only as the stronghold of a privileged few.

Stage by stage, African leaders accumulated ever greater personal power, spreading the tentacles of their control into the further reaches of society. They preferred to rule not through constitutions or through state institutions like parliament but by exercising vast systems of patronage. Parliaments, where they survived, were packed with supporters, chosen for their known obedience. Government bureaucracies were staffed by party loyalists. Trade unions and farmers' organisations were subordinated to the interests of government. The press existed merely as an outlet for government propaganda. Political debate became a matter of platitudes and praise-songs, no longer taken seriously. 'System? What system?' retorted President Bourguiba, when asked about Tunisia's political system. 'I am the system!'

The opportunities for patronage available to African leaders provided them with the 'cement' they needed to consolidate their control. At their disposal were thousands of appointments not only to cabinets, parliaments and bureaucracies, but to new parastatal organisations set up to boost the development of industry and agriculture. In most countries, government was the largest employer, the chief dispenser of jobs and benefits. Many appointments were made not on the basis of merit but of party loyalty or tribal affiliation. The awarding of contracts and licences and the allocation of development projects – roads, schools and hospitals – were influenced by similar considerations. Decisions were often taken as a result of personal ties and obligations or for reasons of personal profit. Fanon likened the leaders of one-party states to 'chairmen of the board of a society of impatient profiteers'. The lines of patronage radiated out from presidencies to regions, districts and villages. At each level, 'big men' worked the system, providing followers and friends with jobs, contracts and favours in exchange for political support; in order to retain support, they had to ensure the distribution of rewards. Throughout Africa, the politics of patronage and patrimonial rule became a common political pattern.

A small elite – no more than about 3 per cent of the population – used their position to great personal advantage. Independence had given them control of land registration, credit, taxation, marketing boards, public investment, import requirements and negotiations with private capital. Politicians lost no opportunity to accumulate wealth and privilege. Many were more preoccupied with their own business deals, with contracts, commissions and quick profits, than with government affairs. Indeed, political activity was seen by ambitious Africans as the most direct way of securing wealth and social standing.

In his study of one-party states in West Africa published in 1965, Arthur Lewis, a distinguished West Indian economist, observed:

> Much of what is going on in some of these countries is fully explained in terms of the normal lust of human beings for power and wealth. The stakes are high. Office carries power, prestige and money. The power is incredible. Most West African Ministers consider themselves to be above the law, and are treated as such by the police. Decision-making is arbitrary. Decisions which more advanced countries leave to civil servants and technicians are in those countries made by Ministers, often without consulting expert advice. The prestige is also incredible. Men who claim to be democrats in fact behave like emperors. Personifying the state, they dress themselves up in uniforms, build themselves palaces, bring all other traffic to a standstill when they drive, hold fancy parades and generally demand to be treated like Egyptian Pharaohs. And the money is also incredible. Successful politicians receive, even if only elected to Parliament, salaries two to four times more than they previously earned, plus per diem allowances, travelling expenses and other fringe benefits. There are also vast pickings in bribes, state contracts, diversion of public funds to private uses, and commissions of various sorts. To be a Minister is to have a lifetime's chance to make a fortune.

Civil servants filling the posts vacated by departing colonial officials insisted on the same high salaries and perks – pensions, housing allowances and cheap loans. Government budgets soon became burdened with the huge cost of salaries, allowances and presidential expenses. Writing in 1962, the respected French agronomist René Dumont noted that a deputy in Gabon was paid more than a British Member of Parliament and earned in six months as much as the average peasant did in thirty-six years. He went on: 'As for the Gabonese presidency, parliament and ministers, with all their supposedly useful trips, it probably represents, in relation to the national income of the country, more than the cost to France of the court of Louis XVI in 1788.' Ministers in Nigeria were rewarded not only with princely salaries but rent-free, air-conditioned residences, replete with stewards, gardeners and drivers, generous car allowances, entertainment budgets, free telephone and free electricity. Senegal's budget for 1964 showed that 47 per cent of the total was allocated to civil service salaries. In the Central African Republic and in Côte d'Ivoire the figure was 58 per cent; in Congo-Brazzaville, 62 per cent; in Dahomey, 65 per cent. A report on Zambia noted: 'Expensive houses built for the emergent elite swallow up the bulk of urban housing investments. Thus the construction of 1,710 high- and medium-cost dwellings and 1,307 servants' quarters absorbed 77.2 per cent of the amount spent on urban housing in 1974. Another 13.4 per cent went into the building of 1,266 low-cost units, 4.7 per cent into 2,000 houses on serviced plots, and the remaining 4.7 per cent into 9,905 shanty houses.'

The wealth the new elite acquired was ostentatiously displayed in grand houses, luxury cars and lavish lifestyles – 'platinum life', it was called in Abidjan. In East Africa a new tribe appeared, cynically known as the WaBenzi, in description of rich politicians, officials and businessmen who drove about in expensive Mercedes-Benz cars. Though ministers in parliament and at public meetings still issued promises about social equality and referred sympathetically to the needs of the common man, the gap between the rich elite living in plush villas, elegant apartment buildings and town houses, and the masses surviving in slums and *bidonvilles* on the fringes of towns became ever more noticeable.

A study of trade figures of fourteen francophone states in 1964 showed that the amount spent on importing alcoholic drinks was six times higher than that spent on importing fertiliser. Half as much was spent on perfume and cosmetic imports as on machine tools. Almost as much went on importing petrol for privately owned cars as on the purchase of tractors; and five times as much on importing cars as on agricultural equipment.

Equally profligate was government spending on prestige projects such as presidential palaces, conference halls, airports, airlines, hotels, grand highways and embassies abroad. The most glaring examples of lavish spending occurred when governments competed for the privilege of holding the annual conference of the Organisation of African Unity, an event renowned for producing little else than bombast and rhetoric from assembled heads of state. Nkrumah set the precedent in 1965 by building a palace containing sixty luxury suites and a banqueting hall capable of seating 2,000 guests. Others followed suit. President Omar Bongo of Gabon, a man much given to gestures of personal grandeur, ordered the construction of several seafront hotels in Libreville especially for an OAU summit and a new palace for himself with sliding walls and doors, rotating rooms and a private nightclub, all costing well over $200 million. President Siaka Stevens spent two-thirds of Sierra Leone's national budget to host an OAU summit meeting. Togo spent $120 million – half of the national budget – on building a thirty-storey hotel and conference centre in Lomé, which included fifty-two presidential suites, in the hope of persuading the OAU to transfer its permanent headquarters from Addis Ababa to Lomé. But the OAU did not agree to the move.

The blight of corruption, meanwhile, spread ever further, most notably in West Africa at first, then to other areas. In many parts of West Africa there had been a long tradition of 'dash' – of gift-giving for services rendered. The bigger the man, the bigger the 'dash' for the favour received. The 'Big Man' became an accepted feature of West African life, a patron fostering his followers by his fame and fortune. Until independence, the opportunities for self-enrichment were limited; the principal beneficiaries of colonial rule were the white elite, officials and businessmen, enjoying a lifestyle which the black elite aspired to emulate but were largely prevented from reaching. Independence unlocked the floodgates. Politicians used their public office to extract 'commissions' at every available opportunity. The bigger the politician, the bigger the political or business manipulation. The common cut on government contracts in West Africa was 10 per cent. Foreign firms and local businessmen alike budgeted for the extra 10 per cent that had to be paid either to politicians or to the ruling party to succeed. In numerous cases, prominent politicians simply looted the state treasury, transferring money to their private accounts; loans and debts to the state were routinely overlooked.

The practice of bribery and embezzlement spread from top to bottom, from politicians to tax collectors, customs officers, policemen, postal clerks and dispensary assistants. It affected everything from job applications to licences, scholarships, foreign exchange and the location of factories. Writing about West Africa in 1961, Frantz Fanon observed: 'Scandals are numerous, ministers grow rich, their wives doll themselves up, the members of parliament feather their nests and there is not a soul down to the simple policeman or the customs officer who does not join in the great procession of corruption.' In time, bribery and corruption became 'a way of life', accepted as a means of getting by, earning a living, obtaining a service or avoiding hassle.

In Ghana, Nkrumah's ministers were well known for pushing through contracts with foreign corporations for a 10 per cent fee. 'It was the order of the day,' one of Nkrumah's officials recalled, 'for every minister connected with a government contract to take a cut for himself.' Ministers flaunted their wealth openly. 'Socialism doesn't mean that if you've made a lot of money, you can't keep it,' remarked Krobo Edusei in 1961. Edusei gained particular notoriety when his wife ordered a £3,000 gold-plated bed from a London store. In the ensuing scandal, she was obliged to send it back. Edusei confessed in later years to owning fourteen houses, a luxurious beach house, a long lease on a London flat, several expensive cars and six different bank accounts.

Nkrumah himself was engaged in the business of collecting bribes, setting up a special company, the National Development Corporation, to facilitate the handling of bribes from foreign businessmen and others seeking government contracts. With control of companies like the National Development Corporation and by using government funds for his personal use when necessary, Nkrumah became a wealthy man. In one example, the price paid by the government for properties purchased from a Greek businessman was deliberately inflated so that £1 million could be turned back to Nkrumah for his own use.

In Nigeria the first years of independence became an orgy of power being turned into profit. The advantages of political office were used at every opportunity by Nigeria's leaders to accumulate empires of wealth and patronage with which to improve both their personal and their party's fortunes. Using public resources, party and government bosses were able to reward their supporters and friends with jobs, contracts, loans, scholarships, public amenities; indeed any favour that came within their purview. Power itself in effect came to rest on the ability to bribe. Parties, once in power, moved quickly to amass a fortune from public funds large enough for them to be able to win the next election; a network of banks, businesses and financial structures were set up to support this objective. Parties which did not command state resources simply stood no chance of winning elections. Between 1958 and 1962, for example, the Action Group government in Nigeria's Western Region invested about £6.5 million in the National Investment and Properties Company, a business which had four party leaders as its directors. In the period between April 1959 and November 1961, one of the directors gave £3.7 million to the Action Group party in the form of 'special donations'. Northern politicians ran a similar spoils system. A study of thirty-nine investment and loan projects of the Northern Nigeria Development Corporation undertaken in 1966 showed that the biggest borrowers had been the big men of the Northern government.

The misuse of public funds in Nigeria had deep roots. During the colonial era, many Nigerians regarded government institutions as *olu oyibo* – whiteman's business, an alien system that could be plundered when necessary. 'Government's business is no man's business,' ran a popular Nigerian saying. Explaining the practice, Eghosa Osaghae, a Nigerian academic, commented: 'There was thus nothing seriously wrong with stealing state funds, especially if they were used to benefit not only the individual but also members of his community. Those who had the opportunity to be in government were expected to use the power and resources at their disposal to advance private and communal interests.' The same attitude prevailed with the coming of independence. The state was regarded as a foreign institution that could be used for personal and community gain without any sense of shame or need for accountability. Plunderers of the government treasury were often excused on the grounds that they had only 'taken their share'. What added to the problem was the notion that the government was, in effect, a reservoir of 'free money'.

Every facet of Nigerian society was eventually permeated by corruption. A senior civil servant summarised: 'You bribe to get your child into school; you pay to secure your job and also continue to pay in some cases to retain it; you pay ten per cent of any contract obtained; you dash the tax officer to avoid paying taxes; you pay a hospital doctor or nurse to get proper attention; you pay the policeman to evade arrest. This catalogue of shame can continue without end.'

It was often said that, because of the internal tensions and rivalries afflicting most African states, only strong government could provide the stability they needed to develop and prosper. Yet in practice, strong governments of the kind employed in Africa – whether personal dictatorships or one-party systems – rarely ensured either political stability or effective administration. Once in power, African leaders became preoccupied with staying in power, employing whatever means were necessary. Much depended on their ability to operate patrimonial systems that kept key supporters loyal to them. Political activity was reduced to 'palace politics', an arena for ruling elites to manoeuvre for their own interests. Rival factions competed for ascendancy. Conspiracies and plots proliferated. The common aim was to gain political office and the power and patronage that went with it. Fanon observed: 'The men at the head of affairs spent two-thirds of their time in watching the approaches and trying to anticipate the dangers which threaten them, and the remaining one-third of their time in working for their country.' Ministers were regularly rotated and reshuffled to keep them off-balance and to prevent them from becoming a threat.

In dealing with political opponents, African leaders resorted readily to arbitrary measures – arrest, detention and other forms of harassment. Within a year of independence, Nkrumah introduced laws allowing the government to detain anyone without trial for up to five years. In theory, the Preventive Detention Act of 1958 and other similar measures that followed were to be employed only at times of emergency; in practice, they were used to silence critics and opponents and even, in some cases, to pay off petty scores. In 1958 thirty-eight people were detained; in 1961, 311; in 1963, 586, in 1965, some 1,200. Among the victims was Dr Danquah, the doyen of the old-guard elite for whom Nkrumah had worked on his return from London. He died in prison in 1965, spending the last year of his life in solitary confinement, a sick and disheartened man, deprived of adequate medical treatment. In Malawi, Banda was characteristically blunt about his intentions: 'If, to maintain the political stability and efficient administration, I have to detain ten thousand or one hundred thousand, I will do it,' he said in 1965. Opposition parties across Africa were routinely banned on grounds of 'national security'; government opponents were routinely imprisoned. Leaders like Nkrumah and Banda relied on fear as an instrument of control.

When the first upheavals occurred, they appeared as random episodes. In 1958, after two years of political squabbling in Sudan, army generals took control, citing the need for 'stable and clean administration'. In 1963 Togo's president, Sylvanus Olympio, was shot dead in Lomé by a group of ex-servicemen led by a 25-year-old sergeant, Etienne Eyadéma, in revenge for refusing to employ them in the Togolese army. The following year, armed African gangs in Zanzibar incited an uprising against the Arab ruling elite, forcing the sultan to flee in his yacht. Some 5,000 Arabs were killed, thousands more interned, their houses, property and possessions seized at will. A revolutionary council, led by Abeid Karume, appealed for assistance from China, the Soviet Union and East Germany. Hundreds of communist technicians duly arrived, prompting Western fears that the island might become another 'Cuba'. On mainland Tanganyika, Nyerere, worried by the prospect of Zanzibar being drawn directly into the Cold War and anxious to exert a moderating influence, proposed a union between Tanganyika and Zanzibar. The union was subsequently named Tanzania.

Former French colonies seemed especially susceptible to disorder and civil strife. French army units stationed in Africa in accordance with defence cooperation agreements which France signed with almost all its former colonies were called upon time and again for help

Farewell the Trumpets: Sir Charles Arden-Clarke standing with Kwame Nkrumah during Ghana's independence ceremonies in March 1957. Six years earlier, Nkrumah made the leap from convicted criminal to prime minister in the course of a day.

Dancing the Highlife: Kwame Nkrumah takes to the floor with Queen Elizabeth II at a ball at State House in 1961. At their first meeting at Buckingham Palace in 1957, Nkrumah was 'agog with excitement'.

A family affair: Nkrumah pictured with his friend Colonel Nasser in 1966. In his first year as Ghana's leader, Nkrumah asked Nasser for help in finding a wife. Nkrumah eventually chose an Egyptian woman he did not meet until his wedding day.

3

4

A hero of the people: Colonel Nasser, together with Sudan's visiting prime minister, Ismail al-Azhari, drives through the streets of Cairo in 1954. Once renowned as a tedious, shy and awkward speaker, Nasser found he could manipulate crowds using the language of the streets.

Before the storm: the only meeting between Nasser and Britain's prime minister, Anthony Eden, took place in the British Embassy in Cairo in February 1955. The following year, Eden became convinced that Nasser was seeking to drive out British influence in the Middle East. In a telephone call to a colleague at the Savoy Hotel in London, he shouted: 'Can't you understand I want him murdered?'

6

5

Suez, 1956. Facing a joint Anglo–French–Israeli assault on Egypt, Nasser promptly sank 47 ships in the canal, blocking all traffic and cutting off the main route for Europe's oil supplies.

Algiers, 1958. General Charles de Gaulle arrives amid civil war to be acclaimed a saviour by white residents convinced he would keep Algeria in French hands.

Algiers, 1961. The French army in revolt. A crowd of white supporters gathers outside government headquarters to hear French generals condemn General de Gaulle's plan to open peace talks with Algerian nationalist fighters. Their *putsch* collapsed after four days.

Algiers, 1962. Algerian women queue up to vote in a referendum on independence. Nearly 6 million Algerians voted in favour; 16,500 said no. In a mass exodus, more than a million white residents fled to France, abandoning homes, farms and livelihoods.

The francophile: as a minister in the French government, Félix Houphouët–Boigny, pictured here in 1959 with President de Gaulle and US President Dwight D. Eisenhower, strove hard to ensure France retained influence in Africa as its empire there was dismantled.

Different approaches: as Côte d'Ivoire's president, Houphouët–Boigny favoured a capitalist strategy, while Tanganyika's Julius Nyerere, pictured at a meeting in Dar es Salaam in 1962, advocated African socialism.

The poet-president: Léopold Senghor, pictured with his wife at celebrations marking Senegal's first year of independence from France. As a Catholic in a predominantly Muslim country, Senghor became adept at building coalitions, without appealing to religious or ethnic affiliation. His inclination for compromise and persuasion became an integral part of Senegal's political tradition.

Dressed in his habitual three-piece suit and black homburg hat, Hastings Banda arrives for a Commonwealth conference in London in 1964. Within weeks of independence in 1964, he dismissed ministers who dared challenge his authority and went on to run Malawi as his personal fiefdom for thirty years.

14 The Moscow-trained revolutionary: Jomo Kenyatta, pictured attending the Pan-African Congress in Manchester in 1945. After twelve years abroad, he was impatient to return to Kenya to engage in the nationalist struggle. 'I feel like a general separated by 5,000 miles from his troops,' he told his English wife, Edna.

Back in Kenya, Kenyatta was accused by the British authorities of being the mastermind behind the Mau Mau rebellion. Lacking evidence against him, the authorities proceeded to rig his trial. In this government photo, taken at his trial at Kapenguria in 1953, the white guard's face has been blotted out as a precaution against Mau Mau reprisals.

16 As prime minister in 1963, Kenyatta offered an amnesty to Mau Mau rebels still at large, like 'Field Marshal' Mwariama. But he remained highly critical of the Mau Mau rebellion. 'Those who built up an organisation of unbridled violence in Kenya were never the political associates or executive colleagues of Kenyatta.'

East Africa's trio: Tanzania's Julius Nyerere, Uganda's Milton Obote and Kenya's Jomo Kenyatta wave to crowds before a government conference in Nairobi in 1964.

The Congo, 1960. His arms roped behind him, the Congo's ousted prime minister, Patrice Lumumba, is hauled off to prison after being captured by Colonel Mobutu's troops. 'If I die, *tant pis*,' he told a friend. 'The Congo needs martyrs.' Badly beaten, he was executed by a firing squad in Katanga under the command of a Belgian officer.

The Congo, 1965. Bored with life as a minister in Fidel Castro's government in Cuba, the Argentinian revolutionary Che Guevara decided on a new adventure, leading a Cuban expedition to the eastern Congo to foment rebellion there. President Nasser warned him not to become 'another Tarzan'. The expedition was a fiasco.

The architect of grand apartheid, Hendrik Verwoerd, a Dutch-born ideological fanatic, cast himself in the role of a leader chosen by God. 'I do not have the nagging doubt of ever wondering whether perhaps I am wrong.'

20

Robben Island, 1964. Sentenced to life imprisonment in 1964 for his involvement in armed rebellion against the South African government, Nelson Mandela, pictured with his life-long friend, Walter Sisulu, endured years of hard labour, working in the island's quarry and collecting seaweed.

22

White rebels: determined to keep Rhodesia in white hands, Prime Minister Ian Smith, surrounded by cabinet colleagues, signed a Unilateral Declaration of Independence from Britain in 1965, claiming to have struck a blow 'for the preservation of justice, civilisation and Christianity'.

in restoring public order or snuffing out anti-government plots. In 1962 French troops were used in Congo-Brazzaville and Gabon to break up fighting between each country's nationals after a disputed football match, while in Cameroon they were actively involved in suppressing the Bamileke rebellion which had erupted before independence. In Gabon in 1964 they were used by de Gaulle to reinstate President Léon M'Ba, who had been briefly deposed by an army coup d'état. A French spokesman explained that it was not possible 'for a few men carrying machine guns to be left free to seize a presidential palace at any time'.

British troops in East Africa were called on in 1964 to suppress a series of army mutinies in Tanganyika, Uganda and Kenya caused by grievances over pay, promotion and continued subordination to British officers. In the case of Tanganyika, soldiers in Dar es Salaam took control of the radio station, the airport, police stations and State House, Nyerere's residence and office, forcing him to go into hiding for two days.

From 1965, however, far from being random events, army interventions became increasingly frequent. In June Algeria's first leader, Ahmed Ben Bella, was deposed by Colonel Houari Boumédienne, his austere, secretive minister of defence, after a prolonged struggle for power. In November the Congo's army commander, General Mobutu, ousted President Kasa-Vubu and assumed the presidency for himself. A spate of coups followed in West Africa. In Dahomey (Benin) after a period of strikes, demonstrations and political deadlock, the army commander, Colonel Christophe Soglo, banned political activity altogether and set himself up in power. Ten days later, Colonel Jean-Bedel Bokassa seized power in the Central African Republic, citing the wholesale corruption prevalent amongst ministers and civil servants in David Dacko's one-party regime. Three days later on 2 January 1966, Colonel Sangoulé Lamizana stepped in to remove Upper Volta's president, Maurice Yaméogo, after crowds of demonstrators in Ouagadougou had implored the army to intervene. Like so many other African politicians of that era, Yaméogo had begun his regime popularly elected, determined to maintain an efficient administration and outspoken in his condemnation of corruption. 'Government is not a gang of old pals having it good on nice food at the expense of the people,' he said. Yet the one-party regime he installed was notorious for corruption. While issuing ringing calls for sacrifice and austerity, Yaméogo lived in a luxuriously furnished presidential palace, ostentatiously married a 22-year-old beauty queen and indulged in other extravagances. He was subsequently convicted of embezzling more than £1 million.

None of the coups in Dahomey, the Central African Republic and Upper Volta attracted much attention. All were desperately poor countries, dependent on French subsidies for survival. Dahomey seemed to be encumbered with every imaginable difficulty: it was crowded, insolvent, beset by tribal divisions, huge debts, mass unemployment, frequent strikes and unending struggles for power among corrupt politicians. All three coup leaders were French army veterans who saw themselves in the tradition of de Gaulle and the Fifth French Republic, replacing ailing regimes with a salutary spell of military rule. 'We had been taught two things by the French army: discipline and how to save the state's finances,' said Lamizana after taking power. 'This lesson we have not forgotten.'

Yet the sequence of coups did not stop there. Like a contagion they spread across the continent, striking not only regimes that were inherently weak and unstable but bringing down even the giants of Africa – Ghana, Nigeria and even Ethiopia's Haile Selassie.

10

FEET OF CLAY

As Ghana's leader, Kwame Nkrumah was accustomed to a diet of endless praise. Every day the press extolled his intellectual brilliance, his foresight, his integrity. 'When our history is recorded,' said the *Evening News* in a typical example in 1961, 'the man Kwame Nkrumah will be written of as the liberator, the Messiah, the Christ of our day, whose great love for mankind wrought changes in Ghana, in Africa and in the world at large.' An official portrait published in 1961 declared:

To millions of people living both inside and outside the continent of Africa, Kwame Nkrumah is Africa and Africa is Kwame Nkrumah. When the question was asked: 'What is going to happen in Africa?' it is to one man that everyone looks for the answer: Kwame Nkrumah. To the imperialists and colonialists his name is a curse on their lips; to the settlers his name is a warning that the good old days at the expense of the African are coming to an end; to Africans suffering under foreign domination, his name is a breath of hope and means freedom, brotherhood and racial equality; to us, his people, Kwame Nkrumah is our father, our teacher, our brother, our friend, indeed our very lives, for without him we would no doubt have existed, but we would not have lived; there would have been no hope of a cure for our sick souls, no taste of glorious victory after a lifetime of suffering. What we owe is greater even than the air we breathe, for he made us as surely as he made Ghana.

As part of his personality cult, Nkrumah assumed grand titles – Man of Destiny, Star of Africa, His High Dedication and, most famous of all, *Osagyefo*, a name which meant 'victor in war', but which was often more loosely translated as 'redeemer'. His presence became inescapable: his profile embellished coins, banknotes, postage stamps; his statue stood outside parliament; his name appeared in neon lights; his birthday became a public holiday; framed photographs adorned offices and shops.

Behind this façade, Nkrumah remained a lonely and isolated figure, distrustful of his colleagues, and suspicious of all the manoeuvres that surrounded him. In her memoirs, Genoveva Marais, an attractive black South African who met Nkrumah at the Independence State Ball in March 1957 and became a confidante, observed: 'The more successful he was politically, the less he seemed capable of trusting his most intimate friends, no matter how loyal they had proved themselves to be. He became so immersed in his own isolation that he withdrew from most people. Instead, he gained the support of party activists who only told him what they thought he wanted to know, to enhance his feelings of superiority.' He sometimes complained to her that he had no one to love and that no one loved him, that he had no one to share his joys, sorrows and anxieties.

In a half-hearted way he tried marriage. Without mentioning a word to any of his closest colleagues, he arranged with Nasser to obtain a bride from Egypt, a woman he had never previously met until she arrived in Ghana on the same day as the wedding. Fathia Rizk spoke only Arabic, with a smattering of French; Nkrumah spoke neither Arabic nor French. The wedding on 30 December 1957 took place in a private ceremony at Christiansborg Castle attended by only a handful of people. When talking to his office staff in the morning beforehand, Nkrumah gave no hint of what he was about to do. Noticing that Nkrumah was looking particularly smart, a senior aide,

Captain Hamilton, remarked: 'Good Lord, PM, you look as if you are going to a wedding.' Nkrumah made no comment.

News of the wedding, announced on the radio, astounded everyone. Market women marched on the castle, others mourned and wept. The marriage produced three children. But Nkrumah ensured his family remained hidden from the limelight. He regarded his wife and children as a 'purely private' matter. When the London publishers of his book *Neocolonialism* prepared notes on the author for the cover, mentioning that Nkrumah was 'married with three children', Nkrumah scored out the passage saying it was totally irrelevant.

As Nkrumah confessed in a letter he wrote to Erica Powell in 1965, marriage did nothing to lighten the sense of isolation he felt.

> Have you noticed over the years that I have known you that I am a very lonely man? Can you say that this and that person is a friend to me? I am friendless and companionless . . . I suffer from intense loneliness which makes me sometimes burst into tears. I am an isolated man – isolated even from life itself. You only know and understand that, Erica, few people know this. They see me in public smiling and laughing, not knowing the burden of loneliness and isolation that I carry. Marriage did not solve it – it has rather intensified and complicated it . . . You know I did not want to get married. You know my views on the subject. Did I ever tell you that I married not for myself but for the presidency?

In her memoir, Erica Powell gave her own verdict on the matter:

> The fact that Dr Nkrumah regretted his marriage was not necessarily, I am inclined to believe, a reflection on the woman he married, although I could never understand how a man of his intelligence could marry a young girl he had never set eyes on and with whom he could not even converse because they had no language in common. I think he would have regretted marriage with *any* woman. He was a loner from choice. People – men, women and children – were drawn to him. When in the mood, he greatly enjoyed the company of women and was amused by their flattery

and the way they vied for his favours. But he did not want to be possessed. He did not like to be organised, to have to follow a routine, to observe conventions. He wanted companionship only when he felt the need for it.

From his lonely perch, Nkrumah built around himself a citadel of power. A new constitution in 1960, establishing Ghana as a republic, enabled him to rule by decree, to reject decisions of parliament, to dismiss any public servant or members of the armed forces or judiciary. He acquired a President's Contingency Fund not subject to parliamentary scrutiny. He maintained a total grip over radio, television and the press. He pursued critics and opponents relentlessly using the Preventive Detention Act and other 'security' measures at will. Of the small band of twelve opposition MPs who tried to block the passing of the Preventive Detention Act in 1958, eleven were to find themselves victims of it over the years, incarcerated in prison. In 1961 it became a criminal offence for anyone to 'show disrespect to the person and dignity of the Head of State'.

Nkrumah also established a vast apparatus of control through the Convention People's Party. Declaring the party to be 'supreme', he compelled existing institutions such as the civil service, the trade unions, farmers' organisations and youth groups to become subordinate to it. From party headquarters, a network of organisations – the Council of Ghana Women, Vanguard Activists, Workers' Brigades, Young Pioneers – spread tentacles across the country. When the Bishop of Accra objected to political indoctrination in the Young Pioneers, he was forced to leave the country.

Incorporating so many disparate interests, however, the CPP soon degenerated into a battleground between rival factions. When Nkrumah asked a journalist, Tawia Adamafio, to become the party's general secretary in 1960, Adamafio was initially reluctant to accept. He recalled : 'I knew the intrigues and jealousies, the vicious whispering campaigns and the rumour mongering, the deliberate name-smearing and wicked mud slinging, the character assassination, the interminable party struggle, the incompetence and greed, the bribery and corruption.' Despite his reservations, Adamafio threw

himself into this can of worms with gusto, ingratiating himself with
Nkrumah and becoming one of his closest confidants.

Along with the tussles for power and influence, the party was consumed by a rising tide of corruption. In his memoirs Adamafio
described the scale of corruption as 'a howling monster threatening to
wreck the whole nation'. Party officials, ministers and members of
parliament spent their time promoting family, clan and community
interests and pursuing their own business activities. While ministers
routinely collected 10 per cent from government contracts, at a lower
level local party officials developed a variety of techniques for extorting money and favours from businessmen, market-women, civil
servants and others, in exchange for 'protection' and other 'benefits'.
An investigation into corruption involving the granting of import
licences found that it was 'organised and systematically operated
through agents at different levels of society'.

Government funds were squandered in every direction. A typical
example concerned the Guinea Press, a company owned by Nkrumah
which received more than £1.8 million from government sources. It
was used, said a report, as 'something of an employment agency with
incompetent and inefficient hands being pushed in on the management by this Minister, the Chief, the Party official, just because that
somebody . . . was the nephew, niece, uncle, brother, son or relative of
somebody'.

In 1961 Nkrumah promised to tackle the problem of corruption.
He denounced party members who combined business interests with
a political career. 'They are tending by virtue of their function and
position to become a new ruling class of self-seekers and careerists.' He
criticised ministers who flaunted wealth. He appointed a committee of
inquiry to investigate the assets and property of party members –
their houses, cars and mistresses. And he gave the guilty a stark alternative – either to resign or to surrender their loot. But the committee
made little headway; its findings were never published; and the corrupt
activities of the party elite went on much as before. Patronage was
what held the system together.

With his plans to turn Ghana into a modern industrial society,
Nkrumah initially made considerable progress. Schools, hospitals

and roads were built at an unprecedented rate; a major hydro-electric scheme on the Volta River was completed, providing a lasting source of cheap energy. Impatient for results on a spectacular scale, Nkrumah pressed on with one project after another – with factories, steelworks, mining ventures and shipyards – almost any idea, in fact, that caught his imagination. Foreign businessmen soon discovered that anyone with a bright idea and a ready bribe stood a good chance of obtaining a deal. Some schemes were started simply for reasons of prestige. Nkrumah wanted, for example, to build the largest dry-dock in Africa, regardless of its viability; once built, it was rarely used. Other schemes were impractical. An enterprising Romanian-born businessman who struck up a friendship with Nkrumah convinced him of the need to build a huge set of concrete silos to store cocoa, so that the price of cocoa could be controlled more effectively; once built the silos were condemned as unusable. One of Nkrumah's expatriate advisers, Robert Jackson, once walked into Nkrumah's office to find a European salesman peddling some far-fetched scheme. Nkrumah had his pen in his hand ready to sign a contract for more than £1 million. 'Shall I just look it over, Mr President?' suggested Jackson. He carefully took the document away and that day saved the exchequer £1 million. The more ambitious the project that was put forward, the more likely it was to gain approval. A simple project for a small and efficient factory to produce urgently needed drugs and pharmaceuticals was turned down in favour of one which cost ten times as much. A footwear factory was set up with luxurious bungalows and a lavish administrative block at a cost eight times higher than the price recommended by an expatriate adviser.

At the same time that the ideas, schemes and instructions were pouring forth from Nkrumah's office, Ghana was heading into economic difficulties. A precipitous drop in the world price for cocoa in 1961 forced the government to introduce new and severe taxes. Protesting against the sharp rise in the cost of living and consumer shortages, dock and railway workers went on strike. Nkrumah's response was to arrest strike leaders and imprison them without trial. In a radio broadcast, one of his ministers denounced the strikers as 'despicable rats'. Through a mixture of force, intimidation and bribery, the strike was eventually broken.

Nkrumah also turned on the hapless opposition, ordering the arrest of leading politicians, and followed through with a purge of his own cabinet, sacking ministers who were showing doubts about the wisdom of his policies. Among them was Komla Gbedemah, an able finance minister who ten years before, while Nkrumah was serving his prison sentence under British rule, had been largely responsible for organising the famous 1951 election victory; prudently Gbedemah went into exile. To control any future disturbances, Nkrumah set up special courts to deal with political offences, with judges appointed by himself, from which there was no right of appeal.

A long visit that Nkrumah made to the Soviet Union, China and other communist countries in 1961 convinced him that what Ghana needed to break through to the industrial uplands was a massive increase in state-operated enterprises. One after another new state corporations were launched: the Ghana National Construction Corporation; the State Steelworks Corporation; the State Gold Mining Corporation; the State Fibre Bag Corporation; the Vegetable Oil Mills Corporation; the Ghana Fishing Corporation; the State Farm Corporation. By 1966 more than fifty enterprises had been set up. Most were badly managed, weighed down by inefficient bureau-cracies and run at a huge loss. The state airline, equipped with a fleet of jet aircraft, was required to fly to destinations such as Cairo and Moscow for which there was hardly any demand; on most flights the only passengers were members of parliament, party officials and their friends whose fares were paid out of public funds.

The government's external debt soared. Officially it reached £184 million in 1963; a year later it stood at £349 million. But no one could ascertain precisely to what extent the government was in debt because complete records of the contracts were not kept in govern-ment files. Nkrumah often awarded contracts personally, without reference to the cabinet, the appropriate minister, or the cabinet's contracts committee. Short of foreign funds, Nkrumah pressed ahead by resorting more and more to using suppliers' credits. In effect, he was mortgaging Ghana's revenues for years ahead. But again, no one was sure, in the absence of proper records, by how much. 'It has not yet been possible to obtain sight of all Foreign Credit Agreements, nor has a solution been found to the problem of verifying goods and services received by the Government under the agreements,' the auditor-general complained in his report for 1962–3. In later years, odd items – a £5 million warship for the navy, a 7,500-ton luxury boat built for Nkrumah himself – kept turning up. In some cases the delivery of goods for which Ghana signed was never made.

Faced with mounting financial difficulties, the government eventually responded by imposing import controls, but they were administered in such random fashion that further chaos ensued. Steadily, the grand industrialisation programme, staffed by corrupt and incompetent managers appointed by the party and hampered by shortages of raw materials and spare parts, ground to a halt. In the words of one expatriate economist, Tony Killick, it became little more than 'a high-cost way of providing what were, in effect, unemployment benefits'.

Nkrumah's agricultural policies were equally disastrous. He favoured mechanised state farms and diverted huge government resources – financial support, technical assistance and import allocations – for their benefit, neglecting the needs of peasant farmers. The index of real producer prices and the index of real value of total payments to cocoa producers fell from 100 in 1960 to 37 in 1965. Government payments to cocoa farmers as a percentage of total export receipts for cocoa fell from 72 in 1960 to 41 in 1965. The index of quantity of insecticide sales to cocoa farmers fell from 100 in 1960 to 2 in 1965. Disgruntled by the low prices offered by the state monopoly of cocoa-buying, farmers reacted by selling cocoa illegally across borders and by refusing to plant more trees. Over a fifteen-year period from 1965, cocoa production halved. The state farms meanwhile, staffed largely by CPP supporters, their families and friends and supplied with imported equipment which frequently broke down, made huge losses, producing yields that were less than one-fifth of peasant agriculture. Most became graveyards of rusting machinery.

The overall result of Nkrumah's handling of the economy was calamitous. From being one of the most prosperous countries in the tropical world at the time of independence in 1957, Ghana by 1965 had become virtually bankrupt: it was saddled with huge debts and beset by rising prices, higher taxes and food shortages. A spending spree of £430 million between 1959 and 1964 had left it encumbered with scores of loss-making industries and a fast-shrinking agricultural sector. Gross national product between 1960 and 1966, despite government spending, actually remained stagnant; over the same period the real value of the minimum wage was halved. An official survey in 1963 showed that the standard of living for unskilled workers in towns had fallen in real terms to the levels of 1939. At a cabinet meeting on 11 February 1963, when the finance minister announced that Ghana's reserves stood at less than £500,000, Nkrumah was so shocked that he sat in silence for fifteen minutes, then broke down and wept.

Nkrumah's dreams of foreign glory fared no better. He invested a huge amount of time and energy campaigning for a United States of Africa, aiming to lead it himself, suggesting the matter was urgent. 'The emergence of such a mighty stabilising force in this strife-torn world should be regarded . . . not as the shadowy dream of a visionary, but as a practical proposition which the peoples of Africa can and should translate into reality . . . We must act now. Tomorrow may be too late.' Yet no other African leader shared his enthusiasm. At a conference of African leaders in 1963, convened to establish the Organisation of African Unity, when Nkrumah proposed 'a formal declaration that all the independent African states here and now agree to the establishment of a union of African States', no one supported him. Nor did they take kindly to the vain and arrogant manner which Nkrumah adopted towards those who disagreed with him. He quarrelled sharply with Julius Nyerere of Tanganyika over his plans for an East African federation, since it conflicted with Nkrumah's own concept of African unity. He also took to denouncing the policies of 'African socialism' which other African leaders favoured after he had decided that 'scientific socialism' was the 'correct road'. In similar fashion, he accused francophone states in West Africa of acting as puppets of French neocolonialism.

Even more serious were the disputes he fell into with his neighbours – Togo, Côte d'Ivoire, Nigeria, Upper Volta and Niger. As well as setting up guerrilla training camps for African exiles from southern Africa, Nkrumah readily supported the activities of subversive groups from neighbouring countries in the hope of helping them to power. After Ghanaian agents were implicated in an assassination attempt on Togo's president, Sylvanus Olympio, seven African heads of state threatened to break off diplomatic relations with Ghana. Nkrumah's support for external subversion nevertheless continued. His Bureau of African Affairs ran subversive agents in nine African countries and organised a host of training camps for anti-government dissidents with the help of East German and Chinese experts. In 1965 an African dissident, trained in Ghana and China, attempted to assassinate President Hamani Diori of Niger. In answering the torrent of criticism of his support for subversion, Nkrumah retorted that there would be no subversion if union government was established.

Despite all the controversies he caused and his increasing lack of success in foreign policy, Nkrumah demanded to play a leading role in all the major African issues of the time – the Congo, Rhodesia and southern African liberation. One of his favourite schemes was to establish an African High Command. In the wider field of foreign affairs, he strove tirelessly to act as a world statesman, offering his services as a mediator in international crises, such as the Sino-Soviet dispute. In support of these ambitions, he built up an extensive diplomatic network which included fifty-seven embassies. But the embassy network achieved little other than to enrich party members who staffed it. Huge sums were spent on diplomatic properties, allowances and expenses of every kind.

Surrounded by sycophants and praised daily by the press, he became increasingly remote from the realities of the crisis that Ghana faced, resenting even mild criticism, refusing to believe that anything had gone wrong. Every setback he attributed to imperialists and neo-colonialists plotting against him. When ministers arrived bearing reports of economic difficulties, he was impatient and dismissive. Palace intrigues swirled around him. An assassination attempt in August 1962 intensified his mood of suspicion and distrust. Convinced that party radicals were responsible, he ordered the arrest of Tawia Adamafio and two other ministers. They were tried on charges of conspiracy before a special court headed by the chief justice. When the chief justice returned a verdict of not guilty and ordered the accused men to be discharged, Nkrumah dismissed him and rushed a new law through parliament enabling him to set aside the verdict of the special court when it was in the state's interest. At a second trial by a handpicked court, all the accused were found guilty and sentenced to death, though Nkrumah subsequently commuted their sentences to life imprisonment. Another assassination attempt was made in 1964 by a police constable. Suspecting this time that the police service at large was involved, Nkrumah ordered the police to be disarmed, sacked several officers and detained the commissioner and his deputy. For protection he relied increasingly on a personal security service recruited from his home district in the south-west corner of Ghana and trained with the help of Soviet advisers.

Tightening his grip even further, Nkrumah decided in 1964 to turn Ghana into a one-party state. A referendum was allowed, but in advance of the vote, the government press threatened reprisals against anyone who did not participate and anyone who did not vote in favour. 'Those who think they can hide under the so-called "secrecy" of the polling booth to fool us must know that the days when we could be fooled are gone,' the *Ghanaian Times* warned. Even then, the result was blatantly rigged. According to official figures, some 96 per cent of the total registered electorate voted, a far higher proportion than had ever voted during any previous election. Some 2,773,900 were said to have voted 'yes'; only 2,452, or 0.1 per cent, voted 'no'. In the Asante region, previously one of the main centres of opposition, not a single 'no' vote was recorded. Students returning to the University of Ghana after the referendum reported that in some areas boxes designated for the 'no' votes had been placed in full view of the returning officer and his party helpers. In one area the 'no' boxes had simply not been provided with slits through which to put voting papers.

In practical terms, the advent of a one-party system made little difference. All opposition had already been silenced. The CPP itself had long ceased to have any serious function. The party consisted of vast networks of committees which never met and organisations which were moribund. At party headquarters the two lifts were frequently out of order; office discipline was lax; a permanent odour emanated from the toilet facilities. From 1964 Nkrumah rarely went there. Even as a vote-gathering machine the CPP no longer served any purpose. In the general election in 1965, all CPP candidates, selected before-hand by Nkrumah and a small party committee, were returned unopposed, without even the formality of a vote. Nkrumah announced over the radio the names of those he had chosen.

Instead of using the party or government machinery, he concen-trated more and more functions of state at Flagstaff House, his main presidential compound in the northern suburbs of Accra, establishing there 'secretariats' which bypassed the work of government ministries and gave him direct control over a wide range of government business. Under his personal auspices came such matters as higher education, foreign trade, internal security, African affairs, parliamentary business, the civil service and defence. At Flagstaff House he also built a well-equipped private zoo, to which various friends made contributions: Emperor Haile Selassie of Ethiopia sent a lion; President Tubman of Liberia, a hippo; and Fidel Castro, a boa constrictor.

But in the months after the assassination attempt in 1964, Nkrumah, moody and introspective, withdrew more and more to the solitude of Christiansborg Castle, cutting himself off even from his most intimate associates, preferring to keep the company of those who simply flattered him or to meditate alone.

The crowning folly of Nkrumah's regime was 'Job 600', the con-struction of a grand complex of buildings for a single conference of OAU heads of state in 1965, costing £10 million, launched at a time when factories were starved of raw materials, food queues in towns were a common sight, hospitals were short of drugs and state cor-porations were bankrupt. Nkrumah's dream was that it would also serve as a future capital for a union government of Africa. The press hailed the event in advance as a moment of great achievement. Nkrumah himself was captivated by the details of Job 600 and proudly boasted of them to parliament – the sixty self-contained suites that would have satisfied the demands of millionaires; the banqueting hall capable of seating two thousand guests; the fountains operated by seventy-two jets with a multi-coloured interplay of light, rising to a height of sixty feet.

Yet the conference turned into an abject failure. Because Nkrumah's foreign policy had alienated so many governments, a large number of African leaders were reluctant to attend. A group of fourteen leaders, led by Félix Houphouët-Boigny, agreed to boycott it in retaliation for Nkrumah's support of subversive activities against their governments. In the end, twenty-eight out of thirty-six members of the OAU attended the meeting, but only thirteen were represented by heads of state. No one supported his call for a union government of Africa. Indeed, the conference even rejected his plea for a sub-committee to consider the issue.

Even in the face of such overwhelming opposition and daily evidence of economic collapse around him, Nkrumah refused to let go of his fantasy. Saying farewell to his faithful secretary, Erica Powell, in December 1965, he remarked: 'To be honest, Erica, what I would really like to do is to resign the presidency and to devote my time to African unity. So much of my daily schedule is taken up by interviews, meetings, courtesy calls – so many time-consuming things that are not really important when weighed against the urgent problems facing the African continent. It is the small things that wear one down, not the big issues.'

Nkrumah's downfall, two months later, came not as a result of Ghana's desperate economic plight, or high-level corruption, or government mismanagement, but because of his fatal decision to interfere with the military. Brought up in the Sandhurst tradition, the army command, though concerned about Ghana's difficulties, had stood aside until the time came when its own interests were threatened. Nkrumah's attempts to subordinate the army to his own purposes, as he had done with so many other parts of the state, to infiltrate the army with party spies and to split its cohesion, produced within the army a deep and dangerous resentment. There was particular anger over the favourable treatment accorded to the President's Own Guard Regiment, an elite unit regarded as Nkrumah's private army, which was equipped with modern weapons and paid at special rates, while the rest of the army suffered from serious shortages.

On 24 February 1966, while Nkrumah was in Beijing on his way to Hanoi, vainly attempting to mediate in the Vietnam War, the army struck. Nkrumah's supporters swiftly deserted him. On the streets of Accra and Kumasi, large crowds gathered to welcome the soldiers and celebrated by ripping down the framed photographs which adorned houses, offices and factories. Outside parliament, Nkrumah's statue was battered to the ground. Some ragged, barefoot urchins were allowed to scamper on top of it. Then it was smashed to bits. Marching through the streets of Accra, youth group members who had been trained on such slogans as 'Nkrumah never dies' and 'Nkrumah is the new Messiah' carried placards proclaiming 'Nkrumah is NOT our Messiah'.

A HOUSE DIVIDED

The hopes that Nigeria would serve as a stronghold of democracy in Africa came to an abrupt halt on 15 January 1966. In a series of coordinated actions, a group of young army officers wiped out the country's top political leaders. In Lagos they seized the federal prime minister, Sir Abubakar Tafawa Balewa, took him outside the city and executed him by the side of the road, dumping his body in a ditch; in Kaduna, after a gun battle, they shot dead the premier of the Northern Region, the Sardauna of Sokoto. In Ibadan they killed the premier of the Western Region, Chief Ladoke Akintola. The wealthy federal finance minister, Chief Festus Okotie-Eboh, a notoriously corrupt politician, was dragged screaming from his house, flung into a car 'like an old army sack', and driven away to be murdered. Several senior army officers were also killed.

The aim of the young majors, as they came to be known, was not just to stage a military coup but to launch a revolution, overthrowing the entire old order. In a broadcast from Kaduna on 15 January, Major Chukwuma Nzeogwu, a Sandhurst-trained officer who had led the assault on the Sardauna's residence, spoke in the name of the Supreme Council of the Revolution:

> Our enemies are the political profiteers, the swindlers, the men in
> the high and low places that seek bribes and demand 10 per cent;
> those that seek to keep the country divided permanently so that
> they can remain in office as ministers and VIPs of waste; the tribal-
> ists, the nepotists; those that made the country look big-for-nothing
> before the international circles; those that have corrupted our soci-
> ety and put the Nigerian political calendar back by their words and
> deeds.

Declaring martial law over the Northern provinces of Nigeria,
Nzeogwu issued a number of proclamations which decreed the death
penalty for offences such as embezzlement, bribery, corruption, rape,
homosexuality and 'obstruction of the revolution'.

But then the revolution faltered and finally failed. In Lagos the
army commander, Major-General John Aguiyi-Ironsi, alerted by the
wife of one of his murdered officers, rallied loyal troops and began to
consolidate his control over the army. Instead of revolution came
army rule and the slide into civil war.

Despite the promising start made at independence in 1960, Nigeria
was soon engulfed by an intense struggle between the country's three
main political parties for supremacy over the federal government.
Control of the federal government determined the allocation of development resources. Because each region produced its own political
party dominated by the major ethnic group based there, the struggle
turned into ethnic combat. Politicians on all sides whipped up ethnic
fear, suspicion and jealousy for their own advantage and to entrench
themselves in power. Tribalism became the ideology of politics.

By nature, Nigerian politics tended to be mercenary and violent.
Political debate was routinely conducted in acrimonious and abusive
language; and ethnic loyalties were constantly exploited. The tactics
employed were often those of the rough-house variety. But the reckless manner in which Nigerian politicians fought for control during
six years of civilian rule was to lead ultimately to a tragedy of monu-
mental proportions.

The independence constitution had left the North with powerful advantages. With three-quarters of the land area and more than half the population, it dominated the federation from the outset and intended to do so indefinitely. In the 1959 federal election the Northern People's Congress (NPC), controlled by Hausa-Fulani, captured 134 of 312 seats, all of them in the North, making it the largest single party. The East's National Council of Nigerian Citizens (NCNC), controlled by Igbo, together with its coalition partners, gained eighty-nine seats; and the West's Action Group, controlled by Yoruba, gained seventy-three seats, spread across three regions. Initially, the NPC was content to run the federal government jointly with the East's NCNC in a coalition that avoided the danger of either the North or the two regions of the South holding power exclusively. The West's Action Group, for its part, settled for the role of parliamentary opposition in the federal parliament in the traditional British manner. At a regional level, each party controlled its own regional government: the NPC ran the North; the NCNC ran the East; and the Action Group ran the West. All were locked in ferocious competition for a larger share from the national treasury. Minority groups were embroiled in the struggle, taking sides against the major parties in their home region, in the hope of advancing the cause of setting up their own states.

In the quest for state resources, political allegiances began to shift. A faction within the Action Group led by Chief Akintola, the premier of the Western Region and the party's deputy leader, argued that the party would do better to join the federal government as a partner rather than stand in opposition against it – a move favoured by the federal prime minister, Balewa. Many in Akintola's faction believed that Yorubas were losing their pre-eminent position in business and the administration to Igbos as a result of the NCNC's decision to participate in the ruling coalition. The opposing faction led by Chief Obafemi Awolowo, the party's leader, argued that there was more to be gained by keeping the Action Group out of the coalition and working to win the next federal election with the aid of a programme of radical reform. In the split that occurred in the Action Group in 1962, Awolowo initially gained the upper hand. The party's executive voted unanimously to remove Akintola as premier and to replace him with a loyal supporter.

But when parliament assembled to approve the change, Akintola's supporters sought to disrupt the proceedings. One member flung a chair across the floor of the chamber; another seized the Mace, attempted to club the Speaker, but missed and smashed the Mace on a table; more chairs and tables were thrown; a minister, hit on the head, was rushed to hospital. Finally, police had to use teargas to clear the chamber. For several hours the Speaker suspended the sitting, hoping for an orderly resumption of business, but when members reassembled, similar scenes of uproar occurred and again the police intervened using teargas.

This crisis in parliament provided a golden opportunity for Balewa and the NPC-led federal government to strike a blow at the opposition and to consolidate their chances of holding on to federal power. Summoning the federal parliament, Balewa imposed a state of emergency in the Western Region, suspended the constitution and appointed a sole administrator to run the region on behalf of the federal government until the end of the year. Thereafter the federal government continued to harass and discredit the Action Group at every opportunity. Leading party members were served with restriction orders and the party's business empire was put under official investigation, revealing to the public a vast web of corruption and malpractice. Awolowo and his senior colleagues were tried, convicted and imprisoned for treasonable felony. Akintola was installed as prime minister of a coalition government, leaving the Action Group in opposition in its former stronghold, shorn of most of its leaders and cut off from the spoils of power with which to maintain its support. As a final blow to its fortunes, the Western Region was carved up into two parts through the creation of a new Mid-West Region.

Yet the federal coalition itself was under stress and strain. The NCNC had joined the coalition in the hope of gaining better access to federal funds and benefits. The pay-offs came with the appointment of party stalwarts to plum positions as ministers, ambassadors and board members of federal institutions and parastatal organisations; Easterners also gained enhanced entry and promotion in the public service and armed forces. But the NCNC was disgruntled by the outcome of a six-year development plan which concentrated the bulk of federal capital expenditure in the North and by the accelerated appointments of less-qualified Northerners in place of Southerners to top political, military and civil service positions. There was also alarm at the increasingly assertive strategy that Balewa and his Northern colleagues were using to maintain their hold over federal affairs, as demonstrated by their handling of the Action Group opposition.

Northerners, for their part, were driven by an ingrained fear of a strong Southern coalition threatening their identity and independent way of life. The principal aim of the North's powerful and autocratic premier, the Sardauna of Sokoto, Sir Ahmadu Bello, was to prevent the influence of skilled and enterprising Southerners from spreading to the North. Above all, Northerners were determined to keep a tight grip over the federal system.

The main hope of Southern politicians wanting a change in the power structure lay with the population census of 1962. Since the North had been able to dominate federal politics by virtue of its huge population, a change in the population balance in favour of the South meant the end of Northern hegemony. Population figures affected not only the distribution of electoral representation in the federal parliament but also the level of revenue allocation among the regions and the allocation of such vital matters as employment quotas. The census itself thus held the potential to determine Nigeria's future.

When the figures were collected, the unofficial results suggested evidence of inflated returns, especially from some Eastern districts. While the North's population was shown to have risen since 1952 from 16.8 million to 22.5 million, an increase amounting to 30 per cent, returns from some Eastern areas claimed increases as high as 200 per cent and rising by an average of 71 per cent; Western returns also gave an increase of more than 70 per cent.

The results were not made public, but what they meant was that the North no longer contained more than half the population in the federation and had thereby lost its position of supremacy in the federal structure. The reaction of Northern leaders was swift. They held a new count and discovered 8.5 million more people in their region, raising the increase since the last census from 30 per cent to 84 per cent and regaining their claim to more than half the population of the federation. In political terms, the census result was a clear victory for the North. All the latent antagonism between the North and the South, never far below the surface, now broke out in a wave of bitter wrangling which wrecked the government coalition.

The 1964 election thus became a battleground between two rival camps. One camp, consisting of the Northern People's Congress, along with its allies like Akintola, was determined to maintain Northern hegemony. The other camp, consisting of a new alliance between the East's NCNC and the West's Action Group, was equally determined to break the Northern stranglehold.

No proper election was held. In scores of constituencies in the North, opposition candidates were prevented from filing nomination papers, enabling NPC candidates to be returned unopposed. In retaliation, the NCNC government in the Eastern Region cancelled the election there altogether. The outcome was a clear majority for the NPC alliance. But when Balewa called on President Nnamdi Azikiwe, a former NCNC leader, to reappoint him prime minister, Azikiwe refused to do so, precipitating a constitutional crisis. Both men vied for the support of the military. In the end a compromise was reached under which Balewa agreed to form another coalition government and the NCNC, preferring to remain close to power and the sources of patronage rather than join the Action Group in opposition, resumed its role as junior partner.

Once again, the South had suffered a severe defeat at the hands of the North, leaving many Southerners in a sullen and frustrated mood. But this time a new factor had been added: by appealing for military support in their struggle for power, Balewa and Azikiwe had given the military cause to consider playing a political role.

Another round of political warfare began in 1965 with elections for the Western Region. The campaign was fought by all sides with brutal tenacity; bribes, threats, assaults, arson, hired thugs and even murder became the daily routine. Akintola's new party – the Nigerian National Democratic Party (NNDP) – used its position in government ruthlessly to rig the election at every stage – blocking the nomination of opposition candidates, kidnapping election officials, destroying ballot papers and falsifying results.

The official result was a victory for the NNDP and hence the Northern strategy. But once Akintola had been reinstated as prime minister, the Western Region descended into lawless turmoil in which hundreds died. Spreading from rural areas to the towns, a wave of riots, arson and political murders gradually engulfed the whole area, bringing administration to the verge of collapse.

Despite the breakdown in law and order, the federal government stood by impassively. Whereas Balewa had been only too ready to intervene in the Western Region in 1962 after a few unruly incidents in parliament in order to crush the Action Group government, when faced with a real emergency, he refused to take any measures that would harm his corrupt ally, Akintola. Both men were high on the death list drawn up by the young majors.

The army coup of 1966, sweeping away a corrupt and discredited regime, was greeted in the South by scenes of wild rejoicing. The coup leaders were acclaimed heroes; the politicians slunk out of sight. Almost overnight, the violence that had gripped the Western Region for three months subsided. By strange coincidence, a prophetic novel by the Nigerian author Chinua Achebe was published in the same week as the coup, telling the story of the rise and fall of an African politician ending with an army takeover. 'Overnight everyone began to shake their heads at the excess of the last regime, at its graft, oppression and corrupt government,' wrote Achebe in *A Man of the People*. 'Newspapers, the radio, hitherto silent intellectuals and civil servants – everybody said what a terrible lot; and it became public opinion the next morning.'

In the North, however, the reaction was more subdued. The former ruling party, the Northern People's Congress, stated that it regarded the transfer of authority 'as the only solution to the many recent problems facing this country'. Traditional emirs came forward with pledges of loyalty to General Ironsi's regime. Radical Northerners and minority groups welcomed the downfall of the Sardauna's autocratic rule. The Northern press too supported the call for an end to corruption and nepotism in Nigeria.

But as Northerners began to weigh up the full impact of what had happened, doubts and suspicions about the motives behind the coup began to take hold. All but one of the seven principal conspirators, it was noted, were Igbo officers. In the murders that they had organised, the North had lost its two most important leaders – Balewa and the Sardauna – and four of its most senior soldiers, and the West had lost one senior politician – Akintola – and two high-ranking officers. Yet no Igbo politicians had been killed. The Eastern Region had been left untouched by the conspirators; the Igbo premier there had been spared; so had the Igbo premier of the Mid-West Region. Only one Igbo officer, the quartermaster-general, had died and that had happened unintentionally, so it was said, because he had refused to hand over the keys of an armoury. Moreover, the result of the coup had been to wrest power away from the North and to install a military government led by an Igbo.

Brooding over their suspicions of these events, Northerners became ever more convinced that the majors' coup, far from being an attempt to rid Nigeria of a corrupt regime, as they claimed, was in fact part of an Igbo conspiracy to gain control. The evidence which undermined this theory was of no account. As more myths and sinister rumours embellished the notion in the following months, fear and resentment in the North steadily mounted. The wound inflicted on Nigeria by the 1966 coup turned septic.

Thrust unexpectedly into a position of power, General Ironsi, a bluff 41-year-old officer who had risen from the ranks of the old colonial army, was ill-equipped to deal with such dangerous undercurrents. Lacking any kind of political instinct himself, accustomed only to military procedures, he set out to clear up the mess left by the politicians by ruling through administrative decree, imposing his own decisions. But one decision after another, taken in what he thought was in the interests of efficiency or sensible administration, served only to alienate Northerners further.

Some of the issues facing Ironsi were unavoidably contentious. Army promotions were needed to fill gaps left by the January events and, since the majority of senior officers were Igbos, Igbo officers benefited substantially from the new appointments, thus raising fears of a growing Igbo takeover among Northerners, already aggrieved by the loss of popular Northern commanders. Ironsi was also caught up in controversy over the fate of January conspirators who were being held in detention. Northerners, especially those in the rank and file of the army, demanded their trial for murder and mutiny. Southerners, regarding them as heroes, demanded their release. Ironsi's answer, pleasing no one, was to prevaricate.

Most fateful of all was Ironsi's decision to tamper with the federal system. Believing that 'regionalism' was the root cause of Nigeria's problems, Ironsi proclaimed himself in favour of a united Nigeria and appointed commissions to inquire into the 'unification' of the regional civil services. Yet for Northerners, control over their own regional civil service was prized as a crucial safeguard against domination by more experienced Southerners. In a united Nigeria, they feared, Northerners would fare badly competing against the Igbo elite for government jobs, and risk losing administrative power.

Without waiting for official reports from his advisory commissions, Ironsi decided arbitrarily to promulgate a new constitution. By Decree no. 34 of 24 May 1966, he abolished the federation, proclaimed Nigeria to be a united state, and announced that the regional civil services were to be unified.

The reaction in the North came swiftly. Civil servants and students staged anti-government demonstrations which soon flared into popular riots against Igbos living in the *sabon garis*, the strangers' quarters sited outside the walls of Northern towns. Several hundred Igbos were killed. '*Araba!*' was the battlecry in the North − 'Let us part!'

At the end of July a group of Northern officers led a counter-coup, killing Ironsi and scores of Eastern officers and other ranks, demanding that the North should secede. In the tense disputes that followed, the army chief of staff, Lieutenant Colonel Yakubu Gowon, a 31-year-old Northerner from a minority tribe in the Middle Belt, opposed to the dissolution of the federation, gained the upper hand and took control as supreme commander. He swiftly rescinded Decree no. 34.

But while the Northerners' coup succeeded in the North, in the West and in Lagos, in the Eastern Region the military governor, Lieutenant Colonel Emeka Ojukwu, refused to accept Gowon's position as supreme commander. An ambitious and clever man, the son of a wealthy Igbo businessman, with an Oxford degree and training in Britain as an army officer, Ojukwu relished the opportunity to exercise political power independently. The July coup, he declared in a radio broadcast, had effectively divided Nigeria into two parts.

As if in confirmation, another upsurge of violence against Easterners erupted in the North on a far more terrible scale than before, and the purpose now was not simply to seek vengeance but to drive Easterners out of the North altogether. All the envy, resentment and mistrust that Northerners felt for the minority Eastern communities living in their midst burst out with explosive force into a pogrom that the authorities made no attempt to stop. Disgruntled local politicians, civil servants and students were active in getting the mobs on to the streets; Northern troops joined in the rampage. In the savage onslaught that followed, thousands of Easterners died or were maimed, and as others sought to escape the violence, a massive exodus to the East began. Abandoning all their possessions, hundreds of thousands of Easterners – traders, artisans, clerks and labourers – fled from their Northern homes. From other parts of Nigeria, too, as the climate of fear spread among Igbos living there, thousands more, including civil servants and academics, joined the exodus. By the end of the year, more than a million refugees, many of them wounded, exhausted and in a state of shock, sought safety in the East.

The fearful sequence of events that had occurred – the downfall of Ironsi, the return of Northerners to power, the murder of Eastern officers, the months of persecution and massacres in the North – produced a mood of anger and outrage that drove the East towards secession. To Ojukwu and his inner circle of Igbo advisers, many of them displaced civil servants and academics, secession seemed an eminently viable proposition. Nigeria's rich oilfields, located in the East, were beginning to produce valuable revenues. Starting production in 1958, the oilfields by 1967 provided Nigeria with nearly 20 per cent of federal revenue; within a few years the figure was expected to double. On that basis alone, the East would prosper far more on its own than by remaining in the federation. To both sides, control of Nigeria's oilfields became a key goal, propelling the country towards civil war.

To rally the population behind the idea of secession, Ojukwu constantly played on fears of genocide. The Eastern government's radio and press were used to keep popular opinion at fever pitch with an unrelenting stream of propaganda, stressing details of the atrocities that had taken place and warning of far worse to come. As the stories were told and re-told, the numbers that had died in the North, once reliably estimated at about 7,000, were raised higher and higher, until in later years, Ojukwu asserted that 50,000 had perished. The effect of the propaganda, as well as binding Igbos together against the Northern threat, was to produce a momentum of its own towards secession.

Yet the East was far from being a united, homogenous area. Minority groups such as the Ibibio, Ijaw and Efik, which altogether represented more than one-third of the East's 13 million population, resented the dominant role played by the Igbo; in the past they had campaigned for their own separate states. In the aftermath of the 1966 massacres in the North, when these minorities had been caught up in the waves of vengeance directed mainly at the Igbo, sympathy and support for the Eastern cause was strong, but this sense of solidarity soon dissipated. Among the minorities there was far less enthusiasm for the idea of an Eastern secession that would leave them permanently under Igbo control. Yet without the minority areas, secession was unviable, for it was in the minority areas that the rich oilfields, the seaports and half of the land lay.

Ojukwu and the Igbo nationalists around him, however, were intent on secession whatever the cost, spurning all attempts at compromise, rejecting concessions offered by Gowon and the federal government that would have given the Eastern Region virtual autonomy. Stage by stage, they severed the East's links with the federation. Decrees were issued ordering the expulsion of all non-Easterners from the region; appropriating all federal revenues collected in the East; and giving the East control of federal corporations, railways, schools and courts. At the same time, they built up a full administration, trained their own armed forces, purchased arms supplies and acquired local sources of revenue. On 30 May 1967, a year after the first riots against Igbos in the North, Ojukwu proclaimed the independence of the new state of Biafra amid high jubilation.

★

The Nigerian civil war lasted for two and a half years and cost nearly a million lives. From an early stage, the prospect of Biafra surviving seemed doubtful. Within a few months it had become an encircled, embattled enclave, bombed and strafed daily by Nigeria's air force and surrounded by an army of 100,000 men that grew ever larger. After a year of fighting it had lost half of its territory, all its major towns and airports, its seaports, its oil refinery and most of its oilfields. Crowded with refugees, short of food, running out of ammunition, its funds all but finished, it seemed on the point of defeat.

Yet despite the appalling suffering of Biafra's population, Ojukwu doggedly held fast to the notion of independence, spurning all attempts at international mediation. A master of manipulation, fond of giving marathon speeches and interviews, he portrayed Biafra as a nation threatened by genocide. For the Igbos, gripped by memories of the Northern pogroms of 1966, the fear of genocide was real enough. In the Igbo heartland, an area of no more than 5,000 square miles, they fought on with extraordinary tenacity and determination, often poorly armed and equipped, believing that otherwise they would be wiped out. Such raw courage on its own, however, was not sufficient to keep Biafra alive, and what prevented imminent defeat, and therefore prolonged the war, was the growing intervention of foreign sympathisers.

The plight of Biafra during 1968 produced waves of alarm and anxiety in Europe and North America. The spectacle of mass starvation among refugees packed into fetid camps as the federal noose slowly tightened galvanised Western opinion. In Europe no other foreign issue aroused such deep emotion. Biafra became a symbol of suffering and persecution, deserving of foreign support. Its very determination to fight on under such terrible conditions lent credence to the fear of genocide.

What followed was the largest privately organised relief operation in history. Church agencies took the lead. At its height in 1969, more than forty relief flights every night made the hazardous journey to a makeshift runway in Biafra, using the same route as gun-runners. The relief operation was vital to Biafra not only in providing food and medical supplies, but also as an invaluable source of revenue for

Ojukwu. By insisting that all the expenses of the relief operation incurred inside Biafra were paid for in foreign currency in Europe, Ojukwu was able to raise funds to buy military supplies and other foreign purchases and thereby stave off collapse. To this extent, the relief effort was used to finance the war and keep Biafra in the field. Ojukwu refused to agree to a supervised land corridor for relief supplies, for this would have rendered unnecessary the airlift that had come to dramatise to the outside world Biafra's plight, as well as deprive the arms flights of their cover.

Foreign governments also assisted in keeping Biafra alive, meddling in the war for their own advantage. Portugal, the last colonial power in Africa, provided vital staging posts for air traffic in Guinea-Bissau and São Tomé, an island 300 miles south-east of the Nigerian coastline. France, partly in response to public opinion, partly because it suited French interests in Africa, authorised the clandestine supply of French arms for Biafra. Thus, for month after month, Biafra endured a terrible war of attrition.

Through it all, Ojukwu remained intransigent, determined to hold on even when there was nothing more to be gained but suffering, presenting himself as a heroic symbol of resistance. Two days before Biafra formally surrendered in January 1970, its people exhausted, demoralised and desperate for peace, Ojukwu fled into exile in Côte d'Ivoire, declaring that 'whilst I live, Biafra lives'.

The aftermath of the war was notable for its compassion and mercy, and the way in which the memories of Biafra soon faded. Quoting Lincoln, Gowon talked of 'binding up the nation's wounds'. No medals for services in the war were awarded; no reparations were demanded. Biafran rebels were reabsorbed in the federal army; civil servants returned to their posts in the federal government; and property belonging to Igbos in the North and other federal areas was restored to them. In this war, said Gowon, there had been 'no victors and no vanquished'.

12

DEATH OF AN EMPEROR

No other African leader during the independence era was revered
so widely as Emperor Haile Selassie of Ethiopia. His defiant
stand against Mussolini's brutal invasion in the 1930s had won him
worldwide fame. Restored to his throne in the 1940s, he stood as the
symbol of an independent Africa that nationalist leaders living under
colonial rule all aspired to achieve. His position as monarch of a state
that traced its origins back to biblical times, that possessed a national
Christian church with a tradition older than that of many European
churches, as well as an ancient liturgical language and a sacred literature, all served to endow him with immense prestige. Adding to the
awe in which he was held was a mystique about the monarchy that
was carefully preserved. According to the Ethiopian constitution, the
emperor was descended directly from the marriage of Solomon and
Sheba, and among the titles with which he was graced was that of
'Elect of God'. His divine right to rule was devoutly upheld by the
Orthodox Church through its multitude of monasteries, churches
and priests. His daily life was surrounded by elaborate traditions of the
royal court and by religious ceremonies performed by patriarchs and
priests. On the world stage he consorted with the great and the good.
In Africa he was universally regarded as an elder statesman, the host of
the founding of the Organisation of African Unity and its first chair-

man. In Jamaica he was worshipped as a living God (Jah) by adherents of Rastafarianism, a religion that emerged in the 1930s and took its name from Haile Selassie's original title, Ras Tafari; during a three-day visit he made to Jamaica in 1966, some Jamaicans were convinced that miracles had occurred.

The sheer duration of his reign was impressive. He had ruled Ethiopia since 1916, first as regent, then as emperor from 1930. In his early years he made considerable efforts to modernise Ethiopia – abolishing slavery; building roads, schools, hospitals and a railway to the Red Sea; authorising the establishment of a parliament. In the postwar era, he laid the foundations of a civilian administration and built up a modern army, the largest in black Africa, with four divisions, an imperial bodyguard and an air force equipped with jet fighters.

But the basic character of his regime remained unchanged. Haile Selassie governed as an autocratic monarch, dispensing titles, appointments and land in return for loyal service, and holding together the empire and its 27 million subjects through a vast network of personal ties. His royal palaces in Addis Ababa constituted the centre of power from where all government affairs were directed. His name was automatically attached to schools, hospitals, roads and bridges, as well as to foundations and prizes. His effigy appeared on coinage and currency. The anniversaries of his birth, his coronation and his return to Addis Ababa from exile were national holidays.

What helped to sustain his power was the considerable extent to which the emperor, together with the Coptic Church and influential aristocratic families in the provinces, owned and controlled land and thereby the livelihood of millions of peasants who worked it. About three-quarters of Ethiopia's peasant farmers were tenants. Under the Civil Code of Ethiopia, promulgated in 1967, tenants were required to pay 75 per cent of their produce to landlords, to provide free labour for the landlord's farm, free transport for his crops, free firewood for his fuel, free service as domestic servants, cooks and guards, and free construction of his granaries. In some places where peasants had special skills in pottery, weaving, tanning or metalwork, they were bound by law to provide these services free as well. Tenants lived in perpetual fear of eviction.

A diminutive figure, outwardly mild-mannered, Haile Selassie was ruthless not only in crushing opposition to his rule in the further reaches of the empire but in extending its boundaries. The inner core of the empire consisted of the mountains and plateaux of central Ethiopia populated by Amharas and Tigrayans bound together by ancient ties of history and religion. But the outer regions had been added by conquest during Emperor Menelik's reign at the end of the nineteenth century. At the same time that European powers were engaged in their Scramble for Africa, Menelik extended Ethiopian rule over Oromo territory to the south and Somali territory to the south-east, notably the Ogaden plateau, doubling the size of the empire. In 1887 one of Menelik's most able generals, Ras Makonnen, occupied the ancient Muslim city of Harar. It was there, five years later, that Makonnen's son, Ras Tafari, was born. Ethiopia's claims to the Ogaden and to Oromo territory were subsequently recognised in treaties with Britain and Italy. But this southern part of the empire, threatened by Oromo and Somali dissidents, was never fully secure. Haile Selassie's authority there was maintained only with the help of the army.

The opportunity for Haile Selassie to expand the empire further came during the 1950s when the future of Eritrea, given to the United Nations to decide, came under discussion. As an Italian colony for fifty years, called Eritrea after the Latin name for the Red Sea, Mare Erythraeum, it had gained a distinct identity of its own. When the Italians were defeated in 1941, the British military administration which provisionally took control of the territory further stimulated a sense of Eritrean identity by encouraging the creation of political parties, labour unions and a free press, none of which was to be found in Ethiopia.

Eritrea's future proved difficult to resolve. Ethiopia, anxious to gain control of the port of Massawa, laid claim to Eritrea on the grounds that historically the territory, or parts of it, had previously belonged to the empire. Arab countries proposed an independent state. The Eritreans themselves, numbering about 3 million, were divided over the issue. The Christian half of the population, mostly Tigrayan, who inhabited the Eritrean highlands surrounding the capital, Asmara, tended to support unification with Ethiopia. The Muslim half of the population, also found in the highlands but mainly occupying the harsh desert region along the Red Sea coast and the western lowlands, tended to favour independence.

The compromise reached by the United Nations was a form of federation linking Ethiopia and Eritrea under which the Ethiopian government was given control of foreign affairs, defence, finance, commerce and ports, while Eritrea was allowed its own elected government and assembly to deal with local affairs. Eritrea was also permitted to have its own flag and official languages, Tigrinya and Arabic.

From the outset, however, Haile Selassie regarded the federation as nothing more than a step towards unification. Ethiopian officials, using a combination of patronage, pressure and intimidation and supported by amenable Christian Tigrayan politicians, steadily consolidated their control. The various freedoms which Eritreans had briefly enjoyed – political rights, trade unions and an independent press – all were whittled away. In 1958 the Eritrean flag was discarded. In 1959 the Ethiopian law code was extended to Eritrea; political parties were banned; the labour movement was destroyed; censorship was introduced; and Amharic replaced Tigrinya and Arabic as the official language. Finally, in 1962, the Eritrean assembly was persuaded to vote for the dissolution of the federation and its own existence in favour of annexation by Ethiopia.

From then on, Haile Selassie's treatment of Eritrea was no different from any of the other thirteen provinces of Ethiopia. Amhara officials were awarded senior posts in the administration. The principle of parity between Christian and Muslim officials, once carefully observed, was abandoned. In effect, Eritrea became simply another acquisition of the empire.

During the 1960s the empire faced revolts on several fronts. An Oromo uprising in Bale province in the south lasted for seven years. Somali insurgents in the Ogaden formed the West Somali Liberation Front aiming to drive out the Ethiopians and restore Somali sovereignty. Periodic clashes between Ethiopian and Somali government forces erupted along the border, culminating in a brief war in 1964 which the Ethiopian army won in a matter of days. In Eritrea guerrilla groups launched a war for independence that eventually required a whole division of Haile Selassie's troops to contain. The brutal methods of repression the Ethiopians employed in Eritrea, burning and bombing villages and inflicting reprisals against the civilian population, served only to alienate increasing numbers of Eritreans and fan the flames of Eritrean nationalism.

Even in his late seventies Haile Selassie showed no sign of willingness to loosen his grip on power. Nor would he discuss the issue of his succession. His favourite son, Leul Makonnen, the Duke of Harrar, had been killed in a car accident in 1957. His eldest son, the crown prince, Asfa Woosen, he never trusted. Everything depended on the emperor's decision. He alone was the arbiter between competing factions and individuals. He alone decided on appointments, promotions and demotions. He in person redressed grievances, received petitions, granted pardons, distributed largesse, cancelled debts and overturned court decisions. He insisted on retaining personal control of even small administrative details, deciding on petty expenditure, ruling on the most minor of ministerial disputes, authorising each trip abroad of his officials. No minister would dare to take any decision of consequence without having first obtained the *fakad* – his approval.

He operated by memory, possessing a formidable ability to recall names, faces and conversations, past events, the particularities of places he visited, the peccadilloes of his ministers, long-forgotten errors and indiscretions, and intrigues that swirled around his palaces and empire. Close by his side or walking a few steps behind him, always in attendance in the course of an audience or an inspection tour, was the Minister of the Pen, ready to take down any order or instruction, to record appointments and dismissals. His signature, rather than the Emperor's, appeared on the publication of all laws, decrees and treaties.

To keep himself informed, Haile Selassie relied on a constant stream of secret intelligence and gossip. In private audiences, ministers were encouraged to report on the activities of their colleagues. Officials competed to provide him with choice titbits of information. At the Jubilee Palace, where he lived, his routine was to take an early morning walk in the park, stopping by the cages of lions and leopards to feed them with chunks of meat handed to him by an aide and listening along the way to intelligence reports from officials who ran his spy networks. One at a time they would approach to pass on their news and rumours, falling in a step behind as he walked on, until each was dismissed by a nod of the head and retreated backwards. Finishing his walk alone, Haile Selassie would feed the dogs.

The seat of his government was the Grand Palace, Menelik's old palace, built on a hill near the Jubilee Palace overlooking parts of the city. It was ringed by successive gates and compounds in the traditional manner of an Ethiopian encampment. At the top stood the Emperor's office. Just below was the imperial *Chelot*, his personal court where, standing on a platform dressed in a black, floor-length robe, Haile Selassie passed judgement on disputes and cases brought before him, pronouncing sentences from which there was no appeal. Close beside was the powerful Ministry of the Pen, which transmitted his orders. Behind were the Council of Ministers chambers and the Crown Council building where the Emperor received petitions. Elsewhere in the grounds were ceremonial buildings such as the Throne Room used for state occasions and the Banqueting Hall.

Constant attendance at the palace was obligatory. Every day, dignitaries and officials appeared at a ritual known as *dej tinat* – 'waiting at the gate' – hoping to accomplish their business or to gain favour. The key to all advancement lay in loyalty and service to the emperor which he was careful to reward. The largesse he distributed came not just in the form of appointments, titles, land grants and salary increases but in gifts of money, houses, cars and other luxury items. Officials who served him well he rewarded with scholarships, free medical treatment and foreign holidays. Those who plotted against him or earned disfavour faced expropriation and ruin.

On his daily routine, as he was driven into the courtyard at the top of the avenue at the Grand Palace, a crowd of dignitaries and officials lined up, hoping to be noticed. In the Audience Hall, all bowed as he entered. As he took his place on the old imperial throne, dwarfed by its size, an official pillow-bearer swiftly slid a pillow under his feet to ensure that his legs were not left hanging in the air. The pillow-bearer, who accompanied the emperor everywhere he went, kept a store of fifty-two pillows of various sizes, thicknesses, materials and colours, to cover every eventuality.

Haile Selassie reached the age of eighty in July 1972, having held absolute power for longer than any other figure in contemporary history, still addicted to pomp, protocol and a system of personal rule that was no longer a viable method of government. The sharpness of his memory was fading. At times he seemed to drift in and out of senility. His long-serving prime minister, Aklilou Abte Wold, found that no matter how many times a problem had been previously discussed, it had to be taken up each time from the beginning. When the minister of public works, Saleh Hinit, appeared at the palace one day, the emperor turned to his aide asking: 'Who is that man? What is he doing here?' At a state dinner in honour of President Mobutu of Zaire (Congo-Kinshasa), Haile Selassie summoned an official to ask, in Amharic, who the guest of honour sitting opposite him was. During his first trip to China in 1973, he made constant references to a previous visit he said he had made there. During an interview at the Grand Palace in early 1974, John Spencer, an American lawyer who had known him for nearly forty years, found a marked deterioration in his demeanour. 'It became apparent to me during the course of our conversation that Haile Selassie was already retreating into a dream world,' he wrote in his memoir. 'He appeared to have become disturbingly inarticulate. I withdrew with the piercing realisation that the curtain of senility had dropped.'

The difficulty now was that Haile Selassie had become too old and infirm to initiate any change in the system of government. Nor was he yet willing to address the issue of succession. In 1973 the crown prince suffered a stroke and repaired to Switzerland to recuperate, leaving the succession in even greater doubt. Even though ministers and leading aristocrats recognised that the system of government was far too archaic to suit the modern needs of Ethiopia, fearful of displeasing the emperor they took no initiative and allowed the government to drift on indeterminately.

When drought and famine overtook the province of Wollo in 1973, claiming the lives of tens of thousands of peasants, the government, though aware of the disaster, made little attempt to alleviate it;

nor did it seek help from international agencies for fear of damaging the country's reputation. When Haile Selassie belatedly paid a visit to the area, he merely referred to the 'natural disasters beyond human control' that had often afflicted Ethiopia and implied that little could be done to prevent them. The government's inertia over the Wollo famine caused a wave of exasperation among the educated Ethiopian elite. But there were no signs of overt opposition to the emperor's rule other than among student groups who were habitually troublesome.

Then, in early 1974, a few small and random incidents occurred that were eventually to culminate in revolution. On 12 January enlisted men at an army outpost in Neghelle in southern Ethiopia mutinied against their officers in protest against poor food and a shortage of water. The soldiers' water pump had broken down; when officers refused to allow them the use of their own well, they were imprisoned. The mutineers sent a petition to the emperor asking for their grievances to be redressed. Haile Selassie responded by sending an army general as his personal envoy to investigate the matter, but he too was detained. Despite the insubordination, Haile Selassie promised an improvement in the mutineers' conditions and decided against any punishment.

News of the Neghelle mutiny spread through the army's network to every unit in the country. On 10 February airmen at an air force base near Addis Ababa staged a similar revolt, holding officers hostage, in protest against pay and conditions. Again Haile Selassie tried to deal with the mutiny by promising salary increases. On 25 February a more serious revolt broke out in Asmara, the capital of Eritrea. Led by a group of seven middle-aged sergeants and corporals, mutineers took control of the radio station and broadcast demands for more pay and improved conditions of service. Messages of support came from other units. In Addis Ababa rebel officers in the Fourth Division took eight ministers hostages, demanding they be sacked for corruption. Haile Selassie responded with more concessions, sacking a bevy of senior officers and further increasing pay and allowances.

Simultaneously, a series of spontaneous civilian protests erupted on the streets of Addis Ababa: students demonstrated over plans for educational reform; teachers went on strike demanding higher pay; taxi drivers struck in protest against fuel price increases; labour unions took to the streets to voice grievances over pay, food price rises and union rights. On 23 February, addressing his 'beloved' people on radio and television, Haile Selassie offered concessions, postponing changes in the educational system, reducing fuel price increases and implementing price controls to check inflation. He also dismissed his prime minister, Aklilou, and agreed to revise the constitution to make the prime minister answerable to parliament, a change that in Ethiopian terms amounted to major reform.

In March a chaotic profusion of strikes and demonstrations burst out in the towns and cities of Ethiopia. One group after another – civil servants, teachers, students, journalists, even priests and prostitutes – took to the streets. A massive demonstration was held in protest against official discrimination against Islam and calling for the separation of Church and state. The most persistent demand was for the arrest and trial of former ministers and palace officials on charges of negligence and corruption. The outbursts were unplanned and uncoordinated, but insistent on the need for widespread reform.

The old aristocratic establishment held out, paying scant heed to the demands other than to permit the arrest of some colleagues and palace officials as a token gesture. They attempted no serious reform but instead turned to loyal units of the army for help in curbing strikes and demonstrations.

Within the armed forces, however, a group of radical junior officers conspired to take control. Meeting at Fourth Division headquarters in Addis Ababa at the end of June, they formed a military 'committee' or 'Derg', comprising 108 representatives chosen by units of the armed forces, to run the country. For many months the Derg remained a shadowy organisation: none of the names of its members was announced and its activities were kept hidden from the public. Moving cautiously at first, unsure of how much resistance it would encounter from the emperor, the aristocracy and loyal units of the armed forces, the Derg issued a statement on 4 July pledging loyalty to the emperor, giving its main goals as the upholding of the Crown and the smooth functioning of civilian government. The slogan adopted – *'Ethiopia Tikdem'*, 'Ethiopia First' – was suitably vague.

But stage by stage, growing in confidence, the Derg began to dismantle the whole imperial structure. During July and August it issued long lists of names of palace functionaries, high government officials and prominent aristocrats, including Haile Selassie's closest advisers, calling on them to give themselves up or face confiscation of their assets. Most surrendered voluntarily; some were arrested by force. Hundreds were incarcerated in the basements of buildings in the Grand Palace, packed so tight that they had to take turns lying down on the bare earthen floor in order to sleep. At the Jubilee Palace, Haile Selassie was left with only a handful of personal servants.

The Derg turned next on the emperor himself. In the government press, on radio and television, a barrage of attacks was unleashed on the *ancien régime*, condemning it for corruption and exploitation. Haile Selassie himself was accused of squandering the country's meagre resources on expensive trips abroad and of being wilfully negligent over the Wollo famine. One by one, the imperial institutions were abolished: the Ministry of the Pen; the Crown Council; the *Chelot*; the emperor's private exchequer. Royal investments in the St George Brewery and Addis Ababa's bus company were taken over. On 25 August the Jubilee Palace was nationalised and renamed the National Palace.

There was to be no dignified exit. At a four-day secret meeting in early September, the Derg voted to dethrone Haile Selassie. On 11 September nine princesses, including the emperor's sole surviving daughter and seven granddaughters, were imprisoned in a dungeon-like cell, their heads shaved, allowed only two mattresses to share between them. On the same day officers from the Derg interrogated Haile Selassie on the whereabouts of his fortune. He vehemently denied possessing any fortune. 'But surely, Your Majesty, you must have put something aside for your retirement?' he was asked. 'For an emperor, there is no retirement,' he retorted. 'Having not provided for our retirement, we have nothing.'

They suggested that he watch a film due to be shown on state television that night. The film, a British television documentary called *The Hidden Famine*, was an exposé examining how thousands of men, women and children had been allowed to starve in Wollo the previous year. It was spliced with scenes showing the emperor and his entourage drinking champagne, eating caviar and feeding meat to his dogs from a silver tray. Sitting in an armchair, Haile Selassie watched the film to the end and then, according to a servant attending him, became lost in thought.

Early the following morning, 12 September, three officers from the Derg, dressed in combat uniforms, entered the chamber where Haile Selassie awaited them. After a preliminary bow, one of them read out the proclamation dethroning him. The proclamation charged that Haile Selassie had 'not only left the country in its present crisis by abusing at various times the high and dignified authority conferred on him by the Ethiopian people but also, being over eighty-two years of age and due to the consequent physical and mental exhaustion, is no more able to shoulder the high responsibilities of leadership'.

Standing before them, Haile Selassie listened impassively, then replied that if the revolution was good for the people then he too supported it and would not oppose his dethronement. 'In that case,' said a major, 'His Majesty will please follow us.' 'Where to?' Haile Selassie asked. 'To a safe place,' replied the major. 'His Majesty will see.'

A green Volkswagen was waiting for them in the palace driveway. The driver, an officer, opened the door and held up the front seat so that Haile Selassie could get in the back. Huddled in the back seat, he was driven through the empty streets of Addis Ababa – where a night curfew was in force – and disappeared through the gates of Fourth Division barracks.

Haile Selassie spent the last months of his life imprisoned in rooms in the Grand Palace. He continued to get up at dawn, attended morning mass and spent much time reading. In a building nearby, members of the Derg met to maintain their grip on power. What had hitherto been a revolution without bloodshed turned increasingly violent. On 23 November the Derg ordered the execution of some sixty prominent prisoners, mostly high officials associated with Haile Selassie's regime, including two former prime ministers and the emperor's grandson. The key figure behind this decision was a young ordnance officer, Major Mengistu Haile Mariam, soon to become infamous.

Haile Selassie died a prisoner on 27 August 1975. According to the Derg, the cause of his death was circulatory failure. According to his followers, he was smothered with a wet pillow. His body was buried beneath a lavatory in the palace, remaining hidden there for sixteen years while the revolution raged on.

13

THE COMING OF TYRANTS

In the first two decades of independence, there were some forty suc-cessful coups and countless attempted coups. In 1967 a 27-year-old Ghanaian army lieutenant, Sam Arthur, finding himself in temporary command of an armoured car unit, decided on an attempt to seize power because, he later confessed, he wanted to 'make history' by becoming the first lieutenant successfully to organise a coup. The coup attempt was given the name 'Operation Guitar Boy'. Arthur's armoured car unit drove into Accra but failed to gain control.

Many coups were accomplished without violence. Some countries even established a tradition of peaceful coups. In Dahomey – later renamed Benin – all six coups after independence were bloodless. In Upper Volta (Burkina Faso), where political activity was confined to such a small elite that incoming ministers tended to be related to those who had just been thrown out, politicians took pride in the fact that no one had ever been killed for political reasons. There was con-siderable disquiet, therefore, when, during the country's fourth coup in 1982, rival army factions clashed; shooting had never occurred before.

Whatever their real reasons for seizing power, coup leaders invari-ably stressed the strictly temporary nature of military rule. All they required, they said, was sufficient time to clear up the morass of corruption, mismanagement, tribalism, nepotism and other assorted malpractices they claimed had prompted them to intervene and restore honest and efficient government and national integrity.

Some attempts were indeed made to return to civilian rule. The generals who overthrew Kwame Nkrumah stayed in power for only three years, taking no serious initiatives other than to increase the pay of soldiers, before handing back control to politicians. The next civilian government, however, encumbered by massive debts from the Nkrumah era, undermined by falling cocoa prices on the world market and pummelled by inflation and strikes, lasted for only three years before the army stepped in again. The next military ruler, General Ignatius Acheampong, ran a regime that was so corrupt that the army eventually removed him, installing another general. Just weeks before new elections were due to be held in 1979, a new phenomenon arose. A group of junior officers led by a 32-year-old air force officer, Flight-Lieutenant Jerry Rawlings, seized power and embarked on what was described as a 'house-cleaning exercise'. Eight senior officers, including three former heads of state, were executed by firing squad; traders accused of profiteering were publicly flogged; the main market in Accra was razed to the ground; and impromptu People's Courts were set up to deal with scores of army officers and businessmen accused of corruption and malpractice. Rawlings then handed power over to the politicians. But only three years later he was back, staging a second coming in 1982. By then, after twenty-five years of mismanagement, plunder and corruption, Ghana had become a wasteland, a society that was crumbling in ruins at every level.

In Nigeria, after thirteen years of military government, General Olusegun Obasanjo presided over elections in 1979 reinstating civilian rule in what seemed to be propitious circumstances. Under a new constitution, Nigeria was divided into a federation of nineteen states, reducing the risk of polarisation between the country's three main ethnic groups and allowing some minority groups their own representation. The new federal structure consisted of four predominantly Hausa-Fulani states, four Yoruba, two Igbo and nine ethnic minority states. Furthermore, the constitution required political parties to demonstrate a broad national presence before they could qualify for registration. Launching the new system, Obasanjo made clear he wanted no return to past practices. 'Political recruitment and subsequent political support which are based on tribal, religious and linguistic sentiments contributed largely to our past misfortune,' he said. 'They must not be allowed to spring up again. Those negative political attitudes like hatred, falsehood, intolerance and acrimony also contributed to our national tragedy in the past: they must not be continued.'

The election in 1979 was held in relatively calm conditions. It was won by the National Party of Nigeria, a northern-based party which drew support from Yoruba, Igbo and minority groups alike. Its leader, Alhaji Shehu Shagari, was a mild-mannered, unassuming and ascetic politician from a northern Fulani family, inclined to seek consensus. Though the election aroused the old ethnic tensions and rivalries that had wrecked the First Republic, they were more diffused than before. What seemed especially promising were Nigeria's economic prospects. By 1979 Nigeria had become the world's sixth largest oil producer, with revenues soaring to $24 billion a year.

Such riches, however, set off a vicious scramble for political office and the wealth that went with it. Access to the government spending process became the gateway to fortune. Patronage politics and corruption reached new heights. The press spoke of 'the politics of bickerings, mudslingings . . . lies, deceit, vindictiveness, strife and intolerance that are again creeping back into the country's political scene'. Addressing the annual conference of the Nigerian Political Science Association in 1981, Claude Ake observed:

We are intoxicated with politics; the premium on political power is so high that we are prone to take the most extreme measures to win and to maintain political power . . .

As things stand now, the Nigerian state appears to intervene everywhere and to own virtually everything including access to status and wealth. Inevitably a desperate struggle to win control of state power ensues since this control means for all practical purposes being all powerful and owning everything. Politics becomes warfare, a matter of life and death.

Foremost in the scramble were Shagari's associates. Renowned for venality, Shagari's administration was termed 'a government of contractors, for contractors and by contractors'. According to Larry Diamond, an American expert on Nigeria, 'the meetings of his cabinet and party councils became grand bazaars where the resources of the state were put up for auction'. The expected kickbacks on contracts rose to 50 per cent. An official enquiry in 1980 established that the cost of government contracts, inflated by kickbacks, was 200 per cent higher than in Kenya. Another enquiry found that the costs of construction in Nigeria were three times higher than in East Africa or North Africa and four times higher than in Asia.

When the oil boom came to an end, the economy plunged into recession, government projects were abandoned, unemployment soared. State governments became unable to pay teachers and civil servants or to purchase drugs for hospitals. But among the elite, the scramble went on. Visiting Nigeria on the eve of elections, Larry Diamond recorded: 'Everywhere one turned in 1983, the economy seemed on the edge of collapse. Still the politicians and contractors continued to bribe, steal, smuggle and speculate, accumulating vast illicit fortunes and displaying them lavishly in stunning disregard for public sensitivities.'

The elections in 1983 were conducted with such massive rigging and fraud that even hardened observers of Nigeria were astonished. Shagari, being the incumbent, won a second term, but as Nigeria descended into anarchy, the generals took control once more. 'Democracy had been in jeopardy for the past four years,' remarked a former army chief of staff. 'It died with the elections. The army only buried it.'

'The trouble with Nigeria,' wrote the Nigerian novelist, Chinua Achebe, in 1983, 'is simply and squarely a failure of leadership. There is nothing basically wrong with the Nigerian character. There is nothing wrong with the Nigerian land or climate or water or air or anything else. The Nigerian problem is the unwillingness or inability of its leaders to rise to the responsibility, to the challenge of personal example which are the hallmarks of true leadership.'

★

There were a few military regimes that were noted for ruling effectively and for their efforts to root out corruption. In Togo, General Eyadéma, the former French army sergeant who had taken part in the assassination of President Olympio in 1963 and who seized power four years later, achieved a degree of stability rare in West Africa. In Niger, Colonel Seyni Kountché, after overthrowing Hamani Diori's corrupt regime in 1974, demanded efficiency and discipline and dealt swiftly with anyone who did not comply, caring little whether his regime was popular or not. But Africa's military rulers generally turned out to be no more competent, no more immune to the temptation of corruption, and no more willing to give up power than the regimes they had overthrown. And amid the hurly-burly of coups and revolutions that afflicted Africa came the tyrants.

In Zanzibar, Abeid Karume's regime, set up after the 1964 revolution against the ruling Arab elite, was bizarre and vindictive from the outset. A former merchant seaman, once proud to have served as an oarsman for the Sultan's ceremonial barge, Karume had little formal education but had gained popularity in the run-up to independence in 1963 as leader of the Afro-Shirazi Party (ASP), drawing support from African labourers, fishermen, farmhands and craftsmen occupying the lower rungs of Zanzibar society. In the last election before independence the ASP gained a majority of total votes cast, taking some 54 per cent, but won only a minority of seats. The result intensified deep-rooted racial animosity between Arab and African inhabitants, culminating in revolution and the emergence of Karume as head of a Revolutionary Council.

Once in power, Karume acted swiftly to crush the Arab community. The Revolutionary Council ordered arrests, imprisonment without trial, torture and execution as it saw fit and seized property and plantations at will. Thousands of Arabs were forcibly deported, packed into dhows, some old and unseaworthy, and sent to the Arabian Gulf. A British port official witnessed how the first three dhows were crammed with 450 Arab deportees given only 600 gallons of water for a journey expected to last anything from three to six weeks. A deserted, forlorn air settled over the narrow streets and alleys of Stone Town, once filled with thriving shops and businesses. A correspondent wrote of the Arab community in 1965: 'They have lost the arrogance typical of their ruling days. Their shyness, their unobtrusive gait as they shuffle along the narrow lanes . . . gives the centre of the town the atmosphere of a ghetto.'

The prosperous Asian community, numbering 20,000, whom the sultan had encouraged to settle in Zanzibar, survived the revolution largely intact, but they too became the target of victimisation. Asian civil servants were abruptly sacked; their special schools were closed. Asians accused of minor offences were publicly flogged. When four young Persian girls refused to marry the elderly Karume, he ordered the arrest of ten of their male relatives for 'hindering the implementation of mixed marriages', and threatened to deport both the men and the hundred-odd members of the Persian Ithnasheri sect to which they belonged. President Nyerere prevailed on him to drop the charges, but a few months later, four other Persian girls were forced to marry elderly members of the Revolutionary Council; and eleven of their male relatives were ordered by a 'people's court' judge to be imprisoned and flogged. 'In colonial times the Arabs took African concubines without bothering to marry them,' said Karume. 'Now that we are in power, the shoe is on the other foot.'

The population at large was subjected to dictatorial control. Ruling by decree, Karume declared a one-party state and ordered all adult Zanzibaris to sign up as members of the ASP. A picture of Karume had to be displayed in every home. His security service, trained by East Germans, was given powers to arrest, torture and imprison without trial. Anyone who complained, even about food or consumer shortages, was liable to be denounced as an 'enemy of the revolution'. Karume also set up his own courts to deal with 'political' offences, appointing judges with powers to hand out death sentences from which the only right of appeal was to himself.

Distrustful of intellectuals and disliking experts, he soon fell out with Marxist members of the Revolutionary Council. Two former members accused of plotting against him were executed. Though given to making long rambling speeches, he never developed a coherent policy. More and more came to depend on his erratic and capricious personality. He banned contraceptives; forced 'volunteers' to undertake farmwork; closed private clubs and abolished private business and trading enterprises. He expelled staff from the World Health Organisation and suspended malaria-control programmes on the grounds that Africans were 'malaria-proof', precipitating a huge surge in malaria.

His attitude towards government expenditure was equally bizarre. As a result of sharp increases in the price of cloves from 1965, Zanzibar gained substantial foreign reserves. But rather than spend the reserves on development projects or on much-needed imported goods like medicines, Karume preferred to hoard them. He insisted that Zanzibar should become self-sufficient. So while the exchequer bulged with funds, hospitals and clinics were chronically short of drugs, and basic supplies of rice, flour and sugar were rationed.

Karume's end came in 1972 when an army officer bearing a personal grudge shot him dead as he was relaxing with friends on the ground floor of party headquarters, drinking coffee and playing *bao*, a Swahili game akin to draughts. Large crowds turned out for his funeral, but they were noticeably subdued.

Jean-Bedel Bokassa's career as dictator of the Central African Republic combined not only extreme greed and personal violence but delusions of grandeur unsurpassed by any other African leader. His excesses included seventeen wives, a score of mistresses and an official brood of fifty-five children. He was prone to towering rages as well as outbursts of sentimentality; and he also gained a reputation for cannibalism.

From an early age, Bokassa's life was affected by violence. When he was six years old, his father, a petty chief in the village of Boubangui, was beaten to death at the local French prefect's office for protesting against forced labour. His distraught mother killed herself a week later, leaving a family of twelve children as orphans. Raised by a grandfather and educated at mission schools, he was constantly taunted by other children about the fate of his unfortunate parents. After completing secondary education, he enlisted in the French army, receiving twelve citations for bravery in combat during the Second World War and in Indo-China, including the Légion d'Honneur and the Croix de Guerre. French officers, while recognising his courage under fire, also knew him to be a vain and capricious personality. But in the rush to independence, Bokassa gained rapid promotion. After serving as a sergeant for seventeen years, he left the French army in 1961 with the rank of captain and was given the task of helping to set up a national army. Three years later, at the age of forty-two, he was appointed chief of staff of the CAR's 500-man army.

Bokassa seized power on 31 December 1965, after learning that President David Dacko, a cousin, intended to replace him. Initially Bokassa's regime was not especially brutal. A former minister was beaten to death because he was deemed not to have shown enough respect to the army in the past. A former head of internal security was executed with extreme cruelty. Dacko was held in solitary confinement for three years. Political prisoners and inmates in Ngaragba prison in Bangui were routinely tortured or beaten on Bokassa's orders, their cries clearly audible to nearby residents. But otherwise Bokassa's preoccupation was to enjoy the pomp and power of office and to amass a fortune for himself.

He liked to describe himself as an 'absolute monarch' and forbade mention of the words democracy and elections. He promoted himself first to the rank of general and then to marshal, for 'supreme services to the State'. For public appearances he insisted on wearing so many medals and awards that special uniforms had to be designed for him to accommodate them. He delighted in naming after himself a host of schools, hospitals, clinics, roads and development projects as well as Bangui's new university. The front page of every school exercise book in the entire country was adorned with his picture. He adored the ceremony of state visits and toured the world a number of times, taking with him large retinues of assistants and distributing gifts of diamonds to his hosts.

His every whim became government policy. He himself held twelve ministerial portfolios and interfered in all the others. He controlled all decision-making, every promotion or demotion, every reward or punishment. Ministers were shuffled with monotonous regularity, as often as six times a year, to ensure that they did not become a threat. As the telephone system in Bangui hardly functioned, all government offices were required to keep their radios switched on in order to hear intermittent instructions sent directly from the presidential office. Development projects were sometimes started with sudden enthusiasm, then abandoned when Bokassa's interest dwindled and the money was needed for another new idea. In a fit of pique about Bangui's poor airline connections, he decided that a national airline should be established: Air Centrafrique was duly set up, then promptly collapsed after a few flights.

Using government funds at will and fortunes he made from diamond and ivory deals, Bokassa acquired a whole string of valuable properties in Europe, including four chateaux in France, a fifty-room mansion in Paris, houses in Nice and Toulouse and a villa in Berne. He built a huge 'ancestral home' at Berengo, fifty miles from Bangui, and ordered a motorway to be built to it. The presidential estate there included private houses and apartments for foreign visitors furnished with reproduction antique furniture and gilt mirrors.

He permitted government ministers to make their own fortunes, occasionally chiding them for excessive greed, but willing to overlook corruption when it suited him. He also pampered the army with large salaries and sophisticated equipment and allowed officers to engage in commercial activities, recognising that his hold on power depended on the army's loyalty. Defence expenditure doubled between 1967 and 1969, and remained the second largest item in the budget. He packed the Presidential Guard with members of his own Mbaka tribe, mainly from his own village, providing them with the best uniforms and equipment. The government's finances were accordingly chaotic. No proper records were kept; budgets were ignored in favour of ad-hoc spending. Civil service salaries were often three or four months in arrears.

His sexual proclivities were voracious. He installed wives and mistresses in separate residences, leaving his palace several times each day to pay them visits, holding up traffic on the way. His principal wife, Catherine, a strikingly attractive woman whom he first spotted at the age of thirteen, lived in the Villa Nasser and owned a fashionable boutique in the city centre. Another favourite, La Roumaine, a blonde cabaret dancer whom he met on a visit to a nightclub in Bucharest, lived in the Villa Kolongo, a palatial residence on the banks of the Oubangui river, surrounded by tropical gardens with courtyards, pools and fountains. Most of his wives tended to be known by their nationality; they included the German, the Swede, the Cameroonian, the Chinese, the Gabonese, the Tunisienne, and the Ivorienne. He was proud of his conquests. 'I did it like everyone,' he said in an interview in 1984. 'In Formosa, for example, I hustled the most beautiful woman in the country whom I later married. In Bucharest, the most beautiful woman in Romania; in Libreville, the most beautiful woman in Gabon . . . and so on. My criterion was beauty.'

He spent considerable effort tracking down a daughter named Martine born to a Vietnamese wife he married in Saigon in 1953. The first Martine to arrive in Bangui turned out to be an impostor. Nevertheless, to show his magnanimity, Bokassa adopted her. Then the real Martine was found working in a cement factory in Vietnam. Bokassa offered both of them in marriage via a kind of public auction. The eventual winners were a doctor and an army officer. Bokassa joyfully presided over a double wedding held in the cathedral, attended by several African heads of state. For the fake Martine, the marriage was to end in disaster. Her husband was involved in an assassination attempt on Bokassa and executed. A few hours after his death, she gave birth to a baby boy. The infant was taken away and murdered.

The French, keen to ensure that the Central African Republic remained within the French orbit, continued to underwrite Bokassa's regime with financial and military support. In wayward moods, Bokassa frequently picked quarrels with them, occasionally threatening to leave the French fold. In 1969 he announced a 'Move to the East' and proclaimed scientific socialism as the government's goal, expecting rewards to flow from the Eastern bloc, but when they failed to materialise, he reversed course. He abruptly converted to Islam, taking the name Salah Addin Ahmed Bokassa, hoping for Arab funds, but disappointed by the result soon reverted to the Catholic Church.

Despite the quarrels, Bokassa's attachment to France remained profound. He worshipped de Gaulle, addressing him as 'Papa' even after he had become president. The greatest moment of his life, he once said, was when he was decorated by de Gaulle in person. During de

Gaulle's funeral, he was inconsolable. '*Mon père, mon papa*,' he sobbed in front of de Gaulle's widow. 'I lost my natural father when I was a child. Now I have lost my adoptive father as well. I am an orphan again.' Bokassa also struck up a warm friendship with President Valéry Giscard d'Estaing – 'a dear cousin' – putting a wildlife reserve at his disposal for him to hunt every year and plying him with generous gifts of diamonds. Bokassa estimated that Giscard personally killed some fifty elephants and countless other animals during the 1970s.

It was during Giscard's presidency that the French indulged Bokassa's greatest *folie de grandeur*. In an attempt to emulate Napoleon, whom he described as his 'guide and inspiration', Bokassa declared the Central African Republic an empire and himself emperor of its 2 million subjects and made elaborate arrangements for his own coronation, using as a model the ceremony in which Napoleon had crowned himself emperor of France in 1804. From France he ordered all the trappings of a monarchy: a crown of diamonds; an imperial throne, shaped like a golden eagle; an antique coach; thoroughbred horses; coronation robes; brass helmets and breastplates for the Imperial Guard; tons of food, wine, fireworks and flowers for the festivities and sixty Mercedes-Benz cars for the guests.

The coronation took place on 4 December 1977 at the Palais des Sports Jean-Bedel Bokassa, on Bokassa Avenue, next to the Université Jean-Bedel Bokassa. To the strains of Mozart and Beethoven, wearing a twenty-foot-long red-velvet cloak trimmed with ermine, Bokassa crowned himself and then received as a symbol of office a six-foot diamond-encrusted sceptre.

The spectacle of Bokassa's lavish coronation, costing $22 million, in a country with few government services, huge infant mortality, widespread illiteracy, only 260 miles of paved roads and in serious economic difficulty, aroused universal criticism. But the French, who picked up most of the bill, curtly dismissed all such criticism. 'Personally,' said the French Cooperation Minister, Robert Galley, who represented Giscard at the coronation, 'I find it quite extraordinary to criticise what is to take place in Bangui while finding the Queen of England's Jubilee ceremony all right. It smacks of racism.' At the end of a state banquet, Bokassa turned to Galley and whispered,

'You never noticed, but you ate human flesh', a remark that prompted his reputation for cannibalism.

Reminiscing in later years about the coronation, Bokassa told the Italian journalist Riccardo Orizio, 'It was the least the French could do to repay me for my services as a soldier fighting for their country, and for all the personal favours their politicians received when I became president.'

The ultimate irony was that less than two years after the coronation, as a result of Bokassa's violent conduct, the French themselves felt obliged to step in and remove him from power. Bokassa's propensity for violence became increasingly evident during the 1970s. In 1972, in a campaign against theft, he published a decree prescribing mutilation for thieves. As part of the campaign, he personally led a bevy of ministers to Ngaragba prison where he ordered guards to beat convicted thieves with wooden staves. As the convicts screamed in agony, Bokassa turned to a foreign newspaper reporter to observe: 'It's tough, but that's life.' Three men died and several others seemed barely alive. The next day, forty-two thieves who had survived the beating, together with the corpses of the three others, were put on display under a blazing sun on a stand in Bangui's main square. When the United Nations Secretary-General, Kurt Waldheim, protested at the atrocity, Bokassa called him 'a pimp', 'a colonialist' and 'dumb as a corpse'. His other exploits included assaulting a British journalist with an ivory-tipped walking stick and attempting to strike a personal representative of Giscard d'Estaing.

The list of Bokassa's victims at Ngaragba grew ever longer. 'From 1976 to 1979,' the prison director subsequently testified, 'I executed dozens of officers, soldiers, diverse personages, thieves, students – under instructions from Bokassa.' Some were beaten to death with hammers and chains. Bokassa was also said to hold kangaroo courts in the gardens of the Villa Kolongo, sentencing men to be killed by lions or crocodiles he kept there.

The events that led to Bokassa's downfall started with student demonstrations in Bangui on 19 January 1979, in protest at an imperial edict that all pupils buy and wear new school uniforms. The uniforms were manufactured by a textile company owned by members of the Bokassa family and sold exclusively in their retail stores. The demonstrations were joined by crowds of unemployed youths and quickly turned into riots; one of Bokassa's stores was ransacked. The riots were brutally suppressed by the Imperial Guard but strikes by teachers, students and civil servants continued.

In April, after further protests, scores of students were rounded up and taken to Ngaragba. One group of thirty students was stuffed into a small cell designed to hold one person; another group of twenty suffered the same fate. By the time the cell doors were opened the next morning, many were dead. Several witnesses claimed that Bokassa himself turned up at the prison and joined in beating and killing other students in detention. An independent judicial inquiry subsequently concluded: 'In the month of April 1979, the massacre of about 100 children was carried out under the orders of Emperor Bokassa and almost certainly with his personal participation.' In France, the media dubbed Bokassa the 'Butcher of Bangui'.

No longer able to stand the embarrassment of propping up Bokassa's regime, the French, after considerable prevarication, decided to remove him. On 20 September while Bokassa was on a visit to Libya, French troops stationed in Gabon and Chad, flew into Bangui, took control and installed David Dacko as president. Among the items they discovered at his residences were several chests full of diamonds, more than 200 cameras and accessories and a collection of pornography. At the Villa Kolongo they also found two mutilated bodies in a refrigerator. One body, with its head, arms and one leg missing, was identified as that of a mathematics teacher. When French troops drained the pond at Villa Kolongo, they came across bone fragments said to have come from some thirty victims eaten by crocodiles. The soldiers were told that other victims had been fed to lions kept in a nearby cage. When pressed by reporters about Bokassa's eating habits, President Dacko readily conceded that human flesh had been a regular item on his menu and had been served on occasion to foreign dignitaries. Bokassa, for his part, always denied charges of cannibalism.

Bokassa sought asylum in France, but was turned away. He found refuge instead in Côte d'Ivoire. At a trial that took place in Bangui in his absence in 1980, he was accused of murder, embezzlement and cannibalism and sentenced to death. After four years in Côte d'Ivoire, he was allowed to settle in his chateau at Hardricourt, west of Paris. In 1986, feeling homesick, he decided to return to the Central African Republic. He was put on trial, found guilty of murder, though not cannibalism, and sentenced to death. The sentence was subsequently commuted, first to life imprisonment, then to twenty years' forced labour. In prison he turned to religion, constantly read the Bible and considered himself an apostle of Christ. After seven years' imprisonment he was released and spent his last years in Bangui in the Villa Nasser, surviving on a French army pension. He died in 1996, at the age of seventy-five, and was buried in an unmarked grave in Berengo.

At the time of Uganda's independence in 1962, Idi Amin was a newly commissioned officer, promoted from the ranks, with a military record that had already given British officials cause for concern. Virtually illiterate, with no schooling and limited intelligence, he had been recruited in 1946 to serve as a trainee cook in the King's African Rifles. A man of huge physique, he had gained attention by excelling at sport and marksmanship and by displaying qualities of stamina and loyalty which British officers admired. For nine years he held the national title of heavyweight boxing champion. Posted to Kenya during the Mau Mau campaign with the rank of corporal, he was nearly cashiered for carrying out interrogations of suspects with undue brutality. British officers nevertheless considered him worthy of promotion as a non-commissioned officer; he duly rose to the rank of sergeant–major, the highest position then open to African soldiers under British rule. But he was never regarded as 'officer material'. In the press of events leading to independence, however, as Britain searched for potential African army officers, Amin was considered an obvious possibility for promotion. Though failing to make much progress on special education courses to which he was sent, he nevertheless was given a commission in 1961 at the age of about thirty-six, one of only two Ugandan officers at the time.

Six months before independence, Amin's proclivity for violent conduct became a matter of controversy. While participating in a military operation in Kenya's Northern Frontier District, Amin was accused of murdering three Turkana tribesmen. British officials in Nairobi dealing with the case wanted criminal charges brought against Lieutenant Amin, but the Governor of Uganda, Sir Walter Coutts, argued that to put on trial for murder one of only two African officers in Uganda shortly before independence would be politically disastrous. He asked instead that Amin should be returned to Uganda to face a court martial or other proceedings.

The decision on Amin's future was left to Uganda's new prime minister, Milton Obote. Obote recommended that Amin should merely be reprimanded. Thus reprieved, Amin continued his climb to the top. In 1964 he was promoted to the rank of lieutenant-colonel, given command of his own battalion and appointed deputy commander of the army. He soon became a familiar figure in the capital, Kampala, introduced into Obote's inner circle, invited frequently to State House, provided with a Mercedes car and other perquisites and clearly trusted by Obote as a bluff, loyal and simple soldier who would do his bidding without too much scruple.

The early years of Uganda's independence were a time of considerable optimism. Between 1960 and 1965, Uganda, with booming exports of coffee, cotton and tea, achieved the highest per capita growth in East Africa. A carefully constructed federal constitution had enabled the ancient kingdom of Buganda to retain a measure of internal autonomy, with its own parliament, the Lukiiko, and monarchic traditions, while allowing the central government in Kampala to maintain effective control nationally. As prime minister of a coalition government, Obote set out to accommodate the disparate ethnic groups on which Uganda was built. The broad division occurred between the Bantu groups to the south, such as the Baganda, and the Nilotic and Sudanic groups of the north, such as the Acholi and Langi, to which Obote belonged; but as much rivalry was to be found among southerners or among northerners as between the north and the south. In the spirit of cooperation that prevailed after independence, Obote supported the appointment of the Baganda king, the Kabaka, Sir Edward Mutesa, as head of state in 1963.

Obote's ambitions, however, were soon to tear Uganda apart. In common with many other African leaders, he set his sights on

establishing a one-party state, arguing that tribal and factional groupings tended to threaten the stability of the country and that a
one-party state was needed to forge a sense of national unity. His style
of government became increasingly secretive and autocratic. Facing
dissent within the cabinet, Obote arranged for armed police to burst
into the cabinet room and haul five leading ministers off to prison. In
what was tantamount to a coup, he then announced he was assuming
all powers, abrogated the constitution, suspended the National
Assembly, dismissed the Kabaka as president and appointed Amin as
the new army commander. Two months later, in April 1966, he published a new constitution installing himself as executive president of a
united state endowed with immense powers.

When the Baganda parliament, the Lukiiko, tried to oppose him
and rallied supporters, Obote ordered Amin to attack the Kabaka's
palace on Mengo Hill, three miles from Kampala's centre. The palace
was shelled and ransacked and several hundred Baganda died. The
Kabaka managed to escape after climbing a high perimeter wall and
hailing a passing taxi. He spent the rest of his life in exile in London,
dependent on the dole and the generosity of friends, and died there of
alcoholic poisoning in 1969. His palace, meanwhile, was turned over
for use by Amin's troops; the Lukiiko was taken over by the defence
ministry; martial law was declared in Buganda; hundreds of Baganda
were detained without trial; and Baganda political parties were outlawed. In 1967 Obote completed the rout by abolishing the kingdom
of Buganda altogether, carving it up into four administrative districts.

Obote's position seemed impregnable. Yet his regime had come to
depend for survival largely on coercion enforced by the army and the
police. Intending to reinforce his control of the security apparatus, he
developed a secret police organisation known as the General Service
Department, recruiting members largely from his own Langi tribe and
giving it a free hand to arrest and imprison suspected opponents. He
also cultivated a personal following among senior army officers and
built up support among the large contingents of Langi and Acholi
troops in the army.

Amin, invariably shrewd and cunning when it came to his own
safety, matched Obote's manoeuvres by enlisting loyal groups of

Kakwa, Madi and Lugbara tribesmen from his home district in the West Nile region; he also recruited heavily from Nubian communities scattered in towns around Uganda, descendants of southern Sudanese mercenaries used by the British authorities to pacify areas of Uganda, who were related directly to Amin's tribal group.

Their suspicions of each other intensified. Amin was implicated in the murder of the army's deputy commander, an Acholi officer who supported Obote. Amin also faced accusations of embezzlement of army funds. Taking advantage of Obote's departure from Uganda for a Commonwealth conference, Amin struck first.

Amin's coup in January 1971 was carried out with remarkably little resistance from within the army and greeted in many parts of Uganda with relief and enthusiasm. Throughout Buganda, the news of Obote's downfall brought rejoicing and popular demonstrations. Enjoying the role of national hero, Amin began by adopting conciliatory measures. He released political prisoners, lifted emergency regulations and made arrangements for the body of the Kabaka to be brought back from England for a traditional burial. He appointed a cabinet consisting mainly of highly qualified civilians drawn from the ranks of the civil service, the legal profession and Makerere University. After the first cabinet meeting, Amin's new ministers came away impressed, so they remarked, by his good nature and common sense. 'He was a model of decorum and generosity,' wrote Henry Kyemba, the cabinet secretary. Amin's early pronouncements encouraged a sense of optimism. He stressed the temporary nature of military rule, disbanded the secret police and promised free elections. He spent much time travelling by helicopter and by car from one district to another, listening to elders and addressing meetings.

Yet Amin never felt secure. Fearing a counter-attack by Obote supporters, he organised death squads to hunt down and kill scores of army and police officers he suspected of opposing him. Within a few months, mass killing of Langi and Acholi began. 'It was impossible to dispose of the bodies in graves,' wrote Kyemba.

Instead, truckloads of corpses were taken and dumped in the Nile. Three sites were used – one just above Owen Falls Dam at Jinja, another at Bujagali Falls near the army shooting range, and a third at Karuma Falls near Murchison Falls. The intention was for the bodies to be eaten by crocodiles. This was an inefficient method of disposal. Bodies were frequently swept to the bank, where they were seen by passersby and fishermen. At Owen Falls many bodies must have been carried through the dam over which the Kampala–Jinja road ran, but many floated into the still waters to one side, near the power station.

In place of the old officer corps, Amin promoted men from his own West Nile district and Nubians, some of them from the ranks of the army, some who were raw civilians, giving them control of special units he set up to snuff out dissent. They owed no loyalty other than to Amin; they were given unlimited powers; and they came to be regarded with utter dread.

Amin's popularity soon dwindled. He had no interest in the business of government, nor indeed any understanding of it. 'His English was poor,' recalled Kyemba. 'He read very badly and clearly had a hard time just signing prepared documents. As his first Principal Private Secretary, I never ever received a handwritten note from him. Amin had no idea how governments were run.' Unfamiliar and impatient with the intricacies of administration, he ruled by whim, broadcasting his orders over the radio and plundering at will what he needed from the treasury. A huge proportion of funds was diverted to military expenditure. When budgets ran out, Amin routinely ordered the central bank to print more currency to 'solve' the problem. Ministers quickly learnt that to argue against him was both unprofitable and dangerous. Explaining his defection in 1975, Andrew Wakhweya, a finance minister, remarked: 'The government is a one-man show. Impossible decisions are taken by General Amin which ministers are expected to implement. The decisions bear no relationship to the country's available resources.' As prices soared and consumer goods became unobtainable, disillusionment with Amin's regime steadily spread.

Hoping to revive his popularity, Amin turned vindictively on Uganda's Asian community. A wealthy, aloof, immigrant minority, controlling much of the country's trade and industry, the Asians were profoundly disliked. In August 1972, in a move that was applauded not only by the African population of Uganda but in other African countries with unpopular Asian communities, Amin ordered Asians with British nationality to leave the country within three months. Their expulsion, however, benefited not the expectant African populace, but Amin's army. The shops, the businesses, the property that the Asians were forced to leave behind, even their personal possessions, were seized as spoils by Amin's cronies. Within a few months, the huge amounts of Asian wealth had vanished. Shops were stripped then left bare; factories broke down; trade was severely disrupted; entire sectors of enterprise collapsed. In the general exodus of the Asian community that occurred – some 50,000 left in all – Uganda lost a large proportion of doctors, dentists, veterinarians, professors and technicians. At a stroke, government's revenues were cut by nearly 40 per cent. The overall impact on government services was disastrous.

Far worse was to come. After an abortive invasion that Obote supporters launched from Tanzania in 1972, Amin took revenge on civilians suspected of opposing him. Thousands died at the hands of his special squads. No one was immune. The chief justice was dragged away from the High Court, never to be seen again. The university's vice-chancellor disappeared. The bullet-riddled body of the Anglican archbishop, still in ecclesiastical robes, was dumped at the mortuary of a Kampala hospital shortly after he had issued a memorandum speaking out about the 'suspicion, fear and hidden hatred' that the civilian population felt towards Amin's forces.

One of Amin's former wives was found with her limbs dismembered in the boot of a car. When Henry Kyemba reported the matter, Amin expressed no surprise and ordered him to have the dismembered parts sewn back on to the torso and then arrange for Amin to view the body together with their children. According to Kyemba, Amin was widely believed to perform blood rituals over the dead bodies of his victims. 'On several occasions when I was Minister of Health, Amin insisted on being left alone with his victims' bodies,' he wrote from exile. 'There is of course no evidence for what he does in private, but it is universally believed in Uganda that he engages in blood rituals.' On other occasions, Kyemba witnessed Amin boasting that he had eaten human flesh.

As, one by one, civilian ministers were dismissed or fled into exile, bearing tales of atrocity and torture, Amin replaced them with military colleagues, mostly untrained and in some cases barely literate. All notion of orderly government ceased to exist.

Constantly needing to demonstrate his power and importance, Amin promoted himself to the rank of field marshal, declared himself president for life, and awarded himself military medals and titles like Conqueror of the British Empire; he also claimed he was 'the true heir to the throne of Scotland'. He took sadistic pleasure in humiliating officials, usually men with wide education and experience, for whom he held an instinctive distrust. His treatment of expatriates living in Uganda, especially the British, was sometimes similarly demeaning. A group of British residents, inducted as army reservists, were required to kneel in Amin's presence when they took the oath of loyalty, as a sign of his power over his former colonial masters. To impress African diplomats at a grand Kampala reception, Amin staged his entrance on a wooden litter borne by British carriers.

He enjoyed too playing a role on the world stage, firing off bizarre cables to foreign leaders. He wished President Nixon 'a speedy recovery from Watergate'; offered Britain's music-loving prime minister, Edward Heath, a post as bandmaster after his election defeat; advised Israel's Golda Meir 'to tuck up her knickers' and run to Washington; suggested to Mao Tse-tung that he should mediate in the Sino-Soviet dispute; and proposed himself as head of the Commonwealth. In a telegram to the United Nations secretary-general, he praised the action of Palestinian guerrillas who had murdered Israeli participants at the Olympic Games, and he went on to extol Hitler's extermination of the Jews. 'Hitler and all German people knew that the Israelis are not people who are working in the interests of people of the world and that is why they burnt over six million Jews alive with gas on the soil of Germany.' By threatening to execute a British lecturer who had written a manuscript describing Amin as a 'village tyrant', he became the centre of world attention. Pleas for clemency arrived from the Queen, the British prime minister, the Pope and some fifty heads of state.

However cruel, capricious and brutal many of Amin's actions may have seemed in the West, in much of Africa he was regarded as something of a hero. By expelling the Asian community and attacking Western imperialism, he was seen to be fearlessly asserting African interests. At meetings of the Organisation of African Unity, of which he was chairman for one year in 1975, Amin's appearances, weighed down with his own medals and gold braid, inspired enthusiastic applause. He was also able to trade on his Muslim credentials, gaining valuable support and generous loans from the Arab world, notably from Saudi Arabia and Libya, in return for agreeing to promote the Islamic cause in Uganda.

The end of Amin's tyranny came in 1979. Faced with internal dissension, squabbling and rivalry within his army, Amin desperately sought a diversion and ordered the invasion of the Kagera Salient in northern Tanzania, allowing his troops to loot and plunder at will in an orgy of destruction. In retaliation, Tanzania launched a force of 45,000 men across the border and then decided to oust Amin altogether. After initial resistance, Amin's army broke and ran. Amin himself abandoned Kampala without a fight, fleeing northwards to his home in the West Nile district, eventually finding refuge in Saudi Arabia.

Amin's rule had left Uganda ravaged, lawless and bankrupt, with a death toll put at 250,000 people. When exiles were reunited with old friends on the streets of Kampala, they greeted each other in their delight with the phrase, 'You still exist!' But there was to be no respite. In 1980 Obote regained power in disputed elections, plunging Uganda into an anarchic civil war. Obote's repression was as bad as Amin's had been; his 'northern' army was accused by human rights groups of being responsible for 300,000 civilian deaths. By the time Obote was overthrown in 1985, Uganda was ranked among the poorest countries in the world.

Equatorial Guinea enjoyed only 145 days of independence before it was pitched into a nightmare of brutality and coercion that lasted for eleven years. A former Spanish colony, comprising the mainland province of Rio Muni and the main island of Fernando Po (Bioko), it achieved independence in October 1968 under a shaky coalition government led by Francisco Macías Nguema. A politician of limited education and low mental ability, Nguema had made his way up the ladder as a result of the support of Spanish administrators who believed he could be turned into a trustworthy collaborator relied upon to do their bidding. On three occasions he had failed to pass examinations qualifying him for a civil service career and *emancipado* status, succeeding the fourth time only because of overt Spanish favouritism. In 1960, under Spanish auspices, he had been appointed *alcade* – mayor – of Mongomo district in the east of Rio Muni and given a seat in the small national assembly on Fernando Po. But while being groomed for office by the Spanish, Nguema harboured intense resentments against them and an abiding hatred of foreign culture and 'intellectuals' in general. Once in power, he lashed out.

The incident that triggered his rage occurred in February 1969 when on a visit to Bata he discovered Spanish flags still flying there. His inflammatory speeches against the Spanish sent youth activists into the streets searching for Spanish victims. Fearing for their safety, thousands of Spaniards fled the country. When the foreign minister, Ndongo Miyone, sought to defuse the crisis, Nguema refused to listen. A few days later Ndongo was summoned to a meeting at the presidential palace, beaten with rifle butts, hauled off to prison with broken legs, and brutally murdered. Scores of other politicians and officials whom Nguema wanted out of the way were killed. A former ambassador died after being repeatedly immersed in a barrel filled with water for more than a week. By the end of March most of the Spanish population of 7,000, including civil administrators, teachers, technicians, professionals and shopkeepers had fled, abandoning their businesses, property and prosperous cocoa and coffee plantations.

Equatorial Guinea steadily sank into a morass of murder and mayhem. Ten of the twelve ministers in the first government were executed. In their place Nguema installed members of his own family and fellow tribesmen from the small Esangui clan from the Mongomo region. His nephew, Colonel Teodoro Obiang Nguema Mbosogo, became commander of the National Guard, military commander of Fernando Po, secretary-general of the ministry of defence and head of prisons. Other nephews were appointed to senior security posts; one simultaneously held the portfolios of finance, trade, information, security and state enterprises; a cousin ran foreign affairs. Officers in the security forces were all linked to Nguema by ties of kinship.

Given unlimited powers to arrest, torture, rape and murder, Nguema's security forces wreaked vengeance on the country's educated classes and took savage reprisals against any hint of opposition. Thousands were incarcerated in prison and murdered there; two-thirds of national assembly deputies and most senior civil servants were killed, imprisoned, or driven into exile. Many were executed on a whim. When the director of statistics published a demographic estimate that Nguema considered too low, he was dismembered to 'help him learn to count'. In two documented cases he ordered the execution of all former lovers of his current mistresses. He also ordered the murder of husbands of women he coveted. Before each state visit that Nguema made abroad, political prisoners were routinely killed to dissuade other opponents from conspiring against him. Death sentences were invariably carried out with extreme brutality. Guineans were liable to be punished merely for failing to attend manifestations of praise and joy or for being '*discontento*'. In 1976 the last remaining senior civil servants, handpicked by Nguema to replace those he had previously murdered, sent him a mass petition asking for a relaxation of the country's total isolationism, hoping there would be safety in numbers. Every one of the 114 petitioners was arrested and tortured, many never to be seen again.

No proper administration survived. The only people to be paid regularly were the president, the army, the police and the militia. Most ministries – including those dealing with education, agriculture, construction and natural resources – had no budgets at all and their offices in Malabo were shut. The central bank too was closed after the director was publicly executed in 1976. All foreign exchange was delivered instead to Nguema who hoarded it along with large amounts of local currency in his various palaces on Fernando Po and Rio Muni. When Nguema was short of money, he resorted to ransoming foreigners: $57,600 for a German woman; $40,000 for a Spanish professor; $6,000 for a deceased Soviet citizen.

In long, rambling and incoherent speeches, Nguema fulminated against his pet bugbears – education, intellectuals and foreign culture. He closed all libraries in the country, prohibited newspapers and printing presses and even banned the use of the word 'intellectual'. All formal education came to an end in 1974 when Catholic mission schools were told to close. Children from then on were taught only political slogans.

In his drive to control organised religion, he ordered church sermons to include references to him as 'The Only Miracle' and decreed that his portrait be displayed in all churches. Under threat of immediate arrest, priests were forced to reiterate slogans such as, 'There is no God other than Macías', and 'God created Equatorial Guinea thanks to Papa Macías. Without Macías, Equatorial Guinea would not exist.' Even this, though, did not satisfy him. In a series of edicts in 1974 and 1975, he banned all religious meetings, funerals and sermons and forbade the use of Christian names. Christian worship became a crime. Virtually all churches were subsequently locked up or converted into warehouses. The cathedral in Malabo was incorporated into the presidential compound and used to store weapons. Foreign priests were expelled. The last Claretine missionary was held as a hostage at the age of eighty-five and released only after a ransom had been paid.

The urban economy collapsed. On a visit to Malabo in 1977, a foreign researcher, Robert af Klinteberg, described it as a ghost town, like 'a place hit by war or plague'. Nearly all shops, market stalls and the post office, along with government ministries, were closed down; consumer goods were unobtainable; electricity supplies were erratic. Trade and commerce were replaced by barter. Goods arriving on the few ships still calling at Malabo mostly went to Nguema's clique; the rest rapidly sold out at exorbitant prices. In rural areas, cocoa and coffee production plummeted. Nigerian plantation workers on contract were treated like slave labour and left in droves. To replace them, Nguema ordered the forced recruitment of 2,500 males from each of the country's ten districts, causing an exodus of tens of thousands to neighbouring Gabon and Cameroon.

In his report on Equatorial Guinea, Klinteberg summed it up as a land of fear and devastation no better than a concentration camp – the 'cottage industry Dachau of Africa'. Out of a population of 300,000, at least 50,000 had been killed and 125,000 had fled into exile. Hardly a single intellectual remained in the country; fewer than a dozen technical school graduates survived.

Presiding over this slaughterhouse, Nguema exhibited many signs of overt madness. His conversation and ideas were increasingly disjointed; his moods swung suddenly from periods of calm to uncontrollable violence. He sometimes carried out lengthy monologues with former colleagues whom he had executed. His movements were often jerky and uncoordinated; he became progressively deaf, shouting loudly in order to hear himself, refusing the use of hearing aids; he consumed large quantities of drugs, local stimulants like bhang and iboga, that visibly affected the pupils of his eyes. He received treatment in Spain for illnesses that were never disclosed.

Ill at ease in Fernando Po, he retreated to the mainland, first to Bata, where a new presidential palace was built for him, then to live in his remote native village in Mongomo where three of his four wives lived. He took with him most of the national treasury, storing huge wads of bills in bags and suitcases in a bamboo hut next to his house. Some of the money rotted in the ground. He also kept the country's pharmaceutical store there. Surrounded by relatives and village elders, he spent hours around a campfire discussing 'state policy' and reminiscing about the good old days before white rule.

Many Guineans believed he was endowed with supernatural powers. His father, a Fang of the Esangui clan, was said to be a much feared sorcerer, and Nguema constantly used his knowledge of traditional witchcraft both to prop up his legitimacy and to keep the local population in terrified submission. At his home in Mongomo he built up a huge collection of human skulls to demonstrate his power. He invented plots, then uncovered them, in order to prove his invincibility. He used clan leaders and elders and itinerant praise singers to spread the dreaded message of his magical powers. 'You may be against Macías as long as the sun shines, but in the night you have to be for him,' one of Klinteberg's informants told him.

Nguema's demise came in 1979 as the result of a clash with his ambitious nephew Colonel Obiang Nguema and other members of his family, who feared that unless he was removed they might be dragged down with him. They were spurred on by an incident in June 1979 when six officers of the National Guard who travelled to Mongomo to ask Macías to release funds for the payment of salaries several months in arrears were summarily shot. On 3 August Obiang led a coup against his uncle. After setting fire to most of the country's fiscal reserves, Macías escaped with two suitcases of foreign currency but was captured two weeks later.

After debating whether to put him on trial or commit him to a psychiatric ward, the family decided on a trial. The trial was held in September 1979 in the Marfil cinema in Malabo. The charges included genocide, paralysis of the economy and embezzlement of public funds. Out of a total of 80,000 murders listed in the original indictment, Nguema was found guilty on 500 counts. He rejected all murder charges, suggesting that his nephew, Obiang, was responsible. 'I was head of state, not the director of prisons.' Along with five of his most brutal aides, he was sentenced to death.

Fearful of his supernatural powers, no local soldier was willing to participate in a firing squad. So the task was given to a group of Moroccan soldiers. Long after his death, Nguema's ghost was believed to be a potent force in Equatorial Guinea. But his successor, Colonel Obiang, settled in comfortably enough.

Major Mengistu Haile Mariam first gained prominence when he harangued the Derg into ordering the execution of some sixty high officials from Haile Selassie's regime. Ambitious, ruthless and cunning, he was impatient from the start for revolutionary action. Coming from a poor background, a private soldier who had worked his way up the ranks to officer training school, his career and character seemed to symbolise the driving force behind the revolution. His mother was the illegitimate daughter of an Ethiopian nobleman, his father a guard at the nobleman's house. With little formal education, he was placed with the army as a 'boy' at the age of fifteen. A dour, secretive figure, whose dark complexion and facial features linked him to one of the empire's conquered peoples of the south, he despised the rich and well-born elite that surrounded Haile Selassie's court. Stationed with the Third Division in Harar province, he acquired a record for insubordination and was constantly in trouble. One reason why he was sent as a representative to the Derg when it was first formed in Addis Ababa in June 1974 was said to be that his divisional commander simply wanted to get rid of him.

As a member of the Derg, Mengistu made common cause with the ordinary soldiers and non-commissioned officers who made up a large part of its membership and who became his power base. He also struck up close links with radical students and Marxist activists, many of whom had returned to Ethiopia from exile in 1974 demanding revolutionary change.

The changes initiated by the Derg came in swift succession. In December 1974 it proclaimed the advent of Ethiopian socialism. In January 1975 it nationalised banks and insurance companies, followed in February by all large industrial and commercial companies. In March it nationalised all rural land, abolishing private ownership and the whole system of land tenancy, thus destroying at a stroke the economic power of the old regime. To spread its message to rural areas, where 90 per cent of the population lived, it despatched the entire body of 50,000 secondary school students, university undergraduates and teachers into the countryside. 'Christ exhorted his apostles to go and teach,' a Derg official told students. 'Today Ethiopia is sending you to the countryside to enlighten the people.' In July the Derg nationalised all urban land and rentable houses and apartments. The monarchy, too, was formally abolished. The climax came in April 1976 when Mengistu appeared on radio and television to proclaim Marxism-Leninism as Ethiopia's official ideology.

As the revolution gathered momentum, Ethiopia was engulfed in strife and turmoil. Landlords and land-owners organised armed resistance; royalists and the nobility raised the banner of revolt; in one province after another, rebellions against the central government over long-held grievances flared up. In the north-western province of Begemdir a conservative opposition party, the Ethiopian Democratic Union, led by aristocrats, raised an army, succeeded in capturing towns close to the Sudan border and advanced towards the provincial capital, Gondar. In the north-east Afar tribesmen formed the Afar Liberation Front and mounted guerrilla attacks on traffic using the main road to the port of Assab on the Red Sea coast, where the country's only oil refinery was located. In Tigray province a large guerrilla force was established by the Tigray People's Liberation Front with the help of the Eritreans. In the south the Oromo Liberation Front was launched with support from Somalia. The Somalis also revived the Western Somali Liberation Front, which had lain dormant for five years, and began to infiltrate arms and equipment into the Ogaden, preparing for a new initiative to recapture their 'lost' lands.

The fiercest struggle occurred in Eritrea. When the Derg decided in November 1974 to prosecute the war in Eritrea rather than seek a negotiated settlement, Eritrean guerrillas launched a massive onslaught. By mid-1976 the guerrillas had gained control of most of the countryside and were laying siege to small army garrisons. In a desperate attempt to shore up the army's hold on Eritrea, the Derg recruited a huge peasant army from other provinces, hoping that sheer numbers would overwhelm the guerrillas. Poorly trained and armed only with ancient rifles, scythes and clubs, the peasant army was routed on the Eritrean border even before it had been deployed.

In Addis Ababa the Derg met growing opposition from radical political groups which wanted civilian control of the revolution. In September 1976 the Ethiopian People's Revolutionary Party (EPRP), drawing support from labour unions, teachers and students, all vehemently opposed to military rule, embarked on a campaign of urban terrorism against the Derg and its civilian ally, the All-Ethiopian Socialist Movement, usually known by its Amharic acronym, Meison. An assassination attempt was made on Mengistu in the centre of Addis Ababa in September, the first of nine such attempts. Scores of officials and supporters of the Derg were murdered. The Derg in turn sent out its own murder squads.

The Derg itself was split between rival factions. Mengistu demanded uncompromising action against the Derg's opponents; other officers favoured a more conciliatory approach. At a meeting of the Derg at the Grand Palace on 3 February 1977, Mengistu and his supporters suddenly left the room, leaving behind seven members he considered his enemies. Mengistu's bodyguards stormed into the room with machine guns and forced them down to the basement. Mengistu joined them there and joined in the executions. He was now in undisputed control.

Mengistu next turned ruthlessly against his civilian opponents, embarking on what he referred to as a campaign of 'red terror', licensing civilian groups – the lumpen-proletariat of the slums – to act on his behalf. 'It is an historical obligation to clean up vigilantly using the revolutionary sword,' he told his supporters. 'Your struggle should be demonstrated by spreading red terror in the camp of the reactionaries.' At a rally in Addis Ababa in April, he smashed three bottles filled with a red substance he said represented the blood of the revolution's enemies, inciting followers to avenge themselves on the EPRP. He ordered arms to be distributed to 'defence squads' formed by urban neighbourhood associations, or *kebeles*, as they were called. Months of urban warfare, assassination and indiscriminate killing followed as supporters of the EPRP, Meison and the Derg struggled for control. From the *kebeles* of the shantytowns, armed gangs hunted down students, teachers and intellectuals deemed to be 'counter-revolutionaries'. Bodies of murdered victims were left lying where they fell with signs attached to their clothing naming them as 'oppositionists' or were dumped in heaps on the outskirts of the capital. Thousands died in the red terror, thousands more were imprisoned, many of them tortured and beaten. By mid-1977 the EPRP was effectively destroyed. In the final phase of the red terror, to establish his own supremacy, Mengistu turned on his Meison allies, destroying them too. The young generation of intellectual activists who had so avidly supported the revolution were all but wiped out.

Mengistu's hold over other parts of Ethiopia was nevertheless precarious. By mid-1977 the Ethiopian army in Eritrea had lost most major towns and controlled little more than Asmara and the ports of Massawa and Assab. In July 1977 Somalia, deciding the time was ripe to take advantage of the Derg's preoccupation with Eritrea and other revolts, launched a full-scale invasion of the Ogaden. By August the Somalis controlled most of the Ogaden. In September they captured

Jijiga, an Ethiopian tank base, and pressed on towards the town of Harar and the rail and industrial centre of Dire Dawa, the third largest city in Ethiopia.

What rescued Mengistu from military defeat was massive intervention by Soviet and Cuban forces, determined to prop up his Marxist regime. In November 1977 the Soviets mounted a huge airlift and sealift, ferrying tanks, fighter aircraft, artillery, armoured personnel carriers and hundreds of military advisers to Ethiopia. A Cuban combat force numbering 17,000 joined them. Led by Cuban armour, the Ethiopians launched their counter-offensive in the Ogaden in February 1978, inflicting a crushing defeat on the Somalis. The full force of the Ethiopian army, supported by the Soviet Union, was then turned on Eritrea.

At the fourth anniversary celebrations marking the overthrow of Haile Selassie in 1978, Mengistu sat alone in a gilded armchair covered with red velvet on a platform in Revolution Square in Addis Ababa watching a procession of army units and civilian groups pass before him. Then he returned to his headquarters at the Grand Palace. Having succeeded in holding the old empire together, he liked to portray himself as following a tradition of strong Ethiopian rulers. Indeed, Mengistu came to be compared with the Emperor Tewodros, a nineteenth-century ruler who started his career as a minor local chieftain, fought his way up to take the Crown and then strove to reunite the empire after a period of disintegration. At official functions at the Grand Palace, while members of the Derg stood respectfully to one side, Mengistu chose to preside from the same ornate chair that Haile Selassie had once favoured.

One of his ministers, Dawit Wolde Giorgis, once a fervent supporter of the revolution, recalled his growing sense of disillusionment.

At the beginning of the Revolution all of us had utterly rejected anything having to do with the past. We would no longer drive cars, or wear suits; neckties were considered criminal. Anything that made you look well-off or bourgeois, anything that smacked of affluence or sophistication, was scorned as part of the old order. Then, around 1978, all that began to change. Gradually materialism became accepted, then required. Designer clothes from the best European tailors were the uniform of all senior government officials and members of the Military Council. We had the best of everything: the best homes, the best cars, the best whisky, champagne, food. It was a compete reversal of the ideals of the Revolution.

He recalled, too, how Mengistu changed once he had gained complete control.

He grew more abrasive and arrogant. The real Mengistu emerged: vengeful, cruel and authoritarian. His conduct was not limited by any moral considerations. He began to openly mock God and religion. There was a frightening aura about him. Many of us who used to talk to him with our hands in our pockets, as if he were one of us, found ourselves standing stiffly at attention, cautiously respectful in his presence. In addressing him we had always used the familiar form of 'you', *ante*; now we found ourselves switching to the more formal 'you', *ersiwo*. He moved into a bigger, more lavish office in the Palace of Menelik. He got new, highly trained bodyguards – men who watched you nervously, ready to shoot at any time. We now were frisked whenever we entered his office. He began to use the Emperor's cars and had new ones imported from abroad – bigger, fancier cars with special security provisions. Wherever he went he was escorted by these cars packed with guards, with more riding alongside on motorcycles.

He concluded: 'We were supposed to have a revolution of equality; now he had become the new Emperor.'

IN SEARCH OF *UJAMAA*

A s the dreams and expectations of independence faded, Julius Nyerere's socialist experiment in Tanzania stood out as a beacon of hope that Africa might yet find a route to the kind of new society that nationalist leaders once imagined. Nyerere was widely regarded as a leader of outstanding ability whose personal integrity and modest lifestyle was in sharp contrast to the extravagance and corruption for which other African presidents had generally become renowned. He possessed both a genuine concern for egalitarianism and an intense dislike for all forms of elitism. A slight, wiry man with a high forehead and a toothbrush moustache, he was known throughout Tanzania affectionately as *Mwalimu*, a KiSwahili word meaning teacher. He dressed simply, took no interest in the spoils of leadership or possessions and pursued his objectives with missionary zeal. Indeed, his speeches often sounded more like sermons than political addresses. He himself once admitted: 'I should have been a preacher in a pulpit instead of the president of a republic.' His intellectual energy was formidable. Articulating his socialist ideals with great clarity, he became the most influential thinker and writer in Africa of his time. On the world stage, he acted as a spokesman for the 'poorest of the poor', demanding a new international economic order that would give them a greater share in the world's wealth. He even found time to translate into KiSwahili two Shakespeare plays, *The Merchant of Venice* and *Julius Caesar*. He had many admirers abroad. In her book *The Colonial Reckoning*, published in 1961, Margery Perham, a British authority on Africa, described him as 'certainly the most poised, confident, extrovert and indeed, radiant of all the African leaders I have met'. His good intentions won him a large measure of uncritical adulation and considerable foreign aid. By the 1970s Tanzania benefited from more foreign aid per capita than any other African country. 'Tanzania became a political Mecca for liberal and socialist progressives from all over the world, anxious to see a challenge to neo-capitalism,' wrote Professor Goran Hyden, an academic at the University of Dar es Salaam.

Nyerere took on the drive for socialism virtually single-handedly. There was no inner group around him committed to socialism; no body of thinking within the ruling party; no working-class agitation; no militant peasantry; no popular expectation of radical change. It was Nyerere's own aspirations, his own ideology, that determined government policy.

For five years he propounded the merits of socialism before taking any initiative, then acted with sudden speed. Alarmed that a new acquisitive African elite was beginning to emerge in Tanzania and that traditional communal values were being eroded, he staged an intellectual coup. On 7 February 1967, he issued a statement of party principles known as the Arusha Declaration that called for national self-reliance, emphasised the need for development to begin at the lowest rural level and asserted the state's right to control all major means of production and exchange. 'Although some economic progress was being made, and although we were still talking in terms of a socialist objective, the nation was in fact drifting without any sense of direction,' he recalled. 'On balance we were drifting away from our basic socialist goals of human equality, human dignity and government by the whole people.'

The need for self-reliance meant that Tanzania would have to rely less on foreign aid, he said. 'There is in Tanzania a fantastic amount of talk about getting money from outside. Our government and different groups of our leaders never stop thinking about methods of getting finance from abroad.' Far too many ministers and civil servants were unable to conceive of a development effort except in terms of attracting foreign aid. Preoccupied with 'money, money, money', Tanzania's leaders had failed to take responsibility for their own development.

> It is stupid to rely on money as the major instrument of development when we know only too well that our country is poor. It is equally stupid, indeed it is even more stupid, for us to imagine that we shall rid ourselves of our poverty through financial assistance rather than our own financial resources . . . Firstly, we shall not get the money. There is no country in the world which is prepared to give us gifts or loans, or establish industries, to the extent that we would be able to achieve all our development targets . . . And even if all the prosperous nations were willing to help the needy countries, the assistance would still not suffice.

Moreover, to rely too much on foreign aid meant that Tanzania would be exposed to donor pressure, undermining its ability to take independent action.

> Independence means self-reliance. Independence cannot be real if a nation depends upon gifts and loans from another for its development. How can we depend upon foreign governments and companies for the major part of our development without giving to those governments and countries a great part of our freedom to act as we please? The truth is we cannot.

The only answer, Nyerere concluded, was slower growth through self-reliance and an emphasis on the development of the peasant agricultural economy. He did not rule out foreign aid but wanted it to be regarded as supplementary to a national development effort.

Attached to the Arusha Declaration was a leadership code designed to prevent the growth of a privileged elite.

> Many leaders of the independence struggle [Nyerere explained] . . .

were not against capitalism; they simply wanted its fruits, and saw independence as the means to that end. Indeed, many of the most active fighters in the independence movement were motivated – consciously or unconsciously – by the belief that only with independence could they attain that ideal of individual wealth which their education or their experience in the modern sector had established as a worthwhile goal.

To general consternation, Nyerere's leadership code stipulated that all senior government and party officials had to be 'either a peasant or a worker and should in no way be associated with the practice of capitalism'. It prohibited them from holding company shares; from holding private directorships; from receiving more than one salary; and from owning houses for rent. Their fringe benefits were cut and restrictions imposed on the importation of luxury goods. Nyerere regarded the wide income differences between the Tanzanian elite and the masses as a major immediate obstacle to an effective socialist strategy. 'Some countries believed they could develop by having a middle class and they measured progress by the number of people in the middle class. We shall be a nation of equals.'

Nyerere followed the Arusha Declaration with announcements of mass nationalisation. Without any detailed planning or legal preparation or proper cabinet discussion, he declared the nationalisation of all private banks and insurance companies, the major food processors and eight major foreign export trading companies; he also proclaimed the government's intention to take a controlling interest in a majority of sisal plantations and manufacturing companies producing cement, cigarettes, shoes and beer. The nationalisation programme later included the entire wholesaling system; and in what Nyerere termed a 'mopping up' operation, all commercial buildings, apartments and even houses – except those lived in by their owners – that were worth more than 100,000 Tanzanian shillings (about £6,000). Compensation was paid only to owners of buildings that were less than ten years old, on the grounds that owners of older buildings had already received an adequate return on their investments. The principal victims were members of the wealthy Asian community.

In September 1967, in a paper entitled *Socialism and Rural Development*, Nyerere laid out his proposals to establish self-sufficient socialist villages across the country as the basis for rural development. He termed this indigenous form of socialism as *ujamaa*, a KiSwahili word he defined in English as 'familyhood'. He believed that in time the idea of 'familyhood' and the values it encompassed could be extended beyond the village community to other ethnic groups, setting a social pattern for the country as a whole.

> Our agricultural organisation would be predominantly that of cooperative living and working for the good of all. This means that most of our farming would be done by groups of people who live as a community and work as a community. They would live together in a village; they would farm together; market together, and undertake the provision of local services and small local requirements as a community. Their community would be the traditional family group, or any other group of people living according to *ujamaa* principles, large enough to take account of modern methods and the twentieth century needs of man. The land this community farmed would be called 'our land' by all the members; the crops they produced on that land would be 'our crop'; it would be 'our shop' which provided individual members with the day-to-day necessities from outside; 'our workshop' which made the bricks from which houses and other buildings were constructed, and so on.

By bringing together the scattered rural population into *ujamaa* villages, Nyerere hoped to raise agricultural productivity; peasant farmers would gain access to modern techniques and equipment; strip farms or shambas would be replaced by large communal units; larger communities would make it easier for the government to provide the rural population with basic services such as roads, schools, clinics and water supplies.

Not only would village communities benefit all round but the *ujamaa* system would help reverse the trend towards the development of unequal classes.

The essential thing is that the community would be farming as a group and living as a group . . . The return from the produce of the farm, and from all other activities of the community, would be shared according to the work done and to the needs of the members, with a small amount being paid in taxes and another amount (which is determined by the members themselves) invested in their own future. There would be no need to exclude private property in houses or even in cattle . . .

Such living and working in communities could transform our lives in Tanzania. We would not automatically become wealthy, although we could all become a little richer than we are now. But most important of all, any increase in the amount of wealth we produce under this system would be 'ours'; it would not belong just to one or two individuals but to all those whose work had produced it.

Nyerere stressed that *ujamaa* villages would be introduced only on a voluntary basis. He was adamant that neither compulsion nor coercion would be used to establish them. 'An *ujamaa* village is a voluntary association of people who decide of their own free will to live together and work together for their common good.'

Despite official encouragement, however, the *ujamaa* campaign made slow progress. By the end of 1968 no more than 180 villages had qualified as *ujamaa* projects. Nyerere therefore set about offering inducements. 'We have to organise our party and government to assist their establishment,' declared Presidential Circular no. 1 (1969). 'We have to give them priority in all our credit, servicing and extension services – at the expense of the individual producer.' By mid-1973 the number of *ujamaa* villages had increased to 5,000, involving some 2 million people, or about 15 per cent of the population. But many were formed merely for the prospect of obtaining a water supply or a school or other government assistance. Few were run on cooperative lines. Most peasants living on the borderline of poverty were reluctant to invest their security on the fortunes of communal farms and preferred to retain their existing landholdings. Indeed, the main beneficiaries in many cases were the host of party officials, agricultural officers and community development officers paid government salaries who settled on to *ujamaa* villages like flies.

Impatient with the results, Nyerere announced the compulsory resettlement of the entire remaining rural population within three years. Explaining his decision in a radio broadcast in November 1973, he reminded Tanzanians of all the benefits his government had brought to the rural population – improving schools, providing clean water supplies, expanding the number of health facilities – and he went on to ask what the peasants had done in return, suggesting that they had done virtually nothing. They had remained idle and evaded their responsibility to make a contribution to the country's socialist development. He concluded by saying that he knew he could not turn people into socialists by force, but what his government could do was to ensure that everybody lived in a village. He wanted that to be completed before the end of 1976. 'To live in a village is an order,' he declared.

Between 1973 and 1977 some 11 million people were placed in new villages, in what amounted to the largest mass movement in Africa's history. Nyerere asserted that the movement of villagers was overwhelmingly voluntary. 'Eleven million people could not have been moved by force in Tanzania; we do not have the physical capacity for such forced movement, any more than we have the desire for it.'

Yet there were numerous reports of coercion and brutality. A university researcher reported from Mara: 'The officials decided that people should move immediately and so the police, army, national service and militiamen were mobilised to move the people. People were ill-treated, harassed, punished in the name of TANU [the ruling party] under socialism, and those who questioned it were told, "This is Nyerere's order".' A senior civil servant reported from Shinyanga: 'In some instances houses were burnt down when it was realised that some people, after having been moved, returned to their former homes again after a few days.' A researcher from Iringa wrote: 'To assure that people remained in the new villages, former houses were usually made uninhabitable by ripping out doors and windows and kicking holes in the mud walls or by setting fire to the thatch roofs. In some cases grain stored in or near the house also caught fire and the family's food supply was destroyed.'

A French writer, Sylvain Urfer, sympathetic towards the Tanzanian experiment, gave this description in his book, *Une Afrique socialiste: la Tanzanie*:

> Between August and November 1974, it was as if a tidal wave had washed over the country, with millions of people being moved in a dictatorial manner, sometimes overnight, on to waste land that they were expected to turn into villages and fields. In many places the army was called in to bring anyone who was reluctant to heel and move them *manu militari*. During the month of October the country seemed to be emerging from some national disaster, with mean huts made from branches and foliage stretching in untidy rows besides the roads.

The Tanzanian press published similar accounts, depicting scenes of people uprooted from their villages and abandoned in the bush, where they were supposed to find planned villages. 'It would be fair to say,' wrote the French agronomist, René Dumont, 'that the operation took place without any planning at all, with the bureaucrats giving orders and "villagising" on paper with no knowledge whatsoever of the regions affected, plus the local leaders' zeal to act quickly and demonstrate their diligence by cramming in the maximum number of people.'

The disruption caused by the 'villagisation' programme nearly led to catastrophe. Food production fell drastically, raising the spectre of widespread famine. Between 1974 and 1977 the deficit recorded in cereals was more than 1 million tons. Drought compounded the problem. The shortfall was made up with imports of food, but the country's foreign exchange reserves were soon exhausted. In 1975 the government had to be rescued by grants, loans and special facilities arranged with the assistance of the International Monetary Fund and the World Bank and by more than 200,000 tons of food aid. Far from helping Tanzania to become more self-reliant and to reduce its dependence on the international market economy, Nyerere's *ujamaa* programme made it dependent for survival on foreign handouts. Nor did the idea of communal farming take root. Although by 1979 some 90 per cent of the peasantry had been moved into *ujamaa* villages, a mere 5 per cent of agricultural output came from communal plots.

Other aspects of Nyerere's socialist strategy were no more successful. His programme of state control spawned a multitude of state corporations that were inefficient, incompetently managed, overstaffed and mired in debt. By 1979 some three hundred parastatal organisations had been set up – state industries, state banks, state farms, state marketing boards, state shops. They were controlled by managers who acted more like bureaucrats than businessmen and ran their domains as civil service bureaucracies, exercising considerable patronage. Workers came to regard their jobs as guaranteed by the socialist state. In a candid speech in 1977 entitled 'The Arusha Declaration Ten Years After', Nyerere complained bitterly of the inefficiency, indifference and laziness of managers and workers in state-run enterprises. 'It is essential that we should tighten up on industrial discipline. Slackness at work, and failure to give a hard day's effort in return for wages paid, is a form of exploitation; it is an exploitation of the other members of society. And slackness has undoubtedly increased since the Arusha Declaration was passed.'

But state enterprises continued to operate in the same manner, incurring huge losses. Among the most notorious were ten state-owned crop authorities. The pyrethrum board, for example, spent more on its administrative costs in 1980 than the total value of the crop it purchased; the sisal board's overheads in 1980 were higher than the amount Tanzania earned from exporting sisal. Farmers meanwhile were offered inadequate prices and faced long delays in payment, sometimes lasting up to one year, and eventually they resorted to using the black market or growing subsistence food. The production of export crops like sisal, cashew nuts and pyrethrum fell drastically in the 1970s.

By the end of the 1970s Tanzania was in dire straits. Its trade deficit was widening all the time: in 1980 exports covered only 40 per cent of the value of imports; its foreign debt had soared. With sharp increases in world oil prices, its terms of trade were constantly deteriorating. Oil imports, which used only 10 per cent of the value of exports in 1972, took 60 per cent in 1980; a ton of exported tea in 1970 bought 60 barrels of oil, but in 1980 only 4.5 barrels. The shortage of foreign currency hampered the running of factories and farms. For want of spare parts and materials, machinery and trucks were idle. Inflation and drought added to the toll. A shortage of basic commodities like soap, sugar and cooking oil and other consumer goods produced black markets, petty corruption and smuggling – *magendo*, as it was called. Manufacturing output in 1980 was reduced to less than one-third of capacity. Agriculture declined by 10 per cent between 1979 and 1982. National output between 1977 and 1982 declined by about one-third. The average standard of living between 1975 and 1983 fell by nearly 50 per cent. In a broadcast in December 1981 to mark the twentieth anniversary of Tanzania's independence, Nyerere admitted: 'We are poorer now than we were in 1972.'

Whatever difficulties Tanzania encountered, however, Nyerere held fast to his socialist strategy, dismissing all suggestions that the strategy itself might be at fault. He acknowledged that the country was neither socialist nor self-reliant, but he argued that government policy had prevented the worst excesses of capitalism, in particular the emergence of a rich and powerful elite. Comparing socialism to a vaccine, he said in 1977: 'We are like a man who does *not* get smallpox because he has got himself vaccinated. His arm is sore and he feels sick for a while; if he has never seen what smallpox does to people, he may feel very unhappy during that period, and wish that he had never agreed to the vaccination.' At a ruling party conference in 1982, Nyerere admitted that Tanzania had many 'very serious' and 'very real' problems, but socialism, he said, was not one of them. 'We have good policies. We have good plans. We have good leadership.'

Throughout Nyerere's tenure as president, few in Tanzania questioned the course on which he had embarked. It was held to be a matter of ideological faith. Indeed, no serious political discussion of any kind occurred. Under Tanzania's one-party system, parliament remained impotent; the press muzzled. Real power lay in State House in Dar es Salaam, in party committees and with a ruling class of bureaucrats, all of them intolerant of opposition. Nyerere himself was by no means averse to using Tanzania's Preventive Detention Act to silence political critics, and Tanzania for many years remained high on the list of African countries with political prisoners.

Much was achieved as a result of Nyerere's efforts, notably in the fields of education, health and social services. Primary school enrolment increased from one-quarter of the school-age population to 95 per cent; adult literacy from 10 to 75 per cent; four in ten villages were provided with clean tap water, three in ten had clinics; life expectancy increased from forty-one years to fifty-one years.

Yet what progress was made was financed largely by foreign aid. During the 1970s Tanzania received no less than $3 billion, mostly from the West. In 1982 the annual level reached $600 million. Without such funds, Tanzania would have plunged into penury. Nyerere's achievement, therefore, was related not to the success of his strategy, but to his ability to persuade foreign sponsors that his objectives were sincere.

15

THE PASSING OF THE
OLD GUARD

On the day after he was overthrown by Ghana's generals in 1966,
Kwame Nkrumah sent a telegram from Beijing to his former
secretary, Erica Powell, in London, saying, 'Take heart. I am well and
determined. You know how happy I am in such times and occasions.'
He remained confident that he would soon return to Ghana, blaming
his downfall on the machinations of imperialism. 'Don't forget that
world imperialism and neo-colonialism hate my guts and all I stand
for. They know I am in the way.'

He was given refuge in Conakry by Guinea's president, Sékou
Touré, settling into an old French colonial-style residence, Villa Syli,
on the seashore about a mile from the town centre. Many visitors
came to see him, some to plot his return to power, some to pay their
respects. Nkrumah liked to portray himself to them as 'Africa's prisoner'. But his wife and children were not among them for Nkrumah
forbade them to come, insisting they should live without him in Cairo.
For several months Sékou Touré allowed him to make broadcasts on
Radio Guinea's *Voice of the Revolution*. 'Stand firm and organise,' he told
Ghanaians. 'Continue your resistance wherever you are. I have faith in
you.' But there was no sign that anyone was listening.

As each year passed, Nkrumah still held on to the belief that an
uprising in his favour would occur. He passed the time drawing up

plans for Ghana after his return to power and devising schemes for 'The African Revolution'. He wrote several books railing against the West, with titles such as *The Handbook of Revolutionary Warfare* and *Class Struggle in Africa*, convinced that his ideas continued to reach a wide audience. He played chess and table tennis, took driving lessons from a Guinean army instructor in an old Peugeot car and in the evenings watched propaganda films provided by the North Korean and Vietnamese embassies, never losing hope that one day the call would come.

But life at Villa Syli steadily deteriorated. The roof leaked; there were power cuts; visitors came less often; his health began to fail. One of his regular visitors, June Milne, an Australian editor who helped with his publications, noticed an air of melancholy about the place. In her memoir of Nkrumah she described how on her last visit to see him in Guinea in July 1970, he asked her to witness a clandestine meeting he was due to hold with two army men from Ghana, by peeping through the keyhole of his bedroom door.

Nkrumah was in considerable pain from what a Russian doctor had diagnosed as acute lumbago but was in fact cancer.

> He could hardly walk. I had helped him to dress, holding his clothes for him and putting on his socks and shoes. He stood erect, but with the bearing not of the physically fit, but of the person who cannot bend without intense pain. He did not want the soldiers to see how incapacitated he was. But he knew he could not conceal from them the fact that he had difficulty walking. So he emerged from his room keeping very erect, but taking short steps . . .
>
> They were tall, tough-looking men, one of them bearded. Nkrumah stood still, smiling and extending his hand to greet them . . . They shook hands. Then Nkrumah raised the stick he was carrying and said: 'You see. I have a stick. I have some small trouble with lumbago!' The men grinned nervously. Nkrumah pointed to the chairs. 'Why don't you sit down?'
>
> He painfully walked to the nearest chair and sat on the edge of it, his back unbending. They were some distance away at the far end of the long sitting room. I did not hear any more what was said.

But the whole scene appeared so dreadful that I felt choked. The very chairs they sat on showed their deterioration since 1966. The stuffing was sticking out through the frayed and faded covers. There was only one electric light bulb which worked . . . It all lasted less than fifteen minutes. Nkrumah stood to see them leave. Then he returned to his room. He looked drained.

In August 1971 Nkrumah flew to Bucharest for medical treatment. He died in hospital there on 27 April 1972. The will that he had prepared began 'I, Kwame Nkrumah of Africa' and charged his executors to 'cause my body to be embalmed and preserved', like Lenin. If this was not possible, then he asked for his body to be cremated 'and the ashes scattered throughout the African continent, in rivers, streams, deserts, savannas, etc'. His body was flown to Ghana in July 1972 and buried in his home village.

The triumphs that Colonel Gamal Abdel Nasser enjoyed during his first years in power were followed by a catalogue of disappointments and disasters. All his Pan-Arab ambitions, his hopes for an 'Arab socialist revolution', turned sour. A merger he arranged with Syria to form a 'United Arab Republic' ended in rancour and recrimination – 'three and a half years of endless troubles', he subsequently described it. On the rebound, he despatched a military expedition to sort out the Yemeni civil war but his intervention resulted only in a ruinously costly adventure there, tying down a third of the Egyptian army for five years. He quarrelled constantly with other Arab governments, retreating more and more into isolation. Most disastrous of all was Egypt's humiliating defeat in the Six Day War against Israel in 1967 which ended with Israel's occupation of Sinai, the loss of the Sinai oilfields and the closure of the Suez Canal. After this debacle Nasser described himself like 'a man walking in a desert surrounded by moving sands not knowing whether, if he moved, he would be swallowed up by the sands or would find the right path'. Anthony Nutting, who met him shortly after the war, found him a changed man. 'Gone was much of the self assurance of bygone years, gone too any pretensions to be the leader of the Arab renaissance,' Nutting wrote. 'As he confided to me with a wan smile, with no army or air force to defend his own country, he could scarcely aspire to the leadership of any other.' Along with all the setbacks, Nasser was dogged by ill-health. As a result of diabetes, he developed a painful arteriosclerosis condition in his upper legs which left him at times severely debilitated. In 1969 he suffered a heart attack. Much of his old drive and energy faded.

He also faced growing disaffection over the tight grip he insisted on maintaining over Egypt. Student demonstrations erupted in 1968 in protest against police interference in university affairs and the suffocating security apparatus that affected every aspect of Egyptian life. Nasser's critics maintained that so much of his regime was designed to enhance his personal control, the rest was in fact hollow. While he expounded enthusiastically about socialism, for example, he never countenanced the presence of socialists nor did he set up institutions needed for the development of a socialist programme. His pronouncements on socialism and economic development were dismissed as muddled and banal. Added to such criticism was discontent over economic difficulties. Though industry's share of national output rose by about 50 per cent, the price for Nasser's over-ambitious economic plans was inflation, shortages of basic essential commodities, debt, an inflated public-sector payroll, stifling controls and urban overcrowding.

Yet whatever disasters befell Egypt, Nasser never lost his popularity with the masses. When, after the 1967 defeat, he announced his resignation, popular protests propelled him back to office. His reputation as the man who had stripped the old ruling class of their power, nationalised their wealth, booted out foreigners, restored to Egypt a sense of dignity and self-respect and led the country towards national regeneration – all of this counted for far more than the setbacks. Nasser skilfully played the populist card at every opportunity, presenting himself as the spokesman for the people, denouncing the foreign imperialists, bourgeois intellectuals, bureaucrats and money-grabbers whom they regarded as the enemy.

His lifestyle was suitably modest. He continued to live in the middle-class house in Manshiet el-Bakri that he had acquired as a young lieutenant-colonel, adding extra rooms and annexes from time to time. He enjoyed a happy family life with his wife Tahia and their five children, preferring to return home for lunch whenever possible. His tastes in food were simple. He devoured newspapers, but took little interest in highbrow literature or the arts. His favourite form of entertainment was the cinema – either Hollywood films or long Egyptian sagas of unrequited love. He listened endlessly to song-poems sung by Um Kulthum, but little else. He liked ties, owned about 250 of them, most of them gifts; he possessed a large number of cameras; but he showed little interest in money-making or acquiring valuable possessions. Nor did he give lavish parties.

There were many paradoxes about Nasser's regime. He was the man who overthrew the Egyptian monarchy but became in effect the uncrowned monarch of Egypt. His form of socialism brought little benefit to the poor whom he championed but allowed the bourgeoisie, whom he despised, to play a greatly expanded role in running industry and commerce that he nationalised.

Yet to the masses he remained an idol. And when he died of a heart attack on 28 September 1970 at the age of fifty-two, there were genuine outpourings of grief. Four million people attended his funeral, many feeling that Egypt had been left an orphaned nation.

In the fifteen years that he presided over Kenya, Jomo Kenyatta enjoyed massive authority. Even critics of his government accorded him due respect. In his old age he ruled not so much by exercising direct control over the government as by holding court with an inner circle of loyal ministers and officials, predominantly Kikuyu from his home district of Kiambu, whom he entrusted with the administration of the country. Kenyatta's court moved with him wherever he chose to stay. His favourite residence was his country home at Gatundu in the hills above Nairobi, where he was born; but he was also to be found at State House in Nairobi or at lodges in Mombasa on the coast and at Nakuru in the Rift Valley. Wherever he was resident, he held regular audiences. His court was open to delegations, petitioners and visitors of all kinds. Sometimes they arrived in huge numbers, accompanied by teams of dancers. For Kenyatta delighted in displays of dancing, and many evenings were spent watching them. He himself performed expertly as a dancer until he suffered from a heart attack in 1972, six years before his death.

In contrast to the socialist programmes fashionable in Africa at the time, Kenyatta adhered to capitalist policies, encouraging both indigenous private enterprise and foreign investment. With government assistance, an expanding African middle class grasped opportunities in the civil service, agriculture, commerce and industry. Senior civil servants were permitted to run their own business ventures. The African share of new companies formed after independence rose from 19 per cent of the total in 1964 to 46 per cent in 1973. Kenyatta's government was also vigorous in promoting local self-help development organisations known as *Harambee* – a KiSwahili word meaning 'pull together' – that were responsible for the construction and operation of schools, health clinics and water provision. 'God', Kenyatta liked to remind his audiences, 'helps those who help themselves.'

With the aid of British funds, the former White Highlands were transferred to African owners, defusing the issue of land hunger that had propelled the Mau Mau rebellion. White farmers were bought out both by smallholders and by other African owners, often members of the Kenyan elite. By 1971 a total of 1.5 million acres had been acquired for settlement schemes involving some 500,000 people; a further 1.6 million acres were sold privately to African owners. By 1977 only about 5 per cent of the mixed-farm area within the former White Highlands remained in expatriate hands. Africans also gained increasing ownership of corporate ranches and coffee plantations. The growth of agricultural incomes resulting from these changes was remarkable. Between 1958 and 1968 the gross farm revenues of smallholders grew by 435 per cent. Within a decade of independence the marketed output of Kenya's smallholder and peasant sector – including cash crops like coffee, tea, pyrethrum and horticultural produce – equalled that of large farms. In the 1970s the annual growth rate of agriculture was 5.4 per cent. The capital, Nairobi, reflected Kenya's growing prosperity. It flourished as an international business and conference centre, its skyline constantly changing with the construction of new hotels and office blocks. Foreign tourists flocked to the country's spectacular wildlife parks and coastal resorts, providing a major source of revenue. Overall, the economic record of the Kenyatta years was impressive. Gross domestic product rose on average by 6 per cent a year in the 1960s and by 6.5 per cent in the 1970s. The annual average growth rate of per capita incomes between 1960 and 1979 was 2.7 per cent.

Yet these figures disguised a wide disparity: while the rich got richer, the level of rural poverty increased. Despite the land transfer programme, the problem of land hunger continued. Less than 20 per cent of Kenya's land was arable, and the large proportion of the population packed into that area grew at one of the fastest rates in the world. In 1962 the population stood at 8 million; by 1978 it had reached 15 million.

Kenyatta's capitalist strategy aroused fierce dissension within Kenya's one-party system. A former Mau Mau leader, Bildad Kaggia, attacked the government for allowing land to pass into the hands of individual Africans, some of whom were able to amass considerable landholdings. He warned of the dangers of letting a new class of African landholders replace white settlers while landless Africans were struggling to survive. Instead of compensating white farmers, he wanted their land to be distributed free to the landless and to ex-Mau Mau fighters.

A more general assault on the direction of government policies was made by a prominent Luo politician, Oginga Odinga, whom Kenyatta had appointed vice-president after independence. As well as free distribution of white-owned land, he advocated a programme of nationalisation of foreign-owned enterprises and a shift in foreign policy away from Kenya's close links with Western countries in favour of new ties to the Eastern bloc.

Kenyatta was ruthless in dealing with any challenge to his authority. Once a Moscow-trained revolutionary himself, he accused Odinga's faction of harbouring communist allegiances. 'Some people try deliberately to exploit the colonial hangover for their own interest, to serve some external force,' he said in 1965. 'To us, communism is as bad as imperialism.' When Odinga resigned from the government and set up an opposition party with a small core of supporters, the government harassed it at every turn. Kenyatta portrayed the opposition as subversive and 'tribalistic'. In 1969 Odinga was arrested and his party banned. Once again Kenya became a one-party state.

In the 1970s Kenyatta faced a more formidable critic. A young, ambitious Kikuyu politician, J. M. Kariuki, who had once been detained by British authorities during the Mau Mau era, emerged as a champion of the poor and landless, with a popular following that came close to rivalling Kenyatta's own. Kariuki's goal, quite openly, was to inherit the presidency after Kenyatta's death. He built his popularity with a sustained attack on the scramble for land and wealth that so occupied the Kenyan elite. 'A stable social order', he declared, 'cannot be built on the poverty of millions. Frustrations born of poverty breed turmoil and violence.'

In truth, Kariuki was not a particularly admirable character. A playboy, an inveterate gambler, he himself owned two farms, a racehorse, a light aircraft and several cars; he also had a reputation for sharp business practices. But he possessed an unerring popular touch and he skilfully exploited the groundswell of discontent that was building up over the greed and corruption clearly evident at the top of Kenyan society.

Kenyatta himself was never a target of such criticism, but members of his own family – 'the royal family', as they were known – aroused strong resentment. The focus of attention rested mainly on the activities of two members in particular: his young wife, Ngina – 'the wife of his old age' – and his daughter, Margaret, the mayor of Nairobi. Both operated business empires and ruthlessly used their link with Kenyatta for personal gain. Ngina Kenyatta became one of the richest individuals in the country with interests that included plantations, ranches, property and hotels. Both were involved in the ivory trade. During the Kenyatta years, high-level corruption cost Kenya half of its elephant population; at least 70,000 elephants were slaughtered.

In his role as champion of the poor, Kariuki persistently attacked the activities of the elite. He called for 'a complete overhaul of the existing social, economic and political systems in Kenya,' claiming that 'a small but powerful group of greedy, self-seeking elite in the form of politicians, civil servants and businessmen has steadily but very surely monopolised the fruits of independence to the exclusion of the majority of our people.' He never mentioned names, but no one was left in any doubt to whom he was referring when he said, 'We do not want a Kenya of ten millionaires and ten million beggars.' Kariuki also dwelt provocatively on the issues over which the Mau Mau rebellion had been fought, a topic that in public was virtually forbidden. 'Our people who died in the forests died with a handful of soil in their right hands, believing that they had fallen in a noble struggle to regain our land . . . [but] . . . we are being carried away by selfishness and greed.' The end result, he warned, would be violence. 'Unless something is done the land question will be answered by bloodshed.'

To the ruling elite, Kariuki represented a clear threat. In March 1975 he was murdered, his body dumped at the foot of the Ngong Hills outside Nairobi. Subsequent investigations implicated members of Kenyatta's inner circle.

In his last years, Kenyatta showed less and less interest in the business of government. Much of his time he spent pottering about his two farms, either at Gatundu or at Rongai in the Rift Valley. In private his thoughts turned to religion; he was given to lecturing visitors on the finer points of theology. And he liked to recall the past – the dour Scottish missionaries who so influenced his childhood. His favourite relaxation, though, was to construct complex riddles – the peculiar delight of the Kikuyu people – in the company of his brother-in-law Mbiyu Koinange. Then at times he would feel lonely and complain with emotion of old friends deserting him. The morning was his best time. He would rise at dawn and occasionally place an early telephone call to his ministers. In the evening he still enjoyed watching tribal dancers. He would retire to bed early, sometimes dropping asleep in the front of the television news. His aides would creep in to switch off the set. He died on 23 August 1978.

Léopold Senghor often said he would prefer to be remembered as a poet than as a politician. As president of Senegal, he continued to write poetry that received acclaim. His collection, *Nocturnes*, published in 1961 won a prize for the best poetry collection in French published by a foreigner. A review in the respected *Figaro Littéraire* in April 1961 called him 'one of our greatest living writers'.

His presidency received less favourable reviews. The close ties he maintained with France prompted accusations from radicals that he was lending himself to neocolonial interests rather than promoting the kind of African socialism he claimed to support. He relied on French advisers, allowed French companies to continue their domination of trade and industry, and kept a French praetorian guard at a military base on the perimeter of Dakar's international airport to ensure national security. He rebuffed demands for the nationalisation of French and other foreign companies, arguing that it would 'kill the goose that laid the golden egg'. French capital, he insisted, was essential to Senegal's economic development. He refused to countenance a more rapid rate of Africanisation – to Africanise at a discount, as he put it – by allowing unqualified Africans to take over jobs from qualified Frenchmen. In Dakar the French population actually grew after independence. He also continued to spend much time in Paris and at his wife's family home in Normandy.

Despite French assistance, Senegal's economy, heavily dependent on groundnut exports, remained largely stagnant. Senghor put an end to a promising programme of rural reform that encouraged peasant cooperatives not because it encountered difficulties but because it threatened the interests of powerful Muslim Brotherhoods who dominated groundnut production and whose political support Senghor needed. A series of droughts affected groundnut production. Exports of groundnuts in shell fell in 1960–70 by 5.5 per cent and in 1970–9 by 8.4 per cent; exports of groundnut oil rose at first by 4.4 per cent, but then fell by 3.5 per cent. When French subsidies for groundnut prices were withdrawn during the 1960s, Senegal had to sell at world market prices that were substantially lower. Its terms of trade were also adverse. A centralised system of groundnut management that Senghor introduced soon became bogged down in incompetence and corruption.

Overall, gross domestic product grew at 2.5 per cent a year from 1960 to 1979, but the average annual growth of population of 2.4 per cent in the 1960s and 2.6 per cent in the 1970s effectively cancelled out the increase. Average incomes for the whole period between 1960 and 1979 declined by 0.2 per cent. At the same time Senegal became increasingly encumbered by external debt. External debt rose from $98 million in 1970 to $738 million in 1979; and debt service from $6.7 million to $130 million. By 1979 Senegal was heavily dependent on foreign aid; net official assistance in that year represented $56 a head – more than 12.5 per cent of total per capita incomes and 13 per cent of gross domestic product.

Senghor steered through these difficulties with a mixture of compromise, coercion and pork-barrel politics. He kept the support of the Muslim Brotherhoods by providing marabouts (religious leaders) with special favours, such as large 'loans' and strategically placed development projects. He bought off political opponents by offering them government posts and material benefits. He reacted to student protests over neocolonialism and corruption with strong-arm tactics – tear gas and arrests.

Approaching the age of seventy, Senghor appeared to have lost the common touch for which he was once renowned. He had become a remote figure, distancing himself from the predicaments of ordinary life, no longer venturing into the countryside except to confer with his supporters, the marabouts, still proclaiming the merits of African socialism and négritude but dealing with dissent with an iron fist. French literary critics who reviewed his poetry in French journals bemoaned the contradiction between his gift for subtle poetry and his authoritarian politics.

But just when it seemed that Senegal was slipping towards being another corrupt one-party state, Senghor rejuvenated the political system by launching an innovative version of multi-party politics. New laws in 1976 authorised the establishment of three political parties, each of which was given a defined ideological framework. Senghor's *Union Progressiste Sénégalaise* occupied the central position as a 'socialist and democratic' party, leaving allocated spaces to its right for a 'liberal and democratic' party and to its left for a 'Marxist-Leninist or communist' party. In explaining this arrangement, Senghor argued that the proliferation of too many small parties would threaten political stability, but that the existence of choice was essential for the needs of African socialism. Two new parties were duly registered. In elections in 1978, Senghor's party, renamed *Parti Socialiste*, won 80 per cent of the vote and 82 seats; the 'liberal democratic' *Parti Démocratique Sénégalaise* won 18 seats; and the Marxists, with just over 3,000 votes, won nothing.

Another innovation was sprung in 1980. At the age of seventy-four, Senghor announced his decision to resign in favour of his protégé, Abdou Diouf, a skilful technocrat. Senghor thus became the first African leader since independence to give up power voluntarily. The tradition of multi-party politics he established in Senegal survived. In 1981 Diouf passed legislation allowing for the legalisation of all political parties – 'an opening up, but with firmness'. By 1983 fourteen political parties had been legally recognised, including five from the far left. Diouf went on to win elections in 1983, 1988, 1993 and 1998, accepting defeat in 2000.

The ultimate accolade for Senghor came after his retirement. In 1984 he was elected to membership of the French Academy, one of forty living 'immortals', as they are called, each considered to have made an enduring contribution to the legacy of French culture and statecraft. It was the highest honour France awarded to its men of letters. Senghor died in France in 2001 at the age of ninety-five.

In neighbouring Guinea, Ahmed Sékou Touré inhabited a world of conspiracies. He spoke frequently of what he called a 'permanent plot' to overthrow his regime, a vast conspiracy, so he claimed, organised by Western powers and other enemies of the 'Guinean revolution'. Some plots were undoubtedly real; some were contrived; others were simply fictitious. Touré used plots as a pretext for liquidating his opponents, whether there was evidence against them or not. Discovering plots became an instrument of government, a device to deal not only with critics and dissenters but ordinary people at times of economic crisis. His regime became notorious for show trials, public executions, arbitrary imprisonment and the use of torture. About one fifth of Guinea's population emigrated to neighbouring African countries, mostly to escape his harsh domestic policies. Few of Touré's close associates escaped unscathed. More than fifty ministers were shot or hanged, or died in detention, or served prison sentences. Among them was Diallo Telli, a distinguished Guinean diplomat who had served as the first secretary-general of the Organisation of African Unity; Telli was imprisoned, tortured and then subjected to '*la diète noire*', a drawn-out form of execution which consisted of depriving a prisoner of food and water until he died. Through all the chaos his regime engendered, Touré battled grimly on, as the historian John Dunn noted, 'like an eighteenth century prizefighter blinded by his own blood'.

The plots and purges started in 1960, only two years after Guinea became independent. Touré announced he had discovered a conspiracy by French nationals and Guinean dissidents to assassinate him, and arrested scores of people; some died under torture. In 1961 he announced the discovery of a 'teachers' plot' after teachers had demanded equal pay for equal work and criticised government policies; prominent teachers and intellectuals were detained, and the Soviet ambassador was summarily expelled, accused of meddling in Guinea's affairs. In 1965, after a group of traders tried to form an opposition party and nominated a candidate to stand in the presidential election against Touré, they were arrested and condemned to death. In 1970, when Portuguese troops from neighbouring Portuguese Guinea launched an abortive invasion aiming to overthrow Touré and destroy the nationalist guerrilla headquarters he allowed to operate from Conakry against the Portuguese, Touré used the occasion to carry out a massive purge. On the pretext that a 'fifth column of internal stooges of imperialism and neocolonialism' was at work, hundreds of people, including ministers, ambassadors and party leaders were arrested and put on trial before a 'supreme revolutionary court'. They were given no opportunity to defend themselves nor to retain lawyers nor even to see or talk to the judges. Some fifty-eight accused were later hanged in public in what the government called a carnival atmosphere. In 1972 a medicine shortage was described by Touré as a 'plot by the physicians to discredit the Revolution'. He also interpreted news of a cholera epidemic in Guinea in 1973 as a counter-revolutionary plot. Even Guinea's defeat in the finals of the African soccer championship in 1976 was viewed as a plot. 'The psychosis of permanent plots instilled fear among the citizenry and coerced them to comply,' wrote Lansiné Kaba, an exile. 'In this inferno, no one was safe, including the party's faithful servants and dignitaries.'

Guinea was potentially a rich country, with well-watered coastal plains and extensive uplands offering huge agricultural potential and vast deposits of bauxite and iron ore. But Touré's economic strategy proved ruinous. To free Guinea from its subordination to France and to prevent the rise of an elite entrepreneurial class in the country, he extended state control to every sector of the economy. Independent traders were denounced as bourgeois traitors to the revolution and replaced by a huge state trading corporation; new state industries were launched as part of an ambitious industrialisation programme; agricultural cooperatives were established; and public works expanded. Yet there was no coherent planning behind the schemes and few trained Guineans to manage them. The result was a string of state corporations that were badly managed, heavily in debt, rife with corruption and crippled by low production. The agricultural cooperatives also failed and, as a result of low crop prices set by the government, food production declined. Whereas at independence Guinea was almost self-sufficient in food, it soon became heavily dependent on food imports.

Despite the chaos and disruption it caused, Touré carried his campaign against small African traders and transporters to even greater lengths. In 1977 a government decree closed all village markets – a major feature of life in Guinea – and accorded state enterprises, run by local party and government officials, a total monopoly on local trade. All farmers were required to deliver their crops to these enterprises. This decree and other grievances over the shortage of goods and the rough treatment dealt out by Touré's 'economic police' led to protest demonstrations by market women, which began in rural centres, then spread to provincial towns and finally erupted in the capital. When market women in Conakry marched on the presidential palace, government troops were instructed to fire on them. The party newspaper, *Horoya*, described the incident as part of the 'historical struggle between revolution and counter-revolution'. Touré himself resorted to blaming 'the fifth column'.

What saved Guinea from complete ruin was the revenue derived from the country's bauxite mines which Touré was careful to leave in the hands of foreign companies. The giant foreign conglomerate at Fria commenced production in 1960 and within a year provided almost three-quarters of total exports and foreign exchange earnings. By 1975, with production running at 9 million tons annually, bauxite and alumina made up 95 per cent of all exports and one-third of gross domestic product.

After twenty years of enforced socialism, Touré began to retreat, permitting some private business and trading firms to operate, and disbanding the 'economic police'. He also began to make overtures to Western investors. 'For the first twenty years we have concentrated on developing the mentality of our people,' he explained in 1979. 'Now we are ready to do business with others.' In 1982 he travelled to New York to appeal to Wall Street financiers for increased private investment in Guinea. He died in 1984, not at the hands of an assassin, as many had expected, but undergoing a heart operation in an American hospital.

16

THE SLIPPERY SLOPE

Given the array of adversities that Africa faced at the time of independence, the advances made in the two decades after 1960 were remarkable. In the field of education, school enrolment in black Africa grew faster than in any other developing region. Primary-school enrolment increased from 36 per cent to 63 per cent of the age group; enrolment at secondary level increased from 3 per cent to 13 per cent; universities turned out thousands of graduates each year. A World Bank study published in 1981 observed: 'The African record is unique: nowhere else has a formal education system been created on so broad a scale in so short a time.' Similar improvements were recorded in the field of medical care. Child death rates fell from 38 to 25 per thousand; life expectancy increased from 39 to 47 years; the numbers of medical and nursing personnel per capita doubled, despite a large increase in the population. New infrastructures were built at a record-breaking pace: ports, railways, roads and buildings. The number of miles covered by all-weather roads tripled, opening up vast areas of the interior for the first time.

Despite the eruption of military coups, civil strife and political instability, a sense of optimism about Africa's future prevailed throughout the 1960s. It was still spoken of as a continent with vast potential. The economic record, though not fulfilling earlier hopes, showed modest progress. The average annual increase in gross domestic product for black Africa in the 1960s was 3.9 per cent; taking population growth into account, the per capita increase amounted to 1.3 per cent.

The scale of Africa's difficulties became clearer, however, when comparisons were made with the world's developing countries as a whole. The increases in gross domestic product and per capita incomes were lower in black Africa than elsewhere: 3.9 per cent compared to an average of 4.5 per cent; and 1.3 per cent compared to an average of 3.5 per cent. As a group, African economies performed poorly in the 1960s by comparison to Latin America and East Asia. School enrolments, despite the massive increases, were still about half the average for low-income countries, and literacy rates were well below the mean for the developing world. Nevertheless, in retrospect, the 1960s came to be seen as halcyon years.

In the 1970s Africa was struck by a series of calamities. A prolonged drought between 1968 and 1973 had a devastating impact on the Sahel region, a thin strip of semi-arid land south of the Sahara desert stretching across parts of Niger, Mali, Chad, Mauritania, Senegal, Upper Volta (Burkina Faso) and Nigeria. In 1972 Mali lost 40 per cent of its cattle and 40 per cent of its food production. In the northern region of Nigeria, where groundnuts were the staple crop, official production dropped from 765,000 tons in 1968–9 to 25,000 tons in 1972–3. Lake Chad shrank to a fraction of its previous size. Areas of eastern and southern Africa too suffered periodically from drought.

In 1973 came the first of the oil shocks. In the wake of the 1973 Arab–Israeli war, crude oil prices increased from about $3 a barrel at the beginning of 1973 to more than $12 in 1974. A second shock came in 1979. As a result of events in Iran and Iraq, the price of oil rose from $19 a barrel in April 1979 to $38 in early 1981. All oil-importing states were adversely affected. World Bank estimates in its 1981 study showed that for a sample of eight oil-importing African states – Ethiopia, Ghana, Kenya, Madagascar, Senegal, Sudan, Tanzania and Zambia – oil imports as a percentage of export earnings rose from 4.4 per cent in 1970 to 23.2 per cent in 1980. The effect was to put a severe strain on their balance of payments, forcing governments to reduce imports of many essential goods and to raise domestic costs and prices. Agriculture was hit by higher fuel and fertiliser costs and shortages of equipment. Industry suffered similar problems, with many factories operating at low levels for lack of imports. As a result of international recession in the 1970s, mineral producers such as Zambia and Zaire (Congo-Kinshasa) faced a slump in commodity prices; both produced copper at a loss.

But the terms of trade did not deteriorate for everyone. The World Bank noted that, apart from mineral producers, most African countries experienced either favourable or neutral terms of trade in the 1970s. Oil-exporting countries such as Nigeria, Gabon, Congo-Brazzaville, Algeria and Libya made spectacular gains and other primary exporters showed a strong upward trend, mainly as a result of a boom in prices for coffee, cocoa and tea between 1976 and 1978. On average, said the World Bank, African oil importers experienced less deterioration in their terms of trade than did most other oil-importing countries in the world. The main causes of Africa's growing economic malaise were not external factors, like the increases in oil costs, but internal factors.

The drive for industrialisation, regarded as the key to economic development by most African governments, had encountered severe difficulties. Most import-substitution industries, protected by high tariff barriers and government subsidies, proved economically inefficient. Many required substantial inputs of imported machinery and raw materials, often costing more in foreign exchange than the value of the imported products they were intended to replace. The markets for their products were often too small to achieve economies of scale. In terms of costs, quality and output, they were generally uncompetitive. Private investors, both foreign and domestic, were deterred by numerous obstacles – bureaucratic obstruction, stringent regulations, import licensing, political risk, the shortage of skilled labour and operational hazards like unreliable electricity supplies and malfunctioning telephone systems. Most state corporations in manufacturing, trade, transport and public utilities, launched in the hope that they would become self-financing enterprises, generating further funds for investment and stimulating modernisation, were inefficiently managed, overstaffed, subjected to frequent political meddling and requiring huge government subsidies to keep them afloat. Few countries possessed enough skilled managers to run them effectively. Mali, a poor country even by African standards, set up twenty-three state enterprises after independence, all of which fell into muddle and chaos, accumulating huge deficits; its list of state enterprises included garages, repair shops, metal works, a printing plant, pharmacies and bookshops. Zambia, rich from copper revenues, squandered its fortunes on a host of high-cost, loss-making, inefficient state corporations. Senegal's parastatal organisations, numbering in all more than one hundred, were estimated to employ four times the manpower they needed. Summarising a series of investigations into parastatal organisations in Benin, Chris Allen, an academic researcher, wrote: 'The institutions were found to be hierarchical, authoritarian and highly bureaucratic, leading to failure to perform essential tasks, to waste and inefficiency. The personnel, apart from being in many cases unqualified or ill-qualified, tended to be idle, undisciplined, arrogant and above all corrupt, so that fraud as well as inefficiency abounded within the parastatal sector.' In many countries, state-owned enterprises were simply badly planned from the start. A sympathetic critic of Guinea's economic policy, Claude Rivière, wrote in exasperation: 'To set up a cannery without products to can, a textile factory that lacked cotton supplies, a cigarette factory without sufficient locally grown tobacco, and to develop . . . a forest region that had no roads and trucks to carry its output – all of these were gambles taken by utopian idealists and ignoramuses.'

State-owned companies became the centre of a web of corruption. Ministers preyed on parastatal corporations under their control for contributions to political funds and foreign trips and for providing jobs for family, friends and kinsmen. Tenders were often awarded to dubious companies that never delivered goods and services. Project costs were grossly inflated to allow for kickbacks, rendering many projects uneconomical. Company assets were routinely stolen. Payrolls were padded with 'phantom' workers – bogus employees. Government-owned banks, a prime target, were obliged to lend large loans to politicians, their wives and associates without any prospect that they would ever be repaid. A report on Uganda's state-owned bank concluded : 'To every regime, the Uganda Commercial Bank was a gravy train. New ministers, army officers and parliamentarians would descend upon it and take out huge loans, often with inadequate or non-existent collateral . . . These people saw the loans as rewards for bringing the government to power.'

The initial spurt of industrialisation soon petered out. Manufacturing output in the 1960s, starting from a low base, expanded by 8 per cent a year, outpacing the average for developing countries. In the 1970s manufacturing growth reached only 5 per cent. By the 1980s much of Africa was facing 'de-industrialisation'. Foreign investors looked to more promising markets in Asia and Latin America. The only segment of industry that continued to attract investment was mining and oil.

The outcome for agriculture was even worse. Agriculture was Africa's principal economic sector. Four out of every five people were engaged in agriculture. Yet African leaders, with their attention fixed on industrial and manufacturing programmes and other enterprises, regarded the agricultural sector as having secondary importance. It was seen as useful primarily for taxation purposes. The marketing boards set up under colonial rule as monopoly purchasers of agricultural crops provided an invaluable source of revenue. Following Nkrumah's example, governments set out to obtain a surplus from the agricultural sector in order to finance urban and industrial development, paying farmers for their export crops a fraction of what they received on world markets. They were far more preoccupied with meeting the needs of urban groups that were politically important to them – civil servants, industrial workers and students – than attending to the inter- ests of scattered rural populations. Above all, they were determined to keep down urban costs for fear of political protest. Governments thus paid low prices for food crops to provide urban consumers with cheap food. They also maintained overvalued exchange rates to reduce both the cost of food imports, like wheat, corn and rice favoured by the urban elite, and the cost of other goods they cherished – like cars, household appliances and fashionable attire. The effect was to penalise farmers at every turn. Farm exporters lost income; food producers found it difficult to compete against subsidised imports. Many farmers obtained less than half of the real value of their crops. In some cases, farmers were not paid enough even to cover their costs of production; cocoa producers in Ghana and sisal growers in Tanzania were two examples. A study completed in 1981 showed that rice growers in Mali were paid by the government 63 francs for a kilo of rice that cost them 80 francs to produce.

The agricultural sector was further burdened with inefficient state-run marketing and distribution agencies which operated at a huge cost but provided a poor service. Farmers were frequently paid months in arrears; crops were not collected in time; fertilisers, seeds and pesti-cides were delivered late; shortages of supplies led to corruption and favouritism. Government support services were both inadequate and overstaffed. The salaries of the Congo-Brazzaville government's agri-cultural staff in 1971 exceeded the incomes of 600,000 peasants. Some governments favoured large, capital-intensive farming schemes, subsi-dising their costs of operations and according them far more favourable treatment than private farmers; but they too suffered from technical and management failures and accumulated heavy losses.

Farming became an increasingly unattractive occupation. Faced with low producer prices, inadequate marketing systems, poor exten-sion services, lack of investment in rural areas and shortages of credit facilities, farmers deserted in droves, some heading for urban areas, some resorting to subsistence agriculture. Farmers considering polit-ical action to demand higher prices faced huge risks. Interviewing a wealthy cocoa farmer in Ghana in 1978, Robert Bates, an academic researcher, asked why he did not organise support among his col-leagues for higher cocoa prices. 'He went to his strongbox and produced a packet of documents: licences for his vehicles, import permits for spare parts, titles to his real property and improvements, and the articles of incorporation that exempted him from a major por-tion of his income taxes. "If I tried to organise resistance to the government's policies on farm prices," he said while exhibiting these documents, "I would be called an enemy of the state and I would lose all these." '

In a number of individual countries the results were disastrous. Ghana's cocoa production, which had once formed the basis of the country's prosperity, fell by half between 1965 and 1979. Nigeria, the world's largest exporter of groundnuts and palm produce at the time of independence in 1960, all but stopped exports of groundnuts, palm oil, cotton and rubber in the 1970s and depended on food imports costing $2 billion. Zambia, blessed with fertile land, reliable rainfall and huge agricultural potential, self-sufficient in food supplies at independence, was also forced to rely on food imports.

The overall results for agriculture showed most of Africa in a perilous state. In the 1960s the volume of agricultural production increased by 2.3 per cent a year, a level which nearly kept pace with the increase in population of 2.5 per cent a year, but food production in that period grew by only 2.0 per cent a year. Agricultural exports, the main source of foreign exchange earnings, grew on average by 1.9 per cent, or 20 per cent over the decade. In the 1970s, when the population growth rate rose on average to 2.7 per cent a year, the deterioration was more marked. Agricultural production fell from a 2.3 per cent increase to a 1.3 per cent increase a year; food production fell from a 2.0 per cent increase to a 1.5 per cent increase a year; and agricultural exports slumped from a 1.9 per cent increase to a 1.9 per cent decrease, an overall fall of 20 per cent over the decade. It was the fall in export growth that largely accounted for Africa's growing financial crisis, rather than deteriorating terms of trade. Another major factor contributing to agricultural decline was the generally low productivity of African agriculture. The average output of cereals per acre was only half the world average.

Africa was the only region in the world during the 1960s and 1970s where food production per capita declined. In statistical terms, according to the World Food Council, the fall amounted to 7 per cent in the 1960s and 15 per cent in the 1970s. Of thirty-nine countries in black Africa, only eight reported an increase in agricultural output per capita during the 1970s; twenty-five countries registered a decline in food production per capita. This decline occurred despite vast sums poured into the agricultural sector. Between 1973 and 1980 about $5 billion in aid flowed into agriculture, half of it from the World Bank. The World Bank calculated in 1985 that one-third of its agricultural projects in West Africa and more than one half of its East African projects had failed. To cover food production deficits, relatively wealthy countries like Zambia paid out huge sums on costly food imports; poorer countries relied on food aid. Imports of grains grew by nearly 10 per cent every year from the early 1960s. Food imports in 1979 amounted to 12 million tons. The need to purchase food imports, coupled with the fall in agricultural exports, depleted foreign exchange reserves and contributed to balance of payments crises.

In growing desperation, African governments tried to meet their commitments by borrowing heavily abroad rather than by adopting austerity measures or policy reforms and currency devaluations that would hit the urban elite. During the 1970s oil-importing countries ran up current account deficits which by 1980 reached an average of 9 per cent of their gross domestic product – twice the figure for oil-importing developing countries in general and conspicuously higher than any other region in the world. Current account deficits rose from a modest $1.5 billion in 1970 to $8 billion in 1980. The deficits were covered to some extent by loans and grants from foreign governments and international agencies which tripled between 1970 and 1980; but otherwise African governments borrowed heavily from private banks at a time when interest rates were fast rising. The average interest rate for new commitments climbed from 5.5 per cent in 1977 to 9.3 per cent in 1981.

Between 1970 and 1980, black Africa's external debts rose from $6 billion to $38 billion. When debt repayments from current earnings became more and more difficult, governments contracted new loans to repay debt in the hope that market conditions would improve. By 1982 external debts had reached $66 billion. A year later they were $86 billion. Some countries ran up debts amounting to 40 per cent or higher of their annual national income. In some cases there was no longer any serious prospect that loans would be repaid. An increasing number of governments were obliged to postpone foreign debt repayments. Arrears in 1982 reached almost $10 billion. Many could not meet debt-servicing costs. Debt-service ratios as a proportion of export earnings rose from 6.5 per cent in 1970 to 28.3 per cent in 1982.

The impact on ordinary life was calamitous. Hospitals and clinics ran short of medicines and equipment; schools lacked textbooks; factories closed through lack of raw materials or spare parts for machinery; shops were plagued by shortages; electricity supplies were erratic; telephone systems broke down; unemployment soared; living standards plummeted.

By comparison to other regions of the world, Africa was dropping further and further behind. Output per person in the 1960s and 1970s rose more slowly than in any other part of the world; in fifteen countries in the 1970s, it actually fell. Life expectancy, despite the improvements, was by far the lowest in the world, still twenty-seven years shorter than in industrialised countries and less than in any other developing region. The African child death rate in 1980 was two-thirds greater than in South Asia, three times higher than in Latin America and twenty-five times higher than in the developed world. The African population was more exposed to endemic diseases like malaria and to other diseases stemming from poor sanitation, malnutrition and poverty. In the field of education, the advances made were still limited: in about one-third of African countries, less than half of the child population received primary education; in only six countries were more than 20 per cent of the age group attending secondary school.

No other country demonstrated the decline of Africa so graphically as Ghana. Once one of the most prosperous tropical countries in the world, it had been reduced by 1980 to a pauper. Its per capita gross domestic product fell by more than 3 per cent a year in the 1970s. Output declined in all major sectors – cocoa, timber, mining and manufacturing. The only sector that flourished was *kalabule* – the black market. The Ghanaian currency, the cedi, traded on the black market at up to twenty times below the official rate. The purchasing power of a labourer's wage fell during the 1970s to one-quarter of its previous worth: a loaf of bread now took two days to earn; a yam sufficient for a family meal cost as much as two weeks' wages. Crime rates soared. Public services disintegrated. According to a World Bank estimate, only one-third of the truck and bus fleet and one-fifth of locomotives were serviceable. Between 1975 and 1981 some 14,000 trained teachers left the government's education service, many heading abroad. Ghana by 1981 had lost half of all its graduates. When Flight Lieutenant Jerry Rawlings took power for the second time in 1982, he railed at how previous administrations had turned 'hospitals into graveyards and clinics into death transit camps where men, women and children die daily because of the lack of drugs and basic equipment'.

The picture was not uniformly bleak. Oil-producing countries such as Nigeria, Gabon, Congo-Brazzaville, Algeria and Libya reaped fortunes from the oil bonanza. But the Nigerian example showed how quickly oil wealth could be dissipated. For a brief period its finances were transformed, with annual revenues soaring from $4 billion to $26 billion. But such riches set off a massive spending spree. Patronage politics and corruption reached new heights. Grand industrial projects were launched – an integrated steel complex, an automotive industry, a petrochemical sector. Contracts were signed for new infrastructure – roads, schools, housing, a new capital city at Abuja. Huge salary increases were awarded to public servants. Vast sums were spent on imported consumer goods. Import scams proliferated. Fraud and corruption cost billions of dollars. Meanwhile, export crops were virtually abandoned; subsistence farming was neglected; local manufacturing suffered; inflation soared.

In 1979 Nigeria had a favourable trade balance of $1.4 billion and gross international reserves of $5.8 billion. By 1982 it had a balance of payments deficit of $7.3 billion and gross international reserves were down to $1.9 billion, about one month's average requirement. Its external debt in 1982 was more than $6 billion. The following year the price of oil fell by 25 per cent; simultaneously Nigeria's quota of oil production under OPEC agreements was cut, reducing daily output by two-thirds. In 1983–4 Nigeria's earnings amounted to only half of the revenue it had earned in 1980, far less than its development plans had envisaged. Its external debt now stood at $18 billion. The boom had turned to bust. The collapse in confidence precipitated capital flight. Nigeria was, in effect, bankrupt for the foreseeable future. In his novel *Prisoners of Jebs*, the Nigerian writer Ken Saro-Wiwa observed: 'Of all the countries who had black gold, Nigeria was the only one that had succeeded in doing absolutely nothing with it.'

Botswana provided a rare example of an African state that used its bonanza of mineral riches wisely. At independence in 1966, Botswana, consisting of large areas of desert, with a population of only half a million, was one of the poorest countries in Africa, heavily dependent on British support. But the discovery of rich seams of diamonds shortly after independence transformed its prospects. By 1980 its per capita income had risen to more than $900 a year. Avoiding extravagant expenditure on prestige projects, Seretse Khama invested in infrastructure, health and education and built up substantial reserves. Private businesses were allowed to grow. Corruption hardly existed. In the 1980s per capita income rose to $1,700 a year.

A handful of countries – Kenya, Malawi, Swaziland, Côte d'Ivoire and Cameroon – developed economies based largely on agriculture that managed to maintain steady growth. Kenya between 1965 and 1989 attained an average rate of per capita increase in gross domestic product of 2 per cent; between the late 1960s and the late 1980s coffee production more than doubled and tea production increased almost fivefold. Malawi, under Hastings Banda's dictatorship, was often cited as an example of how a country that was listed as one of the poorest in the world, that was small, landlocked, heavily populated and lacking in mineral resources, could still achieve progress both in agriculture and industrial development. The most promising example of all was Côte d'Ivoire. In the first two decades after independence, Côte d'Ivoire's annual growth in real terms was more than 7 per cent a year, placing it among the top fifteen countries in the world. The results could be seen in the towering office blocks which dominated the skyline of the capital, Abidjan, in the neat plantations stretching for miles over the countryside, and in the thriving market towns inland. So impressive was Côte d'Ivoire's economic progress that it was termed 'a miracle'. But even there the miracle faded and fell apart.

The strategy adopted by Félix Houphouët-Boigny from the outset of independence was based on close collaboration with France. He relied on French aid, on French personnel and, above all, on French investment to secure economic prosperity. Indeed, the French presence in Côte d'Ivoire became even more noticeable than it was during the colonial era. The number of French residents rose from 10,000 at independence to 50,000, one of the largest French communities living outside France. French advisers and *coopérants* were to be found at every level of government, in the presidency, the security services, the military command, ministries and parastatal organisations. Côte d'Ivoire employed the highest number of French teachers and technicians in Africa and sent the highest number of students to French universities.

French businessmen were given every encouragement to invest in Côte d'Ivoire. An investment code offered foreign investors a five-year tax holiday; ten years' exemption from import duties on capital goods; and no limit to repatriation of profits on capital. A further inducement was Côte d'Ivoire's continued membership of the French franc zone, under which France guaranteed the convertibility of the local currency. The result was an investment bonanza unmatched anywhere else in black Africa.

Houphouët shrugged off criticism about the extent to which Côte d'Ivoire remained dependent on France. His priority, he insisted, was economic growth, and French assistance was required to secure it. He argued that the need for effective management and organisation overrode all other considerations and he willingly turned to the French to provide it if qualified Ivorians were not available. There was no room, he said, for 'cut-rate Africanisation'. Even in the 1980s some 12,000 French personnel were still in government service.

He wasted little time on politics. Public debate and political criticism he viewed as impediments to the business of economic development. Not for twenty years were any contested elections held. Houphouët merely arranged for the country's only political party, *Parti Démocratique de la Côte d'Ivoire*, to present a single list of pre-selected candidates for each constituency. In 1980 he permitted contested elections under a one-party system, but even then his autocratic style hardly changed. Political power was held by a small elite surrounding the president. The party survived mainly as a means of distributing patronage. Yet Houphouët was astute in his use of political power, preferring to draw his critics and opponents into the government system rather than to suppress them, while remaining ever vigilant. 'I am like the crocodile,' he once remarked. 'I sleep with one eye open.' Amid conditions of political stability, the economy flourished.

The boom in agriculture was phenomenal by any standards. With a huge expansion of cultivated land, cocoa production grew from 104,000 tons in 1960 to nearly 300,000 tons in 1980; coffee production doubled. Food production also increased, at an average rate of 4 per cent a year, a higher rate than population growth. Much of the increase was attributable to smallholders thriving on favourable government prices; by 1975 there were about 450,000 peasants growing cocoa and coffee in south-eastern Côte d'Ivoire. Overall, agricultural production tripled between 1960 and 1980. Côte d'Ivoire overtook Ghana as the world's largest producer of cocoa; it became Africa's largest exporter of coffee and a major exporter of pineapples, bananas, palm oil and hardwood.

A similar boom occurred in industrial activity. In 1960 Côte d'Ivoire had almost no industry. Its agricultural exports – coffee, cocoa beans and timber – were exported mostly unprocessed. Primed by French investment, the industrial sector expanded rapidly. Industrial production, mainly by agro-industries and import-substitution enterprises, increased by 11.5 per cent a year in the 1960s and by 10.5 per cent in the 1970s. By 1980 the manufacturing sector consisted of 700 enterprises with a turnover of $3.1 billion, one-third destined for export markets. The government purchased a minority interest in a range of industries but was otherwise content to leave the controlling interest and management in private hands.

The ruling elite profited enormously from the boom. In a remarkably frank speech in 1983, Houphouët boasted how his business activities had earned him 'billions' of francs, listing among his achievements that he was the country's largest producer of pineapples and avocados. He admitted that he operated bank accounts in Switzerland. But he claimed that his wealth had not come 'from the budget'.

These are the fruits of my labours. One of the banks manages my profits from pineapple production. I have 4 billion in turnover from pineapples. I pay some 50 million francs a month for boxes for pineapples. Boats and planes come to 150 million francs a month. I had two sharp falls two years ago when I reached 3,000 tons of pineapples a month, producing a third of the national total. And I asked a bank to manage all this. I have stopped producing coffee. At one time, it brought in very little, perhaps 100 million francs, but that 100 million is today worth billions. I put all this money into my bank accounts in Switzerland, and that produced a lot of interest. My deposits account for a quarter of the deposits in one of the banks in Abidjan. Would I keep all this money here if I didn't have confidence in my country? I have confidence in Côte d'Ivoire. There is even a bank which manages my profits in avocados, of which, I think, I am the main producer in Côte d'Ivoire. There is another bank which modestly manages my profits from poultry farming. But these billions, because this all amounts to billions, are in this country.

Despite Houphouët's claims of propriety, a French investigation disclosed that he kept at least one-tenth of the country's cocoa export revenues in his personal bank account for distribution to his cronies and supporters. He also ensured that members of his family and clan benefited from tax and tariff exemptions, high-level state jobs, and subsidised credit for their businesses.

The high point of the Côte d'Ivoire boom came in the mid-1970s. A price explosion for cocoa and coffee sent state revenues soaring. Gripped by financial euphoria and gambling that commodity prices would remain high, the government embarked on a string of ambitious development projects such as roads, ports and hydro-electric dams, borrowing heavily to do so. It also launched a network of parastatal corporations aiming to promote agricultural and industrial development. The number of parastatal corporations rose from five in 1960 to eighty-four in 1979. Public spending between 1975 and 1978 tripled. External debt rose from $256 million in 1970 to $4 billion in 1980.

Houphouët's favourite scheme was to transform his home village in Yamoussoukro into a new capital city, replete with grand buildings. During the 1960s and 1970s Yamoussoukro received more than one-third of total urban investment outside Abidjan. The presidential palace he built there was sometimes referred to as an African version of Versailles. At the entrance stood two gold-painted rams, Houphouët's personal symbol. Sacred crocodiles were kept in the palace pond, fed daily on live chickens, and a sacred elephant was allowed to wander within the walls. Houphouët also built himself a basilica modelled on St Peter's in Rome, at a cost of $145 million.

The boom soon turned to bust. In the second half of 1978 prices for cocoa and coffee collapsed. By 1981 cocoa prices had fallen to one-quarter of their peak; coffee prices had halved. In 1979–80 state revenues slumped by more than $1 billion. The government was thus left with a huge foreign debt and declining income. For the first time since independence, Côte d'Ivoire in 1980 had an adverse trade balance and an adverse balance of payments. As a result of higher oil prices and the precipitous decline in cocoa and coffee income, the net barter terms of trade between 1978 and 1982 fell by 40 per cent. To make matters worse, most of the parastatal enterprises accumulated large losses. Run as the private fiefdoms of the ruling elite, their products required huge government subsidies: prices for sugar were three times the world price, prices for rice were twice the world price. In 1980 more than half of public external debt was attributable to ten parastatal organisations. Adding to the squeeze, French firms repatriated huge amounts of profit.

Confounding government expectations, the slide continued. Between 1980 and 1983 state revenues dropped by 65 per cent. External debts in 1982 rose to $4.5 billion. The cost of debt-servicing became unmanageable. Debt service grew from $38.5 million in 1970 to $737 million in 1979 to $996 million in 1982. The ratio of debt servicing to annual exports receipts went from 9 per cent in 1975 to 26 per cent in 1981 to 37 per cent in 1983. In 1984 it approached 60 per cent, forcing the government to reschedule its debts. In 1987 Côte d'Ivoire declared itself insolvent. The 'miracle' had been no more than a mirage.

Compounding all the difficulties that Africa faced was an ever-growing population. From a little over 200 million in 1960, the population by 1990 had reached 450 million. On average, African women bore six children. Even with high mortality rates, this meant that Africa's population was growing by more than 1 million a month. The rate of population increase added to pressures on agricultural production, on urban growth and on government spending. Governments were simply unable to cope with the demand for more schools, more clinics, more housing and more basic services like water supply. Indeed, many were not even able to maintain existing infrastructure.

The impact of population growth on land use was especially damaging. By the 1980s arable land was no longer in plentiful supply. Plots of land were divided until they were too small to sustain the occupants. Peasants thus turned to cultivating more and more marginal land, either in areas of unreliable rainfall or on slopes, increasing the problems of soil erosion and degradation, over-grazing and deforestation. Pasture lands were increasingly broken up for cultivation, with adverse results. Between 1973 and 1988 Africa lost as much as 15 million acres of pasture. In Mali and Niger peasants in the 1970s were cultivating land sixty miles north of the limit set two decades earlier. In northern Ethiopia farmers had to cultivate the steepest slopes, suspending themselves by ropes. Arable land was also scarce throughout North Africa and in areas of West African states with large concentrations of population like Igboland. In Kenya, where only 17 per cent of land was suitable for arable agriculture, peasants spread out increasingly into lowveld areas, producing poor crops even in good years. Fallow periods were shortened, weakening the land's productive use. Forests and woodlands were stripped for fuelwood, on which Africans largely depended for cooking and heating. Woodlands were also cleared to provide land for cash crops. Côte d'Ivoire possessed 29 million acres of forest in 1960 but only 3.4 million by 1980. Rain forests were decimated to raise revenues from timber exports. The French agronomist René Dumont estimated that 74,000 acres of rain forest disappeared every day. Each year, the long-term potential of agriculture in much of Africa was diminishing.

The scale of the land crisis was illustrated in its starkest form in the Sahel, a region long accustomed to periods of drought and low rainfall. Until the mid-1960s the region was largely self-sufficient in food.

During the succession of droughts that struck the region between 1968 and 1973, as many as a quarter of a million people may have died; cattle herds were decimated; vast areas of land deteriorated into desert. At first, the Sahel disaster was attributed mainly to the effects of drought. But subsequent studies suggested that drought was only one aspect of the problem. Long before the drought set in, the region was heading for serious trouble. Because of population pressures, peasants were pushing northwards into pastoral areas, tilling soil that was far too arid for permanent cultivation and driving pastoralists and their herds of livestock into even more arid areas. The overall result was over-grazing, over-cultivation and deforestation on a catastrophic scale. Every year some 80,000 square miles of land deteriorated. Food production failed to keep pace with population growth. In statistical terms, the Sahel populations were increasing at the rate of 2.5 per cent a year, while food production was growing, at best, by 1.0 per cent. When drought struck, they were already living too close to the margin of safety.

A massive international rescue operation was launched in an endeavour to reverse the crisis. In the ten years after the 1968–73 drought, some $7.5 billion of aid was poured into the Sahel region. By the late 1970s international aid reached the level of $40 per person a year, compared to $19 per person for Africa as a whole, and only $6 per person for Asia. The region swarmed with experts, commissions and international agencies. In 1981 Upper Volta (Burkina Faso) received no fewer than 340 aid missions. But all the efforts had little lasting impact. Much of the aid was directed towards towns and cities, often in the form of food aid to keep civil servants, soldiers and the police content. Some aid was squandered by local elites in conspicuous consumption of goods and services. The population continued to grow. The process of 'desertification' continued unabated.

By the 1980s a mood of despair about Africa had taken hold. No other area of the world aroused such a sense of foreboding. The sum of its misfortunes was truly daunting. In relentless succession, African states had succumbed to military coups and brutal dictatorships, to periods of great violence and to economic decline and decay. One by one, African leaders had failed to deliver effective programmes to alleviate the plight of their populations. The vast majority of Africans enjoyed neither political rights nor freedoms. More than two-thirds were estimated to live in conditions of extreme poverty. The future was spoken of only in pessimistic terms. 'Our ancient continent', Edem Kodjo, the OAU's secretary-general, told African leaders, 'is on the brink of disaster, hurtling towards the abyss of confrontation, caught in the grip of violence, sinking into the dark night of bloodshed and death . . . Gone are the smiles, the joys of life.'

THE GREAT PLUNDERER

In the tradition followed by African coup leaders, General Joseph Désiré Mobutu explained his motive for seizing power in 1965 as being to prevent the Congo from sliding into chaos and corruption. 'The existence of the nation itself was threatened,' he said. 'Threatened on all sides, from the interior and the exterior. From the interior by the sterile conflicts of politicians who sacrificed their country and their compatriots to their own interests. Nothing counted for them but power . . . and what the exercise of power could bring them. To fill their own pockets, to exploit the Congo and the Congolese, that was their trademark.' The politicians, he said, had ruined the country.

Determined to restore the power and control of the central government in Léopoldville, Mobutu set out to create a 'new Congo' from the shambles it had become after five years of civil war and political strife, acting ruthlessly to suppress disorder and dissent. Four former cabinet ministers were arrested on treason charges, tried by a military tribunal and publicly hanged before a crowd of 50,000 spectators. 'One had to strike a spectacular example, and create the conditions for a disciplined regime,' explained Mobutu. 'When a chief takes a decision, he decides, full stop.' The leader of a rebellion in Kwilu province in 1964, Pierre Mulele, who returned to the Congo from exile under the impression he had been promised an amnesty, was tortured then executed. When units of the former Katangese *gendarmerie* serving with the national army in the eastern Congo turned against Mobutu, they were brutally crushed. A white mercenary revolt also failed. Regional opposition was suppressed. Within five years Mobutu managed to impose law and order of some kind on most parts of the country.

Mobutu's economic strategy initially was equally effective. Inflation was halted, the currency was stabilised, output increased and the government's debts were kept low. The giant copper mining industry was successfully nationalised. By 1970 the Congo under Mobutu was no longer regarded as an object of ridicule and despair but as a viable state which seemed about to realise its vast potential.

Mobutu was regarded as a particularly valuable asset by the United States. Since the Congo's chaotic debut at independence in 1960, Washington had been determined above all to ensure that the country remained a pro-Western bulwark against Soviet ambitions in Africa. During Mobutu's first trip to Washington in May 1963, when he was still army commander, President Kennedy remarked, as he invited his guest to move out into the Rose Garden for photographs: 'General, if it hadn't been for you, the whole thing would have collapsed and the Communists would have taken over.' Mobutu modestly replied, 'I do what I am able to do.' When Mobutu asked for military equipment and training, including six weeks of parachute instruction for himself at Fort Benning and Fort Bragg, Kennedy was only too willing to oblige, but asked apprehensively, 'Can you afford to be away from the Congo that long?' In a gesture of support, Mobutu was given a command aircraft for his personal use and a permanent US Air Force crew to go with it.

After his coup in 1965, Mobutu remained on the CIA's payroll for some time and received regular briefings from Larry Devlin, the CIA station chief in Léopoldville. On successive visits to Washington, he was accorded star status, promised support and constantly flattered. In August 1970 President Nixon described him as a leader of stability and vision. 'Though you are a young man and you come from a young nation,' said Nixon, 'there are things we can learn from you.' Nixon cited Mobutu's handling of the economy as an example. 'Tomorrow I have a meeting scheduled with my cabinet on the budget. I find in studying your administration that you not only have a balanced budget but a favourable balance of trade, and I would like to know your secret before meeting with the cabinet.'

With political stability restored, the Congo's riches excited an increasing number of foreign investors. Its resources of copper, cobalt, industrial diamonds and other minerals provided a glittering basis for economic expansion. Mobutu offered a generous investment code. Further encouragement came from Washington. Twice during Mobutu's visit to the White House in 1970, Nixon extolled the virtues of the Congo as a good place for US investment. In the early 1970s the Congo's prospects seemed ever brighter. The price of copper soared, providing the government with huge revenues. Buoyed up by this new wealth, Mobutu launched a series of grandiose development projects: a steel mill near Léopoldville; a giant dam on the lower reaches of the Congo River at Inga; a long-distance power-line from Inga to Katanga; an ambitious new copper mining project; new manufacturing plants and an array of infrastructure projects. By 1974 American and European financiers were involved in a headlong rush to invest in the Congo, committing more than $2 billion. As a sign of how much the Congo's image had improved, the organisers of the world heavyweight boxing match between Muhammad Ali and George Foreman decided to stage their 'Rumble in the Jungle' there in 1974.

Mobutu's political ambitions grew at the same time. He created a single national political party, the *Mouvement Populaire de la Révolution* (MPR), set himself up as its sole guide and mentor, and laid down an ideology to which everyone was instructed to adhere. The ideology was known at first as *authenticité,* but its official name was subsequently changed simply to 'Mobutuism'. Though never clearly defined, Mobutuism had the full force of law. Any 'deviation' was treated as a constitutional offence. Mobutu's views were clear: 'In our African tradition, there are never two chiefs; there is sometimes a natural heir to the chief, but can anyone tell me that he has ever known a village that has two chiefs? That is why we Congolese, in the desire to

conform to the traditions of our continent, have resolved to group all
the energies of the citizens of our country under the banner of a single
national party.'

Stage by stage, he accumulated vast personal power, ruling by decree,
controlling all appointments and promotions and deciding on the allocation of government revenues. In an endeavour to create an 'authentic'
national spirit, he ordered a wide variety of names to be changed. The
Congo was henceforth called Zaire, a name derived by the Portuguese
from a Kikongo word, *Nzadi*, meaning 'vast river'. Towns with
European names were given local ones: Léopoldville was changed to
Kinshasa; Elisabethville to Lubumbashi; Stanleyville to Kisangani; and
the province of Katanga to Shaba. Zairians with Christian names were
ordered to drop them for African ones. Priests were warned that anyone
caught baptising a Zairian child with a European name would face a
five-year jail sentence. Mobutu himself took the name Mobutu Sese
Seko Kuku Ngbendu Wa Za Banga. In his own Ngbendu translation,
it meant: 'The warrior who knows no defeat because of his endurance
and inflexible will and is all powerful, leaving fire in his wake as he goes
from conquest to conquest.' The more succinct Tshiluba translation
meant: 'Invincible warrior; cock who leaves no chick intact.'

With similar fervour, Mobutu banned Congolese men from wearing European suits. By decree, he ordered that they should be replaced
with a collarless Mao-style tunic, worn without shirt or tie, which
came to be known as *abacost* – *à bas le costume* – literally, down with the
suit. The *abacost* became Mobutu's personal trademark, along with
leopard-skin hats made for him by a Paris couturier and thick, black-
framed spectacles.

The personality cult surrounding Mobutu became all-pervasive.
He assumed grand titles: Father of the Nation; Saviour of the People;
Supreme Combatant; Great Strategist. His deeds were endlessly
praised in songs and dances. Officials took to wearing lapel badges
with his miniature portrait. Much of the adoration took on religious
overtones. The television news was preceded by the image of
Mobutu, with a leopard-skin hat perched on his head, descending, as
it were, through the clouds from heaven. Places where he had worked
and lived were designated as national pilgrimage points – 'high places

of meditation'. His interior minister Engulu Baanga Mpongo told the party faithful: 'God has sent a great prophet, our prestigious Guide Mobutu. This prophet is our liberator, our Messiah. Our Church is the MPR. Its chief is Mobutu. We respect him like one respects a Pope. Our gospel is Mobutuism. This is why the crucifixes must be replaced by the image of our Messiah.'

In his memoir of Mobutu, one of his former prime ministers, Nguza Karl-i-Bond, described the miasma of adulation that surrounded him:

> Nothing is possible in Zaire without Mobutu. He created Zaire. He fathered the Zairian people. He grew the trees and the plants. He brings rain and good weather. You don't go to the toilet without the authorisation of *Le Guide*. Zairians would be nothing without him. Mobutu has obligations to nobody, but everybody has obligations to him. As he said to me on August 13, 1977, in front of three witnesses: 'Nguz', there's nothing I have to do for you; on the contrary, I have made you whatever you are.'

Mobutu next turned to self-enrichment on a scale unsurpassed anywhere else in Africa. In 1973, citing the need to give Zaire greater economic independence, he ordered the seizure of some 2,000 foreign-owned enterprises – farms, plantations, ranches, factories, wholesale firms and retail shops. No provision was made for compensation. Mobutu described his decree as a 'radicalisation of the revolution'. But instead of the state taking control, the enterprises were handed out to individuals as private property. The main beneficiaries were Mobutu and members of his family.

At a stroke, Mobutu acquired free of charge a vast agricultural empire, including fourteen plantations that he merged into a conglomerate called Cultures et Élevages du Zaire (Celza). Celza's plantations produced one-quarter of Zaire's cocoa and rubber output, and employed some 25,000 people, including 140 Europeans, making it the third largest employer in the country. The cattle ranches he obtained were equally extensive. A livestock survey showed that three-quarters of the ranch cattle in the country were in the hands of Celza or other companies controlled by Mobutu or close family members. In grand patrimonial style, Mobutu distributed other valuable properties and businesses to members of his entourage and political allies in return for their loyal service. Official letters assigning assets to them read simply: 'You have been allocated . . .' or 'The State authorises you to take possession . . .' In Équateur province, interior minister Engulu scooped up thirty-five plantations. Mobutu ordered further expropriation of foreign-owned businesses in 1974.

Mobutu's personal fortune grew in leaps and bounds. During the 1970s it was estimated that one-third of total national revenues was in one way or another at his disposal. He used the central bank at will for his own purposes. He also became the largest shareholder in the Banque du Kinshasa, where parastatal companies were required to bank. His other interests included investments in the local operations of multinational corporations such as Fiat, Gulf, Volkswagen and Unilever. He was involved in diamond marketing in conjunction with an American business partner, Maurice Tempelsman. He also had control over the two main parastatal organisations involved in the copper industry and other mining enterprises – Gécamines and Sozacom.

Each year, he funnelled huge sums abroad into his private bank accounts. In one transaction alone in 1976, one of the plantation companies he seized transferred $1 million to his Swiss bank account. The central bank estimated that in 1977 fifty Zairian companies controlled by Mobutu's clique secreted abroad some $300 million in export proceeds. Nguza Karl-i-Bond testified to the US House of Representatives Subcommittee on Africa in 1981 that between 1977 and 1979 Mobutu had withdrawn $150 million in foreign exchange from the central bank and deposited it in his private accounts; that in 1981 he had ordered the central bank to transfer an additional $30 million to his personal account abroad; that at about the same time 20,000 tons of copper, worth about $35 million, was privately sold for Mobutu's benefit; and that quantities of cobalt and diamonds were exported by chartered aircraft to Europe with the proceeds of sale also deposited directly into his personal accounts. 'The budget and the mining revenues are really the private pool of funds for Mobutu and his friends,' an official from the International Monetary Fund observed. 'If Mobutu decides to load a plane with cobalt to sell in Europe, nobody knows about it.' By the end of the 1970s, Mobutu had become one of the world's richest men. In the 1980s his fortune was estimated to total $5 billion.

He spent much of the money assembling a portfolio of luxury houses and estates, mostly in Europe. Among his properties were the Villa del Mar in Roquebrune-Cap Martin on the French Riviera; an 800-hectare estate in Portugal's Algarve; and a converted farmhouse in the Swiss village of Savigny. He also owned a vast apartment on the Avenue Foch in Paris; at least nine buildings in Brussels, ranging from office blocks to mansions and parklands in the residential districts of Uccle and Rhode St-Genèse; and properties in Spain, Italy, Côte d'Ivoire, Senegal, Morocco and Brazil.

His residences in Zaire were similarly lavish. In Kinshasa they included a hilltop mansion with a private zoo in the grounds. He also enjoyed the use of a three-storeyed luxury cruiser, *Kamanyola*, entertaining foreign dignitaries and visiting businessman by taking them on trips along the river; a gracious host, he was assiduous in attending to the comfort of his guests, personally topping up their glasses of champagne.

His favourite residence was a huge palace complex costing $100 million which he built for himself in the depths of the equatorial forest at Gbadolite, a small village 700 miles north-east of Kinshasa that he regarded as his ancestral home. His main palace there, with vast marble-lined salons, sprawled across some 15,000 square metres amid a landscape of ornamental lakes and gardens. A smaller second palace was equipped with a discotheque, an Olympic-sized swimming pool and a nuclear shelter and fitted out with Louis XIV furniture, Murano chandeliers, Aubusson tapestries and monogrammed silver cutlery. Among Gbadolite's other features were luxury guest houses, a hotel and an airport capable of handling supersonic Concordes which Mobutu often chartered for his trips abroad. Mobutu also ordered model farms to be developed in Gbadolite, stocking them with Swiss cows and Venezuelan goats delivered by plane. Four or five times a year, Mobutu would descend on Gbadolite with an entourage of a hundred or so, stay for a few days, drive around in a great cavalcade and then fly off.

While Mobutu was busy accumulating riches, Zaire plunged head-long into crisis. Mobutu's expropriation of foreign businesses proved disastrous. Many quickly went bankrupt; some were simply stripped of their assets and abandoned; others were ruined by incompetent man-agement. The disruption caused to commerce, agriculture and trade in rural areas was severe. In 1976 Mobutu was obliged to reverse his 'revolution' and invite back foreign owners, but few returned.

Simultaneously, the copper bonanza came to an end. After surging to a record high of $1.40 per pound in April 1974, the world price for copper slumped to 53 cents per pound in 1975; in 1977 it reached an all-time low. In 1975 Zaire's exports were worth only half of their 1970 value. At the same time the cost of oil and imported grain soared. As if struck by a tidal wave, Zaire was suddenly beset by an onrush of massive inflation, fuel shortages, falling revenues and huge debts, as well as severe disruption to commerce and agriculture caused by Mobutu's seizure of foreign-owned businesses. In 1975 the gov-ernment fell into arrears on repayments of its foreign debts, which by then amounted to $3 billion. Alarmed by the possibility of financial collapse in Zaire, Western bankers came to the rescue by agreeing to stretch out their loans so as to reduce the immediate burden. Even then, Zaire failed to keep to the revised payment schedule. In 1977 its debt-service liabilities amounted to nearly half of the government's total revenues. More money was lent to Zaire in the hope that the government would eventually bring its finances under control. The banks had reached the point where they could not afford to let Zaire founder.

The grandiose development projects that Mobutu had launched added further difficulty. The steel mill at Maluku near Kinshasa, con-structed at a cost of $250 million, was designed for a capacity of 250,000 tons of steel a year, four times Zaire's requirements. After its opening in 1975, production reached a peak of 25,000 tons a year; after 1978 it never exceeded 10,000 tons a year. The mill produced only low-grade steel at eight times the cost of better-quality imported steel. In 1986 it was shut down.

The Inga hydro-electric project, together with its power-line to Katanga (Shaba), proved an even more costly venture. The first 300-megawatt phase of the dam was built to provide power to the Kinshasa region, including major customers like the steel mill at Maluku. A second phase of the project, providing power to Katanga, was deemed economically feasible because of the planned expansion of the copper industry there. Work on Inga II began in 1973 and was completed in 1977 at a cost of $260 million. Work on the 1,100-mile power-line to Katanga also began in 1973 but it was only completed, six years behind schedule, in 1982 and at a final cost close to $1 billion, four times the initial estimate. By then, the copper industry was in severe difficulties and had abandoned the expansion plans on which Inga II was predicated. Only 18 per cent of Inga II's hydro-electric capacity was used and only about 20 per cent of the power-line's capacity.

The administration, meanwhile, rapidly disintegrated. As corruption spread from the top, permeating every level of society, many government services allocated a budget were never provided. Teachers and hospital staff went unpaid for months. Civil servants and army officers routinely siphoned off state revenues. One informed estimate by foreign bankers suggested that as much as 40 per cent of the government's operating budget was either lost or diverted to purposes other than those intended. It was estimated that two-thirds of the country's 400,000 civil servants who were paid regularly every month were in fact fictitious; their wages were merely pocketed by senior officials. Army officers regularly kept for themselves their soldiers' pay and sold army food supplies on the black market. The soldiers, in turn, extorted money from civilians and set up roadblocks to confiscate farmers' produce being taken to market. Air force officers turned the air force into their own air transport company, undercutting the rates of the national airline by more than a half. Hospital medicines and equipment were sold by staff for their own benefit. Nothing could be accomplished without a bribe.

In a pastoral letter in 1976, Archbishop Kabanga of Lubumbashi issued a devastating critique of the system that Mobutu ran.

The thirst for money . . . transforms men into assassins. Many poor unemployed are condemned to misery along with their families because they are unable to pay off the person who hires. How many children and adults die without medical care because they are unable to bribe the medical personnel who are supposed to care for them? Why are there no medical supplies in the hospitals, while they are found in the marketplace? How did they get there?

Why is it that in our courts justice can only be obtained by fat bribes to the judge? Why are prisoners forgotten in jail? They have no one to pay off the judge who sits on the dossier. Why do our government offices force people to come back day after day to obtain services to which they are entitled? If the clerks are not paid off, they will not be served. Why, at the opening of school, must parents go into debt to bribe the school principal? Children who are unable to pay will have no school . . .

Whoever holds a morsel of authority, or means of pressure, profits from it to impose on people, especially in rural areas. All means are good to obtain money, or humiliate the human being.

Mobutu himself referred to the blight of corruption afflicting Zaire – *le mal Zairois* – and, with brazen hypocrisy, attacked the manner in which government officials were obsessed by the drive for personal enrichment. Addressing delegates at a party congress in 1977, he observed:

In a word, everything is for sale, anything can be bought in our country. And in this traffic, he who holds the slightest cover of public authority uses it illegally to acquire money, goods, prestige, or to avoid all kinds of obligations. Even worse, the citizen who simply asks for his most legitimate rights to be respected is subjected to an invisible tax, which is then openly pocketed by officials. Thus the right to be heard by a public servant, to register one's children in school or to obtain report cards at the end of the year, to obtain medical care, a seat on an airplane, an import licence, a diploma – and I could go on – are all subject to this tax.

Yet Mobutu himself relied on corruption to hold the system together and to keep himself in power. Moreover, he publicly condoned it. 'If you steal, do not steal too much at a time. You may be arrested,' he told party delegates. '*Yibana mayele* – Steal cleverly, little by little.'

The plight of Zaire, after ten years of Mobutu's rule, was pitiful. Hospitals closed for lack of medicine and equipment, deserted by staff unwilling to work unpaid. A fraction of the rural road network remained usable for motor traffic; the river transport system was a wreck. The level of employment was lower than at the time of independence. Because of inflation, the wages of those who could find employment were worth little more than 10 per cent of their value in 1960. Disease and hunger were rife. Relief agencies estimated that 40 per cent of Kinshasa's population suffered from severe malnutrition. In rural areas agricultural production plummeted; only 1 per cent of the land was cultivated. Large imports of food were required to feed the population. The state existed only to serve the interests of the ruling elite, while the mass of the population was left to fend for themselves. '*Débrouillez-Vous!*' – 'Fend for Yourself!' became the guiding principle for surviving Mobutu's regime. Sometimes known as '*Article Quinze*' in a satirical reference to a supposed 'fifteenth' article of the constitution, or '*Système D*', *débrouillardisé* covered everything from embezzlement to smuggling to hawking and petty crime. It was the only way to get by. '*On se débrouille*' was a phrase commonly used. A leading Zairian intellectual, Ilunga Kabongo, described Zaire as having two parts: a zone of existence occupied by the political elite, and a zone of non-existence, for the rest.

In despair at the chaotic state of Zaire's finances, foreign creditors in 1978 forced Mobutu to agree to a series of corrective measures. Foreign officials were placed in key institutions such as the central bank, the customs department and the finance ministry. One of their principal aims was to prevent Zairian companies, with links in high places, from evading taxes, import duties and foreign exchange regulations, as they had been doing at great cost to the exchequer for many years. In November 1978 a retired Bundesbank official, Erwin Blumenthal, who had been given effective control of the central bank, issued a list of fifty individual businessmen and corporations whom he prohibited from engaging in all import and export transactions until all their debts had been repaid and all foreign exchange earned from their past operations, amounting to hundreds of millions of dollars, had been repatriated. Another group of fifty individuals and companies were placed under investigation. Virtually all the names appearing on both lists belonged to Mobutu's inner circle. Blumenthal singled out as the worst offenders two corporations owned by Mobutu's uncle, Litho Maboti.

The effect of Blumenthal's orders was outwardly encouraging. Several companies complied with his requirements; and Mobutu himself announced that 1979 would be a 'year of moralisation'. But ways and means were soon found to circumvent his instructions. In 1979 Blumenthal left in disgust. In a confidential report he compiled about Zaire's prospects, he described 'how gradually the possibilities of control, of intervention, were wrested from the IMF team, its cooperation with honest Zairians inside the bank destroyed, my personal influence diminished, the position of the Central Bank within the administration damaged, its independence threatened'.

On occasion, Mobutu's men used direct methods:

At the end of January 1979, one evening (around 7 p.m.) when I was still in the bank, soldiers of General Tukuzu threatened me with submachine guns when they could not get their hands anymore on the head of the foreign department when they wanted to demand foreign exchange for their general.

Towards the end of his one-year stay, Blumenthal slept with a shotgun under his bed and had a radio that kept him in contact with the West German and American embassies.

He catalogued the lavish spending by members of Mobutu's family, illustrating the way in which Mobutu used the central bank as a private account for himself and his family and associates, listing details of their properties abroad and explaining how Mobutu personally profited from the sale of Zaire's mineral riches.

There just is no effective control over the financial transactions of
the Presidency; one does not differentiate between official and personal expenses in this office . . . All endeavours to improve
budgetary control in Zaire had to stop short before the operations
of the central governing authority: *la Présidence!*

Whatever promises Mobutu made about his commitment to reform,
warned Blumenthal, he had no intention of keeping them.

The corruptive system in Zaire with all its wicked and ugly manifestations, its mismanagement and fraud will destroy all endeavours
of international institutions, of friendly governments, and of the
commercial banks towards recovery and rehabilitation of Zaire's
economy. Sure, there will be new promises by Mobutu, by members of his government, rescheduling and rescheduling again of a
growing public debt, but no – repeat – no prospect of Zaire's creditors to get their money back in any foreseeable future.

He concluded: 'There was, and there still is, one sole obstacle that
negates all prospect: the corruption of the team in power.'

To protect his grip on power, Mobutu relied on a number of elite
military and police units, such as the *Division Spéciale Présidentielle,*
which were commanded by a select group of officers from his own
Ngbendi tribe and which he rewarded with high pay and perks. He
similarly promoted personnel from his own Équateur region when
making other key appointments. He kept ministers and senior officials
in a constant state of flux, rotating them regularly, dismissing them or
imprisoning them to ensure they represented no threat. 'Conventional
wisdom said that besides Mobutu and his family there are only eighty
people who count,' wrote an American journalist, Blaine Harden. 'At
any one time, twenty are ministers, twenty are exiles, twenty are in
jail, twenty are ambassadors. Every three months the music stops, and
Mobutu shuffles the pack.'

The most remarkable example of this *vagabondage politique,* as it was
called, was Nguza Karl-i-Bond. A nephew of the Katanga leader,
Moise Tshombe, he served as Mobutu's foreign minister in 1974, and

as foreign minister again in 1976. To his cost, he was mentioned in the foreign press as a possible successor to Mobutu. Accused of involvement with a rebel group, he was charged with high treason in 1977, tortured, sentenced to death and then pardoned. Named prime minister in 1979, he fled into exile in 1981, called for Western governments to overthrow Mobutu's 'regime of terror', testified against him in US Congressional hearings and wrote a savage denunciation entitled *Mobutu, ou l'Incarnation du Mal Zairois*. Despite all this, in 1985 Mobutu induced him to return to the fold, appointing him first ambassador to Washington, then as foreign minister for the third time and then as prime minister for the second time.

Buying off dissidents was Mobutu's standard practice. 'My father used to say "Keep your friends close, but your enemies closer still",' Nzanga Mobutu recalled. 'Leaving people in exile was a danger, they were making a lot of noise. The game was to neutralise their capacity to damage him.'

But not all Mobutu's critics were willing to play the game. In 1980 a group of fifteen parliamentarians published a fifty-one-page indictment of Mobutu's rule, arguing that he was the root cause of Zaire's difficulties and demanding open elections.

> We know how allergic you are to candour and truth . . . For fifteen years now we have obeyed you. What have we done, during this time, to be useful and agreeable to you? We have sung, danced, animated, in short, we have been subjected to all sorts of humiliations, all forms of subjugation which even foreign colonisation never made us suffer . . .
>
> After fifteen years of the power you have exercised alone, we find ourselves divided into two absolutely distinct camps. On one side, a few scandalously rich persons. On the other, the mass of people suffering the darkest misery.

Mobutu's response was to arrest them and banish them to remote villages. Some subsequently decided to join his regime. Others held out. In 1982 a hard core of dissidents led by Étienne Tshisekedi wa Mulumba, a former minister, formed themselves into an opposition party, *Union pour la Démocratie et le Progrès Social*. The dissidents were accused of attempting to overthrow the government, put on trial before the State Security Court, sentenced to fifteen years' imprisonment, but released after one year. Tshisekedi was arrested time after time again – ten times in eight years – but remained outspoken in his attacks on Mobutu. Describing him as a 'Zairian Caligula', he stressed that Zaire was suffering from something more than just a case of high-level theft. 'Mobutu truly has a malady,' he said. 'He is a kleptomaniac. Zaire is ruled by an uncontrolled thief. It is a kleptocracy.' But in 1988, Tshisekedi, like others before him, tired of the struggle and agreed to quit politics in exchange for his freedom. 'Always arrested, exiled, banished,' he said. 'It's not fun.'

However repressive and corrupt Mobutu's regime had become, he still enjoyed the support of Western governments. His pro-Western, anti-Soviet stance earned him much credit in Western capitals, notably in Washington. In Washington terminology, Mobutu was a 'friendly tyrant', a faithful ally who could be relied upon to support Western interests regardless. The perceived wisdom about Zaire was that the choice was either 'Mobutu or chaos', a theme that Mobutu himself skilfully advanced. When rebels invaded Katanga from Angola in 1977 and 1978, Western governments – the United States, France and Belgium – and African partners such as Morocco were quick to come to Mobutu's aid. US aid between 1965 and 1988 totalled $860 million.

Mobutu sustained direct links to the White House through successive administrations. He regarded George Bush senior as a personal friend, meeting him first when he was CIA director. When Bush visited Kinshasa as US vice-president in November 1982, shortly after Mobutu had imprisoned Tshisekedi's dissidents, he was generous in his praise: 'I have come to appreciate the dynamism that is so characteristic of Zaire and Zairians and to respect your dedication to fairness and reason,' said Bush. 'I have come to admire, Mr President, your personal courage and leadership in Africa.' Mobutu also struck up a warm friendship with President Reagan, regularly visiting him in Washington.

When George Bush became president in 1989, Mobutu was soon

on the plane to Washington for a reunion, the first African head of state to pay an official visit. 'As regards George Bush,' he said, 'I've met him thirteen times. We know each other from way back. He was in charge of the CIA and knew Zaire's problems backwards. He received me at his home in Maine with his mother, wife and children and grandchildren. I met him again recently at the funeral of Emperor Hirohito. He is an intelligent, open and sensitive man, with strong convictions.'

As they stood together on the South Lawn of the White House, Bush was equally fulsome. 'Zaire is among America's oldest friends, and its president – President Mobutu – one of our most valued friends,' he said. 'And we are proud and very, very pleased to have you with us today.'

WHITE DOMINOES

The military commander of Portuguese forces in Mozambique, General Kaúlza de Arriaga, spent Christmas in 1970 with his wife at a small army camp nine miles south of the Rovuma River which marks the border with neighbouring Tanzania. He was in a buoyant mood. After a seven-month offensive, his army had driven thousands of Frelimo guerrillas out of their bases on the Makonde plateau in northern Mozambique and back across the river. For the first time since the war began in 1964, Frelimo had suffered a critical setback in the two northern provinces of Cabo Delgado and Niassa, the main area of guerrilla operations; and de Arriaga, an army engineer appointed commander in 1970, quickly established a reputation as the man who could block the guerrilla advance. 'We are on the right road to success,' he declared.

Similar offensives were launched in Angola and in the small West African enclave of Guinea-Bissau, with similar results. To Portugal's generals it seemed that their new counter-insurgency measures – using airborne assaults, building airstrips and roads in remote regions, constructing fortified villages (*aldeamentos*) to deprive guerrillas of contact with the local population – were having the right effect. They were also encouraged by the large numbers of African recruits willing to serve in the ranks of the army and local militias. In Guinea-Bissau,

African commando units set up by General António Spínola gained a fearsome reputation. In Mozambique, African recruits formed a high proportion of paratroop and commando units and specialist counter-insurgency groups. In the 1970s Africans formed about half of the manpower of Portugal's colonial armies.

The possibility of military defeat or withdrawal was considered to be remote. Only in Guinea-Bissau had nationalist guerrillas managed to gain control of large areas of the country, driving back Portuguese forces to the main towns and a string of fortified camps. But even there they were unable to force a resolution of the conflict. A secret American appraisal of the Portuguese wars, conducted by the National Security Council in 1969, forecast a period of continued stalemate. 'The rebels cannot oust the Portuguese and the Portuguese can contain but not eliminate the rebels,' it concluded.

There was no sign that the Portuguese authorities were willing to consider any form of political compromise. Salazar's successor, Marcello Caetano, who took office in 1968, continued the same colonial strategy as before, holding fast to the notion of an indivisible Portuguese nation. He informed General Spínola that he would prefer defeat in Guinea-Bissau to any negotiation that might provide a precedent for Mozambique and Angola, the main centres of Portugal's African empire.

Yet the drain on Portuguese manpower and morale was considerable. Nearly 100,000 metropolitan troops were needed to contain three simultaneous wars. Most were conscripts, drafted for four years, increasingly disaffected by long spells of service abroad and unwilling to take risks. The officer corps too was stretched to the limit; there were examples of wartime battalions of 600 men being led by no more than three professional officers. In a desperate effort to increase the number of officers, the government in July 1973 passed a decree offering non-career officers with combat experience in Africa the same conditions and privileges as those of professional officers. But the result was an immediate outcry among career officers.

A surge of resentment at Caetano's dictatorship spread through the military, prompting the formation of a 'Captains' movement', then an Armed Forces Movement. Among junior officers there was profound disillusionment with the whole Portuguese regime, its authoritarian government, its economic backwardness and its debilitating colonial wars. A new generation within the army was inspired less by the grandiose ideas of Portuguese nationalism that Salazar and Caetano tried to inculcate than by policies of economic progress that other European states pursued. Africa, even in terms of trade, was of declining importance to Portugal. And the wars there were seen as unwanted legacies from the past.

The military hierarchy, too, no longer believed that the wars could be won. In February 1974, Spínola, now the deputy chief of the general staff, published a book entitled *Portugal and the Future* in which he stated that military victory was not possible. A pre-publication copy was sent to Caetano. According to Caetano's subsequent recollection, 'I did not put the book down until the last page, when it was already dawn. As I closed it, I understood that a coup d'état, the approach of which I had felt for months, was now inevitable.'

Seizing power in Lisbon in the 'carnation revolution' on 25 April 1974, the Armed Forces Movement hoped to bring about an orderly disengagement from Africa. In Guinea-Bissau negotiations were conducted relatively swiftly. A statement issued by the Armed Forces Movement in Guinea-Bissau declared: 'We, Portuguese military troops, who were sent to a war that we did not understand or support, have in our hands a unique opportunity to repair the crimes of fascism and colonialism, to set up the basis for a new and fraternal cooperation between the peoples of Portugal and Guinea.' By September Guinea-Bissau was recognised as an independent republic.

In Mozambique, however, there was confusion and disorder from the start. With the collapse of Caetano's regime, the entire colonial administration fell into disarray. Portuguese troops withdrew from the field, allowing Frelimo to pour guerrillas into central Mozambique unopposed. Hundreds of white settlers in rural areas, fearing revenge by the guerrillas and frightened by Frelimo's revolutionary rhetoric, abandoned their homes and fled to the coast. From early May a mass white exodus from Mozambique began. In negotiations with the Portuguese, Frelimo demanded recognition as the 'sole legitimate representative of the Mozambican people', and the unconditional

transfer of power without prior elections. The negotiations were protracted, but in September 1974 Portugal agreed to hand over power
exclusively to Frelimo after a nine-month transition period. Within
hours of the announcement, right-wing whites launched an abortive
revolt. The white exodus gathered pace. By the time that
Mozambique gained its independence in June 1975, the country had
lost not only most of its administrators and officials, but also managers,
technicians, artisans and shopkeepers. In all, some 200,000 whites
fled Mozambique, abandoning farms, factories and homes.

Undaunted by the crippling loss of skilled manpower, the Frelimo
leader, Samora Machel, set out to transform what had been a struggle
for liberation into a full-scale revolution, using Marxism-Leninism as an
ideological blueprint. In a series of decrees Frelimo nationalised plantations and businesses; introduced central economic planning; ordered
collective agricultural production; and attempted to implement a policy
of 'villagisation' similar to Tanzania's *ujamaa* programme. Groups of
party zealots – *grupos dinamizadores* – were sent into factories, offices,
businesses, hospitals, schools and municipalities to enforce the government's line. In its bid for 'modernisation', Frelimo also sought to root
out 'traditional' customs and land practices and to eliminate the influence of chiefs and headmen. The Catholic Church and its adherents
were another target. Frelimo ordered an end to public religious festivals,
took over church property and terminated church involvement in education and marriage. Traditional religions were similarly denounced.

'Our final aim', declared Machel in 1977, 'is not to hoist a flag that
is different from the Portuguese one, or to hold general elections –
more or less honest – in which blacks instead of whites are elected, or
to have a black president instead of a white governor . . . We affirm
that our aim is to win total independence, to establish people's power,
to build a new society without exploitation for the benefit of all those
who consider themselves Mozambican.'

Such sentiments, however, proved ruinous. Machel's policies provoked widespread discontent that eventually helped fuel civil war.

In Angola the transition from Portuguese rule turned into a major disaster. As the Portuguese administration there disintegrated, three rival

nationalist factions competed for power, transforming a colonial war into a civil war, causing the flight of almost the entire white population and drawing the Soviet Union and the United States into a perilous confrontation by proxy. Neither superpower had a direct strategic interest in Angola. But both were determined, for reasons of their own prestige and because of their preoccupation with the global balance of power, to ensure that the Angolan factions they supported were triumphant. In effect, Angola became a pawn in the Cold War.

All three nationalist factions were weak and disorganised. They made no serious effort to reach a negotiated settlement, but instead tried to gain advantage by appealing for support from foreign interests. It was because of their incessant rivalry that foreign involvement in Angola acquired such crucial importance.

At the time of the Lisbon coup in April 1974, the strongest faction in military terms was Holden Roberto's FNLA. Based in Zaire, it had received support from Mobutu who aspired to play a Pan-African regional role. Roberto and Mobutu also shared a family connection as a result of Roberto's marriage to a kinswoman of Mobutu's wife. On a visit to Beijing in December 1973, Roberto had succeeded in persuading the Chinese government to support the FNLA with military instructors and arms. In June 1974 an advance party of a team of 120 instructors arrived in Kinkuzu, the FNLA's main military base in Zaire, and a consignment of Chinese arms followed shortly afterwards. Roberto also maintained links with the US Central Intelligence Agency. The difficulty facing the FNLA was that its field of operations was confined to northern Angola and its following came only from the Bakongo. From the comfort of his exile in Zaire, Roberto had been content to run little more than a border war against the Portuguese. Nevertheless, by comparison to the other two factions, the FNLA was favourably placed. In September 1974, as Portuguese forces disengaged, newly trained and equipped FNLA troops were able to establish an occupied zone in north-western Angola.

The position of Agostinho Neto's MPLA in April 1974 was precarious. It had fragmented into three rival groups; guerrilla activity was at a standstill; and Soviet arms supplies had been suspended for fear that they would be used for internal fighting. One of the MPLA's most ardent supporters, Nyerere of Tanzania, had become so disillusioned with it that he had used his influence with the Chinese to persuade them to support Roberto and the FNLA instead. But China's involvement with the FNLA and the subsequent deployment of FNLA troops in northern Angola then prompted the Russians in October to resume military supplies to the MPLA, in the hope that it could be rebuilt into a credible armed force. The MPLA also began to make headway mobilising popular support, mainly in urban centres. Luanda, the capital and the key to any bid for power, was regarded from the outset as an MPLA stronghold. The party was firmly rooted, too, in Kimbundu areas lying east of Luanda. Nevertheless, the MPLA remained essentially a regional party. Neither in the north among the Bakongo nor in the south among the Ovimbundu did it acquire much of a following.

The third faction, Unita – *União Nacional para a Independência Total de Angola* – had been launched in 1966 by Jonas Savimbi, one of Holden Roberto's former associates. It had attracted a following among the Ovimbundu, Angola's largest tribe, concentrated in the central highland districts of Huambo and Bié. The only significant foreign support it had received was from China which had supplied small quantities of arms. At the time of the Lisbon coup, Unita consisted of a force of no more than about 1,000 poorly armed men operating in a small base area in the central highlands. But because of its links with the Ovimbundu, it was considered to have considerable potential. Alone among the nationalist leaders, Savimbi had remained with his guerrilla forces in the field during the war and was regarded as a local hero.

Under pressure from the Organisation of African Unity, the three nationalist leaders – Roberto, Neto and Savimbi – met in January 1975 and agreed to form an interim coalition government in conjunction with the Portuguese and to hold elections before independence day, set for 11 November 1975. On 31 January the new transitional government took office in a climate rife with suspicion and mistrust. Clashes between FNLA and MPLA troops soon broke out in Luanda and continued intermittently for months. In February

FNLA forces were joined by Zairian troops. In March the Russians delivered substantial military supplies to the MPLA. After an outbreak of heavy fighting between the two factions in March, thousands of Portuguese civilians, fearing that civil war was imminent, fled the country, causing the collapse of government services and the economy; in the following six months, some 300,000 whites left Angola, the largest exodus of whites from Africa since Algerian days.

The battle for the control of the capital continued for several months. The MPLA armed supporters in Luanda's *musseques* – shantytowns – and recruited a force of about 4,000 Katangese, former Tshombe soldiers based in exile in Angola, with an abiding hatred of Mobutu, whom the Portuguese had used in their war against the FNLA. The MPLA also turned to Cuba for help with training. The Cubans had provided instructors for the MPLA since 1965. In response to Neto's request for assistance made in May, a group of 230 Cuban instructors arrived in Angola in June. Strengthened by the influx of Russian weapons and supported by the Katangese, the MPLA drove the FNLA and Unita out of Luanda in July and gained tentative control of other major towns, including the ports of Lobito, Benguela and Moçâmedes (Namibe). It also held the Cabinda exclave, where the oilfields lay. The transitional government duly collapsed. From then on, the government in Luanda, with Portuguese consent, remained effectively in the hands of the MPLA.

The Angolan civil war, at this point, turned into a major international conflict, drawing in both the United States and South Africa in a determined effort to prevent the Soviet-backed MPLA from gaining power at independence. Hitherto, the Americans had taken only a passing interest in Angola. In July 1974 the CIA resumed some covert funding for the FNLA, but requests for arms from both the FNLA and Unita were ignored. In March 1975 the CIA handed Roberto a covert grant of $300,000, enabling him to acquire a television station and a daily newspaper in Luanda. But still no military supplies were authorised.

By mid-July, however, with the MPLA in control of Luanda, not only had the balance on the battlefield in Angola shifted decisively in its favour, but America's perspective of the Angolan conflict had radically altered. The American defeat in Vietnam in April 1975 had severely damaged its prestige around the world, and it had left Henry Kissinger, the US Secretary of State and head of the National Security Council, anxious to find ways of reasserting American power. The rise of Soviet influence in Angola and Cuban activity there had caught his attention. Warnings about the Soviet role in Angola came from several African leaders, including Mobutu of Zaire and Kaunda of Zambia. Visiting Washington in April 1975, Kaunda privately urged Kissinger and President Ford to counter Soviet activity by supporting Unita as well as the FNLA. In public he spoke openly about the dangers in Africa of 'a plundering tiger and its deadly cubs'. Mobutu was also keen to win greater American support for his intervention in Angola.

Kissinger concluded that unless America countered Soviet activities in cases like Angola, then the larger balance of power between the two superpowers would be impaired. He was convinced that Soviet objectives in Angola were to impose a government of its own choice on the country and to carve out a new sphere of influence. He maintained that if the West allowed that to happen unopposed, then the confidence of pro-Western states like Zambia and Zaire would be severely shaken and US prestige around the world would again be adversely affected. 'Our concern in Angola is not the economic wealth or the naval base. It has to do with the USSR operating 8,000 miles from home when all the surrounding states are asking for our help,' he said. 'I don't care about the oil or the base, but I do care about the African reaction when they see the Soviets pull it off and we don't do anything.'

On 16 July Ford authorised Kissinger to mount a major covert operation supplying arms to both the FNLA and Unita. The first planeload of arms left on 29 July for Zaire, which was used as a rear base for the Angola operation. A vast flow of American arms followed during August and September. Mobutu also committed armoured car units, paratroops and three battalions to the fray.

Simultaneously, the South Africans launched their own intervention. Whereas in Mozambique they had quickly established an amicable working relationship with Frelimo, even though it came to power as a revolutionary party proclaiming Marxist policies, in the case of Angola they saw Soviet and Cuban involvement as part of a communist plan to dominate southern Africa. They believed that Angola, under the aegis of a pro-communist government in Luanda and with Soviet support, was likely to become a springboard for nationalist guerrillas from the South West Africa People's Organisation (Swapo) to attack South West Africa (Namibia) which South Africa controlled. What the South Africans hoped to achieve was the installation of a moderate pro-Western government in Luanda amenable to South African interests. The Angolan theatre also provided South Africa with an opportunity to demonstrate to the US its value as a staunch anti-communist regional power and improve its standing in Washington. At secret meetings with Roberto and Savimbi, South African officials agreed to support the FNLA and Unita with arms and training, and to launch an invasion from South West Africa, disguising it as a mercenary operation. Savimbi had no qualms about his involvement with apartheid South Africa: 'If you are a drowning man in a crocodile-infested river and you've just gone under for the third time, you don't question who is pulling you to the bank until you are safely on it.'

On 14 October a South African column codenamed 'Zulu' crossed the border from South West Africa and advanced rapidly up the coast, supplied en route by air and accompanied by helicopters. The column covered 500 miles, capturing the port of Benguela, before it was checked by the Queve River, north of Novo Redondo, about 120 miles short of Luanda. A second South African column codenamed 'Foxbat' linked up with Savimbi's troops at his headquarters at Huambo in central Angola and moved northwards. The South Africans also supported a northern force of FNLA and Zairian troops moving southwards towards Luanda. Prompted by the CIA, the South Africans then agreed to participate in a joint operation aimed at capturing Luanda for the FNLA before independence day on 11 November. The plan called for Roberto's troops, led by Zairian armoured vehicles and supported by South African artillery, to move southwards across the Quifangondo plain, secure the bridge over the Bengo River, eleven miles north of Luanda, and sweep into the capital.

As independence day approached, the MPLA controlled little more than Luanda and a narrow stretch of territory running eastwards. In the capital there was mounting panic. The Polish journalist Ryszard Kapuściński reported: 'Every so often someone came into the hotel shouting, "They're coming! They're coming!" and announced breathlessly that the armoured vehicles of the Afrikaners were already at the city's edge.'

What prevented the MPLA's defeat was massive intervention from Cuba and Russia. The first Cuban combat troops had arrived in Angola on 27 September. By the beginning of November they numbered about 2,000. When the battle for Benguela was lost, the Cubans decided that only reinforcements on a large scale would prevent the collapse of the MPLA. On 8 November a special forces battalion was flown into Luanda, arriving just in time to take up positions with MPLA forces guarding the Bengo River bridge and the northern outskirts of Luanda.

At dawn on 10 November the South Africans opened with an artillery barrage on MPLA positions and continued with a bombing raid by long-distances bombers, causing MPLA troops to flee. But an FNLA infantry attack that was due to follow was delayed by an hour and forty minutes because Roberto failed to show up on time, and his troops refused to move without him. In the interval the MPLA regrouped. While Roberto, together with his CIA, South African and Zairian advisers, looked on from a nearby hill, a joint force of FNLA and Zairian troops moved out across the Quifangondo plain towards the Bengo River. But facing a sustained barrage of rocket and artillery fire from Cuban troops, they broke and ran, retreating northwards.

In Luanda the Portuguese high commissioner, Admiral Leonel Cardoso, held a brief ceremony at which he announced he was transferring power to 'the Angolan people'; not a single Angolan was present to witness the proceedings. As the cathedral clock struck twelve, Agostinho Neto, standing on a platform in a nearby square, read a text proclaiming the People's Republic of Angola; when the lights on the platform failed, the crowd dispersed into the darkness. At his headquarters at Huambo in the highlands, Savimbi proclaimed his own Democratic People's Republic of Angola. Roberto remained in his base at Ambriz, eighty miles north of Luanda. Thus on 11 November 1975 the Portuguese departed and Angola embarked on independence.

The war was soon over. Thousands more Cuban troops were flown in on a Soviet airlift, along with Soviet tanks and huge quantities of equipment. In a desperate attempt to shore up the FNLA campaign, the CIA organised contingents of French and Portuguese mercenaries for Angola and supplied Roberto with funds to recruit British and American mercenaries. The CIA was thwarted from taking further action when the funds it had available for covert operations ran out. Kissinger was thus obliged to ask Congress for more funds, but Congress proved uncooperative. In December the Senate voted to block all additional covert funds, forcing the CIA to abandon Angola and its allies there.

The FNLA–Unita campaign had long since lost all credibility. Once the extent of South Africa's involvement in the war was realised, African opinion turned swiftly against them. African leaders who had previously been critical of Soviet and Cuban intervention, without knowing at the time of either South Africa's involvement or the CIA's role, now saw the Soviet action in a different, more acceptable light. Far from winning friends in Africa, Kissinger's excursion into the African arena resulted in a humiliating setback for American policies.

In February 1976 the last FNLA stronghold, São Salvador, fell. The Unita capital, Huambo, was also captured, forcing Savimbi to retreat to eastern Angola. French mercenaries suggested that he should escape with them to South Africa to await more favourable circumstances, but Savimbi declined the offer. 'The situation will not change if I wait in some other part of Africa,' he told them, 'but it may change if we stay here.' The scene was set for years of internal strife.

The collapse of Portuguese rule in Mozambique presented Rhodesia with greater dangers than it had ever faced. Since declaring UDI in 1965, Ian Smith had successfully consolidated white control, fending off economic sanctions applied by the British government in a half-hearted manner in the hope that he would be obliged to change his mind. Both Portugal and South Africa helped thwart their impact.

After a few hiccups, the economy continued to expand; by 1972 the level of total exports had climbed higher than in 1965. Favourite brands disappeared from the shops; there was a chronic shortage of Scotch whisky and good brandy; luxury goods became scarce; but there was little unemployment or reduction in earnings, and if the white standard of living did suffer mildly, it was so high as to make the difference bearable. To Smith's delight, thousands of new white immigrants arrived, attracted by an affluent lifestyle and a sub-tropical climate that made everyday life pleasurable. By 1973 the white population had reached 273,000.

The black population, meanwhile, remained relatively quiescent. Smith's UDI provoked only sporadic incidents of violence and sabotage, minor resistance that soon subsided and caused little concern to the government. From their base in Lusaka in neighbouring Zambia, the two rival nationalist groups – Zapu and Zanu – broadcast inflammatory messages exhorting the black population to rise up, but there was no response. Small bands of guerrillas infiltrating across the Zambian border during the 1960s were dealt with swiftly.

A series of negotiations that Smith held with the British government reflected his growing confidence. In 1966 Britain offered Smith a deal that would have postponed majority rule beyond the end of the century, but he rejected it, believing that he could obtain better terms. The following year Britain offered an even more favourable deal, but again Smith turned it down. Then in 1969 he introduced a new constitution that, in his own words, 'sounded the death knell of the notion of majority rule' and 'would entrench government in the hands of civilised Rhodesians for all time'. Even then the British government still considered there was room for a deal. In 1971 the British foreign secretary, Sir Alec Douglas-Home, arrived in Salisbury bearing proposals so favourable to white Rhodesians that Smith accepted them. One constitutional expert estimated the agreement meant that the earliest year by which majority rule was likely to be achieved was 2035.

A British commission set up to test public opinion about the deal concluded, however, that the settlement terms were not acceptable to the black majority and the deal fell through. Leading the opposition, a Methodist bishop, Abel Muzorewa, warned of the deep undercurrents of bitterness rising among the African population, 'the repressed fear, restless silence, forced tolerance and hidden hatred'. But far from paying heed to this new mood of defiance, Smith reacted vindictively, determined to make the black population pay for the lost opportunity of a settlement, enforcing discriminatory measures with ever greater vigour.

The turn of the tide for Rhodesia came as a result of the difficulties the Portuguese found in neighbouring Mozambique in containing Frelimo's war. Zanu guerrillas, instead of having to cross the Zambezi River from Zambia, began to use Mozambique's Tete province as a forward base from which to organise insurgency in north-eastern Rhodesia. The guerrilla war they launched in 1972 was confined at first to border areas in the north-east. The government's counter-insurgency measures were largely successful. Its efforts were shored up by South Africa which despatched large numbers of combat police to the area, regarding the Zambezi rather than the Limpopo as its own front line.

But the coup in Lisbon in April 1974 changed the fortunes of Rhodesia irrevocably. The end of Portuguese rule in Mozambique not only deprived Rhodesia of a long-standing ally and brought to power there a left-wing nationalist movement; it meant that Rhodesia's entire eastern border, some 760 miles long, was potentially vulnerable to infiltration by Zanu guerrillas operating freely from bases in Mozambique. Moreover, Frelimo's accession to power in Mozambique emboldened Rhodesian nationalists to believe that in Rhodesia too guerrilla warfare would succeed in overthrowing white rule.

The South Africans were quick to recognise, in the aftermath of the Lisbon coup, that an entirely new strategy was needed. Hitherto, they had looked on Angola, Mozambique and Rhodesia as a valuable buffer separating them from contact with black Africa, a *cordon sanitaire* which it was in their own interests to strengthen. But with the withdrawal of the Portuguese from Angola and Mozambique, Rhodesia was no longer important as a front-line defence, for the winds of change had finally reached South Africa's own frontier. The South

African prime minister, John Vorster, calculated that in the long run
Smith's position, without an open-ended South African military and
financial commitment, was untenable. White rule in Rhodesia was
ultimately doomed. In this new assessment, Smith, with his long history of intransigence, was no longer a useful partner but a potential
liability. His stubborn resistance to change only served to magnify the
dangers of communist involvement in southern Africa. An unstable
white government in Rhodesia was less preferable than a stable black
government, heavily dependent on South African goodwill.

With this objective in mind, Vorster set out to force Smith to come
to terms with the Rhodesian nationalists. He was obliged to act cir-
cumspectly for fear of antagonising his own electorate and provoking
an outcry in Rhodesia. Fortuitously, he found an ally in Zambia's
President Kaunda, who had become increasingly concerned about the
disruption caused in Zambia by the Rhodesian imbroglio and about
the dangers of a widening guerrilla war there. In conjunction with
other African leaders, Vorster and Kaunda conspired to impose on
Smith and the nationalists their own plan for a Rhodesian settlement.
As a preliminary step, Smith was required, much against his better
judgement, to release nationalist detainees, including Joshua Nkomo
and Robert Mugabe.

In December 1974, after more than ten years in detention, Nkomo
and Mugabe were released. But while Nkomo was willing enough to
engage in negotiation, Mugabe rejected the whole idea. His years of
imprisonment had turned him into a dedicated revolutionary. Alone
among the nationalist leaders, he saw no reason to seek a compromise
with Rhodesia's white rulers that would leave the structure of white
society largely intact and thwart his hopes of achieving an egalitarian
people's state. Armed struggle, he believed, was a necessary part of the
process of establishing a new society.

No sooner had he been released than Mugabe, together with a few
trusted colleagues, set about secretly organising recruits for Zanu's
guerrilla army, despatching them to bases in Mozambique. In March
1975, shortly after his fiftieth birthday, he resolved to head for
Mozambique himself. 'I am going to war, whether I shall return or
not,' he told his mother on a farewell visit to her home at Kutama

Mission, west of Salisbury. Hunted by the Rhodesian security police, he was helped to escape by a white Catholic nun, crossing the border into Mozambique on 5 April with a search party in hot pursuit.

Under pressure from South Africa, Smith went through the motions of attempting a negotiated settlement but, like Mugabe, saw no need to compromise. A conference in August 1975, held under the auspices of Vorster and Kaunda in railway carriages parked on the Victoria Falls bridge on the border between Rhodesia and Zambia, broke up in disarray after the first day. A separate series of negotiations between Smith and Nkomo starting in December 1975 also made no progress. 'I have said we are prepared to bring black people into our government to work with them,' said Smith after the talks had failed, 'and we have to accept that, in future, Rhodesia is a country of blacks and whites, and that it will be governed by blacks and whites. But I don't believe in majority rule, black majority rule, ever in Rhodesia, not in a thousand years.'

In early 1976 the guerrilla war entered a new and more perilous phase. From bases in Mozambique, hundreds of Zanu guerrillas infiltrated into eastern Rhodesia, attacking white homesteads, robbing stores, planting landmines and subverting the local population. When Nkomo's talks with Smith broke down, Zapu guerrillas joined the war, opening a new front in western Rhodesia, along the borders with Zambia and Botswana. Main roads and railways came under attack. White farmers bore the brunt, living daily with the risks of ambush, barricaded at night in fortified homes. A growing number of whites, rather than face military service, emigrated.

Though Rhodesia's army commanders still expressed confidence in their ability to defeat the guerrilla menace, in many parts of the world it seemed that Smith was embarked upon an increasingly risky venture to sustain white rule which endangered the stability of the whole region. Among those whose attention was drawn to the Rhodesian war was Henry Kissinger. In the wake of the Angolan debacle, Kissinger was particularly alert to the dangers of how nationalist guerrilla wars could widen the circle of conflict, drawing in neighbouring countries and providing the Soviet bloc with opportunities for intervention. He found Vorster similarly worried and impatient with

Smith's intransigence. In tandem, they agreed on a plan to force Smith to accept majority rule. To make Smith amenable to the idea, Vorster cut back oil shipments and supplies of arms and ammunition, withdrew helicopter pilots and technicians from Rhodesia and delayed its import and export traffic through South Africa. Kissinger was left to present the terms of surrender.

At a meeting in Pretoria in September 1976, Kissinger handed Smith a typed list of five points that he said must be used as the basis for a Rhodesian settlement. Smith took the document and slowly read aloud the first point: 'Rhodesia agrees to black majority rule within two years.' He looked around the room and said: 'You want me to sign my own suicide note.'

The Kissinger deal was soon mired in controversy, disputed by all sides. A conference the British government convened in Geneva failed to make any progress. As the war spread to every rural area in the country, Smith set out to reach a separate deal – an 'internal' settlement – with the moderate nationalist leader, Bishop Abel Muzorewa, while expressing disdain for the whole exercise. 'Don't let me pretend that I welcome this,' he said. 'Unfortunately I have no option. It had been made clear that even our friends in the world [a reference to South Africa] would abandon Rhodesia unless the undertaking to transfer power was given.' The negotiations were protracted. Smith was determined to gain the most advantageous terms possible for whites, ignoring the dangers that in the process he might undermine the standing and popularity of Muzorewa. By the time they reached an agreement in March 1978, the plight of many isolated farming communities was desperate; health and veterinary services in some areas had collapsed; nearly one-quarter of all black primary schools had closed; ambushes on road traffic were so prevalent that every main road in the country was considered unsafe after dark; and the white exodus was in full flow.

The one hope for the 'internal' settlement was that a new black-led government would be able to undercut the guerrilla campaign and gain international recognition. But though Muzorewa won elections in April 1979 with a substantial majority, there were few signs that the war would abate. Nkomo and Mugabe dismissed Muzorewa as a 'puppet' and made clear they were as determined to bring down Muzorewa's government as they had been to fight against Smith's regime. When Smith finally left the stage as prime minister on the last day of white rule on 31 May 1979, his legacy was a state unrecognised by the international commmunuity, subjected to trade boycotts, ravaged by civil war that had cost at least 20,000 lives and facing a perilous future.

As the war intensified, Britain launched one last initiative to find a solution, calling for negotiations at a conference to be held in London. Muzorewa and Nkomo readily agreed to attend, but Mugabe saw no need. His guerrilla army was planning to embark on a new phase of urban warfare. 'We felt we needed yet another thrust, and in the urban areas, in order to bring the fight home to where the whites had their citadels,' he recalled. The longer the war lasted, the greater were the prospects for achieving his revolutionary objectives.

Only under extreme pressure from Zambia's Kenneth Kaunda and Mozambique's Samora Machel did he eventually agree to attend. Both Zambia and Mozambique had suffered heavily as a result of Rhodesian raids on guerrilla bases and supply lines they harboured. Neither could afford to sustain the war any longer. Machel was blunt in his warnings: if Mugabe refused to go to London and explore negotiations, then Mozambique would withdraw its support.

Mugabe was furious. 'We thought they were selling out,' he recalled. 'The front-line states said we *had* to negotiate, we *had* to go to this conference. There we were, we thought we were on top of the situation back home, we were moving forward all the time, and why *should* we be denied the ultimate joy of having militarily overthrown the regime here? We felt that would give us a better position. We could then dictate terms.'

Mugabe arrived in London in September 1979, a cold, austere figure who rarely smiled and seemed bent on achieving revolution, whatever the cost. While in exile he had repeatedly insisted on the need for a one-party Marxist state, threatened that Ian Smith and his 'criminal gang' would be tried and shot, and warned that white exploiters would not be allowed to keep an acre of land. His main hope was that the conference would break down.

Against all odds, however, the conference stumbled towards agreement. At the final hurdle, when Mugabe balked at accepting the
ceasefire arrangements and made plans to fly to New York to
denounce the whole proceedings at the United Nations, he was given
a direct warning by an envoy from Machel that unless he signed the
agreement, he could no longer count on using Mozambique as a base
for operations; in other words, as far as Mozambique was concerned,
the war was over. Mugabe was resentful about the outcome of the
conference: 'As I signed the document, I was not a happy man at all.
I felt we had been cheated to some extent, that we had agreed to a
deal which would to some extent rob us of [the] victory we had
hoped we would achieve in the field.'

The London agreement, signed on 21 December 1979, involved
Britain sending out to Rhodesia a British governor, supported by a
small team of officials, to hold the ring between an assortment of
armies in the hope that a ceasefire would last long enough for elections to be held. It was a perilous venture, likely to explode at the
point when the elections results were announced.

Returning to Rhodesia in January 1980, nearly five years after his
escape into exile, Mugabe was given a hero's welcome by one of the
largest crowds ever seen in Rhodesia. Banners portraying rocket
grenades, land mines and guns greeted him, and many youths wore T-
shirts displaying the Kalashnikov rifle, the election symbol that Zanu
wanted but the British had disallowed. But Mugabe himself was unexpectedly conciliatory. In Mozambique, shortly before Mugabe's return
to Salisbury, Samora Machel, still struggling to overcome the massive
disruption caused by the exodus of whites at independence in 1975,
had intervened to warn Zanu against fighting the election on a revolutionary platform. 'Don't play make-believe Marxist games when
you get home,' he said. 'You will face ruin if you force the whites into
precipitate flight.' Consequently, Mugabe's manifesto was stripped of
all reference to Marxism and revolution.

The election campaign was fought with ferocious intent on all
sides. British officials judged all three main parties – Mugabe's Zanu-
Patriotic Front, Nkomo's Zapu and Muzorewa's United African
National Council – guilty of using intimidation and violence, but

considered Zanu-PF to be the worst culprit by far. In violation of the ceasefire agreement, Mugabe had withheld several thousand fighters from holding camps to influence the campaign. The scale of intimidation in eastern Rhodesia, according to British officials, was massive. Neither Nkomo nor Muzorewa supporters had been able to campaign there at all. 'The word *intimidation* is mild,' roared Nkomo. 'People are being terrorised. It is *terror*. There is fear in people's eyes.'

But when the election results were announced on 4 March, Mugabe's victory was so overwhelming that arguments over the effect of intimidation became largely irrelevant. With 63 per cent of the national vote, Zanu-PF gained 57 of 80 black seats in parliament, mainly in Shona-speaking areas; Nkomo's showing – 24 per cent of the vote and 20 seats – was confined almost entirely to Ndebele and Kalanga areas of the country; the Muzorewa vote – 8 per cent and 3 seats – simply collapsed.

More than anything else, it was a vote for peace. Muzorewa's failure to bring an end to the war, as he had promised in 1979, destroyed whatever chance he had of being re-elected. The war weariness that gripped the black population had been as much the cause of his victory in 1979 as it was of Mugabe's ten months later. Any other result, as most blacks well knew, would have led almost certainly to a resumption of fighting.

The shock for the whites was all the more profound because they had been convinced, until the last minute, that Muzorewa would win, or that at least an anti-Mugabe coalition would be possible. A black Marxist government had been their greatest dread all along; yet, suddenly, so it seemed, one was upon them. In despair and despondency, many whites prepared to leave. But when Mugabe appeared on television that evening, far from being the Marxist ogre the whites feared, he impressed them as a model of moderation. Even Ian Smith, who, a few weeks beforehand, had denounced Mugabe as 'the apostle of Satan', now found him 'sober and responsible'. So calmly did the transfer of power take place, in fact, that some whites, though their fears about the future remained, wondered at the time why the war had been fought, what the cause was for which there had been so much suffering and grief.

On the eve of Zimbabwe's independence on 18 April 1980, Mugabe marked the occasion with a speech pledging reconciliation. 'If yesterday I fought you as an enemy, today you have become a friend and ally with the same national interest, loyalty, rights and duties as myself. If yesterday you hated me, you cannot avoid the love that binds you to me and me to you.' He said he would 'draw a line through the past' to achieve reconciliation.

> The wrongs of the past must now stand forgiven and forgotten. If ever we look to the past, let us do so for the lesson the past has taught us, namely that oppression and racism are inequalities that must never find scope in our political and social system. It could never be a correct justification that because the whites oppressed us yesterday when they had power, the blacks must oppress them today because they have power. An evil remains an evil whether practised by white against black or black against white.

He called for a new vision and a new spirit.

Zimbabwe, it seemed, was on the threshold of an era of great promise, born out of civil war but now bursting with new ambition. Mugabe himself was widely acclaimed a hero: the revolutionary leader who had embraced the cause of reconciliation and who now sought a pragmatic way forward. Western governments lined up with offers of aid. Amid the jubilation, Julius Nyerere of Tanzania advised Mugabe, 'You have inherited a jewel. Keep it that way.'

PART III

19

RED TEARS

At his headquarters in Emperor Menelik's old palace, Colonel
Mengistu Haile Mariam spent months planning to turn the tenth
anniversary of Ethiopia's 1974 revolution into the most spectacular
celebrations the country had ever witnessed. He intended to use the
occasion to launch his pet project, the Workers' Party of Ethiopia, and
to announce a new Ten Year Plan with confident projections of economic growth. To signify the importance of the event, he ordered the
construction of a new convention hall – the Great Hall of the People –
with seating for 3,500 delegates and the most modern conference
facilities. With the help of hundreds of North Korean supervisors, he
set out to adorn Addis Ababa with triumphal arches bearing revolutionary slogans, with giant stars displaying the hammer and sickle
hoisted high on buildings, and with huge posters of Marx, Lenin
and – Mengistu. Thousands of delegates from communist parties
around the world would be invited to witness the birth of his 'vanguard' Marxist-Leninist party. There would be mass marching and
dancing and banquets. No expense was to be spared.

But while Mengistu became ever more captivated by the details of
the tenth anniversary, Ethiopia was heading for its greatest disaster of
the twentieth century – the famine of 1984. Forewarned of
catastrophe, Mengistu was determined that nothing should be allowed

to get in the way of his celebrations. For months he refused to give the matter any attention. On his orders, relief efforts were obstructed. No mention was made during the celebrations of the masses starving to death north of the capital. When news of the disaster subsequently emerged, it was to inspire an extraordinary surge of compassion and generosity from peoples and governments around the world, prompting the greatest single peace-time mobilisation of the international community in the twentieth century. What was not realised at the time was the extent to which the disaster had been caused by Mengistu's own counter-insurgency wars, wars that he was determined to prosecute even when the full scale of starvation became clear.

Rural life in Ethiopia was generally precarious. Poor rains or droughts were frequent hazards. A leading historian of Ethiopia, Richard Pankhurst, documented at least one famine every decade between the fifteenth and nineteenth centuries. Famines in 1958, 1966 and 1973 killed tens of thousands on each occasion. Even in the best of times peasant families in Wollo and Tigray – the epicentre of the 1984 famine – lived close to the margin of survival. In recent years, population growth had compounded the difficulties of rural existence, resulting in over-cultivation, deforestation, soil erosion and land degradation.

Mengistu's agricultural policies had added to this burden. Though the Derg's land reforms in 1975 had freed peasants from debt and the need to pay rent to landlords, Mengistu's priority was to ensure that the towns and the army were supplied with cheap food at the expense of the peasantry. Peasants were forced to accept low prices dictated by officials from the state-run Agricultural Marketing Corporation (AMC). In 1984 the fixed price set by the AMC was only about one-fifth of the free-market price in Addis Ababa.

A British journalist, Paul Vallely, reporting in *The Times* on an incident in the market town of Areka in Sidamo province, described some of the tactics used by AMC officials:

> The government men were lying in wait for the peasant farmers in
> the market place of the small town of Areka. The harvest of teff,

Ethiopia's staple grain, had not been plentiful in the southern province of Sidamo but at least that meant, the peasants thought, that they would get a good price for what little surplus they had . . .

There was almost a riot in Areka that day. The officials from the Agricultural Marketing Corporation waited until most of the peasants had brought their teff into the dusty marketplace and then made themselves known. They announced the official price they had decided on and told the farmers the AMC would buy their entire stocks.

The price was ludicrously low. The peasants protested. Some even began to gather up their grain, saying they would rather not sell it at such a price. The AMC men then announced that no one would be allowed to withdraw his produce. The farmers began to shout and drag their grain away. The AMC men were jostled. Then the government heavies moved in and the peasants knew they had no choice but to comply.

Peasants were also forced to deliver grain 'quotas' to state officials, regardless of the circumstances they faced. 'Even the poorest of the poor had to sell,' one Wollo farmer told researchers. If they failed to do so, their assets could be confiscated or they could be imprisoned. In numerous cases, peasants had to delve into their own food reserves or sell assets to buy grain on the open market to resell to the AMC at a loss. In Gojjam province in 1983, nearly one-third of farmers failed to grow enough to meet their quotas and had to sell livestock in order to buy grain. In Wollo province in 1984, even though famine was rife, the AMC still insisted on imposing a quota. Other impositions on the peasantry included heavy taxation and mandatory contributions to local development programmes; restrictions on non-farm activities such as petty trading and migrant labour, enforced by a strict system of travel permits; and compulsory unpaid labour on government projects.

Instead of aiding peasant farmers, Mengistu diverted government resources into promoting state farms, mainly commercial farms nationalised after the revolution. Between 1978 and 1983 about 60 per cent of the agricultural budget was devoted to state farms. But they were inefficiently run and, despite huge investment, accounted for less than 4 per cent of total grain production. Mengistu also endeavoured to promote collectivisation, supporting collective farms with every kind of technical assistance and equipment. But they too failed. Indeed, the overall result of Mengistu's agricultural policies was to lower output per capita and to make Ethiopia increasingly dependent on food imports.

But what turned rural hardship into disaster – even before drought struck – were the counter-insurgency measures Mengistu's army employed in dealing with rebel activity, notably in Tigray and northern Wollo where the Tigrayan People's Liberation Front (TPLF) had become firmly entrenched. During the 1970s the army launched five major offensives against the TPLF. A sixth offensive starting in August 1980 in central Tigray lasted for seven months and caused massive disruption. Using scorched-earth tactics, the army destroyed grain stores and houses, burned crops and pastures, killed livestock and displaced about 80,000 farmers. Aerial bombardment created havoc with rural markets and farm life. A seventh offensive began in earnest in February 1983 in western Tigray, a major surplus-producing area. More than 100,000 residents and 375,000 migrant labourers were forced to flee. In addition to outright destruction, the army requisitioned food and enforced blockades of food and people. Food was routinely used as a weapon of war.

Areas of Tigray and Wollo were thus already awash with destitute refugees when the rains failed. Rainfall between 1975 and 1983 had generally been favourable – at average or above-average levels. Indeed, the national crop in both 1982 and 1983 was among the highest on record. In parts of Tigray and northern Wollo, however, there were local droughts.

Officials from the Relief and Rehabilitation Commission (RRC), a government agency set up in Addis Ababa in the aftermath of the 1973 drought, were aware of an impending crisis in Tigray and Wollo. The new head of the RRC, Dawit Wolde Giorgis, a member of Mengistu's central committee, made a tour of the area in July 1983 and witnessed the plight of thousands of refugees crowding into relief centres. He attributed the cause not to the army's campaign of repression but to what he insisted was the long-term failure of rains. Nevertheless, on his return to Addis Ababa, he was determined to press the case for government intervention.

Fortuitously, Mengistu was due to preside over a three-day meeting at Menelik's palace to discuss the annual budget. Dawit took the opportunity to request a ten-fold increase in funds for the RRC. Sitting on an elevated red velvet seat, Mengistu listed the government's achievements and its future goals, but made no mention of the possibility of famine. Dawit's request for more funds was rejected. Instead of challenging Mengistu openly, Dawit decided a private approach might be more effective. In his memoirs, *Red Tears*, he wrote:

> I approached Mengistu respectfully, making a great effort not to anger him. I told him that his comments had been very interesting and doubtless valid for some parts of the country, but what I had personally observed indicated the makings of a terrible famine if the *belg* rains [the short rainy season that usually produced 10 per cent of the annual crop] failed to come in February and March. I explained that we needed more money to prepare for the crisis.
>
> He listened impatiently, then told me not to be so panicky – to stay cool. He said the very name of the agency I was heading invited trouble and encouraged begging. 'You must remember that you are a member of the central committee,' he said. 'Your primary responsibility is to work towards our political objectives. Don't let these petty human problems that always exist in transition periods consume you. There was famine in Ethiopia for years before we took power – it was the way nature kept the balance. Today we are interfering with that natural mechanism of balance, and that is why our population has soared to over forty million.'
>
> He didn't elaborate on this, but I understood what he meant. 'Let nature take its toll – just don't let it out in the open. We need a façade for the outside world, so make it look like we're doing something.' He abruptly ended the conversation, patted my shoulder and walked off.

Except for a few scattered showers, no rain fell in the Ethiopian high-lands between October 1983 and May 1984. The *belg* rains failed altogether, wiping out the spring harvest. Scorching drought, combined with the effects of years of military repression, left Tigray and northern Wollo devastated. Desperate to raise money for food, thousands of farmers sold their livestock, farm equipment and household goods, abandoning their farms and heading with their families towards relief centres in the hope of staying alive. But the relief centres – shelters, as they were called – were soon overwhelmed, their meagre resources used up. In February 1984 the RRC recorded that 10,000 people were dying in shelters each week; in March it put the figure at 16,000. In all, it estimated that 5 million people were at risk.

Travelling up the road from Addis Ababa to Dessie in Wollo province, Dawit witnessed 'miles of starving, ragged people, begging for a bowl of grain, a scrap of cloth, pleading for their lives. Many of them were selling their traditional ornaments, handcrafted from silver long ago.' On his way to Korem, a hill station on the main road to Asmara, he recorded how every village he passed through was in desperate straits. 'Everywhere we saw people carrying corpses, digging graves, grieving, wailing and praying.'

Driving up the escarpment to Korem, he came across columns of starving and exhausted people trudging along the road in the hope of finding food there.

> People who had not eaten for days, weak and deathly ill, were climbing the mountain in an endless, winding stream of suffering. As our cars passed them, we saw their strength failing; saw them collapse and die before our eyes, their lives slipping away where they dropped. Some of the stronger ones carried children, the sick or the aged. We saw the terrible agony of people forced to choose between leaving their dying wives, husbands or children behind, or staying to die with them.

Korem itself was a place of suffering and death. In normal times it was a small town of some 7,000 people, with a church and an army barracks. But the population had grown to 100,000. The shelter there, run by the relief agency Save the Children, could cope with no more than 10,000. The rest were left to fend for themselves.

> Most had only rags to protect them from the chill highland nights. At night they huddled together for warmth as best they could in the open fields. The exhausted relief workers held the power of life and death as they walked through the crowds selecting only the most needy to receive what food there was, while the unlucky thousands watched grimly and waited another day.
>
> The shelters and the open field near the warehouse were packed to overflowing with the sick and dying. We pushed our way through the hordes of groaning people, grieving mothers, whimpering children with the faces of old men and women, listless faces crawling with flies, faces without hope. The smells and sounds of death were all around. There were corpses everywhere, lined up in rows in ragged sackcloth shrouds or still uncovered in the midst of the crowds. Others were dying of slow starvation as we watched. Some bodies twitched helplessly, some writhed in agony as hunger ate away their living tissue, some lay still, alive but barely distinguishable from the dead. It was like walking through an open graveyard.

In view of Mengistu's refusal to take any action or sound the alarm, Western donors felt no inclination to treat the crisis with any sense of urgency. Western governments were distrustful of Mengistu's communist dictatorship, alienated by his constant anti-Western rhetoric and critical of both his lavish spending on the tenth anniversary celebrations and his spending on defence in general – more than half of Ethiopia's budget was directed towards maintaining an army of 300,000 in the field. Western officials were determined to ensure that Western aid was not used in a way that would allow him to concentrate his resources on fighting wars, keeping his regime in power while leaving the West to deal with the consequences of famine. Western relief agencies took a similar view. 'Agencies were tired of helping a government that seemed to do so little to help itself,' remarked Tony Vaux, an Oxfam official.

Donors were also sceptical about Dawit's role, disliking his rude and abrasive manner and his overt antagonism towards the United States. They expressed doubts about the accuracy of his forecasts of the amount of aid that Ethiopia required, the more so since the government itself refused to acknowledge it even had a problem. Dawit's assessment in March was that to get through 1984, Ethiopia needed 900,000 tons of grain. An assessment by the UN Food and Agriculture Organisation put the figure at 125,000 tons.

In April Dawit set off on a month-long tour of Europe and North America to canvass for greater international support. Addressing the United Nations, he spoke of a 'severe drought of unprecedented magnitude' afflicting Ethiopia. 'Starvation is currently the lot of over 5 million of our population.' He gained little attention and returned to find Mengistu livid that he had aired Ethiopia's difficulties so publicly.

I went to his office and truly, he was furious. Anyone who knows Mengistu can tell when he is angry. Before he says anything his cheek bones tremble furiously as he holds in his rage. I nervously braced myself for his attack . . .

He said that imperialist elements would do everything possible to thwart our efforts, to embarrass us, to destroy the gains of the revolution. One way of trying to embarrass us, he said, was by exploiting the drought. The menace in his voice was unmistakable. He told me that I had to be careful not to fall into their trap. My statement to the UN was inaccurate, exaggerated, he said; it showed Ethiopia in a bad light because it told only of disaster and nothing of governmental achievements or efforts to overcome the crisis. I had not emphasised that it was a natural disaster – a drought, not a famine – and that if it were not for this natural setback the Ethiopian people would have made great strides in overcoming food shortages . . .

I tried to tell him the reality as I saw it, as so many others saw it. Mengistu would not listen. He repeated again and again that it was only an ordinary food shortage being used as a ploy. Finally, he angrily ordered me to hold no more public meetings or donor meetings, to go on no more fund-raising tours to Europe or America, but to stay put and to do whatever I could without attracting attention.

Mengistu also ordered famine areas to be closed to all foreign visitors and banned donor representatives and journalists from travelling there. Throughout the summer, while thousands starved to death in Tigray and Wollo each week, no mention was made in the Ethiopian press about the disaster. Newspapers were filled instead with glowing descriptions about preparations for the founding congress of the Workers' Party and the tenth anniversary celebrations. When the summer *meher* rains failed, causing even greater peril, still no alarm was raised. Destitute peasants arriving in Addis Ababa were rounded up and expelled from the city.

In a five-hour televised speech to the Workers' Party congress, delivered in its new convention hall in Addis Ababa on 6 September, Mengistu lavished praise on the achievements of the revolution. He spoke in vibrant terms of 'the success of the measures taken to raise production in the agricultural sector [that] has helped especially to alleviate the shortages of food crops'. But he made no mention of the crisis that Ethiopia faced and made only a passing reference to drought. 'We must put an end to the problem that threatens the lives of millions of our people every time it fails to rain in parts of our country,' he said. 'From now on, our slogan, "We shall control the forces of nature", must be put into action. We must mobilise our collective efforts to free agriculture from the effects of natural disaster.'

On the same day Mengistu unveiled a monument called 'Our Struggle', built around a set of massive bronze friezes depicting the evil times of the old feudal regime that the revolution had overthrown. The central villain was a landlord on horseback, his face partly hidden by a bandit's kerchief, portrayed rejecting the entreaties of his starving tenants, in scenes remarkably similar to the current plight of Ethiopia's peasants.

There followed four days and nights of ceremonies, banquets, parades and gymnastic displays. Slogans abounded everywhere: 'Forward with the Revolutionary Leadership of Comrade Mengistu

Haile Mariam'; 'The oppressed masses will be victorious'; 'Marxism-Leninism is our guideline'; 'Down with American imperialism'; and 'Temporary setbacks shall not deter us from our final objective of building communism'. In all, Mengistu spent an estimated $150 million on the celebrations. Western journalists were invited to Ethiopia for the occasion but when they asked for permission to travel to the north to report on famine conditions, they were refused.

The scale of the disaster, however, had become too great to hide for much longer. At the end of September the Christian Relief Development Association, an umbrella organisation for relief agencies in Addis Ababa, sent a direct appeal to the UN's Disaster Relief Organisation asking for 'immediate and extraordinary action', warning that otherwise 'hundreds of thousands of people will die'. A few days later, realising that his reputation might be damaged, Mengistu finally gave attention to what he called 'the drought problem' and relaxed travel restrictions on donor representatives and foreign journalists. In October a Kenyan television cameraman, Mohamed Amin, arrived in Korem. 'There was this tremendous mass of people, groaning and weeping, scattered across the ground in the dawn mist,' he recalled.

Amin's seven-minute film, together with a commentary by Michael Buerk, broadcast on the BBC on 23 October, had a dramatic impact:

> Dawn, and as the sun breaks through the piercing chill of night on the plain outside Korem it lights up a biblical famine, now, in the twentieth century. This place, say workers here, is the closest thing to hell on earth. Thousands of wasted people are coming here for help. Many find death. They flood in every day from villages hundreds of miles away, dulled by hunger, driven beyond the point of desperation . . . 15,000 children here now – suffering, confused, lost . . . Death is all around. A child or an adult dies every twenty minutes. Korem, an insignificant town, has become a place of grief.

The film was subsequently broadcast by 425 television stations around the world, causing a tidal wave of public horror. Governments and politicians scrambled to respond, pledging aid and dispatching air force transport planes. In Britain an Irish pop singer, Bob Geldof, organised the recording of a fund-raising record, 'Do They Know It's Christmas?', that received massive support. In the United States the singer Harry Belafonte called up a galaxy of stars to record 'We are the World', a song written by Michael Jackson and Lionel Richie and arranged by Quincy Jones. A televised day-long rock concert – Live Aid – staged jointly in Britain and the United States and watched in 108 countries, raised more than $100 million. In just over a year, more than $1 billion was raised and allocated for relief assistance to Ethiopia by government and non-government agencies in the West.

A deluge of visitors descended on Ethiopia on fact-finding missions – politicians, churchmen, singers and actors. But Mengistu himself showed little interest in relief work. He paid just one brief visit to the disaster area, touching down in two locations for a total of thirty minutes. He had devised his own solution to the problem and was far more preoccupied with implementing it.

Mengistu's plan, announced in November, ordered the resettlement of 300,000 families – 1.5 million people – from drought-stricken areas of Tigray and Wollo to more fertile regions in the south-east of Ethiopia, to be carried out within a year. The gradual movement of people from the overpopulated north to the less populated south had been a long established practice, but nothing had occurred on such a scale, over such a short period and with so little previous planning. Mengistu's motives, moreover, were related not so much to any concern for the welfare of famine victims as to his drive to establish new collective farms in the south and his interest in depopulating areas of rebel activity as a means of winning the war.

At a meeting of government and party officials attended by Dawit, Mengistu explained his purpose. Resettlement camps, he said, were to be 'the core of our socialist rural structure'. He continued: 'The future success of collectivisation very much depends on their success.' He was even more explicit about the connection to his war aims.

Almost all of you here realise that we have security problems. The guerrillas operating in many of these areas do so with great help from the population. The people are like the sea and the guerrillas are like fish swimming in that sea. Without the sea there will be no fish. We have to drain the sea, or if we cannot completely drain it, we must bring it to a level where they will lack room to move at will, and their movements will be easily restricted.

Mengistu approached both Western diplomats and Soviet-bloc officials for help with the programme. At a meeting with the French and German ambassadors, he remarked, to their shock, that only the able-bodied would be resettled; the old and young, he said, would be left in drought-stricken areas. Most Western governments shunned the programme. A senior United Nations relief expert, Kurt Jansson, warned: 'It would usually take between five to seven years to get a programme of this size going.' But the Soviet Union responded rapidly with huge Antonov transport aircraft, helicopters and a fleet of 300 trucks with military crews.

Famine victims were told they would be provided with new homes, running water, electricity, in fertile land, capable of producing three harvests a year. Encouraged by such offers, many volunteered to go, but found themselves in an alien environment with little support. When the number of volunteers dwindled, Mengistu ordered forced resettlement. Field workers at the Save the Children shelter in Korem witnessed a battalion of Ethiopian troops surround their camp and seize several hundred people. Tens of thousands were rounded up, weak and emaciated, and packed tightly into Russian transport planes and trucks. Some suffocated; some were crushed to death; pregnant women miscarried; families were split apart. Starving peasants fled in droves from the shelters rather than face deportation. Hundreds of thousands took refuge in Sudan. Thousands tried to escape the resettlement camps despite the risk of being shot. 'If I can go home and spend one night with my family, I'll go, and if they kill me after that it doesn't matter because life here is useless for me,' one deserter told researchers. By February 1986, when the resettlement campaign was stopped, some 600,000 people had been moved; an estimated 50,000 had died in the upheaval. Dawit, given charge of the programme, subsequently wrote that it was 'perhaps the cruellest chapter of the entire famine'. Rather than free people from 'the terror of want', it became 'an even greater cause of terror'.

Perhaps a million people died in the Ethiopian famine of 1984–5. No one knows how many. Western aid helped save the lives of countless thousands of peasants. But much of it was prevented from reaching huge areas of Tigray where TPLF guerrillas held sway. Despite strenuous efforts by Western diplomats, Mengistu adamantly refused to allow 'safe passage' for relief to 3 million civilians living there. In an exchange over the issue with the US chargé d'affaires David Korn, the acting foreign minister Tibebu Bekele blurted out: 'Food is a major element in our strategy against the secessionists.'

For the people of Tigray there was to be no respite. In February 1985, even as the relief operation was struggling to cope with the disaster, Mengistu launched the Eighth Offensive in Tigray, bringing yet more devastation.

20

FAULT LINES

The fault line running across Sudan and Chad around the twelfth parallel, dividing the Muslim north from the non–Muslim south and 'Arab' from 'African', was the cause of endless conflict. At independence in Sudan in 1956, northerners gained control of the central government in Khartoum, eventually precipitating a revolt by southerners. In a reverse sequence in neighbouring Chad, southerners gained control of the central government in Fort Lamy (N'Djamena) at independence in 1960, eventually precipitating revolt by northerners. Like the British in Sudan, the French had treated Chad as a country of two halves: the south they called *le Tchad-utile*; the north, considered *inutile*, was known as *le pays des sultans*. Both conflicts stemmed from ancient hostility between northerners and southerners, dating from the days when Muslim chieftains raided the south for slaves. But they were made infinitely more complex by rivalries and feuds among northerners and among southerners and further aggravated by the way in which foreign governments sought to meddle in the warfare for their own advantage.

The first sign of trouble in Sudan came in the run-up to independence. As British officials departed, they were replaced largely by northerners, enhancing southern fears about northern domination. Out of a total of some 800 senior posts in the civil service filled in

1954, only six were awarded to southerners. The presence of northern administrators, teachers and traders in the south, often abrasive in their dealings with the local populace, soon rekindled old resentments. The Southern Corps of the army, commanded by northern officers but consisting almost entirely of southern troops, mutinied in August 1955. The mutineers, led by southern junior officers and non-commissioned officers in league with disgruntled southern politicians, succeeded in gaining control of the whole of Equatoria province except for the capital Juba, and received widespread local support. Northern officers, administrators, traders and their families were hunted down and killed. The Khartoum authorities re-established control by despatching some 8,000 troops from the north. Some mutineers were caught, tried and executed; most fled south into exile in Uganda.

In the months before independence, northern politicians promised to consider southern demands for a federal constitution that would protect southern provinces from subordination to northern control. But, once in power, northern parties gave the southern case short shrift, arguing that a federal arrangement would be tantamount to a first step towards breaking up Sudan. When the army took control in 1958, General Ibrahim Abboud set out to promote Islam and the use of Arabic in the south in the belief that this would encourage national unity. He considered Christianity an alien religion that foreign missionaries had foisted upon the south and imposed restrictions on their activities. He also expressed contempt for African religions, disparaged indigenous languages and customs and ordered the construction of Muslim religious schools and mosques in the south. The day of rest, previously observed on Sunday in the south, was changed to Friday to concur with Muslim practice in the north. When Christian missionaries objected to Abboud's policies, they were expelled en masse. Southern protests met increasing repression, prompting a number of southern politicians to flee into exile, where they joined ex-mutineers. The exile movement they formed, the Sudan African Nationalist Union, proclaimed their goal as independence for the south. In 1963 armed groups of dissidents, known colloquially as Anyanya, a name derived from a poison concocted in Madi country from snakes and rotten beans, launched a sustained guerrilla attack.

The first civil war lasted for ten years, claiming half a million lives. When General Abboud stepped down in 1964, the northern politicians who succeeded him rejected any form of self-determination or regional autonomy for the south and pursued the same policies of repression. Their goal was the establishment of an Islamic republic.

A military coup in 1969 brought to power a Revolutionary Command Council determined to sweep aside religion-based political groups. It was headed by a 39-year-old officer, Gaafar Numeiri, who had seen service in the south and who advocated a political settlement involving regional self-government rather than military repression. But Numeiri's regime was beset by opposition factions intent on overthrowing him. The first challenge he faced came from conservative forces led by Imam al-Hadi al-Mahdi, a grandson of the fabled Mahdi, Mohammed Ahmad. (In the nineteenth century the Mahdi's Ansar warriors had fought to rid Sudan of the Egyptian army and captured Khartoum in 1885, killing a British general, Charles Gordon, on the steps of the governor's residence. The Islamic state they set up lasted for thirteen years.) Attempting an armed Mahdist uprising in 1970, Imam al-Hadi's Ansar forces were crushed by Numeiri's army and the Imam himself was killed as he tried to escape to Ethiopia. A second challenge came from communist dissidents within the army who staged a brief coup in 1971, imprisoning Numeiri, before being overwhelmed by loyal troops.

Having consolidated his personal control, Numeiri sought an accommodation with the south. At peace negotiations with the Southern Sudan Liberation Movement in 1972, he agreed to allow the south a wide measure of local autonomy. The three southern provinces were linked together as a separate region endowed with its own elected assembly and executive authority, while Anyanya guerrillas were accepted into the ranks of the Sudanese army. A new constitution in 1973 established Sudan as a secular state, with freedom of worship not only for Christians and Jews, designated 'people of the book', but for followers of traditional religions as well – the vast majority in the south – hitherto denigrated by Muslim law as *kuffar* – 'unbelievers'. A secular law governed civilians in civil and criminal matters, while personal and family matters were covered by sharia law for Muslims and customary law for rural populations in the south.

The outcome was a rare example in Africa of a negotiated end to a civil war. But it was not to last. And one of the architects of its demise was Numeiri himself.

Chad's difficulties began soon after independence when its first president, François Tombalbaye, a southerner from the Sara tribe, imposed an increasingly repressive regime from Fort Lamy, dealing particularly harshly with the Muslim population whom he disliked and distrusted. Numbering about half of the population, southerners had gained ascendancy during the colonial era, welcoming French rule as a protection against slave raids from the north, accepting French education and working their way up through the lower ranks of the administration into political life and finally into national government. As peasant farmers, they had also benefited from French development of the cotton trade, the country's sole earner of foreign exchange.

Northerners, by contrast, had preferred their nomadic existence, resisting French endeavours to draw them into the modern world. The authority of the sultans had existed for centuries. In the far north lived the fiercely independent Toubou, black Muslims of the Sahara, who had fought against the imposition of French rule until 1930. Their Saharan zone – the provinces of Borkou, Ennedi and Tibesti, usually referred to as BET – remained under the control of French military officers until 1965, five years after independence.

Once in power, Tombalbaye lost little time in imposing a personal dictatorship. Intolerant of opposition, he banned political parties, enforced a one-party system and arbitrarily arrested opponents. But it was the Muslim population who bore the brunt of his rule. As French officials in Muslim areas were withdrawn, their place was taken by Sara administrators, often poorly qualified, who enforced government measures with a heavy hand, regardless of Muslim traditions. Tax collectors gained particular notoriety for their harassment of the local population. The army, too, recruited mainly from southern tribesmen, became renowned for its brutality and indiscipline. At Tombalbaye's instigation, Muslims were gradually edged out of public life; the authority of their sultans and chiefs was stripped away. Addressing a group of northern dignitaries, Tombalbaye declared: 'The present evolution of our country cannot be judged from the height of a caparisoned saddle, nor does it proceed at the slow pace of a camel. It is time, gentlemen, that you come down from your [high] horse.'

The first revolt, marking the beginning of a prolonged civil war, broke out in Malgamé, an isolated region in central Chad, in 1965. Muslim peasants rioting against tax collectors were fired on by government troops and many fled to take up arms. The rebellion spread eastwards, to the Batha, Ouaddai and Salamat regions. Bands of Muslim dissidents roamed about the countryside, attacking administrative and military posts, murdering government officials and local collaborators, stealing cattle and burning crops. In 1966 Muslim politicians living in exile in Sudan, formed Frolinat, the *Front pour la Libération du Tchad*, with the aim of coordinating rebels in the field. By 1969 the government controlled no more than fifteen *postes administratifs* out of a total of about one hundred in the central and eastern regions of Chad.

In the BET provinces of the far north, popular uprisings erupted soon after French military officers were withdrawn in 1965, handing control to Tombalbaye's army. Sara troops stationed in the north acted as an occupying force. New restrictions were imposed to control the unruly Toubou, including a ban on the wearing of turbans and on meetings of more than three persons. The movement of livestock was regulated. Attempts were made to force nomads into fixed settlements. Both men and women were subjected to humiliating punishment. In 1965 the entire population of the settlement of Bardai was arrested after a soldier had been killed during an affray between Toubou and the army. The following year, a prominent Muslim leader, the Derdeï of Tibesti, fled to Libya with 1,000 followers when government troops were sent to arrest him for protesting against the diminution of his office. In 1968 Toubou Nomad Guards in Aazou mutinied and attacked the small local garrison manned by southern troops.

Having lost control of most Muslim areas, Tombalbaye was compelled to plead for help from France. The French agreed to commit troops to Chad on condition that Tombalbaye implemented measures to restore to Muslim chieftains many of their original powers and broadened his administration by appointing Muslim ministers excluded from office since 1963. After driving back rebel groups in the east and the north, French troops departed.

No sooner had they left than Tombalbaye was beset by plots and intrigues, among the Sara now as well as his northern opponents. Once more, he reacted by ordering arbitrary arrests. He also tried to exert control over the Sara by embarking on a cultural revolution, replacing French customs with a revival of the cult of Yondo, the traditional Sara initiation rites. Yondo ceremonies, involving gruesome ordeals in the bush for weeks on end, were made compulsory for Sara youths and for candidates seeking admission to the civil service or appointment to high public office. Tombalbaye then tried to extend the Yondo campaign by requiring the induction of existing senior civil servants, politicians and high-ranking military officers. In southern Chad Yondo acquired the status of a semi-official religion. All individuals were obliged to assume authentic indigenous names and register them. Tombalbaye changed his first name from François to Ngarta, and the name of the capital from Fort Lamy to N'Djamena. Christians who refused to submit to the Yondo campaign were persecuted.

The eventual result of Tombalbaye's cultural revolution was that he provoked opposition at every level, from urban officials, university students, army officers and Christian missionaries. When he then attempted to purge the army officer corps of suspected opponents, the army struck back. In 1975 Tombalbaye was killed during an army coup. Describing his last moments, the Cameroonian journalist Jérémie Ngansop wrote: 'Tombalbaye had died weapon in hand. He had, in effect, fought to the last cartridge against his attackers, aided by only a few faithful members of his praetorian guard. Everybody had let him down. No one, not his celebrated *Compagnie Tchadienne de Sécurité*, nor his secret police directed by the Frenchman [Camille] Gouvernec, nor the French troops who had a unit stationed not far from the presidency, wished to "get their feet wet" in this reckoning.'

Chad's new military leader, General Félix Malloum, a southern officer whom Tombalbaye had imprisoned two years previously, emptied the jails of political prisoners and pursued a more conciliatory course. But he found his regime harassed by rebel Muslim groups which showed no interest in negotiating a settlement. Added to all Chad's difficulties, a new phenomenon had arisen.

The army coup in Libya in 1969 brought to power a 27-year-old signals officer driven by grand ambitions, fierce hatreds and a pathological penchant for meddling in the affairs of other countries, made possible by the huge flow of oil revenues at his disposal. Muammar Gaddafi was born into a poor Bedouin family. In his student years he had devoured the revolutionary ideas which poured out of Nasser's Egypt, listening avidly to Cairo Radio's 'Voice of the Arabs' and memorising word for word Nasser's speeches urging Arab unity and vilifying Western imperialism. Following in Nasser's footsteps, Gaddafi moved quickly to rid Libya of British and American military bases; he nationalised foreign-owned property and business interests, including the oil industry; and he imposed an austere form of Arab socialism, revising the legal code to conform to sharia law and banning alcohol, prostitution, nightclubs and Christian churches. Like other leaders in Africa – Nkrumah, Nyerere, Kaunda, Mobutu – he devoted much time to devising what he believed was a unique vision of society, publishing three volumes of a 'Green Book' on how to implement it. Based on Islam, it was called the Third Universal Theory and purported to provide an alternative to decadent capitalism and atheistic communism. The 'Green Book' was taught in schools and became required reading for all Libyans.

Gaddafi also issued a stream of proposals designed to forge Arab unity 'from the Atlantic Ocean to the Gulf'. Scarcely three months after he seized power came the Tripoli Charter intended to link Libya's destiny with Nasser's Egypt and Numeiri's Sudan. In 1971 came the Benghazi Treaty linking Libya, Egypt and Syria. In 1973 came the Hassi Messaoud Accords linking Libya and Boumedienne's Algeria. In 1974 came the Djerba Treaty linking Libya and Bourguiba's Tunisia.

None of Gaddafi's schemes for greater Arab unity survived. Soon after Nasser's death, Gaddafi fell out with his successor, Anwar al-Sadat, who scorned his Pan-Arab dreams; his subsequent feud with Sadat culminated in a brief border war in 1977 which left Gaddafi humiliated. In Sudan Numeiri decided that closer involvement with Egypt and Libya, in accordance with the Tripoli Charter, would jeopardise his hopes of reaching an accommodation with Sudan's southerners and dropped the idea. As with Sadat, Gaddafi soon fell out with Numeiri: in 1976 Numeiri accused Gaddafi of involvement in a bloody coup attempt in Khartoum and diagnosed Gaddafi as 'a split personality – both evil'. The arrangements that Gaddafi made with Tunisia and Algeria also came to naught. During the 1973 Arab–Israeli war, Gaddafi, despite his abiding ambition to participate in the annihilation of Israel, was left by Sadat and his Arab allies to sit it out on the sidelines.

'Neither the fire and passion of the Libyan revolution, nor its money could turn history around and revive an exhausted idea,' wrote Fouad Ajami, in his book *The Arab Predicament*. 'The Pan-Arab idea that dominates the political consciousness of modern Arabs has become a hollow claim.'

Thwarted on the diplomatic front, Gaddafi turned increasingly to subversion to achieve his aims, using his oil revenues to support a host of dissident factions and insurgent groups, engaging in plots to overthrow Arab governments opposing him and sending out death squads to murder his opponents living in exile. His readiness to use proxy violence, assassination and bribery made him widely detested and feared, as much in the Arab world as in the West. Among the causes he supported were an array of Palestinian factions; the Irish Republican Army; Basque separatists; and Muslim insurgents in the Philippines and Thailand. In Africa he backed Eritrean guerrillas against Haile Selassie's regime; Polisario guerrillas in the Western Sahara; southern African liberation movements; and opposition factions in Niger and Mali. He also spent heavily getting some thirty African governments to break ties with Israel, striking up a notable alliance with Uganda's Idi Amin, a fellow Muslim. When Amin's army faced defeat in 1979, Gaddafi despatched an expeditionary force to Uganda to try to prop him up, a venture that ended in humiliating failure. In support of his foreign ambitions, Gaddafi built up massive armed forces, including 700 aircraft, submarines and helicopters, relying first on France and then on the Soviet Union as supplier, spending an estimated $29 billion between 1970 and 1985. He also established an Islamic Legion, largely consisting of recruits from African states, to further his aims in Africa.

Gaddafi's greatest endeavour came in Chad, his southern neighbour. The civil war there opened up new opportunities for territorial aggrandisement. In 1971 he began a campaign to infiltrate the Aozou Strip, an elongated stretch of desert about 450 miles long and 90 miles wide extending the full length of the border between Libya and Chad. One of the witnesses to the Libyan campaign in northern Chad was Hissein Habré, a young newly qualified Toubou lawyer recently returned from his studies in France whom President Tombalbaye sent on a mission to northern Chad in 1971 to negotiate with anti-government rebels.

> The Libyans began distributing Libyan identity cards to the inhabitants of Tibesti and Aozou, predating them [Habré told *Le Monde*]. They invited the traditional chiefs to Libya and corrupted them. On the ground, their agents explained that Libyans and Chadians were one and the same people who were only divided by colonialism. At the same time they prepared the minds by distributing food and clothing to the population. When they had enough clients, they came to install themselves in the locality of Aozou and then the whole region.

In 1973 Gaddafi sent troops into the Aozou Strip, claiming that it rightfully belonged to Libya on the basis of an unratified agreement between France and Italy in 1935. He built an airbase at Aozou, set up a civil administration and issued maps showing the Strip as Libya's sovereign territory. He then used the Strip as a forward base for deeper involvement in Chad.

Gaddafi's occupation of the Aozou Strip caused a deep rift among northerners in Chad. One faction, led by Goukouni Oueddeï, the last surviving son of the Derdeï of Tibesti, was willing to accept Libyan involvement. Another faction, led by Hissein Habré, who had abandoned Tombalbaye and joined the rebel movement in Tibesti, was adamantly opposed. Both men were Toubou, but from separate clans. Their rivalry plunged Chad into prolonged conflict.

With Gaddafi's backing, Goukouni succeeded in ousting Habré from northern Chad and moved his forces southwards. In eastern Chad, meanwhile, Gaddafi supported a second insurgent group known as the Volcan army. In a joint offensive in 1978, Goukouni's forces and the Volcan army, supported by Libyan troops, made a rapid thrust towards N'Djamena. To stave off defeat, General Malloum called for help from France. A thousand French troops and combat aircraft were thrown into battle and routed rebel forces on the road to N'Djamena.

In the aftermath of the 1978 clashes, a new alliance was formed between General Malloum and Habré, giving northerners a prominent role in the government for the first time. Since his defeat in the north, Habré had regrouped in eastern Chad, raised a new army with support from Sudan and established a strong enough position in negotiations with Malloum to obtain the post of prime minister in a new 'government of national unity'. The alliance did not last long. In February 1979, in what became known as the first battle of N'Djamena, Habré's forces and Malloum's national army fought for supremacy, precipitating communal violence between northerners and southerners in which thousands died. Encouraged by the southern leader, Colonel Abdelkadar Kamougué, southerners fled en masse southwards, leaving the administration in N'Djamena to collapse. As the cycle of revenge continued, thousands of Muslim traders in the south were killed. Southern officials set up a *comité permanent* to run their own affairs, creating, in effect, a state within a state, levying their own taxes. At a national level, Chad had no government at all.

A host of international mediation attempts – by France, Nigeria, Niger, Sudan and Libya – was launched to try to devise a solution. Eventually, in November 1979, a shaky coalition government was formed, comprising no fewer than ten Muslim factions together with southern representatives. Goukouni was chosen as president, Habré as minister of defence, and Kamougué as vice-president. In N'Djamena, troops from five different armies patrolled the streets. Within a matter of weeks, the bloody struggle for power was resumed. Habré's forces clashed with pro-Libyan factions. Sporadic fighting continued for months. Half of the population fled to neighbouring Cameroon, leaving N'Djamena a ghost city. Finally, in December 1980, Libyan troops, backed by tanks, heavy artillery and units of the Islamic Legion, combined with Goukouni's forces to drive Habré's fighters out of the capital, forcing Habré to seek refuge in Sudan. In January 1981 Gaddafi consolidated his military victory by announcing, at the end of a visit by Goukouni to Tripoli, a merger between Chad and Libya and talked of forming an Islamic Republic of the Sahel.

Gaddafi's takeover caused uproar. In the south the Sara threatened to secede. Kamougué denounced the 'marriage' as 'impossible'; 'black Africans', he said, could not tolerate 'Arabo-Berber' rule. Throughout the region, one government after another lined up to attack Gaddafi, fearing his expansionist schemes and regarding 'unification' as a euphemism for Libyan annexation. Nigeria closed the Libyan embassy and called for sanctions against Libya. Senegal and Gambia broke diplomatic relations claiming Libya was supporting dissident groups. Mali, Mauritania, Niger, Ghana, Guinea and Cameroon took similar action. Egypt and Sudan claimed Gaddafi was acting as a Soviet proxy. Facing universal condemnation, Gaddafi was forced to declare that his agreement with Goukouni was nothing more than an initial move towards a future merger.

After a year's occupation, Gaddafi decided to withdraw his troops from N'Djamena, hoping that it would boost his chances of hosting the OAU's summit in 1982 and gaining the OAU presidency for a year. As the Libyans withdrew, Habré's forces, which had regrouped in Sudan and obtained the support of Egypt and the United States, crossed the eastern frontier, occupied eastern Chad and then took the capital, forcing Goukouni to flee to Libya.

The plight of Chad in 1982 was pitiful. One of the poorest countries in Africa, it had disintegrated into a mêlée of rival factions. All semblance of central authority had collapsed. The north had fragmented into a collection of fiefdoms ruled over by warlords who frequently fought each other, while the Libyans continued to fortify their bases there. In the south Kamougué held sway with his *comité permanent*, but the *comité* itself was torn by quarrels over money. Ex-soldiers in the south, meanwhile, formed their own commando groups – *codos*, as they were known. After successive rounds of fighting, the capital, N'Djamena, was a wreck.

'There was a country, a population, but no state power,' recalled Gali Ngothé, a government minister at the time. 'On the contrary there was a multitude of armed bands who went up and down the country holding the people for ransom . . . the state shattered . . . There were no revenue collection posts any more. Government buildings – schools, hospitals, post offices – were confiscated and turned into lodgings. Even the prisons had become residences. The offices were looted and the equipment sold in neighbouring countries at give-away prices. The archives and museums were sacked and burned down.'

Overshadowing everything, after nearly two decades of civil war, was the prospect of yet more conflict. Having failed to secure his election as OAU chairman, Gaddafi resumed his offensive in Chad in 1983. Goukouni's forces, supported by the Libyans, advanced on N'Djamena once more. In response to Habré's appeals for help, French troops and aircraft were sent to Chad to act as a buffer between the two sides, holding a line against northern incursions on the sixteenth parallel. In 1984 France and Libya agreed to withdraw their forces, but while the French duly left, the Libyans stayed, constructed military bases at Ouadi Doum, Fada and Faya-Largeau, occupied the principal Saharan oases south of the Aozou Strip, issued their own identity cards and prepared their allies for further ventures. In 1986, when Libyan-supported incursions across the sixteenth parallel began again, the French were obliged to return. As part of its wider campaign against Gaddafi, the United States joined in with increased assistance to Habré's forces.

Encouraged by the Americans, Habré sent his forces northwards across the sixteenth parallel in December 1986, overwhelming a major Libyan garrison at Fada. Over the next three months they succeeded in chasing the Libyans out of nearly all of northern Chad south of the Aozou Strip, inflicting a devastating defeat at their base at Ouadi

Doum. Demoralised and poorly trained, Gaddafi's army abandoned vast amounts of equipment, an estimated $1 billion worth, including tanks, aircraft, helicopters and air defence systems. After nearly twenty years of meddling in Chad, Gaddafi's dreams ended in debacle. As a result of a decision by the International Court of Justice in 1994, Gaddafi also lost all claim to the Aozou Strip.

For Chad, there was only more misery. Habré's regime turned into a violent and corrupt dictatorship, relying on death squads to maintain control until his overthrow in 1990. A subsequent commission of inquiry reported that 20,000 people had been killed and thousands more tortured in his jails.

In Sudan the peace agreement between the north and the south survived for eleven years, but came under increasing strain. On both sides there were factions that were never reconciled to the compromises involved in the 1972 agreement. Southerners were aggrieved by the central government's continued control over economic planning in the south and the limited funds it allocated for southern development. The discovery of oil deposits in the south in 1978 became a particular bone of contention: the southern regional government wanted an oil refinery to be built in the south, close to the oilfields; ignoring southern demands, Numeiri ordered the construction of an oil refinery in the north and a pipeline to the Red Sea for the direct export of crude oil. Other disputes broke out over Numeiri's persistent intervention in southern politics. There was further distrust in the south at Numeiri's rapprochement with Islamic factions.

Attempting to broaden the base of his support in the north, Numeiri in 1977 brought into his government two prominent Islamic politicians: Sadiq al-Mahdi, a great-grandson of the nineteenth-century Mahdi, who in 1976 had been involved in a Libyan-backed plot to overthrow him; and Sadiq's brother-in-law, Hassan al-Turabi, leader of the Muslim Brotherhood and founder of the National Islamic Front, a militant Islamic party, whom he had previously imprisoned. Sadiq had a doctorate from Oxford; Turabi, a doctorate from the Sorbonne. Appointed attorney-general, Turabi exerted steady pressure for the Islamic reform of the legal system and promoted the establishment of Islamic banks, enabling them eventually to gain financial dominance. He also led a sustained attempt to redraw the boundaries of the north so as to include both the south's oilfields and the agriculturally productive areas of Upper Nile province. Control of oil resources became a key factor in the contest between the north and the south.

In 1983 Numeiri abandoned the careful balance he had once tried to achieve and declared an 'Islamic revolution'. Sudan was to be an Islamic republic, he decreed, governed by Islamic law. Traditional Islamic law – such as amputation for theft, flogging for alcohol consumption and death for apostasy – would apply on a nationwide basis. Government officials and military commanders were required to give a pledge of allegiance to Numeiri as a Muslim ruler. Numeiri even attempted to take the title of Imam, albeit unsuccessfully. By presidential order, new 'Islamic' laws were added in piecemeal fashion to suit Numeiri's whims, without consultation with the attorney-general or the chief justice. Circumventing the established judiciary, he set up special 'prompt justice' courts. Thousands were arrested and brought before government-appointed judges who routinely handed out punishments such as flogging. To emphasise his dedication to the task, Numeiri poured $11 million worth of alcohol into the Nile and banned European-style dancing.

In the same arbitrary manner, he dissolved the southern regional government and decreed the division of the south into three smaller regions, corresponding to the old provinces under which the south had been governed before 1972, in effect terminating the constitutional arrangements of the peace agreement

Once more, Sudan descended into civil war. Mutinies broke out in garrisons in Bor and Pibor; thousands of southern troops deserted and regrouped across the eastern border in Ethiopia where they formed the Sudan People's Liberation Movement (SPLM). Its leader, Colonel John Garang de Mabior, was a Dinka officer with a doctorate in agricultural economics from Iowa State University and military training at Fort Benning in Georgia. Garang called not for southern secession but for a united, secular and socialist Sudan, free of Islamist rule. He portrayed the SPLM as a national movement striving for 'the liberation of

the whole Sudanese people'. The movement had emerged in the
south, he said, because government repression there was most intense.
'The marginal cost of rebellion in the south became very small, zero
or negative; that is, in the south, it pays to rebel.' During the course
of 1984, SPLM guerrillas spread out from border areas reaching ever
deeper into the interior.

As in the case of Chad, Sudan's second civil war drew in an array of
foreign players. Mengistu's regime in Ethiopia supported the cause of
the southern Sudanese in retaliation for Khartoum's support for
Eritrean secessionists and Tigrayan rebels. In Libya, Gaddafi, who had
once supported the Eritreans but who switched sides when Mengistu
came to power, joined Mengistu in supporting the southern Sudanese.
Numeiri meanwhile supported an anti-Gaddafi Libyan group, the
National Front for the Salvation of Libya, which set up offices in
Khartoum in 1981 and broadcast propaganda programmes attacking
Gaddafi. Numeiri also gave assistance to anti-Gaddafi groups from
Chad. The United States, for its part, despite the repression Numeiri
unleashed in southern Sudan, invested heavily in his regime to bolster
him as a counter-weight to Gaddafi and Mengistu, both of whom it
regarded as pro-Soviet activists; US assistance to Numeiri totalled
$1.5 billion.

With American support, Numeiri was confident he could deal
with any threat posed by rebels in the south. But he was beset by a
host of other difficulties. Hoping to establish Sudan as the 'breadbasket' of the Middle East, Numeiri had encouraged massive investment
in mechanised agriculture, but the overall result was a decline in agricultural production and a foreign debt of $12 billion that Sudan had
no means of repaying. When drought struck in 1983 and again in
1984, causing mass hunger, Numeiri, like Mengistu in Ethiopia,
ignored the consequences, desperately trying to avoid jeopardising
Sudan's image as a suitable destination for agricultural investment.
Only after an estimated quarter of a million people had died was he
prevailed upon to take action. Forced by foreign creditors to accept
austerity measures, Numeiri found his grip on power slipping.
Shortages, inflation, unemployment, deteriorating social services and
rampant corruption caused widespread discontent. The famine itself

provided a rallying point for organised protest. A coalition of trade unions and professional groups, including lawyers, doctors and civil servants, led the opposition. When urban strikes, riots and demonstrations erupted, not even the army was willing to stand by Numeiri. In April 1985, after sixteen years in power, he was overthrown.

An election in 1986 brought to power northern politicians fully committed to the establishment of an Islamic state. As prime minister, Sadiq al-Mahdi, the leader of the Umma Party, pronounced himself in favour of 'the full citizen, human and religious rights' of non-Muslims. But he also declared: 'Non-Muslims can ask us to protect their rights – and we will do that – but that's all they can ask. We wish to establish Islam as the source of law in Sudan because Sudan has a Muslim majority.' The sharia code introduced by Numeiri in 1983 remained in force.

Under Sadiq's regime the north experienced many of the benefits of liberal democracy – parliamentary debate, a vigorous press, an independent judiciary, active trade unions and professional associations. But for the south there was unrelenting warfare. The SPLM refused to accept a ceasefire or to take part in the election, demanding a constitutional convention. Sadiq responded by arming Baggara Arab militias in western Sudan – *murahalin* – licensing them to raid and plunder at will in the Dinka and Nuer areas of Bahr-al-Ghazal, just as their forefathers had done in the nineteenth century. Dinka and Nuer villages were attacked and burned, their livestock stolen, their wells poisoned; men, women and children were killed or abducted and taken back to the north where they were traded or kept as slaves. Atrocities were commonplace. In revenge for an SPLM attack on a Rizeigat militia group in March 1987, Rizeigat survivors attacked Dinka men, women and children in the town of Al Diein in southern Darfur, setting fire to six railway carriages where they were sheltering, killing more than 1,000; those who were not burned to death were stabbed and shot as they tried to escape. A report on the massacre, written by two Muslim academics at the University of Khartoum, blamed the killing on the government. 'Government policy has produced distortions in the Rizeigat community such as banditry and slavery, which interacted with social conflicts in Diein to generate a massacre psychosis . . . Armed banditry, involving the killing of Dinka villagers, has become a regular activity for the government-sponsored militia.' Rizeigat militias, they said, made a practice of selling Dinka women and children to Arab families for use as servants, farm workers and sex slaves. 'All this is practised with the full knowledge of the government.'

Similar tactics were employed elsewhere in the south. In an age-old custom used by the north, the government readily exploited divisions and rivalries among southern groups, arming tribal militias to attack rebel factions. '*Aktul al-abid bil abid*', was the saying – 'kill the slave through the slave.' Garang's SPLM, a predominantly Dinka group, was opposed by a variety of southern factions, some supported by the government, others acting independently. Some sections of the Nuer fought with the SPLM; other sections fought against it. Caught in the middle of this maelstrom was the civilian population. The SPLM struck particularly hard at civilian populations deemed to support hostile militias, acting in places like an army of occupation. But all factions sought to destroy communities presumed to be supporting their opponents. In far-flung, scorched-earth sweeps, heavily armed fighters torched villages, stole livestock and food, planted land mines, conscripted boys and raped women and girls.

The devastation of war culminated in 1988 in the most severe famine in Sudan's modern history. Both sides used food as a weapon. Inflicting hunger became a key military strategy. Army commanders and government officials prevented relief supplies reaching displaced populations and constantly thwarted relief initiatives by foreign donors. In one instance, relief food donated by the European Community sat for more than two years in wagons in a railway siding in Muglad, just a few hundred yards from a refugee camp where Dinka were starving. SPLM units besieged government-held towns, where a million refugees sought refuge, attacking and intercepting relief convoys. An estimated quarter of a million southerners died in 1988 as a result of war-related famine; some three million were displaced, many of them fleeing to the slums of Khartoum.

In an attempt to prevent recurrences of mass starvation, international agencies set up a permanent relief system. Both sides in the war used it to their advantage. The government considered itself absolved from dealing with famine. 'It is no longer a serious problem because international aid has been forthcoming,' Sadiq told an American correspondent. The system provided a regular supply of food for the SPLM's guerrilla army that they were routinely able to commandeer. 'I make deals with Garang,' an aid official explained. 'To get 90 per cent to my people, I let him have 10 per cent. If you don't feed the soldier, you push the soldier to rob the civilian. If you stopped any assistance, it would be the children who would die. It's a vicious circle. You cannot solve it.' Aid workers in the south quickly became cynical about their task. 'They don't care how many people die,' an official remarked. 'The lesson they have learned is that if you keep fighting, the West will keep feeding you.'

By 1989 the tide of war in the south had turned against the government. SPLM guerrillas were able to move without hindrance through much of southern Sudan; government forces were confined to garrison towns. Pressed by the army, facing massive financial difficulties, Sadiq entered into negotiations with the SPLM, agreeing to freeze the implementation of Islamic law as part of a peace process. But the concessions he was prepared to make went too far for Islamic militants. Shortly before Sadiq was scheduled to meet Garang in Addis Ababa, a group of militant officers, supported by the National Islamic Front, staged a pre-emptive coup.

The coup on 30 June 1989 not only scuppered peace negotiations with the SPLM. It placed Sudan in the hands of Islamic militants determined to impose their own brand of Islamic rule on the country. The constitution was suspended, parliament was dissolved, political parties and trade unions were banned and newspapers closed down. Leading politicians, including Sadiq al-Mahdi, were arrested, and the army officers corps was drastically purged. 'Khartoum will never go back to being a secular capital,' declared General Omar al-Bashir.

THE SCOURGE OF AIDS

In January 1985 a team of doctors was despatched by Uganda's ministry of health to investigate an outbreak of unexplained deaths at Kasensero, a fishing village on Lake Victoria, close to the border with Tanzania, frequented by smugglers and bargirls. Over the previous four years more than 100 people had died after succumbing to a mysterious wasting disease which the local population had named 'Slim'. Local explanations for the deaths were varied: some people said they were the result of witchcraft; others claimed they were a punishment from God for greed and loose living; some believed that 'Slim' had been caused by germs released into the atmosphere by the field artillery of the Tanzanian army when it invaded Uganda in 1979 in its counter-attack to drive back Idi Amin's plundering army. Blood samples taken at Kasensero in 1985, however, confirmed the disease to be Aids – Acquired Immune Deficiency Syndrome – a disease transmitted predominantly through sexual activity. Subsequent investigations showed that the causative virus of Aids – Human Immunodeficiency Virus (HIV), a slow-acting retrovirus that infects individuals for up to ten years before serious illness occurs – was rife among the population in the trading centres of Rakai district of southern Uganda and the neighbouring Tanzanian district of Kagera. Long before anyone had realised it, Rakai and Kagera had become the centre of the world's first Aids epidemic to strike a general population.

Originating from viruses carried by two African primates – chimpanzees and sooty mangabey monkeys – Aids had no known cure. It had been active in the human population in Africa, after jumping the species barrier, for at least twenty years before it was first identified as the cause of a series of deaths in the United States in 1981. A set of some 1,800 blood samples taken in Léopoldville (Kinshasa) in 1959, examined by scientists in the 1980s, showed one to be HIV-positive. Another set of blood samples taken from some 800 Kinshasa mothers in 1970 showed two to be HIV-positive – a seroprevalence of 0.25 per cent. A set of blood samples taken from Kinshasa mothers in 1980 showed a prevalence of 3 per cent – a twelvefold increase over ten years.

Across a belt of central Africa, individual cases of Aids occurred during the 1970s without doctors knowing of the disease. The first case in Africa was recognised by Dr Anne Bayley, a professor of surgery at the University Teaching Hospital in Lusaka, the capital of Zambia. On her hospital rounds she noticed a significant rise in the number of patients with Kaposi's sarcoma (KS), a rare type of cancer that had affected Aids victims in New York and San Francisco. 'I had been seeing about eight to twelve cases every year since 1978 – a very steady level,' she recalled. 'And then one day – it was in January of 1983 – I went into my ward to do a round, and I realised that there were nine cases of KS in there at once.' Many of these cases, moreover, were of a different, more aggressive type of KS. 'I realised that I was seeing a new manifestation of the disease.'

In October two teams of European and American doctors, prompted by evidence of Aids among Africans in Europe, travelled to Rwanda and Zaire to ascertain whether the disease had surfaced in Africa. Hitherto, as a result of cases in the United States and Europe, the most vulnerable groups appeared to be active male homosexuals and intravenous drug-users. During four weeks of investigation in Kigali, one team identified twenty-six cases of Aids and prodromal Aids, equally divided between the sexes. Nearly all cases involved employed urban middle-class people. In their report, published in

1984, the doctors concluded: 'Urban activity, a reasonable standard of living, heterosexual promiscuity and contact with prostitutes could be risk factors for African AIDS.' Similar conclusions were reached by the team in Kinshasa where they identified thirty-eight Aids patients, again equally divided between the sexes and coming from affluent backgrounds. In their report, also published in 1984, they discounted homosexuality, intravenous drug use or blood transfusion as risks factors in Africa. 'The findings of this study strongly argue that the situation in central Africa represents a new epidemiological setting for this world-wide disease − that of significant transmission in a large heterosexual population.'

The epidemic then underway in the Rakai district of southern Uganda showed the devastating potential of Aids. By 1984 it had taken root in Kampala, spread there in part by Tanzanian troops during their northwards advance against Amin's army. It moved rapidly along the arterial highways of Uganda, carried by truck drivers and crews stopping off in the bars and brothels for a night's refreshment and entertainment. A survey carried out by Ugandan doctors in 1986–7 at Lyantonde, a truck stop in Rakai district lying astride a major route to Rwanda, Burundi and eastern Zaire, found that 67 per cent of the bargirls there and 17 per cent of all pregnant women in the town were HIV-positive. A survey of the adult population of Lyantonde carried out in 1989 showed that 52.8 per cent were infected by HIV. By the end of the 1980s more than half of the women in their twenties living in trading centres in Rakai and one-quarter of those living in rural areas were HIV-positive. An official survey in 1989 estimated that nearly 800,000 Ugandans were HIV-positive. The death toll steadily rose. By 1988 four sub-districts in Rakai had each recorded more than 1,000 deaths. A 1989 survey of Rakai showed that out of a total population of 354,000, there were nearly 25,000 orphans or 12.6 per cent of the total of all children under fifteen years of age.

A similar pattern occurred in Rwanda. A national serological survey of all age groups from infants to the elderly, conducted in 1986, revealed that 17.8 per cent of urban residents and 1.3 per cent of rural residents were HIV-positive. The capital, Kigali, recorded a 21 per cent prevalence rate. The tally for two small towns in the Hutu heartland of western Rwanda was even higher: Ruhengeri recorded a 22 per cent prevalence rate, and Gisenyi, a lakeside town on the Zaire border, recorded a 31 per cent prevalence rate. In the case of Gisenyi, more than half of all people aged between twenty-six and forty registered HIV-positive.

From its epicentre in central Africa, the main Aids virus – HIV-1 – spread ever further – eastwards to Kenya, southwards to southern Africa and westwards to West Africa. Its advance was hastened by migrant workers; by armies and civil conflict, as in the case of Uganda; by refugee movements; by growing numbers of women and girls forced by poverty into prostitution; by 'sugar daddies' preying on young victims. Figures for cumulative Aids cases from African countries reported to the World Health Organisation in January 1990 showed Uganda's share to be the highest at 20.2 per cent, followed by : Kenya – 16.5 per cent; Zaire – 13 per cent; Tanzania – 11.4 per cent; Malawi – 13 per cent; Burundi – 5.4 per cent; Zambia – 5.2 per cent; Rwanda – 3.7 per cent; Congo-Brazzaville – 3.4 per cent; and Zimbabwe – 3.2 per cent. South Africa's first HIV prevalence survey, conducted in 1990, showed that it had reached there too. Countries in West Africa affected by HIV-1 included Ghana, Nigeria and Côte d'Ivoire. In 1989 some 50 per cent of Abidjan's prostitutes, tested for other diseases, were found to be HIV-1-positive. A second Aids virus, HIV-2, with a lower virulence and infectivity than HIV-1, also affected areas of West Africa, adding to the toll. As an indication of what was to come, surveys in 1990, mainly of pregnant women seeking prenatal care, recorded high HIV prevalence among the adult population in most capital cities in eastern and central Africa. Kampala registered the highest at 27.7 per cent, followed by: Kigali – 25.1 per cent; Lusaka – 24.5 per cent; Blantyre – 22.7 per cent; Harare – 18.0 per cent; Bujumbura – 17.5 per cent; Dar es Salaam – 10.3 per cent; Nairobi – 8.9 per cent; Bangui – 7.4 per cent; Brazzaville – 7.3 per cent; and Kinshasa – 5.3 per cent.

The extent of the epidemic compounded all the difficulties that Africa faced. The groups at greatest risk were those aged between fifteen and fifty, normally the most productive people in society. Typically, half of all people with HIV became infected before they turned twenty-five and died of Aids by the time they reached thirty-five. The loss of so many productive adults through illness and death had a profound impact on every level of society, leaving households and communities struggling to cope with a stream of orphans and cutting into national reservoirs of skilled personnel – teachers, doctors, nurses, administrators and industrial workers. As a result of mother-to-child transmission, infant mortality soared. Generations of children were deprived of childhood, forced to abandon school to undertake work or care for the dying or simply to fend for themselves. With ever-widening consequences, the epidemic overwhelmed health services, impoverished families, disrupted farm work, undermined business, reduced productivity and eroded the capacity of governments to provide public services.

The response of most African leaders to this calamity was to deny or dismiss the problem. African politicians preferred to represent Aids as either a Western import or a Western fabrication, concealing the true picture behind a smokescreen of accusations that it was no more than racist propaganda designed to dampen the sexual ardour and reproductive capacity of Africans. Zimbabwe's minister of health ordered doctors not to identify Aids as a cause of death. Kenya was more concerned to protect its reputation as a thriving tourist destination than to alert its own people about the hazards they faced. Little information appeared in newspapers; public discussion was muted. Many Africans adopted a cavalier attitude to the risks of infection. In Tanzania, Aids was said to stand for '*Acha Inwe Dogedoge Siachi*', a Swahili phrase meaning: 'Let it kill me; I shall never abandon the young ladies.' In Zaire, where Aids was known by the French acronym SIDA, university students translated it humorously as '*Syndrome Imaginaire pour Décourager les Amoureux*', an idea that quickly spread elsewhere.

Only two countries – Uganda and Senegal – launched effective anti-Aids programmes in the 1980s. Uganda's President Yoweri Museveni, after gaining power in 1986, took a leading role in speaking out about the danger posed by Aids, addressing meetings around the country. The disease, he said, was a threat to all Ugandans. He urged people to 'love carefully', to practise monogamy or 'zero-grazing', as it was termed locally, using earthy humour to convey the message. 'If you go into a field and see an anthill full of holes, and then you put your hand into a hole and you are bitten by a snake, whose fault is it?' He instructed every government department to take the problem seriously and established a national Aids control programme, bringing religious leaders – Protestant, Catholic and Muslim – into the campaign and striving to reduce the stigma and shame attached to the disease. An Aids-awareness campaign that initially adopted a 'fear approach' – 'Aids Kills' – was changed to include messages conveying compassion and solidarity – 'Do not point fingers at people with Aids – Anyone can get Aids, even you'. Recognising that the government on its own had few resources to combat Aids – government health expenditure in 1986 amounted to US$0.64 cents per person – Museveni gave free rein to non-governmental organisations to assist the campaign in whatever way they could and encouraged international relief agencies to help.

Senegal too began its own anti-Aids programme in 1986, even before the virus had taken off there in earnest. President Abdou Diouf marshalled government resources and urged religious and civic organisations to join the campaign. Despite the sensitive nature of the subject, Friday prayers in mosques and Sunday services in churches were used as opportunities to promote safe-sex messages. The messages were reinforced in the media and in schools. Sex workers were required to be registered and to undergo regular health checks. The result was that Senegal was able to keep HIV infection rates below 2 per cent.

For the rest of Africa, however, the Aids epidemic was allowed to rage on unchecked while governments remained largely silent. In the 1980s, because of the long time lag before Aids struck down its victims, the death toll was counted in the thousands. Only in the 1990s did the full extent of the disaster become apparent. By then, the death toll was counted in the millions.

THE LOST DECADE

So steep was Africa's economic decline during the 1980s that it became known as 'the lost decade'. In one country after another, living standards plummeted. By the mid-1980s most Africans were as poor or poorer than they had been at the time of independence. Crippled by debt, mismanagement and a collapse in tax revenues, African governments could no longer afford to maintain proper public services. Roads, railways, water, power and telephone systems deteriorated; schools, universities and hospitals were starved of funds; scientific facilities and statistical offices became early casualties. At every level the capacity of governments to function was fast diminishing. A drastic erosion of civil service salaries wrecked what was left of the morale, honesty and efficiency of civil servants; the purchasing power of the civil service in Tanzania, for example, tumbled in real terms between 1969 and 1985 by 90 per cent. Thousands of qualified public employees resigned. The brain drain out of Africa gathered momentum. It was estimated that between 1960 and 1987 some 100,000 trained and qualified Africans chose to work abroad; between 1986 and 1990 alone, some 50,000 to 60,000 middle- and high-level state managers left Africa. Bereft of expertise, African civil services became renowned for pervasive absenteeism, endemic corruption and low morale, incapable of performing basic tasks. A survey of twenty

23

24

'Elect of God': according to the Ethiopian constitution, Emperor Haile Selassie, pictured here in 1954 together with his wife and grandchildren, was descended directly from the marriage of Solomon and Sheba. His daily routine included feeding lions he kept in the grounds of the Jubilee Palace.

25

Feet of clay: Kwame Nkrumah's statue outside parliament was pulled down during the army coup of 1966. Youth groups brought up on the slogan 'Nkrumah is the new Messiah' marched through the streets of Accra carrying placards proclaiming 'Nkrumah is NOT our Messiah'.

Rumble in the jungle: President Mobutu, wearing his trademark leopard-skin hat, poses alongside Muhammad Ali at a reception at his Kinshasa palace on the banks of the Congo River during the World Heavyweight Boxing Championship in 1974.

In Washington terminology, Mobutu was a 'friendly tyrant', a reliable ally during the Cold War years, worth propping up with infusions of aid even though he duly appropriated it for his personal use. He made regular visits to Washington, befriending a succession of US presidents, including Ronald Reagan.

29

'Conqueror of the British Empire': constantly needing to demonstrate his power and importance, Uganda's dictator, Idi Amin, showered himself with military medals and titles, including a claim that he was 'the true heir to the throne of Scotland'. A group of British residents inducted as army reservists were required to kneel in Amin's presence when taking an oath of loyalty.

30

Facing defeat in 1979, Amin abandoned the capital, Kampala, without a fight, fleeing northwards to his home district, but still had time to pose for photographs alongside the remnants of his army.

Folie de grandeur: a former sergeant in the French army for seventeen years, Jean–Bedel Bokassa crowned himself Emperor of the Central African Empire and its 2 million people in 1977 at a ceremony in Bangui costing US$22 million, paid for mainly by France. Less than two years later, he was removed by French troops after the massacre of schoolchildren protesting against his regime.

The pariah: Colonel Gaddafi, pictured in 1972, three years after seizing power. Flush with oil revenues, he spent vast sums on armaments and on subversion around the world. His greatest escapade – a campaign to take control of Chad – ended in failure.

The driving force behind Ethiopia's revolution, Colonel Mengistu urged supporters to spread 'red terror' against his opponents. His friend Fidel Castro despatched 17,000 Cuban combat troops to help defend his regime.

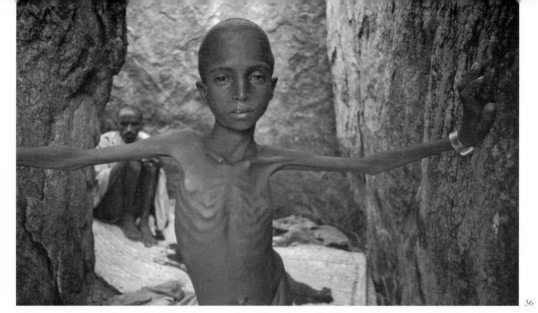

The scorched-earth tactics Mengistu employed against rebellions in Tigray and Wollo led to widespread famine there, prompting a massive international relief effort that included Band Aid and Live Aid. Mengistu continued with his military repression in famine areas even while the relief effort was under way.

Addis Ababa, 1992. Two days after Mengistu fled into exile, Ethiopian workers began dismantling communist-style statues he had erected, including this one of Lenin.

An emotional man, Zambia's President Kenneth Kaunda was prone to weeping in public and habitually carried a white linen handkerchief woven tightly between the fingers of his left hand. His record of economic management was catastrophic.

38

Uganda's president, Yoweri Museveni, was once hailed as representing a 'new breed' of disciplined African leader, but he was later cited by United Nations investigators as an 'accomplice' in looting Congo's mineral riches.

40

3⁹

Publicity stunt: Kenya's president, Daniel arap Moi, sets fire to twelve tons of ivory tusks worth US$2.5 million in a grand gesture in 1989 against ivory trafficking which had decimated Kenya's elephant population. Corrupt politicians and officials in his inner circle had previously made fortunes from the trade.

low-income African countries in 1995 revealed that half had twenty-five or fewer fully qualified accountants in the entire public sector.

As economies failed, large segments of the middle class were impoverished; urban wage-earners were pushed into the informal economy of petty trade and backyard businesses. Public resentment towards the state and its agencies grew apace. Ordinary people, wrote the Nigerian political scientist Claude Ake in 1990, 'see the state as a hostile force to be evaded, cheated or defeated as circumstances permit'. Smuggling, parallel markets and other semi-legal activities were commonly used as a means of survival. In the case of Zaire, its 'second' economy was estimated to be larger than the 'official' economy; much of the country's gold, copper and diamonds was smuggled out of the country illegally. To avoid low producer prices, Ghana's cocoa farmers resorted to large-scale smuggling to Côte d'Ivoire; in 1980 two-thirds of Senegal's groundnut harvest was sold illegally in Gambia; in the early 1980s two-thirds of Tanzania's food crops were sold through unofficial markets; government regulations in Tanzania were flouted so consistently in the informal sector that officials stopped trying to enforce them. Year by year, governments controlled less and less. Everything from currencies to food was managed outside official controls.

Unable to raise funds locally, shunned by commercial banks abroad, African states opted for rescue by the International Monetary Fund and the World Bank. In effect, Western donor institutions took over as Africa's bankers. Senegal in 1979 became the first African state to obtain a 'structural adjustment' loan from the World Bank. One by one, others followed. In the early 1980s the Western donor community believed that they were dealing with a short-term phenomenon and that with expert guidance Africa's difficulties could be overcome within a three-year period. But it soon became apparent that the rot went much deeper than expected and that what Africa faced was not a passing phase but a permanent crisis.

The remedy they devised for Africa's ills was a series of radical economic reforms. Whereas in the 1960s Western development economists had advocated that the state should act as the motor of development and dismissed the role of markets, in the 1980s they regarded the state as a principal cause of development failure and called for market-oriented development strategies in place of government intervention. Where once they had encouraged state ownership, now they sought to enhance the scope of the private sector, contending that private enterprise was more effective. Among the measures they stipulated in return for their assistance, the IMF/World Bank required governments to: devalue currencies; remove subsidies; reduce tariff barriers; raise agricultural commodity prices; cut back bloated bureaucracies; sell or close state enterprises; deregulate prices; reduce budget deficits and public borrowing; and lift restrictions on foreign investment. Overall, the aim was to get governments to shift from consumption, so favoured by elites, to investment.

The conditions set by the IMF/World Bank aroused strong opposition in many quarters. Their insistence on economic efficiency as the criterion for their aid threatened the system of patronage and patrimonialism that underpinned the rule of most African leaders. Africa's bloated bureaucracies and systems of regulation were crucial political assets, the means by which ruling elites provided jobs, contracts and other opportunities for gain for kinsmen and political supporters. As the eminent economist Douglas Rimmer concluded in his study, *The Economies of West Africa*, published in 1984: Africa's political leaders, despite their protestations, had never been primarily concerned with economic growth but rather with the maintenance of political power and the distribution of wealth to themselves and their supporters. They were unaccustomed to restraint. African elites faced losing the perks and privileges that economic control of the state had given them. Public sector labour unions warned against job losses. Most governments, moreover, were still wedded to the ideology of state direction and ownership and regarded public enterprises as a symbol of national sovereignty, however badly they performed; for years, they had treated private-sector entrepreneurs with disdain and discrimination. Many leaders feared that the consequences of lifting food subsidies which had helped keep the lid on urban discontent would be political instability. Tanzania's Julius Nyerere emerged as an eloquent opponent of reform, holding out against IMF conditions until his retirement in 1985, claiming that they would precipitate 'riots on the streets of Dar es Salaam'. Overall, there was widespread resentment about the role of interfering foreigners demanding austerity measures.

Facing bankruptcy, however, African governments had little alternative but to sign up. During the 1980s some thirty-six governments in sub-Saharan Africa entered into stabilisation agreements with the IMF or structural adjustment programmes with the World Bank. In all, a total of 243 loan agreements were made. Foreign aid became an increasingly crucial component in African economies. Dozens of donor institutions and Western non-government organisations were involved, some taking over key functions of the state, notably in health and education. The aid business became a major employer, second only to the state in many African countries. Over the course of two decades, the 1980s and the 1990s, Africa obtained more than $200 billion in foreign aid.

But while accepting donor funds, most governments prevaricated over reform, seeking to protect their own interests, implementing no more than a minimum of measures necessary for them to retain donor support, even though it made economic recovery less likely. Only a few African leaders embraced the cause of reform.

The star performer, unexpectedly, was Ghana's military ruler, Flight Lieutenant Jerry Rawlings. Rawlings stepped onto the stage in 1982, surrounded by Marxist advisers, expressing his admiration for the likes of Castro and Gaddafi and railing against the baneful effects of 'imperialism'. But after launching a series of populist experiments, he recognised the need for a different approach. By 1983 Ghana was close to collapse. Food supplies were unpredictable; production levels were at an all-time low; expenditure on health in real terms was one-quarter of what it had been in 1976; medical facilities were unavailable; infant mortality had risen from 80 per thousand to 120 per thousand in seven years; roads were impassable; inflation had reached 123 per cent; loss-making parastatal organisations devoured 10 per cent of government expenditure – in 1983 the Ghana Cocoa Marketing Board employed more than 130,000 people who handled a crop less than half the size dealt with more efficiently by 50,000 employees twenty years earlier; per capita gross domestic product was declining at the rate of 7 per cent annually. Compounding the crisis, a million Ghanaians were expelled from Nigeria and a severe drought brought power cuts and bush fires.

In 1983, with the support of the IMF/World Bank, Rawlings embarked on wholesale reform, accepting market disciplines and a reduced role for the state. Cocoa producer prices were increased almost immediately, quadrupling in value between 1983 and 1988. 'We are acknowledging the historic debt of the whole nation to the farmer,' declared Rawlings, 'and have thus repudiated the monstrous injustice of a past in which we virtually ran the machinery of the state on the tired backs of rural producers and provided little for their basic needs.'

Stage by stage, the currency was devalued, falling from just under 3 cedis to the dollar in 1983 to 450 cedis in 1992. The import-licensing system was abolished. A determined effort was made to reduce budget deficits and to prune the public sector. According to one investigation into the civil service: 'In some departments you found three typists employed for one typewriter, ten drivers for only one vehicle. And you saw them sitting around all day doing nothing.' During the late 1980s more than 60,000 public sector employees were made redundant. Rawlings also readily endorsed an enhanced role for the private sector. 'The zeal and zest of private ownership is the route to sustained economic growth,' his military council declared. Despite internal opposition, a start was made to privatise parastatal organisations, including Ashanti Goldfields.

The results were outwardly impressive. Cocoa production increased from 155,000 tons to 220,000 tons by 1986. Food production per capita also rose. The manufacturing sector expanded. Inflation fell from 123 per cent in 1983 to about 40 per cent in 1990. Between 1984 and 1989 annual economic growth reached on average 6 per cent.

But what recovery there was came at a price. Between 1983 and 1988 Ghana's foreign debt more than doubled, reaching $3.3 billion. The government's commitment to reform, moreover, brought no end to the crisis. So deep had Ghana sunk into penury that merely to reclaim lost ground was a long-term process. By 1998, after fifteen years of reform effort, Ghana's gross national product was still 16 per cent lower than in 1970.

In Tanzania, once Nyerere had resigned, his successor, Ali Hassan Mwinyi, swiftly reached a deal on reform with the IMF in order to avert collapse. Shortages of consumer goods, materials, equipment and spare parts had brought the economy to its knees; vast parts of the country's medical and educational systems had ceased to function in all but name; primary school enrolment had fallen from 98 per cent in 1981 to 76 per cent in 1988; the debt service ratio by the mid-1980s had climbed to a staggering 66 per cent; food assistance was increasingly needed to ward off disaster; bribery and corruption were rife.

After twenty-three years of socialist experimentation, the Arusha Declaration was formally abandoned as a blueprint for development. Despite Nyerere's warnings about political instability, the public was ready to accept reform. 'There was virtually no visible opposition to the austerity measures that accompanied structural adjustment,' reported Aili Mari Tripp in her study, *Changing the Rules*; the reason, she said, was that more than 90 per cent of households in Dar es Salaam derived their income from informal businesses set up in response to the crisis. Like Ghana, Tanzania made its way onto the donor community's list of 'good pupils'. One World Bank study of the reform process there was even subtitled: 'Resolute Action'.

Most governments, however, were reluctant to make a radical break with the past and soon discovered that there were no serious penalties involved. Aid kept coming. Kenya agreed to undertake the same set of agricultural reforms four times during the 1980s; it failed to reduce the size of the civil service; and it made little effort to liberalise the economy. Yet the grants it received rose from 1 per cent of gross domestic product in 1986 to more than 3 per cent in 1990. In cases where 'non-compliance' went too far, aid programmes were sometimes suspended but always remained open for 'renegotiation'. Under pressure to reduce budgets, governments chose soft targets, preferring to cut investment and maintenance outlays rather than personnel expenditures that sustained their patronage networks. Indeed, governments used donor finance as much to delay reform as to implement it. Aid resources, rather than serving the purposes of structural adjustment, lessened the incentives governments had to undertake policy reforms. Overall, government consumption increased, even as development efforts were pared down. Debt was simply allowed to accumulate, rescheduled again and again. Rescheduling became no more than a ritual. By 1990, thirty countries had negotiated 120 reschedulings. In a majority of cases the most that was achieved from 'structural adjustment' was partial reform that allowed state elites to continue ruling much as before.

Governments also discovered ways to manipulate the reform process to their advantage. Initially hostile to the idea of privatising parastatal organisations which provided them with a major source of patronage, they came to realise that the business of privatisation itself could be used as a means of patronage. As one of the World Bank's favourite causes, funds for privatisation were readily available. Some two-thirds of IMF and World Bank structural adjustment lending to African governments between 1989 and 1991 was directed towards parastatal reform, notably the privatisation of public companies. But donors kept no close control over the process. African leaders were thus given a golden opportunity to sell off government assets to political cronies and select businessmen at minimum prices on highly favourable terms, including low-interest loans and lengthy pay-off periods. Included in the bonanza were parastatal organisations set up with donor support in the 1960s and 1970s and then given project aid for their 'rehabilitation' in the 1980s. Most deals over privatisation were conducted in secret. 'Crony' capitalism flourished.

President Houphouët-Boigny of Côte d'Ivoire used the privatisation process as a way of reasserting his control over client networks. Officials from the World Bank, who had enthusiastically supported his privatisation campaign believing it would enhance local ownership, were horrified to discover that their funding had actually helped develop a larger and less independent parastatal sector. President Biya of Cameroon took the opportunity to strengthen the economic power of his Beti kinsmen. In Nigeria in the late 1980s, military officers acquired a majority of shares in four-fifths of the 100 state-owned firms that were privatised. In Kenya, Uganda, Zaire, Guinea and Senegal, public enterprises were sold to relatives and clients of the political elite. In Congo-Brazzaville a trade union leader complained: 'Really and truly, the people who are lining up to buy the companies up for sale are none other than members of the government.'

By the end of the 1980s, after a decade of structural adjustment, little had changed for the better. Africa was slipping into its own bleak category. Per capita income in black Africa, with a population of 450 million, was lower than it had been in 1960. Growth per capita during the 1980s contracted by an annual rate of 2.2 per cent. External debt tripled, reaching $160 billion, a sum exceeding gross national product. Debt service alone accounted for 25 per cent of exports of goods and services. Only about half of the servicing payments due were actually paid, but even then the outflow exceeded the inflow of foreign aid and investment. Government deficits were running at an average of more than 6 per cent compared with 2 per cent in 1980.

The terms of trade for African commodities continued to decline. Each year during the 1980s the purchasing power of exports fell so that at the end of the decade it stood at only 77 per cent of the level of 1982; in other words, adverse movements in the terms of trade had cost African countries close to 25 per cent of the purchasing power of their exports. In the case of two crops of vital importance, cocoa and coffee, between 1986 and 1989 prices for cocoa fell by 48 per cent and for coffee by 55 per cent. As a result of the fall in commodity prices, Africa lost potential income of $50 billion in the 1986–8 period.

Inflows of private capital – except for oil and mineral investment – were negligible. Foreign businessmen who once regarded Africa as offering high-risk but high-return opportunities now saw it as a place of even higher risk but low return. Foreign aid was needed to fill an ever-widening gap and in some cases became a substitute for government. In 1980 official development assistance constituted less than 4 per cent of black Africa's overall gross domestic product; by 1989 it had grown to nearly 10 per cent. Measured in real terms, foreign aid doubled during the 1980s, growing from $7.6 billion a year to $15 billion. In addition a total of $6 billion of debt was cancelled. But at the same time that public finances had become highly dependent on donor support, the lack of progress in Africa was precipitating 'donor fatigue'.

The World Bank itself had reached the conclusion that economic reform alone would not solve the crisis; political reform too was essential. In a seminal report published in November 1989, *From Crisis to Self-Sustainable Growth*, the World Bank explicitly acknowledged for the first time that Africa's economic malaise had political as well as economic roots. What Africa needed, said the Bank, was not just less government but better government.

> Efforts to create an enabling environment and to build capacities will be wasted if the political context is not favourable . . . Ultimately, better governance requires political renewal. This means a concerted attack on corruption from the highest to the lowest levels. This can be done by setting a good example, by strengthening accountability, by encouraging public debate, and by nurturing a free press. It also means . . . fostering grassroots and non-governmental organizations (NGOs), such as farmers' associations.

In sum, what the Bank advocated was political liberalisation. Economic success, it maintained, depended to a large degree on effective and honest government, the rule of law, open economies and political democracy.

The president of the World Bank, Barber Conable, followed with far more direct criticism:

> The development of many Sub-Saharan African countries has been quite unnecessarily constrained by their political systems. Africans can and must tackle this issue. Indisputably, three decades after independence too many African countries have failed to produce political and economic systems in which development can flourish . . . People need freedom to realise individual and collective potential . . . Open political participation has been restricted and

even condemned and those brave enough to speak their minds have too frequently taken grave political risks. I fear that many of Africa's political leaders have been more concerned about retaining power than about the long-term development interests of their people. The cost to millions of Africans . . . has been unforgivably high.

What this meant henceforth for African regimes in their dealings with the West was that they faced not just economic conditions for Western aid but political conditions.

Simultaneously, there were signs across the continent that African populations were beginning to revolt against the predatory rule of their political leaders.

THE STRUGGLE FOR
DEMOCRACY

'Worshipping a dictator is such a pain in the ass,' complains Ikem Osadi, the editor of the *National Gazette* in Chinua Achebe's novel, *Anthills of the Savannah*, published in 1987. His outburst is prompted by the fickle conduct of a president who has grown from false messiah to monster. 'It wouldn't be so bad if it was merely a matter of dancing upside down on your head. With practice anyone could learn to do that. The real problem is having no way of knowing from one day to another, from one minute to the next, just what is up and what is down.'

Africa, by the end of the 1980s, was renowned for its Big Men, dictators who strutted the stage, tolerating neither opposition nor dissent, rigging elections, emasculating the courts, cowing the press, stifling the universities, demanding abject servility and making themselves exceedingly rich. Their faces appeared on currency notes; their photographs graced offices and shops. They named highways, football stadiums and hospitals after themselves. Their speeches and daily activities dominated radio and television news and government newspapers. They packed the civil service with their own supporters and employed secret police to hunt down opponents, licensing them to detain, torture and murder at will, if necessary. By the end of the 1980s, not a single African head of state in three decades had allowed

himself to be voted out of office. Of some 150 heads of state who had
trodden the African stage, only six had voluntarily relinquished power.
They included Senegal's Léopold Senghor, after twenty years in office;
Cameroon's Ahmadu Ahidjo, after twenty-two years in office; and
Tanzania's Julius Nyerere, after twenty-three years in office.

Some members of the first generation of African leaders still clung
to power even in old age. In Côte d'Ivoire, after twenty-nine years in
office, Félix Houphouët-Boigny, at the age of eighty-four, remained
as adamantly in control as ever. 'There is no number two, three of
four,' he said in 1988. 'In Côte d'Ivoire there is only a number one:
that's me and I don't share my decisions.' Since taking office he had
won all six presidential elections with a reported average of 99.7 per
cent of the vote. A history professor, Laurent Gbagbo, who in 1982
circulated a suppressed speech he had intended to deliver on the
advantages of multi-party democracy, fled soon afterwards to avoid the
risk of imprisonment. When Houphouët offered a general amnesty to
political opponents and exiles in 1988, Gbagbo returned home but
immediately ran into trouble for promoting an opposition party he
had founded in exile. After a spell in a military camp, he was summoned before Houphouët and his entire cabinet to be given a
dressing-down. Asked in 1989 why he wanted to change the system,
Gbagbo replied: 'I take inspiration from President Houphouët-Boigny.
Everything he does is what we should not do. Look around Abidjan
and you have the Houphouët-Boigny stadium, the Houphouët-
Boigny bridge, the Houphouët-Boigny maternity centre. What we
need is decentralisation. That is when people can take their own
affairs into their own hands.'

In Malawi, Banda's dictatorship degenerated into tyranny. Having
appointed himself president-for-life in 1971, he snuffed out any sign
of dissent, incarcerating thousands of Malawians in detention centres
and sending out his secret police and paramilitary Young Pioneers to
deal with opponents at home and abroad. In 1981 Orton Chirwa, a
prominent exile visiting Zambia, and his wife, Vera, were abducted,
charged with treason, paraded at a show trial and given a death
sentence that was commuted to life imprisonment only as a result of
international protest. In 1983 three cabinet ministers and a member of

parliament attempting internal reforms were arrested as they were leaving parliament and bludgeoned to death by the police with sledge-hammers; they were officially described as having died in a car crash. Using his control of government, Banda constructed a huge business empire, Press Holdings, which expanded into tobacco, ranching, transport, property, oil distribution, pharmaceuticals, insurance and banking; it eventually accounted for one-third of Malawi's gross domestic product and employed 10 per cent of the wage-earning work force.

In his old age – in 1988 he was ninety – Banda relied increasingly on two protégés to maintain his rule. One was his constant companion for thirty years, Cecilia Kadzamira, a former nurse he had employed in his surgery before independence, who became his secretary, then progressed to the position of Official Hostess and finally acquired the title of 'Mama' – 'mother of the nation'. The other was Kadzamira's uncle, John Tembo, the chairman of Press Holdings and numerous other organisations and Banda's chief hatchet man, ruthless in eliminating rivals. Between them they controlled access to the president and intended to inherit power on his demise. Despite his old age and growing infirmity, however, Banda showed no signs of being ready to relinquish office. 'I want to be blunt,' he said. 'As long as I am here and you say I must be your president, you have to do what I want, what I like, and not what you like and you want. Kamuzu is in charge. That is my way.'

In Zambia, Kenneth Kaunda's regime was more benign but he was equally adamant about the merits of one-party rule and his own leadership, despite a catastrophic record of economic mismanagement over twenty-five years in office. When Kaunda came up for re-election in 1988, a former minister, Sikota Wina, complained: 'It is impossible to run against Kaunda. It is a watertight system to produce one candidate. There is no way in which anyone can actually challenge the president.' In the 1980s Kaunda was estimated to control 40,000 patronage positions in Lusaka alone.

An emotional man, he was prone to weeping in public and habitually carried a white linen handkerchief woven tightly between the fingers of his left hand. Even with Zambia in such a parlous state, he devoted much of his time to dwelling on world problems such as Palestine and events in the Middle East, Korea and Germany. His speeches were laced with quotations from the Bible and he constantly referred to his philosophy of Humanism on which he published two volumes. But while espousing deep Christian principles, he was not averse to detaining dissidents without trial. A US State Department report on human rights in Zambia noted: 'There are credible allegations that police and military personnel have resorted to excessive force when interviewing detainees or prisoners. Alleged abuses . . . include beatings, withholding of food, pain inflicted on various parts of the body, long periods of solitary confinement and threats of execution.'

In Gabon, Omar Bongo had presided over the country's oil wealth for twenty-two years, making himself one of the world's richest men. A flamboyant, autocratic figure, accustomed to living in style and demanding total obedience, he explained his conversion from Christianity to Islam by pointing out that it removed intermediaries between himself and God. 'I do not have to appear in front of a Monsignor or Bishop in order to render account of what I have done,' he said. The cost of his presidential palace in Libreville ran to $500 million. His business interests ranged from property to manganese and oil exports. In return for substantial tax breaks, he arranged for the French oil company Elf, which managed Gabon's oil resources, to transfer 10 per cent of all petroleum sales into a *Provision pour Investissements Diversifiés,* a thinly disguised slush fund for his own use. The French newspaper *Le Monde* reported in 1989 that during the 1970s and 1980s, one-quarter of public revenues had been diverted into the private hands of the elite, an amount nearly double the national debt that Gabon was struggling to repay. It calculated that 80 per cent of all personal income in Gabon went to 2 per cent of the population, mainly the elite and their extended families.

A number of army coup leaders also dug in for the long term, setting themselves up with one-party systems. Mobutu, by the end of the 1980s, had been in power in Zaire for twenty-four years. General Moussa Traoré had ruled Mali for twenty-one years, winning elections in 1979, 1984 and 1989, in which he stood unopposed. In Togo,

General Gnassingbé Eyedéma, a former French army sergeant involved
in the assassination of President Olympio in 1963, had been in power
for twenty-one years. In Benin (Dahomey), Mathieu Kérékou, a
French-trained paratrooper, had lasted in power for seventeen years,
presiding over what was officially termed a 'Marxist–Leninist' state. In
Ethiopia, Colonel Mengistu, after fifteen years in power, was still
fighting wars against rebels in Eritrea, Tigray and Wollo, employing an
army of half a million men to prop up his regime.

Nigeria's military ruler, General Ibrahim Babangida, took control
in a palace coup in 1985 purporting to favour a return to civilian rule,
but soon acquired a taste for wielding political power himself and set
up an avaricious personal dictatorship more ruthless than anything
Nigeria had previously experienced. His State Security Service
became a law unto itself, notorious for arbitrary arrests, detention, torture and murder. Civilian groups – labour unions, students,
professional associations, human rights organisations and the press –
were denounced as 'extremists' and persecuted. The outspoken editor
of a weekly magazine, *Newswatch*, renowned for its biting commen-
taries and investigative reporting, was assassinated by a parcel bomb.

With increasing abandon, Babangida, his military clique and business associates looted oil revenues, profiteered from drug smuggling
and engaged in systematic commercial fraud on an unprecedented
scale. 'Babangida was seen as the most massively corrupt ruler in
Nigerian history,' wrote the American scholar Larry Diamond. A
sharp increase in the price of oil in 1990 as a result of the Gulf crisis
brought Nigeria a windfall of perhaps $5 billion. Much of it found its
way into the hands of the ruling elite, channelled via 'dedication
accounts' attached to particular projects and ministries. The World
Bank estimated that $2.1 billion in petroleum receipts were diverted
in 1990 and 1991 to extra-budgetary accounts. An official report in
1994 calculated that between 1988 and 1993 about $12.2 billion was
diverted to extra-budgetary accounts. A major portion of Nigeria's
economy involved illegal activity. More than $1 billion a year –
equalling as much as 15 per cent of recorded government revenues –
flowed into smuggling and fraud networks operated with the connivance of the ruling elite.

Babangida worked on the supposition, wrote Segun Osoba, in an essay on corruption in Nigeria, that 'if he corrupted enough Nigerians there would be nobody to speak out on the issue of corruption or public accountability and so the matter would disappear from the national agenda'. He went on:

> To some extent the strategy worked as many university professors and other academics, leaders of the main professions, leading trade unionists, top clerics and evangelists and the shakers and movers of the 'organised private sector' of the national economy scrambled to jump on the Babangida regime's gravy train. Babangida established innumerable commissions, directorates, centres, task forces, committees etc., with open-ended budgets, woolly and indeterminate agendas and arbitrary powers to accommodate his multitudinous army of cronies, lackeys and opportunists.
>
> The main distinguishing feature of corruption in the Babangida regime was the pervasive culture of impunity: any of his acolytes, however high or low in status, could loot the treasury to their heart's content with impunity, provided they remained absolutely loyal and committed to the leader. Those who backslide or waver in their loyalty and commitment . . . were terrorised with all the coercive instruments of state power, even when they had done no wrong.

The lot of the common man, meanwhile, was increasingly grim. The United Nations Development Programme concluded from a survey in 1990 that Nigeria had one of the worst records for human deprivation of any country in the developing world. A World Bank report in 1991 ranked Nigeria as the thirteenth poorest country in the world.

A second generation of political leaders had emerged, with their own ambitions to rule through one-party dictatorships. Among the most notable was Daniel arap Moi, Kenyatta's vice-president for eleven years who inherited power on his death in 1978. Four years into his presidency he turned Kenya into a one-party state by law, scuttling plans for the launch of a new opposition party. He then set up a party disciplinary committee to bar from electoral politics any individual who criticised his policies, boasting of his power to destroy their livelihoods. 'I would like ministers, assistant ministers and others to sing like a parrot after me,' he said in 1984. 'That is how we can progress.' His rule became a litany of Big Man tactics. He curtailed the autonomy of judges and the auditor-general, eliminating their security of tenure; he harassed and imprisoned dissidents, condoning the use of torture; he obliterated press freedoms, muzzled trade unions and turned the civil service into a party machine. He gave party officials police powers to monitor public places, such as bars, hotels and restaurants, to identify opponents. He even abandoned the secret ballot in primary elections, replacing it with a 'queuing' system under which voters were required to line up behind the agents of candidates holding pictures of each contestant, a procedure open to any amount of abuse. Any candidate who obtained more than 70 per cent at this stage of voting was returned unopposed. Elections were commonly manipulated to ensure that only his own placemen were chosen.

An independent analysis of the 1988 election by two academic researchers, David Throup and Charles Hornsby, described it as 'a rigged and shambolic contest in which at least one-third of the electoral contests were rigged and manipulated blatantly to ensure that the "right" candidate won'. A church-funded magazine, *Beyond*, published a special issue documenting electoral malpractice in the 1988 election and was immediately banned by the government, its editor sentenced to nine months' imprisonment. The net effect of the 1988 elections was to eliminate all mildly independent politicians from parliament. Parliament was reduced to functioning as a rubber stamp.

A tribalist at heart, coming from a subgroup of the minority Kalenjin, a language family, Moi handed out key posts to Kalenjin members and promoted Kalenjin interests at every opportunity, using state power to undermine the patronage networks of the old Kikuyu elite established during Kenyatta's regime and to cripple the business interests of his opponents. The business empire he constructed for himself and his sons included assets in transport, oil distribution, banking, engineering and land. His inner circle, known as the 'Karbanet Syndicate' after his home town, became exceedingly rich, obtaining loans from banks and pension funds that they never intended to repay and huge kickbacks from government contracts. Foreign business-men regularly complained of the bribes that Moi's regime demanded to enable them to start up businesses or to win contracts. A Nairobi business magazine, *Financial Review*, which published reports in 1989 of political corruption in the coffee and tea industries, was swiftly banned. A fake export scheme set up by Moi's cronies in 1991 cost the exchequer an estimated $600 million.

Spreading from the top, corruption in Kenya became embedded in the system during the Moi years. 'An ethic of corruption has perco-lated deep into the civil service,' wrote the American journalist Blaine Harden in 1989. 'District commissioners routinely steal cement from donor-funded erosion prevention dams. Court prosecutors routinely demand bribes in return for not opposing bail. The director of motor vehicles has become rich and politically powerful by demanding bribes from everyone who wants to licence a big truck.' The judiciary became notorious for corruption. 'Why hire a lawyer when you can buy a judge?' ran a well-worn Kenyan saying. An investigation carried out in the post-Moi era found that almost half of Kenya's judges and more than one-third of magistrates were corrupt. It revealed that the cost of bribery ranged from up to $190,000 for an Appeal Court judge to $20,000 for a High Court judge to $2,000 for a magistrate. As little as $500 would quash a murder conviction, while $250 would secure acquittal on a rape charge. One judge estimated that at least 20 per cent of prison inmates were wrongfully imprisoned because they could not afford to pay a bribe.

None of this mattered to Moi. He was concerned only for his own interests. To celebrate his one-party regime, he ordered the con-struction of a sixty-storey office tower to house party headquarters and a party-run media centre. A centrepiece of the design was a huge statue of himself.

Out of a list of fifty African countries in 1989, almost all were one-party states or military dictatorships. Opposition parties were illegal in thirty-two states. Elections, when held, served mainly to confirm the incumbent president and his party in power. In twenty-nine countries, over the course of 150 elections held between 1960 and 1989, opposition parties were never allowed to win a single seat. Only three countries – Senegal, the tiny state of Gambia and Botswana – sustained multi-party politics, holding elections on a regular basis that were considered reasonably free and fair. Botswana, in particular, stood out as an example of a liberal democracy, tolerant of opposition activity, where the rule of law was held in respect and where economic development proceeded apace.

Yet a new wind of change was stirring across Africa. It was driven in part by widespread discontent with the corruption, incompetence and stifling oppression of Big Man rule, in part by resentment over rising unemployment, falling living standards and austerity measures that African governments were forced to implement in return for international assistance. Students were at the forefront of a wave of protests that erupted in one country after another, but other urban groups – businessmen, professionals, churchmen, labour unions and civil servants – soon joined in, demanding not just redress of economic grievances but political reform.

Events abroad, in the Soviet Union and Eastern Europe, affected the clamour for change. From the mid-1980s, as a result of Mikhail Gorbachev's 'new thinking', the Soviet Union began to retreat from Africa, no longer willing or able to sustain client states that had relied upon Soviet largesse for survival. With the demise of Marxism–Leninism in Europe came its demise in Africa. When Ethiopia's Mengistu went to Moscow in 1988 to ask for more military hardware, Gorbachev turned him down, telling him he needed to reach a negotiated settlement to the wars in Eritrea and Tigray. Having lost Soviet sponsorship and confronted by rebel advances, Mengistu renounced Marxism–Leninism and embraced the idea of a multi-party system in the hope of avoiding defeat at the hands of the rebels. The outbreak of mass street demonstrations in Eastern Europe starting in the spring of 1989 and culminating in the fall of the Berlin Wall and the departure of European dictators like Ceauşescu in Romania and Honecker in East Germany provided potent examples of what 'people's power' could achieve. One-party regimes now looked outmoded, in Africa as much as in Europe. Even Julius Nyerere, the most articulate spokesman for one-party systems in Africa, felt obliged to modify his support. 'To view a one-party system in almost religious terms is wrong,' he said in February 1990 after visiting Leipzig in East Germany. 'We Tanzanians have one party as a historical necessity. But this is not a kind of divine decree. It is not proper to treat a person who floats the idea of a multi-party system as someone who has committed treason.'

The end of the Cold War, moreover, changed the West's attitudes towards Africa. Western governments no longer had strategic interests in propping up repressive regimes merely because they were friendly to the West. Along with the World Bank, they concluded that one-party regimes lacking popular participation constituted a serious hindrance to economic development and placed new emphasis on the need for democratic reform.

In June 1990 Britain declared that the distribution of its aid programme would henceforth favour countries 'tending towards pluralism, public accountability, respect for the rule of law, human rights and market principles'. At a Franco-African summit at La Baule in June 1990, attended by thirty-three African delegations, twenty-two of which were led by heads of state, President Mitterrand stated that French aid would be dependent on efforts towards liberalisation. He warned: 'French eagerness to offer development aid is bound to cool off in the case of authoritarian regimes which fail to heed the need for democratisation while regimes prepared to embark on the courageous path of democracy will continue to have our enthusiastic support.'

Previously, Franco-African summits had been known as lavish, back-slapping family gatherings, full of empty talk.

The small West African state of Benin became the first to be caught up in the avalanche of protest. Its military ruler, Mathieu Kérékou, and his cronies had looted the state-owned banking system so thoroughly that nothing was left to pay the salaries of teachers and civil servants, some of whom were owed as much as twelve months' back pay. Three state-owned banks had collapsed in 1988 as a result of large unsecured loans awarded to members of Kérékou's inner circle and the bogus companies they had set up, amounting in sum, according to the World Bank, to $500 million. His closest adviser, Mohammed Cissé, a Malian marabout, it was subsequently discovered, had been in the habit of sitting in the manager's office at the Commercial Bank, transferring millions of dollars by telex to his bank accounts in Europe and the United States; in 1988 alone Cissé was estimated to have sent $370 million abroad. With the entire state banking and credit system drained of all liquid funds, normal business activity ground to a halt; companies could not operate, traders could neither sell nor buy.

In January 1989 a student protest over unpaid grants grew into a general mobilisation against Kérékou's regime involving teachers, civil servants, workers and church groups. The army, too, was restless, bubbling with plots; unpaid soldiers hijacked shipments of banknotes sent in from abroad to alleviate the crisis. Only Kérékou's elite Presidential Guard, drawn exclusively from his northern ethnic group, remained loyal. Common to all the strikes and demonstrations that erupted in Benin during 1989 were demands for the payment of salary arrears but the focus turned increasingly on the call for a *renouveau démocratique*.

When Kérékou requested Western aid to pay salary arrears, he was turned down. In December 1989, forced to make concessions, he abandoned Marxism-Leninism as an official ideology and promised constitutional reform. Expecting to be able to manipulate events, he proposed a national conference – '*Conférence Nationale des Forces Vives*' – at which business, professional, religious, labour and political groups, together with the government, would be given an opportunity to draw up a new constitutional framework. In what was intended to be a show of strength, he walked among demonstrators in downtown Cotonou but was booed and jostled. For the first time, government-controlled television screened pictures showing demonstrators waving anti-government placards.

When the national conference duly met for nine days in February 1990, its proceedings, broadcast live on radio and television, turned into a searing indictment of the venality and corruption of Kérékou's military regime. The 488 delegates, presided over by Archbishop Isodore de Souza, declared themselves to hold sovereign power, suspended the constitution, dissolved the national assembly, appointed a former World Bank official, Nicéphore Soglo, as prime minister of an interim government and laid down a schedule for elections. Kérékou was allowed to stay on as interim president.

Benin's legislative and presidential elections in 1991 were the country's first proper contest for power since independence. International observers judged them to have been generally free and fair. In the presidential election Soglo stood against Kérékou, defeating him by a resounding margin of two to one. Following his defeat, Kérékou apologised for abusing power during his tenure of office, pledged his 'deep, sincere and irreversible desire for change' and was granted immunity from prosecution. Benin thus became the first African state in which the army was forced from power by civilians and the first in which an incumbent president was defeated at the polls.

Over a period of four years following Benin's *renouveau démocratique*, a series of intense and protracted struggles for power broke out between Africa's Big Men and opposition groups bent on ousting them. In many cases, the opposition to Big Man rule was led by former ministers or members of the elite motivated not so much by democratic ideals, though that is what they proclaimed, as by determination to get their own turn at the trough of public power and money. Whatever motives were involved, all sides relied heavily on ethnic loyalties for support; neither ideology nor policy nor class counted for much at election time. Even in the case of Benin, where popular support for change was widespread, at election time the electorate voted largely on the basis of ethnic loyalty: northerners plumped in overwhelming numbers for Kérékou (94 per cent); southerners, for Soglo (80 per cent). After seventeen years of 'northern' rule, what many southerners had in mind was not so much the notion of *renouveau démocratique* as the need for *alternance* - a political 'changeover': their turn was due. With so much at stake, elections inevitably brought increased ethnic tensions. In some cases, they were recklessly exploited by politicians for their own advantage.

Ultimately, many Big Men were able to outmanoeuvre the opposition and remain in power; a few succumbed to the tide of protest.

But even in cases where there was a changeover or *alternance*, a sense of disillusionment with *renouveau démocratique* soon set in. In Benin, in 1993, southerners were complaining that 'democracy' had not changed anything; though political life was certainly more open and less repressive, the same elites – 'crooks' was the word usually applied – were still in control. In the north it meant that hated southerners were in charge.

When Houphouët-Boigny's rule was challenged in February 1990 by strikes and demonstrations in protest against austerity measures, he instinctively reacted with repression. Police were used to break up meetings and marches with truncheons, tear gas and stun grenades. A group of 140 students were bludgeoned for trying to hold a meeting in Abidjan's Catholic cathedral, then branded by Houphouët as 'thugs and drug addicts'.

The protests, however, soon took on a political dimension. Demonstrators brandished placards denouncing Houphouët's auto-cratic rule and his lavish spending on a vast basilica at Yamoussoukro and demanding multi-party elections. Houphouët's most persistent critic, Laurent Gbagbo, entered the fray, proposing a national confer-ence similar to the one held in Benin.

Houphouët's initial response was to reject calls for a multi-party system, but the level of discontent was too great for him to resist. In April 1990 he announced that opposition parties would be officially recognised, then moved swiftly to hold elections before they could organise a united front against him. In presidential elections in November 1990, Houphouët, at the age of eighty-five, won a seventh term in office with 82 per cent of the vote, defeating Gbagbo, who was half his age. His party won 163 of 175 seats. The outcome was more Big Man rule, but with a parliamentary opposition for the first time in the country's history. When Houphouët died in December 1993, he had held office as president for thirty-three years.

Zaire's decline had become so precipitate by 1990 that in April Mobutu bowed to pressure to replace his one-party system that had been in place for twenty-three years with multi-party politics. He promised a new era for Zaire and proposed holding a national conference to pave the way. For a brief moment it seemed that Zaire was destined for political change. But Mobutu never had any intention of giving up power. He retained personal control of the central bank, the military and the state security apparatus and proceeded to use brute force in May to crush student dissent at the University of Lubumbashi. The national conference was postponed again and again. Mobutu's commitment to multi-party politics was soon derided in Kinshasa as little more than 'multi-Mobutuism'.

Nevertheless, political activity flourished. More than 200 political parties were launched. Though many of them were fronts for Mobutu and his allies, set up to enable them to manipulate events, significant opposition groups emerged. They included Etienne Tshisekedi's UDPS which formed the nucleus of an alliance of opposition movements taking the name *Union Sacrée de l'Opposition Radicale*; and Nguza Karl-i-Bond's *Union des Fédéralistes et des Républicains Indépendants* which also joined the *Union Sacrée*.

The *Conférence Nationale Souveraine* (CNS) eventually assembled in August 1991. But its proceedings were soon disrupted by an outbreak of looting and violence started by Mobutu's soldiers protesting over low pay that spread from Kinshasa to other towns. One estimate was that the looting destroyed 90 per cent of what remained of the 'modern' economy. Army camps became 'thieves' markets' where looted goods could be purchased. France and Belgium dispatched paratroops to evacuate their nationals and other foreigners.

Under pressure from Western governments as well as his internal critics, Mobutu for the first time agreed to share power with the opposition. In October he appointed Tshisekedi as prime minister. But when Tshisekedi tried to deny Mobutu access to cash at the central bank, Mobutu dismissed him six days after he was sworn in and instructed loyalist troops to lock him and his ministers out of their offices. 'The chief is the chief,' Mobutu told his supporters. 'He is the eagle who flies high and cannot be touched by the spit of the toad.' To replace Tshisekedi, Mobutu turned to Nguza. On Mobutu's orders, Nguza tried to shut down the national conference, but was thwarted by mass protests.

The trial of strength between Mobutu and the CNS continued throughout 1992. As part of his campaign to undermine the opposition, Mobutu stoked up ethnic violence in the provinces. In Katanga he encouraged the governor he had appointed there to drive out Tshisekedi's ethnic group, the Luba of Kasai; 100,000 Luba were forced to flee from their homes. He adopted similar tactics in North Kivu. In August the CNS adopted a new provisional constitution and voted to restore the country's name to 'Congo'. It established a new legislative body, the *Haut Conseil de la République* and elected Tshisekedi as premier. Mobutu simply ignored the CNS and in December ordered it to shut down.

Describing Mobutu's position in 1992, Kengo wa Dondo, a former prime minister, told the journalist Mark Huband:

> He loves power. When I was prime minister, he didn't like discussion . . . He can't see himself sharing the power with somebody that he hasn't nominated. His conception hasn't changed since democracy arrived. Mobutu explains himself very easily: One chief governs. The chief is surrounded by advisers. He consults his college of advisers on decisions. He does consult. But people like him never believe that they take the wrong decisions. Mobutu is a man who is very influenced but he has his opinions. The last word is always his.

The economy, meanwhile, was in free fall. The inflation rate reached 3,000 per cent in 1991, 5,000 per cent in 1992, and 8,828 per cent in 1993. In December 1992 Mobutu ordered the central bank to issue a new high-denomination banknote – five million zaires, worth about US$3 at the time. But Tshisekedi declared the new money null and void and told traders not to accept it. Soldiers who had been paid in the new currency went on the rampage. During another round of violence in Kinshasa, the French ambassador and hundreds of other civilians were killed.

After three years of manoeuvre and obstruction, Mobutu in March 1993 abandoned any further pretence at reform, revived the old constitution and reconvened the old parliament. He became an increasingly remote figure, spending most of his time either on board his luxury yacht in Kinshasa or in isolation in his palaces in Gbadolite. In Washington his old friend President Bush sent him three letters during the course of 1992 urging him to relinquish power, but Mobutu paid no heed. The incoming Clinton administration signified its disapproval of Mobutu by withdrawing the US ambassador to Zaire, Melissa Wells. On her return to Washington, Wells was asked why the US did not simply tell Mobutu to leave. The difficulty, she replied, was that it was not 'as if he were the Wicked Witch of the West and would just melt and disappear. The man won't leave!'

After sustaining Mobutu in power for nearly thirty years, the United States had finally reached the end of the road. Appearing before the Subcommittee on Africa at the House of Representatives in October 1993, a former US assistant secretary of state for Africa, Herman Cohen, summed up what it had all come to:

> To say Zaire has a government today would be a gross exaggeration. A small group of military and civilian associates of President Mobutu, all from the same ethnic group, control the city of Kinshasa by virtue of the loyalty of the 5,000-man Presidential Guard known as the DSP. This same group also controls the central bank which provides both the foreign and local currency needed to keep the DSP loyal. While the ruling group has intelligence information about what is going on in the rest of Zaire, there is no real government authority outside the capital city.

★

The reaction of Ghana's military ruler, Flight Lieutenant Jerry Rawlings, when an opposition movement surfaced in Accra in August 1990 was to dismiss its leaders as a bunch of opportunists seeking to obstruct his 'revolution'. His answer to their demands for open politics, an end to press censorship and the release of political prisoners was to stage-manage a programme of political reform that was kept under his tight control. He established a committee of constitutional experts to formulate proposals for a draft constitution, but stacked it with his own supporters and redrafted its report to include clauses providing amnesty for him and his fellow officers. He waited until May

1992 to lift the eleven-year-old ban on political parties, giving them only six months to prepare for an election and then took full advantage of government resources – money, vehicles, helicopters and the state-owned media – to boost his own campaign. Just prior to the elections he announced a major increase in civil service salaries and launched new job programmes. In presidential elections held in November 1992, Rawlings won 58.3 per cent of the vote to 30.4 per cent for his nearest rival, Adu Boahen, an eminent historian. The election was generally judged by international observers to have been valid, reflecting Rawlings's personal popularity. Opposition parties, however, claimed massive fraud and refused to participate in parliamentary elections the following month, leaving Rawlings and his allies with a clear run. In January 1993 Rawlings was sworn in as president, in effect, of a one-party state.

Nigeria's military ruler, General Babangida, prevaricated for four years before authorising political activity, then imposed rigid restrictions over the electoral process and finally tore up the result when it was not to his liking. By raising expectations about the return of civilian rule, allowing popular momentum to grow, then arbitrarily terminating the whole exercise at the point when an election had been successfully concluded, Babangida created the conditions for riots, demonstrations, strikes and ethnic hostility and raised doubts that Nigeria would ever be able to escape from military dictatorship.

After lifting the ban on political parties in 1989, Babangida proscribed a whole array of political associations he deemed unfit to participate and substituted two news ones of his own making: the Social Democratic Party (SDP) and the National Republican Convention (NRC). Both were dependent substantially on state funding; both were required to adopt emblems and constitutions designed by the government and to stick to centrist manifestos, one veering 'a little to the left', the other ' a little to the right'. Former 'old-breed' politicians and holders of public office were barred from involvement on the grounds that their actions when in office, according to Babangida, had been 'detrimental to the evolution of . . . good government and the assurance of the welfare of the people'. Also excluded were groups deemed by Babangida to be 'extremist'.

Despite Babangida's efforts to regiment the transition, old political loyalties and factional disputes soon surfaced. Though there was much cross-migration, the NRC came to be regarded as 'a little to the North' or the 'Northern Republican Convention', representing con-servative northern interests; and the SDP as 'a little to the South' or the 'Southern Democratic Party', representing southern progressive interests. This perception gained ground as a result of local govern-ment elections in 1990, state legislature elections in 1991 and national assembly elections in 1992. When presidential primary elections in 1992 degenerated into intra-party factional disputes, vote-buying and court challenges, Babangida banned all twenty-three candidates involved and imposed a new nomination procedure.

Two candidates finally emerged to contest presidential elections in June 1993. The most prominent was Chief Moshood Abiola, a Yoruba business magnate and media baron, one of the wealthiest men in Nigeria, with interests in shipping, banking, publishing, agriculture, aviation, oil exploration and communications. A Muslim philanthropist, Abiola had made huge fortunes from his connections with the military hierarchy; in the eight years of Babangida's regime alone, his companies were estimated to have gained government contracts worth some $845 million. The other candidate, Bashir Tofa, by comparison was a colour-less figure, a Muslim business magnate from the northern Hausa heartland of Kano, who was little known even in his home territory.

Both Abiola and Tofa were known to be cronies of Babangida and his coterie. But Tofa, the northerner, was the candidate they favoured. Not only was Abiola a southerner, but his great wealth, when added to the powers of an executive president, was bound to make him more independent of Nigeria's military establishment, in particular the northern elite, long accustomed to wielding power either directly or indirectly through those in office.

With growing signs that Abiola was likely to win, Babangida inter-vened with spoiling tactics. A 'Babangida-must-stay' campaign was launched, with rallies, pamphlets and press advertisements. At the centre of the campaign was a proxy organisation called the Association for Better Nigeria (ABN) set up at Babangida's instigation, which demanded four more years of 'peace, unity and stability' under his leadership. Two days beforehand, the ABN obtained an injunction delaying the election from a High Court judge sitting at the unusual hour of 9 p.m. Despite the ruling, the National Electoral Commission decided to go ahead.

Against all odds, unlike previous occasions, the 1993 election was conducted in an orderly and peaceful manner. An American observer, Peter Lewis, wrote:

> To everyone's surprise, the election of 12 June was possibly the fairest, though hardly the most free in Nigeria's post-independence history. The combined influence of apathy, apprehension and confusion kept many away from the polls – voter turnout was estimated at only 35 per cent. Widespread administrative and logistical problems also prevented a number of intending voters from registering their ballots (including Bashir Tofa, who held an invalid voter registration card), but there was little evidence of systematic fraud or vote-rigging . . . and there were no reports of serious violence or casualties. Despite the narrow choices available to voters, the outcome of the election was eagerly anticipated in the wake of a successful poll.

The unofficial results, published in the press, showed a clear victory for Abiola. He secured 58 per cent of the national vote, leading in nineteen of thirty states and obtaining more than one-third of the vote in all but one state. For the first time in Nigeria's history a southerner had won an election for head of state. His victory was all the more impressive because of the extent of support he managed to gain from across the ethnic, regional and religious boundaries that traditionally divided Nigeria.

However, on 15 June, with half of the election results already published, the ABN obtained a court injunction from a northern court restraining the National Electoral Commission from announcing official results. A torrent of countervailing injunctions followed, ordering the NEC to declare them. The following day the NEC said it had no choice but to suspend the announcement of the results. On 23 June the government declared that in order to prevent 'judicial anarchy' it had annulled the election results. In a televised address three days later, Babangida claimed that the vote had been irreparably tarnished by procedural irregularities and legal haggling. In reality, Babangida's northern military clique had acted to forestall the election of a southern politician who could threaten their interests.

As Nigeria descended into violence, disorder and repression, Babangida's own position became untenable and he resigned as president in August. After a brief interregnum, General Sani Abacha, a northern strongman, staged a palace coup, abrogated the constitution, and demolished all the democratic institutions that had been established over the previous four years – the national legislature, the state legislatures and local governments. His dictatorship was to become more feared than anything that had hitherto occurred.

In Togo, General Eyadéma, facing successive waves of popular protest, made piecemeal concessions to the opposition but ensured that he retained control of the army to decide what the ultimate outcome would be. After months of strikes, demonstrations and violence, Eyadéma agreed in April 1991 to allow opposition parties to operate and in July yielded to demands for a national conference. In a mood of euphoria, suddenly free to speak out, opposition activists used the conference in July and August to denounce the years of brutality and repression they had suffered at the hands of his regime and to demand his prosecution. Many gave harrowing first-hand accounts of detention, torture and murder. Defying Eyadéma's authority, delegates then declared the conference to be sovereign, appointed a High Council of the Republic under the leadership of a Catholic bishop to draft a new constitution, chose a well-known human-rights lawyer, Kokou Koffigoh, as prime minister and scheduled elections for June 1992. Eyadéma denounced what he described as a 'civilian coup' against a constitutional government and refused to recognise the new dispensation.

Though Koffigoh, as head of government and minister of defence, claimed political control of the army, there was never any doubt about where its loyalty lay. Some three-quarters of the army had been recruited from Eyadéma's home region in the north, notably from among his own Kabré tribe. Many had been hand-picked by him during wrestling matches held there every year as part of a traditional festival known as *evala*. Key command posts were filled by his personal protégés, including members of his own family.

Ethnic solidarity was an important factor underlying the struggle. Delegates to the national conference included a disproportionate number of Ewe-speaking southerners interested not so much in *renouveau* as their own turn in power, prompting fears amongst northerners that they might lose their privileged position under Eyadéma and face retribution.

In December 1991 the army seized control, bombarded Koffigoh's residence, took him prisoner and reversed the reforms of the national conference. Koffigoh was eventually allowed to remain as prime minister but he increasingly deferred to Eyadéma. In presidential elections in 1993, Eyadéma won 98 per cent of the vote, standing as sole candidate after an electoral commission disqualified his principal rival, Gilchrist Olympio, a son of Togo's first president, Sylvanus Olympio, whom Eyadéma had assassinated in 1963.

In Gabon a student protest at the Omar Bongo University in January 1990 ignited an outbreak of strikes and demonstrations that continued for weeks, shaking the foundations of Bongo's regime. Bongo responded by setting up a special commission on democracy within the ruling *Parti Démocratique Gabonais* (PDG) which recommended a five-year transition to a multi-party system. But the unrest continued. Bongo therefore agreed to set up a national conference, granting legal recognition to seventy-four political associations that were invited to attend. Manipulated by Bongo, the conference concluded by calling for a multi-party system but asked him to serve out the rest of his term until the end of 1993.

Through a mixture of fraud, force and help from the French government, Bongo managed to maintain his grip on power. In May the death of an opposition leader, Joseph Renjambé, in suspicious circumstances in a Libreville hotel owned by the government, set off an explosion of violence in urban areas; protesters charged that Bongo had ordered the killing. French troops intervened to restore order. In elections in September that were marred by intimidation and irregularity, the PDG gained a narrow victory, winning 63 out of 120 seats. Many Gabonese felt cheated by the result.

In Cameroon, President Paul Biya, presiding over a corrupt one-party regime, at first dismissed calls for a multi-party system as a 'distasteful passing fetish', rolling out familiar excuses that only a one-party system could avoid the hazards of 'tribal and regional allegiances' and ensure 'the efficient running of state machinery'. When Yondo Black, a former president of the Cameroon Bar Association, and a group of colleagues tried to form an independent political party in February 1990, they were arrested. Black's arrest led the Bar Association to strike in demand for his release. It also resulted in the formation of another unauthorised party. Public sector employees and students followed with their own strikes and demonstrations.

In December 1990 Biya agreed to allow the formation of opposition parties, but otherwise tried to crush opposition activity by repression, using the security forces and other means to intimidate activists. Prominent journalists were arrested, opposition newspapers banned and pro-democracy demonstrators violently dispersed. Biya put the army in charge of administering the most troublesome provinces and doggedly rejected the opposition's calls for a national conference.

To force his hand, a coalition of opposition groups in May 1991 mounted *Opération Villes Mortes* – Operation Ghost Town – a campaign of strikes and civil disobedience intended to shut down commerce from Monday to Friday. Supporters were encouraged to stop working completely, to refuse to pay taxes of any kind and to take their money out of the formal banking sector. For a few days the campaign brought the economy to a halt. But it proved difficult to sustain.

The prolonged struggle for control intensified ethnic tensions. Biya had long since favoured his own Beti group, the largest in southern Cameroon, surrounding himself with prominent southern advisers known as the *Beti barons*. Facing ethnic opposition from other regions, he appealed for ethnic solidarity among the Beti. At a rally in Yaoundé, the heart of Beti country, he declared that 'as long as Yaoundé breathes, Cameroon lives'. Beti representatives from the region presented him with a machete, a spear and a drum, a gesture considered highly provocative by the rest of the country.

The final outcome was decided in presidential elections held in October 1992. After a campaign rife with intimidation, violence, fraud and electoral irregularity, Biya won only 40 per cent of the vote, but his two opponents, though gathering between them 55 per cent, split the vote, leaving Biya the victor.

In Kenya the risks of speaking out publicly against Moi's regime were well known. Arrest, detention and other forms of harassment – for journalists, academics, trade unionists and even members of parliament – were the most likely outcome. Senior church figures, however, were treated for the most part with relative lenience. In a New Year's Day sermon in 1990 delivered at St Andrew's Church in Nairobi, the Reverend Timothy Njoya, a Presbyterian cleric, reflected on the changes occurring in Eastern Europe and speculated upon how long it would be before similar pressures erupted in Kenya. He referred to the 'detentions, imprisonments, torture, oppression and deprivations' suffered by Kenyans and suggested that unless the government tackled injustice, corruption and abuse of power, Kenya was heading for a major disaster. His remarks caused uproar. One of Moi's officials described his sermon as 'absolute madness and folly'; a minister called for him to be detained. But another church critic, Henry Okullu, an Anglican bishop, added his voice, openly calling for multi-party politics and a maximum of two terms in office for any future president.

In May 1990 two prominent Kikuyu businessmen, Kenneth Matiba and Charles Rubia, both former ministers who had been ousted in rigged elections in 1988, called a joint press conference to demand an end to the single-party system. Like other Kikuyu businessmen, Matiba and Rubia were aggrieved by Moi's persistent discrimination against Kikuyu business interests and wanted to break the mould. 'We believe our single-party system is the major single contributory factor and almost solely the root cause of the political, economic and social woes we now face,' they said in a statement.

Moi denounced them as 'traitors' and 'tribalists', suggesting they were intent on re-establishing Kikuyu hegemony; he insisted that a multi-party system would divide Kenya along tribal lines. When Matiba and Rubia announced plans to hold a public rally at Nairobi's Kamukunji Stadium on 7 July to state the case for a multi-party system, their application was refused and they were arrested and detained for nearly a year. Their supporters attempted to gather as planned at the Kamukunji grounds on 7 July, but they were dispersed by riot police with batons and tear gas, igniting three days of rioting in the poorer quarters of Nairobi and violence elsewhere in Kikuyuland and the Rift Valley.

Moi's regime, which had once seemed so stable, was rocked by two other incidents in 1990. In February Kenya's foreign minister, Robert Ouko, a highly respected Luo technocrat who had recently compiled a dossier on high-level corruption, was found shot dead near his home in the Kisumu district; his body had been burned so severely that experts had to work for a week to reconstruct the charred remains. News of Ouko's murder set off riots in the capital. The government initially tried to claim it as suicide. But the finger of suspicion pointed to two of Moi's closest associates: Nicholas Biwott, his key 'backroom boy', a hugely wealthy Kalenjin minister and businessman, notorious for corruption; and Hezekiah Oyugi, his senior official in charge of internal security. Both men were named as 'principal suspects' by a British investigator during a commission of inquiry. Shortly afterwards, Moi abruptly dissolved the commission before it had time to complete its business. Biwott and Oyugi were arrested but freed after two weeks in police custody 'for lack of evidence'.

A second death in suspicious circumstances added to the impression of a regime running amok. In August 1990 a prominent church critic, Bishop Alexander Muge, who had spoken out against corruption, accusing government politicians of 'land-grabbing' from the landless, was killed in what was said to be a car accident. He had recently been publicly threatened by another of Moi's ministers.

In an attempt to improve his image, Moi offered a few minor

reforms – abandoning the hated queuing system for voting and restoring security of tenure to High Court judges. But he still resisted all demands for multi-party politics. When the veteran Luo politician Oginga Odinga tried to register a new political party in March 1991, he was blocked. Then in July a small band of lawyers and political activists launched a pressure group they named the Forum for the Restoration of Democracy (Ford), but Moi declared it to be an illegal organisation and warned that its supporters would be 'crushed like rats'. An attempt by Ford's leaders to hold a rally at Kamukunji Stadium on 16 November ended in their arrest.

As the campaign against Moi's regime gathered momentum, a group of predominantly Kalenjin and Maasai ministers involved in his inner circle resorted to ethnic mobilisation in the Rift Valley to fortify their position. The Rift Valley province was occupied mainly by Kalenjin, along with their allies, the Maasai, Turkana and Samburu, and a large population of Kikuyu 'immigrants'. At a series of political rallies, ministers told their supporters that they should regard the Rift Valley as an exclusive zone for the ruling Kenya African National Union (Kanu); those who were not Kalenjin or Kanu supporters or who were 'outsiders' in the Rift Valley province should be required 'to go back to their motherland'. The main target of this attempt at ethnic cleansing were Kikuyu residents and anyone else who favoured multi-party politics.

In October violence erupted between Kalenjin and non-Kalenjin residents, spreading across the province, continuing throughout 1992, with a death toll reaching 800. Tens of thousands were forced to flee their homes. Church leaders accused the authorities of 'complicity' in the clashes. An investigation led by the National Council of Churches of Kenya into the causes of the clashes implicated not only Moi's ministers, but senior government officers and party officials. A parliamentary committee arrived at similar conclusions.

Western donors, meanwhile, had become thoroughly exasperated by Moi's corrupt and repressive regime. Meeting in Paris on 25 November for a two-day conference, they decided to suspend for six months all balance of payments support and other rapid disbursement aid. The psychological effect was dramatic. From being one of the

West's favoured African countries, Kenya had sunk to pariah status. The practical effect was equally significant: foreign aid financed nearly 30 per cent of government expenditure.

Moi swiftly capitulated. On 2 December he convened a party conference in Nairobi attended by 3,600 delegates. Not knowing what to expect, many speakers loyally denounced the idea of a multi-party system. But after several hours of debate, Moi stood up and announced that he intended to lift the ban on opposition parties and hold multi-party elections. A stunned conference unanimously concurred. Moi continued to make clear, however, his opposition to a multi-party system. 'I have not changed my mind – it is because of the Western media set against us, because of the economic setting today.'

Moi's regime had become sufficiently unpopular in much of the country that it seemed at serious risk of defeat at the polls. But in the twelve months leading up to presidential and parliamentary elections in December 1992, instead of presenting a united front, the opposition fragmented into rival tribal factions. Ford split into two: a Kikuyu-based faction named Ford-Asili led by Kenneth Matiba; and a Luo-based faction named Ford-Kenya led by Oginga Odinga. A third party, the Democratic Party, led by Mwai Kibaki, a veteran Kikuyu politician who had served under both Kenyatta and Moi, further split the Kikuyu vote. The contestants were interested not so much in the democratic process or policy issues as the chance to occupy State House.

Moi, moreover, made full use of his control of government machinery to obtain funds, harass the opposition and manipulate the results. The delimitation of constituencies was skewed heavily to favour Kanu strongholds in the North Eastern, Rift Valley and Coast provinces. The number of voters needed to return a single seat in opposition strongholds in some cases was four times higher than in Kanu strongholds. Whereas the North Eastern province, with 1.79 per cent of the electorate, had ten seats, Nairobi province with 8.53 per cent had only eight seats; whereas Coast province with 8.37 per cent of the electorate had twenty seats, Central province with 15.51 per cent had only twenty-five seats. The average size of a secure Kanu constituency was only 28,350 voters, while seats in opposition areas were on average 84 per cent larger with 52,169 voters. The registration process was also manipulated. The government cut short the period allowed for voter registration and delayed the issuing of identity cards needed by young potential voters, effectively disenfranchising at least 1 million people. Opposition areas were under-registered. The highest figures for registration were in the Rift Valley. The independence of the Electoral Commission was also suspect. The man Moi appointed to head it was a former judge who had been declared bankrupt two years previously and removed from the bench for improper conduct.

Government regional officials played a prominent role in Kanu's campaign, controlling licences for meetings, harassing opposition candidates and supporters and even distributing money and food on behalf of Kanu. Police and security forces were used to disrupt opposition meetings. In at least one-third of constituencies, opposition parties were prevented from conducting a viable campaign. In the Rift Valley seventeen constituencies – 'Kanu zones' – went uncontested.

The result, after months of violence, intimidation, rigging, electoral malpractice and propaganda from state-owned radio and television, was a narrow victory for Moi. In the presidential election Moi gained 36.5 per cent of the vote; his three opponents – Kibaki, Odinga and Matiba – split 63 per cent between them. In the 171 contested parliamentary seats, Kanu, with 29.7 per cent of the vote, took eighty-three seats; its three main opponents, with 67 per cent, took eighty-five seats. In Central province, the Kikuyu heartland, Moi secured no more than 2 per cent of the vote. In concluding their study of the 1992 election, Throup and Hornsby observed: 'What began as an apparently national contest based on ideals ended as little more than an ethnic slanging match.'

In Uganda, Yoweri Museveni, whose National Resistance Army seized control in 1986, ruled through a 'no-party' system. Museveni argued that because Uganda was a rural society composed predominantly of peasants with essentially the same economic interests, the only tactics available to political parties to gain support in the past had been to exploit ethnic, regional and religious loyalties, resulting in strife and distracting attention from real issues. 'Tribalism, religion, or regionalism becomes the basis for intense partisanship. There is no healthy basis for honest competition,' he maintained. Therefore, Western-style multiparty democracy was inappropriate for Uganda. The advantage of a 'no-party democracy', he claimed, was that it enabled individual candidates to stand for election on their own merits. 'Everyone who wants to stand for election is free to do so.'

Though political parties were not actually banned, their activities were severely curtailed. They were allowed to issue statements to the press, but they were not permitted to hold public rallies, or organise congresses, or nominate candidates, or campaign for them.

Asked about his 'overly paternalistic attitude to Ugandans' in a BBC interview in July 1992, Museveni replied:

> These people lost 800,000 people in these upheavals. Surely they were not doing that for sport. If they knew how to sort out their matters, why did they have to lose so many people? In the last thirty years, during the time of Amin, during the time of Obote, we lost not less than 800,000 people, murdered for political reasons. So I am not paternalistic, I just simply know the patient. If a doctor says this person may die if you do not give him this treatment, if he does this, that is not paternalism. This is just diagnosis. We should call it a diagnosis. And it is a diagnosis with a history. We are not talking out of the air.

In practice, Museveni's 'no-party' system operated little differently from a 'one-party' system. Candidates supporting Museveni's National Resistance Movement were helped at election times with government cash and cars; candidates known to favour multi-party politics faced harassment and intimidation. In 1996, in the first direct presidential elections in Uganda's history, Museveni, using state resources, secured 75 per cent of the vote. The outcome was said by independent observers generally to reflect popular opinion at the time. But in subsequent years, Museveni became increasingly autocratic, running a patronage system favouring family members and loyal supporters and obstructing any real challenge to his rule – just like other Big Men.

Nevertheless, in the struggle for democracy there were two notable casualties. In Zambia, Kenneth Kaunda, facing demands for a multi-party system, resorted to raising the spectre of ethnic conflict and electoral violence as the reason why he should continue in sole charge. Party competition, he said, would constitute a return to 'stone-age politics'. But popular protest, driven at first by sharp food price rises and other economic grievances, grew apace. In December 1989 the trade union leader Frederick Chiluba called for a referendum on party pluralism, pointing to events in Eastern Europe. 'If the owners of socialism have withdrawn from the one-party system, who are Africans to continue with it?' he asked. 'The one-party system is open to abuse. It is not the people in power who should direct political change, but the ordinary masses.' In June 1990 angry protestors in Lusaka set ablaze a national monument commemorating Kaunda's role in the nationalist struggle. State-owned retail stores were singled out for looting. Demonstrators commonly blamed the one-party system for their economic plight. In July a group of trade unionists, professionals and business leaders established a 'Movement for Multi-Party Democracy' (MMD). Kaunda tried to delay, but faced huge urban crowds chanting the opposition slogan, 'The Hour Has Come!'

Launched as a political party in January 1991, the MMD, led by Chiluba, quickly gained mass support. Conceding multi-party elections, Kaunda used every trick in his arsenal to influence the vote. He kept a lid on maize prices, even though the cost of subsidies had reached $1.5 million a day. He refused to end the twenty-seven-year state of emergency, giving him arbitrary powers, although justification for it had long since disappeared. He refused to update voter registration lists, effectively disenfranchising thousands of potential voters thought to be opposition supporters. He authorised government resources to be used for his own's party purposes. And he tried to block opposition access to the state media, and was thwarted only when the MMD appealed to the courts that his actions were 'illegal, unconstitutional and discriminatory' and won a ruling in its favour.

The result in October 1991 was an overwhelming victory for the MMD. In the presidential election Chiluba gained 76 per cent of the vote. In parliamentary elections the MMD gained 75 per cent of the vote and 125 out of 150 seats.

Kaunda accepted his defeat with grace and dignity. He escorted Chiluba on a tour around State House and gave a generous farewell speech on television. As he left the television studio after his broadcast, he personally detached the presidential pennant from his limousine and, weeping, handed it to his driver, then climbed in and was driven away.

In Malawi the first serious challenge to Banda's dictatorship came from the Catholic Church. On the first Sunday in Lent in March 1992, a pastoral letter, written by all eight Catholic bishops, was read out in every Catholic church in the country. Using a mixture of biblical exegesis and traditional African proverbs, the letter amounted to a scathing indictment of the poverty, corruption, inequality, censorship and political repression that were commonplace in Malawi. It spoke of falling standards and overcrowding in schools; of inadequate health care; of the lack of freedom; of the need for a fair system of justice.

Academic freedom is seriously restricted; exposing injustices can be considered a betrayal; revealing some evils of our society is seen as slandering the country; monopoly of mass media and censorship prevent the expression of dissenting views; some people have paid dearly for their political opinions; access to public places like markets, hospitals, bus depots etc., is frequently denied to those who cannot produce a party card; forced donations have become a way of life.

This is most regrettable. It creates an atmosphere of resentment among the citizens. It breeds a climate of mistrust and fear. This fear of harassment and mutual suspicion generates a society in which the talents of many lie unused and in which there is little room for initiative.

The bishops were taken to police headquarters in Blantyre for questioning and then confined to the house of the archbishop for several days. Their pastoral letter was declared a seditious document. Hundreds of people found in possession of it were arrested. In parliament a resolution was passed condemning the bishops. Young Pioneer thugs burned down the printing press where the letter had been printed. At a meeting on 11 March, according to a tape recording of the proceedings that was subsequently leaked, party officials agreed that 'to make things easier we just have to kill these bishops'.

Other churches, however, spoke out in support of the bishops. The Church of Scotland, of which Banda himself was an elder, called on its members to 'pray for this profoundly lonely man who is locked in the prison house of power'. Students at Chancellor College staged marches singing 'We want multi-party'. Human rights activists used fax machines to saturate Malawi with pro-democracy literature. Strikes erupted, first at Chancellor College, then spreading to factories and agricultural estates. Bank, railway and airline employees joined in. On the streets of Blantyre, violence and rioting broke out. Shops linked to Banda's business empire were looted. Police fired into the crowds killing at least twenty people.

Foreign pressure on Banda also mounted. Disturbed by mass arrests, police shootings and Malawi's long record of human rights abuses, donor governments meeting in Paris on 13 May 1992 suspended all non-humanitarian aid for six months.

Forced to concede multi-party politics, Banda announced in October that a referendum would be held to decide whether Malawi should retain a single-party system, confident that he would win it. At the age of ninety-five, his eyesight failing, he embarked on a punishing schedule of campaign meetings to condemn the 'chaos of multi-partyism', attended by the ever-faithful Mama Kadzimira. His efforts were to no avail. Though the central region, the homeland of Banda's Chewa tribe, voted by a two-thirds majority in favour of a single-party system, at a national level 63 per cent 'voted for change'.

In presidential elections held in 1994, after thirty years in power, Banda was defeated by one of his former ministers, Bakili Muluzi, a Muslim businessman. Like Kaunda before him, Banda accepted defeat gracefully, acknowledged Muluzi 'the clear winner' and promised that his opposition party would contribute to 'building a better, democratic Malawi'.

The following year, in the wake of a commission of inquiry, Banda was charged with involvement in the murder of four politicians in 1983. During his trial he was allowed to stay at Mudi House, the governor's residence in the colonial era, where a British journalist, Alec Russell, interviewed him in 1995, the last to do so. In attendance as ever was Mama Kadzimira, a model of courteous charm, controlling his hearing aid, prompting the odd answer and rephrasing questions. Banda himself, according to Russell, had become a 'tiny, shrivelled' figure. 'His voice was hardly a quaver. It seemed as if it would shatter the delicate bronze parchment which was his skin. His frame was eggshell thin. The giant hearing aid attached to a Heath Robinson-esque contraption heightened the impression that he was near his end.' Much of the interview was a history lesson, rather like the ones Banda used to give to members of his cabinet and to parliament.

'This is the trouble in Africa today – too many ignorant people who do not know anything about history,' he once told Malawi's parliament. 'And if they do know anything about it they do not know how to interpret and apply it. That is why Africa is a mess. That is the tragedy of Africa: too many ignorant people are in a position of power and responsibility.'

Banda was acquitted of conspiracy to murder in December 1996. He died a year later at the age of ninety-nine in a Johannesburg hospital with Mama Kadzimira at his side.

Over a period of five years, most of the one-party systems that had prevailed in Africa for a generation were dismantled. A clutch of military strongmen, like Kérékou in Benin, were swept from office. In Congo-Brazzaville, General Denis Sassou-Nguesso, a hardline Marxist, in power for twelve years, conceded a national conference, was outmanoeuvred by opposition groups and came third in a presidential election in 1992. In the Central African Republic, General André Kolingba blocked demands for a national conference and gambled that, with control of the state media and government resources, he would win an election. When preliminary results of the 1992 election indicated that he was running fourth in a field of five candidates, with as little as 2 per cent of the vote, he abruptly terminated the election process. The following year, however, when he tried to avoid another election defeat, France withdrew economic and military assistance and forced him to concede the presidency. Mali's General Traoré tried to retain control of popular protest through mass arrests and repression, but when he unleashed troops to quell demonstrators demanding his resignation, resulting in scores of deaths, the army overthrew him, convened a national conference and paved the way for elections. In Chad, Hissein Habré was ousted in December 1990 by Idris Déby, a former military commander, who, under pressure from France and other Western powers, established a multi-party system, convened a national conference and went on to be elected as president in 1996. In Ethiopia, Mengistu was driven out of power in May 1991 by a joint army of Eritrean and Tigrayan rebels and fled into exile. A national conference of Ethiopian leaders in July agreed to hold a referendum under United Nations auspices to determine the future of Eritrea that resulted in its independence in 1993, bringing thirty years of warfare to a close.

But while many dictatorships fell in Africa in the early 1990s, as many dictators survived, albeit under different circumstances. Military rulers won presidential elections in Guinea, Mauritania, Equatorial Guinea and Burkina Faso – 'the land of honest men'. A new breed of dictators emerged, adept at maintaining a façade of democracy sufficient for them to be able to obtain foreign aid. Even when regime changes occurred, new governments soon reverted to the same systems of patronage and patrimonialism run by their predecessors; some quickly lapsed into the same autocratic means of rule. In place of Big Man rule came Big Man democracy, with little difference between the two.

Democratic change, moreover, brought no amelioration to the economic crisis that virtually all African states faced. New leaders arriving in office were daunted by the task before them. At his inauguration as Zambia's second president in November 1991, Frederick Chiluba remarked:

The Zambia we inherit is destitute – ravaged by the excesses, ineptitude and straight corruption of a party and a people who have been in power for too long. When our first president stood up to address you twenty-seven years ago, he was addressing a country full of hope and glory. A country fresh with the power of youth, and a full and rich dowry. Now the coffers are empty. The people are poor. The misery endless.

24

A TIME OF TRIUMPH

In the years that Nelson Mandela spent in prison on Robben Island, South Africa became a fortress of white power and prosperity. Throughout the 1960s it experienced one of the highest rates of economic growth in the world, second only to Japan. Its mines produced record amounts of gold and other minerals; factories proliferated as never before. Foreign trade with Western countries rose in leaps and bounds. Foreign investors from the United States, Britain, France and Germany competed vigorously for positions in new industries. The annual net flow of foreign capital into the country in 1970 rose to a level six times above the pre-Sharpeville era. The economic boom also brought to South Africa a flood of white immigrants, mainly from Europe; between 1960 and 1970 there was a net gain of some 250,000. All this gave white South Africans a growing sense of confidence about the future. Black resistance had been crushed; the security apparatus seemed capable of meeting any contingency. A vast bureaucracy existed to ensure government control. Above all, the government had the resources to make white supremacy a success.

The benefits of National Party rule were noticeable particularly among the Afrikaner community. With government assistance, a new class of Afrikaner financiers, businessmen and managers moved into commanding positions in industry, commerce and banking. State enterprises like railways, harbours, steel production, electric power generation and heavy engineering were manned at a senior level almost exclusively by Afrikaners and used as training fields for Afrikaner scientists and business leaders. Government contracts and concessions were frequently steered towards Afrikaner companies. The civil service was virtually an Afrikaner preserve. Afrikaner farmers, consisting of three-quarters of the total number, also fared well under National Party rule, assisted by subsidies, research funds, modernisation programmes and favourable prices fixed by state marketing boards. The Afrikaner working class benefited in particular from the government's policy of white job protection. Almost every skilled trade and craft was reserved for white workers. The English-speaking community, of course, shared in the prosperity; few other communities in the world possessed such a high standard of living. The northern suburbs of Johannesburg, where many English-speakers congregated, were said to have the greatest concentration of swimming pools outside Beverly Hills. But the main beneficiaries were Afrikaners. In 1946 Afrikaner incomes on a per capita basis were just under half that of English-speaker incomes. By 1970, they had passed the two-thirds mark.

Though prosperous, white society under National Party rule became increasingly insular and inbred, isolated from the views and lifestyle of the modern world as well as from the majority of the population. The national radio network served as a propaganda machine; each commentary, each news bulletin conveyed the government's view of the world. All attempts to introduce television were blocked until the government was convinced it could control it. A tight grip was kept on literature and entertainment through censorship laws. The independent press was forced to steer its way through a minefield of legislation, resorting increasingly to self-censorship. White society expected conformity and regarded dissent, however trivial, as a form of treachery. 'Opposing apartheid is worse than murder to some Afrikaners,' observed a prominent Afrikaner critic. 'You endanger the nation by refusing to conform.'

To virtually the entire white population – totalling more than 3.5 million in the 1960s – white rule was an unquestionable virtue.

Outwardly, South Africa could claim many of the trappings of a Western democracy: a parliamentary system of government; an independent judiciary; a vigorous press; a market economy; full churches, generous charities. All this helped to reassure whites that, whatever faults they possessed, South Africa had a rightful place in the Western camp. If harsh police methods were sometimes employed, then they were needed, so it was said, solely to deal with a troublesome minority of the population stirred up by paymasters in Moscow.

The system seemed strong enough to withstand any shock. When Hendrik Verwoerd, the driving force behind grand apartheid, was assassinated in the National Assembly by a deranged parliamentary messenger in 1966, the white community took it in its stride. No shift in policy was considered necessary. Verwoerd's successor, chosen by the National Party, was John Vorster, who as minister of justice had made such a success of smashing black opposition. Immediately upon being elected, Vorster declared, 'My role is to walk further along the road set by Hendrik Verwoerd.'

The full impact of grand apartheid on the African population came with dramatic force during the 1960s and 1970s as the government worked systematically to stem the flow of Africans from rural to urban areas and to destroy all notion that urban Africans could have a permanent place in 'white' towns. With remorseless vigour, the government strove to reduce the urban African population wherever possible, stripping urban Africans of what few rights they possessed and ridding white rural areas of vast numbers of blacks. A government circular in 1967 stated: 'No stone is to be left unturned to achieve the settlement in the homelands of non-productive Bantu at present residing in the European areas.' Among those whom the circular defined as 'non-productive' were 'the aged, the unfit, widows and women with dependent children'. A government minister estimated that of 6 million Africans in white areas, 4 million were 'surplus appendages' suitable for deportation to black homelands.

As the policy took effect, the number of prosecutions under pass laws rose sharply, reaching 700,000 in 1968. Countless thousands found themselves 'endorsed out' of urban areas. In the Transvaal and the Orange Free State a massive urban relocation programme was carried out. African townships considered to be within commuting distance of a homeland were 'de-proclaimed' and their residents moved to new rural townships built in the homelands. In some cases, the entire African population was moved. In other cases, government officials concentrated on removing the unemployed, the elderly and disabled, women and children, leaving behind African workers to live in all-male hostels and visit their families on a weekly or monthly basis.

In place of a stable, urban population, what the government wanted was a workforce composed principally of migrant labour. With migrant workers circulating continuously between black homelands and white-owned enterprises in urban areas, the government saw a means of reconciling the white need for labour with its own determination to prevent permanent black urbanisation. African workers could be turned into commuters, if they lived in homelands close enough to urban areas, or migrants if the distance was too far. Alternatively, African workers could be engaged in the traditional manner on annual contracts, housed in all-male compounds, and released to visit their families in the homelands at the end of a year. In 1970 it was estimated that more than 2 million men spent their lives circulating as migrants between their homes and urban employment. Many of them were deprived of all normal urban family and social life, confined for months on end to a bleak and barren existence in over-crowded barracks notorious for high rates of drunkenness and violence. Others spent hours each day travelling long distances to work in packed buses and trains, rising before dawn and returning home late into the night.

Black townships in 'white' South Africa were kept as unattractive as possible. Few urban amenities were ever provided. Black businessmen were prevented by government restrictions from expanding their enterprises there. No African was allowed to carry on more than one business. Businesses were confined to providing 'daily essential necessities', like wood, coal, milk and vegetables. No banks or clothing stores or supermarkets were permitted. Restrictions were even placed on dry-cleaners, garages and petrol stations. Nor were Africans allowed to establish companies or partnerships in urban areas, or to construct their own buildings. These had to be leased from the local authority. Black housing was rudimentary, consisting of rows of identical 'matchbox' houses. Only a small proportion had electricity or adequate plumbing. Overcrowding was commonplace. In Soweto, the main black urban area serving Johannesburg, the average number of people living in each 'matchbox' house in 1970 was thirteen.

The disadvantages under which the African population laboured in the 'white' economy were legion. Africans were barred by law from skilled work, from forming registered unions, and from taking strike action. In industrial disputes, armed police were often called in by white employers to deal with the workforce. If Africans lost their job, they faced the possibility of deportation. A considerable proportion of the workforce received wages which fell short of providing the costs of family subsistence; an employers' organisation, the Associated Chambers of Commerce, calculated in 1970 that the average industrial wage was 30 per cent below the minimum monthly budget needed for a Soweto family of five.

In its drive for racial separation, the government also turned its attention to excising scores of African settlements surrounded by white farming areas where Africans had lived in relative peace and quiet for generations. In the government's terminology, these settlements were known as 'black spots', small fragments of land in what was deemed to be 'white' South Africa that stood out as irritating blemishes on the apartheid map. Some land was held by title deed, purchased by African farmers in the nineteenth and early twentieth centuries; some was mission land, occupied by generations of African tenants; some consisted of small African reserves that had survived the era of white occupation but were now considered to be 'badly situated'. In all there were an estimated 350 black spots.

The elimination of 'black spots' began in earnest in the 1960s. Whole communities were uprooted and forced to leave their homes. Many were dumped in areas often unsuitable for cultivation, lacking water supplies, far from main roads and out of reach of hospitals or clinics. Any sign of resistance was dealt with by armed police. A Franciscan priest, Father Cosmas Desmond, who made a journey the length and breadth of South Africa to ascertain the full extent of the forced removals policy in 1969, later described how he found a 'labyrinth of broken communities, broken families and broken lives'. By 1970 nearly 100,000 Africans had lost their homes. Many more were to follow.

In white farming areas, where the white population was constantly preoccupied with *die beswarting van die platteland* – the blackening of the white countryside – the government acted with similar vigour to reduce the black population. White farmers were encouraged to adopt more mechanised production methods and to replace permanent black workers with casual employees and single migrant workers. An estimated half a million full-time black workers lost their employment on white farms during the 1960s. Thousands of African tenants – 'squatters' – were also turned off white land. The only Africans whom the government wanted in white farming areas were hired labourers, preferably migrants.

All these changes had a devastating impact on black homelands. Already overcrowded and impoverished, homelands had to cope with an endless flow of displaced Africans – labour tenants, squatters, redundant farm labourers, urban dwellers – 'superfluous' people, as they were described, all scrabbling for survival. Once in the homelands, most African men had no alternative but to offer themselves up to the migrant labour treadmill. The government pronounced itself well pleased with the result.

The years of silence that followed the imprisonment of Mandela and other ANC leaders were broken by a new generation of black activists coming from the ranks of the student population. It was a generation that drew its inspiration not from the concept of multiracial struggle that the ANC had championed but from a sense of black assertiveness more in line with the Africanist tradition of black politics. The black consciousness movement of the 1970s filled the vacuum left by the collapse of the ANC and the PAC. It found an articulate spokesman in Steve Biko, a medical student from the Eastern Cape, who argued that 'group power' would achieve black liberation. Biko was contemptuous of the cowed and submissive attitude of the black population, giving full vent to his views in a student newsletter published in September 1970.

> The type of black man we have today has lost his manhood.
> Reduced to an obliging shell, he looks with awe at the white power
> structure and accepts what he regards as the 'inevitable position' . . .
> In the privacy of his toilet his face twists in silent condemnation of
> white society but brightens up in sheepish obedience as he comes
> out hurrying in response to his master's impatient call. In the home-
> bound bus or train he joins the chorus that roundly condemns the
> white man but is first to praise the government in the presence of
> the police and his employers . . . All in all, the black man has
> become a shell, a shadow of man, completely defeated, drowning in
> his own misery, a slave, an ox bearing the yoke of oppression with
> sheepish timidity . . .

What was needed, said Biko, was a massive effort to reverse the negative image that blacks held of themselves and to replace it with a more positive identity. Black oppression was first and foremost a psychological problem. It could be countered by promoting black awareness, black pride, black capabilities and black achievement. The term 'black' was used to include coloureds and Indians equally with Africans as victims of racial oppression. No help was wanted from white liberals or any other white sympathisers. The slogan used was: 'Black man, you are on your own'.

Abandoning his medical studies in 1972, Biko became a full-time political organiser. As the black consciousness movement gathered momentum, the government struck back. In 1973 Biko and seven colleagues were issued with banning orders. Biko was restricted to King William's Town, forbidden to speak in public or to write for publication or to be quoted or to be present with more than one person at a time. For two years he worked on black community programmes in King William's Town until barred from such work. The security police harassed him endlessly. Over a three-year period he was arrested and detained twenty-nine times.

The government's actions failed to halt the spread of black

consciousness. A dramatic boost to black morale occurred in 1974 when Portuguese rule in Mozambique and Angola collapsed, paving the way for African liberation movements there to take control. When South African troops were obliged to withdraw from Angola in early 1976, having failed to prevent the Marxist MPLA from gaining power, black students again celebrated the defeat of white power.

The issue that finally ignited black anger was the government's system of 'Bantu' education. It had been designed by Verwoerd to limit African education to the needs of the white community. 'What is the use of teaching a Bantu child mathematics when it cannot use it in practice,' Verwoerd had said. 'There is no place for him in the European community above the level of certain forms of labour.' National Party policy had produced a legacy of inferior schooling, poorly trained teachers, overcrowded classrooms and inadequate equipment. Government expenditure had been kept to a minimum: in the early 1970s it spent sixteen times more on white education per pupil than on black education. Because of deliberate restrictions on places in middle and higher schools, hundreds of thousands of children – 'push-outs', as they were known – left school with no greater prospects than menial work or unemployment. Only 5 per cent of African pupils found places in secondary schools and very few completed the fifth and final form successfully. Those who managed to complete secondary school were then faced with a whole range of apartheid restrictions affecting the kind of employment for which they could apply. The difficulties that school leavers faced in 1976 were particularly acute because of an economic recession.

Into this potentially explosive atmosphere the government stumbled with a new regulation: it decided that half of the subjects in secondary school not taught in the African vernacular should be taught in Afrikaans and the other half in English. The practical difficulties involved in this ruling were immense. African teachers in training colleges were taught almost exclusively in English. Many were unable even to converse in Afrikaans. In one protest after another, teachers' organisations, school boards, principals and parents sought to persuade the government to change its mind. But the government remained adamant.

The epicentre of resistance was Soweto. Students, denouncing Afrikaans as the language of the 'oppressor', began to boycott classes in Afrikaans, organised school strikes and then planned a mass demonstration. On 16 June 1976 a dozen columns of students marched through Soweto carrying placards, chanting slogans and singing freedom songs. They were met by armed police who opened fire, killing a 13-year-old schoolboy. As news of the shooting spread, students went on the rampage, attacking government buildings, beer halls, bottle stores, vehicles and buses. Clashes broke out in other townships in the Transvaal. During the first week of the Soweto revolt, at least 150 people were killed, most of them black schoolchildren. Even though the government retreated on the Afrikaans issue, the violence continued. Time and again students returned to the streets, showing remarkable resilience in the face of police firepower and displaying a level of defiance and hatred of the apartheid system rarely seen before. As soon as one set of student leaders was detained or disappeared into exile, others stepped forward, ready to take their place.

Yet for all the courage shown, the student revolt lacked any sense of direction. Marches, demonstrations and arson attacks produced little discernible result other than an endless series of police raids and a high cost in casualties – at least 600 dead and 4,000 wounded. From September onwards the momentum of the revolt began to ebb. By December it had virtually died out.

Despite his banning orders restricting him to King William's Town, Steve Biko continued to travel, to write and to campaign. Returning from a secret meeting in Cape Town in August 1977, he was arrested at a police roadblock outside Grahamstown. For the next twenty days he was held in solitary confinement, kept naked, given no proper washing facilities, and allowed no exercise. He was then taken from his cell to security police headquarters in the Sanlam Building in Port Elizabeth for interrogation, still naked and now held in leg irons and handcuffs. During interrogation he was savagely beaten by a group of white policemen and collapsed from head injuries. Despite his condition, he was chained hand and foot to a metal grille, with his arms stretched out as if on a crucifix, and left like that for the rest of the day while his interrogators waited for him to recover. Although he had visible head injuries and his speech was incoherent, he did not receive any medical attention. During the evening, when night staff took over, the handcuffs holding him against the grille were unlocked, but the leg iron was kept on. He was given some mats to sleep on. Only the next day was a doctor called to examine him, but the doctor reported he could find no apparent injury. Biko was kept at security police headquarters for the rest of the second day before being taken to a prison hospital. The following day, he was found foaming at the mouth and doctors decided he should be removed to hospital for treatment. Though Biko was nearly comatose, the security police arranged for him to be taken to a prison hospital in Pretoria, some 700 miles away. He was put naked into the back of a police van, covered with a prison blanket, and given nothing but a bottle of water for the eleven-hour journey. He died on 12 September, a few hours after arriving in Pretoria, lying on a mat on a stone floor. He was thirty years old.

Two days later the minister of police, Jimmy Kruger, announced that Biko had died after a hunger strike. Kruger provoked laughter at a National Party conference when referring to Biko's death. 'I am not glad and I am not sorry about Mr Biko. It leaves me cold. [*Dit laat my koud*]. I can say nothing to you . . . Any person who dies . . . I shall also be sorry if I die.'

News of Biko's death unleashed a new wave of fury and violence on the streets which the government eventually brought to a halt by detaining dozens of black leaders and outlawing virtually every black-consciousness organisation in the country.

Whatever signs of black discontent there were, the government pressed on with its policies of grand apartheid as determinedly as before. The final solution for the African population, as apartheid's architects saw it, was no longer simply self-government for the home-lands but 'independence'. By bestowing independence on the homelands, the government would be able to remove all claim that the African population had to South African citizenship. It would also provide proof to the international community, so officials in Pretoria believed, that the government had fulfilled its obligations to provide full rights to the African population just as adequately as Europe's colonial powers had done when granting independence to their African colonies.

The geography of the homelands made little sense. Most were made up from scattered and fragmented pieces of land. In the case of two of the most important homelands, KwaZulu in 1975 consisted of forty-eight pieces of land and scores of smaller tracts, and Bophuthatswana of nineteen pieces of land spread across three provinces. Only one homeland, QwaQwa, an area of about 200 square miles, consisted of a single contiguous territory. The economic base supporting the homelands was pitifully inadequate. The home-lands contained few roads or railways, no major ports or cities, poor natural resources and land that was badly depleted by overpopulation and poor husbandry. They remained decaying backwaters, inhabited by an impoverished peasantry and dependent on handouts from Pretoria and on remittances from migrant labour.

Nevertheless, the government found enough willing accomplices among the black population to make its homeland strategy work. For an elite group of African politicians, chiefs, civil servants and traders, self-government had brought substantial rewards. Cabinet ministers, members of legislative assemblies and civil servants gained increasingly from high salaries, loans, land and housing as the South African authorities sought to establish a prosperous middle class that would underpin the homeland system. The prospect of independence seemed even more appealing.

In 1976 the Transkei was duly pronounced to be an 'independent state'. Overnight 1.6 million Xhosas living there and 1.3 million Xhosas living in 'white' areas lost their South African citizenship. Ministers in Pretoria announced that South Africa was henceforth a country of 22 million people, as opposed to 25 million beforehand. Other homelands followed suit. In 1977 Bophuthatswana was made independent, despite evident opposition; in all some 1.8 million Tswana lost their South African citizenship. In 1979 Venda opted for independence, even though the chief minister had lost an election on the issue. In 1981 Ciskei's leader decided to accept Pretoria's offer, ignoring the advice of a distinguished panel of experts and an adverse opinion survey. In all, between 1976 and 1981 an estimated 8 million

Africans lost their South African citizenship. Pretoria was jubilant. 'If our policy is taken to its full logical conclusion as far as the black people are concerned, there will not be one black man with South African citizenship,' declared a government minister.

Despite the apparent success of white supremacy, however, the apartheid system was coming under increasing strain. The economic boom of the 1960s, together with the growing use of advanced production techniques, had produced such a serious shortage of skilled labour that it was hampering further economic growth. The reservoir of white skills had simply run out. White immigration was not sufficient to fill the gap. By 1970 the skills shortage amounted to nearly 100,000 jobs. White businessmen, for reasons of self-interest, argued that the only solution was to scrap the job reservation system giving whites a monopoly of skilled work and to allow blacks to move upwards in the labour market. They were critical of the government's vast apparatus of labour controls that treated millions of workers who passed through it as 'an undifferentiated mass'. What they wanted was a black labour force that was better educated, more highly skilled and stable. They also favoured legal recognition of black trade unions that would allow them to conduct industrial relations on an orderly basis. A rash of strikes in 1973 pointed to the urgent need for improved labour conditions. The Soweto revolt in 1976 intensified all these arguments and added new ones. What employers now feared was the emergence of a new generation of radical activists who, in their hatred of the apartheid system, might turn against the free-enterprise system as well.

Foreign criticism of apartheid, in the wake of the Soweto revolt and Biko's death, was also mounting. The spectacle of armed police shooting schoolchildren in the streets brought worldwide condemnation and calls for economic boycotts and sanctions, endangering South Africa's export markets. Foreign investors no longer looked on South Africa as such a stable and profitable haven. Foreign capital, which had been a vital factor in helping South Africa to achieve high rates of economic growth, began to flow out. Multinational companies with subsidiaries in South Africa faced intense criticism from anti-apartheid groups, some demanding their withdrawal. Several prominent American and British banks terminated their South African business. For the first time, the costs of sustaining apartheid began to affect white interests.

White society itself was beginning to change. More affluent and broad-minded than before, it no longer saw the need for so many of the racial barriers erected since 1948. Petty apartheid, once a key National Party objective, began to fray at the edges. White municipalities exercised their powers to abolish racial restrictions on the use of public amenities. The Johannesburg City Council opened its museums, art gallery and municipal library to all races and removed 'White' and 'Non-White' signs from benches in its parks. Similar action was taken in Cape Town, Durban and East London. The rigid separation of races in government offices was relaxed; post offices which had operated separate windows for blacks and whites were desegregated. White officials, accustomed to abusing blacks at will, were now told to handle them with respect. Restrictions on mixed sporting contests were eased.

In 1978 a new prime minister, P. W. Botha, brought a different style of leadership. Like Verwoerd and Vorster, he was an authoritarian figure, single-minded, ruthless and intolerant of opposition. His commitment to the cause of white supremacy was no less tenacious than theirs. But Botha preferred a pragmatic approach to the conduct of government rather than an ideological one. His objective was to modernise apartheid, to rid it of its more impractical encumbrances, to make it function more effectively. As defence minister for twelve years, he had come to admire the military's methods of planning and coordination and he was close to the military's way of thinking. In the wake of the Soweto revolt, what the military wanted above all were defensible political goals. Botha set out to achieve them.

The air was soon thick with promises of reform. 'We are moving in a changing world,' said Botha. 'We must adapt otherwise we shall die.' He declared himself to be in favour of removing 'hurtful unnecessary discrimination' and suggested that laws banning interracial marriage and sex should no longer be regarded as 'holy cows'. In piecemeal fashion he initiated moves to improve conditions in black urban areas. After thirty years of harsh legislation designed to drive out the black population, the government finally recognised their right to live there permanently, according them property rights. African workers were permitted to join registered unions. Most job reservation laws were scrapped. In the field of education the government committed itself to the goal of providing equal, though separate, education for all population groups.

Botha also announced plans for constitutional change. His aim was to expand the political base of the white population by incorporating the coloured and Indian communities into the white political system, providing them with the right to elect representatives to their own chamber while ensuring that political power remained firmly in the hands of the whites. The terminology he used for describing this exercise was 'a healthy form of power sharing'. Much emphasis was placed on the importance of 'group rights', a term, which, according to the government, meant that each race group was allowed to govern itself without interference or domination by any other group, but which in practice added up to little more than the old system of racial separation run by whites. No representation was accorded to the black population. In Botha's view, blacks had been given sufficient representation through the homeland system. All that he was prepared to concede to urban blacks was elected local councils.

In tandem with his reform programme, Botha began to develop a national security system designed to overcome any challenge mounted against the government either internally or externally. From Pretoria's perspective, the threats to white rule were gathering pace from every quarter. In the southern African region, each of South Africa's white-ruled neighbours, Angola, Mozambique and Rhodesia, had succumbed to guerrilla warfare waged by African nationalist movements with the help of the Soviet Union and adjacent African states. Guerrilla activity was also increasing in South West Africa (Namibia) which South Africa controlled in defiance of United Nations rulings. The collapse of Portuguese rule in Angola and Mozambique in 1974 had left large gaps in the white buffer zone that had once insulated South Africa from black Africa to the north and brought a Cuban expeditionary army into the region. Since 1975 its neighbours there had been Marxist governments friendly to the Soviet Union and willing to provide sanctuaries and training facilities for the exiled African National Congress. The Soweto revolt in 1976 had led to an exodus of some 14,000 black youths from South Africa, providing the ANC in exile with an army of eager new recruits. The capital of Mozambique, Maputo, less than fifty miles from the South African border, had become a key ANC operational centre. ANC groups had also been set up in Botswana, Swaziland and Lesotho to help establish an internal network and to supervise the flow of recruits. From 1977 ANC guerrillas began a low-level sabotage campaign selecting targets mainly with a high propaganda value, intending more to re-establish a political following among the black population and to raise its morale than to threaten the economy or white security. Its targets included police stations in black residential areas, administrative buildings, railways lines and electricity substations. A number of informers, security policemen and state witnesses were assassinated. The advent of black nationalist rule in Rhodesia in 1980 completed South Africa's encirclement to the north by hostile governments.

At an international level too, Pretoria faced an increasingly hostile environment. A United Nations arms embargo had become mandatory in 1977, cutting South Africa off from its last major arms supplier, France. An oil embargo had been imposed by OPEC states; and after the fall of the Shah in 1979, Iran's oil consignments, on which South Africa had traditionally depended, were also stopped. In the United States a new president, Jimmy Carter, had adopted a far more aggressive approach on human rights issues in South Africa. In one country after another, anti-apartheid groups campaigned with increasing vigour for boycotts, sanctions and disinvestment.

Botha's explanation for this tide of events was that it was all part of a master plan by the Soviet Union to achieve global domination. He had a fixed and simple view of world politics, believing that they revolved around a struggle between communist and anti-communist forces, in which South Africa, with its vast mineral resources and maritime facilities, was a glittering prize. Whatever ills befell South Africa, whether it was regional instability, international pressure or domestic unrest, were attributed ultimately to Moscow's grand design.

What made matters worse was that Western states no longer possessed the will to stand up to this challenge.

Botha's answer to this 'total onslaught' was 'total strategy'. He put in place a new security establishment giving it huge powers to coordinate and control all efforts to combat threats to state security and draw upon the expertise of the military, the intelligence community, government administrators and any other experts whenever needed. At the apex of the new structure was the State Security Council, where senior generals and key politicians met regularly to decide what action to take to crush opposition both at home and abroad. From a network of some 500 offices covering the entire country, security officials were employed to ferret out leading activists, detain them and mark them out for elimination, if necessary. A secret police counter-insurgency unit, set up in 1980 on a secluded farm called Vlakplaas, twenty miles from Pretoria, was soon involved in bombing, arson, kidnapping and assassination.

The running battles between ANC guerrillas and the government soon escalated into regional conflict. From 1980 the ANC selected more ambitious targets, destroying fuel storage tanks at industrial plants, firing rockets into a military base, bombing equipment at a nuclear power station. In 1983 a car-bomb attack outside a military building in Pretoria killed sixteen people and injured more than 200 – the most serious sabotage attack in South Africa's history.

The government retaliated against neighbouring states with a combination of military might and economic coercion intended to force them into submission and expel the ANC. Its main target was Mozambique. From bases in the Transvaal, South African military intelligence trained, armed and directed a Mozambique rebel group, Renamo, which it had inherited from Rhodesian intelligence in 1980, and sent it across the border to destroy bridges, railways, agricultural projects, schools and clinics and to terrorise the local population. Direct military raids were made on ANC targets in Maputo. Mozambique was also subjected to economic pressure. In Lesotho commando units struck at ANC residences in the capital, Maseru, and attempted to assassinate its prime minister. The ANC's offices in London were bombed in 1982 by a police team led by a brigadier. In

Angola, South African forces resumed their support for Jonas Savimbi's rebel movement, Unita, in its war against the Cuban-backed MPLA government in Luanda; permanently occupied an area some twenty-five miles deep along Angola's southern border; and launched frequent ground and air attacks against bases used by Swapo guerrillas to attack South West Africa.

Unable to withstand the pressure, South Africa's neighbours capitulated to its demands one by one. In 1982 Swaziland signed a secret security agreement with Pretoria, undertaking to expel ANC personnel from its territory. In 1983 Lesotho, subjected to blockade measures, agreed to expel scores of ANC members. Mozambique, too, decided it had no option but to fall into line. Facing ruin from a combination of drought, cyclones, floods and years of economic mismanagement as well as the havoc wrought by Renamo guerrillas, President Samora Machel at first appealed to his Soviet allies for assistance, but when none was forthcoming, he turned to the United States for help in arranging a rapprochement with South Africa. In March 1984, on the banks of the Nkomati River marking the border between Mozambique and South Africa, Machel and Botha signed a 'good-neighbourliness' agreement in which South Africa promised to withhold support for Renamo and Mozambique for the ANC. In the weeks that followed, Mozambique expelled some 800 ANC members allowing only a mission of ten to remain. Deprived of its most important forward positions, the ANC was forced to operate from headquarters in Lusaka, Zambia, hundreds of miles away from the front line. The South Africans, meanwhile, secretly continued to support Renamo. On the Angolan front, South Africa and Angola signed a ceasefire agreement in 1984 in which South Africa promised to withdraw its forces from Angola while the Angolan government undertook to prevent Swapo guerrillas from crossing the border into Namibia.

At home, Botha's display of *kragdadigheid* – forcefulness – in handling recalcitrant black neighbours was highly popular with the white electorate. But his triumph was to be short-lived.

A new phase of black resistance to apartheid began in the early 1980s. While the black consciousness movement, after bearing the full brunt of government repression, fell into decline, there was a resurgence of interest in the African National Congress, prompted in part by the activities of ANC guerrillas, many of them former Soweto activists infiltrating back into South Africa from training camps abroad. As opinion polls testified, a growing number of blacks accepted the belief that fundamental change could only be brought about by revolutionary violence. Robert Mugabe's victory in neighbouring Zimbabwe, after a guerrilla campaign lasting seven years, provided a potent example. Scores of community associations sprang up around the country campaigning over issues like housing conditions. Radical newspapers appearing in Cape Town, Pretoria and other towns helped bolster community demands. Among the campaigns launched at this time was a petition demanding the release of Nelson Mandela.

For fifteen years, public interest in Mandela's fate had hardly stirred. The government had sought to erase him from the public mind by banning his speeches and his photograph from publication, and he had become a largely forgotten figure. During the early 1970s, as he wrote in his autobiography, when there was no sign of any break in the apartheid system, he and his colleagues on Robben Island had to force themselves not to give up in despair. But in the wake of the Soweto revolt and the repression that followed it, as anti-apartheid protest both at home and abroad gathered momentum, Mandela in prison became a potent symbol of opposition to the government. In March 1980 the Soweto newspaper *The Post* started a campaign demanding his release with the banner headline FREE MANDELA! To many people he seemed linked more to a distant past than of any relevance to the future. But the campaign caught the public imagination, attracting support from white university students and liberal politicians as well as a host of black organisations in South Africa and gaining ground around the world. Millions of people who supported the campaign abroad had little precise idea of who he was. But the tide of hostility towards apartheid was running strongly, making him one of the most famous prisoners in the world. Mandela's presence on Robben Island soon reached mythic proportions. Awards by foreign governments, universities and cities were showered upon him; streets were named after him; songs were written about him. Botha's response to the campaign was to denounce Mandela as an 'arch-Marxist' committed to violent revolution who would have to serve the sentence imposed on him by a court of law. As the clamour for Mandela's release continued, the government decided in 1982 to move him from Robben Island to a prison on the mainland near Cape Town called Pollsmoor. Robben Island itself had become part of the legend the government was anxious to destroy. But Mandela's stature continued to grow. Reports that filtered out about him spoke of a man of immense authority and influence, still resilient after twenty years of prison life.

Botha's plans for constitutional change meanwhile gave political activists an opportunity to stir up national action against apartheid. In 1983 a coalition of more than 300 organisations – church groups, civic associations, trade unions and student bodies – launched the United Democratic Front to oppose the constitutional changes, in what amounted to the broadest display of public opposition to apartheid in nearly thirty years. Cutting across lines of class and colour, the UDF demanded a united, democratic South Africa free from homelands and group areas. While repudiating the use of violence, it represented, in effect, the internal wing of the ANC.

Throughout 1984 a mood of tension spread through black communities. An economic recession, more severe than anything South Africa had known for fifty years, cast thousands into unemployment. The inflation rate climbed, causing a squeeze on black living standards. Rural areas were hit by a devastating drought. Student groups were active once more, protesting at low educational standards. The elections for Coloured and Indian representatives to the new tricameral parliament in August raised the temperature still further. A low turnout of voters suggested massive disapproval of the new constitution. African resentment at being excluded from parliament reached new heights. A new system of local government for African townships also provoked widespread opposition. Rent increases imposed to help finance new councils brought sharp protests. Local councillors, elected in poorly attended polls, were denounced as 'stooges' and 'collaborators'.

In September outbreaks of violence began. They were sporadic at first, ignited by local grievances, flaring up with great intensity, shifting from one area to the next and gradually drawing in more and more of an urban population that was alienated and hostile. At the forefront were groups of black youths – 'comrades' as they came to be known – determined to destroy 'the system' and ready to defy armed police and soldiers in the dusty and decrepit streets of the townships with stones, catapults and petrol bombs. Many saw themselves as shock troops of the revolution and believed that it was within their reach. Students joined the fray, forsaking their classrooms once more. 'Liberation before Education' became their slogan. The townships' revolt, however, was not solely a 'children's war', as it had been in 1976. This time the revolt was part of a popular movement involving entire communities – parents, teachers, workers, churchmen and women. Nor were the aims of black activists confined to resolving particular grievances. This time the objective was to overthrow apartheid.

Urged on by the ANC in exile to mount 'a people's war' and make the townships ungovernable, young comrades enforced consumer boycotts, organised rent strikes, attacked government buildings, set up 'people's courts' and hunted down 'collaborators' – township councillors, local policemen and others deemed to support 'the system'. Their trademark became 'the necklace' method of killing – a tyre filled with petrol thrown over a victim and set on fire.

The government responded with a show of military might, sending troops and paramilitary police into the townships. But other than resorting to repression and letting loose police death squads, Botha had no clear strategy for dealing with the violence. He was prepared to make modifications to the apartheid system, such as abolishing pass laws, but only where they did not diminish white power and privilege.

The daily spectacle of violent protest and government repression, shown on television screens around the world, provoked a chorus of international condemnation and calls for action against Botha's government to force him to undertake major reform and open negotiations with black leaders, including Mandela. Taking fright, foreign investors began unloading their South African shares. American banks decided to stop rolling over loans, starting a chain reaction that pitched South Africa into a severe financial crisis. So strong was the tide of opinion against South Africa that even conservative Western leaders like Ronald Reagan and Margaret Thatcher, previously outspoken in their opposition to sanctions as a means of dealing with South Africa, were obliged to agree to a package of measures. White business leaders, appalled by the unending cycle of black anger, government ineptitude, disinvestment, financial mayhem and international sanctions, lined up to condemn the government's failure to introduce meaningful reforms and demanded urgent action, including the release of Mandela.

Botha's response was to attempt to decapitate all black resistance. Security officials were instructed by the State Security Council to 'identify and eliminate the revolutionary leaders, especially those with charisma' and to destroy their organisations, using 'any means, overt and covert'. Under a state of emergency declared in 1986, the army surrounded whole townships and moved into schools. Prisons were soon filled with community leaders, trade unionists, church workers, students and other anti-apartheid activists. Strict censorship was imposed on the media. Botha declared that South Africa would not 'crawl before anyone' and was quite prepared to 'go it alone'.

His tactics were temporarily successful. With thousands of activists in detention, opposition groups fell into disarray; youth groups lost all vigour. Black leaders who managed to escape the dragnet were forced into an underground existence, often unable to keep in touch with their supporters. As a means of forcing change, random violence in the townships had clear limitations. The white areas of South Africa had emerged virtually unscathed. Barely a ripple had disturbed the placid surface of white society. After two years of strife, all that had been proved was that the black opposition movement was still no match for the government. Its powers of repression had hardly been tested. The security forces were capable of dealing with any threat from either township activists or trained guerrillas. But however much Botha relied on *kragdadigheid* to protect white power, it left South Africa without a viable political strategy, only the prospect of more violence.

From the confines of Pollsmoor prison, Mandela made several approaches to the government, proposing a meeting with Botha as a way of breaking the fearful deadlock that gripped South Africa. Botha ignored the approaches. Responding to calls for Mandela's release, he said he was prepared to release Mandela only if he renounced violence. He was adamant in refusing to open talks with the ANC. Nevertheless, he ensured that the conditions of Mandela's imprisonment were ameliorated. On Christmas Eve in 1986, Mandela was given his first taste of freedom outside prison in twenty-four years: a prison official took him on a car drive around Cape Town. Other trips followed. He was taken to coastal resorts and fishing villages, to the mountains and inland to the edge of the Great Karoo. He walked on beaches, took tea in cafés and ate fish and chips. Once he visited the home of one of his warders, meeting his wife and children. Only a handful of trusted prison staff and guards knew of these secret journeys. No word of them leaked out. Nor was he recognised in public. The last photographs taken of him in the 1960s, for anyone who could remember, showed a heavily built middle-aged man. Now he was a lean, grey-haired, elderly figure, with creases and furrows etched on his face and a slightly fragile air.

Despite misgivings among his prison colleagues, Mandela persisted with his attempts to open a dialogue with the government. He told officials he was not interested in his own release unless it was part of a package of measures that included the lifting of the ban on the ANC. In 1988, two years after Mandela's first approaches, the government agreed to set up a secret committee of senior officials to explore with him a range of political issues. Months of discussions followed. Mandela's grasp of the issues and, in particular, his knowledge and understanding of the Afrikaner people greatly impressed those present. But he became increasingly impatient with the lack of any tangible results. 'You don't have the power,' he told one senior official. 'I want to talk to the man with the power, and that is P. W. Botha. I want to talk to him.'

Mandela's meeting with Botha was finally set for 5 July 1989. In conditions of utmost secrecy Mandela was driven from the prison cottage he had been assigned in Victor Verster prison near Paarl to a basement garage beneath Tuynhuys, the Cape Dutch mansion alongside parliament in the centre of Cape Town that served as the president's official residence. Forewarned of Botha's reputation, Mandela had been expecting to find a grim, cantankerous figure. But as he entered the president's office, Botha walked towards him from the opposite side of the room, his hand outstretched, smiling broadly – 'a charming man indeed', Mandela recalled, unfailingly courteous and friendly. 'The thing that impressed me was that he poured the tea.'

Their conversation amounted to little more than a polite discourse on South African history and culture, lasting for half an hour. When news of the meeting leaked out a few days later, the meeting was described, fairly accurately, as 'a courtesy call'. The symbolic importance of Botha sitting down with a prisoner whom he had hitherto denounced as a 'communist terrorist' was real enough. But Botha was no nearer to addressing the central issue of political reform that Mandela regarded as essential. It was a matter he never seriously contemplated. Six weeks later, after months of friction with his cabinet colleagues, Botha resigned.

On taking office in September 1989, Botha's successor, F. W. de Klerk, began a reassessment of South Africa's prospects. Forty years of National Party rule had left the white population powerful and prosperous; the Afrikaner community, in particular, had fared well, fulfilling its long-held ambition of acquiring wealth, skills and economic strength. The government's ability to defend the apartheid system was still formidable. It possessed the means for totalitarian control and frequently used them. To make the system work, it could depend on a significant number of allies within the black community – homeland governments, urban politicians and vigilante groups. Despite the opprobrium that South Africa aroused around the world, it faced no serious international threat: sanctions were a costly rather than a damaging imposition.

At a regional level, its hegemony over southern Africa remained unchallenged. Under Gorbachev's leadership, the Soviet Union had made clear its intention of disentangling itself from regional conflicts such as Angola. Cuba, tired of endless conflict in Angola, was also looking for an opportunity to withdraw. Negotiations over a deal involving the phased withdrawal of Cuban troops from Angola, in return for South Africa's withdrawal from Angola and the independence of Namibia, were concluded in December 1988. Soviet assistance to Mozambique was also scaled back. In 1989 the Frelimo government, exhausted by years of economic failure and continuing conflict with Renamo rebels, abandoned its position as a Marxist-Leninist state and declared itself in favour of multi-party democracy. Within a matter of months the spectre of 'total onslaught' orchestrated by the communist bloc, which had dominated government thinking throughout the Botha era, began to recede. Moreover, the collapse of socialist governments in Eastern Europe in 1989 deprived the ANC of one of its main sources of financial, logistical and military support. The fear that the ANC could be used as 'a Trojan horse' for advancing Soviet interests fell away.

De Klerk was quick to grasp the importance of these strategic openings. Though a staunch defender of the apartheid system, proud of the achievements of 'separate development', he was essentially a pragmatist, determined above all to protect Afrikaner interests. His close advisers warned him that the modernised form of apartheid he favoured would no longer work. If the whites were to preserve the power and privileges they had enjoyed for so long, a more fundamental change was needed. While the government faced no immediate difficulty, the longer political reform was delayed, the weaker its position would become. Without reform, the cycle of black opposition would intensify. The fate of neighbouring Rhodesia, where Ian Smith had turned down one favourable deal after another, only to find himself embroiled in a seven-year guerrilla war and negotiating a belated settlement that led to the advent of a Marxist government, provided a potent example. 'When the opportunity was there for real constructive negotiation, it was not grasped,' de Klerk concluded. 'We must not make that mistake.' Fortuitously, Mandela's secret talks with government officials had convinced them that he was a man with whom the white establishment could do business.

The mood of much of the white population favoured change. A new generation of white South Africans disliked being treated as pariahs by the rest of the world, subjected to sports boycotts, travel bans, trade sanctions and hostile comments. Businessmen were adamant about the need for a more stable political system that would assist economic growth and rid South Africa of the cost of sanctions. Economic prosperity was becoming more important to white South Africa than racial division. Like other white communities in Africa, they had come to accept the old adage: give them parliament and keep the banks. Further encouragement came from Western governments. From one capital to the next, the advice de Klerk was given was the same: lift the ban on the ANC, release Mandela and other political prisoners and start talks.

Weighing up the balance of risks, de Klerk believed there was a good chance that, if set free, the ANC, poorly organised and ill-prepared for peace, would fall into disarray, leaving the government to forge ahead with a new alliance of conservative black organisations. He also reasoned that the government enjoyed such a preponderance of power that it would be able to set the terms of any settlement.

Despite signs of a right-wing backlash and deep misgivings among the security establishment, de Klerk took the plunge. In a calm, confident manner in parliament in Cape Town on 2 February 1990, he announced that he was lifting the ban on the ANC and releasing Mandela. 'It is time for us to break out of the cycle of violence and break through to peace and reconciliation,' he declared, outlining new aims towards which the government would work. These included a democratic constitution and universal franchise. In effect, de Klerk pronounced the death sentence of apartheid.

The boldness of de Klerk's reforms set South Africa on an entirely new course. In the titanic struggle between white and black, the central issue had always been political power. None of the reforms hitherto implemented by the National Party had come close to addressing the issue. Now, at a stroke, de Klerk had conceded one-person one-vote and opened the way for its attainment.

And so, on 11 February 1990, Nelson Mandela walked through the gates of Victor Verster prison, hand in hand with his wife, Winnie, towards a waiting crowd of supporters and the ranks of the world's media. It was a moment of liberation experienced around the world.

★

Mandela was once asked how different was the man who emerged from prison after twenty-seven years from the one who went in. He replied, with characteristic brevity, 'I came out mature.' Mandela disliked talking about himself and allowed few glimpses of his personal thoughts or emotions. The years of imprisonment had turned him into an intensely private person. Even with his closest friends, his true feelings remained hidden. He was anxious never to betray the slightest sign of weakness either to them or to prison staff, determined to stifle the anger that lay within. He often felt anger about whites, he said, but not hatred. His hatred was directed at the system. His anger was directed at individuals, never against whites as a group. Not once did he express bitterness towards the white community for his ordeal, only against the system they imposed.

While the outside world had expected Mandela to dwell on the suffering he and his colleagues had endured in prison, he himself was more interested in explaining what they had learned there, the understanding they had gained, the reasons for their lack of bitterness, the strength of their commitment to democracy that had sustained them. No matter what personal hardship he had undergone, he was determined never to lose sight of the goal of non-racial democracy, believing that white fear of it could eventually be overcome. The example he set was of profound importance. For if after twenty-seven years in prison, Mandela could emerge insisting on reconciliation, it undermined the demands of those seeking revenge and retribution. His generosity of spirit also had a profound impact on his white adversaries, earning him measures of trust and confidence that laid the foundations for a political settlement.

His homecoming, however, was to bring him little personal happiness. A massive scandal erupted over the criminal activities of his wife, Winnie, once an icon of the liberation struggle, who had become head of a notorious gang called the Mandela United Football Club that had terrorised parts of Soweto in the 1980s. Moreover, Winnie showed no interest in resuming the kind of settled family life that Mandela craved, forsaking him on his return home to Soweto for a lover half her age, flaunting the relationship in public. Mandela's late years of freedom were constantly blighted by her wayward conduct. At the height of his popularity and fame he was often a lonely figure, spending his evenings alone. As with all the other suffering that he had endured, he hid the pain and humiliation behind the mask he had become accustomed to wearing.

It took two years of preliminary skirmishing before multi-party negotiations on the future of South Africa started and another two years of tortuous negotiations before agreement was reached on a new interim constitution, paving the way for national elections. There were many times along the way when it seemed that the whole exercise was doomed. As rival groups competed for ascendancy, South Africa was engulfed in prolonged bouts of violence. A mini civil war broke out between Chief Buthelezi's Inkatha party, a Zulu nationalist movement, and Mandela's ANC, erupting first in the KwaZulu homeland and Natal, then spreading to black townships on the Witwatersrand, South Africa's industrial heartland. Elements of the security forces still wedded to the idea of 'total strategy' aided and abetted Inkatha, determined to thwart any prospect of the ANC coming to power. Massacres by one side or the other became commonplace. All sides used death squads. Armed groups belonging to the Azanian People's Liberation Army, an Africanist faction opposed to negotiations, singled out white civilian targets for attack. White right-wing paramilitary organisations, seeking an Afrikaner *volkstaat*, embarked on their own vigilante action and threatened to wreck the whole negotiation process.

Time and again Mandela and de Klerk clashed over who was to blame for the violence. In public and private their exchanges became increasingly acrimonious. Even on the occasion when the two men were jointly awarded the Nobel Peace Prize in Oslo in 1993, the friction was still evident. In choosing them as 'Men of the Year' for 1993, *Time* magazine noted that 'the mutual bitterness and resentments between de Klerk and Mandela are palpable', and it asked rhetorically, 'How could these two have agreed on anything – lunch, for instance, much less the remaking of a nation?' At a political level, however, Mandela recognised how important de Klerk was to the whole settlement. 'My worst nightmare is that I wake up and de Klerk isn't there,' Mandela told guests at a private dinner party. 'I need him. Whether I like him or not is irrelevant. I need him.'

As the sun rose over the rolling green hills of Natal on 26 April 1994, Nelson Mandela walked up the steps of the Ohlange High School in Inanda near Durban to cast his vote. He emerged from the polling station, his face wreathed in smiles, and spoke of a bright future. 'This is for all South Africans an unforgettable occasion,' he said. 'We are moving from an era of resistance, division, oppression, turmoil and conflict and starting a new era of hope, reconciliation and nation-building.'

In their millions, South Africans made their way to the polls, black and white citizens alike sharing a common determination to make the election a success. Many walked miles to reach a polling station. Some arrived on crutches and some in wheelchairs; some dressed in their Sunday-best clothes and some wore outfits they had made specially for the occasion. Long queues formed outside polling stations, circling around city blocks and winding back along dirt roads and across fields. Many arriving in the early morning were still waiting to vote late in the afternoon, tired and hungry; some in rural areas had to vote by candlelight. Yet, hour after hour, they remained patient. And when they returned home, having voted, it was with a profound sense of fulfilment, not just from participating in the election of a new government, but from exercising a right which had been denied to most South Africans for so long. Time and again, voters leaving polling stations spoke of how their dignity had been restored.

On each of the four polling days, South Africa was more peaceful than it had been for many years. The fever of violence that had afflicted the country for more than a decade abated. Even the killing fields of KwaZulu-Natal, where political warfare had caused more than 10,000 deaths, fell silent. On the Witwatersrand, members of rival factions found themselves joining the same queues in townships, swapping complaints about the long delays.

For many whites the experience of the election was as moving as it was for blacks. Standing side by side with blacks, waiting to vote, they felt a sense of their own liberation. The feelings of relief that the curse of apartheid had finally been lifted were as strong among the white community which had imposed it as among the blacks who suffered under it. The importance of the occasion was all the greater since for so many years it had seemed that a peaceful end to the apartheid system was beyond reach and that a more likely outcome would be revolutionary war.

The victory of the ANC at the polls in 1994 was as much a personal tribute to Mandela as it was to the movement he led. His ordeal of imprisonment had never been forgotten by the people for whom he spoke and was duly acknowledged when the time came for them to vote. Time and again it was said, 'He went to prison for us.' For blacks the election was, above all, about liberation – a celebration of their freedom from white rule – and it was to Mandela's leadership that many attributed that liberation.

The transfer of power was accomplished in an atmosphere of much goodwill. Closing the book on three centuries of white rule, de Klerk chose words of encouragement fitting for such a historic moment. 'Mr Mandela has walked a long road and now stands at the top of a hill. A man of destiny knows that beyond this hill lies another and another. The journey is never complete. As he contemplates the next hill, I hold out my hand to Mr Mandela in friendship and cooperation.'

The day of Mandela's inauguration as president, 19 May 1994, was marked by the greatest celebrations ever seen in South Africa. From all over the world, visiting dignitaries – heads of state, royalty and government leaders representing some 170 countries – gathered in Pretoria to mark South Africa's rite of passage. Taking the oath of office, Mandela promised South Africans a new covenant: 'We enter into a covenant that we shall build a society in which all South Africans, both black and white, will be able to walk tall, without fear in their hearts, assured of their inalienable right to human dignity – a rainbow nation at peace with itself and the world.'

PART IV

IN THE NAME OF
THE PROPHET

In the void that followed the demise of Pan–Arab nationalism in the 1960s, there came a resurgence of radical Islamism that spread across North Africa threatening one regime after another. Its origins lay in the traumatic defeat of the Arab cause in the Six Day War of 1967. It drew inspiration and support from the Islamic Revolution in Iran that brought the downfall of the Pahlavi monarchy in 1979. Within the Muslim world in general, a growing movement sought to revive Islam, demanding stricter adherence to its tenets, believing that religion rather than secular ideology offered a solution to social, economic and political problems. Creeds like nationalism and socialism were condemned as godless Western imports. What mattered more than the world's system of nation-states was the *umma* – the universal community of believers. A central debate within the movement concerned the extent to which the *sharia* – Islamic law – should prevail over the workings of society. Some groups, taking a lead from Saudi Arabia, emphasised the need to apply Islamic law in such traditional areas as family and penal law. Other groups, influenced by Iran, stressed that it should extend to state institutions and economic policy. Moderate intellectuals aimed to 'Islamise modernity', by accepting the West's technology and administrative skills while reforming its moral corruption in accordance with Islamic law and using Islamic institu-

tions as the basis of government. Small radical groups advocated *jihad* –
armed struggle – against the enemies of Islam, including regimes in
the Muslim world they deemed to be impious or apostate, guilty of
permitting Muslim society to be corrupted by Western values and
practices.

The principal architect of jihad ideology, Sayyid Qutb, was an
Egyptian intellectual-activist whose writings influenced generations of
radical Islamists. Once an admirer of the West and Western literature,
he had turned into a formidable critic as a result of a two-year stay in
the United States in the late 1940s, appalled by what he saw as its
moral decadence, its materialism, racism and sexual depravity.
Returning to Egypt in 1951, he became a leading figure in the
Muslim Brotherhood but fell foul of Nasser's repression of the movement. Accused in 1954 of involvement in a failed attempt to
assassinate Nasser, he spent ten years in a concentration camp, developing a revolutionary ideology that rejected not only the West but
governments and societies in the Muslim world. He divided Muslim
societies into two diametrically opposed camps: those belonging to
the party of God and those belonging to the party of Satan. There was
no middle ground. He argued that because of the repressive nature of
un-Islamic regimes, no attempt to change them from within by using
existing political systems would succeed. Hence the only way to
implement a new Islamic order was through jihad. Writing from
prison, he said that the only homeland a Muslim should cherish was
not a piece of land but the whole *Dar al-Islam* – the Abode of Islam.
Any land that hampered the practice of Islam or failed to apply sharia
law was ipso facto part of *Dar al-Harb* – the Abode of War. 'It should
be combated even if one's own kith and kin, national group, capital
and commerce are to be found there.' In 1965, after the Muslim
Brotherhood was blamed for another attempt to assassinate Nasser,
Qutb was executed. Acclaimed a martyr to the cause, he was venerated as a father-figure by Muslim extremist movements around the
world.

Another Egyptian scholar who gained increasing influence among
Islamists was Omar Abdel Rahman, a radical cleric, born in 1938,
blinded by diabetes when he was ten months old. While studying for

a doctorate at Cairo's University of al-Azhar he had been galvanised into becoming a militant activist, like so many others of his generation, by the humiliating Arab defeat in the Six Day War in 1967. In his dissertation – a 2,000-page exposition of a Koranic verse entitled 'Repentance', in which the Prophet Muhammed exhorts his followers to wage war on non-Muslim tribes – he described 'the violence and persecution' the Prophet suffered at the hands of 'infidels', concluding that jihad was 'the only way to vanquish the enemies of Islam'. Posted to the Faiyum Oasis southwest of Cairo, he travelled from mosque to mosque, delivering fiery sermons, alluding to Nasser as an infidel and an apostate. In 1970 he was imprisoned, without charge, for eight months. Appointed a professor of theology at the University of Asyut in Upper Egypt in 1973, he promoted the teachings of Sayyid Qutb, emphasising the need for jihad and martyrdom in driving out infidels. He soon acquired a radical following in university circles and emerged as the spiritual mentor of a network of underground revolutionary organisations, including *Gamaa Islamiyya* and *Jamaat al-Jihad*, that sought to establish an Islamic republic.

The threat that radical Islamists posed in North Africa intensified in the 1980s. In Egypt, Nasser's successor, Anwar al-Sadat, initially tried to cultivate the support of Islamic groups in order to bolster his own position and to escape from Nasser's shadow. He appropriated the title of 'Believer-President', arranged for the mass media to cover his praying at mosques and began and ended his speeches with verses from the Koran. He also encouraged the growth of Islamic student associations, promoted Islamic courses in schools and reached a modus vivendi with the Muslim Brotherhood, allowing it to function publicly once more, as long as it forswore violence.

None of this, however, was enough to satisfy the rising clamour of his Islamist critics. Sadat caused further alienation with new initiatives. His 'open-door' economic policy – '*infitah*' – brought an influx of Western businessmen. His peace accord with Israel in 1978–9, though winning him great praise in the West and a Nobel Peace Prize, was commonly regarded by Muslims in Egypt as an opportunistic capitulation to Israel and the United States that left the occupied Palestine territories of the West Bank and Gaza in the lurch. In protests throughout Egypt, demonstrators denounced the accord as the treasonous act of an 'unbeliever'.

Sadat reacted to growing opposition to his regime by resorting to authoritarian rule and outright repression. His critics – both secular and religious – accused him of acting like a 'pharaoh'. In his most draconian move, in September 1981 he ordered the arrest of more than 1,500 people from across the political spectrum – Islamic activists, lawyers, doctors, journalists, university professors and political opponents. In a television address he maintained he was saving Egypt from political and religious 'sedition'.

A few weeks later, on 6 October 1981, as he was reviewing a military parade from a throne-like chair, Sadat was gunned down by army members of *Jamaat al-Jihad*. As he slumped to the ground, their leader, a 24-year-old lieutenant, cried out: 'I am Khalid Islambuli! I have killed Pharaoh! And I do not fear death!' At a subsequent trial twenty-four men were accused of complicity in Sadat's assassination. They included *al-Jihad*'s principal ideologue, Muhammad al-Farag, the author of a tract entitled *The Neglected Obligation* that maintained that jihad was the sixth pillar of Islam and that armed struggle and revolt was an imperative for all true Muslims so as to rectify the ills of a decadent society: 'There is no doubt that the first battlefield for jihad is the extermination of these infidel leaders and to replace them by a complete Islamic Order.'

Also on trial, sitting next to Lieutenant Islambuli, was the blind cleric Sheikh Omar Abdel Rahman, accused of having issued a fatwa that justified Sadat's assassination, a charge he denied. He was questioned by one of the judges of the military court:

'Is it lawful to shed the blood of a ruler who does not rule according to God's ordinances?'

'Is this a theoretical question?' the sheikh asked.

He was told that it was, and he responded that it was lawful to shed such blood.

'What of Sadat?' asked the judge. 'Had he crossed the line into infidelity?'

Sheikh Omar hesitated, and refused to respond.

In issuing his fatwas, Sheikh Omar never mentioned names, and because the prosecution was unable to prove he had named Sadat, he was acquitted. Along with some three hundred others, he was then charged with organising *al-Jihad* and of conspiring to overthrow the government, but he was eventually acquitted of that too. After spending three years in prison, he sped off to Peshawar on the Pakistan border to participate in the jihad against the Soviet occupation of Afghanistan.

Sadat's successor, Hosni Mubarak, a former air force commander, faced a series of violent challenges by militant Islamists but he managed for the most part to keep the lid on their activities through brute repression and the use of emergency laws. Tunisia, Morocco and Libya also succeeded in crushing radical groups. But in Algeria the struggle turned into a ferocious war that lasted through the 1990s and beyond.

For twenty-six years after independence in 1962, Algeria was run as a one-party dictatorship controlled by a military hierarchy with a monopoly on public life. Having won the liberation struggle against France, the army made itself the country's central institution, wielding power with ruthless determination from behind the scenes. Algerians often remarked sardonically that while every state had an army, in Algeria the army had a state. Every aspect of Algerian society – the economy, religion, language and culture – was subject to state control. A national charter, drawn up in 1976 by the *Front de Libération Nationale* (FLN), declared socialism to be the 'irreversible option', defined Islam as the 'state religion' and insisted that a fusion of political, economic and religious spheres was needed to build a 'fortified state' capable of mobilising economic development. The media, civic and professional associations, student organisations and trade unions, all functioned as part of the state machine. The state also controlled mosques and appointed preachers. A 'cultural revolution', designed to rid Algeria of the legacy of French colonial rule, required schools, universities and the administration to undergo 'Arabisation', making use of modern literary Arabic from the Arab East rather than French, colloquial Arabic or Berber that had been commonly used hitherto. Anyone dissenting from government policy was liable to face imprisonment or exile.

Economic strategy was based on central planning, industrialisation and nationalisation of foreign-owned assets, including the oil and gas sector. Buoyed up by a steep rise in oil revenues during the 1970s, the government poured huge sums into 'industrialising industries' – heavy industry intended to provide the basis for further economic expansion – an iron and steel complex, oil refineries, fertiliser factories, natural gas liquefaction plants. Algeria's investment rate during the 1970s exceeded 35 per cent of national income; per capita gross industrial production increased at an average annual rate of 14 per cent; the total value of industrial production doubled; per capita income rose from $370 to $830; and employment increased from 1.75 million to nearly 3 million. Along with industrialisation came a massive increase in foreign debt; it rose from $2.7 billion in 1972 to $23.4 billion in 1979, with debt-servicing equal to 25 per cent of exports.

Simultaneously, the country's centre of gravity shifted from rural areas to the cities. The agriculture sector was largely neglected. An 'agrarian revolution' decreed the nationalisation of large estates and the establishment of what amounted to a collective-farm sector. For more than ten years, prices and 'salaries' remained frozen to ensure low food costs for the urban population, making agricultural work increasingly unattractive. Each year an estimated 100,000 left rural areas for the cities. Factories were set up on more than 370,000 acres of good agricultural land, further drawing off skilled labour. Food production remained static. With a rapidly rising population, Algeria became increasingly dependent on food imports.

Until the late 1970s there was little overt opposition to the FLN juggernaut. Most Algerians benefited not only from employment opportunities but from an extensive welfare system that gave them free education, free medical care and subsidised food. For as long as the state machine was able to afford distributing largesse, critics of the system remained muted. During the 1980s, however, Algeria faced a growing litany of woes: falling revenues from oil; a bloated bureaucracy; inefficient state companies; declining industrial production; a depressed agricultural sector; a debt-service ratio of 97 per cent of export earnings; inflation soaring to 42 per cent; labour unrest; absenteeism; general unemployment reaching 30 per cent and youth unemployment at 70 per cent. Added to all this was a demographic explosion. With a birth rate exceeding 3 per cent a year, Algeria's population grew from 10 million in 1962, to 18 million in 1980, to 26 million in 1992. The impact was most marked in urban areas. By 1988 half of the population lived in towns afflicted by a desperate shortage of housing; rising crime; water rationing; and food shortages. Millions struggled to survive in wretched *bidonvilles*. Every year 200,000 more young people came on to the labour market. For many the only choice was to become '*hittistes*' – 'those who lean against the walls', whiling away the day in streets and alleyways. Attempts at economic reform brought little benefit.

The gap in social inequality became ever more noticeable. Some 5 per cent of the population earned 45 per cent of national income while 50 per cent earned less than 22 per cent. The ruling elite, meanwhile, living in exclusive neighbourhoods high in the hills above Algiers and profiting from lucrative ties and 'trade commissions' with foreign companies, became renowned for corruption.

Overall, there was a growing sense that the FLN state had lost its authority and its purpose. What remained in place, however, was the group of generals and their business associates – '*Le Pouvoir*' – who controlled political life from the shadows.

The first sign of turbulence came from the Berber community in Kabylia. Constituting nearly one-fifth of the population, Berbers had been alienated by the FLN's determination to promote a 'national' culture and identity by enforcing the use of Arabic at the expense of their own language and culture. Not only did the national charter of 1976 omit all reference to Berber language and culture, it specified that 'the generalised use of the Arabic language and its mastery as a creative functional instrument is one of the primordial tasks of Algerian society'. Two prominent Berber dissidents, Salem Chaker and Saïd Sadi, complained: 'Since independence, the ideological currents of the regime, and especially Arab Islamism, have exerted a monopoly on the cultural and intellectual life of the country, founded on censorship and authoritarianism. They have elaborated an explicit desire to stifle and liquidate the Berber dimension and all autonomous thought.'

In 1980, when the government banned a conference on the use of the Berber language due to be held at the University of Tizi-Ouzou, teachers and students took over the campus in protest; their expulsion precipitated a massive outburst of strikes and riots in Kabylia, known as 'the Berber Spring', a conscious evocation of the Prague Spring of 1968. The disorder was ruthlessly suppressed.

A far more sustained challenge came from radical Islamists. A harbinger of the movement had first appeared in 1964 in the form of an association called *Al Qiyam* – 'The Values'. Though not openly defying the state, *Al Qiyam* presented itself as the champion of the authentic values of Islam, demanded official support for Islamic rites and duties and denounced Western practices such as the wearing of Western clothing by Algerian women. An article in its journal, *Humanisme Musulman*, in 1965 made clear its position on state politics:

> All political parties, all regimes and all leaders which do not base themselves on Islam are decreed illegal and dangerous. A communist party, a secular party, a marxist-socialist party, a nationalist party (the latter putting in question the unity of the Muslim world) cannot exist in the land of Islam.

In 1970, *Al Qiyam* was banned.

Having reasserted its monopoly on religion, the FLN hierarchy adopted a series of measures aimed at enhancing the Islamic character of Algeria while holding fast to its socialist agenda. The day of rest was changed from Sunday to Friday; gambling and the sale of alcohol beverages were banned. But Islamist voices persisted, refusing to subordinate Islam to the state. Writing from exile in Morocco in 1974, Sheik Abdellatif Soltani, a prominent scholar, published a pamphlet condemning the government's socialist strategy and warning against moral decay and 'destructive principles imported from abroad'. Islamist ideas took root in university circles among teachers resistant to Western models of political modernism. Many saw Islam as the only counterculture capable of confronting Western hegemony. The arrival of foreign teachers from Egypt and the Arab East brought in to assist the government's programme of Arabisation helped spread Islamist ideas and literature.

In the early 1980s Islamist groups set out to reconquer the religious sphere and gain autonomy from the state. Hundreds of unofficial mosques were established where 'free imams' spread their message. Thousands of disaffected youths were attracted to the cause. For those excluded or marginalised by 'modernisation', Islam provided a firm moral and social identity. For the poor, it offered salvation. As government services deteriorated, Islamic networks filled the gap, assisting the sick and the poor and imposing their own forms of discipline.

In their struggle for ascendancy, some Islamists were ready to use violence. There were repeated clashes at universities with left-wing and Berberist students. The death of a left-wing student in 1982, killed by blows from a sword, prompted the government to order a wave of arrests. Islamists responded by organising a massive prayer meeting at a university building in downtown Algiers which overflowed onto the streets and paralysed traffic for several hours. A further wave of arrests ensued. Included in the round-up was Sheikh Abdellatif Soltani. When Soltani died when under house arrest in 1984, a crowd of some 25,000 mourners gathered at his funeral. An underground Islamist guerrilla organisation, the *Mouvement Islamique Algérien Armé*, surfaced in 1985, staged a payroll robbery near Algiers and attacked a police barracks, leaving behind a painted slogan on the gate saying, 'Allah the Avenger is with us!' Its leader, Mustapha Bouyali, was a war veteran who used his intimate knowledge of the Atlas mountains to evade capture for sixteen months. Algerian volunteers who had joined the jihad against the Soviet occupation of Afghanistan returned home in the late 1980s as hardened veterans of the struggle, bringing with them militant ideas and a new form of dress. Afghan-style dress when it first appeared in Islamist neighbourhoods in Algiers caused much amusement initially but later unease about the radical fervour it represented.

Though capable of mobilising thousands of supporters on occasions, the Islamist movement remained largely on the fringes of public life. In October 1988, however, the FLN's grip on power was shaken by an outbreak of riots that broke the mould of Algerian politics. Growing spontaneously out of protests in the working-class neighbourhood of Bab el-Oued in Algiers over price rises and consumer shortages, the riots spread to towns and cities across the country. At the forefront were groups of youths, students and the unemployed who attacked public buildings and set up barricades. Islamists joined the throng. In Belcourt a procession of 7,000 Islamist supporters clashed with the police. Called in to suppress the riots, the army acted ruthlessly: some 500 people were killed.

In the aftermath, President Chadli Benjedid, a former army colonel, opted for reform rather than repression. He agreed to separate the FLN from the state and brought an end to the one-party system that had prevailed in Algeria for twenty-six years. A new constitution, opening the way to multi-party politics, dropped all reference to the FLN and to socialism. Almost overnight a host of political parties and civic, professional and cultural associations sprang up. But the most significant new players in the political arena were those affiliated with the Islamist movement. Chadli encouraged the Islamists, hoping that they could be used to underpin support for his regime.

The main contender was the *Front Islamique du Salut* (FIS). Founded in February 1989 and legalised the following September, it was the most politically ambitious Islamist organisation, setting its sights on gaining political power as the prerequisite to reform of society on Islamic lines. It attacked the corruption of '*Le Pouvoir*', advocated strict observance of Muslim law and demanded an Islamic constitution of state. Its leader, Abassi Madani, was a founder member of the FLN who had participated in the attacks launching the war against the French on 1 November 1954. After spending most of the war in prison, Abassi had become a university teacher, earning a doctorate in education from the University of London. A middle-class intellectual, aged fifty-eight, he represented the pragmatic wing of the FIS. His deputy, Sheikh Ali Belhadj, a 33-year-old imam at the Al-Sunna mosque in Bab el-Oued, personified the younger generation of FIS supporters, radical and uncompromising.

Belhadj made clear his disdain for democracy:

> Democracy is a stranger in the House of God. Guard yourself against those who say that the notion of democracy exists in Islam. There is no democracy in Islam. There exists only the *shura* [consultation] with its rules and constraints . . . We are not a nation that thinks in terms of majority–minority. The majority does not express the truth.

He was similarly dismissive of multi-party politics and political pluralism:

> Multi-partyism is not tolerated unless it agrees with the single framework of Islam . . . If people vote against the Law of God . . . this is nothing other than blasphemy. The *ulama* [religious scholars] will order the death of the offenders who have substituted their authority for that of God.

Belhadj's Friday sermons, denouncing liberals, foreign governments, followers of other religions and leaders of other parties, were hugely popular, attracting audiences of up to 20,000 people each week.

Abassi Madani adopted a more moderate line, opposing violence and proclaiming his commitment to democracy, though with some qualifications:

> We will consider that those who have been elected by the people reflect the opinion of the people. In contrast, what we will not accept is the elected member who harms the interest of the people. He must not be against Islam, the sharia, its doctrines and its values. He must not be able to make war on Islam. He who is an enemy of Islam is an enemy of the people.

In the race to establish a new political order between the Islamist movement and secular parties like the FLN, the Islamists made spectacular advances. In provincial and municipal elections in June 1990, the FIS gained control of thirty-one of forty-eight provincial assemblies and 856 out of 1,541 communes, winning landslide majorities in virtually all major cities. Its overall share of the vote was 54 per cent. The FLN came second, with control of 6 provincial assemblies and 487 communes, winning 26 per cent of the vote. A young Algerian explained his support for the FIS in 1990 in these terms: 'You have only four options: you can remain unemployed and celibate because there are no jobs and no apartments to live in; you can work in the black market and risk being arrested; you can try to emigrate to France to sweep the streets of Paris or Marseilles; or you can join the FIS and vote for Islam.'

National assembly elections were due to be held before the end of 1990. But in the intervening period, the Gulf crisis, starting with Iraq's invasion of Kuwait in August and leading to Western military intervention in the region, galvanised public opinion in Algeria, setting off a tidal wave of anti-Western fervour and forcing the FIS to adopt a more militant position. Ali Belhadj appeared at a rally in combat fatigues and called on the government to open training camps for volunteers to go to Iraq. With the onset of war in the Gulf, the elections were postponed until June 1991. Attempts by the government to gerrymander the elections by introducing measures favouring the FLN provoked mass demonstrations. Determined to reassert the authority of the state and cut the Islamists down to size, the army intervened. Two days before the election the army command ordered Islamic slogans to be removed from FIS-controlled town halls and replaced by FLN slogans, and deployed troops in Bab el-Oued and other districts to enforce the change. As pitched battles broke out, the election was postponed once more. Abassi Madani and Ali Belhadj were arrested on trumped-up charges of 'conspiracy against the security of the state' and spent twelve years in prison or under house arrest.

When the first round of national assembly elections finally took place on 26 December 1991, the result was an overwhelming victory for the Islamists. The FIS took 188 out of 231 seats with 47 per cent of the vote; the FLN gained 16 seats with 23 per cent; and the *Front des Forces Socialistes* (FFS), a secular party with deep roots among the Berbers of Kabylia, won 25 seats and 7 per cent. The second round, expected to confirm the FIS's massive lead, was scheduled for 16 January 1992.

But the second round never took place. Even though President Chadli was prepared to work in conjunction with an FIS government, the army – 'les décideurs' – refused to countenance the prospect. Once the Islamists gained power, argued the army command, they could never be trusted to give it up. It would be a case of 'one man, one vote, one time'.

The architect of the 1992 coup was General Khaled Nezzar, the hardline minister of defence. Nezzar was a key figure in a group of senior officers known in Algeria as *hizb França*, the party of France, a coterie of former soldiers in the French army who had deserted to join the FLN midway through the independence struggle in the 1950s and who had since gained a dominant position in the army command. Wedded to a pro-French, anti-Islamist strategy, they enjoyed the support of the French government, sent their children to French schools and maintained profitable links with French business interests. Writing in *El Moudjahid* in 1990, Nezzar had remarked: 'It would be intolerable if men coming to power through democracy led us to dictatorship.'

On 11 January 1992 Nezzar forced Chadli to resign. The following day, the elections were cancelled. Thus Algeria's brief encounter with the democratic process came to an abrupt halt.

The generals next set out to crush the FIS. They began by banning all political activity at mosques and ordering the removal of imams at mosques controlled by the FIS and their replacement by state-approved clergy. When violence erupted, they declared a state of emergency and banned the FIS altogether on the grounds that it had attempted insurrection against the state. Mass arrests of FIS militants followed; thousands were interned in prison camps in the Sahara; newspapers were shut down, town halls closed.

In place of Chadli the army installed a five-man collective presidency known as the *Haut Comité d'État*. To give it a respectable image, they chose as its head Mohamed Boudiaf, one of 'nine historic chiefs' credited with founding the FLN in 1954, a highly regarded modernist who had lived modestly in exile in Morocco for twenty-eight years running a small brickworks. Boudiaf concurred with the banning of the FIS, arguing, like the generals, that 'the FIS wanted to use

democracy to destroy it'; it would, he said, 'stop at nothing to monopolise power'. But he also had ambitions to establish a new political
order, determined to clamp down not just on Islamists but on corruption within the old FLN establishment. 'One has to act against
these people [the mafia] who have monopolised the possessions of the
state . . . We will prosecute them and take all necessary measures to
recover these goods for the state. This is one of my main goals.'

With reformist zeal Boudiaf set out to construct a new political
movement, the *Rassemblement Patriotique Nationale*, intending to win
popular support and gain the presidency in a future election.

'What are the pains that this country is suffering from?' he asked in
a speech in April 1992, one hundred days after his appointment.

> Algeria is suffering from three crises: a moral crisis; a spiritual crisis;
> and an identity crisis. For thirty years our people have been torn
> between East and West, between the French and Arabic languages,
> between Arabism and Berberism and between traditionalism and
> international values . . . After long years during which a single party
> and the dictatorship of a single language prevailed, democratisation
> has become a necessary stage . . . The exploitation of Islam for
> political and partisan aims, and also the resorting to democracy and
> lies, found, for a specific period, listening ears among the deprived
> and marginalised sections of the population.

Boudiaf acquired many enemies. But it was probably his determination to root out corruption within the government and the military
that cost him his life. In June 1992 he was assassinated by one of his
bodyguards while addressing a meeting in Annaba. Popular opinion
blamed the 'Chadli mafia' rather than FIS activists.

With the banning of the FIS, Algeria descended into a nightmare of
violence reminiscent of the colonial conflict. Islamist militants
relaunched the *Mouvement Islamique Armé* and with other pro-FIS
groups waged a campaign of assassination, bombing and sabotage,
aiming to force the government to accept Islamist claims to power.
Scores of policemen, soldiers and government officials were killed.
Killing a policeman became an initiation rite for young *hittiste* recruits.

The ruling elite were divided between '*éradicateurs*' within the army who wanted outright repression and '*conciliateurs*' who advocated a negotiated solution. The army command took the offensive, established special commando forces, used secret detention and resorted to torture and death squads. But the Islamist insurgency continued to spread. A new president, Liamine Zeroaul, a retired general, favoured a dialogue with political parties including the FIS and personally entered into discussions with the imprisoned FIS leaders, Abassi Madani and Ali Belhadj. But he ran into vehement opposition from the *éradicateurs*.

In 1993 the insurrection spawned an extremist wing, *Groupe Islamique Armée* (GIA), dedicated to achieving power solely through revolutionary violence. Its slogan was 'no dialogue, no reconciliation, no truce'. The GIA specialised in the killing of high-profile individuals – writers, journalists, teachers and intellectuals – not just pro-government figures but those perceived to be opposed to the idea of an Islamic state. A GIA leader, Sid Ahmed Mourad, told an underground newspaper: 'Our jihad consists of killing and dispersing all those who fight against God and his Prophet.' He singled out journalists: 'The journalists who fight against Islamism through the pen will perish by the sword.' Another GIA leader, Abdelkader Hattab, issued a leaflet entitled: 'Throat-slitting and murder until the power is God's.'

The GIA also targeted foreign nationals, aiming to drive out the expatriate community. A note handed to three French nationals kidnapped by the GIA warned foreigners: 'Leave the country. We are giving you one month. Anyone who exceeds that period will be responsible for his own sudden death.' Within days some 3,000 foreigners fled the country. Scores were killed.

Regarding itself as the standard-bearer of the Islamist camp, the GIA engaged in internecine warfare with pro-FIS groups, adding to the turmoil. In Algiers it became the dominant armed group. Pro-FIS groups endeavoured to regain the initiative by forming a united armed front, *Armée Islamique du Salut* (AIS). Mixing political violence and criminal activity, Islamist 'emirs' profited heavily from extortion, protection rackets and smuggling on the periphery of major towns where their main support lay.

By the end of 1994 the conflict had claimed 30,000 lives. Without any political process in place, Algeria was adrift in a sea of violence. Trying to find a way through the impasse, a group of opposition parties, including the FIS, the FLN and the FFS, met in Rome in January 1995 to see what common ground they could find. The 'Rome Platform' they signed produced significant advances. Their fourteen-point agreement included: calls for multi-party democracy; an end to military intervention in politics; the release of political prisoners; and an end to the state of emergency imposed in 1992. All were agreed that the ban on the FIS should be lifted and that FIS leaders and activists should be released. For its part, the FIS committed itself to 'political pluralism' and the 'alternation of power through universal suffrage', accepting that any party voted into power could be voted out of power. The FIS further pledged to uphold freedom of religion and full civil rights for members of all faiths. The 'Rome Platform' also dealt with Berber claims, recognising the Berbers (*Imazighen*) and their language (*Thamazighth*) as distinct components of the nation and its culture: 'The constituent elements of the Algerian personality are Islam, Arabism and Amazighism'. Those who signed up to the 'Rome Platform' represented 82 per cent of people who voted in the 1991 parliamentary elections. It was endorsed from prison by the militant FIS leader, Ali Belhadj. But it was rejected out of hand by the *éradicateurs* of Algiers.

Seeking to fill the political void, Zeroaul took the initiative to stage early presidential elections. Presenting himself as a candidate, he hoped to acquire a degree of popular support and legitimacy that would enable him to assert his authority over the army command. Because the main opposition parties – the FLN, the FFS and the FIS – refused to participate, demanding political negotiations in the first place and an end to the state of emergency, Zeroaul was left with an easy victory. Though three other candidates, including the leader of a moderate Islamist party, stood against him in November 1995, Zeroaul was the only plausible candidate. In an official turnout of 75 per cent of the electorate, he obtained 61 per cent of the vote.

With this mandate behind him, Zeroaul pushed through a process of constitutional reform, proposing a series of changes to be put to a referendum. While reaffirming Islam's status as the official religion of the state, he proposed a ban on political parties from seeking to exploit Islam for political purposes by including it in their names or manifestos. The same ban was to apply to the use of Arab and Berber identity. His proposals received a mixed reception. Secular parties were disappointed by the prominent role accorded to Islam. Berberists were bitterly resentful that the Berber language still received no official recognition, leaving Arabic as the sole national language. A referendum in November 1996 endorsed the changes by a wide margin: 85 per cent voted in favour. But figures for the official turnout, put at 80 per cent, had clearly been rigged, undermining the result's authenticity.

The elections for national, provincial and local assemblies that followed in 1997 offered the prospect of establishing a democratic way forward. But once again, lurking in the background, *'les décideurs'* managed and manipulated the outcome. Six main parties were allowed to contest the elections, two representing moderate Islamist parties, two based in the Berber-speaking region of Kabylia, and two that were state-sponsored – the *Rassemblement National Démocratique* (RND) and the FLN. All were essentially middle-class vehicles. There was no party representing the urban poor as the FIS had once done. The principal winners were the RND, which took 155 out of 380 seats in the national assembly, and the FLN which took 64 seats, ensuring a government acceptable to *les décideurs*. The moderate Islamist party, *Mouvement de la Société pour la Paix*, gained 69 seats.

There was considerable evidence of rigging. But the rigging occurred not simply in order to secure a victory for pro-government candidates but to ensure that opposition parties too fared well enough to leave them with a stake in the system, thereby helping to legitimise it. The elections, according to the British scholar Hugh Roberts, essentially reflected 'outcomes of decisions taken by the power-brokers of the regime'.

The evidence of the 1997 elections [wrote Roberts] suggests that the results of the electors' choices have to be 'corrected' in the most systematic way to make them correspond to the backroom bargains struck by the various factions within the regime and so preserve the complex internal equilibria on which the regime rests.

In effect, the army remained the arbiter of the political process.

The Islamist insurgency, meanwhile, degenerated into indiscriminate slaughter. Thousands of civilians were killed in massacres carried out by the GIA during 1997 and 1998. GIA dissidents broke away to form a splinter group – *Groupe Salafiste pour la Prédication et le Combat* (GSPC) – intending to confine their attacks to security forces. But the insurgency had long since lost sight of its original purpose of establishing an Islamic state by force of arms. Abandoning the struggle, the AIS and several smaller groups decided to observe a ceasefire.

A new president, Abdelaziz Bouteflika, elected in 1999 with the approval of the military, set out to promote reconciliation with the Islamists, offering an amnesty to rebels willing to surrender. He also promised an investigation into the cases of some 7,000 Algerians who had 'disappeared', most of them at the hands of the security forces. Hundreds of rebels came forward to hand in their weapons and thousands more – *les repentis* – were released from prison. But both the GIA and the GSPC pledged to fight on, and Bouteflika's peace initiative soon lost momentum. The army command saw it merely as a device to weaken the Islamist opposition. When a new Islamist party, *Wafa*, sought to take the place of the banned FIS, it was refused legal recognition. Abassi Madani voiced his despair at Bouteflika's lack of resolve: 'After he had promised reconciliation as a remedy to the crisis, thereby recognising its essentially political character and, in consequence, implicitly accepting there could be no other kind of solution, the promise simply disappeared,' he said.

Algeria was thus condemned to live with a low-level conflict, year after year. Over a ten-year period more than 100,000 people died. Nor was there any end in sight. The violence seemed to suit both sides – the military and the Islamist rebels. It enabled the military to justify extending the state of emergency and restricting opposition activities, thereby protecting a system of control that had made the ruling elite wealthy and powerful and given them all the patronage they needed to maintain their grip on power. Oil revenues running to $10 billion a year at the end of the 1990s provided them with a comfortable base from which to operate. Privatisation deals were largely confined to elite businessmen linked to the military establishment. For their part, militant Islamists, using the rhetoric of Islam as justification, continued to profit from the business of war. Caught in the middle, the vast majority of Algerians were resigned to a life of poverty.

Compared with the horrors of Algeria, Egypt's Islamist insurgency in the 1990s was more sporadic but it nevertheless made a deep impact. It was initiated in large part by veterans from the jihad in Afghanistan returning home after the Soviet withdrawal in 1989, bringing revolutionary fervour and fighting experience to underground groups like *Jamaat al-Jihad* and *Gamma Islamiyya*. Their targets included government officials, intellectuals, journalists and foreign tourists. They attacked and murdered Coptic Christians and burned Christian shops and churches. They bombed banks and government buildings and theatres, video stores and bookshops that popularised Western culture. Small towns and villages as well as large cities were caught up in the violence. Among the victims was Farag Foda, one of Egypt's best-known writers, an outspoken critic of militant Islam, who was shot dead outside his Cairo home. Egypt's elderly Nobel laureate, Naguib Mahfouz, who had openly criticised the violent tactics of underground Islamist groups, was knifed.

Attacks on foreign tourists had a devastating impact on the tourist industry, worth $3 billion a year. In 1996 seventeen Greek pilgrims were killed outside the Europa hotel in Cairo; *Gamaa Islamiyya* apologised, saying that they had been mistaken for Israeli tourists. Then nine Germans were killed outside the Egyptian Museum. In 1997 fifty-eight foreign tourists visiting the Temple of Queen Hatsheput in the Valley of the Kings, just across the Nile from the city of Luxor, were massacred by *Gamaa* gunmen – students from the University of Asyut – who hunted them down for nearly an hour. Some victims had their throats cut. A note stuffed inside the eviscerated corpse of an old, bespectacled Japanese man read, 'No to tourists in Egypt'; it was signed 'Omar Abdel Rahman's Squadron of Havoc and Destruction'.

Mubarak reacted to the Islamist campaign with a massive crackdown, using emergency laws to detain thousands without trial and setting up military courts to try civilians with no right of appeal. 'Afghan' veterans were hunted down ruthlessly. Suspects were routinely tortured. Family members were held hostage by the dreaded State Security Investigation.

As well as suppressing extremists, Mubarak took the opportunity to curb mainstream Islamic opposition, using the Islamist 'menace' as a cover. His principal target was the Muslim Brotherhood. Since Sadat had allowed it to function openly in 1970, it had transformed itself into a major political, social and economic force in the Islamic cause, advocating evolutionary reform and remaining steadfast in rejecting violence. It was the largest and strongest Islamic organisation in the country. It ran an extensive network of banks, investment houses, factories and agribusinesses. It had gained control of trade unions, student groups, municipalities, university faculties and several professional syndicates – lawyers, doctors, engineers and journalists. Its social service network was often more effective than the government's. Prevented from forming a political party of its own, it had entered into alliances with secular parties to gain a political voice. Campaigning with the slogan 'Islam is the solution', it had stood in the 1987 election under the banner of the Labour Party, taking 17 per cent of the vote.

Insisting that the Muslim Brotherhood was part of the Islamist onslaught, Mubarak used new 'anti-terror' legislation to detain leading members and took action to engineer government control of mosques, preachers and professional syndicates. He was adamant in refusing to allow it to participate in the political arena under its own name. 'I will not permit another Algeria here,' he told an American correspondent. And he blatantly rigged elections to ensure that his National Democratic Party retained its monopoly on power. When a group of disillusioned members of the Muslim Brotherhood joined forces with leftists, Nasserites and Copts to launch a new political party, *Hizb al-Wasat*, aimed at bridging the divide between Arab nationalists and Islamists and advocating a joint role for Muslims and Christians, the government refused to register it. Several of its founders and members were arrested and tried before a military court accused of 'joining an illegal and secret group which aims to over-throw the ruling regime'. Seven were sentenced to prison terms. In the run-up to elections in 2000, the government arrested scores of Muslim Brothers and other Islamist sympathisers to prevent them from standing as candidates and organising campaigns.

Mubarak's strategy of repression largely succeeded in crushing vio-lent Islamist opposition. Both *Gamaa Islamiyya* and *Jamaat al-Jihad* gave up the struggle. But the Islamic tide nevertheless continued to rise. Islamic revival took hold not only among the mass of impover-ished Egyptians but among middle and upper classes. It was no longer a marginal phenomenon. Islamic institutions proliferated across the country, providing an alternative system of schools, clinics, hospitals and social welfare. Islamic values, codes of conduct and dress became part of mainstream society, informing government, the courts and professions. Once renowned for its multicultural, cosmopolitan and secular character, Egypt had turned towards its Islamic roots. Cairo, famous as 'the city of a thousand minarets', by 2004 boasted more than 5,000 mosques, calling the faithful to prayer.

26

BLACK HAWK DOWN

Unlike most African states, Somalia embarked on independence with a strong sense of national identity. The Somalis possessed a common language and a common culture based on pastoral customs and traditions. They also shared a profound attachment to Islam. They were essentially a nation of pastoral nomads, well adapted to surviving in the harsh, arid terrain of the Horn of Africa, enjoying an abiding love of camels and poetry. 'The country teams with "poets",' wrote the British traveller Richard Burton who spent six months in Somalia in 1854.

> Every man has his recognized position in literature as accurately defined as though he had been reviewed in a century of magazines – the fine ear of this people causing them to take the greatest pleasure in harmonious sounds and poetic expressions, whereas a false quantity or prosaic phrase excites their violent indignation . . . Every chief in the country must have a panegyric to be sung by his clan, and the great patronize light literature by keeping a poet.

Yet, by one of those cruel twists of fate that occurred so often during the Scramble for Africa in the nineteenth century, the Somali nation was carved up into five separate territories. The French occupied

French Somaliland, a bleak enclave of lava-strewn desert surrounding the port of Djibouti at the southern entrance to the Red Sea which they wanted as a coaling station; the British acquired northern Somaliland, initially to ensure that the British garrison at Aden was kept regularly supplied with meat; and the Italians established themselves in the Italian colony of Somalia, with a capital at Mogadishu. Further south, Somali communities were incorporated within the boundaries of the British colony of Kenya; and to the west, on the Ogaden plateau, after Emperor Menelik extended the borders of his empire in the late nineteenth century, they came under Ethiopian jurisdiction. At independence in 1960, British Somaliland and Italian Somalia were joined to form the Somali Republic. But it remained the overriding ambition of Somali nationalists to establish a 'Greater Somalia', reuniting Somali communities in the 'lost lands' of Kenya's Northern Frontier District, the Ogaden and Djibouti, where about one-third of the 4 million Somalis lived. This desire for Somali unification was enshrined in the Somali constitution and emblazoned on the Somali flag, which bore as its emblem a five-point star representing the five segments of the Somali people.

Beneath this passionate nationalism, however, lay a complex society based on clan-families, each one subdivided into sub-clans, extending all the way down to lineage segments consisting of close kinsmen and family groups. Somalis asked each other not whence they came but to whom they were related. Every child of eight years was expected to be able to recite their family's genealogy through the male line stretching back some ten or twenty generations or more to a common patriarch. Somalis gave political allegiance first to their immediate family, then to their immediate lineage, then to the clan of their lineage, then to a clan-family that embraced several clans and ultimately to a confederacy of five clan-families – the Darod, the Hawiye, the Isaq, the Dir and the Digil-Mirifleh – that comprised the nation. 'No other single line of communication and common interest connected so directly and incontrovertibly the pastoral nomad of the interior with his kinsmen in the civil service, in the National Assembly, or in the cabinet itself,' wrote the Somali scholar, Ioan Lewis. 'No other bond of mutual interest had so many far-reaching ramifications in all aspects of private and public life.' Each level of segmentation defined the rights and obligations of Somalis as well as their standing in relation to others. But despite such codes of conduct, Somali politics tended to consist more of shifting allegiances and temporary coalitions of lineages, making the system inherently unstable.

For as long as the goal of a 'Greater Somalia' seemed attainable, clan rivalries were held in check. But when the government's irredentist campaign ended in a humiliating military defeat, it set in motion an implosion of the Somali state. Both the United Nations and the United States were caught up in the fallout, with disastrous consequences.

Despite the extreme poverty of Somalia and its lack of resources, the main energies of the Somali government at independence were concentrated on unification. From the outset, Somalia made clear its refusal to accept the validity of any of its existing borders. It actively supported Somali insurgents in Kenya's Northern Frontier District and in the Ogaden. It also opened negotiations with the United States, West Germany and Italy, aiming to establish an army to carry out its own military campaigns; but the most that Western powers were willing to provide was equipment and training for a force of 5,000 men intended to deal with nothing more serious than internal security. In 1963, however, the Soviet Union came forward with an offer to establish an army of 10,000 men, together with a small air force, and the Somalis swiftly accepted it. At the time, the Soviet Union looked for no particular advantage in Somalia; nor did it support the government's plans for a Greater Somalia. A brief full-scale war between Somalia and Ethiopia in 1964 ended in an Ethiopian victory within a matter of days.

But after a military coup in Mogadishu in 1969, Soviet involvement in Somalia increased dramatically. The new Somali leader, General Mohammed Siyad Barre, proclaimed Somalia a Marxist state, embarked on a nationalisation campaign and accepted a large number of Soviet advisers in government ministries and agencies and in the military. As well as adding an African client to their list, the Russians began to take an increasing interest in Somalia for strategic reasons, seeing its value as part of a plan to expand Soviet influence in the Red Sea and the Indian Ocean. In 1972, in exchange for the use of naval facilities in the northern Somali port of Berbera, the Russians agreed to provide Somalia with increased military aid. By 1977 Somalia had acquired an army of 37,000 men, heavy artillery and a modern air force equipped with jet fighters.

Judging that the time was right to take advantage of Mengistu's difficulties in Eritrea, where half of the Ethiopian army was under siege, Siyad committed regular forces in support of Somali insurgents in the Ogaden. Within two months the Somalis had won possession of most of the Ogaden. The war effort galvanised public opinion. Radio reports of the war's progress were followed avidly. Community centres were converted into cottage factories for making uniforms. The dream of restoring 'lost lands' seemed within reach.

But Siyad's Ogaden adventure ran into trouble when the Russians decided to switch sides, preferring to back Mengistu's Marxist regime rather than his own. When Siyad asked for more Russian arms, he was turned down. Siyad's response was to tear up Somalia's Treaty of Friendship and Cooperation with the Soviet Union and expel all Russian personnel, but he was then left without the support of any major arms supplier. Freed from the link with Siyad, the Russians and Cubans committed themselves to Ethiopia on such a massive scale that the course of the wars in the Ogaden and in Eritrea changed dramatically. Facing a strike force of Cuban armour and air support, the Somalis suffered a crushing defeat in the Ogaden in March 1978 and four days later announced their withdrawal.

The impact of the Ogaden defeat reverberated throughout Somalia. Within weeks, officers from the Majerteyn clan of the Darod attempted to overthrow Siyad. The revolt was crushed, but several leaders escaped to Ethiopia where they formed the Somali Salvation Democratic Front (SSDF) and embarked on a guerrilla war against Siyad's regime. A second guerrilla war was started by the Somali National Movement (SNM), a northern group based primarily on Isaq clans in former British Somaliland, also with the support of Ethiopia.

Siyad reacted with harsh military and economic measures and

exploited clan rivalries to keep his opponents divided, distributing money and arms to pro-government groups. He came to rely increasingly on his own clan, the Marehan of the Darod. By 1987 it was estimated that half of the senior officer corps belonged to the Marehan or related clans. Key government positions were given to close family members.

As a result of his anti-Soviet stance, Siyad was also able to obtain Western support to help shore up his regime. During the 1980s the United States provided $800 million worth of aid, one-quarter of it in military assistance, gaining in return military access to ports and airfields. Italy contributed $1 billion, half of it in military supplies. The value of foreign aid to Somalia soared to $80 per person, equivalent to half the gross domestic product. Foreign aid became the main prop of Siyad's regime, used to ensure that his cronies and clan allies were rewarded and enriched. Leading loyalists made fortunes from food aid, appropriating it then selling it on the market. A World Bank study, published in 1988, estimated that the growth of food aid was fourteen times higher than the growth of food consumption. From being a country self-sufficient in food grains, Somalia became dependent on imported food, all to the advantage of the ruling elite.

Looking for ways to undercut rebel support, Siyad in 1988 came to an agreement with Ethiopia under which both sides undertook to cease support for each other's opponents. The aim was to allow Mengistu to move troops away from the Somali border to counter rebel advances in Eritrea and Tigray and to give Siyad an opportunity to crush the SNM in northern Somalia. But Siyad's willingness to make deals with the old arch-enemy was seen as a gross betrayal by many Somalis. The Somali opposition likened the accord to the Hitler–Stalin pact of 1939.

It also led to a rapid upsurge in fighting in northern Somalia. Anticipating Siyad's offensive and no longer subject to Ethiopian restraints, SNM rebels laid siege to several towns, including the regional capital Hargeisa, coming close to capturing it. To stave off defeat, air force fighters made repeated bombing raids on the city, killing thousands of civilians. Siyad, according to one of his close

associates, Hussein Ali Dualeh, was well satisfied with the result. 'I
have never seen Barre so relaxed and happy throughout my long association with him,' he wrote. 'He did not look like a president who had
just destroyed his second capital, causing so much suffering and
anguish. He simply saw himself as a Darod chief who had totally
annihilated an enemy clan.'

Western support, however, dried up. The Americans led the way,
suspending military aid in 1988 and economic aid in 1989. Without
Western support, Somalia began to disintegrate, fragmenting into a
patchwork of rival fiefdoms controlled by clan chiefs, all armed to
the hilt. Ogadeenis of the Darod formed the Somali Patriotic
Movement. The Hawiye, inhabiting central regions of the country,
including Mogadishu, formed the United Somali Congress (USC).
The army splintered into rival factions. Banditry, extortion and lawlessness became commonplace. When a group of prominent Somalis
issued a manifesto proposing the transfer of power to a civilian government, Siyad reacted in fury, ordering the arrest of leading
signatories, including a former president and a former police commissioner. According to Hussein Ali Dualeh, Siyad repeatedly
vowed: 'When I leave Somalia, I will leave behind buildings but no
people.'

By 1990 Siyad's control scarcely reached outside Mogadishu. His
opponents derisively referred to him as 'Mayor of Mogadishu'. But
Mogadishu itself was increasingly threatened. Siyad's main adversary
was General Muhammed Farah 'Aideed', military leader of the USC,
a ferociously touchy character whose nickname meant 'one who does
not take insults lying down'; those who displeased him ran the risk of
summary execution. A former army officer, trained at military acad-
emies in Rome and Moscow, he had been imprisoned without trial by
Siyad for six years. Sent to New Delhi as Somalia's ambassador to India
for five years during the 1980s, he completed work on three books
there, returning to Somalia in 1989. His militia was based on the
Habar Gidir sub-clan of the Hawiye.

In January 1991 the remnants of Siyad's army were driven out of
Mogadishu by Aideed's militia, fleeing southwards in an armoured
convoy loaded down with gold bars, foreign currency and loot

470 THE STATE OF AFRICA

plundered from Western embassies. Rebel soldiers ransacked Siyad's hilltop residence, Villa Somalia, finding miles of magnetic tape recordings from tapped telephone lines and reels of surveillance film. Vast weapons dumps were parcelled out among clan leaders. 'Almost everyone got hold of guns,' a European fact-finding mission reported. 'Armouries are empty. Police have no weapons. There is no army as such. The elders of the clans do not seem to be able to control many of their armed youth, and there are conflicting inter-clan interests which prevent their elders from acting jointly to improve security.'

No sooner had Siyad fled than a protracted struggle for power broke out within the USC between two Hawiye leaders, Aideed of the Habar Gidir, its military boss, and Ali Mahdi Mohammed of the Abgal, a prominent Mogadishu businessman who headed its political wing. While Aideed was still preoccupied with chasing Siyad's forces as they withdrew into southern Somalia, Ali Mahdi proclaimed himself head of a new 'government' in Mogadishu. Their rivalry split the capital into two armed camps, engulfing it in months of conflict that left an estimated 14,000 dead and 40,000 wounded. Mahdi's militias controlled the north, Aideed's militias the south. The city centre was reduced to a wasteland of rubble. Buildings were stripped bare by successive waves of looters and scavengers. Thousands fled from what the Somalis called 'clan cleansing'. 'Death has become too commonplace to matter,' wrote the Somali journalist, Mohamoud Afrah. 'The two greatest products in Mogadishu these days are shooting and rumours: from morning to night they manufacture rumours, from night to morning they manufacture shootings.'

In the north-west of Somalia, meanwhile, the SNM established their own government and in May 1991 declared Somaliland's independence from the rest of Somalia, returning it to its 1960 status. In the north-east, the Majerteyn militia, the SSDF, seized control, setting up their own rudimentary administration in what was later to become known as 'Puntland'. In the south Siyad and Aideed fought for control of the Digil-Mirifleh region, a fertile agricultural belt lying between the Jubba and Shebelle rivers that served as the breadbasket of southern Somalia. Twice Siyad's forces advanced through Digil-Mirifleh in attempts to take Mogadishu, plundering grain stores and livestock, burning villages, murdering and raping as they went. Twice Siyad was beaten back, escaping into exile in 1992, leaving behind a region wracked by famine and starvation.

Somalia's plight attracted the attention of the United Nations Secretary-General Boutros Boutros-Ghali, an ambitious Egyptian diplomat with plans to carve out a more dynamic role for the UN in the post-Cold War era. Boutros-Ghali saw a new potential for UN involvement in preventive diplomacy, peacemaking and peacekeeping, spelling out his doctrine in *An Agenda for Peace*, published in 1992: 'The time for absolute and exclusive sovereignty has . . . passed; its theory was never matched by reality. It is the task of leaders of States today to understand this and to find a balance between the needs of good internal governance and the requirements of an ever more inter-dependent world.' In practice, Boutros-Ghali advocated that national sovereignty should be overridden by the United Nations Security Council in cases where it was deemed necessary for peace enforce-ment.

Yet Boutros-Ghali lacked both the resources and personnel to implement his grand vision with any chance of success. 'The existing UN structures are not at all adapted to the requirements of the new era, especially in apprehending the whole problem of conflict between and within states,' wrote Mohamed Sahnoun, an Algerian diplomat in a post-mortem on the UN Somalia operation. The UN system, he said, dealt with crisis simply through improvisation. 'The UN recruit-ment process does not necessarily respect the criteria of competence and experience . . . Even less regard is given to the criterion of commitment.'

The chaotic conditions in Somalia made foreign intervention espe-cially hazardous. There was no recognised government, only a collection of rapacious militias vying for control, ready too loot and kill at will. After evacuating its staff in December 1990, in the final days of Siyad's collapsing regime, the UN and its agencies had largely turned their backs on Somalia, considering it an environment too dangerous in which to operate. UN 'Somalia' officials worked out of comfortable offices in Kenya. Throughout 1991, as famine in southern Somalia took hold, only the International Committee of the Red Cross, working in partnership with the Somali Red Crescent Society, was willing to risk involvement in a major relief programme, employing gunmen for protection and tolerating high levels of looting. ICRC officials, exasperated by the absence of UN assistance, broke with tradition by criticising the UN publicly. 'How come Unicef [the UN Children's Fund] has thirteen people in Nairobi and no one inside Somalia?' one senior ICRC official inveighed.

A ceasefire in Mogadishu between Aideed and Mahdi in March 1992, however, presented a window of opportunity for intervention. A UN technical mission recommended sending a team of fifty unarmed observers to monitor the ceasefire, accompanied by a force of 500 UN troops to protect them and humanitarian relief supplies. On 24 April 1992 the UN Security Council duly established a United Nations Operation in Somalia (Unosom) under the direction of Mohamed Sahnoun and called for the immediate despatch of observers and the deployment of a security force to be made in consultation with 'the parties in Mogadishu'.

Sahnoun arrived in Mogadishu on 4 May with no budget, no office, no staff and a dearth of background knowledge and intelligence material. He found Aideed deeply suspicious of UN intentions, convinced as a result of previous encounters with UN envoys that the UN favoured Mahdi's claim to leadership. It took two months before Aideed was ready to accept the deployment of ceasefire monitors; and it was not until August that he agreed to the deployment of a security force of 500 Pakistani soldiers.

The streets of Mogadishu, meanwhile, were ruled by groups of gunmen riding around in 'technicals' – stolen pick-up trucks converted into battlewagons – habitually high on *khat*, a narcotic leaf. Various militias controlled access to the port and the international airport, demanding landing fees, holding relief supplies to ransom, running protection rackets, raiding warehouses and fighting among themselves. Relief agencies were obliged to negotiate a series of deals with them to enable food convoys to reach their destination.

'Trucks with food are like trucks full of money,' a German Red Cross convoy chief told a reporter, Scott Peterson, as they were on

their way to a relief centre at Giohar, accompanied by eighty hired
gunmen. On arriving at Giohar, the gunmen threatened to halt food
distribution to the starving unless they were paid seven times the
agreed amount. 'Tense negotiations took all day,' wrote Peterson. 'I
was taken aback by their attitude. There was no sense of community,
no sense of easing a human crisis – just *me*, and what goes into *my*
pocket. In the end, the ICRC had to triple their pay.'

Despite such adverse circumstances, Sahnoun worked assiduously to
gain the trust of militia leaders, engaging in intensive dialogue, earning the respect of both Somalis and the international aid community.
'He would talk with any Somalis who approached,' recalled a Somali
doctor, Hussein Mursal. 'He was the first who came and saw there
were alternatives. He was the first to meet the elders of the Hawiye
clans, the neutral clans, who are not involved in the fighting. Also he
was talking with women. He used to reason like Somalis.'

Preferring a 'soft' approach, Sahnoun tried to make the clan system
'work for Somalis' as a force for cohesion, encouraging inter-clan reconciliation and finding many Somalis willing to help. As he
subsequently wrote:

> What sustained our hope was the encouragement we had received
> from the elders in all regions as well as some former social, politi-
> cal and administrative officials, including former police officers,
> and women leaders at both national and community level. These
> leaders approached us sometimes with tears in their eyes, offering to
> work closely with the UN to bring Somalia out of the mess it was
> in.

Yet the UN operation itself was plagued by bureaucratic infighting,
incompetence and endless delays. Sahnoun's pleas to New York for
more help were frequently ignored. A senior official from the UN's
Department of Humanitarian Affairs, posted to Mogadishu, complained: 'I'm supposed to be creating a database of projects underway.
I'm supposed to provide air support to the aid agencies. I'm supposed
to provide security for both the UN and other relief workers.
The lack of resources means that I can't do any of these things.' In

mid-1992, as the death toll from starvation soared, public criticism of
the UN grew to a crescendo. On a visit to Baidoa, where 'death'
trucks were collecting hundreds of bodies every day for burial, a
senior World Food Programme official, Trevor Page, told a reporter:
'It's so bad because we've let things simmer without paying proper
attention. We've had inexperienced people who don't know what
they are seeing, who don't know what the implications are, and didn't
blow the whistle.' A Unicef official described Somalia as 'the greatest
failure of the UN in our lifetime'. Sahnoun himself became openly
critical of UN incompetence. Addressing a fund-raising conference in
Geneva in October 1992, he said that 300,000 people might have died
from war and famine in Somalia while the United Nations did nothing and Somalia 'descended into hell'. But Sahnoun too became a
victim of its machinations. Later that month, despite the painstaking
progress he had made in winning the trust of all Somali factions, he
was abruptly dismissed by Boutros-Ghali who criticised him for
making high-profile complaints.

In place of the 'soft' approach favoured by Sahnoun came a far more
forceful strategy. At the forefront of the campaign for tougher action,
sounding 'the drumbeat for intervention', was a group of international
aid agencies. Even though the peak of the famine had passed – the
death toll at Baidoa had fallen from 1,700 a week in September to
around 300 in October – senior aid managers agitated for military
intervention. 'The international community, backed by UN troops,
should move in and run Somalia, because it has no government at all,'
declared Philip Johnston, president of Care-US in September. Care
International spoke of 'naked anarchy, wanton destruction and total
collapse of social, economic and political structures'. Johnston was sec-
onded in October to head a UN emergency assistance programme.
'We have to fight the Somalis themselves,' he said. 'There's plenty of
food and the agencies are willing to deliver it. But we have to dodge
firefights to do it and deal with those Somalis who want to rip off the
system and deprive these children.'

At UN headquarters, Boutros-Ghali saw an opportunity both to
expand the UN's role in line with his *Agenda for Peace* and to cover up

its months of failure to deal adequately with Somalia. Lacking resources of his own, he fortuitously found the US ready to flex its muscles on the UN's behalf. In the post-Cold War era, President George Bush envisaged the UN playing a central part in his concept of a 'new world order'. Fresh from its victory in the 1991 Gulf War, the US military was keen to prove that it could undertake 'Operations Other Than War'. The opportunity to sort out a few rag-tag militias in Somalia, while in pursuit of humanitarian objectives, seemed an ideal test case.

Signalling the change to a hardline strategy, Boutros-Ghali chose as a replacement for Sahnoun an Iraqi diplomat, Ismat Kittani, who adopted a confrontational approach from the start. An aloof figure, dismissive of the Somalis, he held no more than two meetings with Aideed and Mahdi throughout his tenure in Mogadishu. 'There was to be no more diplomacy, no balance of intellectual curiosity, no vision and no sincerity which would have commanded respect,' wrote John Drysdale, a Somali-speaking adviser. To advance the case for intervention, Kittani fed Boutros-Ghali with exaggerated reports of conditions on the ground. A despatch he sent to Boutros-Ghali in November, on the eve of a Security Council meeting, claimed that 2 million Somalis faced starvation and that 'in the absence of a government or a governing authority capable of maintaining law and order, Somali "authorities" at all levels of society compete for anything of value'. Most crucially, he reported that between 70 to 80 per cent of relief food was being looted. Sahnoun had estimated the losses at between 15 and 40 per cent. The ICRC put their losses at between 15 and 20 per cent. But both the UN Secretariat and the US State Department picked up Kittani's figures and quoted them as fact, emphasising the case for retaliatory action.

The drumbeat for intervention grew louder. Television and news-paper pictures of starving Somalis added to the pressure. A dispute with militias closed the port at Mogadishu. An incoming relief ship was hit by shellfire. Newspaper columnists in Washington spoke of the need for a 'shoot to feed' policy. Three relief agencies, including Care, threatened to pull out of Somalia unless greater security could be provided. In a letter to the UN Security Council on November 29,

Boutros-Ghali said Somalia was no longer 'susceptible to the peace-keeping treatment'. Meeting in Washington, US army chiefs decided that military intervention was 'do-able'.

On 3 December the UN Security Council authorised a UN force – 'Unitaf' – to use 'all necessary means to establish as soon as possible a secure environment for humanitarian relief operations in Somalia'. Unitaf was to be led by the US military, contributing 28,000 men, with France, Belgium, Canada, Italy, Nigeria and other nations providing additional troops. President Bush, savouring the prospect of a further triumph with which to end his presidency, called the mission 'Operation Restore Hope'.

But there was an immediate source of disagreement between the US and the UN over whether Unitaf's mission was meant to include the disarming of the militias. In a letter to Bush on 8 December, Boutros-Ghali wrote that disarmament of the militias was essential: 'Without this I do not believe that it will be possible to establish the secure environment called for by the Security Council.' The Pentagon, however, was determined to avoid casualties and had no intention of disarming the militias. What Bush envisaged, therefore, in the words of one critical US official, was no more than 'a limited Salvation Army role' – saving the lives of the starving in the run-up to Christmas. 'No one should have to starve at Christmas-time,' Bush reportedly told his officials.

The first US troops landed on the beaches of Mogadishu at night on 9 December in a carefully stage-managed piece of theatre designed to have the maximum impact in the United States. Awaiting them were the massed ranks of the international media but no sign of any Somali militias. Within thirty minutes of landing, US commanders were explaining their mission of mercy in television interviews conducted on the roof of the international airport building.

Most Somalis welcomed the Americans, expecting them to disarm the militias and restore order in the city. The militias for their part indicated that they did not intend to give the Americans any trouble. Both Aideed and Mahdi accepted the American presence as a fait accompli, hoping they could use it to their advantage. Two days after the landing, the chief US envoy, Robert Oakley, a former ambassador to Somalia, engineered a public rapprochement between Aideed and Mahdi. At their first meeting in more than a year, they embraced on an old tennis court in front of the world's media.

From the start, however, the American strategy was inherently flawed. In order to ensure 'zero casualties', they accorded Aideed and Mahdi a prominent role, treating them almost as partners in the exercise, elevating them in status and legitimacy just when their own authority was on the wane. Far worse, instead of using the initial period of goodwill that their arrival had generated to tackle the problem of arms control, they allowed Aideed, Mahdi and other warlords to keep their arsenals intact in designated compounds. No attempt was made to round up heavy weapons, let alone disarm the militias. On Day Two, when an army patrol arrested a group of Aideed's gunmen loading up an arsenal of weapons in a building near the US embassy, army commanders instructed the patrol leader to let them go. From then on, the militia leaders knew they were untouchable. Only piece-meal efforts were ever made to locate and destroy arms caches. Many Somalis concluded that Operation Restore Hope was little more than a cynical deal between the US and the warlords to allow the US to withdraw with minimum difficulty once relief supplies were assured. But it was a strategy that would come to haunt the Americans.

During the five months that the Unitaf mission lasted, it managed to establish relative calm in most of the areas of southern Somalia where foreign troops were deployed. President Bush paid a fleeting visit, promising 'we are not going to leave the people of Somalia naked'.

As a mission of mercy, Unitaf was an undoubted success, though the real impact it made was relatively limited. A post-mortem carried out by the Refugee Policy Group, an independent Washington-based organisation, on behalf of the US government, concluded that between 202,000 and 238,000 had died from famine in Somalia. It put the number of lives lost as a result of 'delays in undertaking decisive action' in 1992, before the arrival of Unitaf, at between 100,000 and 125,000. The number of lives saved after US forces landed in December was estimated to be no more than 10,000.

Nevertheless, Unitaf's presence provided an opportunity for polit-ical negotiations. At a national reconciliation conference in Addis Ababa in March 1993, leading warlords and representatives of various clan movements signed a ceasefire agreement, committed themselves to 'complete' disarmament and empowered UN forces to take strong and effective action against any defaulters. On the eve of his departure, before handing over to a new United Nations mission – Unosom II – Oakley spoke confidently of how the Americans had 'brought Somalia back from the brink of self-destruction'. He claimed that because of the action he had taken in 'plucking the bird', militia leaders could no longer 'fly' – 'You take one feather at a time and the bird doesn't think there's anything terrible going on. Then one day he finds he can't fly.' The result was that 'death and starvation are almost gone now, and clan warfare – which has taken so many lives – is virtually gone'.

Unosom II was a far more ambitious enterprise than Unosom I, ful-filling all Boutros-Ghali's aims of running a fully fledged UN operation. Under the terms of Security Council Resolution 814, Unosom II was given the task of establishing a new government, a new police force and a new justice system, along with rebuilding the economy. Everything from schools to public utilities such as power, water and communication systems were to be reconstructed. The UN goal, said Madeleine Albright, the US ambassador to the UN, was 'nothing less than the restoration of an entire country as a proud, functioning and viable member of the community of nations'.

Unosom's security mandate was no longer confined to securing safe areas for humanitarian relief operations but included 'peace enforce-ment'; this meant, in other words, that Somalia's militias would be required to disarm. In place of Unitaf troops, a new multinational force was set up, consisting in all of 20,000 peacekeeping troops, 8,000 logistical staff and some 3,000 civilian personnel from twenty-three nations; included as part of the force was a contingent of US special forces and 'quick-reaction' units under US command, for use in emergencies. Overall command of Unosom was given to Jonathan Howe, a former US admiral and security adviser to George Bush. Formally, the multinational force was commanded by a Turkish general, but his deputy was an American general. As with Unitaf, Unosom II was effectively an American-run operation.

As the new force assembled, taking over control of Mogadishu on 4 May, Aideed became increasingly convinced that its mandate was directed principally at his own militia rather than any other. Already suspicious of UN intentions, he had been infuriated by an incident in the southern port of Kismayu in February when Unitaf troops had allowed a rival Darod militia, led by Siyad's son-in-law, to occupy the town, ousting a pro-Aideed militia, interpreting it as a partisan move by the UN against him. To signify his anger at what had happened, Aideed sent crowds into the streets of Mogadishu to riot, and prepared to resist any further moves to curb his power. When American officials sought to marginalise Aideed, he launched a propaganda campaign against the UN on his own radio station in Mogadishu — 'Radio Aideed', as it was known — accusing it of 'imperialist designs' and 'colonisation' and calling on Somalis to defend their 'sovereignty'. Rumours were rife that Unosom intended to shut down 'Radio Aideed', a move known to have been urged by his rival, Mahdi. With fateful consequences, Unosom's actions were now to upset the precarious balance of power between rival militias.

On 5 June a detachment of Pakistani troops was sent to inspect one of Aideed's weapons storage sites in Mogadishu. The inspection was authorised by a senior US official. The official reason was that since none of the storage sites belonging to the militias had been inspected since Unitaf's days, they were due for an audit. Aideed's were to be the first. The storage compound chosen for 5 June, however, also housed 'Radio Aideed'. When Aideed's men were informed by letter the day beforehand of Unosom's intention to carry out an inspection, they were immediately suspicious that the real purpose was to seize and destroy 'Radio Aideed'. An Aideed official told Unosom officers: 'This is unacceptable. This means war.' This warning was received by US commanders but not passed on to the Pakistani troops detailed for the job.

While the Pakistanis were inside Aideed's compound, an angry crowd gathered outside. As they emerged, they were attacked. Shots were fired. The Pakistanis fired into the crowd. Three miles away another Unosom patrol was attacked. A third incident occurred at a food distribution centre: a soldier, trying to calm a growing mob, was pulled into the crowd and dismembered. Altogether, twenty-six Pakistani soldiers died that day; many of the bodies were found mutilated, with their eyes gouged out.

The Americans, without waiting for an investigation, instantly blamed Aideed and demanded his arrest. Meeting in New York, the Security Council unanimously adopted Resolution 837 authorising Boutros-Ghali to take 'all necessary measures against all those responsible for the armed attacks . . . to secure the investigation of their actions and their arrest and detention for prosecution, trial and punishment'.

It was, in effect, a declaration of war. Only four weeks after Unosom II arrived with a mandate to 'rebuild' Somalia, its headquarters in south Mogadishu, in the old US embassy compound, were turned into a war centre, surrounded by miles of razor wire, perimeter security lights and sandbagged bunkers. UN civilian agencies retreated into this fortress, cut off from ordinary contact with life outside. Beneath the embassy building a reinforced underground basement was set up as a command post for Admiral Howe, a former submarine commander who seemed quite at home there. A born-again Christian, he pursued the campaign against Aideed with single-minded determination. 'He gave the impression of a crusader with a burning passion to right the wrongs, as he perceived them, of one man, Aideed, at whatever the cost,' wrote John Drysdale, a Unosom adviser.

The cost was huge. For four months Unosom and Aideed's militias fought running battles and intelligence duels inside a labyrinth of narrow alleys and markets with a death toll running into thousands. Combat aircraft and helicopter gunships were used to bombard weapons sites, garages and houses. 'Radio Aideed' was one of the first targets. Howe branded Aideed 'a power-hungry criminal', put a price of $25,000 on his head and, in true Wild West fashion, issued 'Wanted' posters. Day after day, the manhunt continued, but Aideed invariably remained a step ahead, even managing to give occasional media interviews.

On 11 July US commanders received intelligence from a Somali informer that Aideed was planning to attend a meeting the following day at the house of a close associate, Abdi Hassan Awale 'Qaybdiid'. The meeting had been called to enable a large group of Habar Gidir elders, intellectuals, businessmen, clan representatives and other senior figures in Aideed's camp to discuss proposals to open a dialogue with Unosom. Several of those attending had already met Howe in preliminary talks two days earlier. Qaybdiid's house was chosen as the meeting place because it had a large conference hall on the second floor suitable for such a gathering.

Seizing the opportunity to get Aideed, US commanders rapidly assembled a strike force. The plan was for the Somali informer, who was due to attend the meeting, to leave the building giving a prearranged signal to a communications helicopter hovering nearby that everyone was present. Helicopter gunships would then move in to attack the building at three points: the conference hall; the staircase leading from the conference hall to block any escape; and the outside gate so that US marines, landing by helicopter, would have clear access to the building to shoot or capture anyone trying to flee.

Almost everything went according to plan. Once the informer had left the building, Cobra helicopters attacked with missiles and cannons, blasting the building to bits. No warning was given. No attempt was made to obtain surrender. According to the Somalis, American troops on the ground finished off most of the survivors. The Red Cross put the number of dead at fifty-four. The Somalis published the names of seventy-three people they claimed were killed. Among the dead was Sheikh Haji Mohamed Iman Aden, the 90-year-old supreme elder of the Habar Gidir. But not Aideed. He had never been at the house.

Admiral Howe nevertheless pronounced himself satisfied with the result. 'We hit a key military planning cell of key Aideed advisers . . . This is where they have done their plotting for their terrorist attacks. We knew what we were hitting. It was well planned.'

Other officials, however, were horrified that the UN should be involved in such slaughter. The head of Unosom's justice division, Ann Wright, an American lawyer, resigned in protest. In a measured memorandum, she wrote: 'Unosom should anticipate that some organizations and member states will characterize a deliberate attack meant to kill the occupants without giving all the building occupants a chance to surrender as nothing less than murder committed in the name of the United Nations.'

In Somali terminology, the UN headquarters became known as the 'camp of the murderers'.

Still obsessed with finding Aideed, Howe requested reinforcements of US special forces. A team of 400 Rangers and a Delta Force squadron of 130 commandos were duly despatched to Mogadishu. But they had no better luck in hunting down Aideed. Their first night raid ended in fiasco. Tipped off that 'Yogi the Bear' – the Delta codename for Aideed – was hiding in a house at the Lig Lagato compound in south Mogadishu, Delta Force commandos, dressed in black, abseiled from helicopters onto the roof, burst through closed doors, firing from the hip, and arrested nine people. They included the resident representative of the United Nations Development Programme, three international staff members and a senior Egyptian lady dressed in a pink negligee who was forced to lie on shards of broken glass. Colin Powell, chairman of the Joint Chiefs of Staff, said later that he was so angry that 'I had to screw myself off the ceiling'. Subsequent raids were no more successful. In what turned out to be a case of mistaken identity, an assault force stormed the residence of a Somali general who was being groomed by the UN to lead the new police force, arresting him and thirty-eight other members of the Abgal clan. Once more, there were profuse apologies.

Then, on 3 October, an opportunity arose to snatch two of Aideed's closest associates. A Somali informer radioed that they were holding a meeting in a house on Hawlwadig Road not far from the Bakara Market in the Black Sea district of Mogadishu, Aideed's principal stronghold. In mid-afternoon a strike force of sixteen helicopters, including eight troop-carrying Black Hawks, left the international airport, taking only a few minutes to reach the target area three miles away. A ground convoy of twelve vehicles followed. In all, the strike force consisted of 160 Rangers and Delta Force operators with enormous firepower to hand.

A daylight raid into the heart of Aideed's territory, however, was known to be a risky operation. Within seconds, the whole Black Sea district erupted, stirred up like a hornet's nest. Thousands poured on to the street, grabbing weapons, running towards the helicopters and throwing up barricades. Both the helicopter strike force and the approaching ground convoy were engulfed in firefights. Bursting into the target house, snatch squads managed to round up twenty-four Somalis, including Aideed's close associates.

But the mission then went haywire. First, one Black Hawk helicopter was shot down, then another. Two more, badly damaged, managed to limp back to safety. A convoy, carrying prisoners, lost its way in the maze of alleyways and was shredded by gunfire, block after block. Rescue convoys failed to break through the blizzard of gunfire and the barricades, leaving nearly one hundred soldiers, many wounded and dying, stranded for the night in shacks and buildings where they had taken refuge, surrounded by gunmen and running low of ammunition. A mission expected to last one hour turned into a fifteen-hour ordeal. Eighteen soldiers died and seventy-three were seriously wounded before the Americans finally managed to escape from the Black Sea district. After they had gone, the battered corpses of two dead soldiers were dragged as trophies through the streets by angry mobs, scenes shown repeatedly on television.

The Somalis celebrated the battle as *Malinti Rangers* – 'The Day of the Rangers' – though it was a victory won at the cost of at least a thousand Somali lives. For the Americans, it was a catastrophic defeat – elite units of the world's most powerful army humiliated by a few rag-tag militias.

Meeting in the Oval Office of the White House with his senior advisers on 6 October, amid public uproar in the United States, President Clinton called off the hunt for Aideed and decided to terminate US involvement in Somalia. All American forces were to be withdrawn by 31 March 1994. Once the Americans had decided to pull out, other governments lost interest in supporting the Unosom operation and arranged for their contingents to depart while the going was good. With no credible purpose left, Unosom's mission was soon abandoned. After spending $4 billion in the hope of rebuilding

Somalia and fulfilling Boutros-Ghali's grand dream, the UN departed, handing Mogadishu over to its warring factions.

Its final exodus, in March 1995, was marked by massive looting. Amid the ruins of Mogadishu, the UN had constructed a giant fortress for its expatriate personnel, complete with a shopping mall, street lights, satellite communications systems, a modern sewerage network, flower beds and other comforts. Costing $160 million, it had all come from the Somali aid budget. As the UN withdrew, looters swarmed over the area, stripping everything of value. Within a few months even the foundations had disappeared. Nothing remained to mark its intervention, except anger and contempt.

The Somali debacle had repercussions around the world. When President Clinton took office in January 1993, he had high hopes that the United Nations, with the help of the US, could be used as an instrument for world peace. In the wake of the Black Hawk Down episode, he ordered a complete reappraisal of policy. The result was a presidential directive that set strict conditions on any US involvement in UN peacekeeping operations. Henceforth, before offering any military support to the UN, the US had to be satisfied that a vital national interest was at stake; that the mission was clearly defined in size, scope and duration; that a working ceasefire among all local parties was fully evident; and that there was both sufficient political will behind the mission and an identifiable 'exit strategy'.

Just when a far greater catastrophe than Somalia was about to erupt, the US and the UN had been reduced to the role of bystanders.

THE GRAVES ARE NOT
YET FULL

In the tourist literature Rwanda was known as 'the land of a thousand hills', a country of magical beauty tucked away in the heart of Africa, with breathtaking views and crystal-clear lakes, like a tropical version of Switzerland. In the north-west, along the Congo-Nile crest, stood the giant peaks of the Virunga mountains rising to 14,000 feet, a volcanic range covered with thick woodlands, the domain of highland gorillas made famous by the work of the American primatologist Dian Fossey, and her book *Gorillas in the Mist*. Foreign tourists flocked to Rwanda, providing an important source of income.

The people of Rwanda – Banyarwanda – were renowned for being hard-working and orderly. With a high density of population, nearly every available piece of land was cultivated. Banana plantations, eucalyptus groves and coffee farms dotted the landscape. A large majority of Banyarwanda – more than three-quarters – adhered to the Christian religion. Church attendance was high. Church organisations formed a central part of everyday life, running schools and clinics.

A strict hierarchy of government prevailed. The country was divided into eleven *préfectures* led by *préfets*; 145 *communes* led by *bourgmestres*; 1,600 *secteurs* led by *conseillers*; and tens of thousands of *sous-secteurs* comprising small groups of households. At each level

Banyarwanda displayed a high regard for authority. There was almost no crime and little prostitution.

The government's record of economic management was considered impressive. Between 1965 and 1989 gross domestic product increased by nearly 5 per cent a year; inflation was low; despite a high rate of population increase, running to 3.7 per cent a year, there were advances in school enrolment and health care. About two-thirds of rural households were engaged in coffee production providing the mainstay of Rwanda's export earnings. Impressed by the government's commitment to rural development and to law and order, Western donors were generous with aid funds. Belgium, the former colonial power, was the main donor; Switzerland put Rwanda at the top of its list for aid; and France provided technical assistance and military training. Foreign aid constituted an increasing proportion of national income, rising from 5 per cent in 1973 to 22 per cent in 1991.

Yet there was an ugly streak that ran through Rwanda's politics. Ever since the idea of Hutu hegemony had taken hold during the 1950s, Hutu politicians had portrayed the Tutsi minority as an 'enemy' seeking to reimpose their rule over Rwanda. A key part of the ideology they constructed was the myth that the Tutsi were invaders who had overrun Rwanda in the pre-colonial era and enslaved the Hutu – an alien group, therefore, that had no legitimate status in the country. The myth had grown from accounts written by European travellers in the nineteenth century describing the ruling Tutsi aristocracy as being descendants of a 'Hamitic' people, with a culture clearly superior to that of the indigenous Hutu, and claiming they had migrated from distant lands such as the highlands of Ethiopia or the Horn of Africa. The same 'Hamitic hypothesis' was applied to other kingdoms in the Great Lakes region, such as Ankole, Bunyoro and Toro in modern Uganda. It fitted in with the fashionable nineteenth-century European concept of 'historic races'. But in Rwanda, instead of fading away, it became, in the words of the historian Jean-Pierre Chrétien, 'ethno-historic gospel' – a myth incorporated into the history books and seized on by Hutu politicians for their own propaganda purposes. In 1959 the Hutu leader Grégoire Kayibanda described Rwanda as 'two nations in a single state . . . two nations between whom there is no intercourse and no sympathy, who are ignorant of each other's habits, thoughts and feelings as if they were dwellers of different zones, or inhabitants of different planets'.

Though gaining power as a result of the Hutu 'revolution' of 1959–60, Hutu politicians continued to use the language of hatred and division against the Tutsi minority to justify their persecution. They also found it expedient to whip up anti-Tutsi hostility to fortify their own position at times when dissension among Hutu clans was rife. In the early 1990s, when the ruling Hutu clique faced growing political opposition, they sought to maintain their hold on power by rousing Hutu against the Tutsi threat, fomenting a climate of fear and hatred, relying on the Hutu's culture of obedience to ensure their orders were obeyed and preparing for the onslaught well in advance by arming militias and organising death squads. The genocide that followed was caused not by ancient ethnic antagonism but by a fanatical elite engaged in a modern struggle for power and wealth using ethnic antagonism as their principal weapon. Though Western governments knew that massive killing was underway, they failed to take the steps needed to prevent it. The result was slaughter on a scale not witnessed since the Nazi extermination programme against the Jews.

A harbinger of that terrible violence came soon after independence in 1962. The Hutu 'revolution' had led to the exodus of some 130,000 Tutsis to neighbouring countries – Burundi, Uganda, Congo and Tanganyika. In refugee camps there, Tutsi exiles formed small insurgent groups with the aim of restoring the Tutsi monarchy, calling themselves *inyenzi*, a Kinyarwanda word for cockcroach. The border raids they carried out inside Rwanda were largely ineffective. In December 1963, however, a group of 200 men, armed with bows, arrows and home-made rifles, crossed the border from Burundi, linked up with local Tutsi, attacked a military camp, seized weapons and vehicles and headed for the capital, Kigali.

Though the invaders were quickly routed, President Kayibanda took the opportunity to crush Tutsi opposition. Twenty prominent Tutsi politicians were rounded up and summarily executed. Radio Kigali broadcast repeated warnings that Tutsi terrorists were seeking to reimpose their rule. Local officials were instructed to organise 'self-defence' groups. In Gikongoro, Hutu vigilantes, armed with machetes, spears and clubs, set out to kill every Tutsi in sight – men, women and children; some 5,000 Tutsi died. At Shigira, near the border with the Congo, more than 100 Tutsi women and children, rather than face slaughter by Hutu mobs, drowned themselves in the river. The World Council of Churches estimated that in all at least 10,000 Tutsis were killed. Tens of thousands more fled into exile.

The political effect of the *inyenzi* attacks was to give a considerable boost to the flagging popularity of Kayibanda. A Rwandan official confided to the academic, René Lemarchand: 'Before the attacks of the *inyenzi* the government was on the point of collapse. We were faced with enormous dissensions among ourselves. Not only have we survived the attacks but the attacks have made us survive our dissensions.' Tutsi activists in exile soon gave up their plots. But Kayibanda found it useful to resurrect the Tutsi threat when once more his regime was engulfed in political difficulty.

Events in neighbouring Burundi, where the Tutsi minority had managed to hold on to power, provided the opportunity. Since independence in 1962, Burundi's history had been even more turbulent than Rwanda's. Two of the first three prime ministers were assassinated. Seven governments had come and gone in quick succession. In 1965 a mutiny by Hutu army and *gendarmerie* officers led to terrible reprisals against Hutu leaders. An army coup in 1966 brought to power a Tutsi officer, Captain Michel Micombero, who set out to remove the 'Hutu threat' once and for all. The army and government were purged of Hutu members. Leading Hutu politicians and scores of soldiers were executed. Faced with a Hutu uprising in 1972, Micombero exacted revenge on a scale never seen before in independent Africa. Hutus with any kind of education – teachers, church leaders, bank clerks, nurses, traders, civil servants – were rounded up by the army and killed. In a campaign subsequently described as 'selective genocide', the Hutu elite was virtually eliminated. Possibly as many as 200,000 died. Another 200,000 fled into Rwanda.

Using Burundi as an example of the Tutsis' thirst for power and their willingness to kill for it, Kayibanda launched another round of repression, hoping to unite the Hutu behind him. A ruling party pamphlet published in 1972 declared: 'Tutsi domination is the origin of all the evil the Hutu have suffered since the beginning of time. It is comparable to a termite mound teeming with every cruelty known to man.' In what was termed a 'purification' campaign, Kayibanda instructed vigilante committees to ensure that Tutsis were restricted to an ethnic quota of 9 per cent he fixed for schools, the university, the civil service and every sector of employment, including private businesses – a level said to represent their proportion of the population. In some parts of Rwanda, mainly in the west, Tutsis constituted as much as 30 per cent of the population. The result was another mass exodus of Tutsis.

But Kayibanda's hate campaign was not sufficient to save his regime. Ruling through a small group of politicians who came from his home town of Gitarama, giving preference to 'southern' Hutu clans, he lost the support of 'northern' Hutu. In 1973 he was ousted by the army commander, General Juvénal Habyarimana, a 'northerner' from Gisenyi, and thrown into prison, dying there, reportedly of starvation.

Habyarimana installed a one-party dictatorship subjecting the entire population to more rigid control than ever before. Every single Banyarwanda, of whatever age, even babies and the elderly, was required to become a member of his *Mouvement Révolutionnaire National pour le Développement* (MRND). Everyone had to carry an identity card specifying their ethnic group and their place of residence. No one was allowed to move residence without official permission. The party was everywhere; every hill had its cell and its spies.

Tutsis faced the same discrimination as before, but no additional harassment. Habyarimana retained the quota system and limited Tutsi involvement in public life. He allowed one Tutsi into his cabinet, one ambassador in the foreign service, two deputies in the seventy-seat national assembly, and two members in the central committee of his party. In the army Tutsi were disbarred from becoming officers, and Hutu soldiers were not allowed to marry Tutsi women. On a wall in his presidential mansion in Kigali, Habyarimana kept a black-and-white photograph of Tutsi huts in flames, carefully labelled 'Apocalypse Révolution – Nov 1959', a reminder of the origins of

Hutu power. But for most of the Habyarimana years, during the 1970s and the 1980s, the Tutsi factor was of marginal importance.

As the sole candidate standing for office, Habyarimana was elected president in December 1983 and then again in December 1988 with 99.8 per cent of the vote. His main support, however, was confined to Hutu in the north-west, to the Bakiga, who formed a distinct cultural group. Incorporated into the Tutsi kingdom of Rwanda with the help of the Belgians in the 1920s, they had remained deeply attached to their own ruling clans and disdainful of 'southern' Hutu for their less fervent commitment to Hutu nationalism.

Habyarimana favoured his fellow northerners, notably those from his home district of Gisenyi, with cabinet posts, administration jobs, economic opportunities and foreign scholarships. Virtually all senior members of the army and security service were drawn from Gisenyi. A high proportion of development funds was diverted to the north.

A powerful northern clique gathered around his formidable wife, Agathe Kanzinga, the daughter of a Hutu lineage that had ruled an independent principality until the late nineteenth century. Known at first as 'le clan de Madame', then as akazu, a Kinyarwanda word meaning 'the little house', Madame Agathe's inner circle included three brothers, a cousin and a bevy of senior army officers. Wealthy and privileged, they represented the real power behind Habyarimana's throne.

In the late 1980s, after fifteen years of relative prosperity, boosted by large amounts of foreign aid, Habyarimana's regime encountered growing difficulty. A sharp drop in world coffee prices cut farmers' income by half. Drought blighted food production. The government's budget in 1989 had to be slashed by 40 per cent. Gross domestic product in 1989 fell by 5.7 per cent. The shortage of land was becoming ever more acute. From 2 million inhabitants in 1940, the population by 1990 had reached 7 million. Whereas in the 1950s a typical peasant hill community consisted of about 110 people per square kilometre, by the 1970s the number occupying the same area had risen to about 280 and by the early 1990s it had reached an average of 420, with one northern commune registering 820. Adding to land pressures, the elite were quick to buy up land sold because of poverty.

There was growing resentment about Habyarimana's corrupt,

dictatorial rule. In 1988 a Catholic newspaper, *Kinyamateka*, began to publish candid articles about political issues. Though the government responded by arresting several journalists, other newspapers and journalists took up the cause, reporting on corruption and the lavish lifestyle of the ruling elite. In February 1990 Catholic bishops issued a pastoral letter condemning nepotism, regionalism and official corruption. Inspired by Benin's example, other prominent Rwandans began to call for an end to the MRND's monopoly on power, the separation of party and state, the scheduling of a national conference to draft a new constitution and the holding of free and fair elections. Tutsis joined in, complaining about the quota system and restrictions on their employment. Invited to attend the Franco-African summit in La Baule in France, Habyarimana, like other African leaders, was warned that French aid would henceforth depend on political reform. Then, on 1 October 1990, an army of Rwandan Tutsi exiles crossed the northern border from Uganda.

For many Tutsi exiles, thirty years after their exodus had first begun, Rwanda was little more than a mythical country. Thousands had only distant memories of it; thousands more, born in refugee camps, had never even seen it. By 1990 their numbers in Uganda, Burundi, Zaire and Tanzania had reached about 500,000, constituting one of the largest refugee communities in Africa. Most led a settled existence, though their presence often aroused local friction. In southern Uganda, where Rwandan Tutsis were related to the Bahima people, former rulers of the Ugandan kingdoms of Bunyoro and Buha, they were generally welcomed by the Bahima but not by the local Bairu. During Milton Obote's second regime in the 1980s, which was based on 'northern' support, they faced outright persecution. Determined to fight back, hundreds of young Tutsis joined Yoweri Museveni's southern-based National Resistance Army in its campaign to overthrow Obote. Among them was Paul Kagame, the son of a Tutsi family from the hill of Nyaratovu, in Gitarama, a lanky, intelligent figure who, at the age of four in 1961, had witnessed Hutu mobs set fire to Tutsi houses there before escaping into exile with his parents. By the time Museveni took Kampala by force in January 1986, one-quarter of his army – some 3,000 men – were

Tutsi fighters, the sons of exiles, many holding senior positions. The army's deputy commander, General Fred Rwigyema, was a Tutsi who had grown up in the same refugee camp as Paul Kagame. Thousands more Tutsis were recruited into Uganda's army during the early years of Museveni's regime to deal with insurgencies that Museveni faced in Acholi, Teso and West Nile. As a reward for Tutsi support, Museveni announced in July 1986 that Rwandans who had been resident in Uganda for more than ten years would automatically be entitled to Ugandan citizenship.

Exile organisations meanwhile campaigned for the right of Tutsis to return home. Habyarimana's response was to argue that Rwanda was already 'overpopulated' and could not absorb any more people. At a meeting in Kampala in 1987, leading exiles launched the Rwanda Patriotic Front (RPF). Its purpose, they said, was not only to promote the return of Tutsis, by force if necessary, but to support the wider cause of political reform in Rwanda. It sought neither to reimpose Tutsi rule in Rwanda nor to reinstate the Tutsi monarchy but to over-throw a bankrupt regime and establish a democratic government. Its political leaders included Hutu but were predominantly Tutsi; its para-military wing consisted almost entirely of Tutsi, many of them well trained, with combat experience. The movement gained impetus as a result of a growing backlash among Ugandans about the prominent role played by Rwandan exiles. When Museveni decided in 1988 to dispense with the services of General Rwigyema, the RPF acquired a popular and highly respected military leader. In August 1990, after two members of Kigali's elite fled to Kampala, bearing tales of how Habyarimana's regime was on the edge of collapse, split between north and south and drained by corruption, Rwigyema became convinced that the time was right to try to topple it. Overnight, on 30 September, some 4,000 Tutsis deserted the Ugandan army, taking weapons and equipment with them.

The invasion in October was a disaster. Nothing went according to plan. Rwigyema was killed on the second day, leaving fellow officers shocked and demoralised. Moreover, the invasion drew France into the equation.

★

The French had nurtured ambitions about Rwanda since the 1970s. Although Rwanda was a former Belgian colony, they regarded it as a natural member of the Franco-African family – *la francophonie Africaine* – the group of African states that France supported aiming to promote and protect the French language, commerce and culture. The seventeen francophone states in Africa constituted the only region in the world where France retained enough influence to support its claims to medium-power status. What gave Rwanda particular importance was that, along with Burundi, it lay along the borderline between francophone and anglophone Africa.

Ever since an incident in the Sudanese village of Fashoda in 1898, when British forces prevented a French expedition from establishing a band of French territory running eastwards from Dakar to Djibouti, the French had been vigilant in guarding against anglophone encroachment in what they considered to be their own backyard – '*le pré carré*'. In his memoirs, General de Gaulle listed the disasters that had afflicted France in his youth and that had led him to devote himself to upholding France's 'grandeur': the first on the list was the Fashoda incident. The 'Fashoda syndrome', as it was known, formed a basic component of France's Africa policy. To ensure that African issues received due attention, the French presidential office included a special Africa Unit – *Cellule Africaine* – with a wide remit to cover everything from intelligence work to bribery. In 1990 the *Cellule Africaine* was headed by the president's son, Jean-Christophe Mitterrand, popularly known as *Papa m'a dit*, or 'Daddy told me to'.

At first sight the invasion of a group of rebels from Uganda, wearing Ugandan army fatigues and carrying Ugandan army weapons, provided an obvious case for French intervention. It fitted directly into the French notion of an 'Anglo-Saxon' plot. The French took at face value Habyarimana's argument that the real purpose of the invasion was to re-establish Tutsi rule in Rwanda. With little hesitation, President Mitterrand, a personal friend of Habyarimana, authorised the despatch of French troops to Rwanda. Seeking assurance that help was on the way, Habyarimana telephoned the *Cellule Africaine* at the Élysée Palace on 2 October – the day after the invasion – to speak to Jean-Christophe Mitterrand. He was duly reassured. A French political scientist, Gérard Prunier, who was present during the conversation, later recalled Jean-Christophe Mitterrand remarking, with a wink: 'We are going to send him a few boys, old man Habyarimana. We are going to bail him out. In any case, the whole thing will be over in two or three months.'

It was a decision that was to have disastrous consequences. For the French, it meant becoming ever more deeply involved in propping up a regime with genocidal intentions.

The first contingent of French troops arrived in Kigali from their base in the Central African Republic on 4 October, ostensibly to protect French expatriates and organise their evacuation. Habyarimana also managed to secure troops from Belgium and Zaire, whose president, Mobutu, was a close ally. Wanting to dramatise the threat he faced, Habyarimana arranged for government forces to stage a fake attack on Kigali, blaming it on 'enemy troops', prompting the French ambassador to report 'heavy fighting' in the capital. The French government duly responded by despatching more troops to Kigali. With foreign assistance, government forces succeeded in pushing back the rebels to border areas. What threat there was to Habyarimana's regime quickly faded. Mobutu's troops, after going on the rampage, were soon withdrawn. Belgium too, dubious about the whole enterprise, also pulled out its troops. The French, however, remained, taking the opportunity to become the central player in Rwanda's defence.

No sooner had Habyarimana secured the support of foreign troops than he unleashed a wave of repression against his opponents. Using the fake attack by 'enemy troops' on Kigali as a pretext, he ordered the detention of some 13,000 people, imprisoning them without charge. Many were tortured; dozens died. Reverting to the tactics of the 1960s, one of his ministers declared that Tutsis were *ibyitso*, a Kinyarwanda term for 'accomplices' that was to become infamous. 'To prepare an attack on that scale required trusted people [on the inside],' he said. 'Rwandans of the same ethnic group offered that possibility better than did others.' But as well as Tutsis, the term was also applied to Hutu opponents of Habyarimana's regime. On national radio the minister of defence urged the population to 'track down and arrest the infiltrators'. In revenge attacks organised by local officials, hundreds of Tutsis were killed. In a joint report in December 1990, European ambassadors warned: 'The rapid deterioration of the relations between the two ethnic groups, the Hutu and the Tutsi, runs the imminent risk of terrible consequences for Rwanda and the entire region.'

With French assistance, Habyarimana set in motion a huge expansion of Rwanda's armed forces. From the time of the invasion, the army grew from a force of 9,000 men in October 1990 to 28,000 in 1991. France provided training staff, counter-insurgency experts and huge quantities of weapons. It financed, armed and trained a Presidential Guard, an elite force recruited exclusively from Habyarimana's home district. It also facilitated arms contracts with Egypt and South Africa. An estimated $100 million was spent on arms supplies, a vast sum for a tiny, impoverished country. Much of the money came from international funds – quick-disbursing loans under a Structural Adjustment Programme – intended for economic development.

Habyarimana's opponents, meanwhile, undaunted by his campaign of repression, continued to agitate for political reform. Under pressure from Western donors as well as local politicians, Habyarimana eventually agreed to abandon his one-party system. In June 1991 a constitutional amendment was passed making multiple political parties legal. Within months, sixteen opposition parties were launched. Once established, they demanded a role in government. Habyarimana at first resisted, but after massive street demonstrations early in 1992, he was obliged to open talks. The outcome was that in April 1992 Habyarimana formed a coalition government, giving control of key ministries to his own party, but conceding other cabinet positions to opposition parties, including the post of prime minister.

Determined to force through reform and shake up the old MRND administration, opposition parties in the coalition also took the initiative to make contact with RPF rebels. Since retreating to the Virunga mountains, the RPF had regrouped under a new leader, Paul Kagame. At the time of the 1990 invasion, Kagame, a major in the Ugandan army, had been attending a military training course at Fort Leavenworth in the United States. On his return to Uganda, he had quit the army to join the rebels. By the end of 1991 he had managed to turn the RPF into a disciplined guerrilla force of 5,000 men. But though capable of staging hit-and-run raids in areas of northern Rwanda, the RPF had gained little popular support. Kagame was therefore amenable to approaches from members of the coalition for talks. In July 1992 a ceasefire was signed. Under international pressure, Habyarimana agreed to participate in peace talks in Arusha in Tanzania.

All these events – the end of one-party rule, the formation of a coalition government with reform-minded parties, the rapprochement with Tutsi rebels – enraged Hutu supremacists. In secret the northern clique around Madama Agathe, the *akazu*, planned a counter-campaign to regain control. The movement they led became known as Hutu Power. Their aim was not merely to eliminate the Tutsi threat but to rid Rwanda of Hutu *ibyitso*.

A network of supporters, known as '*le réseau zéro*', was established in the army, the security service, the administration, the universities and the media to promote the cause of Hutu Power. Activists launched their own political party, the *Coalition pour le Défence de la Republique* (CDR), using it to attack the government's 'soft' attitude towards Tutsis and their 'collaborators'. Militants in the MRND formed a youth militia, calling it *Interahamwe*, a Kinyarwanda word meaning 'those who work together'. The CDR formed their own youth militia calling it *Impuzamugambi* – 'those with a single purpose'. Youths with no prospect of work were easily recruited with promises of land, jobs and other rewards to be reaped from the campaign. A secret society within the army, *amasusu*, ensured that both militia groups were provided with training and weapons. Death squads went to work.

Much attention was paid to identifying 'the enemy'. An army memorandum, produced in 1992, divided the enemy into two categories: the principal enemy and the accomplices of the enemy. The principal enemy was defined as:

the Tutsi inside or outside the country, extremist and nostalgic for power, who have NEVER recognised and will NEVER recognise

the realities of the 1959 social revolution and who wish to reconquer power by all means necessary including arms.

The accomplices of the enemy were defined as anyone who supported the principal enemy. The groups within which the enemy
were said to recruit included Tutsi refugees, Tutsis inside the country
and Hutu malcontents. The memorandum was sent by the army's
chief-of-staff to all sector commanders, with instructions that it should
be distributed as widely as possible.

Information about the 'zero network' and its objectives was picked
up by Western embassies. The Belgian ambassador reported to
Brussels in the spring of 1992: 'This secret group is planning the
extermination of the Tutsi of Rwanda to resolve once and for all, in
their own way, the ethnic problem and to crush internal Hutu opposition.' In August 1992 the head of the national information service,
Christophe Mfizi, a senior official in the MRND for fifteen years,
resigned, warning of the activities of the 'zero network' in an open
letter. The state, he said, was being ruled by a northern oligarchy,
milking it for private gain.

The press was constantly used to foment ethnic hatred. Of the
forty-two new journals that appeared in 1991, at least eleven had
links with the *akazu*. At the forefront of the hate campaign was the
editor of *Kangura*, Hassan Ngeze, a small-time hustler with a talent
for crude propaganda. In a memorable article published in December
1990, shortly after the RPF invasion, Ngeze laid out a doctrine of
Hutu purity, listing what he called 'The Hutu Ten Commandments'.
The first decreed that any Hutu who married a Tutsi woman,
befriended a Tutsi woman or employed a Tutsi 'as a secretary or a
concubine' was to be considered a traitor since all Tutsi women
worked only for the interest of their own ethnic group. For similar
reasons, any Hutu involved in business dealings with Tutsi was also
deemed a traitor. Hutu were told to be 'firm and vigilant against their
common Tutsi enemy'. Only Hutu should be entrusted to hold
strategic positions in government, in the administration and the
economy. Only Hutu should be employed in the armed forces.
Ngeze's 'Ten Commandments' were widely circulated to popular

acclaim. Habyarimana championed their publication. Community leaders read them out at public meetings. The most frequently quoted commandment was the eighth: 'Hutus must stop having mercy on the Tutsis.'

A central purpose of the propaganda was to stir up the fear that the Tutsi, in order to regain power, were prepared to slaughter Hutu en masse. In December 1990 *Kangura* claimed that the Tutsi were ready for a war that 'would leave no survivors'. A pamphlet produced by Léon Mugesera, a university teacher and MRND official, in February 1991, claimed that the RPF planned 'to restore the dictatorship of the extremists of the Tutsi minority' by 'a genocide, the extermination of the Hutu majority'.

A speech by Mugesera in 1992 to MRND militants at Kabaya, not far from Habyarimana's home in Gisenyi district, inciting murder, gained particular notoriety. Excerpts were broadcast on national radio; cassettes were widely distributed. Mugesera's target was not only the '*inyenzi*', the 'cockroaches' of the RPF but their accomplices, the political parties opposed to Habyarimana, who advocated negotiations with the RPF.

> The opposition parties have plotted with the enemy . . . They have plotted to undermine our armed forces . . . The law is quite clear on this point: 'Any person who is guilty of acts aiming at sapping the morale of the armed forces will be condemned to death.' What are we waiting for? . . . And what about those accomplices (*ibyitso*) here who are sending their children to the RPF? Why are we wait- ing to get rid of these families? . . . I would like to tell you that we are now asking for those people to be put on a list and for them to be brought to court so that they can be judged before us. If they [the judges] refuse . . . we should do it ourselves by exterminating this scum . . . The fatal mistake we made in 1959 was to let them [the Tutsi] get out . . . They belong in Ethiopia and we are going to find them a shortcut to get there by throwing them into the Nyabarongo river [which flows northwards]. I must insist on this point. We have to act. Wipe them all out!

Claiming that the enemy's objective was extermination, he urged his audience to 'rise up . . . really rise up' in self-defence And he ended with this final warning: 'Know that the person whose throat you do not cut now will be the one who will cut yours.'

A series of organised killings occurred during 1992. In Bugesera, groups of *Interahamwe*, *gendarmerie* and Hutu peasants combined to launch an onslaught against Tutsi homesteads. Tutsi were burned in their homes and thrown into rivers. Those who tried to defend themselves were disarmed by government soldiers. In terminology that was to become all too familiar, peasants were told to 'clear the bush'; the slaughter of woman and children was called 'pulling out the roots of the bad weeds'. An estimated 300 people died; more than 3,000 fled the area.

A report into human rights abuses in Rwanda published in March 1993 by a group of international human rights experts from ten countries held Habyarimana and 'his immediate entourage' responsible for a string of massacres, torture, arbitrary detention and other abuses against Tutsis and members of the opposition, carried out over a two-year period. Despite the alarming nature of the report, it caused little international concern. France continued with its programme of support for the army and the Presidential Guard.

After a year of delay and prevarication, Habyarimana was eventually obliged to sign a peace agreement with the RPF. By 1993 Rwanda was effectively bankrupt, awash with refugees and dependent on emergency food supplies. Western donors warned that no more funds would be forthcoming unless Habyarimana signed. The Arusha Accords of August 1993 provided for the establishment of a broadbased transitional government to include Habyarimana and his allies, opposition parties and the RPF, that would remain in place for no more than twenty-two months until elections were held and a democratically elected government was installed. The Rwandan army and RPF forces meanwhile would be pared down and integrated. As a first step, a battalion of 600 RPF soldiers would be stationed in Kigali to provide security for RPF members of government. A United Nations peacekeeping force would be deployed to assist the process.

Habyarimana signed the Arusha Accords only to buy time. The *akazu* were vehemently opposed to them. For army officers and soldiers alike, they meant demobilisation: government troops were to make up only 60 per cent of a reduced army; senior command posts were to be shared equally with the RPF; the Presidential Guard would be abolished. In all, some 16,000 soldiers would be demobilised. For the MRND which had once governed Rwanda unchallenged, the Arusha Accords meant accepting just five cabinet positions out of nineteen, equal to the number allocated to the RPF. During the negotiations in Arusha a senior RPF official encountered Colonel Théoneste Bagosora, a leading member of the *akazu*, standing in a hotel lift surrounded by suitcases. Asked why he was leaving, Bagasora replied that he was going back to Rwanda to prepare '*apocalypse deux*' — the second apocalypse.

What prospects there were for a peaceful outcome in Rwanda were dashed only two months later by events in neighbouring Burundi. After a period of political reform, Burundi had elected its first Hutu president, Melchior Ndadaye, an engineer, in June 1993. Four weeks later in parliamentary elections deemed to have been free and fair, Ndadaye's Frodebu party won 65 out of 81 seats, taking 71 per cent of the vote. A committed moderate, Ndadaye subsequently named a Tutsi economist from the opposition as prime minister and approved a politically and ethnically balanced cabinet. On 21 October he was kidnapped by extremist Tutsi army officers, taken to a military camp and murdered. His death set off massive killings of both Hutu and Tutsi. Some 150,000 died; some 300,000 Hutu fled to southern Rwanda, spreading tales of massacre and torture.

The murder of Ndadaye was taken as irrefutable proof by Hutu supremacists in Rwanda that the Tutsi were bent on total domination. The only choice for the Hutu was to retain power or to face servitude, as in Burundi. Moderate Hutu parties, previously willing to abide by the Arusha Accords, also began to doubt Tutsi intentions, fearing they might be used as a Trojan horse for Tutsi ambitions. Conservative Hutu factions united behind Hutu Power.

The propaganda against Tutsis intensified. A new radio station was launched by the *akazu* — *Radio-Télévision Libres des Mille Collines* — ostensibly to entertain listeners with a mixture of pop music, gossip, rumour and phone-ins, but in reality to prepare them for genocide. Of the fifty original founders, forty were from the three *préfectures* of northern Rwanda. They included Habyarimana, several members of his family, representatives from the MRND and CDR and a popular musician, Simon Bikindi, well known for his virulently anti-Tutsi songs. Although nominally private, *Radio Mille Collines* was allowed to broadcast on the same frequencies as the national radio, Radio Rwanda, between 8 a.m. and 11 a.m., when the latter was not transmitting.

A coordinated plan for 'self-defence' was drawn up. Its principal architect was Colonel Bagosora, the army's head of administration. Born in 1941 into a northern middle-class Hutu family – 'Christian and well-off', as he described it – he had devoted his life to the army, attending training courses in Belgium and France. Like his fellow conspirators, he was driven by an intense hatred of Tutsi. In an essay he wrote in exile in 1995 to justify genocide, he described the Tutsi as 'the masters of deceit', 'dictatorial, cruel, bloody', 'arrogant, clever and sneaky'. They had 'never had a country of their own to allow them to become a people' but had instead arrogantly tried to impose their supremacy over the rightful local inhabitants.

Bagosora set out to establish paramilitary 'self-defence' units in every *commune* in the country. They were trained locally by the military and by communal police and instructed to act in coordination with the military authorities, local councillors, local police and other militias. Bagosora arranged for the distribution of firearms and huge quantities of machetes. Between January 1993 and March 1994 Rwanda imported more than 500,000 machetes, double the number imported in previous years and enough for one for every third adult Hutu in Rwanda. One of the main importers was Félicien Kabuga, a wealthy businessman whose daughter was married to one of Habyarimana's sons, a principal financier of both the *Interahamwe* and the weekly paper, *Kangura*. By the end of 1993 there were hidden stockpiles of firearms, grenades, machetes and axes in most *communes*. Militia groups like the *Interahamwe* were meanwhile busy training and recruiting. A large number of lists were drawn up identifying people regarded as 'the enemy' and their accomplices.

★

While these preparations were underway, the United Nations machinery responsible for peacekeeping operations was slowly stirring into action. The Arusha Accords had envisaged that a peacekeeping force – United Nations Assistance Mission for Rwanda (Unamir) – would be deployed in Rwanda in September, but wrangling over its scope and size caused months of delay. The United States, keen to rein in the UN's burgeoning peacekeeping costs, initially proposed a force no larger than 500. A UN military expert recommended a minimum of 8,000. The Canadian general chosen as Unamir's commander, Roméo Dallaire, asked for 4,500. On 5 October, two days after the Black Hawk Down incident in Somalia, the Security Council authorised a smaller and cheaper version consisting of 2,548 and a reduced mandate. Whereas the Arusha Accords had proposed a force to 'guarantee overall security', the Security Council, mindful of the Somali imbroglio, specified instead a force to 'contribute' to security, not throughout the country, but only in Kigali. Whereas the Accords envisaged that peacekeepers would 'assist in tracking of arms caches and neutralisation of armed gangs throughout the country' and would 'assist in the recovery of all weapons distributed to, or illegally acquired by, civilians', the Security Council deleted these provisions. The Unamir budget was not formally approved until April 1994.

By the end of December, Dallaire had managed to assemble a force of nearly 1,300 peacekeepers in Rwanda. They included 400 Belgian paracommandos, despatched from Somalia. But the bulk of the Unamir contingent was made up of troops from Bangladesh, poorly trained and equipped and lacking operational experience. The Unamir operation quickly turned into a logistical nightmare. Dallaire was short of vehicles, fuel, ammunition, radios, barbed wire, medical support and even petty cash. 'I spent most of my time fighting the heavy mechanical UN system, with all its stupidity,' he recalled. 'We would order torches, and after a long delay they arrived without batteries . . . Seeing to the most immediate needs stopped us from seeing what was reserved for us in the future.'

Even worse, Dallaire lacked any intelligence-gathering capacity. When he asked UN headquarters for intelligence support, his request was turned down. He was told that an intelligence-gathering operation was contrary to peacekeeping policy. The effect was to leave him, as he said, 'blind and deaf in the field'. Though Western diplomats in Kigali were well informed about the momentum towards mass violence, they rarely shared what they knew with Unamir. A CIA analysis in January 1994 predicting that the Arusha Accords would fail, leading to hostilities in which at least half a million people would die, was not passed on until after the genocide was over. 'A lot of the world powers were all there with their embassies and their military attachés,' said Dallaire. 'And you can't tell me those bastards didn't have a lot of information. They would never pass that information on to me, ever.'

The signs were increasingly ominous. After a spate of killings in northern *communes*, a group of dissident officers in the Rwandan army sent a letter to Dallaire warning that more massacres were planned and that prominent opposition politicians had been marked down for assassination. The conspiracy, they said, was led by Habyarimana together with a handful of military officers from his home region. They themselves had once been a part of the plot but now wanted nothing more to do with it. After carrying out his own investigation into the killings, Dallaire reported to UN headquarters on 6 January 1994:

> The manner in which they were conducted, in their execution, in their coordination, in their cover-up, and in their political motives lead us to firmly believe that the perpetrators of these evil deeds were well-organised, well-informed, well-motivated and prepared to conduct premeditated murder. We have no reason to believe that such an occurrence could not and will not be repeated again in any part of the country where arms are prolific and ethnic tensions are prevalent.

His request for reinforcements was turned down.

More details of the conspiracy emerged from a secret meeting on 10 January between the head of the Belgian contingent, Colonel Luc Marchal, and an *Interahamwe* commander, Jean-Pierre Twatzinze, who wanted to defect. A former member of the president's security guard,

Twatzinze described how the *Interahamwe* had trained 1,700 men in three-week sessions at Rwandan army camps. The training had focused on discipline, weapons, explosives, close combat and tactics. He had originally believed that the purpose of the training was to enable the *Interahamwe* to defend Kigali against the RPF. But since the arrival of Unamir in December, he had been ordered to make lists of all Tutsi in Kigali. He was now certain it was for their extermination. Since their training, the *Interahamwe* recruits had been scattered in groups of forty throughout Kigali. They were capable, he said, of killing up to 1,000 Tutsi in twenty minutes. He also claimed there were plans to assassinate Belgian peacekeepers to trigger Belgium's withdrawal from Unamir and precipitate the mission's collapse. He himself had distributed weapons and he knew the location of a stockpile at MRND headquarters. He was willing to show the cache to Unamir and to provide further information, he said, in return for UN protection abroad for himself and his family.

When Dallaire was informed of Twatzinze's offer, he was keen to take the initiative. In a coded cable to New York on 11 January, giving full details of 'Jean-Pierre's' information, Dallaire said he planned to seize the arms within thirty-six hours. 'Where there's a will, there's a way. Let's do it. [*Peux ce que veux. Allons-y.*]' He also recommended that Jean-Pierre should be given safe passage from Rwanda. UN headquarters, however, blocked the move. Dallaire was told that arms seizures went beyond the UN's mandate. As violence increased, he made several further efforts to persuade UN headquarters to authorise weapons seizures, warning again and again that the *Interahamwe* were planning a campaign of 'ethnic cleansing'. On 3 February he told New York:

> We can expect more frequent and more violent demonstrations, more grenade and armed attacks on ethnic and political groups, more assassinations and quite possibly outright attacks on UNAMIR installations. Each day of delay in authorising deterrent arms recovery operations will result in an ever deteriorating security situation and may, if arms continue to be distributed, result in an inability of UNAMIR to carry out its mandate in all aspects . . . and

create a significant danger to the safety and security of UN military and civilian personnel and the population at large.

But UN headquarters adamantly refused. One difficulty was the position taken by the UN Secretary-General Boutros Boutros-Ghali. As Egypt's deputy foreign minister he had developed close links with Habyarimana's regime; he had visited Rwanda twice, negotiated a cooperation agreement with Rwanda and pushed through an arms deal, reversing a previous ban imposed by Egypt. As secretary-general he chose as his special representative in Rwanda a former foreign minister of Cameroon, Jacques Booh-Booh, a personal friend and fellow francophile, who adopted an openly pro-Hutu stance and kept putting an optimistic gloss on events in his reports to New York. Booh-Booh soon clashed with Dallaire, preferring to gather around him a group of Franco-African advisers, and lost no opportunity to undermine Dallaire's credibility in New York. Dallaire was consequently regarded in New York as a maverick inclined to exaggerate the difficulties that Rwanda posed.

Another difficulty was the impact of the Somali debacle. UN staff feared that another failure would produce a UN meltdown. 'We were cautious in interpreting our mandate and in giving guidance because we did not want a repetition of Somalia,' a senior official, Iqbal Riza, subsequently admitted. To Hutu extremists, however, the UN's conspicuous failure to act gave them encouragement to continue. 'It was the worst thing for us, just to stay, and to watch, without reaction,' recalled Colonel Marchal.

The political process had meanwhile stalled. The installation of a new interim government had originally been set for January 1994. But Habyarimana launched one challenge after another to the interpretation of the Arusha Accords, deliberately obstructing any progress. Behind the scenes the *akazu* had no intention of giving up power. The installation was postponed again and again, to February, to March, to early April.

Day after day, *Radio Mille Collines* kept up its broadcasts of incitement and rumour. One announcer openly called for the assassination

of the interim prime minister, Agathe Uwilingiyimana, a pro-democracy Hutu politician critical of Habyarimana's northern clique. A song
by Simon Bikindi beseeching his fellow Hutu – the *bene sebahinzi*, the
'sons of cultivators' – to defend their rights and protect the gains of the
1959 revolution was played again and again:

> . . . the servitude, the whip, the lash, the forced work that exhausted
> the people . . . has disappeared forever. You, the great majority
> [*rubanda nyamwinshi*] pay attention and . . . remember this evil that
> should be driven as far away as possible, so that it never returns to
> Rwanda.

One refrain from the song was repeated endlessly, like a mantra – 'a
heritage that should be carefully maintained . . . and transmitted to
posterity'.

The weekly paper, *Kangura*, added to the climate of fear and suspicion. In January it accused Unamir and the Belgian contingent in
Kigali of siding with the RPF and predicted a war by March. 'If the
RPF have decided to kill us, then let us kill each other. Let whatever
is smouldering erupt,' the paper said. 'The masses will rise with the
help of the army and the blood will flow freely.'

Yet Habyarimana's options were fast diminishing. Western and
African governments alike insisted on implementation of the Arusha
Accords. East African leaders complained that delays in implementation threatened the stability of the whole region. Pro-democracy Hutu
politicians, believing that Unamir's presence would protect them,
became increasingly outspoken in demanding implementation.
Simultaneously, Habyarimana was under attack from extremists in
akazu for agreeing to sign the Arusha Accords in the first place. In
March *Kangura* published a cartoon of Habyarimana carrying the RPF
leader Paul Kagame, telling him: 'I've done whatever I could to get
you Tutsis better off.' In an accompanying article, Hassan Ngeze predicted Habyarimana's imminent death in a public incident. 'Nobody
likes Habyarimana's life better than he does,' wrote Ngeze. 'The
important thing is to tell him how he will be killed.' On 3 April *Radio
Mille Collines* warned that 'a little something' was about to happen.

On 6 April Habyarimana attended a one-day summit meeting of African leaders in Dar es Salaam. Once more, he was confronted with a barrage of criticism for prevaricating over the Arusha Accords. Though he rarely travelled anywhere at night, he insisted flying home to Kigali after the meeting. His Falcon jet, a present from President Mitterrand, flown by a three-man French crew, approached Kigali airport in darkness at about 8.15 p.m. On board, accompanying Habyarimana, were seven senior members of the government and the new president of Burundi, who had asked Habyarimana for a lift. The plane circled once, then, as it came in to land, it was struck by two missiles fired from a hill just outside the airport perimeter and crashed in the grounds of the presidential palace. All on board were killed.

Within minutes, the airport and the palace perimeter were sealed off by a cordon of troops from a nearby military barracks. Militias threw up road blocks across the city. News of Habyarimana's death was broadcast by *Radio Mille Collines*. The killing began.

No conclusive evidence ever emerged about the identity of Habyarimana's assassins. Hutu extremists accused the RPF of his murder and also claimed that Belgian troops were involved. The RPF blamed Hutu extremists. The prime suspects were members of the *akazu* clique determined to wreck any prospect that the Arusha Accords might be implemented, ending their hold on power. Habyarimana's murder was to be the trigger for a genocide that they had long planned. At the centre of the conspiracy was Colonel Bagosora who took charge in Kigali that night, directing operations. At a party to celebrate the national day of Senegal attended by Dallaire and Marchal two nights before, Bagosora remarked that 'the only plausible solution for Rwanda would be the elimination of the Tutsi'.

The first victims were carefully selected. With lists prepared well in advance, soldiers from the Presidential Guard and *Interahamwe* militiamen hunted down prominent moderate Hutus – politicians, senior government officials, lawyers, teachers, human rights activists and independent journalists – all regarded as opponents standing in the way of the *génocidaires*. Among their targets were the president of the

Constitutional Court and a minister who had threatened to close down *Radio Mille Collines*. Within an hour of the plane crash, troops blockaded the home of the Hutu prime minister, Agathe Uwilingiyimana. Friends urged her to go into hiding, but she refused, insisting she wanted to make a broadcast from the national radio station to show that civilian authority was in control and committed to the Arusha Accords. A detachment of Belgian peacekeepers was sent to provide her with an escort from her home to the studios of Radio Rwanda, taking three hours to negotiate their way through roadblocks to reach her. As they arrived at her home, Rwandan soldiers opened fire. Unable to withdraw, the Belgians, together with Uwilingiyimana, waited in vain for reinforcements. After three hours of waiting, the prime minister and her husband fled over a garden wall. They were caught and killed later that day. The ten Belgians were taken prisoner, driven to a military camp, beaten up, tortured and killed.

The slaughter of Tutsis started simultaneously. Hundreds of prominent Tutsis, their names and addresses already listed, were tracked down in their homes and murdered. Gangs armed with clubs, machetes and knives went from door to door searching for Tutsi victims. Thousands were caught at roadblocks by militiamen demanding identity cards, killing Tutsis they found on the spot. Unamir soldiers in Kigali witnessed scores of executions. Describing an incident he saw only yards from the hotel that served as Unamir headquarters, a Unamir peacekeeper recalled: 'He just held him by his shirt and started dragging him . . . and just raised his machete and hacked him on the head . . . he did that twice and we were standing watching him . . . after that he just rubbed his bloodstained machete on his buttocks, and then searched his victim's pockets . . . we all screamed at this.' Not long afterwards a tipper truck came by with a prison detail to collect bodies from the streets. 'Someone flagged it down and dragged the body from under the tree and threw it into the tipper truck which was almost full and people were moaning and crying. You could see that some were not dead.'

In a radio broadcast a Hutu Power leader, Froduald Karamira, told listeners that the war against the Tutsi was 'everyone's responsibility' and called on them to 'assist the armed forces to finish the work'. Thousands of Hutus responded, jogging through the streets of Kigali chanting, 'Let's exterminate them all.' *Radio Mille Collines* broadcast direct incitements to murder: 'The graves are not yet quite full,' it screamed. 'Who is going to do the good work and help us finish them completely?'

Massacres followed in quick succession. Soldiers from the Presidential Guard arrived at the *Centre Christus*, a Jesuit retreat in Kigali, at 7 a.m. on 7 April, demanded identity cards and selected nineteen people for execution, including seven priests and eight young women on retreat. At another church compound in Kigali that morning, sixty Tutsi men and boys were taken away and murdered. At a mission station on a hill in the Kigali suburb of Gikondo, hundreds of Tutsi, terrified by the gunfire and explosions in the capital, sought shelter with Catholic priests. During a mass for some 500 Tutsis, a killing squad burst into the church. 'The militia began slashing away,' a survivor recalled. 'They were hacking at the arms, legs, breasts, faces and necks.' The killing lasted for two hours. Similar massacres broke out across the country.

As the scale of the killing became evident, the RPF leader Paul Kagame warned that his forces would intervene if the slaughter of civilians did not stop. As part of the Arusha Accords, a battalion of 600 RPF soldiers had been stationed in Kigali at the national parliament building, a short distance from central Kigali, to provide security for RPF supporters. The bulk of RPF forces remained in the north. Late on 8 April Kagame announced a return to war and instructed his northern army to advance on the capital.

Amid growing turmoil, Western governments rushed to evacuate their citizens. French troops landed at the airport on 9 April and headed for the embassy. The embassy was crowded not only with French citizens but members of Habyarimana's clique, the *akazu*, whom France had supported for so long and who had been deeply involved in planning genocide. Among them was Madame Agathe Kanzinga, her brother and some thirty other extremists including the director of *Radio Mille Collines*, Professor Ferdinand Nahimana, responsible for organising hate broadcasts. Madame Agathe, her children and the rest of her entourage were escorted on to the first French flight out of Kigali. On arrival in Paris, she received a gift of some $40,000 from the French government, a sum taken from the budget of the ministry of cooperation designated for 'urgent assistance for Rwandan refugees'. Two extremist leaders were subsequently given an audience by Mitterrand. According to a former minister of cooperation, Bernard Debré, Mitterrand remained 'very attached to former President Habyarimana and his family, and to everything that was part of the old regime'. Among those whom the French refused to evacuate were the five children of the murdered prime minister Agathe Uwilingiyimana, and long-standing embassy employees, most of them Tutsis.

A contingent of 250 Belgian paratroops landed on 9 April. Belgium had made strenuous efforts at the United Nations to obtain a strengthened mandate for Unamir enabling UN forces to intervene militarily in Rwanda and stop the killing. Belgium was ready to attach its paratroop contingent to the Belgian peacekeeping force already on the ground. But France adamantly opposed the plan. Belgian paratroops were therefore confined to evacuation duties, passing scenes of slaughter on the street, along with the French. Some Tutsis who managed to board trucks heading for the airport were taken off at militia roadblocks and killed on the spot while French and Belgian troops looked on, under orders not to intervene.

Expatriate doctors from the medical charity *Médecins Sans Frontières* (MSF) joined the exodus on 10 April after fifty wounded people waiting in emergency tents at the central hospital, presumed to be Tutsis, were dragged away and killed. 'We have decided it is no use to work here anymore,' an MSF doctor told an American reporter. 'It is useless to care for someone who is going to be killed.'

By the time the last evacuation plane had left Kigali, the only remaining foreigners were a team from the International Committee of the Red Cross determined to stay on, and a besieged force of ill-equipped Unamir troops restricted to a 'peacekeeping' mandate. Unamir posts were soon crowded with thousands of desperate people seeking shelter from marauding gangs.

The future of Unamir itself was in jeopardy. It had been established to supervise a peace process that had evidently collapsed. UN officials advocated terminating the whole operation. There was considerable confusion about what lay behind the violence. Hutu extremists in the government portrayed the killing as a spontaneous reaction by Hutu to the murder of their president by Tutsi assassins. Western press reports blamed 'the chaos and anarchy' on ancient tribal feuds. UN officials in New York interpreted the killing as a resumption of civil war, about which they could do little. UN Secretary-General Boutros-Ghali saw no reason to break off an extended European tour.

Unamir's commander General Dallaire, however, was in no doubt about the cause of the violence. In a cable to New York on 8 April he described it as a campaign of terror that was well planned and organised, led by the Presidential Guard and directed at opposition leaders, the Tutsi ethnic group and at Unamir and other UN personnel. He also explained how precarious Unamir's position was. His Belgian troops, the backbone of Unamir, were scattered about Kigali isolated by roadblocks. They had no supplies of power or petrol. Ten peacekeepers were dead and he feared for the safety for the rest. Unamir had food for less than two weeks, drinking water in some places for only two days and fuel for at most three days. He was critically short of ammunition and medical supplies.

Dallaire was nevertheless adamant that his men should not withdraw. Three times he was told by UN officials in New York – once by Boutros-Ghali in the only phone call he made – to draw up plans for an evacuation, but he refused to comply. He argued that with reinforcements, he could stop the killing. He was incredulous when French and Belgian troops were sent to rescue expatriates but not used to help restore order. 'We were left to fend for ourselves,' he recalled, 'with neither mandate nor supplies.'

Worse was to come. On 12 April the Belgian government, facing domestic uproar over the death of ten Belgian peacekeepers, announced it intended to pull its contingent out of Unamir. Retreating from their posts, Belgian peacekeepers abandoned thousands of civilians seeking their protection, leaving them defenceless against attacks by the army and militiamen. At the École Technique Officielle, a technical school in the Kigali suburb of Gatonga run by

Salesian Fathers, where 2,000 people were sheltering, a Belgian lieutenant explained that his men were under orders to withdraw and
suggested they slip away under cover of darkness. Some approached
him asking to be shot rather than to be left facing death at the hands
of the militia and their machetes. When the Belgians surreptitiously
began to pull out, a crowd chased after their vehicles, pleading, 'Do
not abandon us.' Within hours nearly all 2,000 were slaughtered.

Watching the Belgians depart on 19 April, Dallaire felt a deep
sense of betrayal. 'I stood there as the last Hercules left . . . and I
thought that almost exactly fifty years to the day my father and my
father-in-law had been fighting in Belgium to free the country from
fascism, and there I was, abandoned by Belgian soldiers. So profoundly did I despise them for it . . . I found it inexcusable.'

Though gravely weakened, Unamir was still protecting some
30,000 civilians at its posts. But meeting in New York on 21 April,
after Boutros-Ghali had produced an anodyne report on the crisis, the
UN Security Council decided that without the Belgian contingent,
Unamir was no longer viable. It passed a new resolution withdrawing
the majority of UN peacekeepers and leaving behind a token force of
270 men with the remit to help secure a ceasefire between the government and the RPF and to assist humanitarian relief operations 'to
the extent possible'. The last hope of reining back the genocide was
gone.

Within two weeks of Habyarimana's death, the *génocidaires* had gained
effective control of the country's administration and its network of
préfets, *bourgmestres* and *conseillers*. A new 'interim government' was
announced consisting entirely of Hutu Power zealots. Officials who
showed no enthusiasm for the cause were removed. The radio was
used to ridicule and threaten administrators and local political leaders
who preached calm. Across the country the call went out for 'self-
defence' against 'accomplices'. Killing became the main business for
an entire hierarchy of control – the army, *gendarmerie*, communal
police, party officials and civilian authorities – all sanctioned by the
'interim government'. Peasants were ordered and cajoled to take up
the 'work'.

Even church leaders connived in the government's campaign, blaming the violence on the RPF and refusing to speak out against the mass murders taking place in their own church buildings. The Catholic archbishop, Vincent Nsengiyumva, a long-standing ally of the Hutu Power movement, who had served as a member of the MRND central committee for fourteen years, was quick to offer his support to the interim government. Anglican bishops followed suit, peddling the government's line.

Many clergy were shocked at the complicity of the church establishment and strove to give what help they could to Tutsi families flocking to them for protection. But some priests actively aided and abetted the *génocidaires*, assisting them in rounding them up for slaughter. The church president at Mugonero, Pastor Elizaphan Ntakirutimana, urged Tutsi refugees to gather at the mission station there. Some 2,000 were packed into the hospital there when soldiers from the Presidential Guard and militiamen sealed off the premises. On the evening of 15 April the refugees were told that the hospital would be attacked the next morning. Seven pastors among them wrote a letter to Ntakirutimana asking for help.

> Our dear leader, Pastor Elizaphan Ntakirutimana,
>
> How are you! We wish you to be strong in all these problems we are facing. We wish to inform you that we have heard that tomorrow we will be killed with our families. We therefore request you to intervene on our behalf and talk with the Mayor. We believe that, with the help of God who entrusted you the leadership of this flock, which is going to be destroyed, your intervention will be highly appreciated, the same way as the Jews were saved by Esther.
>
> We give honour to you.

Ntakirutimana replied:

> There is nothing I can do for you. All you can do is prepare to die, for your time has come.

Across Rwanda, church buildings where Tutsis desperately sought sanctuary became the scene of one massacre after another. More people were killed there than anywhere else.

Some groups tried to organise defences, arming themselves with stones but they were soon overwhelmed as militiamen and the military stormed churches, tossing grenades through the windows and wielding machetes at random. In many churches, because of the thousands crowded there, the killing had to be spread over several days. Those awaiting death had their Achilles' tendons cut to prevent them from escaping. A survivor at a massacre at Ntarama on 15 April recounted her story to researchers:

> A groups of soldiers and *Interahamwe* attacked the church. They made holes in the back walls and threw grenades through the holes. Everyone tried to take cover. The *Interahamwe* then came in with their machetes and began massacring. At least one uniformed soldier continued to shoot into the church to protect the *Interahamwe* until they were right inside the church and had begun their 'work'. The *Interahamwe* included woman and young boys, about eleven to fourteen, carrying spears and sharpened sticks. They used these to beat a lot of children to death.
>
> As they macheted, the militia discussed their work, pointing out wounded people to each other to be finished off. After a while they were arguing as to whether they should continue to machete or if they should start looting. They decided to loot before everyone was dead . . .
>
> I had fallen under some dead. I couldn't move because there were so many dead bodies on top of me. The *Interahamwe* left, thinking everyone was dead.

When researchers from African Rights arrived at Ntarama two months later, the church was still full of decomposing bodies. 'It was impossible to enter the church because corpses were piled so high at the entrance. This made it difficult to estimate the death toll; but looking through the window, every inch of the inside of the church was taken up by corpses who were piled on top of each other.'

Refugees fleeing Ntarama found themselves trapped at a river. A survivor recalled:

> There were *Interahamwe* on both sides of the river bank and they were shooting. The *Interahamwe* on the Ntarama side ordered us to commit suicide by throwing ourselves into the river. In desperation and in the hope of avoiding an even worse death under the machete, very many people jumped and were drowned, including many babies strapped to their backs. Knowing that death awaited them, fathers threw their children into the river as a last gesture of love.
>
> Those of us who refused to commit suicide ran up and down the river bank, playing hide and seek with our attackers.

River banks became a common location for execution, convenient for getting rid of bodies. Some 40,000 bodies washed down the Akagera river into Lake Victoria.

Hospitals were no safer. 'The percentage of doctors who became "killers par excellence" was very high,' concluded *African Rights*. 'A huge number of the most qualified and experienced doctors in the country, men as well as women – including surgeons, physicians, paediatricians, gynaecologists, anaesthetists, public health specialists and hospital administrators – participated in the murder of their own Tutsi colleagues, patients, the wounded and terrified refugees who had sought shelter in their hospitals.' The *British Medical Journal* reported that some of 'the most horrific massacres occurred in maternity clinics, where people gathered in the belief that no one would kill mothers and new-born babies'.

Teachers commonly denounced students to militia groups or killed students themselves. A Hutu teacher told the French journalist Patrick de Saint-Exupéry: 'A lot of people got killed here. I myself killed some of the children . . . We had eighty kids in the first year. There are twenty-five left. All the others, we killed them or they have run away.' Human rights activists were similarly involved. The chairman of one human rights organisation, Innocent Mazimpaka, along with his younger brother, the *bourgmestre* of Gatare, was subsequently charged with responsibility for the slaughter of 12,200 Tutsis in Gatare *commune*.

For week after week, the hunt for Tutsis continued, from hill to hill, in town after town. Survivors told tales of grotesque cruelty. Mothers were forced to watch their children die before being killed themselves; children were forced to kill their families. A mother from Taba described how, after the *Interahamwe* had rounded up her family and killed all the men, the women were made to dig graves to bury the men. The children were then thrown into the graves. 'I will never forget the sight of my son pleading with me not to bury him alive . . . he kept trying to come out and was beaten back. And we had to keep covering the pit with earth until . . . there was no movement left.'

Tutsis were murdered by their friends and neighbours, by schoolmates and colleagues; husbands were forced to kill their Tutsi wives or be killed themselves. A 47-year-old peasant farmer from Kibungo, the father of eight children, was questioned by an American journalist, Bill Berkeley, about the death of his brother-in-law.

> The message from the top was passed down to the local village chiefs, the *conseillers*. The *conseillers* had lists of Tutsis who should be killed. They simply organised their constituents . . .
>
> The leaders of the party and the leaders of the militia rounded up all the men in the village. We were told that we had a mission. We were given a list of people to kill. If we met someone on the list, they would be killed . . .
>
> We would converge on a person. We killed a number of people, but jointly . . .

In his own village, they had killed nine people. He had used a machete; others had used clubs.

> I knew some of them. They were neighbours . . .
>
> I killed because I was forced to. I either had to do it or I would die myself. Many were killed for refusing to kill . . .

And the murder of his brother-in-law?

He did not deserve to die. He was an old man . . . We killed him in his house. He was dragged from the bedroom and killed in the sitting room. Emmanual struck him first. He was the leader of the militia. I could not do it myself. For me, I stood by and watched. There was nothing I could do.

Towards the end of April, Rwanda's holocaust took a new turn. As RPF forces in northern Rwanda advanced southwards, converging on the capital and taking control of eastern areas of the country, the Hutu population in their path fled en masse into neighbouring Tanzania, fearing revenge for the massacres of Tutsis in their home districts. In a single day a quarter of a million people stampeded down the road to the Rusumo Falls bridge to cross the border, leaving huge piles of machetes, knives and spears by the roadside. Among them were Hutu Power leaders and groups of *Interahamwe* determined to keep their hold over the Hutu population. The plight of these displaced Hutu attracted far more attention in the outside world than the genocide in which many of them had participated. A massive relief operation was soon under way.

At the United Nations, members of the Security Council ignored mounting evidence of genocide, reluctant in the wake of Somalia to get involved in another African quagmire. France, still acting to protect its Hutu Power allies, insisted that the violence in Rwanda was not genocide but the result of a civil war. US officials went to extraordinary lengths to avoid using the word 'genocide' for fear that, under the terms of the UN Genocide Convention of 1948, it would create a legal obligation for them to intervene. A draft statement submitted to the Security Council on 29 April warning that 'genocide' contravened international law was watered down to a more acceptable version: 'The Security Council recalls that the killing of members of an ethnic group with the intention of destroying such a group in whole or in part constitutes a crime punishable by international law.'

On 4 May President Clinton, still smarting from events in Somalia, declared: 'Lesson number one is, don't go into one of these things and say, as the US said when we started in Somalia, "Maybe we'll be done in a month because it's a humanitarian crisis" . . . Because there are almost always political problems and sometimes military conflicts which bring about these crises.'

The UN secretary-general, Boutros-Ghali, bungling as badly in Rwanda as he had done in Somalia, added to the confusion. Eight days after the Security Council, on his advice, had voted to withdraw the bulk of Unamir forces, he proposed that Unamir should be reinforced. His proposal was greeted with stunned silence.

On the ground, General Dallaire, endeavouring to find a way through the mire, went to see the RPF leader Paul Kagame, carrying a ceasefire proposal from the 'interim government'. Kagame was scathing. The 'interim government', he retorted, was no more than 'a clique of murderers'. He claimed that the idea of a ceasefire had been devised by France on their behalf.

Meeting again on 17 May, after further evidence of genocide, the Security Council, while still managing to eschew the word 'genocide', approved a new resolution authorising a second Unamir force for Rwanda of 5,500 troops – Unamir 2. But the exercise was largely a sham. There were no troops or equipment yet identified for the operation nor any plan for an airlift to transport them to Rwanda. There was not even agreement over what strategy Unamir 2 should pursue. Dallaire, desperate to stop the killing, proposed that troop reinforcements should land in Kigali where they could be rapidly deployed across the country. American officials, fearing that Unamir could become caught up in combat in Kigali between the RPF and government forces, favoured deploying troops on the periphery of Rwanda where they could establish safe zones to protect civilians. 'Sending a UN force into the maelstrom of Rwanda without a sound plan of operations would be folly,' argued the US ambassador to the UN, Madeleine Albright. The arguments and recrimination continued for weeks. Recalling these events, New Zealand's representative on the Security Council, Colin Keating, observed: 'While thousands of human beings were hacked to death every day, ambassadors argued fitfully for weeks about military tactics.'

On 8 June, two months after the first massacres, the Security Council finally produced an authorisation for Unamir 2. It even managed to mention the word 'genocide', though not in a stark form but wrapped up in the phrase 'acts of genocide'. Asked to explain the American position in the light of previous statements, a State Department spokeswoman replied: 'We have every reason to believe that acts of genocide have occurred.'

'How many "acts of genocide" does it take to make a genocide?' a reporter asked.

'That's just not a question that I'm in a position to answer,' she replied.

But Unamir 2 was stillborn. Before any action was taken, France announced its own intervention. The French had become increasingly alarmed by the prospect that the 'interim government' might be defeated. By late May the RPF had gained control of large areas of Kigali, including the airport, and more than half of the country. The 'interim government' meanwhile had withdrawn to headquarters in Gitarama, taking with them the entire contents of the national treasury, including gold reserves and foreign currency. On 12 June the RPF captured Gitarama, forcing ministers to flee to Gisenyi, the Hutu Power stronghold in the north-west. Mitterrand was determined to prevent an RPF victory in Rwanda even if it meant continuing to collaborate with genocidal killers. According to Human Rights Watch, arms shipments from the French government or French companies operating under government licence were delivered to the Rwandan army at the Zaire border town of Goma on five occasions between May and June.

On 14 June, two days after the fall of Gitarama, Mitterrand authorised a plan to send French troops to Rwanda, dressing it up as a 'humanitarian' mission. 'Whatever happens, we will act. Every hour counts and it is now only a question of hours and days,' he said. 'Increasingly savage fighting is taking place and one can no longer wait.'

Within days, France assembled an expeditionary force – '*Opération Turquoise*' – designed more for military purposes than for 'humanitarian' use. It consisted of 2,500 troops, including commando units and special forces, heavy mortars, one hundred armoured vehicles, ten helicopters, four ground-attack planes and four reconnaissance jet planes. Military officers in Paris talked openly of 'breaking the back of the RPF'. Among the officers appointed to the expedition were former military advisers to Habyarimana's government. Maps were produced delineating a zone of French control that included most of western Rwanda and parts of the city of Kigali still held by the 'interim government'.

When Mitterrand offered to put *Opération Turquoise* at the disposal of the United Nations, Boutros-Ghali leapt at the opportunity. While the Americans were still haggling over peacekeeping costs, France was not only ready to provide troops but willing to pick up the bill. In Kigali, however, Dallaire was hostile to any French intervention, believing their intention was to save the 'interim government' from defeat and split Rwanda into two. Well aware of France's secret arms deliveries to the *génocidaires*, Dallaire remarked in private: 'If they land here to deliver their damn weapons to the government, I'll have their planes shot down.' Despite considerable opposition, the Security Council nevertheless gave its endorsement to *Opération Turquoise* on 22 June.

The following day, French forces crossed into Rwanda from the Zaire border town of Bukavu. They were greeted by the Hutu population and the *Interahamwe* as heroes. Banners proclaimed '*Vive la France*' and praised Mitterrand. French *tricolores* were displayed everywhere, even on Rwandan army vehicles. Broadcasting from Gisenyi, *Radio Mille Collines* called for 'you Hutu girls to wash yourselves and put on a good dress to welcome our French allies. The Tutsi girls are all dead, so you have your chance.'

One detachment of French troops, accompanied by journalists, headed for Nyarushishi, a camp where 8,000 Tutsi refugees had survived under police protection. Largely unnoticed, a second detachment consisting of 200 elite troops crossed from the border town of Goma to Gisenyi, headquarters of the 'interim government', and set up camp there, ready to defend the town from RPF attack. There were no Tutsi left in the area for them to protect. A Hutu resident in Gisenyi told a French journalist: 'We have never had many Tutsi here and we killed them all in the beginning without much of a fuss.'

In some places, the coming of the French set off more killing sprees as militias raced to complete their 'work' before they were stopped.

But the French anyway showed little inclination to disarm the militias or to dismantle their roadblocks. Asked why his troops took no action, Colonel Didier Thibault, a false name used by Colonel Didier Tauzin to cover his role as a former adviser to the Rwandan army, retorted: 'The French army has no authority to disarm the militia or dismantle the roadblocks even though they are a threat to civilian lives.' According to Gérard Prunier, a political advisor to *Opération Turquoise*, Colonel Thibault 'was itching to get at the RPF'.

The original French intention had been to press on to Kigali, but the risks became too great. On 4 July Thibault ordered his troops to draw 'a line in the sand' at Gikongoro, warning that he would give 'no quarter' if the RPF attacked. Having failed to reach Kigali, the French opted to set up a 'secure humanitarian zone' encompassing the south-western quadrant of Rwanda, abandoning the north-west and the 'interim government' in Gisenyi. As the scale of the atrocities in Rwanda became ever more apparent, the French gambit came to an ignominious end. French troops on the ground, disgusted by the evidence of massacres they found, felt betrayed. 'We have not a single wounded Hutu here, just massacred Tutsi,' reported one soldier. 'We have been deceived,' said a sergeant-major, staring at a group of wounded and starving Tutsi refugees. 'This is not what we were led to believe. We were told the Tutsis were killing Hutus. We thought the Hutus were the good guys and the victims.' Initially pleased at the welcome the militias had given them, they now felt revulsion. 'I've had enough of being cheered by murderers,' remarked one soldier. A French officer who had once instructed soldiers of the Presidential Guard broke down and cried, so appalled was he at the crimes committed by men whom he had trained.

On 4 July the RPF took Kigali. Within a few days of the fall of the Rwandan capital, as RPF forces advanced on the last Hutu Power strongholds in the north-west, the *génocidaires* organised a mass exodus of the Hutu population across the border to Zaire. In its last broadcasts from Rwanda, *Radio Mille Collines* spread fear and terror, warning that the RPF were devil-like fighters bent on killing them all. Led by local officials, whole villages decamped. The roads to Zaire became choked with hundreds of thousands of Hutu, in trucks, cars, on bicycles, on foot, taking their livestock and what belongings they could carry. Buildings were stripped of window frames, door handles and corrugated-iron sheets. Watching the exodus at a border crossing near Goma, a relief worker observed: 'It was as though the whole country was emptying.' In two days about a million people crossed into Zaire. 'It was a silent line, a long, long black line of people, all of them walking silently like machines.' Among them were the militias and the remnants of the army, taking with them their weapons and equipment. 'Even if they [the RPF] have won a military victory they will not have the power,' declared a leading Hutu ideologue. 'We have the population. They have only bullets.'

Many prominent *génocidaires*, including Colonel Bagosora, passed through the French 'safe-haven' but the French made no attempt to arrest them. Mitterrand's spokesman explained: 'Our mandate does not authorise us to arrest them on our own authority. Such a task could undermine our neutrality, the best guarantee of our effectiveness.' So, to the end, the French protected the organisers of genocide.

Having largely ignored the genocide, the international aid community, prompted by television pictures of the Hutu exodus, now rushed to assist the mass of Hutu 'refugees' crammed into disease-ridden camps along the Zaire border, without food or shelter. Joining the bandwagon, President Clinton described the 'refugee' camps as the worst humanitarian crisis in a generation. In a publicity stunt, US Air Force planes mounted an air drop of supplies. Some 150 aid organisations arrived on the scene. The United Nations, unable to mount an operation to prevent genocide, now found no difficulty in raising $1 million a day to spend on a refugee crisis organised by *génocidaires* for their own purposes.

On 18 July, after the last Hutu Power stronghold had fallen, Kagame declared the civil war over. The next day a government of national unity was sworn in comprising representatives of all main parties except the MRND. Twelve of the eighteen ministers were Hutu. The new president, Pasteur Bizimungu, was a Hutu relative of Habyarimana who had opposed him; Paul Kagame was installed as vice-president.

The RPF's victory brought an end to the genocide. In the space of

100 days some 800,000 people had been slaughtered – about three-quarters of the Tutsi population. More people had been killed more quickly than in any other mass killing in recorded history. Tutsis who had escaped the holocaust emerged ragged and starving from months of hiding in caves, swamps and forests and crept out from under sheds, inside cupboards and attics. Many had been saved by the help of Hutus. 'When I came out, there were no birds,' said one survivor who had hidden throughout the genocide. 'There was sunshine and the stench of death.'

The entire country had been laid to waste. Hospitals and schools had been destroyed or ransacked, government offices looted; there were no police; the treasury was empty; public utilities such as electricity, water and phone services had collapsed; a year's harvest had been lost. Everywhere there were ditches filled with rotting bodies. Nearly 2 million people inside the country were refugees, uprooted from their homes. According to the World Bank, the genocide had left Rwanda the poorest country on earth.

Yet the conflict was far from over. In their new base in Zaire, supported unwittingly by the international aid effort, the *génocidaires* regrouped and planned their return. The same clique of Hutu politicians, *préfets*, *bourgmestres* and military officers who had organised the genocide now used their control of the refugee camps and food distribution there to raise funds and buy arms for a new offensive. From exile, Colonel Bagosora vowed 'to wage a war that will be long and full of dead people until the minority Tutsis are finished and completely out of the country'.

This new phase of the conflict was to bring further tragedy to Rwanda. It was also to lead to the downfall of Mobutu's regime in Zaire.

WHERE VULTURES FLY

As the cataclysm in Rwanda unfurled, President Mobutu grasped the chance to play a central role in the crisis, hoping to regain some of the international standing he had lost. Zaire was Rwanda's big brother, a giant neighbour long accustomed to acting as a regional power-broker. In times of trouble, Mobutu had readily gone to the aid of Habyarimana, sending him troops to help repel the RPF's invasion from Uganda in 1990. During the civil war, Zaire had facilitated the supply of arms to the Hutu Power government, even after it had been driven out of Kigali. Now that eastern Zaire was host to a million and a half Rwandan refugees, the international aid community needed Mobutu's help to avoid a humanitarian catastrophe.

After thirty years of rapacious government, Mobutu had few foreign friends left. In an age of pro-democracy movements, Mobutu was regarded by many African leaders, such as Uganda's Yoweri Museveni, as a 'dinosaur', a relic from the era of corrupt dictators that Africa was striving to leave behind. Most Western governments and international institutions such as the World Bank had long since given up trying to bail out Mobutu, seeing little result from the $9 billion of foreign aid they had poured into his regime since 1975.

Only France stood by Mobutu, determined above all to bolster a francophone ally and protect its reputation throughout francophone

Africa as a world power able to determine events in its *pré carré* and to thwart 'Anglo-Saxon' schemes. A coterie of French government advisers was actively engaged in promoting Mobutu's cause. Among them was Jacques Foccart, the *eminence grise* of French policy on Africa for forty years, who met Mobutu at his palace in Gbadolite in April 1994 for a summit meeting on Rwanda. In an interview for his memoirs, published in 1995, Foccart told Philippe Gaillard: 'You asked me what was France's interest. On this matter, there is no ambiguity. Congo-Léopoldville, Zaire today, is the largest country in francophone Africa. It has considerable natural resources. It has the means of being a regional power. The long-term interest of France and its African allies is evident.'

The French were especially keen to ensure that Mobutu emerged as central Africa's principal power-broker rather than the 'anglophone' Yoweri Museveni, whom they regarded as an American ally. A confidential Paris newsletter, *La Lettre du Sud*, reflected official thinking in its May issue: 'The region cannot be left in the hands of an English-speaking strongman completely aligned to American views and interests. This is why since 1990 France has supported the late President Juvénal Habyarimana in order to fight the RPF. It did not work out, so now the only choice left is to put back in the saddle the Zairian President Mobutu Sese Seko, the one man capable of standing up to Museveni.'

When African leaders planned to hold a regional meeting on Rwanda in 'anglophone' Tanzania in April 1994, Mobutu and the French blocked the move. Bruno Delaye, head of the *Cellule Africaine* in the president's office in Paris, remarked to Gérard Prunier: 'We won't have any of these meetings in Tanzania. The next one has to be in Kinshasa. We cannot let anglophone countries decide on the future of a francophone one. In any case, we want Mobutu back in. He cannot be dispensed with [the word used in French was '*incontournable*'] and we are going to do it through this Rwanda business.'

At a Franco-African summit in Biarritz in November 1994, Mobutu was accorded a warm welcome while Rwanda's new president, Pasteur Bizimungu, a Hutu opponent of Habyarimana, was refused an invitation. The French minister for cooperation, Bernard

Debré, described the new Kigali government as 'an anglophone Tutsi government coming from Uganda'. One year later the Kigali government was again refused an invitation. The new French president, Jacques Chirac, presided over the opening of the conference with a moment of silence, not for the victims of genocide but in honour of the memory of Habyarimana.

Yet Zaire itself was little more than a rotting carcass. Its formal economy had shrunk by 40 per cent since 1988. The currency was worthless. Per capita gross domestic product in 1993 was $117, some 65 per cent lower than in 1958, two years before independence. Inflation in 1994 reached 9,800 per cent. Copper production, once the mainstay of the economy, had fallen from 450,000 tons during the 1970s to 30,600 tons in 1994; cobalt production had fallen from 18,000 tons to 3,000 tons; diamond production had nearly halved. Gold and diamond smuggling were rife. The state-controlled mining company, Gécamines, had been plundered and looted almost to a standstill. 'Gécamines', recalled Daniel Simpson, the US ambassador at the time, 'was clean as a whistle. Mobutu had not only killed the goose that laid the golden eggs, he'd eaten the carcass and made fat from the feathers.' An American journalist, Carole Collins, observed: 'To visit Zaire in the last years of the Mobutu era was to enter a world of cannibal capitalism, where most banks and public services and any logic of economic growth and expanding productivity had ceased to operate.'

The provinces were largely separate fiefdoms, remote from the reach of central government. Most were afflicted by ethnic tensions, periodically stirred up by Mobutu as part of his divide-and-rule strategy, the last remnant of 'government' that he retained. In 1994, when a million and a half Rwandans suddenly arrived on the doorstep, nowhere was more combustible than the eastern region of Kivu.

With the blessing of Mobutu and the support of a refugee aid budget totalling $800 million over twelve months, Rwanda's *génocidaires* carved out a mini-state in Kivu, setting up their own administration, finances and system of control. Using the same command structure as before, the army – the former *Forces Armées Rwandaise* (ex-FAR) –

established headquarters at Lac Vert, ten miles west of Goma, regrouped its forces in military camps, organised recruitment and training programmes and ordered weapons supplies from abroad. Its ranks grew from 30,000 to 50,000. Heavy weapons originally confiscated by French forces in the 'safe zone' and handed over to Zaire were sold back to the ex-FAR by Zairian officers. Refugee camps were organised by *préfecture*, by *commune* and by *secteur*, led by *bourgmestres* and *conseillers*, just as in Rwanda. Fed and cared for by foreign aid agencies, the population remained in the grip of *génocidaires*, held in camps by a mixture of brute force and propaganda warning that they faced certain death from Tutsis back in Rwanda.

Because aid agencies depended on the Hutu Power administration to assist with the distribution of relief supplies, they turned a blind eye to the system of coercion and abuse prevalent in the camps. With the full knowledge of aid officials, refugee numbers were inflated to enable the *génocidaires* to feed their army and sell surplus food on local markets to finance arms purchases for another war of genocide. Officials who protested faced death threats and other forms of intimidation. Refugees wanting to return home were murdered. A senior US administrator, Richard McCall, described the camps as 'an unfettered corridor for arms shipments' to the *génocidaires*. In November 1994 one agency, *Médecins Sans Frontières*, decided to withdraw from eastern Zaire. 'The situation has deteriorated to such an extent that it is now ethically impossible for MSF to continue aiding and abetting the perpetrators of genocide. Members of the former Rwandan authorities, military and militia exert total control over tens of thousands of civilians.' Most other aid agencies remained.

The camps soon acquired a permanent character. A survey carried out by the United Nations High Commissioner for Refugees in 1995 listed nearly 82,000 thriving enterprises in the camps, including 2,324 bars, 450 restaurants, 589 general shops, 62 hairdressers, 51 pharmacies and 25 butchers. There were photo studios, libraries and cinemas. The camps were so well stocked with cheap supplies that Zairians came from miles to shop *chez les Rwandais*. Aid agencies fattened the coffers of Hutu Power by employing civil servants, doctors, nurses and other professional staff loyal to the cause. They also provided transport, meeting places and office supplies to Hutu Power groups masquerading as community self-help agencies. More than two-thirds of all the foreign assistance provided for Rwanda went not to reconstruction efforts but to the camps of 'Hutuland' and their genocidal bosses.

At their headquarters at Lac Vert, army chiefs planned a two-stage campaign to regain power: the first stage consisted of guerrilla attacks on Rwanda from bases in Zaire designed to disrupt and weaken the RPF's hold on power; the second stage was to engage in open civil war. Sporadic attacks were launched in September 1994 and continued throughout 1995. But the *génocidaires* were intent not only on retaking Rwanda. They also set out to exterminate Tutsi groups living in Zaire. In the process they ignited a revolt that eventually swept them to their doom and brought about the collapse of Mobutu's decaying regime.

The Kivu region had been host to large numbers of Banyarwanda, both Hutu and Tutsi, for many years. In the nineteenth century Tutsi emigrants from Rwanda settled on grazing land around Mulenge in South Kivu. In the 1960s they adopted the name 'Banyamulenge' in order to distinguish themselves from Rwandan Tutsi refugees who arrived after the 1959 massacres and so preserve their political rights and access to land by laying claim to the status of authentic Congolese. Their presence aroused strong local resentment, notably among the Babembe. Wililunga Cosma, a native of eastern Zaire, observed after his field research:

> Babembe consider Tutsi to be good-for-nothings, incapables, lacking in physical strength, uncircumcised, an inferior people who drink all day and bemoan not their dead but their cattle. For their part, Tutsi regard Babembe as trouble-makers, barbaric, haughty, good only for heavy [agricultural] labour in exchange for a calf close to death.

During the 1960s rebellion the Babembe fought against Mobutu's army; the Banyamulenge sided with it.

In North Kivu, Banyarwanda – both Hutu and Tutsi – formed

nearly a majority of the population. During the colonial era, between 1937 and 1955, two successive waves of immigrants arrived from Rwanda, totalling in all some 85,000 people. Local Hunde chiefs regularly complained about the pressure this caused on land, especially grazing land.

Then, between 1959 and 1961, as a result of the Hutu 'revolution' in Rwanda, some 150,000 Rwandan Tutsi fled to Kivu. Most went initially into refugee camps in Masisi, Walikale and Kalehe, then merged into existing communities. More Tutsi refugees followed in 1963–4.

The influx of so many Banyarwanda opened a sharp rift between Kivu's local population – '*autochtones*' or 'natives', as they called themselves – and those they now labelled 'foreigners'. Disputes over land proliferated. In Masisi district, Banyarwanda families constituted three-quarters of the population and controlled nearly 60 per cent of available land; indigenous Hunde found themselves in a minority of 15 per cent of the population. Under pressure from Hunde and Nande politicians in North Kivu, Mobutu decided for electoral reasons in 1981 to repeal a law granting citizenship to Banyarwanda, effectively making them targets for reprisal; a wave of theft, looting and abuse followed. In 1991 Banyarwanda representatives were excluded from the *Conférence Nationale Souveraine*. Reflecting local antagonism, North Kivu's deputy governor declared: 'Rwanda will have to accept the return of its emigrants instead of letting them roam around the world like Palestinians. History has shown that the Tutsi, ever-eager for power, have long been destabilisers. By all possible means they try to subvert established authority . . . The population of the zone of Walikale has elected me to prevent that the zone be invaded by Tutsi.'

In 1993 the Hunde and Nyanga of North Kivu organised local militias to cleanse the fertile Masisi region of Banyarwanda. Their target included both Hutu and Tutsi. Banyarwanda were massacred in Walikale market and in several churches. Thousands on both sides were killed in ethnic fighting and some 350,000 fled their homes. North Kivu was already seething with ethnic tension when a million Hutu descended on Goma, bringing with them their virulent brand of ethnic hatred.

The Banyarwanda community was torn apart. In North Kivu, Zairian Hutu militants, many from communities displaced in 1993, joined forces with Rwandan *Interahamwe* to attack Zairian Tutsi. Thousands of Tutsi were killed; thousands more fled to Rwanda. But Tutsis were not their only target. Seeking land on which to settle, Hutu militias began to take over the rich highland pastures of Masisi from *autochtones*. In December 1995 more than 400 Hunde and Nyanga were killed in Masisi. By February 1996 some 250,000 *autochtones*, mainly Hunde and Nyanga, had been driven from their homes. In retaliation, two *autochtone* militias, Mayi-Mayi and Bangilima, with a long history of warfare against Mobutu's regime, entered the fray, attacking not only Banyarwanda – Hutu and Tutsi alike – but resuming the fight against Mobutu's army, *Forces Armées Zairoises* (FAZ).

In South Kivu, as a result of the influx of Hutu refugees escaping the turmoil that followed the assassination of Burundi's President Ndadaye in 1993 together with the 1994 Hutu exodus from Rwanda, there was a similar outbreak of antagonism towards the Banyamulenge and other Tutsi communities. Stirred up by local Zairian politicians for their own ends, *autochtones* joined forces with Hutu refugee extremists on a campaign of harassment and plunder. Old rivalries between Babembe and Banyamulenge resurfaced. In October 1995 the customary chief of the Bavira, Lenghe III, issued a letter to the effect that 'within his administration, the so-called Banyamulenge are like strangers'.

Threatened by an array of enemies, the Tutsi communities of Kivu – Banyamulenge, Zairian Tutsis, Tutsi immigrants, Tutsi refugees – fashioned the notion of an entire people under attack. The omnibus term they used was 'Banyamulenge', a community now said to number some 400,000, though only about 30,000 were 'original' Banyamulenge. Despairing of any help from Mobutu's regime, they turned to Rwanda's strongman, Paul Kagame, for salvation.

In Kigali, General Kagame had become increasingly frustrated by the turn of events in Kivu. Rwanda was the target of constant cross-borders raids by *génocidaires* using as cover refugee camps sustained by a huge international aid programme. All attempts by United Nations officials to separate *génocidaires* from refugees had been thwarted, leaving the fate of a million Rwandans unresolved. Tutsi communities in Kivu, meanwhile, faced genocidal attacks by Hutu extremists. In July 1996 Kagame visited Washington warning that unless the international community dealt with the *génocidaires*, he would.

Kagame's determination to act was backed up by President Yoweri Museveni of Uganda. Like Kagame, Museveni resented the way in which lawless parts of eastern Zaire were used by anti-government Ugandan militias as a base from which to attack his regime. He also saw an opportunity, in the wake of Kagame's victory in Rwanda, to extend his regional prowess.

Museveni insisted, however, that a Zairian face was needed to cover their intervention. The figurehead they chose was Laurent-Désiré Kabila, a small-time former guerrilla leader whom Che Guevara had once dismissed as lacking 'revolutionary seriousness'. A Baluba from northern Katanga, Kabila had run a minor fiefdom among the Babembe in the mountains of South Kivu until the 1980s, gaining a reputation for greed, brutality and kidnapping Westerners. After abandoning his revolutionary ambitions, he had become a successful trader and smuggler in gold, ivory and leopard skins, maintaining homes in Dar es Salaam and Kampala, where he encountered Museveni. Museveni introduced Kabila to Kagame shortly after the RPF took Kigali in 1994. Though Kabila no longer possessed a following in Kivu, his credentials as a former anti-Mobutu rebel were sufficient for Kagame's purposes.

During the course of 1996, Kagame organised military training for Banyamulenge and Tutsi refugees from Kivu and prepared units of the Rwandan Patriotic Army (RPA) for action in Zaire. The trigger for intervention soon came. On 8 October, following a series of clashes between Banyamulenge and Mobutu's army, the deputy governor of South Kivu, Lwasi Ngabo Lwabanji, ordered all Banyamulenge to leave Zaire within a week or be 'exterminated and expelled'. Kagame's response was immediate: 'We were ready to hit them,' he later told the American journalist Philip Gourevitch, 'hit them very hard – and handle three things: first to save the Banyamulenge and not let them die, empower them to fight, and even fight for them; then to dismantle the camps, return the refugees to Rwanda, and destroy the ex-FAR and militias; and third, to change the situation in Zaire.'

At his palace at Gbadolite, deep in the equatorial jungle, Mobutu was far removed from all these events. At the age of sixty-six, weary of the business of government, he preferred to spend his days roaming around the farms on his estate, talking about crops, soils and rain. 'If I could do it all again, I'd be a farmer,' he often remarked to his close aide Honoré Ngbanda a fellow Ngbandi tribesman who served him as intelligence chief, defence minister and national security adviser. A sinister man, commonly known amongst Zairians as 'the Terminator', Ngbanda recalled in his memoirs the difficulty he had getting Mobutu to focus on national issues rather than play the role of local chief, presiding over village disputes. 'The President of the Republic no longer had an office! We would meet in farms on the outskirts of Gbadolite, in the middle of fields of maize and manioc, amid the commotion of farm machinery and labourers' cries. It was difficult to discuss urgent and sensitive issues in depth.'

Surrounded by members of his family, engulfed in luxury, Mobutu rarely made the journey to Kinshasa, appearing there mainly for ceremonial occasions. Ministers and foreign ambassadors were obliged to fly to Gbadolite for audiences. His Belgian son-in-law Pierre Janssen discovered that the Mobutu household in Gbadolite got through more than 10,000 bottles of champagne each year. For foreign travel, Mobutu tended to charter a Concorde, which could often be glimpsed idling at the airport at Gbadolite. He was once asked by a foreign journalist how he justified the expense. 'I cannot sleep at all on a plane and I am terribly scared of sleeping pills,' he replied. 'To accuse me of wasting money – no, I am sorry. Just think of the time I save.'

Yet Mobutu was a sick man. In August 1996 he was diagnosed as having prostate cancer. Weakened by surgery and radiotherapy, he spent months recuperating in France and Switzerland, dithering over the crisis that erupted in Kivu.

★

Orchestrated by Kagame, led by RPA forces, but presented as a Banyamulenge uprising, the rebellion spread from its origins in South Kivu to the north, along a 300-mile stretch of Zaire's eastern frontier. On 24 October Uvira fell to the rebels; six days later Bukavu, the provincial capital, capitulated. A tidal wave of Hutu refugees fled northwards. On 1 November the rebellion reached Goma, a pretty lakeside town on the black lava foothills of the Virunga mountains, only ten miles from the ex-FAR headquarters and close to one of the main refugee camps at Mugunga.

Appearing in the limelight for the first time as head of his newly formed, custom-built 'liberation movement', *Alliance des Forces Démocratiques de Libération du Congo-Zaire* (AFDL), Laurent Kabila held court for the benefit of the world's press in Mobutu's presidential villa overlooking Lake Kivu on the outskirts of Goma. A portly figure, known for heavy drinking, he presented himself as a freedom-fighter with a long career in opposing Mobutu's dictatorship. 'Our target', he said, 'is to reach Kinshasa.'

The plight of the refugees swiftly became the focus of attention. As AFDL forces advanced, a huge mass of refugees – nearly a million people – crowded into the camp at Mugunga. They were surrounded by a ring of ex-FAR soldiers and *Interahamwe* militias, ready to take on the rebels but effectively holding the refugees hostage. Foreign aid workers fled across the border into Rwanda, leaving them to fend for themselves.

Sounding the alarm, aid agencies, for their own purpose of fund-raising, spread hysteria around the world in their appeals for support. Though Mugunga was well stocked with food and other supplies, the agencies depicted an imminent catastrophe. The British agency Oxfam claimed in an advertisement that 'up to one million people in eastern Zaire are dying from starvation and disease'. The press amplified the warnings. 'Catastrophe! Disaster! Apocalypse! For once the words are the right ones,' declared the Africa editor of *The Economist*.

The French government waged its own campaign, hoping to use the Kivu crisis as a pretext for military intervention in Zaire to protect Mobutu's regime and its Hutu friends, just as it had tried to do in Rwanda. The French foreign minister Hervé de Charette proclaimed

Kivu to be 'perhaps the most disastrous humanitarian crisis the world has seen'. At a Franco-African summit in Ouagadougou, President Jacques Chirac emphasised the need for military intervention. Compounding the hysteria, Boutros Boutros-Ghali at the United Nations spoke of 'genocide by starvation' and backed the French ploy.

Before any foreign intervention was attempted, however, on 13 November AFDL forces resumed their offensive, attacking the ex-FAR headquarters at Lac Vert and the defensive positions around Mugunga. The *génocidaires* broke and ran. Released from their grip, the bulk of the refugees – some 600,000 people – set out on foot to return to Rwanda. Watching them trudge by, day after day, carrying their meagre possessions, pushing bicycles and wheelbarrows, reporters and aid workers marvelled that they appeared to be in good health. Among them mingled groups of *génocidaires*. By the end of November the total number of returnees was said to be around 700,000.

As AFDL forces continued their advance, recruiting child soldiers – *kadogo* – along the way, eastern Zaire became a quagmire of violence. *Génocidaires* and troops from Mobutu's ramshackle army fled in all directions, taking camp followers with them, killing and looting as they went. Caught up in the retreat were an estimated 500,000 Hutu refugees, desperate for sanctuary. Tens of thousands, perhaps as many as 200,000, were massacred in genocidal attacks by AFDL forces. Local militias joined the fray, some fighting alongside the AFDL, some against it. As one town after another fell into rebel hands, it was as if the putrid body of Zaire itself, not just Mobutu, was being consumed by cancer.

Returning briefly to Zaire in December, Mobutu tried to organise a counter-offensive. Despite his illness, on the twenty-mile journey from Kinshasa's airport to Camp Tsha Tshi, the headquarters of his elite *Division Spéciale Présidentielle* (DSP), he managed to stand upright in his open-roofed limousine, holding aloft his presidential cane, waving to crowds who had gathered along the way to welcome him, anxious like him about what the rebellion in the east meant for their future.

But Mobutu's army was as sick as he was. Despite years of effort by the United States, France and Belgium to train and equip a professional corps capable of holding the country together, the FAZ was rotten to the core, top-heavy with officers – fifty generals and 600 colonels – chosen not for competence but for their loyalty to Mobutu and interested above all in the business opportunities available to them. The rank and file were mostly a rabble, poorly trained and often unpaid, used to preying on the civilian population. Twice in recent years – in 1991 and 1993 – mutinous troops had gone on the rampage, inflicting massive damage on shops, factories and homes. Elite units, like the DSP, commanded by Mobutu's cousin, General Nzimba Ngbale, were well-equipped and rewarded with high pay, but showed no inclination to move out of Kinshasa.

Desperate to shore up Mobutu's war effort, but unable to intervene directly, the French intelligence service organised the recruitment of 300 white mercenaries, notably psychopathic Serbs fresh from the killing fields of Bosnia. The French foreign minister Hervé de Charette still claimed that Mobutu was 'undoubtedly the only person capable of contributing to the solution of the problem'. But the mercenary venture made little difference to the wholesale retreat of Mobutu's army.

One province after another joined the rebellion. Not only were Rwanda and Uganda involved in the campaign but Angola too, long resentful of Mobutu's support for the Angolan rebel leader Jonas Savimbi and his Unita movement, decided the time was right to strike back, committing both Katangese auxiliaries in its army and regular troops to help oust Mobutu and eliminate Unita fighters using Zaire as a rear base at the same time. Foreign mining companies, hoping to gain lucrative concessions from a new regime, also gambled large sums on supporting Kabila. In March 1997 Kisangani fell to the AFDL; in April, Mbuji Mayi, the diamond capital, and Lubumbashi, the copper capital, fell. As Mobutu's FAZ retreated to Kinshasa, only Unita rebels and Rwandan *Interahamwe* kept up the fight.

Facing inevitable defeat, Mobutu clung on in Kinshasa, growing increasingly frail but refusing to leave. 'When you are a soldier,' he declared, 'either you surrender or you are killed. But you don't flee.'

As a final refuge he chose to live in a modest grey villa on a hill in Camp Tsha Tshi, with views looking over the river, surrounded by his elite tribal guard, the DSP. On 29 April American negotiators met him there, bearing a letter from President Clinton, trying to persuade him to leave 'with honour and dignity' and spare the capital the orgy of looting and destruction that seemed likely to accompany his downfall. 'It was a very stark presentation,' the US ambassador, Daniel Simpson, later recalled in an interview with the journalist Michela Wrong. 'This was a guy who has worked with the US since the 1950s and he was being told: "You'll be dragged through the streets. These things could happen to you and we are not going to stop them." '

Mobutu still refused to leave but eventually agreed to a meeting with Kabila. After interminable wrangling about the venue, they met on 4 May on a South African navy ship, the *Outeniqua*, moored in Pointe Noire. A special ramp had to be built to enable Mobutu to be driven aboard in his limousine. Posing for an official photo session, Mobutu looked haggard, Kabila beamed. But nothing came of the encounter. A second meeting was arranged on the *Outeniqua* for 14 May. But while Mobutu made the laborious journey to Pointe Noire, Kabila did not bother to turn up.

The following day Mobutu fled with his family to Gbadolite, leaving behind an army of 10,000 elite troops on the brink of collapse. He soon found, however, that Gbadolite no longer provided a refuge. His own troops there were on the verge of mutiny. Exhausted and bewildered, he escaped on board an Ilyushin cargo plane owned by Jonas Savimbi, with bullets ripping into the fuselage as it took off.

Eight months after the rebellion first flared up in South Kivu, Kabila's *kadogo* army walked into Kinshasa. As Mobutu's clique and thousands of DSP soldiers fled across the river to Brazzaville, loaded down with possessions, a city of 6 million people was captured in less than twenty-four hours. In Kigali, Paul Kagame, the mastermind of the campaign, finally admitted his involvement. 'Everywhere it was our forces, our troops,' he said. 'They've been walking for the last eight months.'

On 17 May 1997 Kabila was sworn in as president, renaming the country the Democratic Republic of Congo. Four months later

Mobutu died in exile in Morocco, bitter and resentful at what he considered to be betrayal by his generals. 'It was very, very difficult,' his son, Nzanga told Michela Wrong. 'He began thinking about all the people he trusted who had abandoned him. And seeing the country he'd fought for all his life ending up in such a mess hurt him.'

Soon after Kabila was sworn in, Yoweri Museveni, now considered the regional power-broker, remarked: 'The big mistake of Mobutu was to involve himself in Rwanda. So it's really Mobutu who initiated the programme of his own removal. Had he not involved himself in Rwanda, I think he could have stayed, just like that, as he had been doing for the last thirty-two years – just do nothing to develop Zaire, but stay in what they call power, by controlling the radio station, and so on.'

At his inauguration in May 1997, Kabila was widely hailed as representing a 'new breed' of reform-minded African leader. Such was the relief that Mobutu had finally gone that some saw him as the saviour of central Africa. Museveni proclaimed that the war had 'liberated not only the Congo but all of Africa'. Nelson Mandela joined in the tributes. Kabila himself spoke of how his 'revolution' was an integral part of 'changing the face of Africa'. He portrayed himself as the true successor to Patrice Lumumba, a leader in the Pan-Africanist tradition dedicated to the task of bringing freedom to the Congolese people. 'My long years of struggle were like spreading fertiliser on a field,' he said. 'But now it is time to harvest.'

In reality, Kabila was no more than a petty tyrant propelled to prominence by accident. Secretive and paranoid, he had no political programme, no strategic vision and no experience of running a government. He refused to engage with established opposition groups or with civic organisations and banned political parties. Lacking a political organisation of his own, he surrounded himself with friends and family members and relied heavily for support and protection on Rwanda and Banyamulenge. Two key ministries were awarded to cousins; the new chief of staff of the army, James Kabarebe, was a Rwandan Tutsi who had grown up in Uganda; the deputy chief of staff and commander of land forces was his 26-year-old son, Joseph;

the national police chief was a brother-in-law. Whereas Mobutu had
packed his administration with supporters from his home province of
Équateur, Kabila handed out key positions in government, the armed
forces, security services and public companies to fellow Swahili-speak-
ing Katangese, notably members of the Lubakat group of northern
Katanga, his father's tribe.

Like Mobutu, he used his intelligence apparatus as a means of
political control. Military courts were set up to try civilians accused of
violating his restrictions on political activity. The veteran Kasai politician Etienne Tshisekedi was once more arrested and sent into internal
exile. Others thrown into detention included journalists and editors.
Emulating Mobutu, Kabila even attempted to start a personality cult,
hiring one of Mobutu's chief propagandists for the task.

His relations with Rwanda and the Banyamulenge, however, soon
soured. There was considerable public resentment about the number
of 'Rwandans' within Kabila's close circle of advisers and the presence
of Rwandan troops on the streets of Kinshasa. Congolese hated the
idea of being controlled by Rwanda – 'a country so small you can't
find it on the map'. Hoping to enhance his own popularity and to
prove that he was no Rwandan 'puppet', Kabila began to distance
himself from the Rwandans and to play on anti-Tutsi sentiment.
While promising to grant full citizenship rights to the Banyamulenge
population, he took no action.

In Kigali, Kagame became increasingly disenchanted with his protégé. Despite the change of regime in Kinshasa, *Interahamwe* and
ex-FAR militias continued to use Congo as a base from which to
launch attacks on Rwanda. In Kampala, Museveni had similar complaints: anti-Museveni groups continued to raid Uganda from eastern
Congo. As Kabila sought to assert his independence, Kagame and
Museveni began to plan for another regime change.

Fearing a coup attempt, Kabila decided to recruit *Interahamwe* and
ex-FAR militias – *génocidaires* – to support him. In July 1998 he dismissed the army chief-of-staff, Kabarebe, and all other Rwandan
soldiers and ordered them to return home. A coup attempt failed, but
within days a new rebellion was launched from Kivu to bring Kabila
down.

The rebellion was started in the name of a Congolese group called the *Rassemblement Congolais pour la Démocratie* (RCD). The RCD's leader, ostensibly, was a history professor, Ernest Wamba dia Wamba, previously based in Dar es Salaam. Its military chiefs included Congolese defectors from Kabila's army. Involved in the rebellion were a hotchpotch of former Mobutu politicians and army officers; Congolese Tutsis; Banyamulenge; and former AFDL leaders who had participated in the first rebellion but had since been squeezed out of Kabila's inner circle. But, as with the first rebellion, the driving force was the Rwandan army.

After early successes in Kivu in August 1998, Rwandan commanders organised an audacious airlift of troops from Goma in the east to a military base at Kitona, west of Kinshasa, where thousands of soldiers from Kabila's *Forces Armée Congolaises* (FAC) deserted him and joined the rebellion. A joint force of Rwandan and Congolese troops moved up the main road to Kinshasa, cutting it off from the port of Matadi and seizing control of the Inga hydro-electric plant which supplied power to Kinshasa and much of the rest of Congo. The rebel advance precipitated a wave of attacks on Tutsis living in Kinshasa which Kabila openly encouraged. In an echo of broadcasts once made by Rwanda's *génocidaires*, Congo's state radio urged listeners to use 'a machete, a spear, an arrow, a hoe, spades, rakes, nails, truncheons, electric irons, barbed wire . . . to kill the Rwandan Tutsi'. Thousands of Banyamulenge were killed in pogroms in Kinshasa and Lubumbashi.

What saved Kabila from defeat was massive intervention by Angola and Zimbabwe. Angola's principal concern was to prevent a vacuum in Congo that would allow Unita forces using rear bases there to renew their offensive in Angola. Angola's president, Eduardo dos Santos, also saw an opportunity to play the role of kingmaker and to decide who should rule in Kinshasa. Zimbabwe had no strategic interest in Congo, but like Dos Santos, its president, Robert Mugabe, aspired to become a regional power-broker and also planned to pick up lucrative concessions in Congo. Other African governments entered the fray. Burundi's Tutsi government joined Rwanda and Uganda, aiming to secure its borders against Hutu rebel groups using eastern Congo as a base from which to attack targets in Burundi. Namibia and Chad decided to link up with Angola and Zimbabwe.

Angola's intervention was decisive. Armoured units, striking from behind the rebel front in the west, retook the Kitona base and secured Kinshasa. But simultaneously the rebels captured Kisangani, capital of Orientale province and an important diamond-trading centre. By the end of August Congo was split in half, with Angola and Zimbabwe propping up Kabila in Kinshasa and Rwanda and Uganda in control of the north-east. Zimbabwean troops were hastily despatched to the diamond capital of Mbuji-Mayi to prevent it falling into rebel hands.

Like vultures picking over a carcass, all sides engaged in a scramble for the spoils of war. The Congo imbroglio became not only self-financing but highly profitable for the elite groups of army officers, politicians and businessmen exploiting it. Dependent on Angola and Zimbabwe for survival, Kabila readily handed them contracts and concessions. Angola gained control of Congo's petroleum distribution and production. Angolan generals also grabbed a slice of its diamond business. Zimbabwe established joint ventures in diamonds, gold and timber and was awarded a stake in the state mining company, Gécamines, together with a management contract. A United Nations Panel of Inquiry estimated that over a three-year period $5 billion of assets were transferred from the state mining sector to private companies without payment.

For their part, Rwanda and Uganda, having failed to dislodge Kabila from Kinshasa, turned eastern Congo into their own fiefdom, plundering it for gold, diamonds, timber, coltan, coffee, cattle, cars and other valuable goods. The volume of trade and loot grew in leaps and bounds, becoming the principal reason for them to continue their occupation. Each established separate zones of control and set up Congolese militias as partners in the enterprise.

Rwanda organised its exploitation of eastern Congo through the 'Congo Desk' of the Rwandan Patriotic Army (RPA). The Congo Desk specialised in particular in gaining a grip over the trade in coltan – a tantalum ore used by high-technology industries, notably mobile phone manufacturers. The UN Panel estimated that as much as 70 per cent of coltan production in eastern Congo was mined under the direct surveillance of RPA mining *détachés* and shipped out from airstrips near mining sites. Forced labour was used both for mining and transporting coltan. Another 20 per cent was purchased by *comptoirs* owned by Rwandans, some of them serving army officers, who bought coltan from local *négotiants* at remote coltan sites. The rest was left to Congolese traders. An expatriate *comptoir* owner in Goma complained to a researcher: 'The US *comptoir* is protected by Rwandans, the Egyptian one is associated with Rwandans, and the German one has Rwandans employed there. You can say the same for all of them! . . . The Tutsi in the Masisi are exploiting the stuff there and shipping it straight to Rwanda through their brokers in Goma on to Rwanda. This part of the Congo is just being treated like a Rwandan company!'

The trade in coltan was highly profitable, especially during 2000 when world prices soared from $30 to $240 per pound, triggering a bout of coltan fever. The UN Panel estimated that in an eighteen-month period from 1999 to 2000 Rwanda earned $250 million from Congo's coltan. The Panel commented:

> Here lies the vicious cycle of war. Coltan has permitted the Rwandan army to sustain its presence in the Democratic Republic of the Congo. The army has provided protection and security to the individuals and companies extracting the mineral. These have made money which is shared with the army, which in turn contin-ues to provide the enabling environment to continue the exploitation.

While the Rwandan government exercised direct control over its fief-dom in eastern Congo, Uganda allowed high-ranking army officers a free rein to make private fortunes. Among the key players were mem-bers of Museveni's family, notably his brother, General Salim Saleh. The Ugandan army was used to enforce their business empire and facilitate trade. Aircraft arrived from military airfields in Uganda with consumer goods, foodstuffs and arms and departed with diamonds, gold and coltan in highly profitable ventures. Congo gold became a major Ugandan export. Ugandan officers also trained and equipped

Congolese militias to act on their behalf and set up rebel 'administrations' in towns such as Bunia, Beni and Butembo as a front to collect taxes and other revenues which they then expropriated. The UN Panel concluded:

> The success of the network's activities in the Democratic Republic of the Congo relies on three interconnected features, namely: military intimidation; maintenance of a public sector façade, in the form of a rebel movement administration; and manipulation of the money supply and the banking sector, using counterfeit currency and other related mechanisms.

While this plunder was underway, eastern Congo slid ever deeper into turmoil. The RCD, set up by Rwanda in August 1998 as a front for overthrowing Kabila, splintered into rival factions, some backed by Rwanda, some by Uganda. The entire region became a battleground for competing armies and militias, looting, raping and killing at will. The civil wars that had torn Rwanda and Burundi apart were fought relentlessly on Congolese territory. *Interahamwe* and ex-FAR militias formed a new *Armée de Libération du Rwanda* (Alir) to fight the RPA, helped by Zimbabwe. The Rwandan army based in Congo and its RCD allies retaliated with coercion, torture and massacres. Hutu rebel groups were trained by Zimbabwe troops in Katanga to attack Burundi from bases in Kivu. Burundi rebels served as mercenaries in Kabila's army, along with large contingents of *Interahamwe* and ex-FAR soldiers, to help defend strategic towns like Mbuji-Mayi and Lubumbashi. Banyamulenge fighters split into separate factions, some opposing Rwanda's occupation. Local *Mayi Mayi* militias were embroiled in mini-wars, some fighting against the Rwandans and their Congolese allies, others against the *Interahamwe*.

In Orientale province, rival militias armed by Uganda clashed repeatedly over control of gold, diamonds and coltan sites. A savage tribal war broke out in the Ituri region between Hema pastoralists and Lendu agriculturalists – two groups that harboured long-standing grievances over land rights but both now armed by Uganda for its own purposes. Another Ugandan-backed group, *Mouvement pour la*

Libération du Congo, led by Jean-Pierre Bemba, a millionaire business-man with Mobutu connections, opened up a new front in Équateur province, establishing headquarters in Gbadolite and gaining control of the north.

The scramble for Congo's riches reached a climax in May and June 2000 when Rwanda and Uganda on three occasions fought for control of Kisangani and its lucrative diamond trade. The fighting, so far from their borders, blew apart the pretence both had tried to maintain that their presence in eastern Congo was necessary to protect themselves from rebels based there. Rwanda, once seen by the international community as a victim, now looked more like a predator. Museveni, once hailed as representing a 'new breed' of disciplined African leader, turned out to be just another old-fashioned plunderer.

Outraged by their ill-concealed looting enterprises and the damage they inflicted on Kisangani, the UN Security Council demanded that Rwanda and Uganda withdraw from Congo forthwith. It also ordered an investigation into what it termed the 'illegal exploitation' of Congo's wealth. Both Museveni and Kagame were subsequently cited as 'accomplices' by the UN Panel. Human rights groups campaigned against the trade in coltan using the slogan, 'No blood on my satellite'.

All efforts at negotiations failed, mainly because Kabila obstructed progress. Rather than share power, he preferred to share the country. On 16 January 2001, however, Kabila was shot at close range in his palace by a young member of his bodyguard. The assassin fled the scene but was caught and executed on the spot by Colonel Eddy Kapend, Kabila's cousin, a widely feared figure who acted as the president's chief of staff. Kapend was subsequently convicted of playing the lead role in a palace coup attempt, killing the assassin to silence him.

Unable to agree a successor among themselves, Kabila's cronies settled for his 30-year-old son, Joseph, a shy, unassuming and quietly-spoken man, quite unlike his father, who had been serving as the army chief-of-staff. A political novice with no power base, Joseph Kabila seemed destined to become a mere figurehead for the corrupt 'god-fathers' around him, easy for them to manipulate. But he proved

unexpectedly decisive, lifting the ban on political parties and supporting an 'inter-Congolese dialogue' that his father had persistently
thwarted.

After a series of tortuous negotiations, a peace deal was signed in
July 2002, paving the way for the establishment of an interim coalition
government headed by Kabila and including representatives from the
main Congolese factions. Foreign armies from Rwanda, Burundi,
Uganda, Angola and Zimbabwe were required to withdraw. In four
years of civil war more than 3 million people had died, mostly from
starvation and disease, the largest toll of any conflict in African history.
But in eastern Congo there was to be no respite from violence. Rival
militias, some acting as proxy forces for sponsors in Rwanda and
Uganda and Kinshasa, others controlled by local warlords, continued
their wars of plunder, bringing yet more years of misery to a population desperate for peace. In the words of a KiSwahili proverb, often
cited in Kivu, 'Nyama tembo kula hawezi kumaliza' – 'You never finish
eating the meat of an elephant'.

BLOOD DIAMONDS

In his book *Journey Without Maps*, an account of his travels in Liberia in the 1930s, the English writer Graham Greene recorded that 'Liberian politics were like a crap game played with loaded dice'. It was a game that Liberia's ruling elite – the descendants of some 300 black settler families from the United States who set up an independent republic in 1847 – played among themselves with considerable relish. For more than 100 years – from 1877 to 1980 – Liberia was governed under a one-party system in which the same party, the True Whig Party, controlled by the same elite group, held office continuously, dispensing patronage, deciding on public appointments and retaining a monopoly on power – a record equalled by no other political party anywhere in the world. Elections were nevertheless taken seriously, if only to determine which family – the Barclays, the Kings, the Tubmans – emerged on top. 'The curious thing about a Liberian election campaign,' wrote Greene, 'is that, although the result is always a foregone conclusion, everyone behaves as if the votes and the speeches and the pamphlets matter.' However, he added, the system was more complicated than it seemed. 'It may be all a question of cash and printing presses and armed police, but things have to be done with an air. Crudity as far as possible is avoided.'

As members of a ruling aristocracy, the Americo-Liberians, as they called themselves, were immensely proud of their American heritage. They developed a lifestyle reminiscent of the antebellum South, complete with top hats and morning coats and masonic lodges. They built houses with pillared porches, gabled roofs and dormer windows resembling the nineteenth-century architectural styles of Georgia, Maryland and the Carolinas. They chose as a national flag a replica of the American Stars and Stripes, with a single star, and used the American dollar as legal tender.

Just like white settlers in Africa, the Americo-Liberians constructed a colonial system subjugating the indigenous population to rigid control and concentrating wealth and privilege in their own hands. Despite their origins as descendants of slaves from the Deep South, they regarded black Liberians as an inferior race, fit only for exploitation. The nadir of Americo-Liberian rule came in 1931 when an international commission found senior government officials guilty of involvement in organised slavery.

When other West African states shed colonial rule in the 1960s, the Liberian system stayed much the same. Liberian law stipulated that only property owners were entitled to the vote, so the vast majority of indigenous Africans were effectively left without one. Small numbers were assimilated into the ranks of the ruling elite: 'country boys' adopted by coastal families; girls selected as wives or concubines; ambitious 'hinterlanders' climbing the ladder. During the 1970s a few were co-opted into government. Local administration in the 'hinterland' was largely run by indigenous officials. But essentially Liberia remained an oligarchy where 1 per cent of the population controlled the rest – some 2 million people.

The last of the line of Americo-Liberian presidents was William Tolbert, the grandson of freed South Carolina slaves who had served as vice-president for twenty years. A Baptist minister, he attempted a series of cautious reforms, abandoning the top hat and tail-coat traditions favoured by his predecessor, William Tubman, selling the presidential yacht and abolishing a compulsory 'tithe' of 10 per cent of every government employee's salary that went to the True Whig Party. But much of Tolbert's efforts were also devoted to amassing a personal fortune and promoting the interests of family members in the traditional manner. One brother was appointed minister of finance; another was chosen as president of the senate; a son-in-law served as minister of defence; other relatives filled posts as ministers, ambassadors and presidential aides. The crap game of Liberian politics was as highly profitable in the 1970s as in the 1930s.

Economic development in the 1960s and 1970s helped underpin the system, as well as provide new opportunities for the elite's self-enrichment. The mainstay of the economy had initially been rubber. In 1926 the Firestone Tyre and Rubber Company leased a million acres for ninety-nine years at six cents an acre to meet the American demand for car tyres. But iron ore exports from massive, high-grade deposits in the Bomi hills then overtook rubber as the major source of foreign investment and government income. By 1970 Firestone and the Liberian Iron Mining Company were providing the government with 50 per cent of greatly increased revenues. A third source of income came from registration fees from the world's largest ghost fleet of ships: Liberia possessed only two ships of its own, but allowed more than 2,500 vessels plying the seas to fly Liberia's flag of convenience without the bother of inspection, for a suitable fee.

Liberia's economic advances, however, served only to highlight the growing disparity between the ostentatious lifestyle of the rich elite and the overwhelming majority of impoverished tribal Africans. In 1979 – the same year that Tolbert spent an amount equivalent to half the national budget while acting as host to an OAU heads of state conference – demonstrators took to the streets in protest against a 50 per cent increase in the price of rice, the staple food of most Liberians. The price increase had been authorised by Tolbert in the hope of encouraging local production. But since one of the chief beneficiaries was the president's cousin, Daniel Tolbert, who owned the country's largest rice-importing firm, it was seen as another move to enrich the elite. On Tolbert's orders armed police and troops opened fire on the demonstrators, killing dozens of them.

In the following months Tolbert struggled to contain a rising tide of discontent, colliding not just with the poor but with a new generation of the educated elite. He allowed the formation of an opposition party, but when opposition politicians called for a general strike, he had them arrested on charges of treason and sedition and banned the party.

On the night of 12 April 1980 a group of seventeen dissident soldiers led by a 28-year-old master sergeant named Samuel Doe, scaled the iron gate of the president's seven-storey Executive Mansion, overpowered the guards and found Tolbert in his pyjamas in an upstairs bedroom. They fired three bullets into his head, gouged out his right eye and disembowelled him. His body was dumped in a mass grave along with twenty-seven others who died defending the palace. Ministers and officials were rounded up, taken before a military tribunal and sentenced to death.

Amid much jubilation, watched by a crowd of thousands laughing and jeering and filmed by camera crews, thirteen high-ranking officials were tied to telephone poles on a beach in Monrovia and executed by a squad of drunken soldiers, firing volley after volley at them. A great shout arose from the mob. 'Freedom! We got our freedom at last!' The soldiers rushed forward to kick and pummel the corpses.

Thus the old order ended.

At his first press conference, Sergeant Doe strode into the ballroom of the Executive Mansion wearing a wide-brimmed army ranger hat, crisply pressed fatigues and combat boots. He carried a ceremonial sword, a Magnum revolver and a walkie-talkie radio. In faltering English he read a prepared statement, handled two brief questions and then sat down.

Sergeant Doe was then the youngest and lowest-ranking soldier to seize power in Africa. He was what Americo-Liberians called a 'country boy', a semi-literate tribesman with only basic education and limited intelligence. His tribe, the Krahn, coming from a thickly forested border area in the south-east adjacent to Côte d'Ivoire, were the last to enter the modern sector and stood at the bottom of Liberia's social hierarchy, scorned as backward and uncouth by others. They were, one writer noted, 'the one-at-a-time cigarette sellers, prostitutes and enlisted men'.

What inspired Doe and his group of fellow conspirators to storm the Executive Mansion was not a plan for revolution but simply grievances over poor living conditions in army barracks. They possessed no political objectives, no policy ambitions, no guiding ideology, other than to set themselves up in power. Like other coup leaders, Doe made grand promises about liberating the masses from corruption and oppression, about establishing a more equitable distribution of wealth, about restoring the country to civilian rule. But his first actions as head of the 'People's Redemption Council' was to suspend the constitution, to ban all political activity and to declare martial law. Other than award immediate pay rises for the military, he made few changes. The old America-Liberian business networks remained largely in place. Despite frequent promises about handing back power, Doe continued to rule by decree year after year. 'Same taxi, different driver,' was the verdict on the streets of Monrovia.

Doe's military dictatorship was not noticeably more brutal than many others in Africa. Growing in ambition, he soon fell out with his original colleagues; more than fifty rivals, mostly soldiers, were executed after secret trials. Scores of civilians – student leaders, journalists, opposition figures – were thrown into detention for daring to criticise his regime. Independent newspapers were shut down. Academics had to contend with Decree 2A which banned all academic activities that 'directly or indirectly impinge, interfere with or cast aspersion upon the activities, programs or policies of the People's Redemption Council'. Academics who caused displeasure were flogged.

Bloated with power, Doe changed from being a scrawny sergeant in battle fatigues to a fat-faced general dressed in immaculate suits with a fashionable Afro hairstyle. He believed that he was protected by supernatural powers, and many Liberians believed this too. A leading Liberian writer, Bill Frank Enoanyi, wrote:

Samuel Doe was widely credited with the power not only to be impervious to bullets, but also of disappearing in the face of danger, including plane crashes. He had a coterie of juju men from all over Africa, notably Togo. And some of the rituals he was rumoured to be practising in order to maintain the potency of his powers included drinking the blood and/or eating the fetuses of pregnant

young girls. Once in a while he himself would boast publicly that
no gun had yet been made that could kill him. And the people
believed it.

In ten years in power, Doe claimed to have survived no fewer than
thirty-eight coup or assassination attempts.

Like other dictators, Doe soon found a way to loot state corporations – the Liberian Petroleum Refining Corporation; the Liberian
Produce Marketing Corporation; the Forestry Development
Authority responsible for collecting logging fees. The fortune he
amassed for himself and his cronies during the 1980s was estimated at
$300 million.

But what proved to be disastrous about Doe's regime was the way
in which he promoted his own tribal group, the Krahn. One of the
smallest of Liberia's sixteen tribes, numbering no more than 4 per cent
of the population, Krahn were given key positions in the military and
security apparatus; they also filled the ranks of Doe's elite military unit,
the Executive Mansion Guard, effectively his private militia and personal bodyguard. The dominant role played by the Krahn, particularly
in suppressing dissent, provoked tribal animosities that had long lain
dormant. The eventual consequence was civil war. It was a war that
was not confined to Liberia but spread into neighbouring countries,
engulfing the whole region in conflict.

What was remarkable about Doe's career as a tyrant was the support
he enjoyed from the United States government. American interests in
Liberia were substantial. Liberia was used as a transmission station for
Voice of America broadcasts throughout Africa and a base for the
Omega navigation system for shipping up and down the Atlantic
coast. The American embassy in Monrovia served as a major transfer
point for intelligence gathered in Africa. US military planes had
landing and refuelling rights at Robertsfield, an airfield built by the
Americans as a staging ground during the Second World War. In the
Cold War era all these were considered significant assets.

The Americans took the view that it was worth cultivating Doe in
order to coax him into restoring civilian rule. Doe had received military training in the US from the Green Berets. It was thought that,

with sufficient inducement, he would be pliable enough. The US ambassador, William L. Swing, tutored Doe in the art of statecraft, reporting him to be a good student and referring to him as an 'endearing boy'. A satellite dish was installed on the roof of Doe's mansion so he could watch the speeches of Ronald Reagan, whom he professed to admire deeply. Coached by the Americans, he adopted a strident anti-Soviet line. By 1982 Doe was considered respectable enough to merit a visit to the White House. American aid was increased from $10 million to $80 million a year. Between 1980 and 1985, it accounted for nearly one-third of Liberia's national budget. A sum of $40 million was spent on the construction of military housing. It was seen as part of an 'implicit bargain', in the words of one US official, 'that the military would let go if its needs were looked after'.

Under American pressure, Doe agreed in July 1984 to lift the ban on political activity and to prepare for elections. But despite promises to retire, he also announced that he intended to stand for election as president and he continued to rule in as arbitrary fashion as before, smashing the opposition at every chance. In August 1984 he arrested a popular university professor, Amos Sawyer, and fifteen others, claiming they were plotting a coup. When students protested, Doe sent a detachment of 200 soldiers from the Executive Mansion Guard on to the campus. The soldiers opened fire indiscriminately, stripped students naked, flogged them with rattans, beat them with rifle butts, extorted money from them and raped female students. More than fifty students were killed. Before leaving, the soldiers looted and vandalised campus facilities, causing an estimated $2 million of damage. Doe then fired the entire university administration and teaching staff. Sawyer and his associates were never charged and no details of their alleged plot were ever made public. After two months' detention in a military barracks, they were 'pardoned' and released.

The election campaign degenerated into a crude farce. Doe banned the two most popular opposition parties on the grounds that they advocated 'socialism'. Then he issued Decree 88A, making it a criminal offence to 'create disharmony, spread rumours, lies and disinformation', effectively outlawing criticism of the government. Then he shut down the *Daily Observer*, the most popular independent newspaper. Then he imprisoned key opposition leaders, including Amos Sawyer and Ellen Johnson-Sirleaf, an articulate Harvard-trained economist, who, in a speech delivered in the United States, had assailed 'the many idiots in whose hands our nation's fate and progress have been placed'.

The arrest of Johnson-Sirleaf finally prompted the Reagan administration to take action. Amid a storm of protest, the Americans suspended $25 million in aid to Liberia, demanding the release of Johnson-Sirleaf and other political prisoners. Doe duly released the prisoners and collected $25 million in return. But then he went on to rig the election.

Despite widespread intimidation, massive numbers turned out for the election on 15 October 1985. It was the first election in Liberia based on universal suffrage. Nearly 750,000 voters – one-third of the entire population – participated, many walking for miles to polling stations and waiting for hours in sweltering tropical heat to cast their vote. When preliminary vote counts showed that Doe had decisively lost the presidential election, his election officials suspended the legal vote-counting process and appointed an illegal hand-picked re-count committee stacked with Doe's partisans, many of them Krahn. Thousands of burnt ballots were discovered on a bonfire site outside Monrovia and photographed by the local press. After two weeks sequestered in a Monrovia hotel, Doe's re-count committee announced on 29 October that he had won the election with 50.9 per cent of the vote. A report for the Lawyers Committee for Human Rights, based in New York, described the result as 'one of the most brazen electoral frauds in recent African history'. Monrovia that day was silent and empty.

It was a sign of how pusillanimous the United States government had become in dealing with African dictators it favoured; that while the election was rejected in almost all quarters as fraudulent, US officials alone applauded it as 'generally fair although marked by a few irregularities'. Questioned by the US Senate Committee on Foreign Relations, Chester Crocker, Reagan's senior policy-maker on Africa, praised what he called 'noteworthy positive aspects' about the election. He went on:

There is now the beginning, however imperfect, of a democratic experience that Liberia and its friends can use as a benchmark for future elections – one on which they want to build . . . The prospects for national reconciliation were brightened by Doe's claim that he won only a narrow 51 per cent election victory – virtually unheard of in the rest of Africa where incumbent rulers normally claim victories of 95 per cent to 100 per cent. In claiming only 51 per cent Doe publicly acknowledged that a large segment of society – 49 per cent – supported other points of view and leadership than his own.

But far from marking 'the beginning of a democratic experience', the election marked the beginning of a descent into hell.

One month after the election, on 12 November 1985, an attempted coup to overthrow Doe was launched by his former army commander, Thomas Quiwonkpa, a leading member of the group that had seized power in 1980 who had subsequently fallen out with him and gone into exile. Crossing into Liberia from neighbouring Sierra Leone, Quiwonkpa's insurgents reached Monrovia, seized the main military barracks and the government's radio station and broadcast a recorded message promising free elections. As news of the coup spread, crowds celebrated on the streets of Monrovia, tearing down Doe's billboards along highways and at street junctions. 'The intensity of collective hatred against a regime beats anything I have seen in Nigeria and Ghana,' a Nigerian journalist, Tunde Agbabiaka, reported in an eyewitness account published in the journal *West Africa*.

The celebrations, however, were premature. With the help of the Executive Mansion Guard and other army units, Doe regained control. 'It was as if the nation had been thrown into mourning,' wrote Agbabiaka. 'Many of those who had openly rejoiced . . . now resigned themselves to certain death.'

Quiwonkpa was found by Krahn soldiers hiding in a house outside Monrovia. His body, kicked and pummelled beyond recognition, was taken to the Barclay Training Centre, the main military barracks in downtown Monrovia, directly across the street from a large outdoor market packed with traders and shoppers. As hundreds looked on, his body was castrated, dismembered and eaten. Witnessing these events, Agbabiaka wrote:

> Quiwonkpa's body was chopped up into bits in a macabre canni-balistic ritual by some of Doe's soldiers who, astonishingly in these modern times, still believed that by eating bits of a great warrior's body, some of that greatness would come to them. The heart, of course, was the prize delicacy . . .

Hundreds were executed in revenge for the coup attempt. The main targets were members of Quiwonkpa's Gio tribe from Nimba County. In Monrovia, Krahn soldiers rounded up hundreds of Gio and Mano soldiers and civilians and took them to the grounds of the Executive Mansion and Barclay barracks where they were killed. A soldier who was detained at the Executive Mansion told Bill Berkeley from the Lawyers Committee for Human Rights:

> There were dead bodies all around. The soldiers were in a jovial mood, as if they were conquering heroes, as if they had just won a war. They were openly smoking marijuana, openly drinking. They had bottles of gin. The thing was out of control. The commander had lost control.
>
>   It became like a tribal war. Most of the soldiers were Krahn people. If you were anything else but Krahn or Loma then you had a problem.

Hundreds more Gio were killed in Nimba County and in Grand Gedeh County, Doe's home region, sowing the seeds of a cycle of tribal revenge. A Gio scholar from Nimba County who was detained for two weeks and flogged by Krahn soldiers told Berkeley: 'I'm afraid that if they allow this man [Doe] to be killed, it will be recorded in history that there was once a tribe called Krahn in Liberia.' Talk of revenge was commonplace, a prospect acknowledged among Krahn as well as their rivals. A Krahn farmer in Zle Town confided to Berkeley:

We are in fact living in fear. We know that when power changes hands, everyone will suffer. Whatever happens the way Africans carry out politics, they will not make an exception for us. What I think is that, if there is an eventuality, if you know what I mean, there will have to be revenge. The situation in the country is very grave. We know that something will happen to us. We know that nothing lasts forever. We've got the feeling that something is in the making. When that thing explodes, then God have mercy on us all.

Despite the atrocities, the stolen election, the corruption, US backing for Doe continued as before, lending him a spurious legitimacy. Doe suited American interests. 'We were getting fabulous support from him on international issues,' a senior US policymaker recalled in 1993. 'He never wavered [in] his support for us against Libya and Iran. He was somebody we had to live with. We didn't feel that he was such a monster that we couldn't deal with him. All our interests were impeccably protected by Doe. We weren't paying a penny for the US installations.' In testimony before congressional committees in January 1986, Chester Crocker painted a rosy picture of Liberia, flagrantly ignoring the realities of Doe's regime:

> There is in Liberia today a civilian government based on elections, a multi-party legislature, a journalist community of government and non-government newspapers and radio stations. An on-going tradition among the citizens of speaking out. A new constitution that protects those freedoms, and a judicial system that can help those provisions. The [Liberian] government is committed publicly to that system.

The economic reality, however, was harder to disguise. In Doe's first five years in power, Liberia's economy contracted by 3 per cent a year; domestic investment declined by 16 per cent; foreign debt soared to $1.3 billion. Long-established foreign investors began to wind down their operations. In their place Doe set up commercial deals with a range of dubious businessmen, handing out concessions to keep himself afloat. Attracted by the opportunities for money laundering, the number of banks in Monrovia increased from six to fourteen, even as the formal economy slumped.

In an attempt to sort out Liberia's chaotic finances, the US appointed a team of seventeen operational experts in 1987 to take over financial control of the ministry of finance, the central bank and other key government offices. The 'Opex' team identified numerous scams and the officials running them but their efforts to establish new controls were constantly thwarted and they decided to cut short their work. Doe's Liberia, they concluded in their final report in May 1989, 'was managed with far greater priority given to short-term political survival and deal-making than to any long-term recovery or nation-building efforts . . . The President's primary concern is for political and physical survival. His priorities are very different from and inconsistent with economic recovery . . . President Doe has great allegiance to his tribes people and his inner circle. His support of local groups on ill-designed projects undercut larger social objectives.'

With the failure of the Opex mission, the US, after spending $500 million to prop up Doe for a period of ten years, finally decided to give him no more. Bereft of US support, Doe was vulnerable to new predators.

On Christmas Eve in 1989 a band of 100 insurgents crossed the border into northern Liberia from Côte d'Ivoire. They were members of a newly formed group, the National Patriotic Front of Liberia (NPFL), headed by a Liberian exile, Charles Taylor. Taylor was a relatively obscure figure at the time, but he was to become West Africa's most notorious warlord. Born in 1948 in a small Americo-Liberian settlement outside Monrovia called Arlington, he was the son of a Baptist schoolteacher and circuit judge and a former servant girl from the Gola tribe from north-west Liberia. Like most children of the Americo-Liberian elite, after graduating from high school he was sent to the United States for further education; he earned a degree in economics from Bentley College in Boston and then moved to New Hampshire College for graduate studies. He spent nine years in America, gained a reputation for high living and played a prominent role in Liberian student politics there.

At the time of Doe's coup, Taylor happened to be on a visit to Monrovia. Through his wife's family connections to Thomas Quiwonkpa, one of the coup leaders, he was offered a job as director of the government's procurement agency, a lucrative post enabling him to amass a personal fortune by taking commissions on each contract he arranged. Along with Quiwonkpa, however, he fell out of favour. In 1983 he was accused of embezzling $900,000. He fled to the United States but was detained after Doe issued an arrest warrant and a request for his extradition. For sixteen months he languished in prison while lawyers fought his extradition, then escaped in 1985 by bribing guards, finding his way back to West Africa.

For more than a year Taylor drifted around West Africa, travelling to Ghana, Côte d'Ivoire, Burkina Faso and Sierra Leone, mixing with dissident groups plotting to overthrow Doe and trying to establish his own band of supporters. He found support from Libya, which was always looking for ways to undermine pro-American regimes, and helped organise military training there for a group of 160 Liberian dissidents.

After several false starts, Taylor was ready by late 1989 to launch his rebellion. He received vital assistance from two West African leaders. One was Côte d'Ivoire's Félix Houphouët-Boigny, an old ally of the Tolbert family who had personal reasons for detesting Doe's regime. Houphouët's adopted daughter, Daisy Delafosse, had married Tolbert's son Adolphus. At the time of Doe's coup, Adolphus had sought sanctuary in the French embassy. Daisy rushed to Abidjan pleading for Houphouët to intervene. Houphouët obtained an assurance from Doe that Adolphus would be spared, but he was nevertheless abducted and murdered. Taylor's other main regional supporter was Burkina Faso's military leader Blaise Compaoré, another member of Houphouët's extended family, linked to him by marriage, who had seized power in 1987 with the help of a squad of Liberian exiles. Compaoré provided Taylor with a training base and arms supplies and loaned him some regular soldiers. Taylor's force also included a number of dissidents from Sierra Leone, Nigeria, Ghana and The Gambia, all trained in guerrilla warfare by Libya.

The initial target of Taylor's rebellion was Nimba County, an area occupied by Gio and Mano tribesmen who had suffered terrible repression in the wake of Quiwonkpa's failed coup in 1985. Several key figures in Taylor's NPFL were Gio exiles with a local following. As Taylor had anticipated, Doe despatched a Krahn force to Nimba County to crush the rebels. Repeating its earlier performance, Doe's army unleashed a campaign of terror against the local population, killing, raping and looting at will, burning villages, driving tens of thousands of Gios and Manos from their homes. Doe also sent out Krahn death squads in Monrovia to eliminate prominent opposition figures.

The repression provided Taylor with an army of raw recruits, mainly illiterate teenagers and boys bent on revenge. 'As the NPFL came in,' Taylor recalled, 'we didn't even have to act. People came to us and said: "Give me a gun. How can I kill the man who killed my mother?"' Taylor gave them rudimentary training and sent them into battle with a promise of loot. Orphans were organised into 'Small Boys Units'. To add to their numbers, he opened up prisons in towns he captured, arming the inmates. Marauding gangs swept through the countryside, attacking the Krahn and seizing booty. Bolstered by cane spirit, marijuana and cheap amphetamines, youths and boy soldiers evolved into psychopathic killers, adorning themselves with women's wigs, dresses, fright masks and enemy bones and smearing their faces with white clay and make-up in the belief that this gave them supernatural protection. Many became addicted to the 'Kalashnikov lifestyle'. Taylor's practice of using child soldiers was later followed by other factions in the war. 'It's a children's war,' said a senior United Nations observer. 'Kids get promoted in rank for committing an atrocity. They can cut off someone's head without thinking. The troops move into a village. They take everything and kill and rape. They stay a couple of weeks and then move on.' Doe's forces acted with similar barbarity against the civilian population. Half of the entire population fled their homes.

By May 1990 Taylor's forces had reached the port of Buchanan, eighty miles south-east of Monrovia. They then moved up the coast towards the capital, capturing the Firestone estate and Robertsfield airport, using it to ferry in arms supplies from Burkina Faso. By June

Monrovia was under siege, from the east by Taylor's forces and from the west by a second rebel group led by Prince Johnson, a former army officer from Nimba County who had participated in Taylor's original invasion force but who had split with him shortly afterwards. The city had no power and no water supplies. Unable to escape, short of food, residents ate cats and dogs, then began to starve. The United States deployed a large marine amphibious force but only to evacuate American citizens and other foreign nationals sheltering in the embassy. 'A modest intervention at that point to end the fighting in Monrovia could have avoided the prolonged conflict,' the US assistant secretary of state, Herman Cohen, subsequently admitted. As Doe's ministers fled, Krahn soldiers took control, rampaging through the streets screaming 'No Doe. No Liberia' and looting and executing residents at will. In July they massacred 600 refugees sheltering in St Peter's Lutheran Church, mostly Gio and Mano women and children. The battle for the city swayed back and forth, leaving it in ruins. Amid the anarchy, Doe remained holed up in the Executive Mansion, refusing all pleas for him to go into exile. In between bouts of fighting, he whiled away the time playing draughts with his aides, watching old movies and chatting on a radio-telephone link to the BBC or his wife, Nancy, who had left for England where her children were at school.

In an attempt to halt the carnage, a group of West African states assembled a peacekeeping force intended to separate the combatants. The mastermind behind the plan was Nigeria's General Babangida, keen to assert Nigeria's role as a regional power. Babangida was also worried about the involvement of foreign dissidents in the NPLF, fearing that they could use Liberia as a base from which to launch other campaigns. 'Today it is Liberia,' Babangida told a summit meeting of West African leaders. 'Tomorrow it could be any one of the countries represented here.' Nigeria contributed the bulk of the force, known as Ecomog (Economic Community of West African States Monitoring Group). After a ceasefire had been arranged, an advance party of Ecomog troops arrived in Monrovia on 23 August and set up headquarters in the Freeport. The surrounding area was controlled by Johnson's fighters who often dropped in at the headquarters, unannounced and armed to the teeth, and held impromptu parties.

On 9 September General Doe decided to leave the safety of his Executive Mansion to pay a visit to Ecomog headquarters, accompanied by a bodyguard of seventy Krahn soldiers. Tipped off about Doe's movements, Prince Johnson's rebel group launched a raid on the port to capture him. After a prolonged gun battle, Doe, wounded in both legs, was caught and taken to a bungalow in the residential compound of a mining company in the suburb of Caldwell that Johnson used as his headquarters.

On Johnson's orders, a film was made of Doe's interrogation that later he proudly showed to journalists and that became a bestselling video throughout West Africa. Stripped down to his underpants, Doe stares up at his tormentors, his face bruised and bloody. A strand of protective amulets encircles his waist. 'I want to say something, if you will listen to me,' he says. 'You untie my hands and I will talk . . . I never ordered anybody's execution.' Johnson sits calmly behind a desk, drinking beer. 'Cut off one ear,' he says in a soft voice. Doe is held down flat. A knife slices through an ear. Doe screams. The film shows Johnson holding the ear high above his mouth and then chewing it. The other ear is sliced off. Doe is taken into the garden and questioned further. How much money had he stolen? What did he do with it? Doe refuses to say. The knife comes out again. Doe is told to repeat after his interrogator: 'I, Samuel Kanyon Doe, declare that the government is overthrown. I'm therefore asking the armed forces to surrender to Field Marshal Prince Johnson.'

The following day Doe's mutilated body was paraded through the streets in a wheelbarrow.

With Ecomog troops holding the ring in Monrovia, a new interim government of national unity was announced, headed by Amos Sawyer, the university professor imprisoned by Doe in 1985 who had subsequently gone into exile in the United States. But Sawyer's writ ran no further than parts of the capital. Determined to capture the presidency himself, Taylor refused to participate in the interim arrangements and fought on, attacking Ecomog positions in the eastern suburbs. Ecomog retaliated with air raids on Taylor's positions, joining

A member of the 'dinosaur' generation, Togo's dictator, Gnassingbé Eyedéma, held on to power for thirty-eight years until his death in 2005.

A giant portrait of President Hosni Mubarak hovers over a Cairo street. Through brute repression and the use of emergency laws, Mubarak managed for the most part to keep the lid on the activities of Islamist extremists.

An American soldier on patrol in Mogadishu in December 1992 as part of 'Operation Restore Hope'. The aim was to assist relief efforts for famine victims and to restore order to the streets of Mogadishu where Somali gunmen reigned using 'technicals' – vehicles converted for combat use. But the US involvement in Somalia was to end in disaster.

Land of a Thousand Hills: once renowned for its magical beauty, a highland country tucked away in the heart of Africa, Rwanda became the setting for Africa's worst genocide. In the space of a hundred days, some 800,000 people were killed – about three-quarters of the Tutsi population.

Facing defeat, Rwanda's *génocidaires* ordered the exodus of the Hutu population to neighbouring Zaire (Congo) to enable them to continue their campaign. In two days, about one million Hutu crossed the border. 'It was as though the whole country was emptying,' said an observer.

Desperate to find sanctuary, Tutsi families sought refuge in churches, but to no avail. They were slaughtered there en masse, sometimes with the cooperation of Hutu priests.

The return journey: released from the grip of the *génocidaires*, Hutu refugees trudge back to Rwanda from Zaire.

West Africa's most notorious warlord, Charles Taylor, won the election in Liberia in 1997 using as his campaign slogan: 'He killed my ma, he killed my pa, but I will vote for him.' Forced to step down amid civil war in 2003, he made his farewell speech dressed in a virginal white suit, drawing parallels between himself and Jesus Christ. 'I would be the sacrificial lamb,' he said. He went into comfortable retirement in Nigeria.

Shortly after seizing power in an Islamist coup in Sudan in 1989, General Omar al-Bashir pledged to purge the country of 'enemies' – 'Anyone who betrays the nation does not deserve the honour of living'. In his jihad against African tribes in the south he ordered ethnic cleansing costing hundreds of thousands of lives.

When rebels in Darfur launched a guerrilla war against his regime in 2003, Bashir used the same tactics of ethnic cleansing, arming Janjaweed militias to drive out the civilian population. More than a million refugees fled to neighbouring Chad.

The graduate: during the eleven years he spent in Ian Smith's prisons, Robert Mugabe collected three university degrees to add to the three he already possessed. As Zimbabwe's president, he boasted of a seventh degree – 'a degree in violence' – which he used ruthlessly to crush his opponents.

53

A moment of liberation experienced around the world: Nelson
Mandela walks free in 1990 after twenty-seven years' imprisonment
in the Cape, hand-in-hand with his wife, Winnie.

5

South Africa's election, 1994. In their millions, voters queued patiently for hour after hour,
determined to make the elections a success, and on leaving for home spoke of how their
dignity had been restored.

The world's last hero: Nelson Mandela rides with Queen Elizabeth in a carriage procession during a state visit to Britain in 1996.

Passing the baton: Nelson Mandela with his successor Thabo Mbeki, pictured in 2003.

Western leaders like Tony Blair and George Bush admired President Olusegun Obasanjo's commitment to democracy. But Nigeria, after squandering an oil bonanza of US$280 billion, remains in a pitiful state.

the war as yet another faction in it. Like other factions, Ecomog was heavily involved in looting, arms trading and contraband. Senior officers in Ecomog supplied various factions with weapons and other war matériel in return for looted goods. So notorious did its dealings in cars, consumer goods and scrap metal become that Liberians dubbed it as standing for 'Every Car Or Moving Object Gone'.

Thwarted in his bid to take the capital, Taylor established his own regime outside Monrovia in what became known as 'Greater Liberia', setting up a commercial empire there, trading in gold, diamonds, iron ore and timber. He quickly came to an accommodation with Firestone and arranged a string of deals with other foreign companies. A British firm paid Taylor $10 million a month for permission to ship out stockpiled iron ore through the deepwater port of Buchanan. France became Taylor's main customer for timber. Foreign firms were also required to help with the purchase of fuel oil and vehicles and pay for the costs of 'security force' protection. An American researcher, William Reno, calculated that during the first two years of the war, the total yield of Taylor's warlord economy reached $200 million a year. Added to this was the trade in looted goods – stolen cars, building materials, office equipment and street lighting. Taylor's brother, Nelson, netted $10 million in three months from gold and diamond mining in his own corner of south-west Liberia. Another brother made a fortune from selling mining machinery.

Taylor's ambitions, however, were not confined to Liberia. He set his sights on neighbouring Sierra Leone whose government had provided Ecomog with a rear base at Lungi airport, just north of the capital, Freetown, and sent troops to Liberia in support of Ecomog's operation there. What particularly attracted Taylor to Sierra Leone were the rich alluvial diamond fields of Kono, less than 100 miles from the Liberian border.

It was now Sierra Leone's turn to be caught up in the horrors of civil war.

The diamond fields of Sierra Leone were its most valuable asset. For three decades in the postwar era, diamonds had provided the government in Freetown with more than half of its revenue. But during the

1970s President Siaka Stevens turned the diamond industry into his personal preserve, setting up a private network of Lebanese dealers and local traders to run it for him. His one-party dictatorship was subsequently remembered as a 'seventeen-year plague of locusts'. By the time he retired in 1985, at the age of eighty, he had amassed a personal fortune estimated at $500 million. Sierra Leone, however, was left decrepit and bankrupt.

Stevens chose as his successor his sycophantic army commander, Joseph Momoh, an inept man who presided over the same corrupt one-party system and ruled the country through an ethnic cabal. The diamond fields remained in the hands of private entrepreneurs, producing a trade worth at least $300 million a year, most of it smuggled out of the country, leaving the government with minimal income. When the government stopped paying teachers, the education system collapsed. Thousands of unemployed youths – 'rarray boys' – roamed the streets of Freetown and other towns, an alienated underclass, angry and resentful, addicted to a lifestyle of gambling, drugs, petty theft and violence. Unpaid civil servants ransacked their offices, stealing furniture, typewriters and light fixtures, anything that would provide an income to keep their families fed. Much of the professional class emigrated to Europe and the United States, leaving the country to slide inexorably towards ruin.

Worse was to come. On 23 March 1991 a group of about 100 fighters, armed and financed by Taylor, crossed the border from 'Greater Liberia' and captured several border villages. Calling themselves the Revolutionary United Front (RUF), they included Sierra Leonean dissidents, hardened NPFL units and a number of mercenaries from Burkina Faso. Their leader, Foday Sankoh, was a 54-year-old former corporal in the Sierra Leone army whom Taylor had met in a training camp in Libya. Sankoh had previously spent seven years in Freetown's Pademba Road Prison for participating in an abortive coup attempt against Siaka Stevens in 1971. Discharged from the army, he had worked as a commercial photographer in diamond districts before leaving for Libya. Announcing its existence in a communiqué in early April, the RUF set out a vaguely populist agenda, claiming to be fighting against government officials and their business associates in Freetown engaged in plundering the country's resources, but its principal purpose was to gain control of the diamond fields of Kono for itself and for Taylor. To destroy the existing system of authority, the RUF seized and summarily executed chiefs, village elders, traders, agricultural project workers and other government employees. Within a few weeks it succeeded in overrunning a string of towns and diamond-producing areas in the east of the country. Taylor duly proclaimed Sankoh 'governor of Sierra Leone'.

Sankoh's rebellion gained local support from urban 'rarray boys' and from illicit diamond diggers – 'san-san boys', as they were known – all hoping to profit from a new order. Following Taylor's lead, Sankoh also forcibly recruited children, abducting them during raids on villages. The children were subjected to a period of indoctrination, provided with drugs and trained to kill. In some cases, they were required to kill their own parents and relatives. Girls were frequently forced to become 'soldiers' wives'.

Child soldiers became a prominent feature of Sierra Leone's war, used by all sides. It was estimated that at one stage half of all RUF combatants were in the age range of eight to fourteen years. Once involved, many found it impossible to leave, risking summary execution by the RUF if they were caught or revenge killing by their enemies. Some, however, preferred the life of fighters. 'Many under-age combatants joined up voluntarily, some looking for revenge, others to survive,' two researchers, Krijn Peters and Paul Richards, wrote in a study on Sierra Leone's boy soldiers published in 1998. 'Joining a militia group is both meal ticket and substitute education. The pay may be derisory, but weapon training pays quicker dividends than school ever did; soon the AK47 brings food, money, a warm bath and instant adult respect. The combat group substitutes for lost family and friends.'

Officers rated highly the use of both male and female child soldiers. 'Under-age irregulars fight without inhibitions and kill without compunction, sometimes casually, sometimes as an extension of play,' wrote Peters and Richards. 'They are good in ambush situations, one of the main combat tactics and – separated by war from their kin – are fiercely loyal to their bra [Krio for 'big brother'], the officer responsible for recruiting and training them.'

The RUF also routinely conscripted civilians to work as slave labour in mines or as porters, beating or killing anyone who resisted. A civilian 'mule' described to an American journalist, Greg Campbell, how he had spent two years hauling weapons and equipment from the Liberian border to RUF camps inland, fearful of death every day. 'The mules were required to carry up to 100 kilos of equipment each, and a twisted ankle, fatigue, or even a slow pace was enough of an excuse for the RUF captors to shoot them and dump their bodies in the woods,' wrote Campbell. 'The life span of a mule was not long.'

RUF 'town commanders' were given free rein to inflict any punishment they saw fit – hacking off hands and feet became a RUF trademark. Insurgents looted whatever they wanted from the civilian population as their reward. There was no ideology, no political strategy, behind the RUF, only the use of brute force. Hundreds of thousands fled their homes to escape its campaign of terror.

To stave off the rebellion, Momoh asked Nigeria and Guinea to provide troops. He also tripled the size of the Sierra Leone army to 14,000 troops, recruiting 'rarray boys' and common prisoners to make up the numbers. 'Not much time was given to screening entrants,' Momoh subsequently admitted. 'The result is that a large number of undesirables, waifs, strays, layabouts and bandits may now be in the nation's military uniform.' He also encouraged Liberian exiles living in Sierra Leone – former Krahn soldiers and dispossessed Mandingo traders – to form their own rebel group – the United Liberation Movement for Democracy in Liberia (Ulimo) – both to combat the RUF and to carry the war back into NPFL territory in Liberia. In eastern areas local Mende communities formed self-defence militias, based on traditional hunting guilds known as Kamajors, to ward off RUF attacks.

But Momoh had no adequate means to pay his expanded army or to provide them with support and equipment in the field, provoking subaltern unrest. Army discontent was aggravated by the tendency of commanders to 'lead' operations from the rear and to divert soldiers' pay into their own pockets and siphon off army rice supplies for sale on the open market.

In April 1992 a group of dissident junior officers led by a 27-year-old captain, Valentine Strasser, drove to Freetown to make their grievances known and ended up seizing power. In his first interview, Strasser described how he had had to fight the RUF with 'obsolete guns that will not fire'. Wounded with shrapnel in his leg, he had had to endure an operation in hospital without anaesthetic because there were no supplies available. The military then refused to send Strasser and other injured soldiers for treatment abroad on the grounds that the country could not afford it.

In standard coup-time fashion, Strasser denounced the 'nepotism, tribalism, gross mismanagement and total collapse of our economic, education, health, transport and communications system' and promised a 'clean-up exercise'. But after a brief period of populist sloganeering, Strasser and his colleagues began to engage in their own scams and line their own pockets. Like their predecessors, they also tried to muscle in on the diamond trade. The diamond fields became the centre of an increasingly chaotic struggle between mining gangs, rogue military units, rebel warlords and criminal business interests.

Sankoh's use of terror tactics eventually won him control of a large part of the diamond fields and the $300 million traffic in diamonds from eastern Sierra Leone. Advancing further afield, in 1994 the RUF overran bauxite and titanium mines, cutting off the government from its last reliable source of income. The bauxite operation on its own had accounted for nearly 60 per cent of total export earnings. By 1995 the RUF was poised to strike at the capital, Freetown.

Desperate to avoid defeat, protected only by a ramshackle army, Strasser made a deal with a South African security firm, Executive Outcomes, to provide him with a mercenary force in exchange for concessions to mine diamonds in areas where Executive Outcomes regained control. In effect, Strasser subcontracted the government's defence to a foreign company and mining operations to one of its associates. Within one week, Executive Outcomes cleared the Freetown area of rebels. The company then set about retraining army units, integrating them into its own operations. It also helped organise Kamajor self-defence groups into well-armed militias. By August

1995, though much of the country was still afflicted by civil war, the diamond fields were back under Freetown's control.

Under pressure from civic organisations and the donor community, Strasser agreed in 1995 to hold elections. But simultaneously he signalled his intention to retain power by announcing he would stand as a candidate for the presidency. When he subsequently threatened to fire his colleagues if they did not support him, he was deposed in a palace coup in January 1996 by his deputy, General Julius Maada Bio, and sent in handcuffs to neighbouring Guinea. Though Maada Bio harboured ambitions to make himself president, he allowed the election campaign to proceed.

In an attempt to disrupt the election, the RUF attacked villages in the north and east, indiscriminately hacking off hands, arms and legs of helpless villagers – men, woman and children alike – as a warning to the civilian population to steer clear of the polls. Despite the RUF's atrocities, 1 million people turned out to vote in March 1996, electing by a decisive margin Ahmed Tejan Kabbah, the leader of the Sierra Leone People's Party, a 64-year-old Mende politician from the Siaka Stevens era.

Kabbah's difficulties were formidable. His government had no money and few foreign friends. It was bogged down in a civil war, dependent on an army that was poorly trained and ill-disciplined. Many soldiers were involved in banditry, looting and extortion no different from the rebels. Though Kabbah initiated peace overtures to Foday Sankoh, their talks made little real progress. Sankoh demanded seats in the government and the expulsion of all foreign forces including Executive Outcomes and troops from Nigeria and Guinea on whom Kabbah relied to protect strategic installations. A peace deal swiftly ran into difficulties. Foreign donors proved reluctant to commit funds. As a result of foreign pressure, notably from the International Monetary Fund, Kabbah was obliged to terminate the services of Executive Outcomes and its mercenary force in exchange for aid. Deprived of reliable defence, he turned increasingly to the Kamajor militias for help with security, arousing discontent in the army. Despite popular support, his position seemed increasingly precarious. 'It is strange to say,' reflected Desmond Luke, a prominent Freetown lawyer, 'but I believe without diamonds this country couldn't have been in this state of exploitation and degradation.'

In Liberia, meanwhile, Charles Taylor suffered a series of reverses. The Liberian exile group Ulimo began to make headway in the north-west corner of 'Greater Liberia'. It was led by a former Doe minister, Alhaji Kromah, who used the Guinean capital Conakry as a base and ran diamond-mining operations in border areas of Sierra Leone to finance his campaign. Ulimo became an integral part of Ecomog's alliance against Taylor. It was provided with weapons and intelligence by Nigerian officers in exchange for a percentage of diamond profits.

Taylor launched a frontal assault in October 1992 to gain control of Monrovia, bombarding the heart of the city and residential neighbourhoods with mortar and rocket fire, but it ended in failure. When his forces came close to capturing Ecomog headquarters, the Nigerians poured in reinforcements from their base in Sierra Leone, and eventually drove the NPFL back. Taking the offensive, the Nigerians bombed NPFL-occupied towns; imposed a naval blockade of ports shipping goods from Taylor's territory; and succeeded in capturing Buchanan which they comprehensively looted, dismantling and exporting industrial equipment worth some $50 million. Greater Liberia began to shrink.

The setbacks persuaded Taylor that he would never attain power through military means alone. He therefore set out to reach an accommodation with Ecomog and its Nigerian backers, believing that he could manipulate his way to the top through negotiation. The wrangling took more than two years to resolve. A series of peace accords came and went before a deal was finally struck in the Nigerian capital in August 1995. Under the terms of the Abuja agreement, signed by eight faction leaders, Liberia was to be run for an interim period before elections by a Council of State consisting of six members, including Taylor representing the NPFL, and two other warlords. Two weeks later Taylor entered Monrovia for the first time since launching his invasion in 1989, after two devastating attempts to take the city by force and a civil war that had cost 150,000 lives.

Neither the wrangling nor the scramble for spoils stopped, however. A struggle for control of the diamond trade soon turned violent. In April 1996 Taylor's forces and Krahn factions fought for control of Monrovia once more. Fighters on both sides engaged in cannibalism, ripping out hearts and eating them. One group known as the 'Butt Naked Brigade' fought naked in the belief that this would protect them against bullets. Ecomog soldiers joined in a looting spree. Aid workers and other foreigners fled. Once more, Monrovia was reduced to a wrecked city.

Four months later, in August 1996, Liberia's warlords assembled in Abuja again to sign a new peace accord – the fourteenth. This time West African governments demanded rigorous compliance, threatening them with penalties, including a freeze on their assets, a travel ban and the possibility of war crimes prosecution. Western governments warned that it was the last peace initiative they were willing to underwrite. Having regained considerable chunks of territory, Taylor now saw the peace process as a means to legitimise his climb to power and fell more readily into line. Along with other warlords, he converted his militia into a political party and agreed to participate in demobilisation and disarmament schemes.

In elections in July 1997 Taylor's National Patriotic Party (NPP) gained a decisive victory, securing 75 per cent of the vote, 49 out of 64 seats in the National Assembly and 21 out of 26 seats in the Senate. The resources he was able to pour into his campaign were far greater than any other party, and included control of Liberia's only nation-wide short-wave radio station; the use of a helicopter; and widespread distribution of T-shirts and rice. Taylor also made it clear that if he did not win, he would resume the war, emphasising his warlord credentials with the slogan: 'He killed my ma, he killed my pa, but I will vote for him.' Many Liberians voted for him just for the sake of peace. The result was endorsed as fair by foreign observers, including a former US president, Jimmy Carter. But though the election marked the fulfilment of Taylor's ruthless ambition to rule Liberia, it did not put an end to the schemes he still harboured for extending his writ further afield.

★

In Sierra Leone, Kabbah's government lasted no longer than fourteen months. On 25 May 1997 a group of twenty soldiers stormed Freetown's Pademba Road Prison, released Major Johnny Paul Koroma, a dissident officer being held in connection with a coup plot, seized the radio station and announced the formation of an Armed Forces Revolutionary Council (AFRC). In fierce fighting that followed, government buildings in the city centre, including the ministry of finance and the central bank, were wrecked. Thousands of soldiers wearing red shirts and bandannas roamed Freetown, looting, raping and shooting at will. Adding to the mayhem were 600 prisoners set free from Pademba Road Prison at the same time as Koroma. Marauding gangs ransacked supermarkets, offices, banks, shops and private houses. Kabbah fled to Guinea; foreigners were evacuated; thousands of civilians headed for exile. Just like Monrovia, Freetown became a derelict city.

Koroma's group had no clear strategy other than to seize power. Like many others in the army, Koroma was poorly educated. An awkward, rebellious student from the northern Limba tribe, he had left school without any qualifications, joined the army and gained rapid promotion. His main grievance concerned the army's low status and the precedence that Kabbah accorded to the Kamajors tribal militias. In its first broadcast the AFRC declared: 'No more Kamajors. No more civil defence groups. We are the national army. We have to fight for this country.'

The civilian population showed their anger at the coup by keeping offices and schools closed. African leaders and Western governments too expressed their opposition. Western attempts to persuade the junta to step down and leave the country with guarantees of safety came to an abrupt halt, however, when the AFRC decided instead to come to a deal with Sankoh's rebels. The RUF was offered four places on the AFRC; Sankoh himself, though held in detention by Nigeria since March, was made vice-chairman in his absence. After five years of savage rural conflict, RUF fighters, recognisable by their matted hair and red headbands, walked into Freetown.

Just as had happened in Monrovia, the Nigerians, acting in the name of Ecomog, decided to intervene. Reinforcements were sent to the international airport at Lungi and the local airport at Hastings which they held. On 1 June the Nigerians bombarded the army's Cockerill headquarters, expecting the AFRC to flee. Their intervention, however, precipitated a massive RUF attack on a small contingent of Nigerian troops guarding the perimeter of the Mammy Yoko Hotel where more than 800 foreigners had taken shelter. After ten hours of heavy fighting, with part of the hotel on fire, a truce was arranged, enabling the foreigners to escape.

For seven months Freetown remained in the hands of the AFRC and the RUF, subjected to blockades by air and sea imposed by Nigerian forces. While desultory negotiations took place, both sides prepared for a final battle. A British security firm, Sandline, linked to Executive Outcomes, supported the Nigerian effort and helped train and supply Kamajors militias engaged in combat with the RUF. Taylor's fighters from Liberia helped bolster the RUF. In February 1998 the second battle for Freetown broke out as Nigerian forces advanced on the city centre. After several days of heavy fighting the AFRC/RUF abandoned the capital, destroying houses, killing civilians and looting as they retreated. In March Kabbah returned from exile in Guinea to a ruined city.

Propped up by international aid and protected by Nigerian forces, Kabbah tried to restore some semblance of government. Army officers who had supported the AFRC were tried for treason and sentenced to death. In July the Nigerians sent Foday Sankoh back to Freetown to be tried for treason. The RUF warned that unless he was released, it would intensify its campaign of terror against civilians. In October Sankoh was convicted of treason and sentenced to death. While he waited on death row for the outcome of an appeal, the RUF launched 'Operation No Living Thing', massacring and mutilating civilians and abducting children en masse. Resupplied from Liberia and Burkina Faso, RUF forces advanced once again on Freetown.

In January 1999 the third battle for Freetown began. In a period of four days the RUF captured the city centre and most of the suburbs. With terrifying violence they massacred some 6,000 civilians, amputating hands and feet at random, destroyed hundreds of buildings and thousands of homes, and brought the Nigerians to the brink of defeat before retreating, taking hundreds of captured children with them.

In the aftermath of the RUF assault, both sides eventually agreed to conduct ceasefire negotiations. Worn down and weakened by the war and dependent on the Nigerians for survival, Kabbah offered Sankoh a power-sharing deal. Among the terms of the agreement was a clause giving Sankoh and his rebels full amnesty for war crimes. In July 1999, amid considerable fanfare, they signed a peace agreement at a ceremony in Lomé, Togo, attended by a panoply of African leaders including Liberia's Charles Taylor and Burkina Faso's Blaise Compaoré. 'Kabbah wanted peace, Sankoh wanted power,' commented a Western diplomat. Sankoh was appointed vice-president and given charge of the Strategic Minerals Resources Commission – the diamond mines. In exchange the RUF promised to demobilise and disarm to a UN peacekeeping force. After eight years of butchery, the RUF had finally bludgeoned its way to power.

The peace deal, however, soon ran into trouble. Sierra Leone remained divided between areas under Nigerian (Ecomog) control and RUF control. Kabbah's government held more territory, but the RUF kept possession of the Kono diamond fields, providing it with ample funds to continue the war. Plans to disarm the RUF and Kamajors militias made little progress. A UN peacekeeping force – Unamsil – was introduced to replace Ecomog, but, as had happened in Rwanda, it was deployed with inadequate resources, equipment, logistics and intelligence capacity. When Unamsil announced in May 2000 its intention to move into the diamond fields, the RUF retaliated by seizing 500 Kenyan and Zambian peacekeepers.

To prevent Freetown from being overrun by the RUF and Unamsil from humiliation and defeat, Britain intervened in May 2000 with a fully armed expeditionary force – paratroops, special forces, combat aircraft, attack helicopters and warships. As the first troops arrived, civic groups in Freetown organised a mass demonstration demanding the release of the UN peacekeepers. When a crowd of 30,000 people advanced on Sankoh's house on Spur Road, Sankoh's bodyguards opened fire indiscriminately, killing seventeen civilians and injuring dozens more. Amid panic and confusion, Sankoh escaped over a back wall dressed in woman's clothing, but he was captured nearby ten days later. After being stripped and paraded naked in the streets, he was

handed over to the government. Taylor's attempts to arrange his transfer to a third country were quickly rebuffed.

In the aftermath of Britain's military intervention, a major international effort was launched to restore order to Sierra Leone and bring
an end to the war. British personnel took up key posts in government,
the central bank and the police and began the task of rebuilding a
national army. The UN peacekeeping force was increased to 18,000,
one of its largest operations in the world. Following Sankoh's arrest
the RUF fragmented into rival groups, losing momentum. In
November 2000 a ceasefire was signed, enabling Unamsil to deploy
throughout the country. In January 2002 Kabbah formally declared
the war over.

Over a period of eleven years some 50,000 people had died, 20,000
were left mutilated and more than three-quarters of the population
had been displaced. And, according to a UN report, of all the world's
countries Sierra Leone had reached the very bottom of the league for
human development.

Charles Taylor did well out of the war in Sierra Leone. Most of the
country's diamond production during the war years was smuggled
through Liberia and handled by traders acting on Taylor's behalf. In
addition to Sierra Leone's diamonds, Monrovia acted as a major centre
for laundering diamonds from other African conflicts such as Angola.
Liberia's 'official' exports during the mid-1990s ranged from $300
million to $450 million a year, far in excess of its own production.
'Unofficial' diamond exports added to the total. In effect, Taylor was
a running a gangster economy, well attuned to enhancing his private
fortune.

As well as his involvement with the RUF, Taylor dabbled in other
regional rebellions, hoping to profit from them. He liked to boast that
Liberia possessed the most effective guerrilla fighters in Africa. He
sponsored a rebel group from Guinea aiming to overthrow President
Lansana Conté, providing it with bases in northern Liberia. But his
meddling soon backfired. Conté, in turn, began supporting Liberian
dissidents aiming to overthrow Taylor. In 1999 a new group calling
itself Liberians United for Reconciliation and Democracy (Lurd), an

assortment of anti-Taylor factions, gained a foothold in Lofa County in north-west Liberia, using Guinea as a rear base.

Exasperated by the havoc that Taylor continued to wreak in West Africa, Western governments imposed an arms embargo and trade sanctions on Liberia and a travel ban on government officials. Taylor himself was labelled a pariah. A United Nations Panel of Experts was set up to investigate and monitor his activities. A UN-backed tribunal indicted him for war crimes in Sierra Leone. American officials openly spoke of the need for 'regime change'.

The end of the Taylor era was as chaotic and violent as its beginning. During the course of 2003 Lurd made rapid advances towards Monrovia, looting, raping and abducting children as it went, in similar fashion to Taylor's forces. A second rebel group, the Movement for Democracy and Elections in Liberia (Model) gained control of the south and east. For weeks fighting raged on the outskirts of Monrovia. Tens of thousands of residents sought refuge in the city centre, without food or water. Child soldiers roamed the streets, dressed in bizarre outfits, high on 'Blue Blue' barbiturates and marijuana, sometimes carrying AK-47s in one hand and toys in the other. Ministries were looted by their own staff. The government ceased functioning. Hundreds died from cholera and starvation.

Taylor repeatedly promised to stand down as president, but prevaricated from one week to the next. The shelling of Monrovia continued. In August, after protracted wrangling over money, a West African peacekeeping force led by the Nigerians arrived in the capital, amid scenes of popular rejoicing among the civilian population desperate for an end to their ordeal

In an elaborate ceremony on 11 August, attended by a gospel choir and a trio of African presidents, Taylor made his farewell speech, perched on a velvet throne and dressed in a virginal white suit, drawing parallels between himself and Jesus Christ. 'I would be the sacrificial lamb,' he said. 'God willing, I will be back.' Accompanied by his wife, Jewel, he boarded a plane for Nigeria, where he had been granted sanctuary and a sumptuous villa, to enjoy a comfortable retirement.

NO CONDITION IS
PERMANENT

Even by the standards that Nigeria's military dictators had set, General Sani Abacha reached new levels of notoriety. From his fortified presidential complex at Aso Rock in Abuja, he relished the use of raw power to crush all opponents and to amass a personal fortune, acting with a degree of ruthlessness that outstripped that of all his predecessors. A reclusive figure, he rarely appeared in public or travelled abroad. Not once during his time as president in the 1990s did he visit Lagos, the country's commercial capital. Shielded by security personnel and a presidential guard, he remained inaccessible even to most of his ministers and to the ruling military council, preferring to deal with a handful of key civilian advisers and business cronies. Yet from his headquarters at Aso Rock he spawned a climate of fear that Nigerians had never before experienced. The civilian population, angry and resentful that the military had once again thwarted efforts to establish democratic rule, discovered that opposing Abacha's dictatorship carried a high cost. 'Abacha is prepared to reduce Nigeria to rubble as long as he survives to preside over a name,' Wole Soyinka, the Nobel Prize laureate, wrote in 1995 after leaving for exile.

Within months of his coup in November 1994, Abacha faced rising public clamour for him to step down. Much of the agitation came from southern political groups still furious that the June election won by the Yoruba tycoon Chief Abiola, had been stolen from them by northern generals. Vigorous campaigns against military rule were waged by the 'opposition' press. In May 1995 the National Democratic Coalition (Nadeco), a loose alliance of mainly southern groups, issued an 'ultimatum' to Abacha to hand over power to Abiola on May 31. Members of the disbanded Senate and House of Representatives voiced their support.

On 11 June Abiola declared himself president and was 'sworn in' in a brief ceremony in Lagos. 'Let the heavens fall,' he told a press conference. Abacha ordered his arrest on charges of treason, but the result was an explosion of dissent. Oil workers declared an indefinite strike. They were joined by bank employees, teachers and nurses. The oil sector strike, paralysing refineries, terminals and other installations, led to acute shortages of petroleum products throughout the country. Oil exports were reduced by a third.

To break the strikes, Abacha tried bribes, threats, arrests, thuggery and eventually outright repression. The oil workers' unions were shut down; pro-democracy activists were detained; Nadeco was banned; and independent newspapers – *The Concord, The Guardian* and *Punch* – were proscribed. Critics spoke of a new 'dark age'.

In March 1995 Abacha instituted a new purge, claiming evidence of a coup plot. Among those arrested were two former generals, Olusegun Obasanjo and Shehu Yar' Adua, both of whom had spoken out against military rule. Obasanjo had held power for three years from 1976 to 1979 before handing over to an elected civilian government; a born-again Christian from Yorubaland, he had since retired to his farm fifty miles north of Lagos and taken up chicken and pig farming. Yar' Adua, a multimillionaire Katsina prince, ran a powerful political machine in the north and harboured presidential ambitions. In all, more than forty people – military officers, journalists and human rights activists – were convicted in secret trials held by a special military tribunal and sentenced to death or long prison sentences. Obasanjo was given life imprisonment; Yar' Adua was sentenced to death. After international protests, both sentences were reduced.

In dealing with dissident minority groups from the Niger Delta region, the location of Nigeria's oil wealth, Abacha acted with similar ferocity. The main grievance of Delta activists was that oil revenues produced by the Delta were used largely to benefit ethnic-majority areas of the country while their own region suffered from neglect. The Delta region was one of the poorest, least developed parts of Nigeria, lacking basic amenities; there was little provision of electricity or pipe-borne water supplies, and schools and hospitals were inadequately funded. Moreover, the Delta had to contend with the burden of environmental degradation: oil spills from pipelines polluted the land and waterways; gas flaring polluted the air; fishing and farming were contaminated, destroying the livelihood of farmers and fishermen.

During the 1970s and 1980s various Delta communities launched sporadic protests at multinational oil companies. In the early 1990s, however, more organised resistance emerged, directed not just at the companies but at the government. A host of community organisations sprang up – the Organisation for the Restoration of Actual Rights of Oil Communities; the Conference of Traditional Rulers of Oil Producing States; Concerned Youths of Oil Producing States. Many were founded to represent ethnic interests: the Ijaw National Congress; the Urhobo Progress Union; the Isoko Development Union. Foremost among them was the Movement for the Survival of Ogoni People (Mosop) founded in 1990.

The principal founder of Mosop, Ken Saro-Wiwa was a writer, television producer and business entrepreneur, born in Ogoniland in 1941. A diminutive figure, with a vituperative turn of phrase, he was best known in Nigeria as the creator of *Basi & Co*, a television soap opera watched by 30 million Nigerians each week that lampooned the country's get-rich-quick mentality. In his novel *Prisoners of Jebs* he turned his fire on the oil-boom folly. 'Nigeria was full of inflation, corruption, injustice, murder, armed robbery, maladministration, drug-trafficking, hunger, knavery, dishonesty and plain stupidity . . . But it still remained a blessed country.'

In the 1980s he became increasingly preoccupied with the plight of Ogoniland, an area of no more than 400 square miles in Rivers State with a population of 500,000 Ogonis. It was the fifth largest oil-producing community in Rivers State. Since 1958 its wells had

produced about $30 billion worth of oil, yet hardly a trickle had fil-
tered down to the people living there. Saro-Wiwa blamed both the
government and the Anglo-Dutch company Shell, which operated
most of the oil wells and pipelines there, for Ogoniland's poverty and
degradation. In a newspaper article for the *Sunday Times* in 1990, he
demanded a reallocation of oil money in favour of local people. The
article was entitled: 'The Coming War in the Delta'.

The opening salvo came in 1990 with the publication of an *Ogoni
Bill of Rights*. Drawn up by Mosop and approved by the traditional
heads of five Ogoni clans, it demanded political autonomy for
Ogoniland, local control of its economic resources and protection
from further environmental degradation. Nigeria's military rulers dismissed the demands, but Mosop's grievances found a more receptive
audience abroad, notably among environmental and human rights
groups. In December 1992 Mosop wrote to Shell, Chevron and the
state-owned Nigerian National Petroleum Corporation, the three oil
companies operating in Ogoniland, demanding payment of $6 billion
for accumulated rentals and royalties for oil exploration dating back to
1958; payment of $4 billion for damages and compensation for envi-
ronmental pollution; and negotiations to decide 'acceptable terms' for
future oil exploration. The companies were given thirty days to meet
these demands and threatened with mass action if they failed to do so.
The time had come, said Mosop, in their letter to the oil companies,
for 'the Ogonis to fight for their own salvation . . . because there is no
government to deliver us'.

The government responded by sending troops to protect oil installations and announcing a ban on all public gatherings and
demonstrations. It also issued a decree declaring that demands for
self-determination and disruptive activities affecting oil production
would be considered as acts of treason punishable by death.

Defying the threat, Mosop organised mass 'Ogoni Day' rallies,
focusing on the demand for self-determination. 'We are not asking for
the moon,' Mosop's president, Garrick Leton, told demonstrators in
Bori in January 1993, 'but the bare necessities of life – water,
electricity, roads, education and a right to self-determination so
that we can be responsible for our resources and our environment.'

Saro-Wiwa called on the international community to come to the
rescue of Ogonis before they were driven 'to extinction' by 'the
multinational oil companies and their protectors'. He urged the crowd
to 'rise up now and fight for your rights'.

The 'Ogoni Day' rallies, attended by tens of thousands of Ogonis,
marked the peak of Mosop's fortunes. Traditional leaders took fright
at the growing confrontation with the government. After an outbreak of violence in April, they issued a statement apologising for the
disorder and supporting a crackdown on dissidents. The Ogoni
movement became divided between a conservative faction anxious to
reach an accommodation with the government and a radical wing of
youth activists led by Saro-Wiwa, determined to pursue the campaign. The conservatives accused Saro-Wiwa of employing 'an army
of trained thugs' to ensure that he emerged as 'the one Ogoni
leader'. To add to the disarray, the government stirred up tribal strife
between the Ogonis and their neighbours the Andonis, another oil-
producing community, supplying them with arms and expertise.
More than 1,000 Ogonis were killed and some 30,000 left homeless.
A similar conflict broke out between Okrikas and Ogonis in Port
Harcourt.

The end of the movement came in May 1994 after four conservative leaders meeting in the chief's palace at Gokana were killed by a
local mob. Saro-Wiwa and other prominent activists were arrested,
and government forces unleashed fearful repression throughout
Ogoniland, killing at least fifty Ogonis. A Human Rights Watch
report described the carnage:

> Troops entered towns and villages shooting at random, as villagers
> fled to the surrounding bush. Soldiers and mobile police stormed
> houses, breaking down doors and windows with their boots, the
> butts of their guns and machetes. Villagers who crossed their paths,
> including children and the elderly, were severely beaten, forced to
> pay 'settlement fees' [bribes] and sometimes shot. Many women
> were raped . . . Before leaving, troops looted money, livestock and
> other property.

Saro-Wiwa was held in detention for nine months, without access to lawyers, before being charged with incitement to murder. He was then brought before a special tribunal, consisting of two judges and a military officer, with no right of appeal. He denied the charge and no credible evidence was ever produced linking him to the murders. He was nevertheless found guilty and, along with eight other defendants, sentenced to death. Within eight days Abacha's Provisional Ruling Council confirmed the sentence. Despite worldwide calls for clemency, the Ogoni Nine were executed two days later, on 10 November 1994.

Abacha remained indifferent to the barrage of condemnation that came from abroad. The execution of the Ogoni Nine had served its purpose of warning critics of the costs of opposing him. Other notable victims included Kudirat Abiola, the wife of Chief Abiola, a tireless campaigner for her husband's cause, who was gunned down in her car in Lagos by security agents; and General Yar' Adua, who was murdered in prison. The army too was purged of dissidents. Abacha's deputy, General Oladipo Diya, and other Yoruba officers were charged with plotting a coup and executed.

Maintaining his vice-like grip on power, Abacha next turned his attention to obtaining a popular mandate for his rule. He allowed the registration of five political parties, all of which were closely identified with members of his regime and its supporters. Other groups suspected of opposing him or likely to become 'too powerful' were denied registration and proscribed. All five political parties duly assembled conventions, each selecting Sani Abacha as their presidential candidate.

His plans, however, were cut short. On 8 June 1998 Abacha died while in the arms of a pair of Indian prostitutes. His successor, General Abdulsalami Abubakar, swiftly reversed direction. Within weeks he freed scores of prisoners, including General Obasanjo, human rights activists, oil union chiefs and Ogoni dissidents. Negotiations over the release of Chief Abiola were underway when Abiola suddenly died of a heart attack. Abubakar also declared his intention to return Nigeria to civilian rule, setting out a new schedule for elections. Local elections were held in December 1998, state elections in January 1999 and elections for the national assembly and for the presidency in February 1999. Obasanjo won the presidential election, taking 63 per cent of the vote, mainly through the support of northern power-brokers; and his People's Democratic Party gained control of the national assembly. The elections in February were riddled with fraud, bribery and other irregularities. However, independent election observers, while judging the elections to be neither 'free nor fair', according to standard criteria, nevertheless concluded that they generally reflected 'the will of the people'. At an elaborate ceremony in Abuja in May 1999, Obasanjo was sworn in as president, ending sixteen years of military rule.

Forty years after independence, Nigeria presented a sorry spectacle. Wole Soyinka described his own country as 'the open sore of a continent'. Despite an oil bonanza of $280 billion, the economy was derelict; public services were chronically inefficient; schools and hospitals were decaying; higher education had virtually collapsed; roads were pitted with potholes; the telephone system hardly functioned. There were frequent power cuts; even shortages of domestic petroleum supplies. On average, Nigerians were poorer in 2000 than they had been at the start of the oil boom in the early 1970s. Income per head at $310 was less than one-third of that in 1980. Half of the population lived on less than 30 cents a day; half of the population had no access to safe drinking water. Almost one-fifth of children died before their fifth birthday; nearly half of under-fives were stunted because of poor malnutrition. Millions of people lived in slums surrounded by rotting mounds of garbage, without access to basic amenities.

The record of successive governments had been abysmal. Leading institutions such as the civil service swallowed huge sums of money but delivered few services; embezzlement and bribery were rife. The military were widely hated. The police acted as an occupying force, routinely extorting money from civilians and sometimes colluding with criminal gangs; the paramilitary Mobile Police were so notorious for brutality that they were nicknamed 'Kill and Go'. Police numbers had been kept deliberately low to prevent them from emerging as rivals to the military. Lagos, a city of about 10 million inhabitants, had no more than 12,000 policemen on its payroll. Underfunded, ill-equipped and poorly trained, the police were no match for criminal gangs.

The justice system was chaotic. Prisoners were often locked up without trial for years on end. A government commission investigating overcrowded prisons found that half of the inmates had never been legally sentenced; some had sat in their cells for ten years without ever seeing a judge. Court proceedings were often determined by bribes rather than by justice. Many criminals were safe from prosecution because they came from prominent families or enjoyed the patronage of powerful politicians. Anyone with sufficient money and influence was able to make use of state institutions to harm opponents, whether in land or business disputes or in personal vendettas.

Vast sums had been spent on prestige projects, to no advantage. A total of $8 billion had gone on constructing a steel industry complex based at Ajaokuta that had yet to produce a single bar of steel. Billions more had been sunk into an ultra-modern capital at Abuja, complete with glittering hotels and office towers, that the ruling elite enjoyed using but that brought little benefit to ordinary Nigerians.

Even worse were the vast sums siphoned off through corruption. Abacha's greed exceeded that of all his predecessors. It was estimated that he stole more than $4 billion, taking money either directly from the treasury, or from government contracts, or through scams like the Petroleum Trust Fund that he set up ostensibly to channel extra revenue from an increase in the domestic fuel price into infrastructure and other investments. The looting continued right through to the end of General Abubakar's regime. In the last months of military rule a flurry of public contracts went to well-connected firms. Foreign exchange reserves shrank by $2.7 billion between the end of December 1998 and the end of March 1999.

Abroad, Nigeria was ranked as one of the most corrupt countries in the world. It was renowned for commercial fraud, in particular an advance-fee fraud known locally as a '419 scam', after the article in the penal code that outlawed it. Nigerian syndicates also played a central role in the world's drug trade, controlling a large share of heroin and cocaine imported into the United States.

Compounding all the difficulties that Nigeria faced was a resurgence of ethnic and religious rivalry, held in check by years of repressive military rule. 'Everybody is sharpening his knife,' warned the governor of Anambra State in a press interview. One underlying cause was the collapse of government institutions, their failure to provide even basic services. Ethnic and religious groups turned their back on the state, resorting to a primary loyalty for aid and protection. Politicians exploited the despair and disillusionment with central government for their own ends. Competition between rival groups was fierce. For what was at stake were the revenues of the state and the ability of politicians to deliver them to their constituents.

A host of ethnic groups sprang up, some demanding self-determination, some wanting control over local economic resources, some setting out cultural and social objectives. Militant groups formed their own militias and used vigilante forces to combat rising levels of crime that the police failed to curb. Outbreaks of ethnic violence became increasingly common. More than 200 clashes were recorded between January 1999 and January 2000. A Nigerian quoted by the United Nations Development Programme's Human Development Report for 2002 remarked: 'When we were in the military regime, we didn't get anything from the government but we had peace. Now we are in a democracy, we don't get anything from the government and we do not get peace.'

Yoruba activists rallied to the Oodua People's Congress (OPC), convinced of a northern conspiracy to marginalise them. Not only had the Yoruba leader Chief Abiola been deprived by northern officers of his 1993 election victory, but he had then been left to rot in prison without adequate medical care. His subsequent death was regarded as suspicious. Nor were they mollified by the installation of Obasanjo's government. Though a Yoruba himself, Obasanjo was viewed as a stooge of northern interests. In the 1999 election Yorubas voted overwhelmingly against him, favouring the Yoruba-based opposition party, Alliance for Democracy.

Communal violence between Yoruba and Hausa flared soon afterwards. In Sagamu, a major centre of the kola-nut trade, thirty-six miles from Lagos, where Hausas had lived and traded for generations, fighting broke out as the result of the murder of a Hausa woman after she was caught allegedly watching traditional Yoruba religious rites known as *Oro*. More than fifty people were killed; homes, shops, mosques and markets were destroyed both in Yoruba neighbourhoods and in the Hausa quarter of Sabo. When fleeing Hausa traders arrived in Kano, bearing news of their ordeal, reprisals were launched against Yoruba residents there. Four months later, Yoruba and Hausa traders clashed over control of the strategic Mile 12 Market in Ketu, Lagos. The violence in Ketu prompted Hausa to set up a northern counterpart to the OPC, the Arewa People's Congress. OPC activists were also involved in clashes with Ijaw dockworkers in Lagos which sparked pitched battles between residents in the Lagos slum of Ajegunle. Obasanjo ordered police to shoot rioters on sight and told a national television audience that, 'When people decide to behave like animals, they must be treated like animals.'

Militia groups in the east were equally active. One of the most prominent was the Ijaw Youth Council (IYC), a confederation of youth associations in the Ijaw homeland in the Niger Delta region which included an armed wing called the Niger Delta Volunteer Force, more popularly known as the Egbesu Boys. Like the Ogoni, the Ijaw demanded control of local oil resources, focusing their campaign on multinational oil companies. In December 1998 the IYC issued the Kaiama Declaration giving oil companies a nineteen-day ultimatum to vacate 'Ijawland' – an area covering parts of Rivers, Bayelsa and Delta States – and warning that any oil company that sought protection from government forces would be regarded as 'an enemy of the Ijaw people'. Carrying out their threat, Ijaw militias sabotaged oil installations and pipelines and kidnapped oil company employees for ransom, prompting massive government repression. They were also involved in clashes with Urhobos and Itsekiris over control of the oil city of Warri. Kidnapping and hostage-taking subsequently became a routine for company employees in the Delta, normally settled by oil companies quietly making payments.

Igbo activists launched the Igbo People's Congress supporting demands for the self-determination of ethnic areas. A more extreme group – the Movement for the Actualisation of the Sovereign State of

Biafra – agitated for the dismemberment of Nigeria and the formation of a separate Igbo state. Its members openly hoisted the old flag of Biafra. 'Nothing good can ever come out of Nigeria,' said a spokesman. 'What you hear are power outages, shortage of water, armed robbery and other evils. We don't want to be part of that evil.'

As well as ethnic mobilisation, some ethnic groups ventured into the business of crime control, despairing of police assistance. An Igbo vigilante force known as the Bakassi Boys became infamous for its use of 'jungle justice' but was widely popular. Originally set up by traders in the market town of Aba in Abia State in 1999, after years of extortion, theft and thuggery by criminal gangs unhindered by the police, the Bakassi Boys swiftly gained a reputation as effective enforcers and found other towns pleading for their services. Within a few weeks they succeeded in 'cleaning' the entire state of criminal gangs. Local traders in neighbouring Anambra State persuaded the authorities to let them fight crime there too. The results were impressive. During the first weeks of their operations in the market town of Onitsha in 2000, they caught and executed 200 alleged criminals.

A former lecturer at the University of Nsukka, Johannes Harnischfeger, described, in a research paper on the Bakassi Boys, how prisoners were handled:

> At first . . . they remain for some days imprisoned in the Bakassi Centre, where they are investigated by an investigation committee. Only once their guilt has been established are they taken out on to the street and then to a road junction that is sufficiently large for hundreds of spectators. They are driven along the streets by a succession of blows, so that they have no time to turn to the bystanders, bewail their fate, or appeal to onlookers' feelings of compassion. Nor do the Bakassi Boys announce the sentence, or attempt to justify their actions. On arriving at the place of execution, they simply throw the bound victims on the ground and chop away at them for minutes on end with their blunt machetes – a silent bloodbath, because the victims do not scream, even though some are still writhing on the ground when the Bakassi Boys finish their task by tossing tyres on top of them and dousing them with petrol.

I was unable to find anyone among the crowd of spectators who voiced any disapproval or disgust. All that I occasionally noted was a slight feeling of apprehension. A number of women, for instance, scurried past on the way to do their shopping at the market, and merely cast brief glances at the horrifying scene while quickly crossing themselves. Others held cloths before their mouths, as the smoke drifting over from the charring bodies was poisonous. But otherwise no regret was shown towards the victims.

According to a report by the Civil Liberties Organisation in 2001, the Bakassi Boys were estimated to have executed as many as 3,000 people in Anambra State over an eighteen-month period – with a dramatic impact on crime levels. A committee of journalists awarded Anambra a prize in 2001 as 'the most crime-free State in Nigeria'.

Northern Nigeria, meanwhile, was torn apart by endemic bouts of religious strife between Muslims and Christians. Since the 1980s militant Muslim groups had agitated for the introduction of more sharia measures in northern states. A Muslim sect led by Muhammadu Marwa, popularly known as 'Maitatsine' – 'the one who curses' – mobilised the young urban poor in a series of uprisings in the early 1980s, first in Kano and later in Yola, Kaduna and Maiduguri, in which thousands died. In 1982 a wave of violence erupted in Kano spreading from Muslim anger at reconstruction work on a church sited close to a mosque. Christian resentment was fuelled in 1986 after Babangida announced that Nigeria would join the Organisation of Islamic Conference as a full member, a move that some Christian leaders interpreted as a step towards establishing an Islamic state. In 1987 a quarrel between Christian and Muslim students in southern Kaduna led to riots in which scores of churches and mosques were destroyed. Riots broke out in Kano in 1991 when a Christian evangelist from Germany attempted to stage a revivalist rally at the racecourse there. In Bauchi there were riots as a result of a feud between a Christian governor and a local Shiite leader. In 1992 a land dispute between Christian Katafs and Muslim Hausas in southern Kaduna escalated into wider religious violence in which hundreds died.

The cause was often as much to do with mass poverty, unemployment and crime and the government's failure to alleviate them as with religious belief. A contributing factor to rising demands in the north for the implementation of sharia law was the collapse of the judicial system and inadequate law enforcement. Youths invoked piety and joined vigilante groups to enforce sharia law not out of religious conviction but as political acts. Politicians for their part exploited religious loyalty as a means of gaining mass support in their own struggles for power.

Religious tensions in the north flared up once more after Obasanjo, a southern Christian, was installed as president in 1999. The northern power-brokers who helped elect him were disgruntled to find that he was not as amenable to their bidding as they had expected him to be. Soon after his inauguration, Obasanjo acted to remove hundreds of senior army officers who had been closely involved with the previous military regime, most of them northerners. Smarting from the loss of political power, northern leaders raised fears of a Christian 'hidden agenda' and used sharia as a weapon to reassert northern solidarity.

In October 1999 a newly elected governor, Ahmed Sani, announced that Zamfara, an impoverished state in the far north, would adopt sharia law as its only legal system in January 2000, citing Saudi Arabia as his model. Hitherto, about three-quarters of the northern penal code had been based on sharia, including such matters as marriage and divorce. Sani's intention was to extend sharia to all criminal cases and to apply it as well to sentencing, with penalties that would include flogging and stoning. Sharia, he said, was necessary to restore clean living to a decadent society. He claimed that sharia would affect only the Muslim population, though he proposed bans on alcohol, prostitution and the local cinema. Minority Christian groups in the north were outraged and fearful. The southern press accused Sani of leading Zamfara back into the dark ages. The Christian Association of Nigeria announced legal action in the courts. Delegates in the Cross River assembly in the south-east threatened to declare a 'Christian state' if Zamfara made the change.

Other northern states, however, decided to follow Sani's lead – twelve in all. A Christian protest in the city of Kaduna in February

2000 resulted in bloody clashes leaving hundreds dead. Entire neighbourhoods were 'religiously cleansed'. Many of the victims were Igbo. In revenge, Igbo vigilante groups in southern Nigeria – including the Bakassi Boys – killed hundreds of Hausa migrants from the north living there. As thousands of refugees and emigrants fled from the far north, religious tensions increased in other areas. Jos, the capital of Plateau State, hitherto renowned for its peace and quiet, was engulfed in clashes between Christian and Muslim groups in 2001 in which 3,000 died.

So many violent disputes broke out in the early years of Obasanjo's regime – over land, politics, religion, ethnicity, money – that at times it seemed that Nigeria was ungovernable. With a population of 120 million divided into some 250 ethnic groups, each with its own agenda, the potential for disorder was unlimited. 'The frequency and ferocity with which these clashes have spread across the country have made many Nigerians wonder to what extent the generality of Nigerians are appreciative of our hard-won democracy,' Obasanjo remarked in 2002.

Obasanjo struggled valiantly to keep a lid on ethnic strife and to get to grips with the myriad of problems that Nigeria faced. But he made little headway. The decay in Nigeria was too deep-rooted, its system of corruption too deeply embedded, to allow for easy solutions. Nigerian politics, moreover, remained an arena for an elite group on the look-out for money-making opportunities, not a vehicle for pursuing economic and social reform.

In 2003 Nigerians went to the polls once more, electing Obasanjo for a second term, but more disillusioned with politicians than ever before. It was a measure of how little was expected of Nigeria that the holding of a second election in four years in relatively peaceful circumstances was itself regarded as a major achievement. Nigerians, however, remained profoundly sceptical about their prospects. One of their favourite admonitions, carried on the side of trucks and buses, was: 'No condition is permanent'.

THE HONOUR OF LIVING

Shortly after seizing power in Sudan in 1989, General Omar al-Bashir addressed a rally holding a copy of the Koran in one hand and a Kalashnikov rifle in the other. 'I vow here before you to purge from our ranks the renegades, the hirelings, enemies of the people and enemies of the armed forces,' he declared. 'Anyone who betrays the nation does not deserve the honour of living.'

Bashir's coup marked the beginning of an Islamist dictatorship that dealt ruthlessly with Muslim and non-Muslim opponents alike. His guide and mentor in this enterprise was Hassan al-Turabi, founder of the National Islamic Front (NIF) and head of the Muslim Brotherhood, who had played a prominent role in promoting Islamist ideology during Numeiri's regime earlier in the 1980s. A diminutive man, with a white wisp of a beard, educated at universities in England and France, bespectacled, erudite and charming, he saw himself at the centre of an Islamic revival that would transform not only Sudan but other countries in the region. An Islamic scholar of world renown, he represented the genteel face of Bashir's totalitarian rule.

One institution after another – the civil service, the army, the judiciary, the universities, trade unions, professional associations, parastatal organisations – was purged of dissent. Prominent Muslim sects such as the Khatmiyya and Ansar movements were silenced; much of their property and assets, including mosques and shrines, were taken over by the state. Christian activities were curtailed and suppressed. The press was rigidly controlled. Hundreds of politicians, journalists, doctors and trade unionists were detained without trial. Many were taken to 'ghost houses' – houses whose existence the government denied – where they were tortured. According to a report published by the UN Commission on Human Rights in 1994, detainees were subjected to burnings, beatings, electric shocks and rape to extract confessions from them.

A new Islamic penal code promulgated in 1991 provided for public hanging or crucifixion for armed robbery; execution by stoning for adultery; and death for apostasy. A public order act introduced by the Khartoum state authorities restricted music, dance and wedding celebrations and banned men and women from dancing together. Police broke up concerts and wedding parties for violating the act. Women were hounded out of public life. A presidential decree in 1991 limited women's activities and required them to abide by strict dress codes that were enforced by the NIF's Guardians of Morality and Advocates of the Good. In a further bout of zeal in 1996, Khartoum state authorities introduced regulations that separated men and women on public transport, in theatres, cinemas, parties and picnics; enjoined Muslims not to look at members of the opposite sex; and forbade men from watching women playing sports. Religion became in effect a method of repression. As well as enforcing their own brand of Islamic rule, the government promoted Arabisation, insisting on the use of Arabic in education and denigrating the culture of non-Arabic peoples.

Bashir also formed his own Islamic militia, the People's Defence Force (PDF), modelling it on Iran's Revolutionary Guards. PDF training was made compulsory for civil servants, teachers, students and higher-education candidates; youths were seized off the streets and taken to training camps. PDF numbers eventually reached 150,000. They were used to suppress civilian demonstrations in northern towns and sent to the south as part of the war effort against rebel forces. The war itself officially became a jihad, a sacred duty for all Muslims to support. Bashir declared soldiers who died in battle there as martyrs 'irrigating the land of the south with their blood so that the land may sprout dignity and honour'.

Turabi meanwhile pursued his ambition to turn Sudan into a hive of pan-Islamic activity. In 1991, in the wake of the Persian Gulf crisis that brought Americans troops to the region, he established the Popular Arab and Islamic Conference (PAIC) in Khartoum as a pan-Islamic front to resist America's 'recolonisation of the Islamic world'. A throng of militant groups were invited to inaugural conferences in Khartoum, effectively marking the start of the 'war on America' and its allies. Many set up bases in Sudan. Islamist activists from Algeria, Tunisia and Egypt were offered sanctuary and provided with diplomatic passports. The blind Egyptian cleric Sheikh Omar Abdel Rahman, on trial in Egypt *in absentia* for political incitement, was given a government villa before heading for the United States on a tourist visa, intending to set up a base for Islamist groups there. By the end of 1991 Sudan hosted a thousand Egyptian insurrectionists. Palestinian leaders, including Abu Nidal, were also welcomed. Even the notorious terrorist Ilich Ramírez Sánchez, better known as Carlos the Jackal, was given temporary protection, after failing to find sanctuary in Iraq and Libya.

Among those who chose Sudan as a convenient new abode was the wealthy son of a Saudi construction magnate, Osama bin Laden, inspired, like Turabi, by the idea of establishing an 'Islamist International'. For ten years bin Laden had been involved in the jihad against the Soviet occupation of Afghanistan, first as a fundraiser in Saudi Arabia and the Middle East, then as an organiser based in Peshawar on the Pakistan border. Together with a Palestinian academic, Abdullah Azzam, he had established the *Maktab al-Khidamat* or Afghan Service Bureau, overseeing the recruitment and training of foreign *mujahidin* (guerrilla fighters). Following the Soviet withdrawal in 1989, he had returned to Saudi Arabia, rejoined the family business and founded a welfare organisation for veterans of the Afghanistan war. When Iraq invaded Kuwait in August 1990, he offered to mobilise 10,000 mujahidin to defend the Saudi kingdom, but, to his fury, the Saudi royal family turned to the United States for protection, inviting American troops to establish bases on Saudi soil. After denouncing the royal family, bin Laden was confined to Jeddah. Looking for a new base, he eagerly accepted an offer to relocate to Khartoum.

Shortly after his arrival in Khartoum in 1991, at the age of thirty-six, bin Laden dined with Turabi. They had much in common. Turabi had long been a supporter of the Afghan jihad, travelling to Peshawar on at least six occasions. He had been a close friend of bin Laden's associate there, Abdullah Azzam, and also of Sheikh Omar Abdel Rahman, another dedicated supporter of the Afghan cause. He also shared bin Laden's antipathy towards the Saudi royal family, condemning them not only for allowing American troops on Saudi soil but for straying from what he regarded as the true path of Islam. Over dinner, Turabi promised to give bin Laden all the help he needed and to provide him with an office and security guards. He was keen to assist bin Laden's plans for investing in Sudan and arranged to exempt his construction company from customs duties on the import of trucks and tractors. Bin Laden moved into a villa in the Riyadh district of Khartoum, next door to Turabi's spacious home.

In return, bin Laden was generous with his support for Turabi's pan-Islamic ambitions. By his own account, he paid $5,000 on arrival to become a member of Turabi's National Islamic Front and contributed $1 million to his PAIC. He also launched a wide variety of businesses. His construction company was involved in building a new highway from Khartoum to Port Sudan; a new airport outside Port Sudan; and several other government projects. He invested in banking and agriculture and traded in agricultural commodity exports.

He was equally active in organising insurgent networks. He claimed to have spent $2 million to fly Arab mujahidin from Pakistan to Sudan. He also built and equipped at his own expense twenty-three training camps in Sudan. By the summer of 1994 at least 5,000 mujahidin had been trained in Sudan, often while working on bin Laden's construction and agricultural projects.

Sudan soon became notorious as a rogue state supporting terrorist causes. Egypt accused Sudan-trained assassins of murdering the speaker of parliament. Tunisia claimed that Turabi and Sudanese government officials had conspired with Tunisian activists to smuggle weapons into the country in a plot to assassinate the president. In Algeria the Islamist insurrection against the military government was started by Algerian veterans of the Afghan war who had trained in Sudan. Libyans who had trained in Sudan attempted to assassinate Gaddafi in 1993 and launched attacks inside Libya in 1995. Palestinian Hamas activists trained in Sudan organised suicide bombings on Israeli civilian buses in Gaza. Sudan was also involved in supporting Aideed's militia in Somalia and Islamist groups in Eritrea and Ethiopia. In 1993 Turabi's old friend Sheikh Omar was implicated in the bombing of the World Trade Center in New York. Six of those convicted in the plot were Sudanese; two Sudanese diplomats at the United Nations were accused of helping the conspirators. Though he was never brought to trial for the World Trade Center bombing, Sheikh Omar was convicted in 1996 of seditious conspiracy to wage 'a war of urban terrorism against the United States' including the bombing of various New York landmarks, and sentenced to life imprisonment.

The climax of Sudan's involvement with terrorist causes came in June 1995 with an assassination attempt in Ethiopia on Egypt's president, Hosni Mubarak, as he drove from the airport at Addis Ababa on his way to the city to attend a summit meeting of the Organisation of African Unity. The attackers were Egyptian activists who had prepared for the mission on a 'safe farm' in Sudan before crossing the border into Ethiopia. Most were captured, but three escaped back to Sudan. The plot was traced to Turabi and senior figures in Sudan's security service. Egypt and Ethiopia accused Sudan of organising the attack. Mubarak, badly shaken, denounced Turabi and Bashir as 'thugs, criminals and crackpots'. The UN Security Council weighed in, imposing a package of sanctions on Sudan and demanding the extradition to Ethiopia of the three wanted Egyptians.

Exposed as a supporter of terrorism, reviled by neighbouring governments and shunned by the West, Bashir's government began to change course. Turabi's PAIC was disbanded; foreign fighters were expelled. One casualty was bin Laden who was told in March 1996 to leave for Afghanistan along with his followers. According to Turabi, he left Sudan 'angry at being banished'. Sudan nevertheless had provided him with an invaluable opportunity to incubate terrorist networks over a period of five years and to position his own group, al-Qa'eda, at the centre of jihad activity.

The repercussions of Sudan's alliance with Islamist extremists reverberated for many years. In August 1998 'sleeper' cells planted by al-Qa'eda in East Africa in 1994 bombed American embassies in Kenya and Tanzania, killing 263 people and injuring more than 5,000. President Clinton retaliated by ordering a missile strike against a pharmaceutical factory in Khartoum, claiming it was being used to manufacture chemical weapons. No credible evidence was ever provided to support the claim but Sudan lost a large part of its capacity to produce medical supplies.

Bashir's jihad in the south was meanwhile prosecuted with ever greater zeal and ruthlessness. A new area of conflict developed in the Nuba mountains of southern Kordofan where the local population, both Muslim and non-Muslim, resentful of land-grabbing by northern merchants, joined the SPLM campaign. As Muslims were now included as targets for reprisal, a fatwa was issued by religious scholars in 1992 setting out the status of all who opposed the government: 'An insurgent who was previously a Muslim is now an apostate; and a non-Muslim is a non-believer standing as a bulwark against the spread of Islam; and Islam has granted the freedom of killing both of them.'

The 'freedom of killing' involved slaughter in the south on a massive scale. Villages and relief centres were bombed indiscriminately from the air; PDF units and government-sponsored militias massacred civilians and plundered their property and cattle at will. Thousands of women and children were captured as war booty and forced into slavery. Uprooted from their homes, much of the population faced starvation, depending for survival on international relief supplies reaching them through war zones.

The misery of the south was made even worse by a resurgence of internecine warfare between rival southern factions. In August 1991 a Nuer guerrilla commander, Riek Machar, attempted to seize control of the SPLM from John Garang, the Dinka leader who had run the movement in dictatorial fashion since 1983. Machar wanted independence for the south rather than a united secular Sudan favoured by

Garang. Their struggle for power brought about a tribal split between Dinka and Nuer lasting for years. Tens of thousands were killed in this secondary war; several hundred thousand starved to death in the resulting famine. Both sides conscripted boy soldiers. Profiting from the split, the Khartoum government reached an accommodation with Machar, supplying him with weapons to fight Garang and steering clear of combat in areas under Machar's control. Adding to the turmoil, fighting erupted between rival Nuer factions.

The war in the south was further complicated when neighbouring governments, alarmed by Bashir's vision of a regional jihad emanating from Khartoum, retaliated by supporting the southern rebellion. Uganda acted as a major conduit for arms and ammunition for Garang's forces. In reprisal, Bashir began to support rebel movements in northern Uganda, notably the Lord's Resistance Army led by a messianic psychopath, Joseph Kony, whose speciality was abduction, rape and mutilation of children. The US government responded by providing increased aid to Museveni's government in Kampala. Other players dabbling in southern Sudan included Christian fundamentalist groups from the West involved in 'redemption' programmes to buy back the freedom of African slaves.

Though reduced to a wasteland, southern Sudan still possessed the ultimate prize for both sides: oil. After discovering oil north of Bentiu in Upper Nile province in 1978, the American company Chevron spent about $1 billion on exploration, identifying two main oilfields in the area – 'Unity' and 'Heglig' – but suspended its activities in 1984 as a result of rebel attacks. Bashir's government was determined from the outset to develop Sudan's oil potential. Oil, as much as Islamist ideology, dominated its strategy. In 1992 it prevailed upon Chevron to sell its 42 million-acre concession, subdivided the area into smaller blocks and introduced new oil partners.

The oilfields lay mostly in Nuer and Dinka territory. To protect the area from rebel attacks, the government initiated a campaign of ethnic cleansing, using the army and Baggara militias to drive out the local population and establish a *cordon sanitaire* around the oilfields. It also employed Riek Machar's Nuer faction as a proxy force to ward off the SPLM, hinting at a sharing of oil revenues. The deal with Riek

Machar was formalised in 1997 with the signing of a peace agreement in Khartoum that the government hoped would convince foreign investors that the oilfields were now secure. A new oil consortium was set up – the Greater Nile Petroleum Operating Company – involving state-owned companies from China and Malaysia. Within two years it completed the construction of a 1,540-kilometre pipeline from the Nile oilfields to a new marine port for oil supertankers on the Red Sea. The opening ceremony was presided over by Turabi and Bashir in May 1999; and the first exports of crude oil began in August 1999. Bashir described the exports as a reward from God for 'Sudan's faithfulness'. He called for Islamist volunteers to join a special brigade to help protect the oilfields. By 2001 Sudan was producing 240,000 barrels a day. Oil revenues that year contributed more than 40 per cent of the government's total revenue. With new funds at his disposal, Bashir embarked on a military spending spree, purchasing helicopter gunships and armoured combat vehicles. Defence spending between 1998 and 2000 increased by 96 per cent. As new areas of exploitation in the Western Upper Nile were opened up, more of the local population were driven from their homes.

Several peace initiatives were launched during the 1990s but never made any real progress. The ruling NIF clique in Khartoum participated for tactical reasons, with no intention of making concessions to the rebels. A protracted power struggle between Bashir and Turabi culminated in Turabi's arrest in 2001 but did not alter the NIF's commitment to its Islamist agenda. Nevertheless, Bashir was keen to shed Sudan's status as a 'pariah state' and break out of the isolation imposed on it both by neighbouring states and by Western governments.

The combination of Sudan's record of supporting international terrorism, its savage conduct of the war in the south and its repression of all opposition had made Bashir's government one of the most reviled in the world. Year after year, the UN General Assembly and the UN Commission for Human Rights issued condemnations over the war. In 2000 a new US government agency, the Commission for International Religious Freedom, concluded that 'the government of Sudan is the world's most violent abuser of the right of freedom of religion and belief'. Right-wing Christian organisations in America became increasingly vociferous in denouncing Sudan's involvement in slavery and religious persecution, urging sanctions to punish Bashir's government. In 2001 the US House of Representatives passed legislation – the Sudan Peace Act – proposing a package of sanctions that would be imposed if the Khartoum government failed to engage in meaningful negotiations to end the war or continued to obstruct humanitarian relief efforts. In September 2001, after al-Qa'eda's attack on the World Trade Center's Twin Towers in New York and the Pentagon in Washington, desperate to avoid retaliation, Bashir hastened to denounce terrorism and to pledge cooperation with US measures aimed at al-Qa'eda and other terrorist organisations.

He was also far more amenable to the idea of negotiations to end the war. President Bush appointed a special envoy for peace in Sudan, Senator John Danforth, with the remit to ascertain whether the two main protagonists in the conflict – the NIF government and Garang's SPLM – were ready to negotiate. 'For nearly two decades,' said Bush in September 2001, 'the government of Sudan has waged a brutal and shameful war against its own people. And this isn't right, and this must stop. The government has targeted civilians for violence and terror. It permits and encourages slavery. And the responsibility to end the war is on their shoulders. They must now seek the peace, and we want to help.'

Danforth proposed four tests for the two sides. He wanted: a cease-fire agreement in the Nuba mountains, an area north of the old 1956 border between Northern and Southern Sudan; an agreement not to attack or target civilians or civilian structures and property; an agreement to respect 'zones of tranquillity' in the conflict area to enable medical humanitarian agencies to carry out immunisation programmes; and agreement to appoint a commission to investigate slavery in Sudan.

There was early progress on establishing a slavery investigation and 'zones of tranquillity'. A ceasefire in the Nuba mountains was signed by both parties in Switzerland in January 2002. But agreement over the issue of civilian immunity from attack proved more difficult to resolve; Bashir at first flatly rejected a halt to aerial bombing. In February 2002, however, after a helicopter gunship attack on a World

Food Programme feeding centre at the village of Bieh killed twenty-four civilians, the international furore that followed forced the government to issue an apology and suspend air attacks.

In his report to President Bush in April 2002, Danforth concluded that a negotiated end to the war was possible in the near term and recommended that the US pursue its role as an intermediary vigorously. Together with Britain and Norway, the US consequently played a central part in driving the peace process forward. To underline the consequences of failure, Bush signed into law the Sudan Peace Act. Its key provision was that if, after six months, the president certified that the Sudanese government was not negotiating in good faith or was obstructing humanitarian relief efforts, he was empowered to impose sanctions on Khartoum and give assistance to the SPLM. No action would be taken against the government if the SPLM was deemed not to be negotiating in good faith.

The peace process that emerged contained inherent flaws. No one in Sudan other than the two main protagonists was involved. The NIF government represented only a relatively small northern faction that over a period of twelve years had successfully suppressed all opposition in the north, relying on security agencies to keep itself in power, using imprisonment without trial as a principal weapon and enforcing rigid media control. Opposition groups such as the Umma Party and the Democratic Unionist Party that commanded far greater support than the NIF were left out of the process. Other northern groups – in Darfur in the west and in Beja territory in the Red Sea hills in the east – were openly hostile to the NIF government, engaged in subversion in their own regions. None concurred with the Islamist brand of government that the NIF was determined to maintain.

The SPLM, for its part, was a Dinka-led organisation dominated by Garang but riven by shifting rivalries. It aimed to establish a united secular state but otherwise lacked an ideological base. A large proportion of southern opinion, meanwhile, harboured an abiding hatred of Arab and Islamic rule and favoured independence for the south. But southerners possessed little sense of national identity; their attachment to tribe and clan was far stronger. Not only was there considerable animosity between government-supported Nuer factions and SPLM Dinka supporters but a host of other tribal militias – the Murle in Jonglei; the Mundari and Toposa of eastern Equatoria; the Fartit of western Bahr-al-Ghazal – opposed the SPLM.

Nevertheless, the peace process at least held out the prospect of some respite from a conflict that by 2002 had resulted in 2 million dead and 4 million displaced. Meeting for five weeks in the sleepy Kenyan town of Machakos, the NIF government and the SPLM reached agreement on several key issues. Under the terms of the Machakos Protocol, signed in July 2002 and finalised in 2004, the south was accorded the right to self-determination. After a six-year interim period beginning in January 2005 when a final peace settlement was signed, southerners would choose in a referendum whether to remain in a united Sudan or set up an independent state. The question of religion was dealt with by treating the north and the south separately. Sharia was confirmed as the source of law in the northern two-thirds of the country, outside Khartoum, while the south was free to be run as a secular part of Sudan. Thus some 5 million non-Muslims living in the north would still be subject to sharia law. No consideration was given to the option of establishing a secular state for the whole of Sudan – an aim that many northerners as well as southerners shared.

But just as one war was winding down, another broke out in the western region of Darfur, threatening disaster of a magnitude that had not occurred since Rwanda. Its origins lay in an age-old conflict over land between nomadic Arab pastoralists and settled 'African' agriculturalists that intensified during the 1980s as a result of drought and increasing desertification. Arab pastoralists moving southwards from the arid northern part of Darfur into areas occupied by black Muslim tribes – the Fur, Masaalit and Zaghawa – were involved in a series of violent clashes. Rather than working to defuse tensions, the Khartoum government sided with Arab pastoralists, providing them with arms.

In February 2003 a rebel group calling itself the Sudan Liberation Army, encouraged by the deal that southern Sudan's rebels had won, launched its own insurgency citing both Khartoum's neglect of the region's development and its failure to provide protection against Arab raiders. Its leaders demanded a share in central government. A second rebel group, the Justice and Equality Movement, joined the fray. Khartoum reacted with a savage campaign of ethnic cleansing intended to drive out the local population and replace it with Arab settlers, just as it had done in oil-producing areas of the south and the Nuba mountains. The air force bombed villages; the army launched ground attacks; and Arab militias known as *janjaweed* were licensed to kill, loot and rape at will. They burned to the ground hundreds of villages, killed thousands of tribesmen, raped women en masse, abducted children and stole cattle. Refugees were left with no means of survival. By February 2004 a million people had fled their homes. When UN agencies attempted to intervene, the Khartoum government obstructed outside investigation and blocked relief efforts. Fearful of jeopardising the hard-won peace agreement in the south, Western governments dithered in their response, reluctant to impose sanctions, even after UN officials described Darfur as 'the worst humanitarian crisis in the world'. The US government eventually declared Khartoum's actions as 'genocide'. Under the spotlight of world attention, Bashir reined in the *janjaweed*. The violence subsided, but the conflict remained unresolved.

There seemed little prospect of Sudan finding a durable peace. The stark fact about its existence as an independent state since 1956 was that it had spent more than thirty years at war.

BLACK GOLD

The first glimpse of peace in Angola's interminable civil war came in 1990 as the Cold War drew to a close. Throughout the 1980s Angola had remained a pawn in the Cold War, a theatre in which the United States and the Soviet Union used proxy forces to compete for ascendancy. While the Russians and the Cubans continued to prop up the MPLA's Marxist regime in Luanda, the Americans, along with the South Africans, sustained Jonas Savimbi's rebel Unita movement. Angola featured as part of President Reagan's strategy of 'bleeding' Soviet resources by fuelling insurgencies in countries he regarded as Soviet 'client states'. During his first term in office, Reagan, thwarted by the 1976 'Clark Amendment' banning direct US assistance to Unita, used third parties to arm Savimbi. During his second term he succeeded in overturning the Clark Amendment, enabling him to provide direct covert military aid to Unita. Year by year the amount increased.

American officials dealing with Savimbi gave him high marks for leadership. 'It was difficult not to be impressed by this Angolan, who combined the qualities of warlord, paramount chief, demagogue and statesman,' wrote Chester Crocker, a former Assistant Secretary of State for African Affairs, in his 1992 book *High Noon in Southern Africa*. Noting that Savimbi was fluent in three African languages and four European ones, Crocker considered him to possess 'a world-class strategic mind'. In 1986 Savimbi was invited to the White House and presented to the American public as a 'champion of democracy'.

With American as well as South African support, Savimbi's forces gained control of much of southern and central Angola and spread northwards to the border with Zaire, overrunning the diamond fields of the Lunda region that provided three-quarters of Angola's diamond production. With the collusion of Mobutu, Savimbi used Zaire as a base for guerrilla activity in northern Angola, a conduit for receiving American arms supplies and an entrepôt for selling diamonds.

To fend off the Unita threat, the MPLA government relied on 50,000 Cuban troops and spent heavily on Soviet arms, drawing on revenues from the offshore oil fields being developed by American companies. Between 1987 and 1990, the Soviet Union supplied more than $3 billion worth of military equipment. One of the paradoxes of the Angolan conflict was that Cuban forces were given the task of defending American-owned oil installations from attacks by American-backed rebels. The overall cost of the war was huge. During the 1980s more than 350,000 died and a million more – deslocados – were uprooted from their homes.

Though a deal involving South Africa's withdrawal from Angola and Namibia in return for the phased withdrawal of Cuban troops from Angola was reached in December 1988 it still left the war unresolved. Mobutu, anxious to win favour in Washington, attempted to broker a local peace deal and in June 1989 invited Savimbi and the MPLA leader, Eduardo dos Santos, to his palace at Gbadolite where they met for the first time and frigidly shook hands. Seven days later Savimbi's commandos attacked Luanda's electricity supply.

Meeting during Namibia's independence celebrations in March 1990, American and Russian officials initiated their own discussions for peace in Angola. Portugal, the former colonial power, joined the initiative, mediating at a first round of direct talks between the MPLA and Unita in Portugal in April. Thirteen months later, at a meeting in Lisbon on 31 May 1991, dos Santos and Savimbi signed a sixty-page package of agreements intended to bring an end to sixteen years of civil war. Dos Santos was stiff and silent; Savimbi was charming and exuberant, brimming with confidence. American and Russian officials attending the ceremony simultaneously declared an end to the Cold War in Africa. A key role was accorded to a United Nations mission led by a British-born UN diplomat, Margaret Anstee, which was charged with monitoring the peace process and verifying elections scheduled for 1992. In the sand slums of Luanda – the *musseques* – where 2 million residents lived, the 1991 accord was gratefully known as 'Margaret's peace'.

Despite the appearance of goodwill, the two sides viewed each other with intense distrust. The MPLA was an authoritarian party in the hands of a small elite – an oil *nomenklatura* – long accustomed to wielding power in an arbitrary manner and to enriching themselves from the business of government. It had relied heavily on a security apparatus developed with East German assistance to ensure control and to suppress any sign of opposition. An internal coup attempt in 1977 had been put down with the help of Cuban forces with extreme violence, instilling a mood of fear that still prevailed. Since taking office in 1979 on the death of Agostinho Neto, dos Santos, a Soviet-trained petroleum engineer, had accumulated more and more personal power, developing a personality cult. Eulogising his leadership, a MPLA congress in 1985 declared: 'His prestige, authority and respect and admiration of militants and the people are becoming increasingly evident, owing to his consistency and honesty in respect of the principles of the revolution and his intelligence and modesty in analysing and solving the party's central problems.'

In reality, the MPLA's policies had proved disastrous. For fifteen years it had enforced a Soviet-inspired system of centralised planning and nationalisation, causing the collapse of both industrial and agricultural production. Oil revenue was the only source of wealth. Oil enabled the government to prosecute the war against Unita, to pay for food imports for the urban population and to provide the *nomenklatura* with extravagant lifestyles. The rural population was meanwhile left to fend for itself. Even in Luanda there were constant shortages. While the MPLA elite enjoyed the use of their own supermarkets, well stocked with Italian chocolates, Scotch whisky and red meat, ordinary people spent hours each day in queues – *bichas* –

hoping for a modicum of rice or potatoes. Street trade was mainly conducted not with currency but by bartering eggs, six-packs of lager in aluminium cans or other items. When public services disintegrated, the elite used education and health facilities abroad, paid for by public funds.

At his presidential headquarters at Futungo de Belas, a modern complex built for him by the Cubans on a promontory overlooking the sea, dos Santos resided in luxury, rarely leaving the compound, remaining remote from the squalor of Luanda, its decrepit buildings, its power shortages, its outbreaks of cholera, its stench and decay. Though the MPLA still proclaimed itself to be a Marxist-Leninist party, its commitment to socialism was entirely bogus.

In 1990, after the Russians had lost interest in Angola, the MPLA formally abandoned Marxism-Leninism and pronounced itself in favour of economic reform. The reforms it instituted, however, provided yet more business opportunities for the elite, notably the privatisation of state assets. What the MPLA had come to represent by then was little more than a front for a cabal of wealthy inter-related families linked to the presidency – the *futungos* – whose central purpose was self-enrichment. None of them had any intention of putting their business interests at risk for the sake of a peace deal.

As for Unita, it was Savimbi's personal fiefdom, a vehicle for his relentless drive for power. For all the praise heaped on him by President Reagan and other Western admirers, Savimbi was a ruthless dictator with a messianic sense of destiny, insistent on total control and intolerant of dissent and criticism from anyone in his movement. He purported to represent the 'African' people of Angola, portraying the MPLA as a coastal party dominated by whites and *mestiços* in Luanda. Yet he himself had survived only as a result of assistance from South Africa's white rulers as part of their crusade to sustain white supremacy. For thirteen years his headquarters at Jamba, a remote spot in the south-east corner of Angola, within easy reach of South African bases in South West Africa and the Caprivi Strip, had been supplied and protected by South African forces, keeping his rebellion alive. Foreign journalists ferried there were invariably impressed by Unita's discipline and efficiency, comparing it favourably with the incompetence and corruption for which the MPLA was renowned. Adept at public relations, Savimbi readily represented himself as a staunch anti-communist defending Western values. He relished his image in Western circles as a heroic guerrilla leader who in the 1970s had endured a 'long march' into the bush to continue the fight against Marxist tyranny. Yet, like the MPLA, Savimbi relied heavily on an extensive security apparatus to maintain his grip, using fear as a method of control. He systematically purged Unita of rivals and critics, ordering death sentences not only for party dissidents but for members of their families as well. Human rights groups reported incidents of how women and children, accused of witchcraft, had been publicly burned to death, on a bonfire. According to his biographer, Fred Bridgland, Savimbi was also reputed to have a voracious sexual appetite. 'Savimbi's sexual practices went beyond most usual concepts of lust. He chose wives for his senior officers and slept with them in a bizarre rite of passage before they were married.' He had even seduced his own teenage niece, Raquel Matos, and made her one of his concubines. 'Raquel's parents protested and were executed,' said Bridgland.

An inside glimpse of Savimbi's methods came in February 1992, as Angola was preparing for elections. Two of Savimbi's closest colleagues – his 'foreign minister' Tony da Costa Fernandes and his 'interior minister' General Miguel N'Zau Puna – announced that they had quit Unita after discovering that Savimbi had ordered the death of two prominent officials, Tito Chigunji, and his brother-in-law, Wilson dos Santos, together with their families. Chigunji came from a distinguished Ovimbundu family which Savimbi was said to regard as potential rivals; several members had previously died in suspicious circumstances. According to the two defectors, Chigunji's two children, one a baby, had died with their heads smashed against a tree.

The disclosures inflicted enormous damage on Savimbi's reputation both in Angola and in the West. Chigunji and Wilson dos Santos had served as Unita representatives abroad and were well known in Washington. The US Secretary of State, James Baker, wrote to Savimbi demanding a full account of what had happened to the two men. Savimbi denied any involvement in their deaths and rode out the storm. He remained convinced he was on course to win the election. In Luanda he set up headquarters in a magnificent white villa on the heights of Miramar, a diplomatic quarter overlooking the bay, repeatedly telling journalists who went to interview him there that he could only lose as a result of fraud.

Shortly after arriving in Angola in February 1992, the UN chief, Margaret Anstee, went to introduce herself. 'Everything about him was larger than life – his hypnotic piercing eyes, his hands, even his immaculately polished leather boots,' she wrote in her memoir. 'The man simply exuded charisma. On that occasion he also exuded charm and sweet reasonableness . . . Superficially it was a highly civilised and modern occasion. Yet my overwhelming sensation was of being a guest at a medieval court.'

Despite rising tensions, Angola experienced its first dance of freedom. New shops and bars opened; foreign volunteers – *cooperantes* – arrived in droves; ambitious plans for reconstruction were drawn up; foreign businessmen came in search of contracts; residents painted their houses. 'Angola in 1992 was like a Rip Van Winkle yawning and stretching awake after the moribund days of socialist deprivation,' wrote Judith Matloff, an American journalist. 'The days of spies and using eggs as a bartering currency were over.' Overall, there was widespread relief at the respite from war, but scepticism about whether it would last. 'Will it be like 1975?' a market trader asked. 'It is not the people who make war, but the leaders.'

The peace process itself was in considerable difficulty. The 1991 accords envisaged that the two rival armies, amounting in all to some 200,000 soldiers, would be confined to cantonments, demobilised and reconstituted as a new national army of 50,000 men – all in the space of sixteen months, before the election was held. The logistical problems alone were immense. Two-thirds of all roads in the country were unusable as a result of landmines or destroyed bridges; air transport was limited. On top of that, an estimated 5 million voters had to be registered.

The United Nations mission assigned to verify demobilisation and to monitor the electoral process – Unavem – was given a limited mandate and few resources. The Security Council, when authorising the mission under resolution 747, insisted on keeping expenditure to a minimum. 'I have been given a 747 to fly with only fuel for a DC3,' Anstee told a journalist jokingly after her arrival in Luanda. Whereas the UN's election exercise in Namibia had been run on a budget of $430 million and in Cambodia on $2 billion, Anstee's budget was $132 million. To keep the mission on track, she had to resort to begging individual Western governments for more supplies and equipment. A team of 350 military observers was expected to cover a demobilisation plan fraught with danger. 'The world's cheapest peacekeeping operation' was Anstee's description. A total of 800 election observers were assigned to monitor 5,820 polling stations in an area larger than the combined territories of France, Germany and Italy. Watching the drama unfold, Judith Matloff summed up the exercise as 'a UN peace mission of absurd incompetence'.

Every aspect of the peace process was soon far behind schedule. By September 1992 only about half of the MPLA's army had been demobilised and no more than about one-quarter of Unita's army. The new national army – *Forças Armadas Angolanas* – consisted of only 8,800 troops. Each side feared the other was holding back forces to resume the war if it lost the election. Disputes proliferated, intensifying the miasma of distrust. Unita was infuriated by a government decision to form a new 'anti-riot' police force – *ninjas*, as they commonly came to be known – whose members, dressed in navy blue uniforms, wearing dark glasses and carrying AK47s and Uzi machine guns, began to appear on the streets of Luanda. Savimbi claimed it was 'a parallel army'.

The election campaign was conducted by both sides with increasing belligerence. Savimbi excelled at angry rhetoric, threatening that he would not accept an election result that did not give him victory. 'If Unita does not win the elections, they have to be rigged. If they are rigged, I don't think we will accept them.' On the streets, a popular saying at the time was: 'The MPLA steals, Unita kills.' The elections nevertheless proceeded in a calm and orderly manner. When the polls closed on 30 September, there had been almost no incidents of violence. Whatever the machinations of Angola's politicians, the electorate had shown their determination to vote with an estimated 90 per cent turnout, desperately hoping for peace.

The trouble began when the state-run radio began broadcasting preliminary results, mainly from urban constituencies where the MPLA was known to be well entrenched, showing that the MPLA had a commanding lead. A battle of the air waves ensued. Unita's Vorgan radio station – 'Voice of the Resistance of the Black Cockerel' – insisted that Unita was ahead by a two-to-one margin. Without warning on 3 October, as official results were still awaited, Savimbi broadcast a 'Message to the Angolan Nation' on Vorgan radio, warning of violence if the MPLA was declared the winner.

It is a pity for me to tell you that the MPLA wants to cling to power illegally, tooth and nail, by stealing ballot boxes, beating up and deviating polling-list delegates and distorting facts and numbers through its radio and television network . . . Right now the MPLA is cheating. In all provinces, Unita is ahead both in the presidential and parliamentary elections . . .

The National Electoral Council will have to take into consideration that its manoeuvres through the falsification of numbers and tampering with the computers will all lead Unita to take a position which might deeply disturb the situation in this country . . .

The National Electoral Council is manipulated by the Futungo de Belas presidential palace and we are not afraid of Futungo de Belas. If Futungo wants the process to halt and the situation in the country to deteriorate, then it should continue telling lies, stealing ballot boxes and distorting the figures. Just as we said in 1975 to the late president, Dr Agostinho Neto, 'It is easy to start a war, but to prolong and win it is difficult.' If the MPLA wants to opt for war, it knows that such a war will never be won.

We would like to draw the MPLA's attention to the fact that there are men and women in this country who are ready to give up their lives so that the country can redeem itself. As far as we are concerned, it will not depend on any international organisation saying that the elections were free and fair . . .

Leaving no doubt about his intentions, two days later Savimbi ordered Unita's generals to withdraw from the new national army. Savimbi himself left Luanda for Huambo in the central highlands, Angola's second largest city, which he had used as his headquarters in 1976. Striving to keep the peace process alive, Anstee went to see him there and undertook to investigate Unita's allegations of fraud before official election results were declared. The investigations concluded that although irregularities had occurred, there was no evidence of fraud on a major scale.

After repeated delays, the official results were finally announced on 17 October. In the presidential elections dos Santos obtained 49.57 per cent of the votes, compared with Savimbi's 40.07 per cent. Since a 50 per cent vote was needed to win, a second round of voting would have to be held. In the parliamentary elections the MPLA gained 53.7 per cent, taking 129 seats, compared with Unita's 34.1 per cent, with 70 seats. Anstee gave the results her imprimatur, declaring that despite the 'deficiencies', the UN mission considered the elections had been 'generally free and fair'.

An analysis of the results showed that the MPLA had swept the board in its Mbundu 'home territory', winning 81 per cent of the presidential vote and 85 per cent of the parliamentary vote in Luanda and the surrounding provinces of Bengo, Kwanza Norte and Malange. Similarly, Unita had triumphed in its Ovimbundu heartland, winning 80 per cent of the presidential vote and 76 per cent of the parliamentary vote in the three provinces of Benguela, Bié and Huambo and a fourth sparsely populated province in the south-east, Cuando Cubango. What made the difference was the MPLA's success in attracting support beyond Mbundu territory. In the ten provinces outside the two parties' core zones, the MPLA won 72 per cent of the presidential vote and 77 per cent of the parliamentary vote. Many voters who might have supported Unita were deterred by Savimbi's belligerent election campaign, his menacing rhetoric threatening a return to war if he did not win.

Though Anstee's team and other foreign delegations made prodigious efforts to salvage the peace process, both sides prepared for another war. Unita's forces decamped from their cantonments and took control of large parts of the interior, including the diamond-producing areas of Lunda, forcing government administrators to flee. In Luanda the MPLA government began handing out weapons to its supporters in the *musseques*. Clashes broke out in several towns. Unita troops attacked the radio and television stations in Huambo and attempted to occupy the government's palace.

On 31 October the battle for Luanda erupted. In three days of fighting Unita's forces were driven from the capital. Its offices, residences and hotels were destroyed. In what one senior United Nations official described as 'wholesale butchery', government *ninjas* and armed vigilantes from the *musseques* hunted down Unita supporters in a 'cleansing operation' – *limpeza* – intended to eliminate them from Luanda.

The battle for Luanda was followed by similarly vicious contests for possession of other towns in which some 300,000 people died. Once more, Angola was partitioned into government- and rebel-held areas. This time, however, the war was no longer a sideshow of the Cold War nor an adjunct of South Africa's struggle over white supremacy. It was a war to satisfy the ambition of one man to hold absolute power.

As Angola's peace efforts collapsed, a similar exercise was launched to bring an end to Mozambique's civil war. Over a period of fifteen years it had reduced the country to a wreck. By the early 1990s more than 1 million people had died and 5 million others had been uprooted from their homes out of a total population of 18 million. More than 90 per cent of the population lived below the poverty line, and 60 per cent of those lived in absolute poverty. To prevent mass starvation, Mozambique relied on foreign aid.

Under international auspices, the Frelimo government and the Renamo rebel movement were drawn into protracted negotiations. Since starting life as a proxy force, first for white Rhodesia then for South Africa, Renamo had gained a reputation for extreme brutality, carrying out exemplary massacres and mutilations and conscripting child soldiers; but it had also managed to tap into a deep groundswell of discontent with Frelimo's authoritarian policies, winning control of large parts of central and northern Mozambique. Offered the prospect of participating in a new political order, Renamo agreed in 1992 to disband its army, transform itself into a political party and compete in an electoral contest. The peace deal was signed in Rome on 4 October, a few days after Angola's elections were held.

Mindful of the debacle of Angola's peace initiative, the UN decided to pour resources of men, money and matériel into Mozambique, in effect setting up a parallel government there. Most key functions ranging from demobilisation and disarmament to the resettlement of refugees and combatants were carried out by UN agencies or by non-governmental organisations acting on their behalf. Demobilisation began in January 1994 and was completed by September, in advance of the election. Presidential elections in October gave Frelimo's Joaquim Chissano 53 per cent of the vote and Renamo's Alfonso Dhlakama 33 per cent; in parliamentary elections Frelimo won 44 per cent of the vote, taking 129 seats, and Renamo won 38 per cent, taking 112 seats. Renamo accepted the result and settled for the role of a 'loyal' opposition.

In Angola the war of the cities, as it was known, lasted for two years, causing destruction on a scale that it had never before experienced. Changing the guerrilla strategy he adopted in the 1980s, Savimbi focused his campaign on trying to retain control of key urban centres. Driven out of Luanda, Lobito and Benguela, Unita managed to seize five out of eighteen provincial capitals including Huambo which Savimbi used as a headquarters. The battle for control of Huambo lasted for fifty-five days, leaving much of the city in ruins. After retreating from the city, government forces continued to bomb it from the air. Unita also laid siege to government-held towns, trying to starve them into submission. Kuito, the capital of Bié province, was bombarded relentlessly for nine months until a temporary ceasefire was arranged; by the time fighting finally stopped six months later there was little left standing. Both sides planted millions of landmines, leaving behind a new generation of *mutilados* among the civilian population.

Though Savimbi no longer had the support of his former

sponsors – the United States and South Africa – his supply routes through Mobutu's Zaire remained open, enabling him to trade diamonds for arms. Unita's earnings from diamonds, ranging from $300–500 million a year, gave him considerable purchasing power. Mobutu provided Savimbi with end-user certificates for arms deals and allowed him to stockpile weapons in Zaire, in return for diamonds and cash. Savimbi also reached deals with the presidents of Congo-Brazzaville and Togo for support facilities; President Eyadéma in Togo provided sanctuary for Savimbi's children.

Savimbi's hold on territory, however, began to slip. In 1993 he controlled more than two-thirds of Angola's territory. But during 1994, as the government reorganised its forces, spending half the national budget on arms, Unita steadily lost ground. In November 1994 government forces recaptured Huambo, forcing Savimbi to fall back on his home town of Bailundo, once the seat of Ovimbundu kings. Eleven days later, for tactical reasons, Unita agreed to a new peace deal at negotiations in Lusaka.

Unlike the 1991 peace deal, the Lusaka Protocol gave direct responsibility for overseeing implementation of the peace process to a new United Nations mission. A contingent of 7,000 UN troops was assigned to the tasks of assisting demobilisation and the formation of a new national army. UN officials hoped to copy the example of Mozambique. But though Savimbi was offered a transitional period of power-sharing, from the start he resorted to prevarication and delay to obstruct implementation, playing for time to amass a war chest from diamond production in areas he still controlled. He sent more than 70,000 men to UN-administered 'quartering areas', but most of them were village reservists rounded up to boost numbers. His real army he held in reserve, together with their equipment and supplies. He also turned down an offer from dos Santos to give him the post of vice-president in a future government of national unity. When a foreign journalist questioned him about the offer, he roared back: 'Do I look like a puppet?'

A government of national unity, including Unita ministers, was eventually established in April 1997. The UN was sufficiently optimistic about the peace process by then to withdraw most of its peacekeeping force and to replace it with a residual mission with only 1,500 troops. But Savimbi still refused to allow the government to extend its authority to many of the areas under his control, in particular the diamond fields. He was brazen enough to hold auctions close to mining areas, inviting foreign buyers to fly in from abroad. By 1997 his income from diamonds over the previous five years had reached an estimated $2 billion.

In exasperation at Savimbi's obstruction of the peace process, the UN Security Council imposed sanctions on Unita in August 1997, banning leading officials from international travel, closing Unita's offices abroad and prohibiting all aircraft from flying into Unita-controlled areas. After further prevarication, the Security Council in June 1998 ordered a ban on the purchase of Angolan diamonds without official certificates of origin and a freeze on Unita's bank accounts and other financial assets.

Savimbi's position in Bailundo appeared increasingly vulnerable. The collapse of Mobutu's regime in May 1997 deprived him of his last dependable foreign ally. When Congo-Brazzaville was convulsed by civil war in June 1997, he lost another diamond outlet. Unita ministers and members of parliament in Luanda, frustrated with his policy of obstruction, decided to break away. Yet the war chest Savimbi had accumulated had enabled him to re-equip his army in preparation for another push for 'victory'.

The government too spent vast sums on military purchases, determined to crush Savimbi by force if he continued to thwart the terms of the Lusaka Protocol. Finally losing patience, dos Santos declared in December 1998 that war was the only option and ordered a military offensive against Unita's strongholds in the central highlands. As the peace process collapsed, the UN closed its observer mission, having spent $1.5 billion on Angola since 1994 to no avail.

The 1998 war lasted for more than three years. Both sides used forced recruitment, destroyed villages, looted property, murdered civilians and raped women and children. Nearly one-third of the entire population – about 4 million people – were listed as *deslocados*, left homeless and destitute. After losing control of Bailundo and his last remaining large airfields in 1999, Savimbi moved his headquarters

to the eastern province of Moxico, abandoning his strategy of capturing towns and reverting to guerrilla strikes on government targets.
Weakened by government offensives, Unita's fighting capacity steadily
diminished. In the final stages of the war the government resorted to
scorched-earth tactics, forcibly deporting the rural population from
Unita areas and burning their crops. The end came in February 2002
when Savimbi was trapped and killed in a firefight in the remote
region of Luva near the Zambian border. Within days, Unita sued for
peace.

Throughout the rollercoaster years of war and peace, dos Santos and
his entourage prospered greatly. From his headquarters at Futungo de
Belas, dos Santos ran a presidential patronage system that rewarded his
family, friends and colleagues – the *futungos* – with government contracts, business opportunities, diamond concessions, land titles, import
licences, trade monopolies and cheap credit. Arms purchases for the
war provided a favoured few with large kickbacks. The government's
privatisation programme enabled high-ranking army officers and
senior officials to acquire state-owned properties, farms and businesses
for nominal sums or sometimes for no payment at all. Allowed access
to foreign exchange, some *futungos* made fortunes from the dual
exchange rate, 'round-tripping' between markets.

Elite families also benefited from state scholarships for their children
to study abroad, in secondary schools as well as university level, and
from state provision of foreign medical treatment. Between 1997 and
2001 overseas scholarships accounted on average for 18 per cent of
total government expenditure on education, more than was spent
within the country on technical education and higher education combined. Foreign medical expenditure consumed 13 per cent of total
government spending on health, almost as much as was spent on primary health care. Ministers and officials who proved their loyalty
were awarded generous 'Christmas bonuses' far in excess of their
annual salaries.

A large proportion of Angola's oil wealth was siphoned off for private purposes. Oil production rose sixfold after 1983. Between 1997
and 2002 the oil sector generated $17.8 billion. Yet what happened to

the income was shrouded in secrecy. An International Monetary Fund report in 2002 showed that 22 per cent of government expenditure between 1996 and 2001 was 'unexplained'; a further 16 per cent was listed as 'extra-budgetary'. Using IMF figures, a Human Rights Watch report published in 2004 calculated that between 1997 and 2002 an amount of $4.2 billion went 'unaccounted for' – an average of $700 million a year, nearly 10 per cent of gross domestic product, roughly equivalent to the total sum spent on education, health and social services over the same period. What had occurred, said the report, was gross mismanagement and corruption on the part of Angola's rulers.

> When a government is the direct beneficiary of a centrally controlled major revenue stream and is therefore not reliant on domestic taxation or a diversified economy to function, those who rule the state have unique opportunities for self-enrichment and corruption, particularly if there is no transparency in the management of revenues. Because achieving political power often becomes the primary avenue for achieving wealth, the incentive to seize power and hold on to it indefinitely is great. This dynamic has a corrosive effect on governance and, ultimately, respect for human rights. Instead of bringing prosperity, rule of law and respect for rights, the existence of a centrally controlled revenue stream – such as oil revenue – can serve to reinforce and exacerbate an undemocratic or otherwise unaccountable ruler's or governing elite's worst tendencies and enrich itself without any corresponding accountability . . . This has happened in Angola.

Dos Santos went to extraordinary lengths to ensure that the government's oil accounts were hidden from scrutiny. A State Secrecy Act passed in 2002 classified as secret 'financial, monetary, economic and commercial interests of the State', authorising terms of imprisonment for anyone caught divulging information. When an IMF team, attempting to unravel the government's oil accounts, asked for an explanation about a discrepancy of up to $215 million between what the government said it had received in oil exploration fees from oil companies and what the oil companies said they had paid,

government officials said they 'could not provide any supporting documentation on those payments because of confidentiality agreements
with the oil companies'. When British Petroleum, responding to
demands for greater transparency, announced in 2001 that it would
publish its payments to Angola, the government threatened to cancel
its multibillion dollar contracts and threw in a warning to all other oil
companies: 'In the hope of maintaining good relations that we have
always had with the oil companies that operate in Angola, we strongly
discourage all our partners from similar attitudes in the future.'

Despite the government's determination to maintain secrecy,
glimpses of some of dos Santos's dealings came as a result of a series of
investigations in Europe into what colloquially became known as
'Angolagate'. In July 2000 a former oil company executive, André
Tarallo, testified to French authorities that dos Santos was one of the
beneficiaries of a multimillion-dollar slush fund that Elf-Aquitaine
kept to pay African leaders in exchange for influence and oil deals.
Dos Santos denied the allegation. 'The Cabinet of the President of
Angola believes that Mr Tarallo's attitude to be unacceptable and
unfair, given that the Angolan authorities granted him, in good will,
all manner of assistance to ensure the success of Elf's operations in
Angola and its good performance, which allowed France to occupy
the second position in the Angolan oil industry, with obvious benefits.'

Dos Santos was also named as a beneficiary in a murky deal involving the rescheduling of Angola's $5 billion debt to Russia for arms
purchases. In 2002 a Swiss magistrate, Daniel Devaud, ordered a freeze
on $700 million held in a Geneva bank account while he investigated
transactions involving 'Russian and Angolan dignitaries' connected to
the debt deal, one of whom was dos Santos. The MPLA leader was
livid. In a letter of protest to the Swiss president, dos Santos claimed
that Swiss judges had no right to get involved in a bilateral matter
between Angola and Russia and threatened to withdraw his ambassador from Switzerland. He denounced Devaud's action as 'arrogant and
an abuse of power and a violation of the principles of international
law'. However, in June 2002 Angola's minister of the interior admitted in Luanda's parliament that government funds had indeed been
placed in private bank accounts, but justified this as commonplace in

countries facing exceptional situations. When IMF staff asked for details of the Russian debt deal, the government refused to comply on the grounds that 'it would infringe on national sovereignty'.

An indication of how wealthy the *futungos* had become was provided by the Economist Intelligence Unit in 2003. It reported that there were thirty-nine individuals in Angola worth at least $50 million and another twenty reportedly worth at least $100 million. Six of the seven wealthiest people on its list were longtime government officials, and the seventh was a recently retired official. Overall, the combined wealth of these fifty-nine people was at least $3.95 billion. By comparison, the total gross domestic product of Angola, with a population of about 14 million, was about $10.2 billion in 2002.

The stark contrast between the rich elite and the mass poverty of the rest of the population was nowhere more evident than in Luanda. Its streets were packed with the latest models of Mercedez-Benz and Toyota Land Cruisers; jet skis circled the bay; prices in air-conditioned shopping malls were equivalent to those in London. But milling around on street corners were groups of street children and *mutilados* begging from the passing traffic. Half of the city's population of 4 million had no access to clean water and survived on untreated water from the Bengo river bought by the bucketful from informal vendors. Most Angolans subsisted on less than seventy cents a day.

A DEGREE IN VIOLENCE

The sense of hope and optimism that accompanied the birth of Zimbabwe as an independent state in 1980 survived for several years. In keeping with his promises about reconciliation, Robert Mugabe strove to build a good working relationship with his former white adversaries. He appointed two white ministers to his cabinet and retained the services of the former Rhodesian armed forces commander, General Peter Walls, as the country's military chief. He even kept in place the head of intelligence, Ken Flower, who had previously spent considerable effort trying to organise Mugabe's assassination. At one of their first meetings in Mugabe's office, Flower was anxious to explain about the various attempts the Rhodesians had made to kill him, to ensure that Mugabe was fully informed about his background. But Mugabe simply laughed. 'Yes, but they all failed, otherwise we would not be here together,' he remarked. 'And do not expect me to applaud your failures.' In his memoirs, Flower recalled: 'It was a strange experience working for an African leader whom whites had been taught to hate and whose assumption of power we had forecast to be catastrophic.'

Equally remarkable, Mugabe struck up a cordial relationship with the former Rhodesian leader, Ian Smith, inviting him round for a series of meetings. Smith was duly impressed. 'When I got back home,' Smith recorded after their first encounter, 'I said to Janet that I hoped it was not an hallucination. He behaved like a balanced, civilised Westerner, the antithesis of the communist gangster I had expected. If this was a true picture, then there could be hope instead of despair.' In subsequent encounters, Smith left feeling ever more confident, remarking in his diary on Mugabe's 'maturity, reasonableness and sense of fair play'.

Mugabe also went out of his way to reassure white business about the future, stressing the importance of foreign investment and the need to pursue development on capitalist lines before moving on to socialist measures. 'We shall proceed to bring about changes, but changes in a realistic manner,' he said. 'We recognise that the economic structure of this country is based on capitalism, and that whatever ideas we have, we must build on that. Modifications can only take place in a gradual way.'

He was particularly keen to win the trust of white commercial farmers. One of the most privileged groups in the country, numbering no more than 6,000 in all, they owned nearly 40 per cent of all agricultural land and two-thirds of the best land. Their role was regarded as crucial to the economic welfare of Zimbabwe. They accounted for three-quarters of the output of the agricultural industry and produced a multitude of crops and commodities using sophisticated techniques and equipment. They grew 90 per cent of marketed maize, the main staple; 90 per cent of cotton, the main industrial crop; and virtually all tobacco and other export crops, including wheat, coffee, tea and sugar, accounting in all for one-third of total exports. They employed about one-third of the wage-earning labour force – some 271,000 people in 1980.

Mugabe saw the need to treat white farmers as 'royal game', ensuring that the industry was rewarded with generous price rises and other financial incentives and that technical services and support were maintained at a high standard. As a result of his careful patronage, white farmers, nervous and depressed by the 1980 election results, soon rebounded with confidence, even applauding him as 'Good old Bob!' In its first two years of independence, moreover, Zimbabwe was blessed with good rains and record harvests.

The honeymoon of independence brought many benefits to the white community. No longer did they face military call-up or economic sanctions or petrol rationing. Now they were free to take up old leisure pursuits abandoned during the war. As well as owning most commercial farmland, they dominated commerce, industry and banking, possessed a virtual monopoly of high-level skills and retained for the most part considerable property and personal wealth. In the economic boom that followed the end of the war – growth of 24 per cent in two years – the whites were major beneficiaries.

Buoyed up by a huge influx of Western aid – nearly £900 million was pledged during the first year of independence – Mugabe was also able to embark on ambitious programmes to extend education and health services to the entire population and to finance the start of a land redistribution scheme. Land reform was a pressing issue. Four million people lived on communal land that was overcrowded, overgrazed and rapidly deteriorating. Three-quarters of all peasant land lay in areas where droughts occurred frequently and where even normal levels of rainfall were inadequate for intensive crop production. The population density in communal areas was more than three times that of 'white' areas and the number of people living there double their carrying capacity. Land shortage and land degradation were deeply entrenched problems, left unresolved over decades of white rule and mounting inexorably as a result of population pressures. Each year the communal areas produced an additional 40,000 families.

Assisted by funds from Britain, Mugabe's government initiated a programme to resettle 18,000 families over a three-year period on some 2.5 million acres of former white land, mainly farms in the north-east that had been abandoned during the war. The programme was elaborately designed and required an infrastructure of roads, fencing, dip tanks, housing, schools and clinics. It represented only a preliminary step in tackling the land issue, but Mugabe was precluded from taking more radical measures by a constitutional agreement lasting for ten years after independence stipulating that land transactions could only be conducted on a willing-seller willing-buyer basis. And to reassure white farmers about their land rights, Mugabe insisted he would observe the agreement for its full term.

But while he was willing to accommodate the interests of the white community, on whom economic prosperity largely depended, Mugabe showed no such tolerance towards his black opponents.

Mugabe's objective, as he repeatedly stated from the outset of independence, was to establish a one-party state run by Zanu-PF. As became evident, he had fought the war not to achieve democracy but to gain total control. In an interview after he became prime minister in 1980, he made clear his disappointment that the peace negotiations in London in 1979 had deprived him of the chance of a military victory – 'the ultimate joy' – and thus the opportunity 'to dictate terms'. For the sake of expediency, urged on by Britain, he had agreed to a coalition government with his rival Joshua Nkomo, the Zapu leader, while their two guerrilla armies – Mugabe's Zanla and Nkomo's Zipra – were integrated into a new national army. But from the start, Mugabe showed his impatience with the arrangement, licensing his closest colleagues – Edgar Tekere and Enos Nkala – to scorn and denigrate Nkomo and his Ndebele supporters. Within weeks of independence, despite the risk of provoking conflict, both Tekere and Nkala spoke openly of the need to 'crush' Zapu. Nkala, a Ndebele politician with an abiding hatred of Nkomo, derided him as a 'self-appointed Ndebele king'. Tekere went further: 'Nkomo and his guerrillas are germs in the country's wounds,' he said, 'and they will have to be cleaned up with iodine. The patient will have to scream a bit.'

In secret, Mugabe planned for a showdown. In October 1980, only six months after independence, he signed an agreement with North Korea, a brutal communist dictatorship, for assistance in training a new army brigade with the specific remit to deal with internal dissidents. Recruits for the new brigade were drawn almost entirely from Shona-speaking former guerrilla forces loyal to Mugabe. Kept separate from the rest of the national army, 5 Brigade, as it came to be known, wore different uniforms, with distinctive red berets; it used different equipment, transport and weaponry. Its codes and radios were incompatible with other units. And its chain of command bypassed the intermediate levels observed by the rest of the army, answering directly to Mugabe's army commanders. Not until August 1981, after a team of 106 North Korean instructors had started work in Zimbabwe, did Mugabe disclose the existence of the new brigade.

Mugabe's henchmen meanwhile kept up their campaign against Zapu. At a political rally in November 1980 in Nkomo's stronghold of Bulawayo, Nkala denounced Zapu as 'the enemy' and called on Zanu-PF supporters to mount what he called a general mobilisation. 'Organise yourselves into small groups in readiness to challenge Zapu on its home ground. If it means a few blows, we shall deliver them.' After the rally, rival party supporters clashed in the streets, and in the Bulawayo suburb of Entumbane, rival guerrilla groups fought a pitched battle that lasted two days. The incident led to tension and distrust at other military bases, including newly integrated units of the defence force. In a second round of fighting in Entumbane in February 1981, more than 300 people died. Fearing for their safety, large numbers of Zipra soldiers deserted their units, taking their weapons with them.

By early 1982 Mugabe felt secure enough to stage a split with Nkomo. The pretext he used was arms caches. Though a joint high-level committee had been set up to deal with the problem of arms caches left over from the war, Mugabe claimed that a number of arms caches found on farms belonging to Zapu provided clear evidence of plans by Zapu's leadership to instigate a military coup. 'These people were planning to overthrow and take over the government,' he declared. He likened Nkomo's role in the cabinet to having 'a cobra in the house' and went on: 'The only way to deal effectively with a snake is to strike and destroy its head.' Nkomo was duly sacked from the government; his party's businesses, farms and properties were seized, ruining thousands of ex-combatants who had invested their demobilisation payments in them; and two former Zipra leaders, including the deputy commander of the national army, were arrested on charges of treason. Nkomo denied all Mugabe's accusations. 'The arms were not the real issue,' he said. 'This was the trigger-point of a political move against me, for pushing ahead the one-party state.'

As a result of Mugabe's accusations, former Zipra soldiers in the national army were picked out for reprisal. Many were killed, beaten or otherwise victimised. Hundreds fled, taking their arms with them. Groups of ex-Zipra 'dissidents', as they were called, roamed Matabeleland, robbing stores, holding up buses and attacking isolated farmhouses and villages. They had no clear goal. 'In the 1980s, no one was recruited,' said one ex-Zipra fighter subsequently interviewed by researchers. 'We were forced by the situation. All of us just met in the bush. Each person left on his own, running from death.'

The growing lawlessness in Matabeleland provided South Africa with an opportunity to meddle in the conflict, just as it had done in neighbouring Mozambique. Small groups of dissidents, trained at a base in northern Transvaal, infiltrated back into Matabeleland to add to the mayhem. No more than a hundred men were involved, but in the terminology the South Africans used at the time, they were enough 'to keep the pot boiling'. Mugabe blamed dissident activity on Zapu, claiming that it was acting in league with South African-based groups to overthrow the government, and used the violence as a pretext to unleash repression across the whole of Matabeleland and to eliminate Zapu in the process. 'Some of the measures we shall take are measures that will be extra-legal,' he told parliament in 1982. 'An eye for an eye and an ear for an ear may not be adequate in our circumstances. We might very well demand two ears for one ear and two eyes for one eye.'

The task was given to 5 Brigade. Mugabe called the new brigade *Gukurahundi*, a chiShona word defined as meaning the rain that blows away the chaff before the spring rains. He had used the term during the war, naming 1979 as *Gore reGukurahundi* – 'The Year of the People's Storm' – signifying the culmination of the people's struggle against white rule. In Matabeleland *Gukurahundi* acquired a more sinister meaning: there it was interpreted as 'the sweeping away of rubbish'.

From the moment it was deployed in Matabeleland North at the end of January 1983, 5 Brigade waged a campaign of beatings, arson and mass murder deliberately targeted at the civilian population. Villagers were rounded up, harangued and beaten for hours on end. The beatings were often followed by public executions. The initial targets were former Zipra soldiers and Zapu officials whose names were read out from lists, but often victims were chosen at random and included women. Villagers were then forced to sing songs in the Shona language praising Zanu-PF while dancing on the mass graves of their families and fellow villagers killed and buried minutes earlier. A string of massacres occurred. Within the space of six weeks at least 2,000 civilians were killed, hundreds of homesteads destroyed and tens of thousands of civilians beaten. In addition, 5 Brigade imposed stringent curfews, banned all forms of transport, closed shops and blocked drought relief supplies for villagers starving to death.

Mugabe was blunt about his approach to counter-insurgency. 'We have to deal with this problem quite ruthlessly,' he told an audience in rural Matabeleland. 'Don't cry if your relatives get killed in the process . . . Where men and women provide food for the dissidents, when we get there we eradicate them. We do not differentiate who we fight because we can't tell who is a dissident and who is not.'

In 1984 Matabeleland South became the focus of the *Gukurahundi* campaign. The area was already suffering from a third year of drought. The local population there, numbering 400,000, was heavily depend- ent on relief deliveries and food supplies from local stores. In a move that was bound to lead to widespread starvation, the government closed all stores, halted all food deliveries to the area, including drought relief, and enforced a blanket curfew, restricting all movement in and out of curfew zones. Hundreds of thousands of ordinary civil- ians were quickly reduced to a desperate state. Churchmen pleaded with Mugabe to lift the measures, warning that mass starvation was imminent. But for two months the measures were kept in place. An officer in 5 Brigade, explaining the army's food policy at a meeting with local Ndebele, said: 'First you will eat your chickens, then your goats, then your cattle, then your donkeys. Then you will eat your children and finally you will eat the dissidents.' Troops pillaged the land of what food remained and looted cattle, sneering that they were cattle the Ndebele had stolen during raids against the Shona in the nineteenth century. Many villagers were reduced to eating insects and grass seeds trying to stay alive. Untold numbers died.

When the Bishop of Bulawayo charged the government with employing a policy of systematic starvation, Mugabe retorted that the bishop was more interested in worshipping Nkomo than God. The security forces, he claimed, had performed 'a wonderful duty'. Priests should stay out of politics. 'It is not when the bishop sneezes that we all catch a cold. No, we are a government and we run our affairs as we see fit . . . The fact that bishops speak should not get us running around. What for?'

As well as enforcing the food embargo, 5 Brigade, together with Mugabe's secret police, the Central Intelligence Organisation, rounded up thousands of men, women and children, even the elderly and infirm, taking them to interrogation centres where they were held sometimes for weeks on end. Army camps such as Bhalagwe became notorious as places of torture and brutality. As many as 2,000 Ndebele were held there at a time, trucked in from all over Matabeleland South. Inmates of Bhalagwe spoke of daily deaths from beating and torture; survivors were given the task of digging graves. Bodies were also taken away by the truckload and dumped in local mine shafts. In a period of four months in 1984, an estimated 8,000 passed through Bhalagwe. At Stops Police Camp in Bulawayo, detainees were held in 'cages' open to all weather and spattered with blood and faeces from previous occupants. The cages were close to interrogation cells which meant that detainees could hear the screams and moans of those being interrogated day and night.

In the run-up to the 1985 election, Matabeleland was subjected to further violence. Zanu-PF Youth Brigades, modelled on China's Red Guards, were unleashed on the local population, coercing them into buying party cards, forcing thousands on to buses to attend party rallies and beating anyone who stood in their way. Scores of Zapu officials and councillors – perhaps as many as 400 – were abducted from their homes at night, many of them never seen or heard from again. At an election meeting in Bulawayo, Mugabe issued his own thinly veiled threats to those thinking of voting for Zapu. 'Where will we be tomorrow?' he asked. 'Is it war or is it peace tomorrow? Let the people of Matabeleland answer this question.'

Despite all the violence and intimidation, Nkomo's supporters held firm: Zapu won all fifteen parliamentary seats in Matabeleland. Determined to exact revenge, Mugabe appointed Enos Nkala as his new police minister. Nkala himself had stood as a Zanu-PF candidate in Matabeleland South but had received less than 10 per cent of the vote and was obliged to find another constituency. Within a week of Nkala's appointment, the police raided Nkomo's home and arrested his aides and bodyguards. Several hundred Zapu officials were detained, including five members of parliament, along with eleven councillors on Bulawayo's city council, the mayor, the mayor-elect, the town clerk and some two hundred council employees. Nkala made his intentions clear: 'We want to wipe out the Zapu leadership. You've only seen the warning lights. We haven't yet reached full blast. I don't want to hear pleas of mercy. I only want encouragement to deal with this dissident organisation.'

Stage by stage, Nkala managed to grind Zapu down. He banned all Zapu rallies and meetings, then ordered the closure of all Zapu offices. District councils which Zapu controlled were dissolved. 'Zanu-PF rules this country,' said Nkala, 'and anyone who disputes that is a dissident and should be dealt with.' There was no longer any pretence that the aim was to crush armed dissidents. It was to crush Zapu, as Mugabe had intended all along.

On 27 December 1987 Mugabe and Nkomo signed a Unity Accord. It merged Zapu and Zanu-PF into a single party which was henceforth known as Zanu-PF. Offered an amnesty, the remaining 122 dissidents handed themselves over to the authorities. An amnesty was also granted to all members of the security forces.

In Mugabe's drive for a one-party state, at least 10,000 civilians were murdered, many thousands more were beaten and tortured, and an entire people were victimised. Mugabe's stock-in-trade had long been violence. Given Smith's intransigence, it was ultimately the only method of gaining majority rule. But during the war against white rule he had become fixated by the power that came from the gun. In a radio broadcast from Mozambique in 1976, summing up his view of electoral democracy, he had remarked: 'Our votes must go together with our guns. After all, any vote we shall have, shall have been the product of the gun. The gun which produces the vote should remain its security officer – its guarantor. The people's votes and the people's guns are always inseparable twins.' It was a creed to which he held fast.

Once in office, Mugabe continued to use violence to achieve his objectives. Indeed, in later years he was to boast that he had 'a degree in violence'. For Zimbabwe, it was to prove ruinous.

While the Matabeleland campaign was underway, the aura of goodwill between Mugabe and the white community evaporated. Whites were irritated by the way in which radio and television, once the vehicles for Rhodesian Front propaganda, were swiftly turned into the propaganda arm of Zanu-PF, with frequent disparaging references made to 'racist' whites. Mugabe's ministers also took to criticising the white community in speeches that were reported prominently by the government-controlled media. In his private talks with Mugabe, Ian Smith protested time and again at what he called 'the ongoing campaign of recrimination against our white community'. At a meeting in 1981 he tackled Mugabe about his open support for a one-party state, pointing out the adverse effect it had on foreign investors. It was their last meeting. 'He was obviously displeased, and our parting, unlike previous occasions, was cool,' Smith recorded in his memoirs. 'He stood his distance.'

White members of parliament, elected separately on a special roll to represent white interests for the first seven years of independence, adopted an increasingly abrasive attitude, carping at the government at every available opportunity. Smith weighed in, suggesting that the new government should display proper gratitude for the benefits of ninety years of white rule. He became perpetually gloomy, telling all and sundry that Zimbabwe was sliding towards a one-party Marxist dictatorship.

A series of sabotage attacks carried out by South Africa with the intention of keeping Zimbabwe in a weak and defensive position widened the rift. Mugabe accused disaffected whites in Zimbabwe of acting in collusion with South Africa. After a massive bomb blast tore apart Zanu-PF headquarters in December 1981, he declared the 'honeymoon' over. 'What baffles my government is that reactionary and counter-revolutionary elements, because of their treason and crimes against humanity in Zimbabwe we could have put before a firing squad, but which we decided to forgive, have hardly repented.' He broadened his attack to include not just spies and saboteurs but the white community as a whole, focusing his anger on the wealth they enjoyed. Their monopoly on economic power, he said, must be broken.

What lingering hopes there were for racial harmony gave way to mutual mistrust and suspicion. A growing number of whites decided to leave. Within three years of independence, about half of the white population emigrated. What was left was a rump of 100,000 whites who retreated into their own world of clubs, sporting activities and comfortable living. In the 1985 election, when whites voted for their own representatives for the last time before the end of the seven-year period allowed them, they chose overwhelmingly to vote for Smith and his band of die-hard colleagues rather than moderate candidates.

Mugabe reacted with fury, seeing their victory as a betrayal. Denouncing Smith and the 'racists' who had voted for him, he threatened reprisals. The trust shown to the white community at independence had been completely undeserved, he said.

> The voting has shown that they have not repented in any way. They still cling to the past and support the very man . . . who created a series of horrors against the people of Zimbabwe. We wish to make it very clear that it is going to be very hard for the racists of this country . . . Those whites who have not accepted the reality of a political order in which the Africans set the pace will have to leave the country. We are working with those whites who want to work with us. But the rest will have to find a new home.

Speaking in chiShona, he promised: 'We will kill those snakes among us, we will smash them completely.'

Having demolished his Zapu rivals and established a de facto one-party state, Mugabe went on to accumulate huge personal power. At a ceremony on 30 December 1987, accompanied by the refrain *You Are The Only One*, he was declared executive president by parliament, combining the roles of head of state, head of government and commander-in-chief of the defence forces, with powers to dissolve

parliament and declare martial law and the right to run for an unlimited number of terms of office. He ruled through a vast system of
patronage, controlling appointments to all senior posts in the civil
service, the defence forces, the police and parastatal organisations,
gaining a virtual stranglehold over government machinery. One by
one, the civil service, the state media, the police and parastatal organisations were subordinated to his will.

Under Mugabe's auspices, a new ruling elite emerged – ministers,
members of parliament, party officials, senior civil servants, defence
and police chiefs, select businessmen, aides and cronies – whom he
allowed to engage in a scramble for property, farms and businesses, as
a means of ensuring their loyalty and underpinning support for his
regime. 'I am rich because I belong to Zanu-PF,' boasted one of
Mugabe protégés, Phillip Chiyangwa, a millionaire businessman. 'If
you want to be rich you must join Zanu-PF.' The scramble became
ever more frenetic, spawning corruption on a massive scale. One after
another, state corporations – the national oil company, the national
electricity supply company, the posts and telecommunications corporation – were plundered. In the most notorious case, a state fund set
up to provide compensation for war victims was looted so thoroughly
by Mugabe's colleagues that nothing was left for genuine war victims.
An official inquiry into the scandal named prominent politicians,
including cabinet ministers, among the culprits, but no action was
ever taken against them.

Mugabe himself became an increasingly remote and authoritarian
figure. His official residences in Harare were heavily fortified. He
travelled only in large motorcades surrounded by retinues of armed
bodyguards with screaming sirens heard for miles around. He spoke
openly of his admiration for dictators such as Nicolae Ceauşescu of
Romania, praising him the day before he was overthrown by popular
revolution. Party advertisements in newspapers paid homage to
Mugabe as 'our Consistent and Authentic Leader', emulating the style
of communist personality cults. He lectured endlessly on the merits of
communism, insisting that Zimbabwe's future was 'better guaranteed
under one single, monolithic and gigantic political party'. Much of his
time he spent on foreign travel, trading on his image as a revolutionary

hero and cultivating a reputation as a key figure in the international campaign to defeat apartheid. His interest in domestic issues steadily waned.

For all the foreign glory Mugabe enjoyed, there was growing resentment back home at the corruption and high living of the ruling elite. Mugabe's promises of a new socialist era appeared increasingly bogus. Although there was a major expansion in education and health services, there was no increase in employment. Tens of thousands of youths left school each year with a reasonable education but no prospect of finding a job. While the elite could afford expensive private education and health facilities, the vast majority of the population faced declining standards in government schools and hospitals, for there were not enough resources available both to fund an increase in services and to maintain them. As inflation rose, wage-earners found that the gains they had made in the early years of independence were soon eroded.

In rural areas the land resettlement programme proceeded so slowly that only a fraction of the peasant population benefited. By the end of the first decade of independence a total of 52,000 families, some 416,000 people, had been resettled on 6.5 million acres of former white land. This was a worthy enough achievement, but it came nowhere near to tackling the scale of the problem. A far greater effort was made by Zanu-PF politicians to acquire farms of their own. By 1990 a new class of landowners was firmly established: ministers, members of parliament, senior civil servants, police and defence officials and parastatal managers. In all, they had managed to acquire 8 per cent of commercial farmland since independence, though little of it was put to productive use.

The plight of thousands of ex-combatants was particularly striking. Many had left school early to join up and possessed neither education nor skills. After demobilisation in 1980 they had been paid monthly stipends for two years, but were then left to their own devices. Some set up cooperatives, but these soon collapsed. Some scratched a living in communal areas; others roamed towns searching for work, feeling cheated and disillusioned. Many were destitute. In all, an estimated 30,000 were unemployed. Newspapers took up their cause, accusing the government of wilful neglect. 'How frustrating and disillusioning it must be to the thousands of ex-combatants in dire straits to observe those with whom they shared the perils of the war of liberation now virtually wallowing in the lap of luxury, while they live in poverty,' commented the Bulawayo *Chronicle*. The government promised to set up a special committee to investigate the problem but nothing was done.

With few demonstrable benefits to show after ten years of independence, Mugabe decided to whip up support in the run-up to the 1990 election by focusing attention on the land issue. 'It makes absolute nonsense of our history as an African country that most of our arable and ranching land is still in the hands of our erstwhile colonisers, while the majority of our peasant community still live like squatters in their God-given land.' Without consulting farmers, rural communities or even his own agricultural specialists, he announced a 'revolutionary' programme to redistribute some 13 million acres – more than half of the remaining white-owned land – to peasant farmers. Amid singing and dancing, parliament passed a constitutional amendment empowering the government to confiscate land, fix the price it paid and deny the right to appeal to courts for fair compensation.

Mugabe's land plans provoked a storm of protest, not only from white farmers but from Britain, the United States, the World Bank and the International Monetary Fund, all outraged by the idea of a land grab without fair payment. Many white farmers – nearly half of them – had purchased their farms since independence, obtaining government approval to do so. Mugabe portrayed the issue as an historic reckoning between the land-hungry majority and 'a greedy bunch of racist usurpers' determined to thwart the popular will. And he declared that he would disregard any court decision that might stand in the way of his land acquisition programme. 'I, Robert Mugabe, cannot be dragged to court by a settler.'

After months of argument Mugabe backed down, agreeing to allow the courts to intervene to determine a fair price for confiscated land. His minister of agriculture, Witness Mangwende, tried to mollify white farmers by assuring them that the targets the government had in mind were not productive farms but under-utilised land, foreign-owned derelict land, land owned merely for speculative purposes, absentee landlords and 'people with more farms than are considered necessary'.

The implementation of Mugabe's land reforms was chaotic from the start. Without warning or consultation, the government in 1992 'designated' for acquisition thirteen farms totalling 17,000 acres. Farmers learned of the decision from newspapers. Most farms were productive; they included a large dairy farm and a major tobacco producer. As an indication of how much planning had gone into the decision, seven of the thirteen farms were subsequently 'undesignated'. In 1993 the government designated another seventy farms. Again, many were highly productive. The list included a number of farms belonging to the government's political opponents, arousing the suspicion that the land acquisition programme was being used to settle old political scores. When a group of white farmers went to court to challenge the legality of the government's policy, Mugabe reacted in fury. 'We will not brook any decision by any court from acquiring any land,' he said in July 1993. 'We will get land we want from anyone, be they black or white.'

To Mugabe's acute embarrassment, however, the land resettlement programme was soon engulfed in scandal. In April 1994 an independent newspaper discovered that a 3,000-acre farm that the government had forcibly purchased against the objections of the white owner had been used not for the resettlement of thirty-three landless peasants but leased out to Mugabe's own minister, Witness Mangwende. Further investigations revealed that some 300 farms intended for resettlement had been handed out to ministers and senior officials, including the commissioner of police and the air force commander, in many cases for nominal rent and in some cases for no rent at all.

Bowing to popular outrage, Mugabe agreed to cancel a batch of farm leases. Yet once the furore had died down, the black elite continued to get their hands on government land, leaving the redistribution exercise mired in corruption. Britain, having spent £44 million on land resettlement since independence, decided to cut off further support for it.

The land scandal added to the government's growing unpopularity. While Mugabe and his cronies were seen to be using every opportunity to enrich themselves, the population at large faced rising unemployment, high inflation and deteriorating social services. Mugabe's reaction to the groundswell of discontent was to blame the country's economic woes on the whites. Anti-white abuse became the centrepiece of his strategy. He had nothing else to offer in answer to Zimbabwe's decline.

Isolated from ordinary reality and surrounded by sycophantic ministers and aides, he had little idea of how much disaffection there was with his regime. At the funeral of a popular war veteran, Mukoma Musa, in December 1996, a serving army officer, Brigadier Gibson Mashingaidze, delivered a forthright attack on Zanu-PF, questioning its commitment to the ideals and principles it had set for itself during the war. While the politicians had enriched themselves, said the brigadier, veterans like Musa had been ignored. He told mourners that he had had to spend his own money to give Musa a decent burial because he was so poor. 'Some people now have ten farms to their names and luxury yachts and have developed fat stomachs when ex-combatants like Comrade Musa lived in abject poverty. Is this the Zanu-PF I trusted with my life? Is this the same party which promised to care for us in our old age?'

War veterans, once considered the most loyal of Mugabe's supporters, took to the streets in 1997 in a series of demonstrations in protest against the government's neglect of their grievances, singing revolutionary songs, banging drums, waving placards and denouncing the president himself. When Mugabe refused to meet them, they became increasingly aggressive, demanding gratuities, pensions and land and threatening war if they did not get them. After weeks of prevarication, Mugabe capitulated to their demands, promising a package of benefits, including land for resettlement. The estimated cost was more than $400 million, money that the government, already overspent, did not have. Mugabe said the government would use any means to get the money, borrowing it, if necessary, dismissing concerns about a financial collapse. 'Have you ever heard of a country that collapsed because of borrowing?' he asked. The World Bank was sufficiently worried to suspend its lending programme. And when Mugabe announced in November that the war veterans would be paid out by Christmas the value of the Zimbabwe dollar plunged.

The war veterans crisis reignited the land issue. With demands for land ringing in his ears, Mugabe resumed his attacks on white farmers. 'We are going to take the land and we are not going to pay a cent to any soul.' The only payment that the government would make, he said, was for 'infrastructure' – buildings, roads and dams – but nothing for 'the soil itself'. It was up to Britain, as the former colonial power, to provide other compensation. In November 1997 the government published a list of 1,503 farms to be expropriated, amounting to about 12 million acres.

The shockwaves from this nationalisation of half the country's commercial farmland reverberated throughout Zimbabwe and beyond. Economists, bankers and businessmen, white and black alike, warned that such a hasty, ill-planned move to seize so much of the country's productive assets would send it into an economic tailspin. The stock exchange, where more than a third of companies listed were heavily dependent on agriculture, plummeted. Britain rejected demands for further aid for the land resettlement programme, saying the funds previously committed had failed to benefit poor blacks as had been intended.

As Zimbabwe sank ever deeper into an economic quagmire, Mugabe faced mass resistance. Protesting against his proposals to impose new taxes and levies to pay for his largesse towards the war veterans, trade unions organised a nationwide strike, bringing many towns to a halt. A series of food price increases in 1998 provoked riots. To quell them, Mugabe had to turn to the army for help, bringing troops on to the streets for the first time since independence. Desperate for loans from the International Monetary Fund, the World Bank and the European Union to keep the country afloat, he agreed to shelve plans to expropriate white-owned farms.

A major international effort was made in 1998 to find a workable solution to the land issue. Representatives from United Nations agencies, the World Bank, the IMF, the EU and twenty-three foreign governments, including Britain, the United States, China and Cuba, gathered for a three-day conference in Harare, along with delegates from the Commercial Farmers Union and other local non-governmental organisations. Mugabe opened the conference outlining ambitious plans for massive change. In the eighteen years since independence the government had resettled some 70,000 families on about 9 million acres of land. What Mugabe now proposed was to acquire a further 12 million acres on which to settle 150,000 families over a five-year period at a cost estimated at $1 billion.

The conference delegates considered Mugabe's proposals to be far too ambitious, well beyond the government's ability to implement. In view of the scandals which had been uncovered about the previous land programme, they also insisted that any new programme was strictly supervised to ensure land was directed towards peasant settlement. Moreover, they stipulated that land had to be bought at market-related prices and on a willing-seller willing-buyer basis. And instead of a massive programme of acquisition, they wanted a limited initial phase, carried out step-by-step, to ascertain its viability. What was finally agreed by all parties involved in the conference, including the Zimbabwe government, was a resettlement plan beginning with 118 farms, covering about 700,000 acres, already offered for sale by their white owners. Twelve foreign donors agreed to contribute funds for the first stage. It was the greatest opportunity that Mugabe had ever been given to make real progress on the land issue.

But nothing happened. Mugabe made no effort to pursue the initiative. Land for Mugabe was more useful as a political weapon. With a population growing ever more disgruntled and restless after eighteen years of his rule, it was the last political card he had to play.

By the end of the 1990s Zimbabwe was in dire straits. The unemployment rate had risen to more than 50 per cent. Only one-tenth of the number of pupils leaving school were able to find formal employment. Inflation had reached 60 per cent. The value of wages in real terms had fallen over ten years by 22 per cent. On average, the population of 13 million was 10 per cent poorer at the end of the 1990s than at the beginning. More than 70 per cent lived in abject poverty. Hospitals were short of drugs and equipment; government schools were starved of funds; state corporations were bankrupt; the public transport system was decrepit; fuel supplies were erratic; scores of businesses had closed. Harare, once renowned as one of the cleanest cities in Africa, was noted now for debris on the pavements, cracked cement pavings, broken street lights, potholes, uncollected refuse and burst pipelines. Street crime was endemic.

Despite the ruinous state of the economy, Mugabe still pursued dreams of foreign glory. Without consulting parliament or the cabinet, he sent an expeditionary force of thousands of troops, combat aircraft and armoured vehicles to Congo in August 1998 to prop up the tottering regime of Laurent Kabila, hoping to establish himself as the region's principal power-broker. When questioned about the cost to Zimbabwe, estimated to be at least US$1 million a day, Mugabe retorted: 'Don't talk of resources as if resources are more important than the security of the people and the sovereignty of the country. The people must survive. The only way to bring peace to the country is to confront the rebels.'

For a select group of defence officials and businessmen, the Congo offered rich pickings. In return for military support, Kabila was prepared to hand out mining and timber concessions and offer favourable deals in diamonds, cobalt and other minerals. Though the intention was said to be to allow Zimbabwe to recoup some of the cost of the war, the real beneficiaries were Mugabe's cronies. Zimbabwe was left with ever increasing debt. Both at home and abroad, Mugabe's intervention was seen as a sign of his growing megalomania.

The Congo escapade helped galvanise opposition to Mugabe's regime. In September 1999 an alliance of trade unions, lawyers and civic groups launched a new political party, the Movement for Democratic Change (MDC), aiming to oust Zanu-PF at the next parliamentary elections scheduled for 2000. Its leader, Morgan Tsvangirai, a trade union official who had turned the labour movement into a cohesive force, had long been an outspoken critic of Mugabe's rule. In conjunction with human-rights groups and church organisations, Tsvangirai threw his weight behind a campaign for constitutional reform, hoping to prevent Mugabe from standing for a third term of office as president.

Mugabe's response was to set up a constitutional commission, giving it the task of drawing up a new constitution to be put before the electorate in a national referendum. Packed with his own supporters, the commission duly produced a draft constitution that left untouched the vast powers and patronage that Mugabe had acquired as president over twenty years. Although the draft proposed that in future the president would be restricted to two terms of five years, this was not to apply retrospectively, giving Mugabe the right to hold office for an additional ten years. Without consulting the commission, Mugabe inserted an amendment to the draft allowing land expropriation without compensation, believing that it would help secure the rural vote. The amendment declared that Britain, as the former colonial power, was responsible for the payment of compensation for land seized. If Britain defaulted, said the amendment, then the government would have no obligation to pay compensation. The Commercial Farmers Union made clear their opposition to the draft constitution, mobilising the white farming community against it.

The referendum campaign during January and February 2000, coming at a time of mass unemployment, growing poverty, fuel shortages, factory closures, crumbling public services, corruption scandals and an unpopular war in the Congo, centred as much on the government's record as on the draft constitution. Mugabe blamed the economic crisis on farmers and industrialists, on hoarders and speculators, on Britain, the IMF and the World Bank, stirring up anti-white sentiment. Government-controlled newspapers, radio and television followed suit. 'While 20 years ago we fought [the whites] using AK rifles, today we are using a pen and ballot paper,' said the *Sunday Mail*. 'But the war is no less important than in the 1970s. The enemy is the same.' Whites were said to be the masterminds behind the MDC, using it to protect their own interests. They were warned that if they encouraged their employees to vote 'No' they would face repercussions. A massive propaganda blitz was launched to persuade the electorate to vote 'Yes'.

The result was a stunning defeat for Mugabe. The draft constitution was rejected by 55 per cent of the voters. Despite promises of land, rural voters largely abstained. Shaken to the core, the ruling elite suddenly saw their grip on power slipping and with it all the wealth, the salaries, the perks, contracts, commissions and scams they had enjoyed for twenty years. Mugabe attributed his defeat principally to the whites and was determined to make them pay for it.

In a carefully coordinated campaign, starting ten days after the referendum result was announced, gangs armed with axes and machetes invaded white-owned farms across the country. Government and army trucks were used to transport them to the farms and to keep them supplied with rations. They were called war veterans, but the majority were too young to have participated in the war twenty years earlier. Large numbers were unemployed youths paid a daily allowance. They assaulted farmers and their families, threatened to kill them and forced many to flee their homes, ransacking their possessions. They set up armed camps and roadblocks, stole tractors, slaughtered cattle, destroyed crops and polluted water supplies. The police refused to take action, leaving the farmers defenceless.

The land invasions were directed from Zanu-PF headquarters in Harare. Senior Zanu-PF officials, army officers and police agents all played a leading role. Among the most prominent was Chenjerai Hunzvi, a corrupt opportunist who had gained control of the War Veterans Association. Addressing the press at Zanu-PF headquarters on 15 March, Hunzvi disclosed that he had been given substantial party funds both to organise farm invasions and to campaign for Zanu-PF in the forthcoming parliamentary elections. The land invasions, he said, would deter whites from organising against Mugabe, as they had done in the referendum.

As well as white farmers, farm employees and their families living on white-owned farms became the target of the terror campaign. Some 400,000 workers were employed by white farmers. Together with their wives, they constituted a sizeable portion of the electorate, as much as 15 per cent. Convinced that they had helped defeat him in the referendum, Mugabe regarded them as part of the enemy camp. On one farm after another, they were subjected to violence and intimidation by gangs acting with impunity. Workers were assaulted, kicked and whipped; men were abducted, women raped; their homes were destroyed, their possessions looted. Thousands were rounded

up en masse and taken in convoys of stolen trucks, tractors and trail-
ers to 're-education centres' on farms deserted by their owners. At
indoctrination sessions lasting sometimes for days and nights on end,
lists of workers said to be MDC supporters were read out before large
gatherings, then the individuals named were hustled to the front to be
beaten and whipped.

Farmers went to the High Court to seek protection and won orders
declaring the farm invasions illegal, but Mugabe simply shrugged off
the orders and instructed the police to ignore them. He told party
supporters that if any white farmer resisted the takeover of their land,
he would retaliate. 'Then I will declare the fight to be on and it will
be a fight to the finish I can tell you and they won't win the fight, we
will win it.' His rhetoric became increasingly belligerent. Referring to
farmers who had dared to oppose him in the referendum, he told the
state radio: 'For them to have banded together to the man in opposition to the government and, for that matter, to have gone much
further in mobilising, actually it's coercing, their labour forces on the
farms to support the one position opposed to [the] government, has
exposed them as not our friends but our enemies.' Making the point
even clearer, he went on: 'Our present state of mind is that you are
now our enemies, because you really have behaved as enemies of
Zimbabwe and we are full of anger. Our entire community is angry
and that is why we now have the war veterans seizing their land.'

At this critical juncture the British government intervened, believing that what was required was tough talk. Sparking off a war of
words, an ambitious British minister, Peter Hain, suggested that
Mugabe had lost touch with reality. He portrayed Zimbabwe as a
country close to collapse and talked openly of Britain's contingency
plans for an evacuation of 20,000 of its nationals, adding to the sense
of alarm and fear spreading through the white community. But his
remarks served only to enrage Mugabe and to enable him to portray
the crisis as a struggle by Zimbabwe to gain its rightful heritage against
a former colonial power acting on behalf of the white community to
protect their interests. Referring to British residents in Zimbabwe,
Mugabe retorted: 'They are free to go. We can even assist them by
showing them the exit.'

Throughout the election campaign Mugabe kept up his angry tirades against his opponents, effectively licensing violence against them. 'Those who try to cause disunity among our people must watch out because death will befall them,' he warned at the opening ceremony of a Swedish-financed water project in Manicaland. He branded Tsvangirai 'a traitor' and 'a puppet' serving the interests of Britain and white settlers, and issued what he called 'a declaration of war' against the opposition. 'The MDC will never form the government of this country, never ever, not in my lifetime or even after I die.' MDC candidates, officials and supporters were attacked and assaulted while the police often stood by watching. Some forty opposition supporters were murdered, including three prominent white farmers who were active MDC members; and though in many cases the police knew the identity of the killers, no action was taken against them. Three weeks before the election in June 2000, the MDC reported that only in twenty-five constituencies was free and safe campaigning possible; in forty-six constituencies campaigning was affected by high levels of intimidation; and in forty-nine constituencies the level of violence and intimidation was so high that no campaigning was possible at all. 'What Mugabe wants,' said Tsvangirai, 'is to intimidate the whole country into submission.' In a pre-election report the National Democratic Institute, a Washington-based organisation, concluded that 'conditions for credible democratic elections in Zimbabwe do not exist'.

After months of systematic intimidation, Zanu-PF managed to secure a narrow victory. With 48 per cent of the votes cast, it won sixty-two seats in parliament. The MDC, with 47 per cent, won fifty-seven seats. After only nine months in existence, the MDC won all the seats in Harare and Bulawayo, and ten of the twelve constituencies in Matabeleland; it also performed strongly in towns in the Midlands and in Manicaland. Zanu-PF was reduced to a party entirely dependent on rural Shona votes; it retained only one urban constituency in the entire country. Without intimidation, Zanu-PF would almost certainly have been defeated.

Though the election was over, there was to be no respite from Mugabe's tyranny. Showing increasing signs of paranoia, he insisted that the strength of the opposition against him was due to a conspiracy by his old enemies – Britain, the West, the old Rhodesian network, white farming and business interests, even the churches – all trying to overthrow his 'revolution'. During a post-mortem session on the election results in July, Mugabe told members of Zanu-PF's central committee that it would be a serious miscalculation 'to underestimate the forces ranged against us'. The MDC, he said, was not an ordinary opposition party, as some assumed. It was the manifestation of 'the resurgence of white power' – 'a counter-revolutionary Trojan Horse contrived and nurtured by the very inimical forces that enslaved and oppressed our people yesterday'. All these forces had been mobilised for the 2000 election campaign and they had now set their sights on the presidential election in 2002. It was the task of Zanu-PF to defeat them, using whatever methods were necessary.

The brunt fell at first on white farmers. Mugabe initiated a 'fast-track' land resettlement programme listing thousands of farms for expropriation. They included large cattle ranches, flower farms, dairy estates, game ranches, tobacco farms, safari properties, abattoirs and smallholdings. Farmers were issued with eviction notices giving them thirty days to leave. They were promised payment for 'improvements' to their properties at some unspecified date in the future, but nothing for the land, even though many had bought their farms with government approval in the years after independence.

According to Mugabe, the 'fast-track' programme was intended to assist the resettlement of landless peasants, but it quickly degenerated into a chaotic land grab. Soldiers, policemen, air force officers, war veterans, government and party officials and peasants descended on commercial farms in their thousands in a wild scramble for land, building shacks, cutting down trees, hunting wildlife and looting buildings. Farms were occupied whether they were listed for expropriation or not. Any hint of resistance was dealt with by assaults, death threats and forced eviction. Party bosses and military and police commanders led the action, taking prize properties for themselves. MDC supporters were explicitly banned from receiving any 'fast-track' land.

In an attempt to stop the mayhem, the Commercial Farmers Union sought protection from the Supreme Court. The Supreme Court duly declared the fast-track programme unlawful; for good measure, it added that the rule of law in commercial farming areas had clearly been overthrown. 'Wicked things have been done and continue to be done. They must be stopped.' Mugabe's response was to launch a campaign of vilification against white judges, singling out the white chief justice, Anthony Gubbay, whom he had appointed to the post in 1990. In November 2000, while five Supreme Court judges were assembled to hear an application from the Commercial Farmers Union, a mob of two hundred government supporters invaded the Supreme Court building, in full view of the police, waving placards and shouting 'Kill the judges'.

At a Zanu-PF conference the following month, in a speech laden with crude racist rhetoric, Mugabe denounced white landowners as 'white devils', vowing to take all they owned.

> The courts can do whatever they want, but no judicial decision will stand in our way . . . My own position is that we should not even be defending our position in the courts. This country is our country and this land is our land . . . They think because they are white they have a divine right to our resources. Not here. The white man is not indigenous to Africa. Africa is for Africans, Zimbabwe is for Zimbabweans.

At a subsequent meeting with Gubbay, Mugabe's minister of justice, Patrick Chinamasa, asked for his resignation, telling him that, if he refused to go, the government 'could not guarantee his safety'. After receiving death threats, Gubbay resigned. In his place Mugabe appointed a party loyalist. He also increased the number of judges in the Supreme Court, packing it with his placemen. One of their first actions was to declare his land programme lawful.

Mugabe next turned his attention to white business. He accused whites of sabotaging the economy by closing factories and companies and blamed them for causing unemployment, rising prices and fuel shortages. 'Many people blame us, the government, our party, for all the economic ills that affect our country. But those who control the

economy are a racial group,' he told a party conference. His answer to
this 'onslaught' was to licence yet more terror. To wild cheers and
applause from party delegates, he declared: 'Our party must continue
to strike fear in the hearts of the white man, our real enemy.'

Operating from Zanu-PF headquarters, party gangs stormed into
white-owned factories and offices, just as they had done during the
land invasions. They assaulted and abducted managers and staff, seized
equipment and set up kangaroo courts. They even invaded a private
hospital in Harare, where fifteen operations were underway,
threatening managers: 'We will march you to Zanu-PF headquarters
and put you in a room with no door.' In a matter of weeks some three
hundred businesses had been invaded, including shops, restaurants,
hotels and foreign-owned companies. Growing ever more ambitious,
the war veterans' leader Chenjerai Hunzvi announced plans to extend
the action to foreign embassies and aid agencies, which Mugabe regularly accused of assisting the MDC. Among the targets they selected
were aid agencies involved in civic education programmes, food relief
and the care of orphans. Only after an international uproar did
Mugabe call off the raids.

In the run-up to the presidential election of March 2002, Mugabe
left no doubt about the lengths to which he would go to win. 'What
we are now headed for is real war, a total war,' he told delegates at a
party conference in December 2001. 'You are soldiers of Zanu-PF for
the people. When we come to your province, we must see you ready
as the commanders. When the time comes to fire the bullet, the
ballot, the trajectory of the gun must be true.' He warned that the
presidential election campaign would present a tougher challenge
than the election campaign of 2000. 'Last year we never spoke of the
command centre, but now we are talking about it, and that shows the
battle ahead of us. We should move like a military machine.' At one
point during his address, making a contemptuous reference to
Tsvangirai, he shouted: 'Death to the tea boy!'

A new round of violence and intimidation was unleashed on the
electorate. From militia bases across the country, youth squads were
deployed to hunt down opposition supporters. They raided shops,
destroyed houses and set up roadblocks, dragging people out of buses

and cars, demanding party cards. Whole swathes of the country were turned into 'no-go' areas, sealed off to prevent the MDC from campaigning there. MDC officials were abducted, beaten, tortured and sometimes murdered; rallies were disrupted; party offices attacked.

Mugabe's campaign objective was to ensure a high turnout in rural areas where Zanu-PF retained its main following and to undermine support for the MDC in urban areas by harassing and disenfranchising voters there. On Mugabe's orders the election authorities used every possible device to obstruct urban voters. New rules were introduced impeding voter registration. Changes to citizenship laws effectively deprived thousands of residents of the right to vote. An estimated 1 million Zimbabweans living abroad were prevented from voting. The government further insisted that voters, instead of being allowed to vote in any constituency in the country as before, were now required to vote in their home constituencies, thereby effectively disenfranchising thousands of voters who had fled violence and intimidation in their homes areas, such as farm workers and opposition supporters. The election authorities allowed the names of thousands of new Zanu-PF supporters to be added in secret to the voters' rolls after the deadline for registration had passed, to boost their numbers.

New security legislation was introduced making it a criminal offence to criticise the president, empowering the police to ban political rallies at will and prohibiting the courts from granting bail to suspects in politically motivated crimes, in effect enabling the government to detain people without trial. Radio, television and the government press meanwhile poured out a relentless torrent of propaganda denigrating his opponent, Morgan Tsvangirai. Tsvangirai was denounced as a puppet of white Rhodesians intent on overthrowing the government; an agent of the British government seeking to recolonise Zimbabwe; a traitor said to be involved in a plot to assassinate Mugabe. A regular Zanu-PF advertisement in *The Herald* urged: 'Don't let him sell your birthright, don't let him sell your soul, don't let him sell your country, don't let him sell your land.' Adding to the climate of intimidation, the defence force commander, General Vitalis Zvinavashe, declared the military would not recognise the result of the election if Mugabe lost.

The election itself was riddled with fraud and malpractice. To prevent a large urban vote from being cast, the election authorities drastically cut the number of polling stations normally allocated to urban areas. In the case of Harare, where about one-sixth of the entire population lived, some 880,000 registered voters were allocated no more than 167 polling stations, only half the number previously allocated for the parliamentary elections. Election officials were deliberately obstructive, keeping the flow of voters at some polling stations to as low as twenty an hour. Huge numbers queued for hours without getting a chance to vote.

The official result showed that Mugabe gained 1,685,000 or 56 per cent of the vote while Tsvangirai trailed behind with 1,258,000 or 42 per cent. The turnout in the three provinces of Mashonaland, Zanu-PF's rural stronghold, was declared to be far higher than during the 2000 parliamentary elections – 62 per cent – providing Mugabe with the bulk of his vote, while Harare's turnout was put at 47 per cent and Bulawayo's at 45 per cent.

At a victory party at his home in Zvimba, Mugabe warned that he would deal with any protests against his government with an iron fist. 'We will not brook any protests, any attempt to cause problems,' he said. 'Those who want to rebel and to cause lawlessness will be beaten to the ground like they have never been beaten.'

Across Zimbabwe, another campaign of repression began. Opposition activists were hunted down, beaten, tortured and in some cases murdered. Thousands fled their homes. Tsvangirai was charged with treason. All the courage that Zimbabweans had shown in resisting Mugabe's dictatorship had proved in vain.

Then came the final onslaught against white farmers. In May some 3,000 white farmers – the bulk of those remaining on the land – were given forty-five days to stop all production and then a further forty-five days to vacate their properties without compensation or face imprisonment. When the August deadline arrived, hundreds tried to defy the order to leave but were duly arrested. 'The game is up,' declared Mugabe. Many valuable farming enterprises were taken over by Mugabe's clique – his wife, his brother-in-law, other relatives, ministers and senior officials.

The farm seizures spelt the end of commercial agriculture as a major industry. Hundreds of thousands of farm workers and their families were left destitute; many were driven off the land by Zanu-PF youth militias. The impact on food supplies was calamitous, compounding the effects of drought. With vast areas lying fallow, crop production plummeted. To survive, Zimbabwe became increasingly dependent on food imports and foreign relief supplies – a once prosperous country reduced to taking handouts.

With 7 million people at risk of starvation – half of the population – Mugabe turned food into a political weapon to coerce support for Zanu-PF, just as he had done in Matabeleland in the 1980s. A government order gave the state-controlled Grain Marketing Board the sole right to import and distribute maize supplies, enabling party and government officials to give priority to Zanu-PF supporters and to block distribution to opposition areas. 'As long as you value the government of the day you will not starve,' a government minister, Abednico Ncube, told villagers. 'But we do not want people who vote for colonialists and then come to us when they want food. You cannot vote for the MDC and expect Zanu-PF to help you . . . You have to vote for Zanu-PF candidates . . . before [the] government starts rethinking your entitlement to this food aid.' One of Mugabe's closest colleagues, Didymus Mutasa, was even more explicit: 'We would be better off with only 6 million people, with our own people who support the liberation struggle.'

As opposition areas ran increasingly short of food, Bulawayo's Catholic archbishop, Pius Ncube, issued an outright condemnation of Mugabe's government. 'It is criminal what this government is doing,' he said. 'They don't care if people die. For the sake of political power the government is willing to sacrifice the lives of thousands. The government is starving areas that voted for the opposition in recent elections. It is the work of devils.'

Through the use of brute force, Mugabe managed to retain his grip on power. But the cost was enormous. Over a five-year period, from 1999 to 2004, the economy shrank by one-third. Hundreds of thousands left Zimbabwe, desperate to escape economic collapse and political repression. The exodus included not only much of the

remaining white community but a large part of the black middle
class – doctors, nurses, teachers, accountants and other professionals –
who saw no future for themselves while Mugabe's regime lasted.
Mugabe shrugged off the cost. He was equally indifferent to the
vortex of murder, torture and lawlessness he had created, for that is
what kept him in power. In a speech in 2003 he warned he would use
even worse violence if necessary, threatening to act like a 'black Hitler'
against the opposition. 'If that is Hitler, then let me be a Hitler ten-
fold. Ten times. That is what we stand for.'

SOMEWHERE OVER THE
RAINBOW

At the official launch of his autobiography in Johannesburg in December 1994, seven months after his inauguration as president, Nelson Mandela joked, in his customary self-deprecating manner, that such were the rigours of office that he sometimes longed for the relative calm of prison. The magnitude of the task of transforming South Africa into a fully fledged democracy after centuries of white-minority rule was indeed daunting. The entire system that Mandela inherited had been designed largely to serve white interests. Other than parliament, all the main institutions – the civil service, the security forces, the business community, the universities, the media, the stock exchange, the banks and agriculture – were dominated by whites. As Mandela publicly acknowledged, South Africa's fortunes still depended heavily on the skills, expertise and capital of the white community. Yet while recognising the need to reassure whites about their future under black rule, he also faced an avalanche of black expectations. In the aftermath of his election victory, the black electorate was impatient for change. Mandela's pledges during the election campaign – of more jobs, more housing, better education and health services – still reverberated across the country. All at once, there were so many demands, so many priorities. At the age of seventy-five, after fifty years as a political activist in the titanic struggle to defeat apartheid, Mandela confronted yet another challenge, as formidable as anything that had come before. 'I have discovered the secret that after climbing a great hill, one only finds that there are many more hills to climb,' he concluded in his autobiography.

What was required was not just a new administration capable of undertaking major programmes of economic and social development but a whole new structure of provincial and local government, involving the incorporation of former homeland territories into nine new provinces and the redesign of some 800 segregated local authorities into 300 multiracial bodies. The police service, once at the forefront of enforcing apartheid laws, required a complete overhaul to make it more acceptable to local communities. The new national defence force required reorganisation to absorb units from the ANC's guerrilla army and former homeland armies. The entire education system, where each race group had previously been segregated, required restructuring. While white public education offered high standards, black public education had suffered from decades of deprivation: many buildings were derelict, one-third had no electricity, a quarter had no water, a half had no sanitation, one-third of teachers were unqualified and many more were under-qualified.

The legacy of apartheid included a massive disparity in wealth. The average white income was eight times greater than that of the average black. Whites, comprising 13 per cent of the population, earned 61 per cent of total income. Although the black middle class was growing apace, its share of total income was still comparatively small. Barely 2 per cent of all private-sector assets were black-owned. According to calculations published in the United Nations Human Development Report for 1994, if white South Africa was treated as a separate country, its standard of living would rank twenty-fourth in the world, just below Spain's; black South Africa on the same basis would rank one hundred and twenty-third, below Lesotho and Vietnam. Overall, in terms of human development, South Africa ranked only ninety-third in the world. Out of a population of 40 million, 22 million lacked adequate sanitation, including 7.5 million in urban areas; 12 million lacked clean water supply; 23 million had no access to electricity; and some 2 million children were without schools. Almost half of all households in South Africa lived below the poverty line; a quarter lived on an income of less than half of the poverty-line income; some 8 million were estimated to be 'completely destitute'. One-third of the population was illiterate.

The assets that South Africa possessed to help it overcome this legacy were considerable. They included one of the world's richest stores of minerals, with 44 per cent of world diamond reserves, 82 per cent of manganese reserves and 64 per cent of platinum-group metal reserves. It was the world's largest producer of gold, mining one-third of world production. Its financial, banking and legal systems were well established and efficient; the Johannesburg stock exchange was the tenth largest in the world. Its manufacturing base, though over-protected and uncompetitive by world standards, was capable of major expansion. The infrastructure of roads, railways, ports and airports was well developed. Telephone and electricity services were reliable. Universities and technical colleges turned out a ready supply of competent graduates. In statistical terms, South Africa, with a gross domestic product of $120 billion, ranked as one of the world's twenty-five largest economies. In Africa, it stood out as a giant.

What Mandela discovered on taking office, however, was that South Africa's economy was in dire straits. The ANC had expected to inherit an economic cornucopia; its ambitious development plans were based on that notion. But the coffers, in fact, were nearly empty. The previous government had run up a record budget deficit of 8.6 per cent of gross domestic product, and gross foreign exchange reserves were down to less than the equivalent of three weeks of imports. The government's domestic debt, moreover, was huge. The cost of debt service together with current expenditure consumed 92 per cent of government revenue, leaving only 8 per cent for capital spending. 'There was simply no money to do what we had planned,' recalled one of Mandela's key ministers, Mac Maharaj. 'We had to dump our blueprints and start from the beginning.'

The unemployment figures on their own represented a sizeable crisis. Only about half of the economically active population had formal-sector jobs. Several million more earned a living in the informal sector – hawkers, small traders, domestics and backyard businesses.

Even so, the official unemployment rate was calculated as 33 per cent. A high proportion of the estimated 5 million unemployed possessed no skills or training and had little prospect of ever finding a job. Of the 450,000 new entrants to the labour market in 1994, only 27,000 were expected to be able to find a job. On average, the formal sector of the economy could absorb no more than 6 per cent of new entrants to the labour market. When the new government advertised civil service vacancies for 11,000 managers, clerks and cleaners, more than 1.5 million people applied.

Economic growth in recent years had been dismal. In the longest recession in its recorded history, South Africa's GDP fell by 0.5 per cent in 1990; by 0.4 per cent in 1991; and by 2.1 per cent in 1992, a drop caused mainly by drought disrupting agricultural production. Over the four-year period from 1990 to 1993, the aggregate fall in GDP amounted to 1.8 per cent. Formal employment between 1989 and 1993 fell by more than 350,000. Merely to absorb the annual number of new entrants into the labour market required an annual growth rate of 6 per cent. To make any inroads into the rate of unemployment required a growth rate of between 8 and 10 per cent.

Not only was the economic legacy none too healthy, but, as Mandela recognised, his ability to make progress on his development objectives depended heavily on attracting foreign capital. Even with the support of the private sector, local resources were not sufficient to raise the annual growth rate much above 3 per cent. Yet foreign investors were wary of the ANC's long history of advocating nationalisation and state control of the economy and reluctant to commit themselves until they could see something of the new government's track record. Mindful of the need to convince foreign and local investors about the government's determination to pursue fiscal discipline and sound economic management, Mandela stuck to a cautious and conservative approach to economic policy. But the slow pace of change led to increasing restlessness. Labour unions, which had helped put the ANC in power, began to flex their muscles, wanting rewards for their endeavours. Within the ANC too, there was frustration at the compromises the government was required to make. 'Are we in power or just in office?' asked Tokyo Sexwale, premier of the Gauteng region, the country's industrial heartland, in November 1994.

Mandela also had to contend with the legacy of protest politics from the apartheid era. The culture of protest ran deep. Township residents accustomed to years of boycotting rent and service-charge payments in protest against apartheid policies showed little inclination to start paying their dues even though a new government was in power. Outbreaks of lawlessness were commonplace. Students seized teaching staff as hostages, vandalised buildings and looted shops. Striking policemen set up roadblocks. Prison warders allowed dangerous prisoners to escape. Former ANC guerrillas in the defence force absconded without leave. Taxi drivers blockaded central Johannesburg. Squatters invaded vacant houses. Shop workers went on a looting rampage. Added to all this was an epidemic of violent crime.

The scale of disorder was serious enough to prompt Mandela to read the riot act. Opening the second session of parliament in February 1995, he launched into a tirade against workers and students who resorted to acts of anarchy and disruption to secure their demands. 'Let it be clear to all that the battle against the forces of anarchy and chaos has been joined,' he said. He was equally blunt about those who demanded immediate benefits from his government:

The government literally does not have the money to meet the demands that are being advanced. Mass action of any kind will not create resources that the government does not have. All of us must rid ourselves of the wrong notion that the government has a big bag full of money. The government does not have such riches. We must rid ourselves of the culture of entitlement which leads to the expectation that the government must promptly deliver whatever it is we demand.

It was a sober message to deliver after so much euphoria over the coming of majority rule. What Mandela was demanding was discipline and belt-tightening from a population which had been led to expect something different.

★

The lead that Mandela took in promoting national reconciliation proved far more rewarding. National reconciliation became his personal crusade. From the moment of his inauguration he strove to establish a new racial accord, constantly reassuring the white minority of their well-being under majority rule and stressing the importance of building a 'rainbow nation'. Addressing a huge crowd on the lawns below Union Buildings in Pretoria on inauguration day, he urged a spirit of forgiveness. '*Wat is verby is verby*,' he said in Afrikaans. 'What is past is past.'

Towards his old political adversaries, he remained magnanimous. He welcomed F. W. de Klerk into his cabinet, praising him for his contribution to establishing democracy and commending him as 'one of the greatest sons of Africa'. He was assiduous in cultivating right-wing Afrikaner politicians, determined to avert the risk of right-wing resistance. He ensured that statues, monuments and streets names commemorating events and heroes from Afrikaner history remained untouched. He regularly spoke in Afrikaans, describing it as 'a language of hope and liberation'. When appealing to civil servants to support government reforms, he addressed them in Afrikaans. In changing the name of his official residence in Cape Town from Westbrook, he chose an Afrikaans word, *Genadendal*, meaning 'Valley of Mercy', the name of the first Christian mission in the Cape.

His gestures of goodwill were manifold. He organised what he called 'a reconciliation lunch', bringing together the wives and widows of former apartheid leaders and leading black activists. He made a special trip to visit the widow of Hendrik Verwoerd, the architect of apartheid, who was living in a small town on the banks of the Orange River which Afrikaner *bittereinders* had preserved as a whites-only colony. Even more remarkable was the lunch he arranged for Percy Yutar, the prosecutor in the Rivonia trial who had argued for Mandela to be given the death sentence and expressed regret when this did not happen.

The climax to Mandela's efforts came when South Africa hosted the Rugby World Cup tournament in 1995. Rugby was a sport embraced with almost religious fervour by Afrikaners, but regarded as a 'Boer game', a symbol of white supremacy, by much of the black population. White enthusiasm for the rugby festival was overwhelming but Mandela was determined to turn it into a national event. He arrived at the Springbok training ground near Cape Town, gave his personal blessing to the squad, all but one of them white, and urged blacks to rally behind them. 'We have adopted these young men as our boys, as our own children, as our own stars. This country is fully behind them. I have never been so proud of our boys as I am now and I hope that that pride we all share.'

In the final match between South Africa and New Zealand, as the two teams took to the field, Mandela emerged on to the pitch wearing the green and gold number 6 jersey of the South African captain and a Springbok cap, sending the overwhelmingly white crowd into a frenzy of enthusiasm and excitement. When the Springboks went on to win the match, in one of the most intense afternoons of physical endeavour and emotion that any of those present were ever likely to witness, the whole of South African erupted in celebration, blacks as joyful as whites. It was a moment of national fusion that Mandela had done much to inspire.

There were critics within the black community who argued that Mandela devoted greater effort to reassuring whites than to addressing black grievances. But Mandela dismissed such criticism: 'We had to allay the fears of whites to ensure the transition process took place smoothly. If we had not done so, the civil war that was threatening would have broken out.' Reassuring whites, he said, involved no cost.

The honeymoon period came to an end over differences of how to deal with South Africa's violent past. Mandela was determined that human rights violations during the apartheid era should be investigated by a truth commission, not for the purpose of exacting retribution but to provide some form of public accounting and to help purge the injustices of the past. Unless past crimes were addressed, he said, they would 'live with us like a festering sore'. De Klerk, a deputy president in Mandela's government of national unity, denounced the whole idea, arguing that a truth commission would result in a 'witch-hunt' focusing upon past government abuses while ignoring ANC crimes. It was, he said, likely to 'tear the stitches of wounds that are beginning to heal'.

In the national debate that followed, some argued, as the ANC had once done, in favour of Nuremberg-style trials, claiming that apartheid was 'a form of genocide' equivalent to Nazi atrocities during the Second World War, atrocities for which Nazi leaders were subsequently prosecuted. Some demanded reparations from the white community on the grounds that they were the main beneficiaries of the apartheid system. Others argued that the best way to improve the chances of peace and reconciliation would be to grant a general amnesty to all sides. A large proportion of the white community, like de Klerk, opposed the whole process, maintaining that the only result would be to open old wounds and revive old animosities still close to the surface. A common theme in the Afrikaans-language press was: 'Atrocities were committed on both sides, so let us just forgive and forget.'

There were conflicting views about what the central purpose of a truth commission should be. Some argued that the overriding imperative was the need to achieve justice and to bring to account those guilty of gross human rights violations. Others maintained that truth was at least as important as justice and that knowledge of the truth alone would contribute significantly to the cause of peace and stability; avoiding trials would also reduce the risk of a backlash from security forces, still largely under the control of whites. Mandela himself once remarked privately that if he were to announce a series of criminal trials, he could well wake up the following morning to find his home ringed by tanks.

The Truth and Reconciliation Commission (TRC) that emerged in 1995 was born inevitably of compromise. Its remit was limited to the investigation of gross violations of human rights – murder, abduction and the use of torture – in the thirty-four-year period from 1960, starting with the massacre at Sharpeville. Thus the wider injustices of the apartheid system – such as the forced removal of some 3 million people from their homes, the imprisonment of millions for pass-law offences and the widespread use of detention without trial – would not be addressed. Only the extremes of apartheid would be examined, not its normality.

The TRC was given powers of subpoena and of search and seizure and it was supported by its own investigative unit. It was required to pay as much attention to violations committed by liberation movements as by the security police. But it was not a judicial body or a court of law. It could not carry out prosecutions or hand out punishment. Its aim was not so much to reach a judgement about culpability as to establish a process of disclosure. In exchange for telling the truth, perpetrators who came forward were to be granted amnesty from prosecution on an individual basis provided the commission was satisfied that they had made full disclosure of their crimes and that their actions had been carried out with a political objective. If they failed to come forward, they would remain at risk of prosecution.

Few people at the time believed that the TRC would establish either truth or reconciliation let alone help solve murders and disappearances that had occurred as far back as ten or twenty years beforehand. The old security police network, the prime suspect in most cases, had long since covered its tracks and was determined to thwart any investigation. There was no shortage of victims or members of their families willing to testify to what they knew, but little solid evidence about the identity of the culprits or those who gave them their orders. TRC officials expected few perpetrators to take advantage of the offer of amnesty.

Against all odds, however, the commission eventually succeeded in breaking through the barriers of silence. In October 1996 five former members of a police death squad based in northern Transvaal, fearful of prosecution as investigators closed in, asked for amnesty for a tally of sixty murders. Their actions, they said, had all been carried out for political reasons, namely 'to uphold the National Party government and apartheid, to fight communism and to resist liberation'. Members of other death squads followed suit. Stage by stage, the secret world of the security police was exposed, and many of the killers and torturers were forced out into the open.

What was even more unexpected was that once the security police network began to unravel, the TRC found it possible to probe higher and higher up the chain of command, reaching the highest levels of government. At the apex of the security establishment was the State

Security Council, where senior generals and key politicians met regularly to decide what action to take to crush opposition both at home and abroad. It was here that P. W. Botha's policy in the 1980s of 'total strategy' was fashioned. Summoned to appear before the commission, the generals and politicians of the apartheid era struggled to explain away documents obtained by TRC investigators authorising the 'elimination', 'neutralisation' and 'removing from society' of targets they selected. When Botha himself, a former chairman of the State Security Council for twelve years, was issued with a subpoena by the TRC, he adamantly refused to attend.

De Klerk made three appearances before the TRC. As the most prominent Afrikaner leader of the time, he was presented with an opportunity to shoulder responsibility for past crimes on behalf of his community. But he turned out to be a petty politician, concerned only with trying to absolve himself from personal blame. Although he offered a fulsome apology for all the hardship and suffering caused by apartheid, he rejected all notion of responsibility for security force abuses, blaming 'rogue elements' for taking 'unauthorised action' and 'lower ranks' for 'misinterpreting' government policy.

The ANC's appearances before the commission were of even greater significance, for how it accounted for its own involvement in murder, bombing and torture, had an immediate bearing on its fitness for government. The ANC was called upon to answer for the activities not just of its combatants but also of supporters who had carried out 'necklace' murders and other human rights violations. It also had to account for its role in the internecine conflict with Inkatha, in which thousands had died.

The position the ANC adopted from the outset was that there was little for which it had to answer. In his first submission to the commission, Thabo Mbeki, Mandela's deputy, argued that the ANC had been engaged in a 'just war' against an evil system of government. It would be 'morally wrong and legally incorrect', he said, to equate resistance to apartheid with defence of it. The ANC had resorted to violence as a 'last resort', only after the apartheid regime had blocked all possibilities of non-violent resistance. It had set out to avoid civilian casualties, but the brutal activities of the security forces in the mid–1980s had inevitably led it to broaden its range of targets. Some actions might have occurred 'outside the established norms', but they had to be understood in the context of irregular warfare.

The ANC's penchant for self-exoneration caused the TRC serious difficulty. When senior ANC officials declared that ANC members need not seek amnesty for bombings and killings on the grounds that their fight against apartheid had been part of a 'just war', the TRC chairman, Archbishop Desmond Tutu, threatened to resign. 'If parties are able to grant themselves amnesty, what is the point of having a truth commission?' The legislation setting up the TRC was quite clear, he said. It made no provision for a moral distinction between gross violations of human rights. 'A gross violation is a gross violation, whoever commits it and for whatever reason. There is thus legal equivalence between all perpetrators. Their political affiliation is irrelevant.'

In its second submission, the ANC was more forthcoming about details of its armed operations but remained ambivalent about issues like 'necklace' murders, by which at least 400 people had died. When it came to dealing with its internecine warfare with Inkatha, the ANC evaded virtually all responsibility. Mbeki delivered a long, rambling explanation notable for its misleading answers. Indeed, many of the answers Mbeki gave were as self-serving as those given by de Klerk.

The TRC's report, completed in 1998, after nearly three years of investigation, delivered some damning verdicts. It concluded that it was Botha's government in the late 1970s that had entered 'the realm of criminal misconduct'. Whereas previous governments had ruled by repression, Botha's government had adopted a policy of killing its opponents. It was also responsible for the widespread use of torture, abduction, arson and sabotage. Botha, said the report, by virtue of his position as head of state and chairman of the State Security Council, had 'contributed to and facilitated a climate in which . . . gross violations of human rights could and did occur'.

The 'realm of criminal misconduct', the report continued, extended into de Klerk's period in office. It criticised de Klerk for failing to tackle the activities of the 'third force' – the network of security force members and right-wing groups seeking to wreck any transition that would lead to an ANC government. It also accused him of failing to make a full disclosure to the commission of gross human rights violations committed by senior members of his government and senior police officers. 'His failure to do so constitutes a material nondisclosure, thus rendering him an accessory to the commission of gross human rights violations.'

The TRC was no less forthright in dealing with the ANC. During its armed struggle, said the report, the ANC had engaged in bombing and land-mine campaigns resulting in civilian casualties. In fact, the TRC pointed out, its armed actions had 'ended up killing fewer security force members than civilians'. While accepting that targeting civilians had not been ANC policy, the TRC concluded: 'Whatever the justification given by the ANC for such acts . . . the people who were killed or injured by such explosions are all victims of gross violations of human rights perpetrated by the ANC.' It also censured the ANC for regarding state informers and state witnesses as legitimate targets for assassination. Their killing, it said, constituted gross violations of human rights. Furthermore, the ANC was held 'morally and politically accountable' for creating a climate during the armed struggle that allowed its supporters to regard violence against opponents – urban councillors, rural headmen, members of Inkatha and others perceived to be collaborators of the system or enemies of the ANC – as a legitimate part of a 'people's war'. During the period from 1990 to 1994, it added, the ANC was responsible for the death and injury of hundreds of its opponents. It had also contributed to the spiral of violence by creating and arming 'self-defence units' that 'took the law into their own hands' and committed atrocities.

Two months before its report was due to be published in October 1998, the TRC, in accordance with its statutory obligations, sent summaries of its findings to some 200 individuals and organisations that it had named in connection with human rights abuses. Their reaction was uniformly hostile. De Klerk was livid that he had been named 'an accessory to human rights violations' and applied to the High Court for an interdict preventing publication of a thirty-line passage referring to him.

Far more of a shock was the ANC's reaction. Outraged that it had been roundly condemned for war crimes, the ANC insisted on a meeting with the TRC, intending to get it to rewrite its findings. The TRC invited the ANC to make a written submission but refused a meeting. The ANC retaliated by accusing the TRC of 'criminalising' the anti-apartheid struggle. Its findings were 'capricious and arbitrary'. The TRC had 'grossly misdirected itself'.

In an astonishing lapse of judgement, Thabo Mbeki went to the High Court, just like de Klerk, to apply for an urgent interdict to block publication of the report. Unable to conceal his anger and frustration, Archbishop Tutu conducted a series of media interviews warning of the dangers of a new tyranny in South Africa. 'We can't assume that yesterday's oppressed will not become tomorrow's oppressors. We have seen it happen all over the world, and we shouldn't be surprised if it happens here.' He urged all South Africans to be on their guard against government abuse and corruption.

Though nothing came of Mbeki's ill-fated attempt to muzzle the commission, it caused severe damage to the ANC's reputation and serious misgivings about his leadership ability. When the TRC finally presented its five-volume report to Mandela in October 1998, it was a sombre occasion, overshadowed by the ANC's wrecking manoeuvre. Mandela himself made clear his support for the TRC and its work. 'We are confident that it has contributed to the work in progress of laying the foundation of the edifice of reconciliation.' But there was a cacophony of contrary voices. Mbeki continued to insist that the TRC was 'wrong and misguided'. De Klerk accused the TRC of seeking vengeance not reconciliation.

Obscured by the furore, the achievements of the TRC were considerable. It had established beyond all doubt that death squads had operated not as aberrations but as part and parcel of the system of government repression; that torture had been used systematically and in effect condoned as official practice; and that violence between rival black factions had been officially encouraged, supported and financed. It had established the chain of command leading directly to the highest levels of government. It had helped solve many of the murders and disappearances that for so long had troubled so many families. It had confronted the liberation movements with their own crimes of murder, torture and necklacing, refusing to judge these crimes any differently from government crimes. It had also provided a hearing for thousands of victims and their families, affording many people relief from their burden of suffering and grief for the first time. As Lukas Sikwepere, a victim blinded by police gunfire, summed up the experience: 'I feel that what has been making me sick all the time is the fact that I couldn't tell my story. But now it feels like I got my sight back by coming here and telling you the story.'

All this, however, had come at a high price: amnesty. Though the amnesty process had persuaded many perpetrators eventually to come forward, throwing light on past atrocities, the disturbing consequence was that guilty men who had been seen and heard to confess to appalling crimes then walked entirely free.

Moreover, there were few signs that the proceedings of the TRC had advanced the cause of reconciliation. The white community would have preferred to let the past slip by into amnesia. Few whites attended TRC hearings, watched them on television, or listened to the radio broadcasts. What most heard were mere fragments of evidence. Many whites were genuinely shocked when they learned of the activities of death squads and other atrocities, but they believed them to be no more than one part of the picture, the part on which they claimed the TRC was concentrating. The more shocking the disclosures became, the more they felt able to distance themselves from them.

Opinion polls consistently showed white distrust and resentment about the TRC. In a survey carried out in July 1998, some 72 per cent of whites felt that the TRC had made race relations worse; almost 70 per cent felt that the TRC would not help South Africans to live together more harmoniously in the future; and some 83 per cent of Afrikaners and 71 per cent of English-speaking whites believed the TRC to be biased. In effect, it was a massive vote of no confidence.

The black community, by contrast, followed the proceedings of the TRC with avid interest. Writing in the *Sowetan* at the end of the exercise, Mathatha Tsedu recalled:

We were moved by the testimony, the fears, the sobs and the wailing of survivors and relatives who could not take the memories and the revelations. We cried a little too in our homes.

We also sat glued to the radio and television screens as killers of our patriots spoke of the murders they committed to defend white hegemony.

We hissed as the men, with no visible remorse, spoke of the pyres and burning of human bodies alongside the lamb chops and steak barbecues on the banks of various rivers of our land.

We got even more angry as the men walked away scot-free after such testimony.

Indeed, the work of the TRC provoked as much anger in parts of the black community as it did among the whites, particularly over the way that security force operatives responsible for heinous crimes were given freedom in exchange for a bit of truth-telling, while victims and their families were denied access to the courts. What many wanted more than truth was justice – prosecutions and prison sentences.

Opinion polls reflected nearly as much disillusionment with the work of the TRC among the black population as among the white community. The survey carried out in July 1998 showed that though a majority of blacks – 60 per cent – believed that the TRC had been fair to all sides, some 62 per cent thought that its work had made race relations worse. Significantly, however, blacks were more optimistic than whites about the future: nearly 80 per cent felt that as a result of the TRC's work people in South Africa would now live together more harmoniously.

In answering criticism levelled at the TRC, Tutu argued that the truth often turned out to be divisive. 'Reconciliation is not about being cosy; it is not about pretending that things were other than they were. Reconciliation based on falsehood, on not facing up to reality, is not true reconciliation and will not last.' Though truth might not always lead to reconciliation, there could be no genuine reconciliation without truth.

★

However much Mandela tried to focus attention on the poorer sections of society, the immediate beneficiaries of the new South Africa
were the black middle class. In the civil service and parastatal corporations, blacks rapidly gained positions of status and responsibility from
which they had been barred for so long. The business sector followed
suit, anxious to be seen redressing the legacy of inequality. Only 10
per cent of managerial posts were held by blacks, despite years of talk
about the need for black advancement. The opportunities for those
with skills and qualifications were vast. Yet the reservoir of trained and
experienced blacks was all too small. Out of a total of 14,000 char-
tered accountants, for example, only 65 were black. One consequence
was that in one business deal after another, as white-owned corporations sought to promote the development of black capitalism, a small
group of successful black entrepreneurs made all the running, enriching themselves hugely in the process. The black middle class were also
the main beneficiaries of the government's corrective discrimination
measures that accorded preferential treatment for 'previously disad-
vantaged' groups in hiring, promotion and the award of government
contracts.

What the Mandela years witnessed, in fact, was a significant widening of the income gap within the black community. The gap had been
growing since the late 1970s. During the 1980s, while the poorest half
of the population slid ever deeper into poverty, the black middle class
fared well, their rising incomes making them the most upwardly
mobile group in the country. During the 1990s the black elite – politicians, bureaucrats, entrepreneurs, managers, businessmen – prospered as
never before, many acquiring the lifestyle and status symbols so prized
in South Africa – executive cars, swimming pools, domestic staff, pri-
vate-school education, golf handicaps and foreign holidays. Perhaps 5
per cent of the black community reached middle-class status. But for
the majority, the same struggle against poverty continued.

From an early stage in his presidency, Mandela began to prepare South
Africa for the post-Mandela era. He was adamant that, regardless of
popular demand, he would not stay in office for a second term after
1999. 'At the end of my term, I'll be eighty-one,' he said. 'I don't

think it's wise that a robust country like South Africa should be led by an octogenarian. You need younger men who can shake and move this country.'

Indeed, there was a noticeable lack of decisiveness about Mandela's administration, a tendency to let government business drift. It was as though the sheer size of the agenda it faced was too daunting. Mandela himself contributed to the muddle and confusion into which the government sometimes fell. In his old age he was prone to act as impetuously as in the days of his youth. On occasions, he wielded his massive authority unwisely. His bouts of stubbornness and quick temper were legendary. When ministers he had appointed proved incompetent or corrupt, he rode to their rescue out of perverse loyalty rather than sack them. Despite the overwhelming need to attract Western investment, he persisted with personal initiatives to develop close ties with dictators like Gaddafi and Castro likely to deter Western investors.

Nevertheless, whatever the faults and failures of his administration, Mandela managed both to sustain his popularity among the black population and to retain the respect and admiration of the white community. As a mark of his standing, the name by which he became affectionately known, by black and white alike, was Madiba, his clan name dating from an eighteenth-century chief. National sporting victories in rugby, soccer and cricket were sometimes attributed to 'Madiba magic' – the effect of his presence among the spectators.

Mandela enjoyed the fame but remained unmoved by it. A patrician by nature, he possessed a common touch rare among African leaders. He often stopped to talk to children or youths with genuine interest. He greeted workers and tycoons with the same civility. He was invariably courteous and attentive to individuals, whatever their status or age. Amid an endless stream of meetings, speeches and official functions, he nevertheless found time to respond to individual requests, readily accepting invitations from schoolchildren and from ordinary citizens, telephoning strangers when the occasion arose and making himself available for snapshots. Despite the ailments of old age, he brought to his years as president remarkable energy, as if anxious to make up for lost time.

Indeed, so much confidence, so much trust came to be placed in Mandela that there were deep apprehensions about the prospect of his departure from government. He was seen not only as the founding father of democracy but also the guarantor of its stability. Rumours of his ill-health were enough to send the stock exchange and the currency into a tailspin. Mandela sought to minimise his own importance in government, emphasising the talent and ability of his cabinet colleagues. 'Many of my colleagues are head and shoulders above me in almost every respect. Rather than being an asset, I'm more of a decoration.'

He kept the prospect of retirement firmly in view, using his remaining time in office to foster a climate of tolerance in the hope that it might take root permanently. 'I am nearing my end,' he told Afrikaner students. 'I want to be able to sleep till eternity with a broad smile on my face, knowing that the youth, opinion-makers and everybody is stretching across the divide, trying to unite the nation.'

His legacy was a country which had experienced greater harmony than at any previous time in its history.

His successor, Thabo Mbeki, arrived with a new set of priorities. While Mandela had placed the need for reconciliation above all else, Mbeki put far greater emphasis on the need to transform South African society. 'You cannot find reconciliation between blacks and whites in a situation in which poverty and prosperity continue to be defined in racial terms,' he said. 'If you want reconciliation between black and white, you need to transform society. If we have an economy that is geared to benefit the whites and disadvantage the black majority, and you do not address that, you will not have reconciliation.' What Mbeki feared most was what he described as the 'mounting rage' of millions of blacks denied the opportunity of advancement. 'What happens to a dream deferred?' he asked, quoting the black American poet Langston Hughes. 'It explodes.'

There was also a marked change in the style of leadership. While Mandela had presided over South Africa as a benign patriarch, floating above the political hurly-burly, Mbeki was known as a back-room operator, a shrewd intellectual who enjoyed quoting Shakespeare and

Yeats but who lacked the common touch and who played his cards close to his chest. While Mandela took a broad-brush approach to government, Mbeki immersed himself in detail.

Mbeki had been nurtured in the business of nationalist politics from an early age. His father, Govan Mbeki, a hardline communist and ANC stalwart, had dedicated his life to political struggle and expected Thabo, his eldest son, to follow suit. A studious, introverted boy, who spent much of his spare time reading his father's books at the family home in rural Transkei, he joined the ANC Youth League at the age of fourteen, launched a pro-ANC student organisation at the age of nineteen, then joined the Communist Party a year later. In 1962, at the age of twenty, he was sent abroad by the ANC, along with twenty-six other students, to further his studies and he did not return until 1990. In his years in exile he earned a degree in economics from the University of Sussex in England, underwent military training in the Soviet Union, became a member of the Communist Party's polit-buro and represented the ANC in a series of foreign postings.

During the 1980s, when Western leaders like Britain's Margaret Thatcher regarded the ANC as 'a typical terrorist organisation', Mbeki came to be seen in the West as its acceptable face – a soft-spoken, articulate pragmatist, who favoured a negotiated settlement to end apartheid rather than revolutionary violence. He was particularly skilful in handling contacts with the stream of white South Africans – businessmen, academics, churchmen and opposition politicians – who travelled from South Africa to talk to the ANC, in defiance of the government, seeking a way through the impasse. Dressed in a tweed jacket and puffing his ubiquitous pipe, Mbeki spoke more the language of the middle class than the rhetoric they expected of revolutionaries. Once back in South Africa, he performed much the same task, pacifying businessmen alarmed by talk of nationalisation, right-wing Afrikaners demanding a separate *volkstaat*, and Zulu nationalists threatening civil war. 'He can be diplomatic to the point where many people regard him as weak,' Mandela once observed.

As Mandela's deputy, Mbeki took over much of the routine business of government, acting in effect as his chief executive. He was given particular responsibility for fashioning economic policy. The outcome was a policy document called *Growth, Employment and Redistribution* (Gear) that endorsed an orthodox free-market strategy. Published in 1996, it advocated strict fiscal discipline, lower government deficits, privatisation, trade liberalisation and export-driven growth. Its stated aim was to stimulate economic growth to reach 6 per cent a year and to create 500,000 jobs by 2000. A key part of Mbeki's strategy was to promote black business and foster the development of a black middle class. Addressing a conference of black business leaders, he declared: 'As part of the realisation of the aim to eradicate racism in our country, we must strive to create and strengthen a black capitalist class.' Blacks had no need to be embarrassed about the emergence of a successful and prosperous black bourgeoisie, he said. It was part of the process of the 'deracialisation' of the economy and society. The benefits would spread to the poor.

Mbeki's free-market strategy won him the approval of foreign investors and the business community but infuriated the ANC's traditional allies – the trade unions and the Communist Party. He was accused of betraying the revolution, of selling out to international capital, of forsaking 'the soul of the ANC'. At a conference of the Communist Party in 1998, after listening to one speaker after another denounce the ANC's 'treachery', he hit back, accusing its leaders of 'fake revolutionary posturing', describing them as 'charlatans' and 'confidence tricksters' attempting to build their organisation 'on the basis of scavenging on the carcass of a savaged ANC'. They were, he claimed, trying to 'propagate the understanding that our government has failed, as all other African governments have failed'.

By the time Mbeki took over as president in 1999, he had acquired a mixed reputation. His critics portrayed him as an arch-manipulator, ruthless in disposing of rivals and trusting only a small cabal of loyal advisers. He was known as a dedicated workaholic who insisted on mastering detail, but bungled a number of assignments Mandela gave him and showed abysmal judgement when handling the TRC report. The press noted how hostile, even paranoid, he had become about criticism and pointed to his tendency to react to criticism with accusations of racial malice. When Mbeki was elected unopposed to succeed Mandela as the ANC's leader at the party's fiftieth conference in 1997, Mandela expressed his own concern, his remarks prompting applause. 'There is a heavy responsibility for a leader elected unopposed,' he said. 'He may use that powerful position to settle scores with his detractors, to marginalise or get rid of them [applause] and surround themselves with yes-men and yes-women [applause]. His first duty is to allay the concerns of his colleagues to enable them to discuss freely without fear within internal structures.'

Mbeki's first term as president started well enough. He was bolstered by an election victory in 1999 won by the ANC with an even larger majority – 66 per cent of the vote – than in 1994. In his inaugural address, after paying tribute to the older generation for rescuing South Africa from the abyss, he spoke of the hope of a better future for the millions still living in misery. Quoting a proverb of the Tswana people, he said the country was at the stage of 'the dawning of the dawn', when only the tips of the cattle's horns could be seen etched against the morning sky. But within a year Mbeki had become embroiled in a senseless controversy over Aids which not only damaged his authority but called into question his fitness for office.

Like other African states, South Africa reacted lethargically to the onset of the Aids crisis. The first significant batch of HIV-positive cases was reported among migrant mineworkers from Malawi employed on Rand gold mines in 1986. By 1990 the adult HIV infection rate, measured in an ante-natal survey, stood at 0.7 per cent; by 1992 it had trebled to 2.2 per cent. But when the apartheid government eventually stirred into action, launching Aids education and prevention programmes, it met considerable resistance. Anti-apartheid activists claimed the programmes were a government plot to control population growth by convincing black people to have less sex and produce fewer babies and thereby check the advance of African liberation; they lampooned the Aids acronym saying it stood for 'Afrikaner Invention to Deprive us of Sex'. Others interpreted the epidemic as the product of malevolent individuals employing witchcraft.

Mandela's government purported to give the Aids campaign a high priority, but with so many other causes demanding attention – housing, education, jobs and wider health problems – it achieved little.

Though designating it a 'Presidential Lead Project', Mandela found the topic uncomfortable and failed to throw his weight behind it. An expensive musical show, *Sarafina II*, that the Department of Health commissioned intending to take Aids education to the masses, became mired in controversy and caused a rift with Aids-prevention field workers. There was further controversy when the health minister, Dr Nkosazana Dlamini-Zuma, announced in 1998 that an anti-retroviral drug, Azidothymidine (AZT), which tests had shown could cut vertical transmission from infected mothers to babies by 50 per cent, would not be made available on the grounds of cost, even though AZT's manufacturer had drastically cut the price. By the time Mandela stood down in 1999, official estimates of the number of HIV-positive cases stood at 4 million people – 10 per cent of the population; the number who had already died of Aids was put at 500,000.

Despite the gravity of the crisis, Mbeki became increasingly obsessed with the view of a small group of maverick scientists who questioned whether HIV existed at all or, if it did, whether it was not simply a harmless 'passenger' virus. They challenged the orthodox view of the causes of Aids, accepted by the vast majority of the world's medical establishment, claiming it was part of a conspiracy by large pharmaceutical companies to profit from the misery of Africa's poor. Anti-retroviral drugs, they argued, were not only expensive, they were toxic, more lethal than the disease they were supposed to be treating. Aids was not contagious; it was the result of poverty aggravating old disease patterns.

Early in 2000 Mbeki decided to set up a 'Presidential International Panel of Scientists on HIV/AIDS in Africa' to establish what he called 'the facts', suggesting that the orthodox view of the causes of Aids was no more than a 'thesis'. To the outrage of the scientific and medical fraternity, he invited a number of well-known 'dissidents' to take part, even though their theories had long since been discounted. In a letter sent in April 2000 to world leaders, including UN Secretary-General Kofi Annan, US President Bill Clinton and Britain's prime minister, Tony Blair, he explained that he had included the dissidents because he believed all opinions needed to be considered in the search for a response to the epidemic. He then went on to make an alarmingly intemperate defence of the dissidents' position, portraying them as victims of intimidation similar to that which had occurred during the apartheid era. 'Not long ago in our country people were killed, tortured and imprisoned because the authorities believed that their views were dangerous,' he wrote. 'We are now being asked to do the same thing that the racist apartheid tyranny did, because there is a scientific view against which dissent is prohibited.'

In Washington the White House was so astonished at this piece of chicanery that officials checked to see whether the letter was a hoax. The president of the Medical Research Council in South Africa, Professor Malegapuru Makgoba, a renowned microbiologist, complained of the 'lengthening list of politically-driven decisions regarding the South African AIDS crisis' and warned that the country was 'rapidly becoming a fertile breeding ground for the types of pseudo-science embraced by politicians'.

Apart from the confusion and paralysis the controversy caused in South Africa, it took on a worldwide significance. In July 2000 South Africa was due to host an international Aids conference. Hoping to keep the atmosphere calm, the conference chairman, Professor Hoosen Coovadia of the University of Natal, urged Mbeki to steer clear of scientific debates. Mbeki's response, however, was to authorise his ministers to make personal attacks on Coovadia and other critics, questioning their academic credentials and suggesting they were operating as 'frontline troops of the pharmaceutical industry'. When 5,000 scientists, including Nobel Prize winners and directors of leading research institutions and medical societies, signed a declaration, in advance of the conference, stating that HIV was the direct cause of Aids, Mbeki's health minister, Manto Tshabalala-Msimang, dismissed it as an 'elitist document' signed only by health scientists. 'You can't have a certain exclusive group of people saying this is what we believe about HIV and Aids.' Mbeki's spokesman, Parks Mankahlana, warned that if the drafters of the declaration gave it to the president or the government, it would find 'its comfortable place among the dustbins of the office'.

Opening the conference in Durban, Mbeki made no attempt to pull back into the mainstream. He reiterated his doubts about the gravity of the epidemic and dwelt on the findings of a 1995 World

Health Organisation report which argued that the world's biggest killer was extreme poverty – a theme favoured by the dissidents. Following the conference he retreated further into semantics, conspiracy theories and pseudo-science, continuing to ridicule the link between HIV and Aids. 'Aids is Acquired Immune Deficiency Syndrome,' he told parliament. 'I don't believe it's a sensible thing to ask: "Does a virus cause a syndrome?" It can't. A virus will cause a disease.' His office issued a statement accusing anti-Aids activists who wanted the government to provide anti-retroviral drugs in public hospitals of trying to poison black people. 'Our people are being used as guinea-pigs and conned into using dangerous and toxic drugs,' said the statement; it likened this to 'the biological warfare of the apartheid era'. He told the ANC's parliamentary caucus that criticism of his Aids policies was a plot by the CIA acting in alliance with drug companies to discredit him as the leader of efforts by the developing world to obtain a better deal in the international economic system. Interviewed by a Cape Town television station, he said he was not prepared to set an example by taking a public HIV test because it would send a message that he supported a particular scientific viewpoint – the dominant medical 'paradigm'. In a lecture he gave at Fort Hare University, he suggested that medical scientists and anti-Aids activists engaged in public campaigns had racial motives. 'It does happen that others who consider themselves to be our leaders take to the streets carrying their placards to demand that because we are germ carriers and human beings of a lower order that cannot subject its passions to reason, we must perforce adopt strange options, to save a depraved and diseased people from perishing from self-inflicted disease.' In other words, the explanations of the causes of the epidemic as set out by Mbeki's critics were part of a racial conspiracy against Africans. The effect of Mbeki's embrace of dissident arguments was to increase public resistance to Aids education.

Whatever contorted reasoning Mbeki tried to use, the evidence of catastrophe continued to mount. The UN Aids agency estimated that 250,000 people in South Africa died of Aids in 2000. The World Health Organisation estimated that one in five South African adults in 2000 was HIV-positive. The South African paediatric association estimated that 70,000 babies were born with HIV in 2000. Health Department surveys in 2001 showed that one-quarter of all South African women receiving support from public ante-natal clinics were HIV-positive. A study by the Medical Research Council concluded that, in the period from 1999 to mid-2001, Aids had become the leading cause of death. In 2000 40 per cent of deaths among those aged from fifteen to forty-nine, and 25 per cent of total deaths, including children, were from Aids-related illnesses. It warned that if the epidemic went unchecked it would claim between 5 and 7 million South Africans by 2010; 2 million children would be left as orphans; life expectancy would have plunged from a pre-epidemic high of sixty-five years to forty-one years; and the annual death toll from Aids would have reached 800,000.

Mbeki's obduracy over Aids caused considerable dissension within the upper echelons of the ANC. A senior ANC official told a reporter that Mbeki had 'exposed a side of his personality which some of us were aware of: terrible conceit and paranoia'. Mandela made clear his disapproval and demanded government action. 'This is a war, it has killed more people than has been the case in all previous wars,' he told a newspaper. 'We must not continue to be debating, to be arguing, when people are dying.' Professor Makgoba accused Mbeki of a 'Soviet-style' attempt to intimidate his critics and warned doctors and scientists against remaining silent in the face of 'genocide'. Trade unions called for the epidemic to be declared a national emergency. Provincial governments, on their own account, began authorising the use of a new anti-retroviral drug called nevirapine, helped by an offer from its manufacturer of five years of free supply. Comedians jumped in on the act, ridiculing Mbeki's attitude. 'Not everyone regards you as a pretentious, arrogant, paranoid, heartless, ruthless Stalinist,' wrote Evita Bezuidenhout, the alter ego of satirist Pieter-Dirk Uys, in a letter to the *Cape Times*. Her son Izan, she said, serving a prison term for racist crimes, had become a big fan of Mbeki because official confusion over Aids meant that the disease, by killing off the black majority, 'will succeed where apartheid failed'.

In August 2001 an activist organisation, the Treatment Action Campaign, which had spent four years trying to persuade the president to change course, started legal proceedings aimed at forcing the government to provide nevirapine to help reduce mother-to-baby transmission. The government argued that the courts had no right to make policy decisions. But it lost its case, first in the High Court and then in the Constitutional Court. In July 2002 the Constitutional Court ordered the government to provide nevirapine to all HIV-positive pregnant mothers at all public hospitals free of charge 'without delay', leaving Mbeki humiliated.

Even then, Mbeki continued to drag his feet. His health minister, Manto Tshabalala-Msimang, a crony from exile days, recommended quack remedies such as eating garlic, beetroot or olive oil which she claimed had produced 'astounding results'. Only when further court action was threatened did the government finally respond with an Aids drugs programme. By then, 1 million people had died from Aids; the number of people infected by HIV had reached 5.3 million; an estimated 2,000 were infected with HIV every twenty-four hours; and some 600 people were dying from Aids each day.

Mbeki's handling of Zimbabwe's dictator Robert Mugabe further damaged his reputation. South Africa possessed a unique ability to bring pressure to bear on its landlocked northern neighbour. It provided transport links, electricity supplies and other services vital for Zimbabwe's welfare. In the 1970s the South African government, for reasons of self-interest, used these means to force Ian Smith to concede black majority rule. In 2000, when Mugabe began his sustained campaign of terror to stay in power – crushing political opponents, violating the courts, trampling on property rights, rigging elections, suppressing the independent press and precipitating economic collapse – the reaction of Western governments was to issue a torrent of condemnation and eventually a package of personal sanctions, but Mbeki chose what he termed 'quiet diplomacy'.

There were, initially, sound enough reasons for Mbeki to take a cautious approach. Britain's attempt at megaphone diplomacy had merely exacerbated the problem and enabled Mugabe to portray Britain as a neo-colonial power throwing its weight around to protect the interests of white settlers. Mbeki hoped that discreet persuasion offered a better prospect. His efforts, however, failed again and again. On one occasion, after holding discussions with Mbeki, Mugabe pledged at a televised news conference, with Mbeki sitting beside him, that the 'war veterans' would be removed from all commercial farms they had occupied and resettled elsewhere. The following day Mugabe claimed he had been 'misquoted' and ordered land seizures to be speeded up. Time and again, Mugabe promised Mbeki that he would negotiate a solution with the opposition but never made any attempt to do so. Despite numerous other examples of Mugabe's perfidy, Mbeki continued to insist that 'quiet diplomacy' would produce results. Not once did he speak out in defence of human rights in Zimbabwe. Indeed, he began to parrot Mugabe's argument that the root cause of the trouble was Britain's failure to honour its commitment to finance land redistribution and its interference in supporting its own 'white kith and kin' in Zimbabwe. The only reason why such a fuss had been made about Zimbabwe was 'because white people died and white people were deprived of their property'. The fact that Mugabe's tyranny had inflicted violence, hardship and misery on millions of blacks did not seem to Mbeki sufficient cause to protest. As the lawlessness continued, Mbeki, far from becoming more critical of Mugabe, acted to shield him against the onslaught of Western outrage, making strenuous efforts to overturn Zimbabwe's suspension from the Commonwealth.

Mbeki's determination to back a brutal African dictator, rather than stand up for human rights, followed a long tradition by leaders in Africa of turning a blind eye to the nefarious activities of their peers for the sake of group solidarity. It won him support in Africanist circles in South Africa who celebrated Zimbabwe's example of giving the whites a good kicking and hoped for something similar in South Africa. But it caused apprehension among foreign investors, nervousness among the white population and aroused further misgivings about Mbeki's commitment to democratic values. Moreover, it sullied the reputation of the ANC, which had received so much help in its own struggle for human rights and now remained indifferent to the struggle that others in the neighbourhood faced. In a thinly veiled rebuke, Archbishop Tutu, forever the voice of conscience in South

Africa, pronounced himself 'baffled' by African leaders who supported dictators like Mugabe. 'Human rights are human rights and
they are of universal validity or they are nothing,' he said.

In its first ten years as a democracy, South Africa recorded significant
achievements. It established a high degree of political stability, all the
more remarkable after such a prolonged and violent contest for power.
It held a series of orderly elections – in 1994, 1999 and 2004 –
generally acknowledged to be free and fair. It produced a new constitution robust in its protection of individual rights. And it enjoyed an
independent judiciary, an assertive press and a vigorous civil society.

Moreover, its siege economy was transformed into an internationally competitive one, no longer dependent on gold-mining profits but
including flourishing sectors in manufacturing, tourism, banking and
insurance. The economic growth rate more than doubled, averaging
2.8 per cent a year. National finances were restored to good order.
Inflation and interest rates fell. Education rather than debt repayments
took the largest share of government spending. A poll of business
confidence in 2004 touched a fifteen-year high. Major strides were
made in the provision of housing, sanitation, electricity, primary medical care and pension benefits.

But the magnitude of the problems that South Africa faced still
remained daunting. Despite economic growth, unemployment rates
stood at more than 40 per cent. The number of job-seekers continued
to outpace the growth in jobs. Fewer than 7 per cent of school-
leavers could expect to find jobs in the formal economy. In some rural
areas the unemployment rate was as high as 95 per cent; sometimes a
dozen people survived on one old-age pension. Out of a population
of 45 million, more than 3 million lived in squatter camps or informal
settlements, many enduring abject poverty, with little or no sanitation,
clean water or power and no visible means of support. In all, 18 million people lived without any sanitation; 5 million lacked safe water
supplies; and 7 million struggled below the national poverty line.
Crime for many was the only means to survive; South Africa suffered
from one of the highest crime rates in the world.

Indeed, during the first ten years of democracy, the gap between rich and poor grew ever wider. It no longer marked the boundary between white and black, as it had done during the apartheid years. For, by 2004, blacks constituted 10 per cent of the top fifth of earners; more than 700,000 were employed in professional or managerial positions. In all more than 7 million South Africans earned a regular wage in the formal economy. The rest, however, faced a precarious existence. It was among them that Mbeki feared 'mounting rage'.

35

OUT OF AFRICA

In the euphoria that followed the advent of democracy in South Africa in 1994, Nelson Mandela spoke optimistically of how not only South Africa but the whole continent stood at the threshold of a new era. Addressing an OAU summit meeting in June 1994, he recited a litany of suffering and subjugation that Africa had experienced since Roman times, acknowledging that many modern African leaders had added to the toll of misery. 'We must face the matter squarely that where there is something wrong in how we govern ourselves, it must be said that the fault is not in our stars but in ourselves that we are ill-governed.' The time had now come for 'a new birth', he said. 'We know that we have it in ourselves, as Africans, to change all this. We must assert our will to do so. We must say that there is no obstacle big enough to stop us from bringing about an African renaissance.'

The idea of an African renaissance was not new. It had been a common theme in the 1950s and 1960s during the era of African emancipation from colonial rule. But the addition of South Africa to the wider community of African states, bringing an economic output nearly equal to the rest of sub-Saharan Africa and a new impetus to democratic rule, seemed a propitious moment.

The idea was taken up by Thabo Mbeki during his term as president and turned into a personal crusade. Mbeki's aim was to improve the image of Africa in order to attract foreign investment and make the new South Africa an important global trading nation. In a speech given to a Japanese audience in Tokyo in 1998, he opened by quoting the Roman historian Pliny the Elder: '*Ex Africa semper aliquid novi*', Pliny wrote. 'Out of Africa always something new.' Mbeki referred to the past glories for which Africa was renowned: the pyramids of Egypt; the Benin bronzes of Nigeria; the obelisks of Aksum in Ethiopia; the libraries of Timbuktu in Mali; the stone fortresses of Zimbabwe; the ancient rock art of South Africa. 'When I survey all this and much more besides, I find nothing to sustain the long-held dogma of African exceptionalism, according to which the colour black becomes a symbol of fear, evil and death.' Since the advent of independence, said Mbeki, Africa had had to contend with the problems of 'neo-colonialism' and the Cold War. But that era had now passed. The fall of dictators like Mobutu in 1997 marked 'the death of neo-colonialism on our continent'.

A new era – the African renaissance – had already begun. One-party states and military dictatorships were no longer considered acceptable forms of government. Democracy was now the lodestar. During the 1990s, Mbeki claimed, at least twenty-five countries had established 'multi-party democracies'. South Africa's own emergence as a democracy was part of 'this African movement'. New economic policies had been introduced to attract investors, encourage the growth of the private sector and reduce state intervention. Africans had learned from past mistakes and were better able now to implement their own reforms. 'The African renaissance, in all its parts, can only succeed if its aims and objectives are defined by Africans themselves, if its programmes are designed by ourselves and if we take responsibility for the success or failure of our policies.' Nevertheless, international assistance was an essential component. 'We believe that it is important that the international community should agree that Africa constitutes the principal development challenge in the world.'

Mbeki's vision of an African renaissance won applause in Western circles. During his second term of office, President Bill Clinton was keen for the US to develop a more dynamic approach to Africa and readily seized on the idea. In March 1998 he embarked on the most comprehensive tour of Africa ever undertaken by a sitting American president – a ten-day trip covering six nations starting with Ghana.

'One hundred years from now your grandchildren and mine will look back and say this was the beginning of an African renaissance,' he told an exuberant crowd in Accra's Independence Square. 'By coming and going a bird builds a nest. We will come and go and do all we can to help you build a new Africa.' He was similarly effusive in South Africa. 'It used to be that when US policymakers thought of Africa – if they thought of Africa – they said: "What can we do for Africa, or about Africa?" They were the wrong questions. The right question is: what can we do *with* Africa? Yes, Africa still needs the world, but more than ever the world needs Africa.'

Clinton's strategy for Africa involved selecting a small group from the 'new generation' of African leaders who passed American tests for their commitment to democracy, economic renewal and civil rights. Besides Mbeki, the group included Uganda's Yoweri Museveni; Rwanda's Paul Kagame; Ethiopia's Meles Zenawi; Eritrea's Isaias Afwerki, and Ghana's Jerry Rawlings. The risks inherent in such a strategy were quickly evident. Within three months of Clinton's visit to Africa, Ethiopia and Eritrea embarked on a futile border war in which 100,000 people died, one-third of Eritrea's population was displaced and hundreds of millions of dollars were squandered on arms. Two months after the start of their war, Rwanda and Uganda plunged headlong into another round of war in Congo and then began fighting among themselves over the spoils of their occupation there. American support for the idea of an African renaissance rapidly dwindled.

Mbeki persevered with his call for an African renaissance, but with increasing difficulty. In addition to wars in Angola, Congo, Sudan, Liberia, Sierra Leone, Ethiopia and Eritrea, a host of other conflicts bedevilled Africa. Congo-Brazzaville was convulsed by tribal strife that brought an end to its experiment with multi-party politics and wrecked parts of the capital. The Central African Republic was also torn apart by tribal strife. In Côte d'Ivoire, renowned for its stability during Houphouët-Boigny's reign, a succession of leaders stirred up ethnic and religious divisions for their own purposes, setting Christian southerners against Muslim northerners, eventually precipitating civil war that engulfed parts of Abidjan and split the country apart. In Uganda, while Museveni's army commanders were busy plundering in Congo, Joseph Kony's atavistic cult, the Lord's Resistance Army, continued its campaign of murder and abduction in Acholiland, enslaving thousands of children in its cause each year. In 2000 there were more than ten major conflicts underway in Africa. One-fifth of all Africans lived in countries battered by war. Some 12 million were classified as refugees – 40 per cent of the world's total. The cause of democracy and development, as *The Economist* said, seemed 'hopeless'. When Abdou Diouf of Senegal accepted defeat in an election in March 2000, he was only the fourth African president to do so in four decades.

In an attempt to give the idea of an African renaissance some concrete form, Mbeki, in conjunction with a group of other African leaders – Nigeria's Olusegun Obasanjo; Algeria's Abdelaziz Bouteflika; Egypt's Hosni Mubarak; and Senegal's Abdoulaye Wade – produced an initiative known as the New Partnership for African Development or Nepad. Launched in 2001, Nepad contained a large amount of familiar rhetoric. The fifteen governments that signed its founding documents pledged themselves, individually and collectively, to promote democratic principles, popular participation, good governance and sound economic management. They agreed to set up an African peer review mechanism to monitor their performance and punish defaulters. In exchange they asked industrialised states for an improved package of trade, investment, aid and debt relief measures. In particular they wanted Western governments to dismantle trade barriers directed against African products such as textiles and agricultural goods; to increase their development aid to an equivalent of 0.7 per cent of their GDP, in accordance with United Nations targets; and to encourage greater Western private-sector investment. The hope was to channel $64 billion a year to Nepad's partner states for a period of fifteen years, lifting annual growth to 7 per cent and reducing poverty by half by 2015. The slogan for this endeavour was 'Better Africa, Better World'.

Linked to the drive for renewal was a plan to overhaul the Organisation of African Unity, hitherto regarded as little more than a club for dictators. The leading figures behind the plan were Mbeki and Obasanjo. The OAU needed to be strengthened, said Mbeki in 1999, 'so that in its work, it focuses on the strategic objective of the realisation of the African renaissance'. Simultaneously, Colonel Gaddafi sought to use the OAU as a means both to rehabilitate himself after years of international isolation and to create for himself a new leadership role in Africa. In 1999 he invited African leaders to a special summit in Sirte where he revealed his plan for a 'United States of Africa', complete with a continental presidency, a single military force and a common African currency, all to be approved then and there.

The outcome was that in 2001 the OAU was replaced by the African Union, an organisation adorned with a plethora of new institutions, including a Pan-African parliament, a Pan-African Court of Justice, an African central bank and a Peace and Security Council. It was also granted greater powers. Whereas the OAU was required by charter to refrain from interference in individual states, the African Union was given the right to intervene, without consent, in a member state in order to 'restore peace and stability'; to 'prevent war crimes, genocide and crimes against humanity'; and in response to 'a serious threat to legitimate order'.

In July 2002 the leaders of fifty-three African states gathered in Durban for the inaugural conference of the African Union. There was a carnival mood, with grand speeches, sumptuous banquets and a succession of pageants – Zulu dancers, Senegalese footballers, marching bands and gospel choirs. 'This is a moment of hope for our continent and its peoples,' declared Mbeki. 'The time has come that Africa must take its rightful place in global affairs. The time has come to end the marginalisation of Africa . . . Through our actions, let us proclaim to the world that this is a continent of democracy, a continent of democratic institutions and culture. Indeed, a continent of good governance, where the people participate and the rule of law is upheld.'

But the occasion served as much as a reminder about Africa's ugly past as about its hopes for the future. As well as modernisers like Mbeki and Obasanjo, there was a large contingent of megalomaniac dictators with little interest in democracy or good governance. Some presidents – like Liberia's Charles Taylor, who had won election with the slogan, 'He killed my ma, he killed my pa, but I will vote for him' – were no more than gangsters. Others – like Kenya's Daniel arap Moi – were grotesquely corrupt. Many were 'dinosaurs' who had entrenched themselves in power for decades. Togo's Gnassingbé Eyedéma, a former army sergeant who had participated in the assassination of President Olympio, had maintained his grip since 1967; Gabon's Omar Bongo since 1967; Libya's Gaddafi since 1969; Kenya's Moi since 1978; Equatorial Guinea's Teodoro Obiang Nguema since 1979; Zimbabwe's Robert Mugabe since 1980; Egypt's Hosni Mubarak since 1981; Cameroon's Paul Biya since 1982.

Mbeki's attempts to endow the occasion with a sense of gravitas as well as pageantry were soon overshadowed by the antics of Gaddafi, who arrived in Durban with an entourage of 600 officials and a cavalcade of sixty armoured cars. Determined to steal the limelight, Gaddafi stood up in front of a crowd of 30,000 spectators in King's Park stadium, shaking his fists in the air, and insisted on making an unscheduled, impromptu speech in English. 'Africa for Africans! The land is ours! Africa is our land! You are the masters of the continent! You are proud! You are marching to glory! No more slavery! No more colonisation! It's a new dawn!' Referring to the whites of South Africa and Zimbabwe, Gaddafi declared: 'My brother, Mr Mandela! My brother Mbeki! Forgive! My brother Mugabe! Forgive the whites. They are now poor. You are your own masters. Forgive them. You are free. We are bigger than them. We are mighty! . . . If they want to serve us, okay. If they want to go back, okay. Goodbye. You tell them goodbye.' It was left to the UN Secretary-General Kofi Annan, himself a Ghanaian, to sound a more sombre note: 'Let us be careful not to mistake hope for achievement,' he warned.

In reality, fifty years after the beginning of the independence era, Africa's prospects are bleaker than ever before. Already the world's poorest region, it is falling further and further behind all other regions of the world. Its average per capita national income is one-third lower than the world's next poorest region, South Asia. Most African countries have lower per capita incomes now than they had in 1980 or, in some cases, in 1960. Half of Africa's 880 million people live on less than US$1 a day. Its entire economic output is no more than $420 billion, just 1.3 per cent of world GDP, less than a country like Mexico. Its share of world trade has declined to half of what it was in the 1980s, amounting to only 1.6 per cent; its share of global investment is less than 1 per cent. It is the only region where per capita investment and savings has declined since 1970. It is the only region where school enrolment is falling and where illiteracy is still commonplace: two in five Africans – and half of all African women – are illiterate, compared to one in every eight adults in East Asia or Latin America. It is also the only region where life expectancy is falling. On a list drawn up by the United Nations Development Programme, all twenty-five countries that rank lowest in terms of human development are African. Africa has also found itself on the losing side of globalisation, lacking both the skills and the infrastructure to attract the multinational corporations that drive it.

The scourge of Aids has inflicted a terrible additional burden. Sub-Saharan Africa is home to just 10 per cent of the world's population but bears more than 70 per cent of the world's HIV/Aids cases. With the pandemic still in its infancy, by 2004 some 20 million people had died from Aids; 30 million were infected by the HIV virus and their number was rising by an estimated 3 million new cases each year. Southern Africa is the worst affected region. Botswana has the highest infection rate in the world: more than 37 per cent of its population of 1.6 million are HIV-positive; in the age group of fifteen to forty-nine, the infection rate is 40 per cent. By 2010 average life expectancy in Botswana is expected to fall to twenty-seven years; half of all children in the country are likely to be Aids orphans. Other countries in the region – Zambia, Zimbabwe, Malawi, Mozambique and Swaziland – are similarly affected. The disease not only tears apart family structures but wrecks government efforts to provide public services. Teachers die at a faster rate than replacements can be trained. The skills shortage grows worse.

The prospects of Africa escaping from precipitous decline, as Mbeki acknowledged, depend heavily on Western assistance. The magnitude of the crisis is too great for African states to resolve by themselves. Most states are effectively bankrupt, weighed down by debt, barely able to raise sufficient funds on their own account to provide a mini-mum of public services. By the late 1990s more than half already relied on Western aid to fund as much as 50 per cent of government budgets and 70 per cent of public investment.

Yet Western governments, while applauding the objectives set out by Nepad and by the African Union, remain sceptical of Africa's abil-ity to deliver its side of the bargain. So many previous initiatives have failed. Since independence Africa has received far more foreign aid than any other region in the world. More than $300 billion of Western aid has been sunk into Africa, but with little discernible result. Aid fatigue has become a permanent condition. During the 1990s inter-national government aid for Africa fell from an average of $28.6 billion a year to $16.4 billion. There has been scant enthusiasm for increasing it. US officials in the Bush administration argued that aid had all too often been wasted. Japan, a major aid donor, was hampered by its own economic crisis. Britain's prime minister, Tony Blair, was one of the few Western leaders to advocate a significant increase in aid. 'The state of Africa is a scar on the conscience of the world,' he said in 2001, with a touch of missionary zeal. 'But if the world focused on it, we could heal it. And if we don't, the scar will become angrier still.'

When Mbeki led an African delegation to plead the case for sup-porting Nepad at the G8 summit of the world's richest nations in Canada in 2002, he received no more than a lukewarm response. His own reputation had been tarnished by his reluctance to take a stand against Mugabe's tyranny, in accordance with the commitments that he himself had made under the terms of the Nepad contract. For many Western governments, Mugabe was the test of Nepad's credi-bility, a test that Mbeki was deemed to have failed. Nor were they impressed by his grievous mishandling of South Africa's Aids crisis. At the very moment that Mbeki sought 'a new partnership' with the West, the West no longer regarded him as a safe pair of hands. All that the Africans obtained from the G8 summit was a pledge of $6 billion of extra aid a year and a relatively small increase in debt relief. Aid agencies like Oxfam derided the offer as 'peanuts'.

Nor are Western governments inclined to amend their trade and agricultural policies for the sake of Africa's revival. Determined to protect their own producers, industrialised countries operate a system of subsidies and tariff barriers that have a crippling effect on African producers. The total value of their agricultural subsidies amounts to 1 billion dollars a day – $370 billion a year – a sum higher than the gross domestic product of the whole of sub-Saharan Africa. The European Union subsidy for each of its cows is about $900 a year – more than the average African income; the Japanese subsidy is $2,700 per cow. Western surpluses produced at a fraction of their real cost are then dumped on African markets, undermining domestic producers. Simultaneously, African products face tariff barriers imposed by industrialised countries, effectively shutting them out of Western markets.

The case of cotton illustrates the hurdles that Africa has to surmount. Africa is the world's third largest producer, turning out high-quality cotton at competitive prices. In West Africa cotton provides a living for a million farmers. Cotton production in francophone West Africa has soared from 100,000 tons a year at independence in 1960 to 900,000 tons. In Benin, Burkina Faso, Chad, Mali and Togo, cotton represents between 5 and 10 per cent of GDP, more than a third of export income and more than 60 per cent of agricultural export income. Production costs in West Africa are about 38 cents a pound. By comparison, production costs in the United States are more than twice as high. But the US provides its 25,000 cotton farmers with an annual subsidy of $4 billion – more than the value of the entire crop. US farmers have therefore been able to export cotton at one-third of what it costs them to produce. Over a period of fifteen years, they have gained nearly one-third of the world market. A study by Oxfam in 2002 calculated that, as a result of the US subsidy, the world price was 25 per cent lower than it would otherwise have been. It estimated that the cost to Burkina Faso was 1 per cent of its GDP or 12 per cent of its exports; to Mali, 1.7 per cent of GDP or 8 per cent of exports; and to Benin, 1.4 per cent of GDP or 9 per cent of exports. According to Oxfam, the trade losses associated with US farm subsidies that West Africa's eight main cotton exporters suffered outweighed the benefits they received from US aid.

In addition to US subsidies, the European Union supports its cotton producers with a subsidy amounting to about $1 billion a year. A World Bank study estimated that it would be three times cheaper for Europe to import cotton than to grow it in Spain or Greece, where the subsidy paid to farmers is far more than the market price of cotton. China spends more than $1 billion a year on cotton subsidies. The overall impact on world prices has been huge. Though West African cotton production rose by 14 per cent between 1998 and 2002, receipts fell by 31 per cent. The World Bank estimated that eliminating cotton subsidies altogether would raise West Africa's export income by $250 million a year. In similar fashion, African farmers have struggled to compete against a wide range of other sub-sidised agricultural products – European sugar, Asian rice, Italian tomatoes, Dutch onions; many have been forced out of business.

A number of Western initiatives have been launched in an attempt to lift Africa out of crisis. Debt relief schemes have been put in place for highly indebted countries. In 2000 the US approved the African Growth and Opportunity Act, which focuses on the promotion of free markets and the expansion of two-way trade and investment, offering trade preferences and other economic benefits to countries pursuing market-reform measures. In 2002 President Bush announced the Millenium Challenge Account directing funds towards African states selected for their record on promoting good governance and economic reform. The following year he promised to spend $15 bil-lion over five years to fight Aids in Africa and the Caribbean. Britain has campaigned vigorously for debt relief programmes and drawn up proposals for an International Financing Facility aiming to use global fund markets to double aid spending. In 2004, prompted by the former Irish pop singer Bob Geldof, Britain's Tony Blair set up a Commission for Africa, asking experts to devise a new agenda for change, warning that 'the scale of the problem is growing'.

Yet Western governments have frequently lagged far behind the commitments they made and the rhetoric they used. During a visit to Africa in 2003, Bush stressed the importance of Africa to the US agenda. In terms of aid, however, the US ranks at the bottom of all donor countries in relation to the size of its economy, contributing no more than 0.1 per cent of national income to foreign aid worldwide; one hundredth of 1 per cent of the US budget is spent on aid to sub-Saharan Africa. Most other Western governments fall far short of the UN target of spending 0.7 per cent of national income on aid.

But even given greater Western efforts, the sum of Africa's misfortunes – its wars, its despotisms, its corruption, its droughts, its everyday violence – presents a crisis of such magnitude that it goes beyond the reach of foreseeable solutions. At the core of the crisis is the failure of African leaders to provide effective government. Few countries have experienced wise or competent leadership. South Africa, in the post-apartheid era, has emerged as a well-managed democratic state, with strong institutions and a system of checks and balances firmly entrenched in a modern constitution. Botswana stands out as a unique example of an enduring multi-party democracy with a record of sound economic management, that has used its diamond riches for national advancement and maintained an administration free of corruption.

But for the most part, Africa has suffered grievously at the hands of its Big Men and its ruling elites. Their preoccupation, above all, has been to hold power for the purpose of self-enrichment. The patrimonial systems they have used to sustain themselves in power have drained away a huge proportion of state resources. They have commandeered further riches by acting as 'gatekeepers' for foreign companies. Much of the wealth they have acquired has been squandered on luxury living or stashed away in foreign bank accounts and foreign investments. The World Bank has estimated that 40 per cent of Africa's private wealth is held offshore. Their scramble for wealth has spawned a culture of corruption permeating every level of society. A report prepared for the African Union in 2002 estimated that corruption cost Africa $148 billion annually – more than a quarter of the continent's entire gross domestic product. Veteran oil-producing states, like Nigeria, Angola and Gabon, rank highest for the sums dissipated by their ruling elites. But new oil producers are no different. Equatorial Guinea's oil revenues rose to $700 million in 2004, but remained the private preserve of its brutal dictator Obiang Nguema and members of his family; like dos Santos in Angola, Obiang insisted that the use of oil revenues remained a 'state secret'. Sudan's Islamist rulers spent its first oil revenues on arms to suppress their opponents.

Even when regimes have changed hands, new governments, whatever promises they made on arrival, have lost little time in adopting the habits of their predecessors. When Kenya's Daniel arap Moi was eventually obliged to stand down at the end of 2002 after twenty-four years in power, investigators estimated that he and his cronies had looted as much as $3 billion. Moi's successor Mwai Kibaki spoke of inheriting 'a country badly ravaged by years of misrule and ineptitude' and he pledged to root out corruption. 'Corruption will cease to be a way of life in Kenya,' he declared. But no sooner had Moi's 'Karbanet Syndicate' of Kalenjin politicians departed than they were replaced by Kibaki's 'Mount Kenya mafia' of Kikuyu politicians who moved swiftly to set up their own lucrative deals. After little more than a year in office, the level of corruption had become so noticeable once more that it provoked the British High Commissioner in Kenya, Edward Clay, into making a memorable outburst. The names of honest ministers and senior officials, he said in a speech to business leaders in Nairobi in July 2004, would fit on the back of a postage stamp.

> It is outrageous to think that corruption accounts for about 8 per cent of Kenya's GDP. Kenya is not a rich country in terms of oil deposits, diamonds or some other buffer which might featherbed a thoroughgoing culture of corruption. What it chiefly has is its people – their intelligence, work ethic, education, entrepreneurial and other skills.
>
> Those assets will be lost if they are not managed, rewarded and properly led. One day we may wake up at the end of this looting spree to find Kenya's potential is all behind us and it is a land of lost opportunity.
>
> We never expected corruption to be vanquished overnight. We all recognised that some would be carried over to the new era. We hoped it would not be rammed in our faces. But it has: evidently the practitioners now in government have the arrogance, greed and perhaps a sense of panic to lead them to eat like gluttons. They

may expect we shall not see, or will forgive them, a bit of gluttony because they profess to like Oxfam lunches. But they can hardly expect us not to care when their gluttony causes them to vomit all over our shoes.

The same lament applies throughout Africa. Time and again, its potential for economic development has been disrupted by the predatory politics of ruling elites seeking personal gain, often precipitating violence for their own ends. 'The problem is not so much that development has failed,' observed the Nigerian academic Claude Ake, in his essay on *Democracy and Development in Africa*, 'as that it was never really on the agenda in the first place.' After decades of mismanagement and corruption, most African states have become hollowed out. They are no longer instruments capable of serving the public good. Indeed, far from being able to provide aid and protection to their citizens, African governments and the vampire-like politicians who run them are regarded by the populations they rule as yet another burden they have to bear in the struggle for survival.

CHAPTER NOTES

The broad nature of this book has meant that I have relied on the work of many other authors. Included in these chapter notes are references to some of the books which I found to be of particular interest and value. A more complete list can be found in the select bibliography.

Introduction

The collection of general histories of Africa includes the eight-volume *Cambridge History of Africa* and single volumes by Philip Curtin et al; John D. Fage; John Iliffe; Roland Oliver; and John Reader. Thomas Pakenham writes vividly about the Scramble for Africa. On the decolonisation period, the two volumes of essays edited by Prosser Gifford and Roger Louis and the account by John Hargreaves are especially useful.

Chapter 1

Sir Charles Arden-Clarke spoke of his Gold Coast experiences at a joint meeting of the Royal African Society and the Royal Empire Society in London in November 1957; his address was published in *African Affairs*, Vol. 5, 226, January 1958. David Rooney makes extensive use of Arden-Clarke's private papers in his biography. Nkrumah's autobiography, written with the help of Erica Powell, was published to coincide with Ghana's independence. Erica Powell gives a vivid account of working with Nkrumah over a period of more then ten years in *Private Secretary (Female)/Gold Coast*. The outstanding account of the period is Dennis Austin's *Politics in Ghana*.

Chapter 2

William Stadiem writes about Farouk's colourful life. Three leading conspirators – Nasser, Neguib and Sadat – published accounts of the 1952 coup. Among the biographies of Nasser I consulted were those by Anthony Nutting; P. J. Vatikiotis; Jean Lacouture; and Robert Stephens. In his book *No End of a Lesson*, Nutting, for reasons of discretion, toned down the word that Eden used about Nasser – 'I want him destroyed, can't you understand?' In an interview recorded for Granada's television series, *End of Empire*, produced by Brian Lapping, Nutting recalled that Eden had, in fact, used the word 'murdered'.

Chapter 3

Some 3,000 books and more than 35 films have been produced about France's Algerian war. Even though today it is more than forty years since the end of the war, it remains an issue that continues to divide France. Until 1999, French politicians could not even agree on whether to give it the formal label of a 'war'. Previously, it carried the euphemism of a law-and-order operation and was referred to as *les événements en Algérie*. When the French National Assembly met in 2002 to consider a bill designating the date of the Evian peace agreement as a 'national day of remembrance', delegates split on the vote, with 278 in favour and 204 against. Such was the passion aroused that it was decided to drop the bill. The outstanding account in English is Alistair Horne's *A Savage War of Peace*.

Chapter 4

Senghor's life and work are covered by Janet Vaillant; Jacques Hymans; and Irving Markovitz. Houphouët-Boigny was born plain Houphouët, but in the wake of his 1945 election victory, to celebrate his success, he added Boigny to his name. In the Baulé language it means 'ram' and is said to reflect stubborn determination. Paul-Henri Siriex writes favourably about Houphouët. Marcel Amondji is far more critical. The quotation from *West Africa* about Houphouët's palace in Abidjan is taken from the 26 August 1961 issue.

Chapter 5

The official British government report by F. D. Corfield, *Historical Survey of the Origins and Growth of Mau Mau* (HMSO, London, 1960) is still of interest mainly because it illustrates, seven years after the rebellion, how little the colonial authorities understood of what had happened. Personal accounts by Bildad Kaggia; Waruhiu Itote; and J. M. Kariuki provide valuable insights from the rebel perspective. Fred Kubai gave his version of the central committee's encounter with Kenyatta in an interview for Brian Lapping's series, *End of Empire*. Jeremy Murray-Brown follows Kenyatta's career. Academic researchers have covered the ground extensively. Among the most useful accounts are those by Tabitha Kanogo; Frank Furedi; David Throup; Greet Kershaw; John Lonsdale (in Berman and Lonsdale); David Anderson; and the collection of essays edited by E. S. Atieno Odhiambo and John Lonsdale.

Chapter 6

Ever since Joseph Conrad's novel *Heart of Darkness* was first published in 1902, a legion of writers and historians have been drawn to the Congo and its turbulent history. The fascination remains as strong in modern times as ever. Adam Hochschild's vivid account of King Léopold's Congo Free State was published in 1998. That same year the American novelist Barbara Kingsolver produced *The Poisonwood Bible*, the story of an American missionary who in the fateful year of 1960 takes his wife and four young daughters into the heart of Africa to save Congolese souls. In 2000 Michela Wrong published a brilliant account of the last years of Mobutu's ailing regime and the American journalist Jeffrey Tayler wrote of his remarkable journey down the Congo river. In 2001 the Haitian filmmaker Raoul Peck produced a memorable film recreating Lumumba's brief and tumultuous career. The film includes a line from Lumumba's last letter to his wife,

Pauline: 'I know that history will have its say some day, but it will not be history as written in Brussels, Paris or Washington, it will be our own.'

Ludo De Witte's groundbreaking investigation into the murder of Lumumba was published first in Dutch in 1999, then in French in 2000, then in English in 2001. Drawing on personal testimonies and a series of official documents, De Witte placed primary responsibility for the murder on the Belgian establishment, causing a public furore in Belgium. For forty years, officials had insisted that Congolese were entirely to blame. De Witte's evidence prompted the Belgians to set up a parliamentary investigation in 2000. Written in measured terms, the parliamentary report, published in November 2001, concluded that 'certain members of the Belgian government and other Belgian participants were morally responsible for the circumstances leading to the death of Lumumba'. The parliamentary investigation also uncovered the memorandum of 19 October 1960 incorporating King Baudouin's remarks in the margin.

The evidence about Mobutu's role as a police informer comes from Frederic Vandewalle, a former head of the *Sûreté* in the Congo who was interviewed by Sean Kelly in 1985. Mobutu remained on the Belgian payroll from the time he left the army in 1956. He regularly provided the Belgians with detailed reports on the activities of fellow Congolese, particularly those of his own generation who, like himself, were beginning to become involved in politics. Vandewalle said that under his administration the *Sûreté* developed a policy of employing many such Congolese as paid informers. 'They were not spies in a Cold War sense, but simply informants who could tell us about the new Congolese leaders, and what we might expect from them. We were very short of this type of information in those days.'

In 1958 the Belgian colonial government sent Mobutu to Brussels where he studied journalism and continued reporting to the *Sûreté*. He also began working for Lumumba's MNC, ending up in charge of its Brussels office. Lumumba was apparently aware of Mobutu's connection to the *Sûreté* and decided it was an innocent activity by a struggling journalist designed to bring in some badly needed income. According to Vandewalle, Mobutu's political reporting to the *Sûreté* was routinely passed to the CIA station at the US embassy in Brussels. Lawrence Devlin, who was serving in Brussels at the time, first met Mobutu during an American embassy reception in early 1960. As the CIA's station chief in Léopoldville, appointed shortly after the Congo's independence in June 1960, Devlin developed a close relationship with Mobutu, providing him with funds to secure the loyalty of his troops.

From her interviews with Devlin, Michela Wrong describes an incident in which he foiled an assassination attempt on Mobutu. Devlin rejected any notion that Mobutu was an American puppet. 'He was never a puppet. When he felt it was against the interests of the Congo, he wouldn't do it, when it didn't go against his country's interests, he would go along with our views. He was always independent, it just happened that at a certain point we were going in the same direction.'

Catherine Hoskyns provides a detailed account of the Congo during 1960 and 1961. Madeleine Kalb explores the American role. Also useful is the Report of the Senate committee investigating the CIA: *Alleged Assassination Plots Involving Foreign Leaders*, United States Senate, Washington, US Government Printing Office, 1975. Devlin and Gottlieb both appeared before the Senate committee using pseudonyms.

Chapter 7

South Africa's apartheid system has been examined exhaustively in a vast range of literature. Leonard Thompson's writings stand out for their clarity and balance. Nelson Mandela's career is covered by his autobiography and by biographies by Anthony Sampson and Martin Meredith.

Rhodesia's road to rebellion has also been studied in detail. Useful accounts are provided by James Barber; Robert Blake; Larry Bowman; Frank Clements; and Kenneth Young.

Portugal's colonial record is described by Malyn Newitt. John Marcum's two-volume study of Angola provides a wealth of detail. The date on which the MPLA was founded has been the subject of prolonged controversy. At the heart of the dispute lies the question of which group started the anti-colonial movement. The 'official' MPLA version is that it was founded on 10 December 1956. A contrary version claims that no mention was made of the MPLA until 1958 or even later and that its origins were subsequently backdated to shore up its credibility. Fernando Guimarães examines both sides of the controversy.

Chapter 8

One of the most influential economists promoting industrialisation was W. Arthur Lewis who for a period in the early 1960s served as an adviser to the government of Ghana. He argued consistently that African countries could not achieve economic growth by seeking to increase their production of tradable agricultural commodities. He believed that world markets were simply saturated with the products that African countries were seeking to exploit – tea, coffee, cocoa and sugar. Increased production would only result in a lowering of the world price, thereby eliminating any prospect of gain.

Chapter 9

The title, 'The First Dance of Freedom' is taken from a quotation from Lord Byron's *Detached Thoughts*, 1821–2. 'I sometimes wish I was the Owner of Africa; to do at once, what Wilberforce will do in time, viz – sweep Slavery from her desarts, and look on upon the first dance of their Freedom'. In his book *The Soccer War*, the Polish journalist Ryszard Kapuściński told of how in the course of one month at the end of 1965, he drove through five countries in West Africa – Guinea, Ghana, Togo, Dahomey and Western Nigeria – in four of which there were states of emergency. One president had just been overthrown, another had saved himself by chance, a third was afraid to leave his house which was surrounded by troops. Two parliaments had been dissolved, two governments had fallen, scores of people had died in political conflicts, scores more had been arrested. 'Over a distance of 520 kilometres, I had been checked twenty-one times and subjected to four body searches. Everywhere there was an atmosphere of tension, everywhere the smell of gunpowder.' The example of Action Group corruption in Western Nigeria is taken from the *Report of the Coker Commission of Inquiry into the Affairs of Statutory Corporations in Western Nigeria* (Ministry of Information, Lagos, 1962). The study of trade statistics of fourteen francophone states by Gérard Chaliand was published in a special issue of *Partisans* – '*L'Afrique dans l'Épreuve*', May–June, 1966.

Chapter 10

After Nkrumah's overthrow, the military's National Liberation Council appointed a commission of inquiry headed by Justice Fred Apaloo to investigate Nkrumah's assets. It was the first of more than forty commissions, committees, special audit teams and other investigative bodies charged with probing the public and private activities of Nkrumah's regime. There was no doubt that the military's intention in exposing the depth of corruption to which Ghana had sunk was to discredit Nkrumah and legitimise its seizure of power. Yet the evidence uncovered was solid and substantial. The Apaloo Commission found that at the time of the coup, Nkrumah possessed cash and property worth £2,322,000. An American scholar, Victor LeVine, concluded that Nkrumah 'clearly was involved in a variety of corrupt transactions'. Trevor Jones gives a detached account of Nkrumah's last years.

Chapter 11

Chinua Achebe's novels run the gamut of African experience from colonial rule to Big Man politics. For the crises that engulfed Nigeria's First Republic, see: James Coleman (1958); Richard Sklar (1963); John P. Mackintosh et al. (1966); Robin Luckham (1971); Kenneth Post and Michael Vickers (1973); Billy Dudley (1973); and Larry Diamond (1988). John de St Jorre gives the best overall account of the civil war. John Stremlau examines international involvement. Michael Crowder provides a standard history of Nigeria.

Chapter 12

Haile Selassie's regime is covered by Christopher Clapham; Patrick Gilkes; and John Markakis. John Spencer, an American lawyer familiar with Haile Selassie's court over a forty-year period gives a personal account. Ryszard Kapuściński interviewed former palace officials after Haile Selassie's overthrow, compiling a vivid picture of life at the old imperial palaces in his last months as emperor; critics claimed it was a little too imaginative.

Chapter 13

In his book *Talk of the Devil*, the Italian journalist Riccardo Orizio recorded interviews with Amin, Bokassa and Mengistu after their downfall. Amin was living comfortably in exile in Jeddah, courtesy of the Saudi government; Bokassa was living in retirement in the Villa Nasser in Bangui, after serving seven years in prison; and Mengistu was living in Harare as a guest of Robert Mugabe.

Henry Kyemba's account of Amin's regime is of particular interest. Kyemba served Amin as principal private secretary, cabinet secretary, head of the civil service and minister before fleeing into exile in 1977. Iain Grahame, a former British army officer, also knew Amin well. Tony Avirgan and Martha Honey give an eyewitness account of the Tanzanian invasion. Amin died in exile in Jeddah in 2003 at about the age of eighty. At the time of his death, Uganda's economic output had recovered to the level it was in 1971 – the year Amin came to power.

Mengistu's revolution is covered by David and Marina Ottoway; Fred Halliday and Maxine Molyneux; John Markakis and Nega Ayele; René Lefort; Christopher Clapham; and Andargachew Tiruneh. Dawit Wolde Giorgis provides a valuable insider's account. Samuel Decalo, in his book *Psychoses of Power*, examines the careers of Amin, Bokassa and Nguema. Brian Titley gives a more balanced account of Bokassa. Robert Af Klinteberg's report on Equatorial Guinea was published in 1978 by the International University Exchange Fund, Geneva.

Chapter 14

Nyerere's single-handed effort to pursue socialism is explained with great clarity in his own collection of writings and speeches. His *ujamaa* experiment excited particular interest in academic circles. Cranford Pratt examines its origins. Other useful accounts include those by Andrew Coulson; Goran Hyden; Dean McHenry; and Michaela von Freyhold.

Chapters 16 and 22

A valuable body of work has been produced on Africa's economic decline. Particularly useful are accounts by Robert Bates; David Fieldhouse; Douglas Rimmer; Tony Killick; Ralph Austen; Richard Sandbrook; John Ravenhill; Nicolas van de Walle; Roger Tangri; and the collection of essays edited by Thomas Callaghy and John Ravenhill. Two works published in 1981 had a marked influence on the analytical debate about African economies. One was the World Bank's *Accelerated Development in Sub-Saharan Africa*, popularly known as the Berg Report after its principal author, Elliot Berg; the other was Robert Bates's *Markets and States in Tropical Africa*. Both pointed to government intervention as a major cause of Africa's economic decline. Robert Bates's work, demonstrating how well-organised urban interest groups dominated national politics, had a significant impact on academic and policy circles.

Chapter 17

The extent of Mobutu's fortune and what happened to it has been the subject of prolonged speculation. According to his biographer Francis Monheim, in Brussels at the end of 1959 Mobutu had no more than $6 to his name. In 1988 he told US Representative Mervyn Dymally:

> Clearly, I would be lying if I said I do not have a bank account in Europe; I do. I would be lying if I said I do not have considerable money in my account; I do. Yes, I do have a fair amount of money. However, I would estimate it to total less than 50 million dollars.

What is that for twenty-two years as head of state in such a big country?

In 1987, a team of editors and reporters from *Fortune* magazine, involved in a year-long project to rank the world's richest people, placed Mobutu in a category 'hard to prove and impossible to trace'. They said Mobutu was 'reportedly' worth $5 billion. The US television programme *Sixty Minutes*, in a report on Zaire in 1984, used the same figure. The London *Financial Times* in May 1997 estimated his fortune at $4 billion. A glimpse of his family's wealth came from litigation papers in the US involving the assets of his uncle, Litho Maboti, who died in 1982, said to be worth $1 billion.

Certainly, Mobutu enjoyed flaunting his wealth. On one memorable occasion in 1982, he arrived in the United States for a vacation accompanied by nearly one hundred Zairians and in the space of two weeks, during visits to hotels, stores, a dude ranch and Disney World, spent an estimated $2 million.

But at the end of it all, after Mobutu's downfall, apart from his properties scattered around the world, investigators found difficulty in locating his fabled private wealth. A paltry $4 million was discovered in Swiss banks. It seems likely that, although Mobutu acquired vast sums, much of it was used to sustain his system of personal rule.

A US Treasury estimate in the early 1990s came up with a figure of $40–$45 million. 'When we tried to get a hold on what we had, we found to our surprise that Mobutu was having serious cash flow problems,' an official told Michela Wrong. 'He was having problems paying his bills, maintaining his French properties and keeping his entourage happy. It suggested that his ability to plunder various state mechanisms had shrunk enormously as Gécamines and Miba [the state diamond corporation] had decayed. He had squandered huge amounts and not squirreled it away as was supposed.'

Larry Devlin retired from the CIA in 1974 and became the personal representative of Maurice Tempelsman in Kinshasa. Tempelsman, scion of an Antwerp diamond-trading family which had moved to New York before the Second World War, remained a Mobutu confidant for more than two decades. Devlin had direct access to Mobutu, continuing to function as an intelligence channel. According to a former US deputy assistant secretary of state who visited Zaire in 1979, Devlin was 'the true representative of the United States Government' in Mobutu's eyes, 'having much better access than the ambassador'.

In his testimony about the political and economic situation in Zaire to the Subcommittee on Africa, House of Representatives in Washington in September 1981, Nguza described in chilling detail the torture he had experienced in 1977 after he was dismissed as foreign minister and sentenced to death for 'high treason' at a summary trial. Mobutu, according to Nguza, threatened to shoot him personally. During Nguza's subsequent interrogation by security personnel, a metal tube was inserted into his penile shaft, through which jets of air were introduced, rupturing blood vessels and causing intense pain. Electric shocks were applied to his testicles at the same time. Despite all this, Nguza returned to work for Mobutu. Erwin Blumenthal's IMF report was published in *Info-Zaire*, No. 36, October 1982.

Among the numerous accounts of the Mobutu era, those of particular merit include the work of Michela Wrong; Sean Kelly; Crawford Young and Thomas Turner; Collette Braeckman; Jean-Claude Williame; Blaine Harden; Bill Berkeley; and Mark Huband. Michael Schatzberg vividly describes the acute suffering of peasants in rural Zaire. A number of intrepid journalists recorded memorable journeys through the Congo during the Mobutu era. They include: David Lamb; Jeffrey Tayler; and Helen Winternitz. Winternitz interviewed Tshisekedi in Kinshasa in 1983 and describes her subsequent ordeal with Mobutu's security police.

Chapter 18

Norrie MacQueen describes the collapse of Portugal's African empire from the Portuguese perspective. John Stockwell, the head of the CIA's Angola task force, gives an insider's account, repenting his own involvement. Fernando Guimarães unravels the competing interests of Cuba, the Soviet Union, China, the United States and South Africa and examines the timetable of Cuban involvement, concluding that

Cuban military intervention in Angola had probably been planned during the first half of 1975. In *Another Day of Life*, Ryszard Kapuściński gives a vivid eyewitness account of the weeks leading up to independence. Professor Spies writes the official history of South Africa's intervention, *Operation Savannah*. Fred Bridgland provides a favourable portrait of Savimbi. Martin Meredith writes about Rhodesia's UDI years and the eventual outcome.

Chapter 19

The title 'Red Tears' is taken from the memoir by Dawit Wolde Giorgis, who fled into exile in 1985. Alex de Waal provides the most comprehensive account of war and famine in Ethiopia over a thirty-year period. Other useful accounts are by David Korn, the US chargé d'affaires in Addis Ababa at the time; and by Peter Gill who looks at international aspects of the relief operation.

Chapter 20

On Chad, Robert Buitenhuijs's two volumes provide a comprehensive overview of Chad's civil wars in the 1970s and 1980s. Also useful are works by Virginia Thompson and Richard Adloff; Sam Nolutshungu; and Michael Kelley.

On Libya, Gaddafi's regime is examined by Jonathan Bearman; John Cooley; Lillian Craig Harris; and David Blundy and Andrew Lycett. Gaddafi's intervention in Chad is covered by John Wright; and by René Lemarchand.

On Sudan, Douglas Johnson explains the complexities of the wars in the south. An account of the Al Diein massacre by Dr Ushari Ahmad Mahmud and Suleyman Ali Bado was published by the University of Khartoum in 1987. Deborah Scroggins describes the plight of Dinka refugees in Darfur in 1988 in *Emma's War*. Other valuable eyewitness accounts are provided by David Lamb; Robert Kaplan; Scott Peterson; Mark Huband; and Bill Berkeley. The quotes from aid officials are taken from Bill Berkeley's account.

Chapter 21

Most scientists believe that Aids jumped the species barrier from African primates to humans by 'natural transfer', the result, for example, of a hunter infected by a chimpanzee. A competing theory claims that Aids was caused in the 1950s when thousands of Africans were given contaminated polio vaccine from chimpanzee kidneys. This theory is argued at length by Edward Hooper in his book *The River*. Tony Barnett and Alan Whiteside provide a global perspective on the Aids pandemic but concentrate mainly on Africa. Ezekiel Kalipeni et al. focus on the ramifications of Aids in Africa. A report in 2000 by ActionAid, London, entitled *Open Secret: People facing up to HIV and AIDS in Uganda*, provides an account of Uganda's strategy for dealing with Aids.

Chapter 23

Between 1990 and 1996, 37 out of 48 African states in sub-Saharan Africa held multi-party elections. More than half of the elections resulted in a former dictator remaining in office. The most useful accounts of the 'democratisation' period are those by Michael Bratton and Nicolas van de Walle; Jennifer Widner (ed.); David Apter and Carl Rosberg (eds.); and John Wiseman. Segun Osaba's essay on corruption in Nigeria was published in the *Review of African Political Economy* (1996), No. 69, 371–86. Peter Lewis's observations on the 1993 election in Nigeria were published in *African Affairs* (1994), 93, 323–40.

Chapter 24

The rise of black consciousness is dealt with by Gail Gerhart; Steve Biko's role is described by Donald Woods. Evidence about Biko's ordeal at the hands of the security police is taken from testimony to the Truth and Reconciliation Commission; the role of Winnie Mandela as head of the criminal gang known as the Mandela United Football Club was also examined at length by the Truth and Reconciliation Commission: see Martin Meredith's *Coming to Terms*.

The series of secret negotiations between Mandela and the South African government and South Africa's subsequent odyssey to democratic elections are best covered by Allister Sparks; and by Patti Waldmeir.

Chapter 25

For an explanation of the ideas and work of Sayyid Qutb, see Gilles Kepel; on Sheikh Abdullah Abdel Rahman, see Mary Anne Weaver; and on the conspirators behind the assassination of Sadat, see Johannes Jansen.

On Algeria's conflict, Hugh Roberts's collection of essays, *The Battlefield*, provides valuable insights. Other useful accounts are by Michael Willis; and by Luis Martinez. While the massacres of the 1990s are generally attributed to the GIA, there is evidence implicating the security forces as accomplices if not perpetrators in some of them. A civilian eyewitness account of the massacre at Bentalha, a township ten miles south of Algiers, on the night of 22 September 1997, in which more than 400 people – men, women and children – were slaughtered, points to security force involvement. The account – *Qui a tué à Bentalha: chronique d'un massacre annoncé* – was written by Nesroulah Yous, with Salima Mellah, and published by La Découverte, Paris, in 2000. In *La Sale Guerre*, published by La Découverte in 2001, a former special forces officer, Habib Souaïdia, gives a scathing account of the counter-insurgency campaign, claiming he witnessed his army comrades engaging in torture, rape and wanton killing. A report by Human Rights Watch, *Time for Reckoning*, published in 2003, deals with the issue of 7,000 'disappearances', mostly at the hands of the security forces.

Chapter 26

Professor Ioan Lewis provides the historical context, and in the fourth edition of his *Modern History of the Somali*, follows through until 2002. A number of individual accounts stand out, including those by John Drysdale; Scott Peterson; Mark Huband; and Keith Richburg. Mohamed Sahnoun gives his version in *Missed Opportunities*. Mark

Bowden reconstructs the US operation on October 3–4 , 1993 in gripping detail. John Hirsch and Robert Oakley present a narrative account largely from Oakley's point of view. Ann Wright's memorandum, 'Legal and Human Rights Aspects of UNOSOM Military Operations', was sent to the special representative of the secretary-general on July 13, 1993, two days after the 'Qaybdiid' raid. A comprehensive after-action aid report, *Hope Restored? Humanitarian Aid in Somalia, 1990–1994*, was published in November 1994 by the Center for Policy Analysis and Research on Refugee Issues, Washington.

Chapter 27

No accurate assessment of the number of people killed during Rwanda's genocide is possible. Human Rights Watch estimate the figure as at least half a million. The figure most generally cited is 800,000. Other estimates put the number at 1 million. A census carried out in 2000 established the names of 951,000 victims. But entire families were sometimes wiped out leaving no knowledge of their existence. A report published the following year by the Rwandan government cited a figure of just over 1 million. Kagame's army was responsible for the massacre of some 50,000 Hutus during and immediately after the genocide – war crimes that Kagame eventually admitted had occurred.

More than one hundred books have been written about the genocide. The most comprehensive account is provided by the Human Rights Watch report, *'Leave None to Tell the Story': Genocide in Rwanda*, written by Alison des Forges and published in 1999. A 1,200-page report by African Rights contains testimony from scores of witnesses. Gérard Prunier provides an invaluable overall history, including revealing insights into French policy. Linda Melvern looks at the broader international role in Rwanda; in *Conspiracy to Murder*, she incorporates testimony given at the International Criminal Tribunal for Rwanda. Among a number of outstanding accounts by journalists are those by Fergal Keane; and by Philip Gourevitch. Gourevitch uncovers the role of Pastor Elizaphan Ntakirutimana. Elizabeth Neuffer portrays the difficulties of seeking justice in Rwanda.

Chapter 28

Michela Wrong provides a vivid account of the end of Mobutu's regime. Other accounts of interest are by Mobutu's close aide Honoré Ngbanda, and his son-in-law Pierre Janssen. Reports by the United Nations-appointed panel of experts on the Illegal Exploitation of Natural Resources and Other Forms of Wealth from the Democratic Republic of Congo were published in 2001, 2002 and 2003.

Chapter 29

After visiting Liberia in 1953, John Gunther wrote: 'I could use any of several adjectives about it: "odd", "wacky", "weird".' The upkeep of President Tubman's 463-ton yacht, he noted, cost 1 per cent of the total national budget. Bill Berkeley's report for the Lawyers Committee for Human Rights provides a detailed description of Doe's regime, including atrocities perpetrated in Nimba County. He writes again about Liberia in *The Graves Are Not Yet Full*. Mark Huband's eyewitness account of the Liberian civil war includes portraits of Charles Taylor and Prince Johnson. Anthony Daniels gives a guided tour of the ruins of Monrovia in 1991. William Reno delves into the murky world of warlord finances in Liberia and Sierra Leone and examines the extent of corruption in Siaka Stevens's regime. Stephen Ellis explores the religious dimension of Liberia's war. Aminatta Forna gives a vivid portrait of her father, Mohamed Forna, a medical doctor and former minister, who stood against Stevens's tyranny and was executed after a rigged trial in Freetown. Greg Campbell provides an eyewitness account of the diamond fields of Sierra Leone. Paul Richards looks at the social background of the war in Sierra Leone. The essay by Krijn Peters and Paul Richards, '"Why We Fight": Voices of Youth Combatants in Sierra Leone', was published in *Africa* 68 (2), 1998.

Chapter 30

Karl Maier writes perceptively about modern Nigeria in his book *This House Has Fallen*. The title is taken from a quotation by Chinua

Achebe : 'This is an example of a country that has fallen down; it has collapsed. This house has fallen.' Ken Wiwa provides an affectionate portrait of his father, Ken Saro-Wiwa. Johannes Harnischfeger's paper on the Bakassi Boys was published in the *Journal of Modern African Studies* 41, 1 (2003), 23–49.

Chapter 31

The UN Commission on Human Rights report, published in February 1994, was compiled by Gaśpár Bíró. Other useful reports include those by Human Rights Watch: *Denying the Honour of Living: Sudan, a Human Rights Disaster*, New York, March 1990; and *Sudan, Oil and Human Rights*, New York, 2003. African Rights deals with the plight of the Nuba. In *Slave*, Mende Nazer tells her moving story of how as a young Nuba girl she was abducted by Baggara raiders and sold into slavery. Other useful accounts include those by Ann Mosley Lesch; and by Donald Petterson, a US diplomat stationed in Khartoum.

Riek Machar became famous internationally not just for being a warlord but because of his marriage to an English aid worker, Emma McCune. Deborah Scroggins tells the tale in *Emma's War*. Scroggins reports McCune's remark to a friend that it was 'an incredible high' to get up from lovemaking to draft constitutions for an independent southern Sudan. McCune died in a car accident in Nairobi in 1993.

Chapter 32

Tony Hodges gives a detailed analysis of modern Angola. Valuable eyewitness accounts are provided by Judith Matloff; Karl Maier; and Pedro Rosa Mendes. Margaret Anstee gives an inside account of the ill-fated 1992–3 peace process. Fred Bridgland, a British journalist, wrote a favourable biography of Savimbi, but later became disillusioned with Unita's totalitarianism. Bridgland relates an anecdote told to him by Savimbi about his school days in the 1940s at a Protestant mission station. The missionaries there arranged a football game between black students at Savimbi's school and white pupils from a nearby town. The white visitors brought along their own Portuguese referee who, according to Savimbi, disallowed every score by the black team. This infuriated Savimbi, especially because they were playing with his ball. So he stopped the game and walked off with the ball. The game had to be abandoned.

Chapter 33

A detailed account of the Matabeleland atrocities – *Breaking the Silence* – was published in 1997 as a joint venture by the Catholic Commission for Justice and Peace and the Legal Resources Foundation, using testimony from more than a thousand witnesses. In two books, *African Tears* and *Beyond Tears*, Cathy Buckle, a white Zimbabwean farmer, chronicles the disruption and terror of the land invasions and the tragic outcome. Martin Meredith covers Mugabe's career.

Chapter 34

The report of the Truth and Reconciliation Commission on South Africa was published in five volumes in October 1998. Accounts of its work include those by Desmond Tutu; Alex Boraine; Antjie Krog; and Martin Meredith. On Aids in South Africa, see Kyle Kauffman and David Lindauer.

SELECT BIBLIOGRAPHY

Achebe, Chinua, *Things Fall Apart*, Heinemann, London, 1958
—— *A Man of the People*, Heinemann, London, 1966
—— *The Trouble with Nigeria*, Heinemann, London, 1983
—— *Anthills of the Savannah*, Heinemann, London, 1987
Adamafio, Tawia, *By Nkrumah's Side*, Collings, London, 1982
Adamolekun, Ladipo, *Sékou Touré's Guinea*, Methuen, London, 1976
Adamson, Kay, *Algeria: A Study in Competing Ideologies*, Cassell, London, 1998
Adelman, Howard and Govind C. Rao (eds.), *War and Peace in Zaire/Congo*, Africa World Press, Trenton, 2004
Adelman, Howard and Astri Suhrke (eds.), *The Path of a Genocide: the Rwanda Crisis from Uganda to Zaire*, Transaction Press, New Brunswick, 1999
Adwok, Peter, *The Politics of Liberation in South Sudan: An Insider's View*, Fountain Publishers, Kampala, 2000
Afrah, Mohamoud M., *Mogadishu: A Hell on Earth: A Journalist's Diary About the War in Mogadishu*, Copos, Nairobi, 1993
African Rights, *Facing Genocide: The Nuba of Sudan*, London, 1995
Aissaoui, Ali, *Algeria: The Political Economy of Oil and Gas*, Oxford University Press, 2001
Ajami, Fouad, *The Arab Predicament: Arab Political Thought and Practice Since 1967*, Cambridge University Press, 1992
Ake, Claude, *Democracy and Development in Africa*, Brookings Institution, Washington, 1996
Alden, Chris, *Mozambique and the Construction of the New African State: from Negotiations to Nation-Building*, Palgrave Macmillan, Basingstoke, 2001
Alexander, Jocelyn, Joann McGregor and Terence Ranger, *Violence and Memory: One Hundred Years in the 'Dark Forests' of Matabeleland*, Currey, Oxford, 2000
Allen, Charles, *Tales from the Dark Continent*, Deutsch, London, 1979
Allen, Chris, Michael S. Radu, Keith Somerville and Joan Baxter (eds.),

Benin, The Congo, Burkina Faso: Politics, Economy and Society, Pinter, London, 1988

Amin, Samir, *Neo-Colonialism in West Africa*, Penguin, London, 1973

Amondji, Marcel, *Félix Houphouët et la Côte d'Ivoire: L'envers d'une légende*, Karthala, Paris, 1984

Andargachew Tiruneh, *The Ethiopian Revolution, 1974–1987: A Transformation from an Aristocratic to a Totalitarian Autocracy*, Cambridge University Press, 1993

Anderson David, *Histories of the Hanged: Britain's Dirty War in Kenya and the End of the Empire*, Weidenfeld & Nicolson, London, 2005

Anderson, David M. and Richard Rathbone (eds.), *Africa's Urban Past*, Currey, Oxford, 2000

Anstee, Margaret, *Orphan of the Cold War: The Inside Story of the Collapse of the Angolan Peace Process, 1992–3*, Macmillan, Basingstoke, 1996

Anstey, Roger, *King Leopold's Legacy: the Congo under Belgian Rule, 1908–1960*, Oxford University Press, 1966

Andereggen, Anton, *France's Relationship with Subsaharan Africa*, Praeger, Westport, 1994

Appiah, Kwame Anthony, *In My Father's House: Africa in the Philosophy of Culture*, Oxford University Press, 1992

Armah, Ayi Kwei, *The Beautyful Ones Are Not Yet Born*, Heinemann, London, 1969

Apter, David E., *Ghana in Transition*; Second Revised Edition, Princeton University Press, 1972

Apter, David E. and Carl G. Rosberg (eds.), *Political Development and the New Realism in Sub-Saharan Africa*, University Press of Virginia, Charlottesville, 1994

Attwood, William, *The Reds and the Blacks: A Personal Adventure*, Hutchinson, London, 1967

Atieno Odhiambo, E. S. and John Lonsdale (eds.), *Mau Mau and Nationhood: Arms, Authority and Narration*, Currey, Oxford, 2003

Austen, Ralph, *African Economic History: Internal Development and External Dependency*, Currey, London, 1987

Austin, Dennis, *Politics in Ghana, 1946–1960*, Oxford University Press, 1964

Avirgan, Tony and Martha Honey, *War in Uganda: The Legacy of Idi Amin*, Lawrence Hill, Westport, 1982

Awolowo, Obafemi, *Path to Nigerian Freedom*, Faber and Faber, London, 1947
—— *Awo: The Autobiography of Chief Obafemi Awolowo*, Cambridge University Press, 1960

Ayittey, George B. N., *Africa Betrayed*, St Martin's Press, New York, 1992
—— *Africa in Chaos*, Macmillan, Basingstoke, 1998

Azevedo, Mario J. and Emmanuel U. Nnadozie, *Chad: A Nation in Search of its Future*, Westview, Boulder, 1998

Azikiwe, Nnamdi, *My Odyssey, An Autobiography*, Hurst, London, 1970

Bach, Daniel C., *Regionalisation in Africa: Integration and Disintegration*, Currey, Oxford, 1999

Bahru Zewde, *A History of Modern Ethiopia, 1855–1991*, Currey, Oxford, 2001

Baker, Bruce, *Escape from Domination in Africa; Political Disengagement and its Consequences*, Currey, Oxford, 2000

Barber, James, *Rhodesia: The Road to Rebellion*, Oxford University Press, 1967

Barkan, Joel D. (ed.), *Beyond Capitalism vs Socialism in Kenya and Tanzania*, Rienner, Boulder, 1994

Barnett, D. L. and Njama Karari, *Mau Mau from Within*, Macgibbon and Kee, London, 1966

Barnett, Michael, *Eyewitness to Genocide: The United Nations and Rwanda*, Cornell University Press, 2002

Barnett, Tony and Piers Blaikie, *AIDS in Africa: Its Present and Future Impact*, Belhaven Press, London, 1992

Barnett, Tony and Alan Whiteside, *AIDS in the Twenty-First Century: Disease and Globalization*, Palgrave Macmillan, Basingstoke, 2002

Bates, Robert H., *Markets and States in Tropical Africa: The Political Basis of Agricultural Policies*, University of California Press, 1981

—— *Essays on the Political Economy of Rural Africa*, University of California Press, 1987

—— *Beyond the Miracle of the Market: The Political Economy of Agrarian Development in Kenya*, Cambridge University Press, 1989

Bayart, Jean François, *L'État au Cameroun*, Presses de la Foundation Nationale de Sciences Politiques, Paris, 1985

Bayart, Jean François, Stephen Ellis and Béatrice Hibou, *The Criminalization of the State in Africa*, Currey, Oxford, 1999

Baynham, Simon (ed.), *Military Power and Politics in Black Africa*, Croom Helm, London, 1986

Bearman, Jonathan, *Qadhafi's Libya*, Zed, London, 1986

Behrend, Heike, *Alice Lakwena and the Holy Spirits: War in Northern Uganda, 1986–97*, Currey, Oxford, 1999

Beinart, William, *Twentieth Century South Africa*, Oxford University Press, 2001

Beinart, William and Saul Dubow (eds.), *Segregation and Apartheid in Twentieth-Century South Africa*, Routledge, London, 1995

Bello, Sir Ahmadu, the Sardauna of Sokoto, *My Life*, Cambridge University Press, 1962

Bender, Gerald J., *Angola under the Portuguese: The Myth and the Reality*, Heinemann, London, 1978

Benson, Mary, *Nelson Mandela*, Penguin, London, 1986

Berkeley, Bill, *Liberia: A Promise Betrayed*, Lawyers Committee for Human Rights, New York, 1986

—— *The Graves Are Not Yet Full: Race, Tribe and Power in the Heart of Africa*, Basic Books, New York, 2001

Berman, Bruce, *Control and Crisis in Colonial Kenya*, Currey, Oxford, 1990

Berman, Bruce, Peter Eyoh and Will Kymlicka (eds.), *Ethnicity and Democracy in Africa*, Currey, Oxford, 2004

Berman, Bruce and John Lonsdale, *Unhappy Valley: Conflict in Kenya and Africa*, 2 vols, Currey, London, 1992

Berry, Sarah, *No Condition Is Permanent: The Social Dynamics of Agrarian Change in Sub-Saharan Africa*, University of Wisconsin Press, 1993

Beshir, Mohamed Omer, *The Southern Sudan: Background to Conflict*, Hurst, London, 1968

—— *Revolution and Nationalism in the Sudan*, Collings, London, 1974

—— *The Southern Sudan: From Conflict to Peace*, Hurst, London, 1975

Bhebe, Ngwabi and Terence Ranger (eds.), *Soldiers in Zimbabwe's Liberation War*, Currey, London, 1995

—— *Society in Zimbabwe's Liberation War*, Currey, Oxford, 1996

Bigo, Didier, *Pouvoir et obéissance en Centrafrique*, Karthala, Paris, 1988

Biko, Steve, *I Write What I Like*, Bowerdean Press, London, 1986

Birmingham, David and Phyllis M. Martin (eds.), *History of Central Africa: The Contemporary Years Since 1960*, Longman, London, 1998

Blair, David, *Degrees in Violence: Robert Mugabe and the Struggle for Power in Zimbabwe*, Continuum, London, 2002

Blake, Robert, *A History of Rhodesia*, Eyre Methuen, London, 1977

Blundell, Sir Michael, *So rough a wind*, Weidenfeld & Nicolson, London, 1964

Blundy, David and Andrew Lycett, *Qaddafi and the Libyan Revolution*, Weidenfeld & Nicolson, London, 1987

Boraine, Alex, *A Country Unmasked: Inside South Africa's Truth and Reconciliation Commission*, Oxford University Press, 2000

Boutros-Ghali, Boutros, *An Agenda for Peace*, United Nations, New York, 1992

—— *Unvanquished: A U.S.–U.N. Saga*, Random House, New York, 1999

Bowden, Mark, *Black Hawk Down: A Story of Modern War*, Atlantic Monthly Press, New York, 1999

Bowman, Larry, *Politics in Rhodesia: White Power in an African State*, Harvard University Press, 1973

Braeckman, Colette, *Le Dinosaure: le Zaire de Mobutu*, Fayard, Paris, 1992

—— *Rwanda: Histoire d'un génocide*, Fayard, Paris, 1994

—— *Terreur africaine: Burundi, Rwanda, Zaire, les racines de la violence*, Fayard, Paris, 1996

—— *L'Enjeu Congolais: l'Afrique Centrale après Mobutu*, Fayard, Paris, 1999

Bratton, Michael and Nicolas van de Walle, *Democratic Experiments in Africa: Regime Transitions in Comparative Perspective*, Cambridge University Press, 1997

Bredon, Miles, *Blood on the Tracks; a rail journey from Angola to Mozambique*, Picador, London, 1994

Bretton, Henry, *The Rise and Fall of Kwame Nkrumah: A Study of Personal Rule in Africa*, Pall Mall Press, London, 1967
—— *Power and Politics in Africa*, Longman, London, 1973
Bridgland, Fred, *Jonas Savimbi: A Key to Africa*, Macmillan South Africa, Johannesburg, 1986
Brittain, Victoria, *Death of Dignity: Angola's Civil War*, Pluto, London, 1998
Brown, Richard, *Private Wealth and Public Debt: Debt, Capital Flight and the IMF in Sudan*, Macmillan, London, 1992
Buckle, Cathy, *African Tears: The Zimbabwe Land Invasions*, Covos Day, Johannesburg, 2001
—— *Beyond Tears: Zimbabwe's Tragedy*, Jonathan Ball, Johannesburg, 2003
Buijtenhuijs, Robert, *Mau Mau: Twenty Years after the Myth and the Survivors*, Mouton, The Hague, 1973
—— *Le Frolinat et les Révoltes Populaires du Tchad, 1965–1976*, Mouton, The Hague, 1978
—— *Essays on Mau Mau*, African Studies Centre, Leiden, 1982
—— *Le Frolinat et les Guerres Civiles du Tchad (1977–1984): la révolution introuvable*, Karthala, Paris, 1987
Burgat, François, *The Islamic Movement in North Africa*, University of Texas, 1993
Burr, J. Millard and Robert O. Collins, *Requiem for the Sudan: War, Drought and Disaster Relief on the Nile*, Westview, Boulder, 1995
—— *Revolutionary Sudan: Hasan Al-Turabi and the Islamist State, 1989–2000*, Brill Academic Publishers, Leiden, 2003
Callaghy, Thomas M., *The State–Society Struggle: Zaire in Comparative Perspective*, Columbia University Press, 1984
Callaghy, Thomas M. and John Ravenhill (eds.), *Hemmed In: Responses to Africa's Economic Decline*, Columbia University Press, 1993
Cambridge History of Africa, see Oliver and Fage (eds.)
Campbell, Greg, *Blood Diamonds: Tracing the Deadly Path of the World's Most Precious Stones*, Westview, Boulder, 2004
Carr, Rosamond Halsey, *Land of a Thousand Hills; My Life in Rwanda*, Penguin, New York, 2000
Carter, Gwendolyn and Patrick O'Meara, *African Independence: The First Twenty-Five Years*, Indiana University Press, 1985
Cartwright, John R., *Political Leadership in Sierra Leone*, Croom Helm, London, 1978
—— *Political Leadership in Africa*, St Martin's Press, New York, 1983
Caute, David, *Under the Skin: The Death of White Rhodesia*, Allen Lane, London, 1983
Chabal, Patrick, *Amilcar Cabral: Revolutionary Leadership and People's War*, Cambridge University Press, 1983
Chabal, Patrick (ed.), *Political Domination in Africa: Reflections on the Limits of Power*, Cambridge University Press, 1986

Chabal, Patrick and Jean-Pascal Daloz, *Africa Works: Disorder as Political Instrument*, Currey, Oxford, 1999

Chabal, Patrick, David Birmingham, Joshua Forrest, Malyn Newitt, Gerhard Seibert and Elisa Silva Andrade (eds.), *A History of Postcolonial Lusophone Africa*, Hurst, London, 2003

Charlick, Robert B., *Niger: Personal Rule and Survival in the Sahel*, Westview, Boulder, 1991

Charlton, Michael, *The Last Colony in Africa: Diplomacy and the Independence of Rhodesia*, Blackwell, Oxford, 1990

Chazan, Naomi, *An Anatomy of Ghanaian Politics: Managing Political Recession, 1969–1982*, Westview, Boulder, 1983

Chazan, Naomi, Robert Mortimer, John Ravenhill and Donald Rothchild, *Politics and Society in Contemporary Africa*, Lynne Rienner, Boulder, 1992

Chazan, Naomi, Peter Lewis, Robert A. Mortimer, Donald Rothchild, and Stephen John Stedman, *Politics and Society in Contemporary Africa*, 3rd edn, Rienner, Boulder, 1999

Chipman, John, *French Power in Africa*, Blackwell, Oxford, 1989

Chomé, Jules, *L'Ascension de Mobutu: du Sergent Joseph Désiré au Général Sese Seko*, Editions Complexe, Brussels, 1974

Chrétien, Jean-Pierre, *Le Défi de l'ethnisme, Rwanda et Burundi, 1990–1996*, Karthala, Paris, 1997

—— *The Great Lakes of Africa: Two Thousand Years of History*, Zone Books, New York, 2003

Chrétien, Jean-Pierre, Jean-Francois Dupaquier, Marcel Kabanda and Joseph Ngarambe, *Rwanda: Les Médias du Génocide*, Karthala, Paris, 1995

Clapham, Christopher, *Haile-Selassie's Government*, Longman, London, 1969

—— *Transformation and Continuity in Revolutionary Ethiopia*, Cambridge University Press, 1988

—— *Africa and the International System: The Politics of State Survival*, Cambridge University Press, 1996

Clapham, Christopher (ed.), *Private Patronage and Public Power: Political Clientelism in the Modern State*, Pinter, London, 1992

—— *African Guerrillas*, Currey, Oxford, 1998

Clark, John F. (ed.), *The African Stakes of the Congo War*, Palgrave Macmillan, New York, 2002

Clark, John F. and David E. Gardinier (eds.), *Political Reform in Francophone Africa*, Westview, Boulder, 1997

Clarke, Peter, B., *West Africa and Islam: A Study of Religious Development from the 8th to the 20th Century*, Arnold, London, 1982

Clay, Jason W. and Bonnie K. Holcomb, *Politics and the Ethiopian Famine, 1984–1985*, Cultural Survival, Cambridge, MA, 1985

Clayton, Anthony, *The Zanzibar Revolution and its Aftermath*, Hurst, London, 1981

Clements, Frank, *Rhodesia: The Course to Collision*, Pall Mall Press, London, 1969

Cohen, Herman, *Intervening in Africa: Superpower Peacemaking in a Troubled Continent*, St Martin's Press, New York, 2000

Coleman, James, *Nigeria, Background to Nationalism*, University of California Press, 1958

Coleman, James, and Carl G. Rosberg (eds.), *Political Parties and National Integration in Tropical Africa*, University of California Press, 1958

Collier, Ruth Berins, *Regimes in Tropical Africa: Changing Forms of Supremacy, 1945–1975*, University of California Press, 1982

Connell, Dan, *Against All Odds: a Chronicle of the Eritrean Revolution*, Red Sea Press, Trenton, 1993

Conrad, Joseph, *The Heart of Darkness*, Penguin, London, 1976

—— *Last Essays*, Dent, London, 1926

Cooley, John K., *Libyan Sandstorm: The Complete Account of Qaddafi's Revolution*, Sidgwick and Jackson, London, 1983

Cooper, Frederick, *Africa since 1940: The Past of the Present*, Cambridge University Press, 2002

Coquery-Vidrovitch, Catherine, *Afrique Noire: permanences et ruptures*, Editions Payot, Paris 1985 (English edn: *Africa: Endurance and Change South of the Sahara*, University of California Press, 1988)

Coquery-Vidrovitch, Catherine, Alain Forest and Herbert Weiss (eds.), *Rébellions-Révolution au Zaïre, 1963–1965*, 2 vols, L'Harmattan, Paris, 1987

Cosma, Wililunga, *Fizi, 1967–1986: le maquis Kabila*, L'Harmattan, Paris, 1997

Coulson, Andrew, *Tanzania: A Political Economy*, Clarendon Press, Oxford, 1982

Coulson, Andrew (ed.), *African Socialism in Practice: The Tanzanian Experience*, Spokesman, Nottingham, 1979

Cowen, Michael and Liisa Laakso (eds.), *Multiparty Elections in Africa*, Currey, Oxford, 2002

Cox, Thomas S., *Civil-Military Relations in Sierra Leone*, Harvard University Press, 1976

Crocker, Chester A., *High Noon in Southern Africa: Making Peace in a Rough Neighbourhood*, Norton, New York, 1993

Crowder, Michael, *The Story of Nigeria*, 4th edn, Faber and Faber, London, 1978

Cruise O'Brien, Conor, *To Katanga and Back*, Hutchinson, London, 1962

Cruise O'Brien, Donal, *The Mourides of Senegal: The Political and Economic Organization of an Islamic Brotherhood*, Clarendon Press, Oxford, 1971

Cruise O'Brien, Donal B., John Dunn and Richard Rathbone (eds.), *Contemporary West African States*, Cambridge University Press, 1989

Cruise O'Brien, Rita (ed.), *The Political Economy of Underdevelopment: Dependence in Senegal*, Sage, Beverly Hills, 1979

Crummey, Donald (ed.), *Banditry, Rebellion and Social Protest in Africa*, Currey, London, 1996

Curtin, Philip, Steven Feierman, Leonard Thompson and Jan Vansina, *African History: From Earliest Times to Independence*, 2nd edn, Longman, London, 1995

Dallaire, Lt-Gen Roméo, *Shake Hands with the Devil: The Failure of Humanity in Rwanda*, Random House, Canada, 2003

Daly, Martin and Ahmad Alawad Sikainga (eds.), *Civil War in Sudan*, Tauris, London, 1993

Daniel, John, Roger Southall and Morris Szeftel (eds.), *Voting for Democracy: Watershed Elections in Contemporary Anglophone Africa*, Ashgate, Aldershot, 1999

Daniels, Anthony, *Monrovia Mon Amour: A Visit to Liberia*, John Murray, London, 1992

Davenport, T. R. H. and Saunders, Christopher, *South Africa: A Modern History*, 5th edn, Macmillan, London, 2000

Davidson, Basil *The African Awakening*, Cape, London, 1955

—— *In the Eye of the Storm: Angola's People*, Longman, London, 1972

—— *Black Star: A View of the Life and Times of Kwame Nkrumah*, Allen Lane, London, 1973

—— *Africa in Modern History: The Search for a New Society*, Allen Lane, London, 1978

—— *No Fist is Big Enough to Hide the Sky: The Liberation of Guinea-Bissau and Cape Verde*, Zed, London, 1981

—— *The Black Man's Burden: Africa and the Curse of the Nation-State*, Currey, London, 1992

Dawit Wolde Giorgis, *Red Tears: War, Famine and Revolution in Ethiopia*, Red Sea Press, Trenton, 1989

Dayal, Rajeshwar, *Mission for Hammarskjold: The Congo Crisis*, Oxford University Press, 1976

Deng, Francis M., *The Dinka of Southern Sudan*, Holt, Rinehart and Winston, New York, 1972

—— *War of Visions: Conflict of Identities in the Sudan*, Brookings Institution, Washington, 1995

de Klerk, F. W., *The Last Trek: A New Beginning – The Autobiography*, Macmillan, London, 1998

de Waal, Alex, *Evil Days: Thirty Years of War and Famine in Ethiopia*, Africa Watch, London, 1991

—— *Famine Crimes: Politics and the Disaster Relief Industry in Africa*, Currey, Oxford, 1997

—— *Food and Power in Sudan: A Critique of Humanitarianism*, African Rights, London, 1997

de Waal, Alex (ed.), *Islamism and its Enemies in the Horn of Africa*, Hurst, London, 2004

De Witte, Ludo, *The Assassination of Lumumba*, Verso, London, 2001

Decalo, Samuel, *Psychoses of Power: African Personal Dictatorships*, Westview, Boulder, 1989

—— *Coups and Army Rule in Africa*, 2nd Edn, Yale University Press, 1990

Den Tuinder, Bastiaan A., *Ivory Coast: The Challenge of Success*, Johns Hopkins University Press, 1978

Des Forges, Alison, *'Leave None to Tell the Story': Genocide in Rwanda*, Human Rights Watch, New York, 1999

Desmond, Cosmas, *The Discarded People: An Account of African Resettlement in South Africa*, Penguin, London, 1971

Destexhe, Alain, *Rwanda and Genocide in the Twentieth Century*, Pluto, London, 1995

Diamond, Larry, *Class, Ethnicity and Democracy in Nigeria: The Failure of the First Republic*, Macmillan, Basingstoke, 1988

Diamond, Larry, Anthony Kirk-Greene, and Oyeleye Oyediran (eds.), *Transition Without End: Nigerian Politics amd Civil Society Under Babangida*, Rienner, Boulder, 1997

Diamond, Larry and Marc Plattner (eds.), *Democratization in Africa*, Johns Hopkins University Press, 1999

Douglas-Home, Charles, *Evelyn Baring: The Last Proconsul*, Collins, London, 1978

Drysdale, John, *Whatever Happened in Somalia? A Tale of Tragic Blunders*, Haan Associates, London, 1994

Dualeh, Hussein Ali, *From Barre to Aideed: Somalia – the Agony of a Nation*, Stellagraphics, Nairobi, 1994

Dudley, B. J., *Instability and Political Order: Politics and Crisis in Nigeria*, Ibadan University Press, 1973

Duigan, Peter J. and L. H. Gann (eds.), *Colonialism in Africa 1870–1960*, vols, 2, 3, 4, Cambridge University Press, 1970–75

Duignan, Peter and Robert Jackson (eds.), *Politics and Government in African States*, 1960–85, Hoover Institution Press, 1986

Dumont, René, *L'Afrique Noire Est Mal Partie*, Le Seuil, Paris, 1962 (English edn: *False Start in Africa*, Deutsch, 1966)

Dumont, René and Marie-France Mottin, *L'Afrique Étranglée*, Editions du Seuil, Paris, 1980 (English edn: *Stranglehold on Africa*, Deutsch, London, 1983)

Dungia, Emmanuel, *Mobutu et L'Argent du Zaire*, L'Harmattan, Paris, 1992

Dunn, John (ed.), *West African States: Failure and Promise – A Study in Comparative Politics*, Cambridge University Press, 1978

Dunn, Kevin C., *Imagining the Congo: The International Relations of Identity*, Palgrave Macmillan, New York, 2003

Dutfield, Michael, *A Marriage of Inconvenience: The Persecution of Seretse and Ruth Khama*, Unwin Hyman, London, 1990

Eden, Anthony, *Full Circle: The Memoirs of Anthony Eden*, Cassell, London, 1960

El-Affendi, Abdelwahab, *Turabi's Revolution: Islam and Power in Sudan*, Grey Seal Books, London, 1991

Ellis, Stephen, *The Mask of Anarchy: The Destruction of Liberia and the Religious Dimension of an African Civil War*, Hurst, London, 1999

Ellis, Stephen (ed.), *Africa Now: People, Policies & Institutions*, Currey, London, 1996

Englebert, Pierre, *Burkino Faso: Unsteady Statehood in West Africa*, Westview, Boulder, 1996

Enoanyi, Bill Frank, *Behold Uncle Sam's Stepchild*, Sanmar, Sacramento, 1991

Esposito, John L., *Political Islam*, Rienner, Boulder, 1997

—— *Islam and Politics*, 4th edn, Syracuse University Press, 1998

—— *The Islamic Threat: Myth or Reality?* 3rd edn, Oxford University Press, 1999

—— *Unholy War: Terror in the Name of Islam*, Oxford University Press, 2002

Esposito, John L.(ed.), *Voices of Resurgent Islam*, Oxford University Press, 1983

—— *Political Islam: Revolution, Radicalism or Reform?*, Rienner, Boulder, 1997

Étienne, Bruno, *L'Islamisme radical*, Hachette, Paris, 1992

Fage, J. D. with William Tordoff, *A History of Africa*, 4th edn, Routledge, London, 2001

Fanon, Frantz, *L'An Cinq de la Révolution Algérienne*, Maspero, Paris, 1959

—— *The Wretched of the Earth*, Penguin, London, 1967 (French edn: *Les Damnés de la Terre*, first published in Paris in 1961)

—— *For the African Revolution*, Penguin, London, 1967

—— *A Dying Colonialism*, Penguin, London, 1970

Fatton, Robert, *The Making of a Liberal Democracy: Senegal's Passive Revolution*, Rienner, Boulder, 1987

—— *Predatory Rule: State and Civil Society in Africa*, Rienner, Boulder, 1992

Fauré, Yves A. and Jean-Francois Médard, *Etat et Bourgeoisie en Côte d'Ivoire*, Paris, Karthala, 1982

Fieldhouse, David, *Black Africa, 1945–80, Economic Decolonisation and Arrested Development*, Allen and Unwin, 1986

Finnegan, William, *Crossing the Line: A Year in the Land of Apartheid*, Harper and Row, New York, 1986

—— *A Complicated War: The Harrowing of Mozambique*, University of California Press, 1992

Fitch, Bob and Mary Oppenheimer, *Ghana: End of an Illusion*, Monthly Review Press, New York, 1966

Flower, Ken, *Serving Secretly: An Intelligence Chief on Record, Rhodesia into Zimbabwe, 1964–1981*, John Murray, London, 1987

Foccart, Jacques and Philippe Gaillard, *Foccart Parle: Entretiens avec Phillipe Gaillard*, 2 vols, Fayard, Paris, 1995, 1997

Forna, Aminatta, *The Devil That Danced On The Water*, HarperCollins, London, 2002

Forrest, Joshua, *Lineages of State Fragility: Rural Civil Society in Guinea-Bissau*, Currey, Oxford, 2003

Freund, Bill, *The Making of Contemporary Africa: The Development of African Society Since 1800*, Macmillan, London, 1988

Fuller, Alexandra, *Don't Let's Go to the Dogs Tonight; an African Childhood*, Picador, London, 2002

Furedi, Frank, *The Mau Mau War in Perspective*, Currey, London, 1989

Furley, Oliver W. (ed.), *Conflict in Africa*, Tauris, London, 1995

Gann, L.H. and Duigan, P. (eds.), *Colonialism in Africa 1870–1960*, vol. 1, Cambridge University Press, 1969

Garang, John, *The Call for Democracy in Sudan*, KPI, London, 1992

Gauze, René, *The Politics of Congo-Brazzaville*, Hoover Institution Press, Stanford, 1973

Geffray, Christian, *La cause des armes au Mozambique: Anthropologie d'une guerre civile*, Karthala, Paris, 1990

Gellar, Sheldon, *Senegal: An African Nation Between Islam and the West*, Westview, Boulder, 1995

Gérard-Libois, Jules, *Sécession au Katanga*, CRISP, Brussels, 1963. (English edn: *Katanga Secession*, University of Wisconsin Press, 1966)

Gerhart, Gail M., *Black Power in South Africa: The Evolution of an Ideology*, University of California Press, 1979

German, Emmanuel, *La Centrafrique et Bokassa, 1965–1979; force et décline d'un pouvoir personnel*, L'Harmattan, Paris, 2000

Gifford, Prosser, and Wm. Roger Louis (eds.), *The Transfer of Power in Africa: Decolonization, 1940–1960*, Yale University Press, 1982

—— *Decolonization and African Independence*, Yale University Press, 1988

Gilkes, Patrick, *The Dying Lion: Feudalism and Modernization in Ethiopia*, Friedmann, London, 1975

Gill, Peter, *A Year in the Death of Africa: Politics, Bureaucracy and Famine*, Paladin, London, 1986

Glaser, Antoine and Stephen Smith, *L'Afrique sans Africaines: Le Rêve Blanc du Continent Noir*, Stock, Paris, 1994

Godwin, Peter, *Mukiwa: A White Boy in Africa*, Macmillan, London, 1996

Godwin, Peter, and Ian Hancock, *Rhodesians Never Die: The Impact of War and Political Change on White Rhodesia, c. 1970–1980*, Oxford University Press, 1993

Goldsworthy, David, *Tom Mboya: The Man Kenya wanted to forget*, Heinemann, London, 1982

Gombeaud, Jean-Louis, Corinne Moutot and Stephen Smith, *La Guerre du Cacao: histoire secrète d'un embargo*, Calmann-Lévy, Paris, 1990

Gordon, Nick, *Murders in the Mist*, Hodder and Stoughton, London, 1993

Gould, David, *Bureaucratic Corruption and Underdevelopment in the Third World: The Case of Zaire*, Pergamon, New York, 1980

Gourevitch, Philip, *We wish to inform you that tomorrow we will be killed with our families: Stories from Rwanda*, Picador, London, 2000

Graf, William D., *The Nigerian State: Political Economy, State, Class and Political System in the Post-Colonial Era*, Currey, London, 1988

Grahame, Iain, *Amin and Uganda: A Personal Memoir*, Granada, London, 1980

Gran, Guy, (ed.), *Zaire: The Political Economy of Underdevelopment*, Praeger, New York, 1979

Greene, Graham, *Journey Without Maps*, Heinemann, Bodley Head, London, 1978

Greenfield, Richard, *Ethiopia: A New Political History*, Pall Mall Press, London, 1965

Griffiths, Ieuan Ll., *The Atlas of African Affairs*, 2nd edn, Routledge, London, 1994

—— *The African Inheritance*, Routledge, London, 1995

Guest, Robert, *The Shackled Continent, Africa's Past, Present and Future*, Macmillan, London, 2004

Guevara, Ernesto 'Che', *The African Dream: The Diaries of the Revolutionary War in the Congo*, Harvill, London, 2001

Guimarães, Fernando Andresen, *The Origins of the Angolan Civil War: Foreign Intervention and Domestic Political Conflict*, Macmillan, Basingstoke, 1998

Gunther, John, *Inside Africa*, Hamish Hamilton, London, 1955

Gutteridge, W. F., *The Military in African Politics*, Methuen, London, 1969

—— *Military Regimes in Africa*, Methuen, London, 1975

Gyimah–Boadi, E. (ed.) *Democratic Reform in Africa*, Rienner, Boulder, 2004

Hadland, Adrian and Jovial Rantao, *The Life and Times of Thabo Mbeki*, Zebra, Johannesburg, 1999

Hall, Margaret and Tom Young, *Confronting Leviathan: Mozambique since Independence*, Hurst, London, 1997

Hall, Richard, *The High Price of Principles: Kaunda and the White South*, Hodder and Stoughton, London, 1969

Halliday, Fred and Maxine Molyneux, *The Ethiopian Revolution*, Verso, London, 1981

Hamdi, Mohamed Elhachmi, *The Making of an Islamic Political Leader: Conversations with Hasan al-Turabi*, Westview, Boulder, 1998

Hancock, Graham, *Ethiopia: The Challenge of Hunger*, Gollancz, London, 1985

Hanley, Gerald, *Warriors and Strangers*, Hamish Hamilton, London, 1971

Hansen, Holger Bernt and Michael Twaddle (eds.), *Uganda Now: Between Decay and Development*, Currey, London, 1988

—— *Changing Uganda: The Dilemmas of Structural Adjustment and Revolutionary Change*, Currey, London, 1991

—— *From Chaos to Order : The Politics of Constitution-Making in Uganda*, Currey, London, 1995

—— *Religion and Politics in East Africa: The Period Since Independence*, Currey, London, 1995

—— *Developing Uganda*, Currey, Oxford, 1998

Harbeson, John W., Donald Rothchild and Naomi Chazan (eds.), *Civil Society and the State in Africa*, Rienner, Boulder, 1994

Harden, Blaine, *Africa: Dispatches from a Fragile Continent*, HarperCollins, London, 1991

Harding, Jeremy, *Small Wars, Small Mercies; Journeys in Africa's Disputed Nations*, Penguin, London, 1993

Hargreaves, John, *Decolonisation in Africa*, 2nd edn, Longman, London, 1996

Harris, Lillian Craig, *Libya: Qadhafi's Revolution and the Modern State*, Croom Helm, Beckenham, 1986

Harrison, Graham, *Issues in the Contemporary Politics of Sub-Saharan Africa: The Dynamics of Struggle and Resistance*, Palgrave Macmillan, Basingstoke, 2002

Harrison, Paul, *The Greening of Africa*, Penguin, London, 1987

Hartley, Aidan, *The Zanzibar Chest: A Memoir of Love and War*, HarperCollins, London, 2003

Hastings, Adrian, *A History of African Christianity 1950–1975*, Cambridge University Press, 1979

—— *The Church in Africa, 1450–1950*, Oxford University Press, 1994

Henrikson, Thomas H., *Mozambique: A History*, Collings, London, 1978

—— *Revolution and Counter-Revolution: Mozambique's War of Independence, 1964–74*, Greenwood, Westport, CT, 1983

Hepple, Alexander, *Verwoerd*, Penguin, London, 1967

Herbst, Jeffrey, *The Politics of Reform in Ghana, 1982–1991*, University of California Press, 1993

—— *States and Power in Africa: Comparative Lessons in Authority and Control*, Princeton University Press, 2000

Hill, Justin, *Ciao Asmara*, Abacus, London, 2002

Hirsch, John L., *Sierra Leone: Diamonds and the Struggle for Democracy*, Lynne Rienner, Boulder, 2001

Hirsch, John L. and Robert B. Oakley, *Somalia and Operation Restore Hope: Reflections on Peacemaking and Peacekeeping*, US Institute of Peace, Washington, DC, 1995

Hochschild, Adam, *King Leopold's Ghost. A Story of Greed, Terror and Heroism in Colonial Africa*, Macmillan, London, 1999

Hodges, Tony, *Angola: Anatomy of an Oil State*, Currey, Oxford, 2004

Hodgkin, Thomas, *Nationalism in Colonial Africa*, Muller, London, 1956

Holm, John D. and Patrick P. Molutsi (eds.), *Democracy in Botswana*, Macmillan, Botswana, 1989

Holt, P. M. and M. W. Daly, *A History of the Sudan*, 5th edn, Pearson, Harlow, 2000

Hooper, Edward, *Slim: A Reporter's Own Story of AIDS in East Africa*, Bodley Head, London, 1990

—— *The River: A Journey Back to the Source of HIV and AIDS*, Allen Lane, London, 1999

Hopkins, A. G., *An Economic History of West Africa*, Columbia University Press, 1973

Horne, Alistair, *A Savage War of Peace: Algeria, 1954–1962*, Papermac, London, 1987

Hoskyns, Catherine, *The Congo since Independence, January 1960–December 1961*, Oxford University Press, 1965

Huband, Mark, *The Liberian Civil War*, Cass, London, 1997

—— *The Skull Beneath The Skin: Africa After the Cold War*, Westview, Boulder, 2001

Human Rights Watch, *Sudan, Oil and Human Rights*, New York, 2003

—— *Angola: Some Transparency, No Accountability. The Use of Oil Revenue in Angola and Its Impact on Human Rights*, New York, 2004

Hyden, Goran, *Beyond Ujamaa in Tanzania: Underdevelopment and an Uncaptured Peasantry*, Heinemann, London, 1980

Hyden, Goran and Michael Bratton (eds.), *Governance and Politics in Africa*, Lynne Rienner, Boulder, 1992

Hyland, Paul, *The Black Heart: A Voyage into Central Africa*, Gollancz, London, 1988

Hymans, Jacques Louis, *Léopold Sédar Senghor: An Intellectual Biography*, Edinburgh University Press, 1971

Iliffe, John, *A Modern History of Tanganyika*, Cambridge University Press, 1979

—— *The Emergence of African Capitalism*, Macmillan, London, 1983

—— *The African Poor*, Cambridge University Press, 1987

—— *Africans: The History of a Continent*, Cambridge University Press, 1995

Ingham, Kenneth, *Obote: A Political Biography*, Routledge, London, 1994

Isaacman, Allen and Barbara Isaacman, *Mozambique: From Colonialism to Revolution, 1900–1982*, Westview, 1983

Itote, Waruhiu, *'Mau Mau' General*, East African Publishing House, Nairobi, 1967

Iyob, Ruth, *The Eritrean Struggle for Independence: Domination, Resistance, Nationalism, 1941–1993*, Cambridge University Press, 1995

Jackson, Robert H. and Carl G. Rosberg, *Personal Rule in Black Africa: Prince, Autocrat, Prophet, Tyrant*, University of California Press, 1982

Jacobs, Sean and Richard Calland (eds.), *Thabo Mbeki's World: The Politics and Ideology of the South African President*, University of Natal Press, 2002

James, Alan, *Britain and the Congo Crisis, 1960–1963*, Macmillan, London, 1996

James, Wendy, Donald L. Donham, Eisei Kurimoto and Eisei Triulzi (eds.), *Remapping Ethiopia: Socialism and After*, Currey, Oxford, 2002

Jansen, Johannes J. G., *The Neglected Duty: The Creed of Sadat's Assassins and the Resurgence of Islamic Militance in the Middle East*, Macmillan, New York, 1986

Janssen, Pierre, *À La Cour de Mobutu*, Lafon, Paris, 1997

Jansson, Kurt, *The Ethiopian Famine*, Zed, London, 1987

Jennings, Christian, *Across the Red River: Rwanda, Burundi & The Heart of Darkness*, Phoenix, London, 2001

Johnson, Douglas, *The Root Causes of Sudan's Civil Wars*, Currey, Oxford, 2003

Jones, Trevor, *Ghana's First Republic, 1960–1966*, Methuen, London, 1976

Joseph, Richard, *Radical Nationalism in Cameroun: Social Origins of the UPC Rebellion*, Clarendon Press, Oxford, 1977

—— *Democracy and Prebendal Politics in Nigeria: The Rise and Fall of the Second Republic*, Cambridge University Press, 1987

Joseph, Richard (ed.), *State, Conflict and Democracy in Africa*, Rienner, Boulder, 1999

Kaggia, Bildad, *Roots of Freedom*, East African Publishing House, Nairobi, 1968

Kalb, Madeleine G., *The Congo Cables: The Cold War in Africa – From Eisenhower to Kennedy*, Macmillan, New York, 1982

Kalck, Pierre, *Central African Republic: A Failure in Decolonisation*, Pall Mall Press, London, 1971

Kalipeni, Ezekiel, Susan Craddock, Joseph R. Oppong and Jayati Ghosh (eds.), *HIV and AIDS in Africa: Beyond Epidemiology*, Blackwell, Oxford, 2004

Kamarck, Andrew M., *The Economics of African Development*, Praeger, New York, 1967

Kanogo, Tabitha, *Squatters and the Roots of Mau Mau, 1905–63*, Currey, London, 1987

Kanza, Thomas, *Conflict in the Congo: The Rise and Fall of Lumumba*, Penguin, Harmondsworth, 1972

Kaplan, Robert D., *Surrender or Starve: The Wars behind the Famine; Travels in Ethiopia, Sudan, Somalia and Eritrea*, Westview, Boulder, 1988

Kapuściński, Ryszard, *The Emperor: The Downfall of an Autocrat*, Quartet, London, 1983

—— *Another Day of Life*, Pan, London, 1987

—— *The Soccer War*, Granta, London, 1990

—— *The Shadow of the Sun*, Allen Lane, London, 2001

Karis, Thomas, Gwendolyn M. Carter and Gail M. Gerhart (eds.), *From Protest to Challenge: A Documentary History of African Politics in South Africa, 1882–1990*, 5 vols, Hoover Institution, Stanford, Indiana University Press, 1972–97

Kariuki, J. M., *'Mau Mau' Detainee*, Oxford University Press, 1963

Kasfir, Nelson, *The Shrinking Political Arena; Participation and Ethnicity in African Politics*, University of California Press, 1976

Kasfir, Nelson, (ed.), *Civil Society and Democracy in Africa: Critical Perspectives*, Cass, London, 1995

Kauffman, Kyle D. and David L. Lindauer (eds.), *Aids and South Africa: The Social Expression of a Pandemic*, Palgrave Macmillan, Basingstoke, 2004

Keane, Fergal, *Season of Blood: A Rwanda Journey*, Viking, New York, 1995

Keké, I. Baba, *Sékou Touré: Le Héros et le Tyran*, Jeune Afrique, Paris, 1987

Keller, Edmond J., *Revolutionary Ethiopia: From Empire to People's Republic*, Indiana University Press, 1988

Kelley, Michael, *A State in Disarray: Conditions of Chad's Survival*, Westview, Boulder, 1986

Kelly, Sean, *America's Tyrant: The CIA and Mobutu of Zaire*, American University Press, Washington, 1993

Kennedy, Paul, *African Capitalism: The Struggle for Ascendancy*, Cambridge University Press, 1988

Kenney, Henry, *Architect of Apartheid: H. F. Verwoerd – An Appraisal*, Jonathan Ball, Johannesburg, 1980

Kenyatta, Jomo, *Facing Mount Kenya*, Secker and Warburg, London, 1938

—— *Suffering Without Bitterness*, East African Publishing House, Nairobi, 1968

Kepel, Gilles, *Muslim Extremism in Egypt: The Prophet and the Pharoah*, University of California Press, 1986

—— *Jihad: The Trail of Political Islam*, Belknap Press, Cambridge, MA, 2002

Kershaw, Greet, *Mau Mau from Below*, Currey, Oxford, 1997

Khalid, Mansour, *Numeiri and the Revolution of Dis-May*, KPI, London, 1985

Killick, Tony, *Development Economics in Action: A Study of Economic Policies in Ghana*, Heinemann, London, 1978

Killingray, David and Richard Rathbone (eds.), *Africa and the Second World War*, Macmillan, London, 1986

King, Preston, *An African Winter*, Penguin, London, 1986

Kingsolver, Barbara, *The Poisonwood Bible*, Faber and Faber, London, 1999

Kirk-Greene, Anthony and Daniel C. Bach (eds.), *State and Society in Francophone Africa since Independence*, Macmillan, London, 1995

Klinghoffer, Arthur Jay, *The Angolan War: A Study in Soviet Policy in the Third World*, Westview, Boulder, 1980

Korn, David, *Ethiopia, the US and the Soviet Union*, Croom Helm, London, 1986

Kriger, Norma, *Zimbabwe's Guerrilla War: Peasant Voices*, Cambridge University Press, 1992

Krog, Antjie, *Country of My Skull*, Random House, Johannesburg, 1998

Kyemba, Henry, *State of Blood*, Corgi, London, 1977

Kyle, Keith, *Suez*, Weidenfeld & Nicolson, London, 1991

—— *The Politics of the Independence of Kenya*, Macmillan, Basingstoke, 1999

Lacouture, Jean, *Nasser*, Secker & Warburg, London, 1973

—— *De Gaulle: The Ruler, 1945–1970*, Harvill, London, 1991

Laitin, David D. and Said S. Samatar, *Somalia: Nation in Search of a State*, Westview, Boulder, 1987

Lamb, David, *The Africans: Encounters from the Sudan to the Cape*, Bodley Head, London, 1983

Lan, David, *Guns and Rain: Guerrillas and Spirit Mediums in Zimbabwe*, University of California Press, 1985

Lapping, Brian, *End of Empire*, Granada, London, 1985

Larkin, Bruce D., *China and Africa, 1949–1970*, University of California Press, 1971

Leakey, M. D., *Olduvai Gorge: My Search for Early Man*, Collins, London, 1979

Lefort, René, *Ethiopia: An Heretical Revolution?*, Zed, London, 1981

Lelyveld, Joseph, *Move Your Shadow: South Africa Black and White*, Joseph, London, 1986

Lema, Antoine, *Africa Divided*, Lund University Press, 1993

Lemarchand, René, *Political Awakening in the Belgian Congo*, University of California Press, 1964

—— *Rwanda and Burundi*, Pall Mall Press, London, 1970

—— *Burundi: Ethnocide as Discourse and Practice*, Cambridge University Press, 1994

Lemarchand, René (ed.), *The Green and the Black: Qadhafi's Policies in Africa*, Indiana University Press, 1988

Lesch, Ann Mosely, *The Sudan: Contested National Identities*, Currey, Oxford, 1999

LeVine, Victor, *Political Corruption: The Ghana Case*, Hoover Institution Press, Stanford, 1975

—— *Politics in Francophone Africa*, Rienner, Boulder, CO, 2004

Levtzion, Nehemia and Randall L. Pouwels (eds.), *The History of Islam in Africa*, Currey, Oxford, 2000

Lewis, I. M., *A Pastoral Democracy: A Study of Pastoralism and Politics Among the Northern Somali of the Horn of Africa*, Oxford University Press, 1961

—— *A Modern History of Somalia: Nation and State in the Horn of Africa*, 4th edn, Currey, Oxford, 2002

Lewis, I. M. (ed.), *Islam in Tropical Africa*, Hutchinson, London, 1980

Lewis, W. Arthur, *Politics in West Africa*, Allen and Unwin, London, 1965

Leys, Colin, *Underdevelopment in Kenya: The Political Economy of Neocolonialism*, Heinemann, London, 1975

—— *The Rise and Fall of Development Theory*, Currey, London, 1996

Liebenow, J. Gus, *Liberia: The Quest for Democracy*, Indiana University Press, 1987

Linden, Ian, *Church and Revolution in Rwanda*, Manchester University Press, 1977

Liniger-Goumaz, Max, *Small is Not Always Beautiful: The Story of Equatorial Guinea*, Hurst, London, 1986

Little, Peter D., *Somalia: Economy Without State*, Currey, Oxford, 2003

Lodge, Tom, *Black Politics in South Africa Since 1945*, Longman, London, 1983

—— *Politics in South Africa: From Mandela to Mbeki*, David Philip, Cape Town, 2002

Lofchie, Michael, *Zanzibar: Background to Revolution*, Princeton University Press, 1965

Lofchie, Michael F., *The Policy Factor: Agricultural Performance in Kenya and Tanzania*, Rienner, Boulder, 1989

Logiest, Guy, *Mission au Rwanda: Un blanc dans la bagarre Tutsi-Hutu*, Didier-Hatier, Brussels, 1988

Louis, W. R., *Ruanda–Urundi, 1884–1919*, Clarendon Press, Oxford, 1963

Luckham, Robin, *The Nigerian Military: A Sociological Analysis of Authority and Revolt 1960–67*, Cambridge University Press, 1971

Lumumba, Patrice, *Le Congo, terre d'avenir – est-il menacé?*, Office de Publicité S.A., Brussels, 1961 (English edn: *Congo, My Country*, Pall Mall Press with Barrie and Rockcliff, London, 1962)

Macey, David, *Frantz Fanon: a Biography*, Granta, London, 2000

MacGaffey, Janet, *Entrepreneurs and Parasites: The Struggle for Indigenous Capitalism in Zaire*, Cambridge University Press, 1987

MacGaffey, Janet, et al., *The Real Economy of Zaire: The Contribution of Smuggling and Other Unofficial Activities to National Wealth*, Pennsylvania University Press, 1991

MacGaffey, Janet and Rémy Bazenguissa-Ganga, *Congo-Paris: Transnational Traders on the Margins of the Law*, Indiana University Press, 2000

Mackintosh, John P., et al., *Nigerian Government and Politics*, Northwestern University Press, Evanston, 1966

Macmillan, Harold, *Pointing the Way, 1959–61*, Macmillan, London, 1972

MacQueen, Norrie, *The Decolonization of Portuguese Africa: Metropolitan Revolution and the Dissolution of Empire*, Addison Wesley Longman, Harlow, 1997

Mahoney, Richard D., *JFK: Ordeal in Africa*, Oxford University Press, 1983

Maier, Karl, *Angola: Promises and Lies*, Serif, London, 1996

—— *Into the House of the Ancestors: Inside the New Africa*, Wiley, New York, 1997

—— *This House Has Fallen: Nigeria in Crisis*, Allen Lane, London, 2000

Malan, Rian, *My Traitor's Heart*, Bodley Head, London, 1990

Maliyamkono, T. L. and M. S. D. Bagachwa, *The Second Economy in Tanzania*, Currey, London, 1990

Malkki, Liisa H., *Purity and Exile: Violence, Memory and National Cosmology Among Hutu Refugees in Tanzania*, University of Chicago Press, 1995

Maloba, Wunyabari, *Mau Mau and Kenya: An Analysis of a Peasant Revolt*, Indiana University Press, 1993

Mamdani, Mahmood, *Citizen and Subject: Contemporary Africa and the Legacy of Late Colonialism*, Currey, London, 1996

—— *When Victims Become Killers: Colonialism, Nativism and the Genocide in Rwanda*, Currey, Oxford, 2001

Mandela, Nelson, *No Easy Walk to Freedom*, Heinemann, London, 1965
—— *Long Walk to Freedom: The Autobiography of Nelson Mandela*, Little, Brown, London, 1994
Manning, Patrick, *Francophone Sub-Saharan Africa, 1880–1995*, 2nd edn, Cambridge University Press, 1999
Marais, Genovava, *Kwame Nkrumah as I knew him*, Janay, Chichester, 1972
Marchal, Colonel Luc, *Rwanda: la descente aux enfers. Témoinage d'un peace-keeper, December 1993–Avril 1994*, Labor, Brussels, 2001
Marcum, John, *The Angolan Revolution: Vol. 1. The Anatomy of an Explosion (1950–1962). Vol 2. Exile Politics and Guerrilla Warfare (1962–1976)*, MIT Press, Cambridge, MA, 1978
Maren, Michael, *The Road to Hell: The Ravaging Effects of Foreign Aid and International Charity*, The Free Press, New York, 1997
Markakis, John, *Ethiopia: Anatomy of a Traditional Polity*, Oxford University Press, 1974
—— *National and Class Conflict in the Horn of Africa*, Zed, London, 1990
Markakis, John and Nega Ayele, *Class and Revolution in Ethiopia*, Spokesman, Nottingham, 1978
Markakis, John and Michael Waller (eds.), *Military Marxist Regimes in Africa*, Cass, London, 1986
Markovitz, Irving Leonard, *Léopold Sédar Senghor and the Politics of Negritude*, Heinemann, London, 1969
Martens, Ludo, *Pierre Mulele ou la Seconde Vie de Patrice Lumumba*, Edn EPO, Antwerp, 1985
Martin, David, *General Amin*, Faber, London, 1974
Martin, David and Phyllis Johnson, *The Struggle for Zimbabwe: The Chimurenga War*, Faber, London, 1981
Martinez, Luis, *The Algerian Civil War, 1990–1998*, Hurst, London, 2001
Matloff, Judith, *Fragments of a Forgotten War*, Penguin, Johannesburg, 1997
McHenry, Dean, *Tanzania's Ujamaa Villages: The Implementation of a Rural Development Strategy*, University of California Press, 1979
—— *Limited Choices: The Political Struggle for Socialism in Tanzania*, Rienner, Boulder, 1994
Médard, Jean-François (ed.), *États d'Afrique Noire: Formation, mécanismes et crises*, Karthala, Paris, 1994
Meldrum, Andrew, *Where We Have Hope: A Memoir of Zimbabwe*, John Murray, London, 2004
Melvern, Linda, *A People Betrayed: The Role of the West in Rwanda's Genocide*, Zed, London, 2000
—— *Conspiracy to Murder: The Rwandan Genocide*, Verso, London, 2004
Mendes, Pedro Rosa, *Bay of Tigers: a journey through war-torn Angola*, Granta, London, 2003
Meredith, Martin, *The Past Is Another Country: Rhodesia, UDI to Zimbabwe*, Pan, London, 1980

—— *The First Dance of Freedom: Black Africa In the Postwar Era*, Hamish Hamilton, London, 1984

—— *In the Name of Apartheid: South Africa in the Post War Period*, Hamish Hamilton, London, 1988

—— *Nelson Mandela: A Biography*, Hamish Hamilton, London, 1997

—— *Coming to Terms: South Africa's Search for Truth*, Public Affairs, New York, 2001

—— *Fischer's Choice: A Life of Bram Fischer*, Jonathan Ball, Johannesburg, 2002

—— *Mugabe: Power and Plunder in Zimbabwe*, Public Affairs, London, 2003

Milne, June, *Kwame Nkrumah: A Biography*, Panaf, London, 2000

Miners, N. J., *The Nigerian Army, 1956–1966*, Methuen, London, 1971

Minter, William, *Apartheid's Contras: An Inquiry into the Roots of War in Angola and Mozambique*, Zed, London, 1994

Monheim, Francis, *Mobutu, l'homme seul*, Editions Actuelles, Brussels, 1963

Morgenthau, Ruth Schachter, *Political Parties in French-Speaking Africa*, Clarendon Press, Oxford, 1964

Morris-Jones, W. H. and G. Fischer (eds.), *Decolonisation and After: the British and French Experience*, Cass, London, 1980

Mortimer, Edward, *France and the Africans, 1944–1960*, Faber, London, 1969

Morton, Andrew, *Moi: The Making of an African Statesman*, O'Mara, London, 1998

Mphahlele, Ezekiel, *Down Second Avenue*, Faber, London, 1959

Mudimbe, V. Y., *The Invention of Africa: Gnosis, Philosophy and the Foundation of Knowledge*, Indiana University Press, 1990

Mugabe, Robert, *Our War of Liberation: Speeches, Articles, Interviews, 1976–1979*, Mambo Press, Gweru, Zimbabwe, 1983

Munslow, Barry, *Mozambique: The Revolution and its Origins*, Longman, London, 1983

Murray-Brown, Jeremy, *Kenyatta*, Allen and Unwin, London, 1972

Museveni, Yoweri, *Sowing the Mustard Seed: the Struggle for Freedom and Democracy in Uganda*, Macmillan, London, 1997

Mutesa II, the Kabaka of Buganda, *Desecration of My Kingdom*, Constable, London, 1967

Nafziger, Wayne E., *Inequality in Africa: Political Elites, Proletariats, Peasants and the Poor*, Cambridge University Press, 1988

Naipaul, Shiva, *North of South: An African Journey*, Deutsch, London, 1978

Naipaul, V. S., *A Bend in the River*, Penguin, London, 1980

Nasser, Gamal Abdel, *The Philosophy of the Revolution*, Public Affairs Press, Washington, DC, 1955

Nazer, Mende and Damien Lewis, *Slave*, Virago, London, 2004

Neguib, Mohammed, *Egypt's Destiny*, Gollancz, London, 1955

Neuffer, Elizabeth, *The Key to My Neighbour's House: Seeking Justice in Bosnia and Rwanda*, Bloomsbury, London, 2002

Newbury, Catherine, *The Cohesion of Oppression: Clientship and Ethnicity in Rwanda, 1860–1960*, Columbia University Press, 1988

Newitt, Malyn, *Portugal in Africa*, Hurst, London, 1981

—— *A History of Mozambique*, Hurst, London, 1995

Ngbanda Nzambo-ku-Atumba, Honoré, *Ainsi sonne le glas! Les Derniers Jours du Maréchal Mobutu*, Gideppe, Paris,1998

Nguza Karl-i-Bond, *Mobutu, ou l'Incarnation du Mal Zairois*, Collings, London, 1982

Niblock, T., *Class and Power in Sudan: The Dynamics of Sudanese Politics, 1898–1985*, Macmillan, London, 1987

Nkomo, Joshua, *The Story of My Life*, Methuen, London, 1984

Nkrumah, Kwame, *Ghana: The Autobiography of Kwame Nkrumah*, Thomas Nelson, Edinburgh, 1959

Nolutshungu, Sam C., *Limits of Anarchy: Intervention and State Formation in Chad*, University Press of Virginia, Charlottesville, 1996

Nordstrom, Carolyn, *A Different Kind of War Story*, University of Pennsylvania Press, 1997

Nugent, Paul, *Africa Since Independence; A Comparative History*, Palgrave Macmillan, Basingstoke, 2004

Nugent, Paul and A. I. Asiwaju (eds.), *African Boundaries: Barriers, Conduits and Opportunities*, Pinter, London, 1996

Nutting, Anthony, *No End of a Lesson: The Story of Suez*, Constable, London, 1967

—— *Nasser*, Constable, London, 1972

Nyerere, Julius K., *Freedom and Unity: A Selection from Writings and Speeches, 1952–65*. Oxford University Press, 1966

—— *Freedom and Socialism: A Selection from Writings and Speeches, 1965–67*, Oxford University Press, 1968

—— *Ujamaa: Essays on Socialism*, Oxford University Press, 1968

—— *Freedom and Development: A Selection from Writings and Speeches, 1969–1973*, Oxford University Press, 1973

Nzongola-Ntalaja, Georges, *The Congo From Leopold to Kabila: A People's History*, Zed, London, 2002

Odinga, Oginga, *Not Yet Uhuru*, Heinemann, London, 1967

Ogot, B. A. and W. R. Ochieng' (eds.), *Decolonization and Independence in Kenya 1940–93*, Currey, London, 1995

Ogunsanwo, Alaba, *China's Policy in Africa, 1958–1971*, Cambridge University Press, 1974

Okello, John, *Revolution in Zanzibar*, East African Publishing House, Nairobi, 1967

Oliver, Roland, *The African Experience*, Weidenfeld & Nicolson, London, 1991

Oliver, R. and J. Fage, *A Short History of Africa*, Penguin, London, 1988

Oliver, Roland and J. D. Fage (eds.), *Cambridge History of Africa*, 8 vols, Cambridge University Press, 1975–86

Omaar, Rakiya, *Rwanda: Death, Despair and Defiance*, African Rights, London, 1995

Orizio, Riccardo, *Talk of the Devil: Encounters with Seven Dictators*, Secker & Warburg, London, 2002

Osaghae, Eghosa, *Crippled Giant: Nigeria Since Independence*, Hurst, London, 1998

O'Toole, Thomas, *The Central African Republic: The Continent's Hidden Heart*, Westview, Boulder, 1986

Ottoway, Marina and David, *Ethiopia: Empire in Revolution*, Africana Publishing, New York, 1978

Pakenham, Thomas, *The Boer War*, Weidenfeld & Nicolson, London, 1979

—— *The Scramble for Africa, 1876–1912*, Weidenfeld & Nicolson, London, 1991

Palmer, Robin, *Land and Racial Discrimination in Rhodesia*, Heinemann, London, 1977

Pankhurst, Richard, *The Ethiopians: A History*, Blackwell, Oxford, 1998

Parsons, Neil, Willie Henderson and Thomas Tlou, *Seretse Khama*, Macmillan Boleswa, Johannesburg, 1995

Parsons, Raymond, *The Mbeki Inheritance: South Africa's Economy 1996–2004*, Ravan Press, Johannesburg, 2004

Perham, Margery, *The Colonial Reckoning*, Collins, London, 1961

Peterson, Scott, *Me Against My Brother: At War in Somalia, Sudan and Rwanda*, Routledge, London, 2001

Petterson, Don, *Revolution in Zanzibar: An American's Cold War Tale*, Westview, Boulder, 2002

—— *Inside Sudan: Political Islam, Conflict and Catastrophe*, Westview, Boulder, 2003

Poku, Nana K. and Alan Whiteside (eds.), *The Political Economy of AIDS in Africa*, Ashgate, Aldershot, 2004

Pool, David, *From Guerrillas to Government: The Eritrean People's Liberation Front*, Currey, Oxford, 2001

Post, Kenneth W. J. and Michael Vickers, *Structure and Conflict in Nigeria, 1960–1966*, Heinemann, London, 1973

Pottier, Johan, *Re-Imagining Rwanda: Conflict, Survival and Disinformation in the Late Twentieth Century*, Cambridge University Press, 2002

Powell, Erica, *Private Secretary (Female)/Gold Coast*, Hurst, London, 1984

Pratt, Cranford, *The Critical Phase in Tanzania, 1945–1968: Nyerere and the Emergence of a Socialist Strategy*, Cambridge University Press, 1976

Prunier, Gérard, *The Rwanda Crisis: History of a Genocide*, Hurst, London, 1995

Quandt, William B., *Between Ballots and Bullets: Algeria's Transition from Authoritarianism*, Brookings Institution Press, Washington, 1998

Ranger, Terence, *Peasant Consciousness and Guerrilla War in Zimbabwe*, Currey, London, 1985

Ravenhill, John (ed.), *Africa in Economic Crisis*, Macmillan, London, 1986

Reader, John, *Africa: A Biography of the Continent*, Penguin, London, 1998

Reno, William, *Corruption and State Politics in Sierra Leone*, Cambridge University Press, 1995

—— *Warlord Politics and African States*, Lynne Rienner, Boulder, 1998

Reyntjens, Filip, *L'Afrique des Grands Lacs en Crise: Rwanda, Burundi, 1988–1994*, Karthala, Paris, 1994

—— *La Guerre des Grands Lacs: Alliances Mouvantes et Conflits Extraterritoriaux en Afrique Centrale*, L'Harmattan, Paris, 1999

Richards, Paul, *Fighting for the Rain Forest: War, Youth and Resources in Sierra Leone*, Currey, London, 1996

Richburg, Keith B., *Out of America: A Black Man Confronts Africa*, Basic Books, New York, 1997

Rimmer, Douglas, *The Economies of West Africa*, Weidenfeld & Nicolson, London, 1984

—— *Staying Poor: Ghana's Political Economy, 1950–1990*, Pergamon Press, Oxford, 1992

Rimmer, Douglas (ed.), *Africa 30 Years On: The Africas of 1961 and 1991*, Currey, London, 1991

Rivière, Claude, *Guinea: Mobilization of a People*, Cornell University Press, 1970

Roberts, Hugh, *The Battlefield: Algeria, 1988–2002; Studies in a Broken Polity*, Verso, London, 2003

Rooney, David, *Sir Charles Arden-Clarke*, Collins, London, 1982

—— *Kwame Nkrumah: The Political Kingdom in the Third World*, Tauris, London, 1988

Rosberg, Carl G. and John Nottingham, *The Myth of 'Mau Mau': Nationalism in Kenya*, Praeger, New York, 1966

Rosberg, Carl G. and Thomas M. Callaghy, *Socialism in Sub-Saharan Africa*, University of California, 1979

Rothchild, Donald (ed.), *Ghana: The Political Economy of Recovery*, Rienner, Boulder, 1991

Rothchild, Donald and Naomi Chazan (eds.), *The Precarious Balance: State and Society in Africa*, Westview, Boulder, 1988

Russell, Alec, *Big Men, Little People: Encounters in Africa*, Macmillan, London, 1999

el-Sadat, Anwar, *Revolt on the Nile*, Wingate, London, 1957

Sahnoun, Mohamed, *Somalia: The Missed Opportunities*, United States Institute of Peace Press, Washington, DC, 1994

Samatar, Said S., *Somalia: A Nation in Turmoil*, Minority Rights Group, London, 1991

Sampson, Anthony, *Mandela: The Authorised Biography*, HarperCollins, London, 1999

Sandbrook, Richard, *The Politics of Africa's Stagnation*, Cambridge University Press, 1985

—— *The Politics of Africa's Economic Recovery*, Cambridge University Press, 1993

—— *Closing the Circle: Democratization and Development in Africa*, Zed, London, 2000

Schatzberg, Michael G., *Politics and Class in Zaire: Bureaucracy, Business and Beer in Lisala*, Africana Publishing, New York, 1980

—— *The Dialectics of Oppression in Zaire*, Indiana University Press, 1988

—— *Mobutu or Chaos? The United States and Zaire, 1960–1990*, University Press of America, Lanham, 1991

Schatzberg, Michael G. (ed.), *The Political Economy of Kenya*, Praeger, New York, 1987

Schatzberg, Michael G. and I. William Zartman (eds.), *The Political Economy of Cameroon*, Praeger, New York, 1986

Scott, Ian, *Tumbled House: The Congo at Independence*, Oxford University Press, 1969

Scroggins, Deborah, *Emma's War: Love, Betrayal and Death in the Sudan*, HarperCollins, London, 2003

Shelley, Toby, *Endgame in the Western Sahara: What Future for Africa's Last Colony?*, Zed, London, 2004

Shivji, Issa G., *Class Struggles in Tanzania*, Heinemann, London, 1976

Short, Philip, *Banda*, Routledge and Kegan Paul, London, 1974

Siriex, Paul-Henri, *Félix Houphouët-Boigny; homme de la paix*, Seghers, Paris, 1975

—— *Houphouët-Boigny ou la sagesse africaine*, Fernand Nathan, Paris, 1986

Sklar, Richard, *Nigerian Political Parties: Power in an Emergent African Nation*, Princeton University Press, 1963

Smith, Ian D., *The Great Betrayal*, Blake, London, 1997

Smith, Stephen and Antoine Glaser, *Ces Messieurs Afrique: Le Paris-Village du continent noire*, Calmann-Lévy, Paris, 1992

—— *Ces Messieurs Afrique 2: Des réseaux aux lobbies*, Calmann-Lévy, Paris, 1997

Smith, William E., *We Must Run While They Walk: A Portrait of Africa's Julius Nyerere*, Random House, New York, 1971

Sorrenson, M. P. K., *Land Reform in the Kikuyu Country*, Oxford University Press, 1967

Soyinka, Wole, *The Open Sore of a Continent: A Personal Narrative of the Nigerian Crisis*, Oxford University Press, 1996

Sparks, Allister, *The Mind of South Africa*, Heinemann, London, 1990

—— *Tomorrow Is Another Country: The Inside Story of South Africa's Negotiated Revolution*, Heinemann, London, 1995

—— *Beyond the Miracle: Inside the New South Africa*, Jonathan Ball, Johannesburg, 2003

Spencer, John, *The Kenya African Union*, KPI, London, 1985

Spencer, John H., *Ethiopia at Bay: A Personal Account of the Haile Selassie Years*,

Reference Publications, Algonac, 1984

Spies, F. J. du T., *Operasie Savannah, Angola, 1975–1976*, Suid-Afrikaanse Weermag, Pretoria, 1989

St Jorre, John de, *The Nigerian Civil War*, Hodder and Stoughton, London, 1972

Stadiem, William, *Too Rich: The High Life and Tragic Death of King Farouk*, Robson, London, 1992

Stephens, Robert, *Nasser, A Political Biography*, Allen Lane, London, 1971

Stockwell, John, *In Search of Enemies: A CIA Story*, Deutsch, London, 1978

Stone, Martin, *The Agony of Algeria*, Hurst, London, 1997

Stora, Benjamin, *Algeria, 1830–2000, A Short History*, Cornell University Press, 2001

Stremlau, John J., *The International Politics of the Nigerian Civil War 1967–1970*, Princeton University Press, 1977

Sundkler, Bengt and Christopher Steed, *A History of the Church in Africa*, Cambridge University Press, 2000

Swainson, Nicola, *The Development of Corporate Capitalism in Kenya, 1918–1977*, Heinemann, London, 1980

Tangri, Roger, *The Politics of Patronage in Africa: Parastatals, Privatization and Private Enterprise*, Currey, Oxford, 1999

Tayler, Jeffrey, *Facing the Congo: A Modern-Day Journey into the Heart of Darkness*, Abacus, London, 2001

Tekeste Negash and Kjetil Tronvall, *Brothers At War: Making Sense of the Eritrean–Ethiopian War*, Currey, Oxford, 2000

Theroux, Paul, *Dark Star Safari: Overland from Cairo to Cape Town*, Hamish Hamilton, London, 2002

Thompson, Leonard M., *The Political Mythology of South Africa*, Yale University Press, 1985

—— *A History of South Africa*, Yale University Press, 1994

Thompson, Virginia and Richard Adloff, *French West Africa*, Allen and Unwin, London, 1958

—— *The Emerging States of French Equatorial Africa*, Oxford University Press, 1960

—— *Conflict in Chad*, Hurst, London, 1981

Thompson, W. Scott, *Ghana's Foreign Policy, 1957–1966: Diplomacy, Ideology and the New State*, Princeton University Press, 1969

Throup, David, *Economic and Social Origins of Mau Mau, 1945–53*, Currey, London, 1987

Throup, David and Charles Hornsby, *Multi-Party Politics in Kenya: The Kenyatta and Moi States and the Triumph of the System in the 1992 Election*, Currey, Oxford, 1998

Timberlake, Lloyd, *Africa in Crisis: The Causes, the Cures of Environmental Bankruptcy*, Earthscan, London, 1988

Titley, Brian, *Dark Age: The Political Odyssey of Emperor Bokassa*, Liverpool

University Press, 1997

Tordoff, William, *Government and Politics in Africa*, 4th edn, Palgrave Macmillan, Basingstoke, 2002

Toulabor, Comi, *Le Togo sous Eyadéma*, Karthala, Paris, 1986

Tripp, Aili Mari, *Changing the Rules: The Politics of Liberalization and the Urban Informal Economy in Tanzania*, University of California Press, 1997

Tutu, Desmond, *No Future Without Forgiveness*, Random House, Johannesburg, 1999

Unesco, *General History of Africa*, 8 vols, Currey, Oxford, 1990–99

United Nations, *The United Nations and Somalia, 1992–1996*, United Nations Blue Book Series, vol. 8, UN Department of Public Information, New York, 1996

Urfer, Sylvain, *Une Afrique socialiste: la Tanzanie*, Editions Ouvrières, Paris, 1976

Vail, Leroy (ed.), *The Creation of Tribalism in Southern Africa*, Currey, London, 1989

Vaillant, Janet G., *Black, French and African: A Life of Léopold Sédar Senghor*, Harvard University Press, 1990

van de Walle, Nicolas, *African Economies and the Politics of Permanent Crisis, 1979–1999*, Cambridge University Press, 2001

Vatikiotis, P. J., *Nasser and his Generation*, Croom Helm, London, 1978

—— *The History of Egypt*, 3rd edn, Weidenfeld & Nicolson, London, 1985

Verschave, François-Xavier, *La Françafrique; Le plus long scandale de la République*, Stock, Paris, 1998

Villalón, Leonardo A. and Phillip A. Huxtable (eds.), *The African State at a Critical Juncture: Between Disintegration and Reconfiguration*, Rienner, Boulder, 1998

Voll, John O. (ed.), *Sudan: State and Society in Crisis*, Indiana University Press, 1991

Von Freyhold, Michaela, *Ujamaa Villages in Tanzania: Analysis of a Social Experiment*, Heinemann, London, 1979

Waldmeir, Patti, *Anatomy of a Miracle: The End of Apartheid and the Birth of a New South Africa*, Viking, London, 1997

Wasserman, Gary, *Politics of Decolonisation: Kenya Europeans and the Land Issue, 1960–1965*, Cambridge University Press, 1976

Watson, Catherine, *Exile from Rwanda, Background to an Invasion*, US Committee for Refugees, Washington, 1991

Weaver, Mary Anne, *A Portrait of Egypt: A Journey through the World of Militant Islam*, Farrar, Strauss, New York, 2000

Weiss, Herbert, *Political Protest in the Congo: The Parti Solidaire Africain During the Independence Struggle*, Princeton University Press, 1967

Weiss, Herbert and Benoît Verhaegen (eds.), *Les Rébellions dans l'est du Zaire, 1964–1967*, Centre d'Étude et de Documentation Africaines, Brussels, 1986

Weissman, Stephen R., *American Foreign Policy in the Congo, 1960–1964*, Cornell University Press, 1974

Werbner, Richard, *Tears of the Dead: The Social Biography of an African Family*, Edinburgh University Press, 1991

White, Dorothy Shipley, *Black Africa and de Gaulle: From the French Empire to Independence*, Pennsylvania State University Press, 1979

Widner, Jennifer A., *The Rise of a Party-State in Kenya: From 'Harambee!' to 'Nyayo'*, University of California Press, 1992

Widner, Jennifer (ed.), *Economic Change and Political Liberalization in Sub-Saharan Africa*, Johns Hopkins University, 1994

Williame, Jean-Claude, *Patrimonialism and Political Change in the Congo*, Stanford University Press, 1971

—— *Zaire, L'épopée d'Inga: chronique d'une prédation industrielle*, L'Harmattan, Paris, 1986

—— *Patrice Lumumba: la Crise Congolaise Revisitée*, Karthala, Paris, 1990

—— *L'Automne d'un Despotisme: Pouvoir, Argent et Obéissance dans le Zaire des Années Quatre-Vingt*, Karthala, Paris, 1992

Willis, Michael, *The Islamist Challenge in Algeria: a Political History*, Ithaca Press, Reading, 1996

Wilson, Richard A., *The Politics of Truth and Reconciliation in South Africa: Legitimizing the Post-Apartheid State*, Cambridge University Press, 2001

Winternitz, Helen, *East Along the Equator: A Journey Up the Congo and into Zaire*, Atlantic Monthly Press, New York, 1987

Wiseman, John, *The New Struggle for Democracy in Africa*, Ashgate, Aldershot, 1996

Wiseman, John (ed.), *Democracy and Political Change in Sub-Saharan Africa*, Routledge, London, 1995

Wiwa, Ken, *In the Shadow of a Saint*, Doubleday, London, 2000

Woods, Donald, *Biko*, Paddington Press, London, 1978

Woodward, Peter, *The Horn of Africa: Politics and International Relations*, Tauris, London, 2003

World Bank, *Accelerated Development in Sub-Saharan Africa: An Agenda for Action*, Washington, DC, 1981

—— *Towards Sustained Development in Sub-Saharan Africa: A Joint Program of Action*, Washington, DC, 1984

—— *Sub-Saharan Africa: From Crisis to Self-Sustainable Growth*, Washington, DC, 1989

—— *Governance and Development*, Washington, DC, 1992

—— *Adjustment in Africa: Reforms, Results and the Road Ahead*, Washington DC, 1994

—— *Assessing Aid: What Works, What Doesn't and Why*, Oxford University Press, New York, 1998

—— *Can Africa Claim the 21st Century?*, Washington, DC, 2000

—— *Economic Causes of Civil Conflict and their Implications for Policy*,

Washington, DC, 2000

Woronoff, Jon, *West African Wager: Houphouët versus Nkrumah*, Scarecrow Press, Metuchen, 1972

Wright, John, *Libya, Chad and the Central Sahara*, Hurst, London, 1989

Wrong, Michela, *In the Footsteps of Mr Kurtz: Living on the Brink of Disaster in the Congo*, Fourth Estate, London, 2000

—— *I Didn't Do It For You: How the World Betrayed a Small African Nation*, Fourth Estate, London, 2005

Young, Kenneth, *Rhodesia and Independence*, Eyre & Spottiswoode, London, 1967

Young, Crawford, *Politics in the Congo: Decolonization and Independence*, Princeton University Press, 1965

—— *Ideology and Development in Africa*, Yale University Press, 1982

—— *The African Colonial State in Comparative Perspective*, Yale University Press, 1994

Young, Crawford and Thomas Turner, *The Rise and Decline of the Zairian State*, University of Wisconsin Press, 1985

Young, John, *Peasant Revolution in Ethiopia: The Tigray People's Liberation Front, 1975–1991*, Cambridge University Press, 1997

Yeros, Paris (ed.), *Ethnicity and Nationalism in Africa: Constructivist Reflections and Contemporary Politics*, Macmillan, Basingstoke, 1999

Zack-Williams, Tunde, Diane Frost and Alex Thomson (eds.), *Africa in Crisis: New Challenges and Possibilities*, Pluto, London, 2002

Zartman, I. William and Christopher L. Delgado (eds.), *The Political Economy of Ivory Coast*, Praeger, New York, 1984

Zartman, William (ed.), *Collapsed States: The Disintegration and Restoration of Legitimate Authority*, Lynne Rienner, Boulder, 1995

Zolberg, Aristide R., *Creating Political Order: The Party-States of West Africa*, Rand McNally, Chicago, 1966

—— *One-Party Government in the Ivory Coast*, Princeton University Press, 1969

INDEX

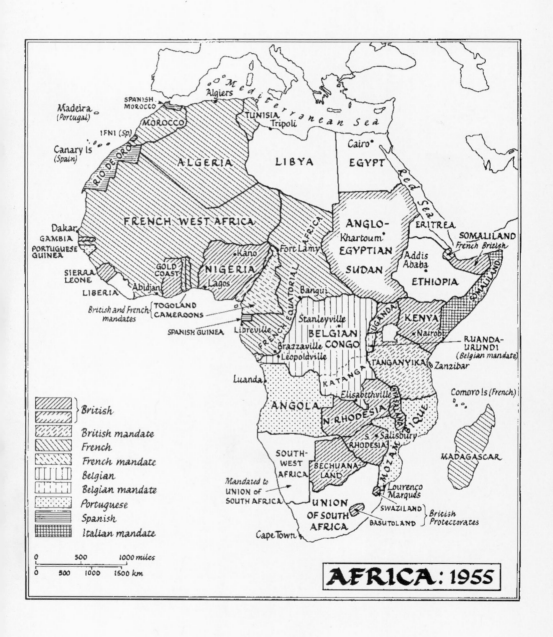

Madeira
(Portugal)

SPANISH
MOROCCO

IFNI (Sp.)

Canary Is
(Spain)

RIO DE ORO

MOROCCO

Algiers

TUNISIA
Tripoli

Mediterranean Sea

ALGERIA

LIBYA

EGYPT

Cairo

Red Sea

ANGLO-
Khartoum
EGYPTIAN

ERITREA

SOMALILAND
French British

FRENCH WEST AFRICA

Dakar
GAMBIA
PORTUGUESE
GUINEA

SIERRA
LEONE

LIBERIA

Kano

Abidjan

GOLD
COAST

British and French
mandates

TOGOLAND
CAMEROONS

SPANISH GUINEA

NIGERIA

Lagos

A.E.C.

Fort Lamy

Bangui

SUDAN

Addis
Ababa

ETHIOPIA

SOMALILAND

KENYA

Nairobi

FRENCH EQUATORIAL

Libreville

Stanleyville

BELGIAN
CONGO

UGANDA

RUANDA-
URUNDI
(Belgian mandate)

Brazzaville
Léopoldville

TANGANYIKA

Zanzibar

Luanda

KATANGA

Elisabethville

Comoro Is (French)

ANGOLA

N. RHODESIA

MADAGASCAR

MOZAMBIQUE

Salisbury
S.
RHODESIA

SOUTH-
WEST
AFRICA

BECHUANA-
LAND

Mandated to
UNION of
SOUTH AFRICA

Lourenço
Marques

SWAZILAND

British
Protectorates

UNION
OF SOUTH
AFRICA

BASUTOLAND

Cape Town

British

British mandate

French

French mandate

Belgian

Belgian mandate

Portuguese

Spanish

Italian mandate

0   500   1000 miles
0   500   1000   1500 km

AFRICA: 1955